The Psychopath:
Theory, Research, and Practice

The Psychopath:
Theory, Research, and Practice

Edited by

Hugues Hervé
Forensic Psychiatric Hospital

John C. Yuille
University of British Columbia

LEA LAWRENCE ERLBAUM ASSOCIATES, PUBLISHERS
2007 Mahwah, New Jersey London

Editorial Director: Steve Rutter
Editorial Assistant: Nicole Buchmann
Cover Design: Kathryn Houghtaling-Lacey
Full-Service Compositor: MidAtlantic Books & Journals, Inc.

This book was typeset in 10/12 pt. Palatino, Italic, Bold, and Bold Italic.

Lawrence Erlbaum Associates, Inc., Publishers
10 Industrial Avenue
Mahwah, New Jersey 07430
www.erlbaum.com

CIP information for this volume can be obtained from the Library of Congress.

ISBN   0-8058-5053-8 (case)
ISBN   0-8058-6079-7 (pbk)

Books published by Lawrence Erlbaum Associates are printed on acid-free paper, and their bindings are chosen for strength and durability.

Printed in the United States of America
10   9   8   7   6   5   4   3   2   1

This volume is dedicated to the memory of Cheryl Wynne Hare, whose life and death touched all who knew and loved her.

Contents

Preface

In 2000, John and I had the honor of organizing a festschrift for (a tribute to) Dr. Robert D. Hare in light of his retirement (at least on paper) from academia. To celebrate this momentous occasion, we invited experts from all over the world, all doing research on some aspect of psychopathy. Our aim was to have not only renowned scholars but individuals who, in one way or another, had been influenced by Dr. Hare, either directly via supervision and collaborative enterprises or indirectly by the enormous contribution that Dr. Hare had made to this area of study throughout his illustrious career. Not surprisingly, a list of speakers was not difficult to find. In fact, it was hard to think of any expert who had, to one degree or another, not been influenced by Dr. Hare and his research. Moreover, invitations were, almost without exception, enthusiastically accepted.

In light of the response we received, the festschrift quickly evolved into a conference which was held in October of 2000 and attended by many. *The Hare Psychopath: Past, Present, and Future* was, by all accounts, a great success. In light of the quality and breadth of topics covered, as well as the many other topics informally discussed, it became apparent that it was time for an edited volume that reflected the changing face of psychopathy theory, research, and practice. This was the impetus for this book. Most of the conference presenters eagerly agreed to author chapters; others regrettably could not. To ensure that topics of importance were addressed, we expanded our list of contributors beyond conference presenters. As a result, this volume consists of scholarly pieces from leading figures in the field. We are most appreciative of their involvement.

This book is intended for academics, researchers, theorists, practitioners, lawyers, judges, law enforcement personnel, students, and other professionals interested in or working within forensic psychology. In addition, this text is of interest to other mental health law professionals who study and/or treat psychopathology (e.g., criminologist, sociologist, etc.), especially those interested in personality disorders. Given its depth and scope, it will make interesting supplementary reading for graduate students within programs specializing in Forensic Psychology and Criminology.

We have organized this volume to parallel the manner in which we believe one's understanding of psychopathy should evolve. The book begins with a historical view of psychopathy, then examines measurement issues, followed by etiological theories and practical considerations. The chapters have been grouped to reflect this organization.

In light of psychopaths' socially destructive nature, the study of psychopathy is of critical importance. Fortunately, this area of enquiry has come a long way and promises to evolve into new and exciting arenas. Dr. Hare introduces this volume by discussing the current state of psychopathy research, highlighting its advancements, potential pitfalls or impediments, and future trajectory. The remaining chapters draw attention to these various topics.

In Part I, Dr. Hervé discuss the evolution of the construct throughout the ages, following which Drs. Harris and Rice provide a specific example of how the construct evolved within a correctional treatment facility.

In Part II, the implications of statistical advances in recent years for refining our understanding of psychopathy are discussed. The chapters by Drs. Neumann, Kosson, and Salekin and by Dr. Bolt provide new insights into Item Response Theory and Factor Analysis, highlighting its implication for the construct of psychopathy, as defined by the PCL-R. Dr. Hemphill then tackles methodological issues related to psychopathy-related risk research.

In Part III, three models addressing the nature and etiology of psychopathy are described. Dr. Newman and his colleagues outline a neurocognitive theory in which attention-related deficits play a central role. Dr. Patrick describes his emotion-based theory of psychopathy. Finally, Dr. Herba and her colleagues review neurobiological research, with a specific focus on emotion processing. By contrasting these three models within one volume, we hope to allow readers to easily compare each theory's strengths and weaknesses.

In Part IV, the socially destructive aspects of the disorder are reviewed. Dr. and Mrs. Porter focus specifically on the nature of psychopathic violence. The implication for Violent Crime Scene Analysis is then discussed by Dr. O'Toole. This section concludes with Ms. Spidel and her colleagues discussing the emerging research in the area of domestic violence.

In Part V, the generalization of the construct of psychopathy across populations and settings is reviewed. The construct of psychopathy, as defined by the Hare PCL-R, was initially validated on incarcerated male offenders. Given the implications of this line of research, a concerted effort was made to see if this construct applies to other arenas. Dr. Frick reviews how the construct of psychopathy can be useful to understand behaviorally challenging children. In a similar vein, Drs. Forth and Book review the research on psychopathy in adolescent offenders, highlighting its strengths and weaknesses. Drs. Jackson and Richards review the empirical and clinical implications of psychopathy for women offenders. This section concludes with Dr. Babiak's research and experience with psychopaths in the work place. Each chapter focuses on measurement issues, practical implications, and ethical considerations.

Part VI focuses on the newly revived notion of psychopathic subtypes. Dr. Hervé reviews the history of subtypes and proposes a taxonomy that reflects clinical and research findings. Drs. Wong and Burt then address the implications of subtypes of psychopathy for the management and treatment of incarcerated psychopaths.

Finally, in Part VII, two main and largely understudied areas of practice are reviewed. First, the importance and implications of psychopathy for credibility assessment is discussed by Drs. Cooper and Yuille. Second, Drs. Thornton and Blud provide a detailed clinical perspective of the impact of psychopathy upon therapy, with special emphasis placed upon how the unique diagnostic features of this disorder disrupts the therapeutic process.

We know that there will be considerable advancements in the area of psychopathy in the 21st century and hope this volume will help set its foundation. By bringing together academics and practitioners, this volume offers a unique combination of breadth and depth in the study of psychopathy. In addition to having direct application to current research and practice, these chapters directly and indirectly address the current limitations of our knowledge and provide a challenge for theory development in the future.

We would like to acknowledge the Social Sciences and Humanities Research Counsel (SSHRC) of Canada for helping fund the conference that initiated this work, Teresa Howell without whom the conference would not have materialized, and the many UBC volunteers who helped make sure the conference ran smoothly. We are also grateful to Teresa Howell and Kristin Kendrick for their help in preparing this volume, from soliciting authors to administrative duties. Many thanks to our editors for their patience and helpful insights.

Contributors

Editors:

Hugues Hervé, PhD, RPsych, Forensic Psychiatric Hospital, Psychology Department, Port Coquitlam, British Columbia, Canada; hherve@forensic .bc.ca.

John C. Yuille, PhD, Full Professor, University of British Columbia, Psychology Department, Vancouver, British Columbia, Canada; jcyuille@ interchange.ubc.ca.

Contributors

Paul Babiak, PhD, Industrial-Organizational Psychologist, New York, NY; Babiak@HRBackOffice.com.

Nigel Blackwood, MRCPysch, Institute of Psychiatry, Denmark Hill, London, United Kingdom; N.Blackwood@iop.kcl.ac.uk.

Linda Blud, PhD, Director of LMB Consultancy Ltd, Forensic Psychology Services, Broseley, Shropshire, United Kingdom; Lmbconsultancy@aol.com.

Daniel M. Bolt, PhD, Department of Educational Psychology, University of Wisconsin–Madison, Madison, Wisconsin; dmbolt@facstaff.wisc.edu.

Angela S. Book, PhD, Department of Psychology, Brock University, St. Catherines, Ontario, Canada; Angela_book@hotmail.com.

Chad A. Brinkley, PhD, Staff Psychologist, Psychology Services, Federal Detention Center, Houston, Texas; mourn@houston.rr.com.

Grant Burt, PhD, Youth Forensic Psychiatric Services, Burnaby, British Columbia, Canada; Grant.Burt@gov.bc.ca.

Barry S. Cooper, PhD, Correctional Service of Canada, Kent Institution, Psychology Department, Agassiz, British Columbia, Canada; CooperBS@ CSC-SCC.GC.CA.

Don Dutton, PhD, University of British Columbia, Department of Psychology, Vancouver, British Columbia, Canada; dondutton@shaw.ca.

Adelle Forth, PhD, Associate Professor, Department of Psychology, Carleton University, Ottawa, Ontario, Canada; adelle_forth@carleton.ca.

Paul J. Frick, PhD, Research Professor, Director, Applied Developmental Program, Department of Psychology, University of New Orleans, New Orleans, Louisiana; pfrick@uno.edu.

Robert D. Hare, PhD, Emeritus Professor of Psychology, University of British Columbia, Psychology Department, Vancouver, British Columbia, Canada; rhare@interchange.ubc.ca.

Grant Harris, PhD, Director of Research, Mental Health Centre, Penetanguishene, Ontario, Canada; Associate Professor of Psychology, Queen's University at Kingston, Ontario, Canada; Associate Professor of Psychiatry, University of Toronto, Ontario, Canada; gharris@mhcp.on.ca.

James F. Hemphill, PhD, RPsych, Psychologist, Youth Forensic Psychiatric Services, Burnaby, British Columbia, Canada; Adjunct Professor of Psychology, Simon Fraser University, Burnaby, British Columbia, Canada; james_hemphill@sfu.ca.

Catherine M. Herba, PhD, Institute of Psychiatry, Denmark Hill, London, United Kingdom; C.Herba@iop.kcl.ac.uk.

Kristina D. Hiatt, MS, Department of Psychology, University of Wisconsin–Madison, Madison, Wisconsin; kdhiatt@wisc.edu

Sheilagh Hodgins, PhD, Institute of Psychiatry, Denmark Hill, London, United Kingdom; S.Hodgins@iop.kcl.ac.uk.

Matthew T. Huss, PhD, Creighton University, Department of Psychology, Omaha, Nebraska; mhuss@creighton.edu.

Rebecca Jackson, PhD, Assistant Professor, Director, Forensic Psychology Certification Program, Pacific Graduate School of Psychology, Palo Alto, California; bjackson@pgsp.edu.

David S. Kosson, PhD, Department of Psychology, Rosalind Franklin University of Medicine and Science, North Chicago, IL; David.Kosson@rosalindfranklin.edu.

Veena Kumari, PhD, Institute of Psychiatry, Denmark Hill, London, United Kingdom; V.Kumari@iop.kcl.ac.uk.

Amanda R. Lorenz, PhD, The Psychology Center, Douglasville, Georgia; drarlorenz@yahoo.com.

Donal G. MacCoon, PhD, Waisman Laboratory for Brain Imaging and Behavior, Madison, Wisconsin; dgmaccoon@wisc.edu.

Kris H. Naudts, CCSTPsych, MD, Institute of Psychiatry, Denmark Hill, London, United Kingdom; K.Naudts@iop.kcl.ac.uk.

Craig S. Neumann, PhD, Associate Professor, University of North Texas, Psychology Department, Denton, Texas; csn0001@unt.edu.

Joseph P. Newman, PhD, Professor and Director of Clinical Training, Department of Psychology, University of Wisconsin–Madison, Madison, Wisconsin; jpnewman@wisc.edu.

Mary Ellen O'Toole, PhD, Supervisory Special Agent, Federal Bureau of Investigation, Behavioral Analysis Unit II FBI Academy, Quantico, Virginia; meotoole@fbiacademy.edu.

Christopher J. Patrick, PhD, Starke R. Hathaway Distinguished Professor; Director, Clinical Science and Psychopathology Research Training Program; Director, National Institute of Mental Health Neurobehavioral Training Program; Department of Psychology, University of Minnesota, Minneapolis, Minnesota; cpatrick@tc.umn.edu.

Mary Phillips, MRCPsych, MD, Institute of Psychiatry, Denmark Hill, London, United Kingdom; M.Phillips@iop.kcl.ac.uk.

Sasha Porter, BSc (Hons), Springhill Institution, Springhill, Nova Scotia, Canada; sashaporter2@hotmail.com.

Steve Porter, PhD, Associate Professor, Dalhousie University, Department of Psychology, Halifax, Nova Scotia, Canada; sbporter@dal.ca.

Marnie Rice, PhD, FRSC, Scientific Director, McMaster University and MHC Penetanguishene, Centre for the Study of Aggression and Mental Disorder, Penetanguishene, Ontario, Canada; Professor of Psychiatry and Behavioural Neuroscience, McMaster University, Ontario, Canada; Professor of Psychiatry, University of Toronto, Ontario, Canada; Associate Professor of Psychology, Queen's University at Kingston, Ontario, Canada; riceme@mcmaster.ca.

Henry Richards, PhD, Director, Special Commitment Center, P.O. Box 88450, Stellacoom, Washington; richahj@dshs.wa.gov.

Randy T. Salekin, PhD, Associate Professor, Department of Psychology, The University of Alabama, Tuscaloosa, Alabama; rsalekin@bama.ua.edu.

Alicia Spidel, MA, University of British Columbia, Psychology Department, Vancouver, British Columbia, Canada; aliciaspidel@aol.com.

Lindsey Thomas, MA, University of British Columbia, Psychology Department, Vancouver, British Columbia, Canada; lindsey.thomas@shaw.ca.

David Thornton, PhD, Sand Ridge Secure Treatment Center, Mauston, Wisconsin; thorndm@dhfs.state.wi.us.

Gina Vincent, PhD, Department of Psychiatry, Law & Psychiatry Program, University of Massachusetts Medical School, Worcester, Massachusetts; gina.vincent@umassmed.edu.

Jason Winters, MA, University of British Columbia, Psychology Department, Vancouver, British Columbia, Canada; jwinters@interchange.ubc.ca.

Stephen C. P. Wong, PhD, Director of Research, Regional Psychiatric Centre, Saskatoon, Saskatchewan, Canada; Adjunct Professor, University of Saskatchewan, Saskatchewan, Canada; s.wong@sasktel.net.

The Psychopath:
Theory, Research, and Practice

INTRODUCTION

Forty Years Aren't Enough: Recollections, Prognostications, and Random Musings

Robert D. Hare

Some 20 years ago I wrote a chapter that described my recollections and experiences in the field over the previous two decades (Hare, 1986). Now, another 20 years down the road, it is time to provide an update, but this time with more emphasis on my impressions of the important trends in theory and research over that period, coupled with what I see for the future. My hope, unrealistic I know, is that I will be able to repeat the exercise in another 20 years.

I begin with a brief account of my early experiences in the field, not because they are particularly interesting but because they are a reflection of the theories, areas of interest, and paradigms that characterized psychology in the 1960s. In those days, there was great interest in learning theory, motivation, and in the new field of psychophysiology. The early research on psychopathy was an extension of these interests, just as current research interests are heavily influenced by cognitive psychology, information-processing, general personality theory, psychobiology, and neuroimaging. Admittedly, many students are not overly impressed by the historical antecedents of their discipline, but a sense of what preceded their own research cannot hurt them and may even be of some use (e.g., see Hervé, chap. 2, this volume). It might also help to counteract a recent trend for some new and established researchers to overvalue the importance and significance of their work, largely because they fail to put it into a historical context. I am particularly bemused by authors who confidently conclude from a single study of a specific sample and a specific paradigm that their results "call into question" some well-established theory or findings, or that clinicians should now rethink how they view and deal with psychopathic patients and offenders or that public policy needs to be changed to accommodate the findings. The tendency to overgeneralize results is exacerbated by an apparent disinterest in putting them into the larger context of historical and current research and theory from diverse areas of interest.

EARLY DAYS

Before I started the doctoral program in experimental psychology at the University of Western Ontario (UWO) in the early 1960s, I had worked for 8 months as the only psychologist in the maximum security British Columbia Penitentiary (BCP) near Vancouver. Unfortunately, my background in psychology had not prepared me for what turned out to be an interesting but daunting experience. As I have outlined elsewhere (Hare, 1998a), things got off to a rocky start when the first inmate appeared in my office, located on the top floor of the administrative block. Later, I realized that the inmate probably was a psychopath, but at the time he baffled and worried me with his piercing stare and casual accounts of his predatory, cold-blooded behaviors. Fortunately, several prison-wise classification officers befriended me and made things a lot easier for me. One, Tom Taylor, went on to a career in probations, while the other, John Maloney, became warden of the penitentiary.

The doctoral program at UWO was rather broad in scope and involved comprehensive examinations in several areas, including general experimental psychology, philosophy of science, personality, social psychology, abnormal psychology, learning, motivation, perception, psychobiology, psychometrics, mathematical models, and statistics. In those days, the only way to research the literature and to prepare for the comprehensives was to read the books and journals in the departmental library or in the university library "stacks," hundreds of long rows of academic books and of bound and unbound journals. Compared with today, the process was tedious and time consuming, but it had the great advantage of exposing students to a wide array of material on a variety of topics.

I was Alan Paivio's first doctoral student (John Yuille was his fourth). He was just beginning his ground-breaking work on imagery, not a very popular topic in a behavioristic era. Rather than imagery, I chose to do a dissertation on the effects of punishment on human behavior (Hare, 1965a). After completion of the Ph.D. program, I took up an academic position at the University of British Columbia (UBC) in Vancouver, not far from the BCP. Because of my earlier experiences and contacts at the penitentiary and its proximity to the university, it was the ideal place to begin research on a topic that had begun to intrigue me while I was a student at UWO. During my extended periods in the library stacks, I had come across the third (1956) edition of Cleckley's *The Mask of Sanity*, as well as the extensive clinical (mostly psychodynamic) literature on psychopathy by Benjaman Karpman, Silvano Arieti, Robert Lindner, and William and Joan McCord, among others. As an empirically oriented psychologist, I was impressed by the research and writings on the topic by Harrison Gough, Herb Quay, and David Lykken.

My first papers on psychopathy appeared soon after I had arrived at UBC (Hare 1965b, 1965c, 1965d). The framework for this research reflected the dominant themes of the time in psychology, as well as my attempt to integrate several disciplines that I considered relevant for understanding psychopathy. For the next 20 years my research on psychopathy made use of learning, motivation, and cognitive theory, mostly with a psychophysiologi-cal slant. For a long time I took the view that the most valuable research on psychopathy involved the concurrent measurement of cognitive, behavioral, and biological processes. I still am sympathetic to this view. However, the early use of autonomic/somatic variables such as skin conductance, heart rate, and vasomotor, respiratory, and electromyographic activity gradually gave way to the use of electrocortical activity (electoencephalogram; event-related potentials [ERPs]) and, more recently, to cognitive/affective neu-roscience and neuroimaging. Nonetheless, as the research of many investi-gators has shown, highly informative research on psychopathy can be conducted without the systematic inclusion of psychobiological variables.

TWENTY YEARS AGO

As a way of indicating what I and others thought was important 20 years ago, it may be helpful to list the section headings in the chapter referred to ear-lier (Hare, 1986): Early Days; Temporal Gradient of Fear Arousal; Ratings of Psychopathy; Patterns of Autonomic Activity; Modulation of Sensory Input; Behavior Under Stress; Perceptual-Cognitive Factors; Detection of Deception; A 22-Item Checklist For Psychopathy; A 20-Item Revised Psychopathy Checklist; Comparisons Among Assessment Procedures; and Cerebral Spe-cialization for Language.

Some of the topics covered are still of interest to the research community, but any attempt to describe and evaluate them and the many new avenues of research would prove a lot more difficult than it was 20 years ago. So much has happened since then that whole volumes now are required to summarize and describe recent advances in theory and research. The scope of the current interest and activities is reflected in the establishment of the first formal soci-ety devoted solely to research in psychopathy, *The Society for the Scientific Study of Psychopathy* (SSSP), which held its inaugural meeting in Vancouver on July 28–30, 2005. In this chapter, I will confine myself to some comments about the notable developments in recent years and to a few speculations about what the future might hold for the burgeoning field of psychopathy. My approach and comments are more impressionistic than scientific, and the coverage of developments is far from exhaustive.

ASSESSMENT

There is general agreement that a useful development in the assessment of psychopathy was the introduction to the research and applied communities of the Psychopathy Checklist (PCL; Hare, 1980), its revision, the Psychopathy Checklist–Revised (PCL–R: Hare, 1991, 2003), and its derivatives. The latter include the Psychopathy Checklist: Screening Version (PCL:SV; Hart, Cox, & Hare, 1995) and the Psychopathy Checklist: Youth Version (PCL:YV; Forth,

Kosson, & Hare, 2003), as well as the Antisocial Process Screening Device (APSD; Frick & Hare, 2001). The events leading up to the construction of these instruments, as well as descriptions of their structural properties, are covered in detail elsewhere (Hare & Neumann, 2005, 2006; Bolt, chap. 5, this volume; Neumann, Kosson, & Salekin, chap. 4, this volume).

The rapid and widespread adoption of the PCL–R and its derivatives has been very gratifying. It helped to fill a diagnostic and assessment void by providing researchers and clinicians with a common metric that has demonstrated reliability and validity in an array of populations and contexts. Indeed, the success of the PCL–R has led to its description as "the gold standard" but also to occasional plaints that its popularity has led to its reification and that the "measure has become the construct." Such plaints voice little apparent appreciation or acknowledgment of the important role played by the PCL–R in getting us where we are today.

The remedy for concerns about the dominance of a single measure of psychopathy is to develop and validate other measures of psychopathy, including those that use a variety of methods to tap the construct. The procedure involves what Cronbach and Meehl (1955) described as the concept of the nomological network as a theoretical framework for understanding construct validity (see Benning, Patrick, Salekin, & Leistico, 2005, for an outline of the concept to psychopathy). Some recent efforts of researchers along these lines are beginning to broaden the repertoire of assessment tools and show promise of helping us to understand better the construct they purport to measure. These mostly consist of self-report scales, including the *Psychopathy Personality Inventory* (PAI; Lilienfeld, 1990; Lilienfeld & Andrews, 1996), the *Self-Report Psychopathy* (SRP) scale, and its latest revision (the SRP–III; Paulhus, Hemphill, & Hare, in press), and the *Youth Psychopathic Traits Inventory* (YPI; Andershed, Kerr, Stattin, & Levander, 2002). Behavior rating scales, which are widely used in developmental and educational psychology and in psychopathology, have also emerged. They require that the ratings be made by qualified professionals or by knowledgeable informants. Two such scales for the assessment of psychopathy, each based on the PCL–R, are the APSD and the *Childhood Psychopathy Scale* (CPS; Lynam, 1997). They clearly are playing an important role in delineating and elucidating the behavioral genetics and early antecedents of psychopathy.

In addition to these specialized (for psychopathy) self-report and behavioral rating scales, there is increasing use of more general, omnibus self-report inventories that measure personality dimensions presumably relevant to psychopathy. These include the *Multidimensional Personality Questionnaire* (MPQ; Tellegen, in press) and the various instruments used in the five-factor model of personality (Costa & McCrae, 1992; Costa & Widiger, 2002; Lynam, 2002a).

There are several advantages and disadvantages to using specialized and general scales of this sort for the study of psychopathy (Lilienfeld & Fowler, 2006; Westen & Weinberger, 2004). They make it possible to use very large samples, in both forensic and other populations. They broaden the nomological network by extending to the general population some of the research paradigms found useful in experimental and laboratory research with forensic populations. Further, by viewing psychopathy from different perspectives, including that of the individual under study (self-reports), these scales may lead to a more complete and accurate conceptualization of the construct when combined with other measures. And of course they also make the researcher's task much easier, because most of the assessment work is done by the study participants, who provide their own managed view of themselves.

However, we should take pains to ensure that the nomological net is not cast too wide or in the wrong place and that the construct putatively under investigation really is what we think it is. As Rutter (2005) put it in his introduction to a special journal issue on adolescent psychopathy, some of the core features of psychopathy ". . . may not be best represented by scores on personality dimensions that are designed to pick up rather different features" (p. 500). We also should be concerned that the rapid proliferation of assessment tools does not result in a partial return to the conceptual and measurement confusion that held sway some 20 years ago. In those days, we had a number of procedures described as measures of psychopathy or as psychopathy-related: clinical impressions, *Diagnostic and Statistical Manual of Mental Disorders*, 2nd ed. (*DSM–II*), rating scales, and self-report inventories. Most were only weakly associated with one another, and there was little systematic evidence for the validity of the construct they purportedly measured. The PCL was developed to overcome these problems, and soon morphed into the PCL–R and its derivatives. The development and use of alternate conceptualizations and measurements of psychopathy certainly are good things, but we should ensure that the convergence we perceive is not more apparent than real. One approach, suggested by Benning et al. (2005), is to use the PCL–R as an "anchor for the burgeoning nomological network of psychopathy" (p. 271).

As a final point here, it seems likely that current methods for the assessment of psychopathy eventually will be supplemented (not replaced) with cognitive/affective, biochemical, and neuroimaging variables. The early and continuing paradigm for psychophysiology is to view individuals in terms of patterns of interacting behavioral, cognitive, and biological processes. A similar paradigm is used in cognitive/affective neuroscience, with some indications that a psychobiological marker for psychopathy might be feasible. For example, Kiehl and his colleagues have identified a component in the ERPs of psychopaths that consistently appears while they perform a variety of laboratory tasks (Kiehl, Bates, Laurens, Hare, & Liddle, in press; Kiehl, Hare, McDonald, & Brink, 1999). At some point, it may be possible, or even mandatory, to supplement structured-clinical ratings and self-reports with a number of indices derived from cognitive/affective neuroscience, behavioral genetics, and/or biochemistry. Even now, it might prove interesting to do structural equation modeling with data sets made up of some of these variables.

Les Arcs

I might note that this early measurement confusion not only led to the development of the PCL but also probably played a role in the evolution of antisocial personality disorder (APD), as described in *Diagnostic and Statistical Manual of Mental Disorders*, 3rd ed. (*DSM–III*). As outlined in Hare and Neumann (2006), in 1975 I directed (with the late Daisy Schalling) a NATO Advanced Study Institute (ASI) in Les Arcs, France. Ostensibly on psychopathy, the 10-day ASI rapidly became a conceptual and diagnostic free-for-all. A psychiatrist likened the situation to the parable of several blind men whose description of an elephant was determined by what part of the animal they touched. Hans Eysenck replied that, "Psychopathy is a white elephant and ought to be dumped into Lake Annecy." Tony Gale wondered if I were a psychopath, given that my late invitation for him to be a speaker reflected a lack of planning ability. Things went downhill from there. Fortunately, some of the graduate students at the ASI, including Sheilagh Hodgins, Robert Cloninger, David Cox, and Cathy Widom, were not permanently scarred by the experience.

The confusion at Les Arcs played an important role in the subsequent efforts by my laboratory to improve upon the assessment procedures then used in research and clinical practice. Indeed, the development of the PCL items and the *DSM–III* criteria for APD followed much the same time course. However, whereas *DSM–III* was carefully planned, the publication of the PCL items (referred to then under the rubric of a "research scale for the assessment of psychopathy in criminal populations") was the result of an invitation by Hans Eysenck to submit a conference paper for the first issue of his new journal, *Personality and Individual Differences*. At the same time, Janice Frazelle and I began to circulate a 17-page mimeographed outline of rudimentary scoring instructions for each of the 22 PCL items.

One of the Les Arcs participants was Lee Robins, whose work and recommendations played an important role in the planning for *DSM–III*, then underway. No doubt her view that psychologists and psychiatrists could not assess personality traits reliably was reinforced by the spectacle. The result was the *DSM–III* criteria for APD which, though reliable, constituted what Ted Millon aptly described as a laundry list of trivial antisocial behaviors. In one sense then, I must bear some of the responsibility for this list. As we know, the field trial for the *Diagnostic and Statistical Manual of Mental Disorders*, 4nd ed. (*DSM–IV*) (Widiger et al., 1996) did not support Robins' pessimism about the ability of clinicians to measure traits reliably. Nevertheless, the criteria for APD in *DSM–IV* remained heavily weighted with antisocial behaviors (Hare, Hart, & Harpur, 1991).

Parenthetically, at the International Congress on Personality Disorders, held at Harvard University in 1993, I gave an address on the nature and measurement of psychopathy. Following the presentation Robert Spitzer noted that the picture painted was compelling, and he wondered why psychopathy was not to be more influential in the forthcoming *DSM–IV*. I said that I could not answer the question, whereupon Tom Widiger, director of the APD Field

Trial, responded that had they "started from scratch" the APD criteria would contain many of the psychopathy items my students and I had put together for the Field Trial (see Hare et al., 1991; Widiger et al., 1996). Later, one of the major figures in the development of *DSM–IV* approached me and said, "Bob, I hear you are unhappy with *DSM–IV*," to which I replied, "I'm only unhappy about APD." His response was, "Bob, everyone knows you've won the war, but the timing is not right." Perhaps it will be right for *Diagnostic and Statistical Manual of Mental Disorders*, 5th ed. (*DSM–V*), particularly now that there is evidence for the dimensionality of the PCL–R and its components. In any case, it is important to keep in mind that APD and psychopathy are related but not identical constructs (see Hare, 1996a; Hare & Hart, 1995; Rogers, Salekin, Sewell, & Cruise, 2000; Widiger, 2005).

Of interest, in *DSM–IV* selected items from the diagnostic criteria of several personality disorders (e.g., narcissistic and antisocial) might have been combined to describe something very much like psychopathy. For example, cluster analyses of the criteria for *DSM–III* histrionic, antisocial, borderline, and narcissistic personality disorders revealed a dimension strongly indicative of psychopathy (Harpur, Hare, Zimmerman, & Corryell, 1990). Similar analyses of the *International Classification of Diseases*, 10th revision (ICD–10) personality disorders identified a clear psychopathy dimension (Ullrich & Marneros, 2004). These authors commented, "Although suggestions to replace ASPD in *DSM–IV* with the construct of psychopathy were previously rejected, its importance within forensic contexts is established. Against the background of our findings, we conclude that specific dimensions of personality disorders are strongly interrelated and show remarkable similarities to the personality features constituting psychopathy" (pp. 211–212). Much the same results are obtained with dimensional analyses of personality inventories (e.g., Livesley & Schroeder, 1991).

Alvor

In 1995 I organized a second NATO ASI, held in Alvor, Portugal. The co-directors were Adelle Forth, Joseph Newman, and David Cooke. Unlike the first ASI, the Alvor ASI was very successful (see Cooke, Forth, & Hare, 1998; Hare, 1997). Many of today's leading researchers on psychopathy, some of whom have authored chapters in this volume, and founding members of SSSP were in attendance.

STRUCTURAL PROPERTIES OF PCL–R PSYCHOPATHY

The factor structure of the PCL–R and its derivatives has been the subject of much (some would say too much) analysis and debate (see Hare & Neumann, 2005, 2006; Neumann et al., chap. 4, this volume). The original two-factor model, based on exploratory factor analysis, has been replicated several times and has proven useful in research delineating correlates of psychopathy and its components, as well as in conceptualizations of psychopathy in terms of both personality traits and externalizing or undercontrolled psychopathology. More recent work, using confirmatory factor analysis has revealed between two and four factors, depending on the statistical programs used and on the number of items included in the analyses. The three-factor model (Interpersonal, Affective, and Lifestyle) proposed by Cooke and Michie (2001) is based on a selected set of 13 items. The authors claimed that these particular items were core personality traits, whereas the remaining 7 items were "downstream" manifestations of the core traits and therefore of little use in the conceptualization and measurement of psychopathy. These claims are at odds with their earlier conclusion that an item response theory (IRT) "analysis confirms that the PCL–R is a good measure of psychopathic personality disorder because all the items contribute to the estimate of the trait and there are different items that function efficiently, at different points, along the whole length of the trait" (Cooke & Michie, 1997, p. 10). It is unclear why some of the retained items and their scoring criteria (e.g., Impulsivity, Irresponsibility, and Pathological Lying) are more trait-like or less "antisocial" than are two excluded items, Early Behavior Problems and Poor Behavioral Controls. One possibility is that Cooke and Michie (2001) excluded these two items after a number of iterations because they did not fit the three-factor model they sought, a modern version of the Procrustean bed. Had they used factor analytic procedures that treated the PCL–R items as ordinal scales (which they are), these two excluded items would have loaded quite nicely on the Lifestyle factor (see Neumann et al., chap. 4, this volume). The resulting 15-item, three-factor model might be referred to as the *Big-3*, and the 13-item model as the *Small-3*.

In any case, the literature on the developmental correlates of antisocial and psychopathic behavior and recent work by Neumann and his colleagues, clearly indicate that asocial, antisocial, and other socially disruptive behaviors (not necessarily criminal) are important components of psychopathy, and that an 18-item, four-factor model (Interpersonal, Affective, Lifestyle, and Antisocial) clearly is tenable, not only for the PCL–R but also for the PCL:SV and the PCL:YV (Hare & Neumann, 2006; Neumann, Vitacco, Hare, & Wupperman, 2005; Vitacco, Neumann, & Jackson, 2005). Of interest, Early Behavior Problems and Poor Behavioral controls, which are part of the Big-3 model, are even more comfortable as part of the fourth (Antisocial) factor in the four-factor PCL–R model. The statistical and conceptual issues concerning the factor structure of the PCL–R are thoroughly discussed by Neumann et al. (chap. 4, this volume). Among other things, they argue that statistical analyses and structural models of the PCL–R and its derivatives should take into account the ordinal nature of its items. They also emphasize that the factor structure of the PCL–R and its derivatives is of more than academic interest. For example, the pattern of correlations between the factors and outcome variables (e.g., predicted violence) and the conclusions drawn, may be quite different when four factors are used than when the Antisocial factor is excluded. The article by Vitacco et al. (2005) illustrates the point rather well. They calculated the correlations between the PCL:SV and 20-week follow-up reports of violence and aggression in the MacArthur risk assessment study of civil psychiatric patients (Steadman et al., 2000). Vitacco et al. found, with the Small-3 model, that violence/aggression was uncorrelated with the Interpersonal factor but significantly correlated with the Affective (.34) and Lifestyle (.11) factors. With the four-factor model, violence/aggression was uncorrelated with the Interpersonal and Lifestyle factors, whereas the correlation with the Affective factor increased to .41, and the correlation with the Antisocial factor was .40.

Of course, factor analysis is not the only way of looking at the structural properties of the PCL–R and the construct it measures. For example, clinicians and researchers long have wondered whether psychopathy is better represented as a dimension or as a discrete category, or taxon. I have been more or less neutral on the issue, but my "gut feeling" always has been that it is the latter, a feeling that found some support in a PCL–R study by Harris, Rice, and Quinsey (1994). However, the study was based on the use of file reviews to score the PCL–R, and it seemed likely that their taxon was more a reflection of antisociality than of psychopathy. More recent analyses of a large set of PCL–R scores obtained from interview and file reviews provided evidence that the PCL–R and its four factors reflect dimensional constructs (Guay, Ruscio, Knight, & Hare, 2005). The issue is far from settled, however. It will be interesting to see, for example, if some of the dependent variables in laboratory research (e.g., ERPs, cerebral activation, autonomic arousal, biochemistry, indices of learning, and information-processing) are linearly related to PCL–R scores (suggesting dimensionality) or if there is a point (or range) at which discontinuity occurs (suggesting taxonicity). If the latter is found and if the Guay et al. findings should be replicated, this would suggest that the dimensionality of the PCL–R scores might reflect rater test characteristics rather than the "nature" of psychopathy.

IRT has proven useful in helping to understand the structure of psychopathy and the PCL–R. As indicated by Bolt (chap. 5, this volume), IRT provides information about the ways in which items and test scores relate to the latent trait they purport to measure. Each item can be described in terms of its discriminating value with respect to the latent trait, and the level or threshold at which it discriminates. IRT studies of the PCL–R (Bolt, Hare, Vitale, & Newman, 2004; Cooke & Michie, 1997) and the PCL:SV (Cooke, Michie, Hart, & Hare, 1999) indicate that the original Factor 1 items are more discriminating of psychopathy than are the original Factor 2 items, but that all items contribute to the measurement of the construct. IRT can also help to determine the extent to which items and test scores have scalar equivalence across groups. When one is comparing different groups for scalar equivalence, IRT provides information about group differences in the item–trait relationship. When a difference occurs, the item is said to exhibit differential item functioning (DIF). IRT also provides information about the scalar equivalence of total test scores, depicted by test characteristic curves (TCCs). Multigroup studies indicate that most Factor 1 items show less DIF than do Factor 2 items. Several large-sample studies (using as anchors items that do not show DIF) revealed that the TCCs are similar for male and female offenders, male forensic psychiatric patients, African-American and Caucasian offenders, and various ethnic and cultural groups, indicating considerable metric equivalence across various populations (generalizability) at the total test score level (Bolt et al., 2004; Cooke, Kosson, & Michie, 2001; Cooke, Michie, Hart, & Clarke, 2005a). However, it is important to be cautious about the limitations of IRT in testing for metric equivalence. The procedures and rationale used to select anchor items influence the observed metric equivalence of different groups or cultures. For example, Cooke, Michie, Hart, and Clarke (2005b) used only three anchor items to argue that a given PCL–R score for United Kingdom (UK) offenders represented a higher level of the trait of psychopathy than did the same score for North American (NA) offenders. However, as Bolt, Hare, and Newman (2006) have pointed out, the procedures for selecting the anchor items seemed somewhat arbitrary. The use of more appropriate sets of anchor items clearly indicated that there was good metric equivalence between UK and NA offenders, with a given PCL–R score reflecting the same level of psychopathy in each group (similar analyses are reported in appendix B of the 2nd Edition of the PCL–R Manual). The issue is of more than academic interest; the Cooke et al. (2005b) analyses identify considerably more UK offenders as psychopathic than do the Bolt et al. (2006) analyses.

Meanwhile, the recent use of multidimensional scaling (MDS) as a nonlinear supplement to factor analysis provides an additional perspective on the structure of psychopathy. A multidimensional scaling analysis of the PCL–R by Bishopp and Hare (2005) indicated that the emergent structure of the PCL–R psychopathy can be interpreted in more than one way and at different levels of specificity. Multidimensional scalograms revealed a set of facets consistent with the two- and four-factor solutions that emerged from the same data set. They suggested that the structure of the PCL–R can be interpreted, through personality theory, as a set of core traits and behavioral manifestations, consistent with an evolutionary basis for psychopathic tendencies. The analyses provided support for a multidimensional structure within the PCL–R, consistent with the four-factor model and suggested that psychopathy can be viewed as an extreme variant of multiple dimensions of personality. Similar suggestions emerge from research in which psychopathy is viewed from the perspective of general personality theory (e.g., Harpur, Hart, & Hare, 2002; Lynam, 2002a; Skeem, Miller, Mulvey, Tiemann, & Monahan, 2005; Widiger, 2006; Widiger & Lynam, 1998).

Of course, the full meaning of these structural analyses of the PCL–R will not become clear until they are integrated with a body of data external to the PCL–R (and other measures of psychopathy).

ETIOLOGY AND DEVELOPMENTAL COURSE

"I do not believe obvious mistreatment or any simple egregious parental errors can justifiably be held as the regular cause of a child's developing this complex disorder" (Cleckley, 1976, p. 24).

There is little doubt that a large proportion of criminals come from seri-ously dysfunctional and disruptive family backgrounds. Many might be described as *sociopathic* (Lykken, 1995), a term that has been applied to indi-viduals whose antisocial attitudes and behaviors largely are molded by their early experiences, role models, and peer groups. Unlike psychopaths, who cannot be understood solely in terms of adverse social forces, they have a capacity for empathy, remorse, and loyalty to their own group.

A major problem in uncovering the developmental precursors of psy-chopathy has been the failure to include, at an early age, measures of the personality traits that might be relevant to psychopathy. Until recently, researchers would apply such measures *after* the individuals had matured, making it difficult to unravel cause and effect. For example, the study by Weiler and Widom (1996) often is cited as providing evidence for an asso-ciation between child abuse and adult psychopathy. In a prospective cohorts design, they followed into adulthood 652 children for whom there was documented evidence of child abuse or neglect, and 489 matched con-trol subjects. The PCL–R was scored from interview and available collateral information approximately 20 years after the abuse or neglect. The mean PCL–R score was 9.2 ($SD = 6.9$) for the abuse group and 6.8 ($SD = 5.9$) for the control group. Some commentators have taken these findings to indi-cate that abuse and neglect are *causal* factors in psychopathy. However, the authors acknowledged that they could not determine whether the psycho-pathic traits preceded or followed the abuse. Further, in view of the low PCL–R scores for each group, the findings may have less to do with the development of psychopathy as a clinical construct than with the correlates of a few psychopathic features. Clearly, the only way to unravel this prob-lem is to obtain information about relevant traits at the beginning of a prospective study.

Research along these lines is well under way, with downward extensions of psychopathy to adolescence and childhood (see Forth & Book, chap. 14, this volume; Frick, chap. 13, this volume; Frick & Marsee, 2006). This work is greatly facilitated by the availability of reliable and valid scales for the assessment of psychopathic traits and behaviors in adolescence and child-hood, including the PCL:YV, the CPS (Lynam, 1998, 2002b), Frick's Psy-chopathy Screening Device, formally published as the APSD (Frick & Hare, 2001), and the self-report YPI (Andershed et al., 2002).

Although it is clear that adult psychopathy has to come from *somewhere*, the idea of looking for its roots in childhood and adolescence is controversial. Aside from the potentially serious issues associated with labeling, most of the concern has to do with measurement issues and with the stability of psycho-pathic traits from adolescence to adulthood. Good progress has already been made with respect to measurement, but resolution of the stability issue will require extensive longitudinal research. The information available thus far is encouraging for those who believe that potentially psychopathic traits emerge early and are stable from childhood into adulthood. For example, Frick and his colleagues (Frick, chap. 13, this volume; Frick & Marsee, 2006) have shown that callous–unemotional (CU) traits, as measured by the APSD, can be observed at a very early age and that these traits have considerable explanatory and predictive value. They also appear to be reasonably stable across periods of 3 or 4 years. Lynam (2004) has used the CPS in an accelerated, multiple cohort, longitudinal design (three large cohorts of 7-, 10-, and 13 year olds) to investigate the stability of psychopathic traits from adolescence. He concluded that juvenile psychopathy can be measured at an early age, that it provides predictive utility and is quite stable from adolescence into early adulthood and that it is unlikely that developmentally normative change will masquerade as psychopathy (also see Forth & Book, chap. 14, this volume).

Behavioral genetics researchers are providing new insights into the etiology of psychopathy. Blonigen, Hicks, Krueger, Patrick, and Iacono (2005) used the MPQ (Tellegen, in press) to estimate psychopathic traits in 17-year-old monozygotic (MZ) and dizygotic (DZ) twins in the Minnesota Twin-Family Study. They concluded that the interpersonal–affective (Fearless Dominance) and antisocial (Impulsive Antisociality) traits of psychopathy, as measured by the MPQ "are equally and substantially heritable, with each accounting for roughly half of the total variance in both men and women" (p. 644). Larsson, Andershed, and Lichstenstien (in press) administered the YPI to Swedish MZ and DZ twins, all 16 or 17 years old. They concluded that "A genetic factor explains most of the variation in the psychopathic personality." Viding, Blair, Moffitt, and Plomin (2005) used items similar to those in the APSD to assess heritability of antisocial behaviors and CU traits in a very large sample of English 7-year-old twins. They concluded that genes account for 70% of the individual differences in CU traits, that the core symptoms of psychopathy are strongly genetically determined, and that the genetic contribution is highest when CU traits are combined with antisocial behaviors.

Thus far, the evidence for genetic determinants of psychopathy is based on research using self-reports and simple observer ratings of psychopathic (or psychopathy-related) traits and behaviors. It is very likely that similar findings will be obtained when structured assessments are used to assess psychopathy. Meanwhile, the increasing evidence that psychopathic traits have a substantial genetic basis may lead to the belief that some individuals are destined to become psychopaths. However, both the environment and environmental–genetic interactions also are very important in shaping personality and its behavioral manifestations, as well as "subtypes" of psychopathy (see Hervé, chap. 17, this volume; also see Poythress & Skeem, 2005). As twins are followed into adulthood, we will gain new insights into the etiological and developmental factors of psychopathy. I might note that the early results from behavioral genetics research are consistent with the evolutionary psychology view that psychopathy is less a result of a neurobiological defect than a heritable, adaptive life-strategy (Harris & Rice, 2005). In this view, the early emergence of antisocial behavior, including aggressive sexuality, is central to psychopathy.

NEUROIMAGING

In the past decade, researchers concerned with the psychophysiological correlates of psychopathy began to add a powerful new tool to their armamentarium—neuroimaging. To my knowledge, the first functional brain-imaging
study of psychopathy was conducted by Intrator et al. (1997) at the Bronx VA
Center. We used single-photon emission computerized tomography to monitor cortical and subcortical relative blood flow while psychopathic substance
abusers and control subjects performed a lexical decision task. This was an
extension of the study by Williamson, Harpur, and Hare (1991), who found
that nonpsychopaths differentiated between neutral and negative words
(decision times and event-related brain potentials), whereas psychopaths did
not. Intrator et al. found that psychopaths showed *greater* activation to the
emotional words than to the neutral words in frontal–temporal cortical
regions and contiguous subcortical areas, whereas nonpsychopaths showed
the opposite effect. We speculated that this unexpected finding was an indication that in normal individuals, the neurophysiological processes involved
in decoding the affective information contained in words are so overlearned
and automatic that metabolic demands are less than for the processing of
neutral words. For psychopaths, we reasoned that emotional words were difficult for them to process, much like trying to communicate in a poorly
learned second language and thus were less automatic and required more
cortical and subcortical activation than was the case for neutral words. Interestingly, this interpretation of our results is consistent with a more recent
functional magnetic resonance imaging (fMRI) study by Schneider et al.
(2000). They found that in a differential classical conditioning paradigm normal individuals showed a *decrease* in the activity of the amygdala and dorsolateral prefrontal cortex, whereas psychopaths showed an *increase* in the
activity of these areas. The authors suggested that this was a result of "an
additional effort put in by (the psychopaths) to form negative emotional associations, a pattern of processing that may correspond to their characteristic
deviant emotional behavior" (p. 192).

    Since the original study by Intrator et al. (1997), there have been several
dozen imaging studies, both structural and functional, of persons with psychopathy. Although this research has not uncovered any significant or consistent signs of brain damage or structural defects, several studies have indicated that psychopathy might be associated with slight anomalies in some
limbic and cortical structures (see reviews by Hare, 2003; Raine & Yang, 2006;
Rogers, 2005). More consistent results have been obtained with fMRI (see
review by Raine & Yang, 2006; also see Blair, 2006; Kiehl et al., 1999, 2001,
2004; Müller et al., 2003; Schneider et al., 1998; Söderström et al., 2002; Veit
et al., 2002). I think it is becoming clear that psychopathy will not be understood as a defect or anomaly in any one brain region. Rather, it is probably
the result of poor or abnormal integration of many regions. It also is possible that many of the functional differences observed are related to the use of
unusual cognitive and affective processing strategies, perhaps the result of

some interactions between genetically based dispositions and life experiences. In any case, the neuroimaging studies of brain-personality-behavior relationships will provide remarkable new insights into the problem of psychopathy over the next few years, particularly when combined with behavioral genetics (Waldman & Rhee, 2005), neurochemistry (Minzenberg & Siever, 2006), and cognitive processing (Hiatt & Newman, 2006).

THEORIES AND MODELS

Some investigators have wondered why I have not developed a theory of psychopathy. I suppose one reason is that I simply am not a theorist. Another might have to do with my traumatic exposure to the grand theories and model-building fever that dominated the field of psychology when I was a graduate student. Then, most research endeavors were directed more to generating and testing formal, theory-driven hypotheses than to accumulating as much information about a topic as possible. Few of these theories have survived intact, most being replaced by more modest, circumscribed efforts. Much of my research has been guided by various *mini-theories* of psychopathy, including those having to do with cerebral specialization and cognitive–affective integration. Fortunately, there are some investigators with the talent and interest in integrating the mini-theories and developing more general theories of psychopathy. Several have chapters in this volume (see Newman et al., chap. 7, this volume; Patrick, chap. 8, this volume; Herba et al., chap. 9, this volume; also see Patrick, 2006). I am particularly impressed with the systematic and insightful theoretical and empirical work of Joseph Newman and his colleagues, and with their response modulation model of psychopathy (Newman et al., chap. 7, this volume; Hiatt & Newman, 2006). The model is more general than most and accounts rather well for many of the clinical and laboratory findings on psychopathy.

CRIMINAL JUSTICE

The PCL and the PCL–R had their origins in research with criminal populations, not because I was particularly interested in criminals but because it was much easier to study psychopathy in a group in which its prevalence was high and there was sufficient information to conduct assessments. As my students, colleagues, and I accumulated PCL and PCL–R scores, we began to think about using criminal variables as part of the construct validation of these instruments. The subsequent explosion of research in the criminal justice system was unexpected. In general, this research has provided strong support for the validity of the PCL and PCL–R, particularly with respect to the prediction of recidivism and violence (see Harris & Rice, chap. 3, this volume; Hemphill, chap. 6, this volume; O'Toole, chap. 10, this volume; & Spidel, chap. 12, this volume).

Risk Assessment

Perhaps the most common criminal justice use of the PCL–R and its derivatives is in the risk assessment business, in which they typically are referred to as *risk scales*. However, it is important to keep in mind that these instruments were designed as measures of the construct of psychopathy, not as risk tools. If the construct is relevant in a particular context, then we might expect the PCL–R and its derivatives to facilitate understanding and prediction. However, their validity is not determined solely, or even largely, by their explanatory and predictive role in the criminal justice system. Construct validation involves exploring a network of associations between an instrument and a wide variety of variables, including diverse self-reports and ratings of personality, attitudes, and behaviors, other clinical assessments, behavioral genetics, developmental factors, and laboratory findings from studies of cognition, information processing, learning, emotion, psychophysiology, neuroimaging, and so forth.

Some investigators and commentators believe that purpose-built actuarial scales generally are superior to the PCL–R (and other structured clinical instruments) in predicting recidivism and violence and that the PCL–R therefore is not useful for the assessment of risk. Actuarial scales were developed to maximize predictive efficiency in a particular context, but their performance tends to be context-specific. They may work well with the population and for the purpose for which they were developed but not so well in other populations and contexts. In contrast, the PCL–R and its derivatives were developed to maximize assessment efficiency of a clinical construct. Their predictive power is generalizable to a variety of populations (e.g., criminal, forensic psychiatric, civil psychiatric, noncriminal, adult, and adolescent) and contexts (e.g., general, violent, and sexually offending, nature of the violence, treatment outcome, institutional behavior, and spousal abuse), in which the construct of psychopathy has theoretical or empirical relevance. An advantage of actuarial scales is that they can be scored by technicians and clerks, whereas assessments of psychopathy and other clinical constructs require considerable time and effort by qualified psychologists and psychiatrists. However, psychological and psychiatric assessments are a large part of what clinicians do for a living, and actuarial scales may tell them little about the nature of the individual offender, patient, or client, beyond his or her level of risk. As one of my former students put it, ". . . psychopathy is such a robust and important risk factor for violence that failure to consider it may constitute professional negligence" (Hart, 1998, p. 133).

Because of the importance of psychopathy, some actuarial scales, such as the Violence Risk Appraisal Guide (VRAG; Quinsey, Harris, Rice, & Cormier, 1998) and the classification tree (CT) model developed in the MacArthur Risk Assessment Study of civil psychiatric patients (Steadman et al., 2000) include the PCL–R or the PCL:SV (as the most potent predictors) in their assessment of risk. The same is true of some sophisticated structured-clinical scales, including the HCR-20 (Webster, Douglas, Eaves, & Hart, 1997). Some clinicians may wish to omit the assessment of psychopathy because it requires training and experience and is too time-consuming. However Webster, Müller-Isberner, and Fransson (2002, p. 46) urged that "the PCL–R and PCL:SV be recognized as pivotal measures." In the VRAG, CT, and HCR-20, "psychopathy stands out. . . . It therefore makes no sense to exclude it. . . . When the stakes are high, both for the individual under assessment and for the members of society in general, omission of the psychopathy item cannot easily be justified." I might note that the time required to complete a PCL–R assessment often is exaggerated and is predicated on the assumption that one must do so "from scratch." But clinicians generally base their evaluation of a client on the integration of as much interview and collateral information as possible, most of which can also be used in a PCL–R assessment.

Actuarial risk tools and the PCL–R differ primarily in their source of information and their method of measurement. The former rely heavily upon the aggregation of scores derived from simple counting, scoring, or low-level inferences, whereas the latter aggregates scores derived from structured clinical reports of judgments and inferences. Both are what Westen and Weinberger (2004) describe as *statistical/actuarial* methods for aggregating information and can be contrasted with informal and unstructured clinical methods of aggregation. They state that ". . . clinician reports are likely to be most useful when responses require experience with psychopathology. They are also useful when the domain being assessed, even if inaccessible to self-report, has manifestations in behavior that can be decoded (implicitly or explicitly) by an experienced observer; when the population of interest is represented among patients seen in clinical practice settings or can be represented using targeted sampling strategies (e.g., collecting data from clinicians who work in forensic settings to study psychopathy); and when the clinician knows the patient relatively well" (p. 602). Westen and Weinberger (2004) further note that

> . . . there is no substitute for clinical experience in generating hypotheses and devising clinically relevant items for use in research. Consider the concept of psychopathy, a precursor to the *DSM–IV* antisocial PD [personality disorder] diagnosis. The psychopathy construct is currently experiencing a renaissance (and a likely return in some form to a future *DSM*) because it tends to be more predictive of outcomes than the antisocial diagnosis, which focuses more on antisocial behaviors and less on underlying personality dispositions (e.g., Hare, 1998; Lorenz & Newman, 2002). Virtually all current research on psychopathy, however, presupposes the observations of a brilliant clinical observer (Cleckley, 1941), whose clinical immersion among psychopaths over 60 years ago still provides the foundation for the measure considered the gold standard in psychopathy research (Hare et al., 1991). Had Cleckley not identified and aggregated a set of important variables in the best sense of "clinical" intended by Meehl, we would *have* no statistical prediction. (p. 599)

Further, when "clinical observations are quantified using standard psychometric procedures . . . clinical description becomes statistical prediction"

(p. 595). I might add that clinical description and statistical prediction are necessary prerequisites to the management and reduction of risk in psychopathic individuals.

Law Enforcement

Almost 15 years ago two agent/instructors with the Federal Bureau of Investigation (FBI), Anthony Pinizzotto and Edward Davis, conducted an interesting study on the characteristics of the killers of police officers (Pinizzotto & Davis, 1992). Almost half of the killers had personality and behavior features virtually identical with psychopathy. Their findings are consistent with more recent data on the instrumental, cold-blooded nature of psychopathic violence and murder (Porter & Porter, chap. 10 this volume; Woodworth & Porter, 2002).

In the past few years, interest in psychopathy has sharply increased among law enforcement personnel, particularly with respect to crime-scene analysis, interviewing, and hostage negotiations. A good example is the use of psychopathy by Special Supervisory Agent Mary Ellen O'Toole of the FBI's National Center for the Analysis of Violent Crime to help understand crime-scenes (chap. 11, this volume). Mary Ellen has a Ph.D., is one of the FBI's top "profilers," and works on many of their most important murder and serial murder cases. She and I first met at the 1998 conference in Seattle on psychopathy by the Most Dangerous Offender Project, King County Prosecuting Attorney's Office. We were speakers at the conference, with an audience that consisted of prosecuting attorneys and homicide investigators. While I was giving my presentation, several participants in the front row kept saying, "Oh shit," as they made copious notes. I wondered at the time if this was an editorial comment on my presentation. The next day, Mary Ellen gave her presentation, a real eye-opener for me. She described how she used the literature on psychopathy to aid in her investigation of homicide crime scenes, often involving serial murder. When she and I met with the people who had made the comments during my talk, we learned that they were homicide investigators who had spent many fruitless hours trying to get a suspect, already implicated in several murders, to confess to a series of other murders. Later, we received a letter from the King County Prosecutors Office thanking us for helping to get the suspect to confess to the other murders. They had realized that the suspect may be a psychopath and that the interrogation procedure ("Think about the family of the victims;" "You'll feel better if you tell us about it") was counterproductive. Their new tactic was to appeal to his sense of importance and grandiosity ("If you give these murders up you won't be Ted Bundy but you'll be the big man on campus"). It worked.

Since then I have spent a considerable amount of time consulting with the FBI and sit on the Research Advisory Board of the FBI Child Abduction and Serial Murder Investigative Resources Center (CASMIRC). Mary Ellen, her colleagues at the FBI, and I have been working to develop procedures that will help criminal investigators to apply psychopathy to their work. We have been joined by Matt Logan and his colleagues at the Behavioral Sciences Group of the Royal Canadian Mounted Police (RCMP). Matt has been an RCMP officer for more than 20 years, and several years ago completed a Ph.D. in psychology, while working in a Federal prison where he did many PCL–R assessments. He does hostage negotiations and directs an innovative study for the RCMP in which high-risk sex offenders are identified, assessed with a battery of instruments (including the PCL–R), and tracked in the community after their release from prison. Our plan is to develop a shortened version of the *P-Scan* (Hare & Hervé, 1999), a tool designed to help criminal investigators generate useful hypotheses about the likelihood that a suspect is psychopathic. The new tool will provide investigators with information about the "subtype" of psychopathy that might be involved and with a range of possible response scenarios. Law enforcement personnel have shown particular interest in subtypes of psychopathy (Hervé, chap. 17, this volume) and in the motivations for psychopathic violence (Porter & Porter, chap. 10, this volume). We propose to codify some of this information in a form that will be useful to investigators.

Of course, there is nothing new about the role played by psychologists in law enforcement. What is new is the specific use of *psychopathy* to help law enforcement, security, and intelligence personnel to understand better the people with whom they deal. This is a trend that probably will continue and expand into related areas of the criminal justice system.

EXTENSIONS TO SOCIETY

Although most of the theory and research on psychopathy over the years has been focused on the offender and psychiatric populations, there is increasing interest in extending this work to the general population. This enterprise is facilitated by the development and validation of instruments, many of them self-report, that permit the acquisition of data from samples for which little collateral information is available. It also is encouraging to see general personality theorists paying more attention to the topic. Their attempts to understand psychopathy as extreme variants of personality dimensions is consistent with recent findings on its dimensionality (Bishopp & Hare, 2005; Guay et al., 2005).

Recently, there has been a great deal of interest in the role of psychopathy in organizations, largely because of the large number of recent corporate scandals and frauds. Babiak (1995, 2000, chap. 16, this volume) has used the PCL:SV in his study of corporate executives and has described in detail how psychopathic management personnel enter and function in an organization. Based on the P-Scan principles and format, we developed the *B-Scan-360* (Babiak & Hare, 2005) as a research tool for use in identifying and managing corporate personnel with many psychopathic features.

TREATMENT AND MANAGEMENT

Perhaps one of the most frustrating experiences for clinicians is the gap between what they would like to do and what they actually accomplish in psychopathy treatment programs. The intractability of psychopathic offenders and patients is well known. Despite occasional claims to the contrary, there is no credible empirical evidence that "anything works." Nor is there evidence that "nothing works." The issues involved in the treatment, intervention, and management of psychopathic offenders and patients have been well-described elsewhere (see Harris & Rice, 2006; Wong & Hare, 2005; Wong & Burt, chap. 18, this volume; Thornton & Blud, chap. 20, this volume).

Some historical anecdotes may be useful here. In 1990 the Director of Research and Statistics (DRS) for the Correctional Service of Canada (CSC) commissioned me to develop a treatment/management program for psychopathic offenders. I put together an international team of researchers, clinician, and treatment experts and submitted a report to CSC in 1992. After receiving no response for about 6 months, an old and well-connected friend arranged a luncheon meeting for us with the Assistant Attorney General of the United States. We discussed what we did with violent psychopathic offenders in the United States and Canada, and the report I had submitted to CSC came up. The Assistant Attorney General then asked for a copy, but I replied that I first would have to check with the DRS. When I did so, he and a small team from CSC flew to Vancouver several days later. We had intensive meetings with the warden and staff of a CSC prison near Vancouver and concluded with a detailed plan to implement the program. Six months passed, with no further progress, until a local reporter doing a story on the treatment of psychopathic sex offenders asked me what advice I might give her. I said that she should contact CSC. She did so, and several days later the DRS and his team again appeared in Vancouver. This time, we expanded on our previous meeting and arrived at a new, improved plan, as well as a budget. Soon after, the DRS left his position with CSC, and it was taken up by a psychologist with little interest in psychopathy or in the differential treatment of psychopathic offenders. Apparently, my report was put on a shelf and disappeared. Later, because of some media concerns about the correctional treatment of psychopaths, CSC asked me for a copy.

I mention all of this because even in the early 1990s my colleague, Stephen Wong, a psychologist with CSC and a major contributor to the report, and I were concerned that the one-treatment-fits-all philosophy was partly responsible for the poor outcomes of treated psychopaths (see Harris & Rice, 2006). We continued to work on a treatment program and recently published the *Guidelines for a Psychopathy Treatment Program* (PTP; Wong & Hare, 2005).

Some 10 years ago a major treatment initiative began to take shape in England and Wales under the auspices of the Offending Behavior Programmes Unit (OBPU), Her Majesty's Prison (HMP) Service. David Thornton (see

Thornton & Blud, chap. 20, this volume) was the driving force behind the initiative, which included several clinical and research Advisory Panels charged with helping to develop a treatment program for psychopathic offenders and a series of PCL–R Workshops conducted by Adelle Forth and me. Among the Advisory Panel members were Adelle Forth, Stephen Wong, James Blair, and I. The meetings were organized and directed by David Thornton, Linda Blud, and Gill Attrill. An important aspect of the initiative established by David Thornton and maintained and developed by Gill Attrill and her team at OBPU is the requirement that all HMP psychologists be well trained on the PCL–R and on the issues and problems associated with attempts to work with psychopathic offenders in a therapeutic context. Versions of the OBPU program are now in use in HMP prisons and in the Dangerous and Severe Personality Disorder program in England and Wales. Outcome data should be available in the near future.

The philosophy behind these programs is that rather than giving up on psychopathic offenders and patients, it makes more sense to search for ways in which their propensity for offending and violence can be managed, without futile attempts to produce fundamental changes in their personality. Many correctional administrators and treatment providers seem to believe that all any offender needs to become a productive citizen is a hug, a musical instrument, and a puppy dog. In contrast, I believe that psychopathic individuals will agree to adhere to prosocial norms only if they realize that it is in their own best interest to do so (see Wong & Hare, 2005).

WHERE DO WE GO FROM HERE?

Things certainly are not what they used to be! Forty years ago there were few researchers in psychopathy and a relatively small body of literature on the topic. On the one hand, this made the job of we few in the area much easier because the literature was not difficult to summarize and integrate. I started out with a small box of 4 × 6 index cards, a system of filing that worked well for quite a few years. The lack of empirical data also made it easy for some researchers to theorize and speculate. On the other hand, it was hard to build a credible edifice without bricks.

Today we have a lot more bricks and no shortage of talented people who know what to do with them. The field has exploded over the past few years, not only in terms of applied areas, such as the mental health and criminal justice systems, but in terms of the search for basic mechanisms and processes. The quantity and quality of theory and research now available are truly awe-inspiring, especially to one who is familiar with the early efforts in the field. If the recent trend continues, there is a good chance that scientific and applied work in psychopathy will increase exponentially over the next decade. We will see the range and sophistication of research and theory increase even further, in large part because of the influx of new researchers and students who are at once highly motivated, questioning, and equipped with a remarkable armamentarium of skills and talents. We also will see a great increase in multidisciplinary programs of research, more attention being paid to concordant research on a variety of "spectrum" disorders and conditions (e.g., autism, Asperger's disorder, attention deficit hyperactivity disorder (ADHD), alexithymia, and so forth) that may have some psychobiological commonalities with psychopathy, and perhaps even the establishment of an International Psychopathy Research Institute, a long-time dream of mine.

Ten years ago one of my articles described psychopathy as a "clinical construct whose time has come" (Hare, 1996b). If I were to write a similar paper today I might refer to psychopathy as a "clinical construct here to stay."

ACKNOWLEDGMENT

I thank the many outstanding students and colleagues with whom I have been associated over the past 40 years. Our research has been facilitated by the cooperation and participation of the staff and inmates of the Correctional Service of Canada and by generous grants from the Medical Research Council of Canada, the Social Sciences and Humanities Research Council, and the Canadian Mental Health Association. I also thank John Yuille and Hugues Hervé for organizing the Festschrift that honored me and that was the impetus for this volume. Averil, my wife and best friend, whom I met in the back row of a class in abnormal psychology, continues to play a pivotal role in my life and research career. I could not have persisted this long without her wise counsel, her incisive discussions about what I was trying to do, and her loving presence. Our daughter and only child, Cheryl, enriched our lives and taught us about the courage, grace, and dignity of the human spirit in the face of adversity.

REFERENCES

Andershed, H., Kerr, M., Stattin, H., & Levander, S. (2002). Psychopathic traits in non-referred youths: A new assessment tool. In E. Blauuw & L. Sheridan (Eds.), *Psychopaths: Current international perspectives* (pp. 131–158). The Hague: Elsevier.

Babiak, P. (1995). When psychopaths go to work: A case study of an industrial psychopath. *Applied Psychology: An International Review, 44*, 171–178.

Babiak, P. (2000). Psychopathic manipulation at work. In C. Gacono (Ed.), *The clinical and forensic assessment of psychopathy: A practitioner's guide* (pp. 287–311). Mahwah, NJ: Lawrence Erlbaum Associates.

Babiak, P., & Hare, R. D. (2005). *The B-Scan 360: Research version*. Toronto, Ontario, Canada: Multi-Health Systems.

Benning, S. B., Patrick, C. J., Salekin, R. T., & Leistico, A. M. R. (2005). Convergent and discriminant validity of psychopathy factors assessed via self-report: A comparison of three instruments. *Assessment, 12*, 270–289.

Bishopp, D., & Hare, R. D. (2005, July). *A multidimensional scaling analysis of the PCL–R*. Poster presented at the inaugural meeting of the Society for the Scientific Study of Psychopathy, Vancouver, British Columbia, Canada.

Blair, R. J. R. (2006). Subcortical brain systems in psychopathy: The amygdala and associated structures. In C. J. Patrick (Ed.), *Handbook of psychopathy* (pp. 296–312). New York: Guilford Press.

Blonigen, D. M., Hicks, B. M., Krueger, R. F., Patrick, C. J., & Iacono, W. (2005). Psychopathic personality traits: Heritability and genetic overlap with internalizing and externalizing psychopathology. *Psychological Medicine, 35,* 1–12.

Bolt, D. M., Hare, R. D., & Newman, J. P. (2006). *Score metric equivalence of the PCL–R across North American and European criminal offenders: A critique of recent practice and a new analysis.* Manuscript under review.

Bolt, D. M., Hare, R. D., Vitale, J. E., & Newman, J. P. (2004). A multigroup item response theory analysis of the Psychopathy Checklist–Revised. *Psychological Assessment, 16,* 155–168.

Cleckley, H. (1941). *The mask of sanity.* St. Louis: Mosby.

Cleckley, H. (1956). *The mask of sanity* (3rd ed.). St. Louis: Mosby.

Cleckley, H. (1976). *The mask of sanity* (5th ed.). St. Louis: Mosby.

Cooke, D. J., Forth, A. E., & Hare, R. D. (Eds.). (1998). *Psychopathy: Theory, research, and implications for society.* Dordrecht, The Netherlands: Kluwer.

Cooke, D. J., Kosson, D. S., & Michie, C. (2001). Psychopathy and ethnicity: Structural, item, and test generalizability of the Psychopathy Checklist–Revised (PCL–R) in Caucasian and African American participants. *Psychological Assessment, 13,* 531–542.

Cooke, D. J., & Michie, C. (1997). An item response theory analysis of the Hare Psychopathy Checklist–Revised. *Psychological Assessment, 9,* 3–14.

Cooke, D. J., & Michie, C. (2001). Refining the construct of psychopathy: Towards a hierarchical model. *Psychological Assessment, 13,* 171–188.

Cooke, D. J., Michie, C., Hart, S. D., & Clark, D. (2005a). Searching for the pan-cultural core of psychopathic personality disorder. *Personality and Individual Differences, 39,* 283–295

Cooke, D. J., Michie, C., Hart, S. D., & Clark, D. (2005b). Assessing psychopathy in the UK: Concerns about cross-cultural generalisability. *British Journal of Psychiatry, 18,* 335–341.

Cooke, D. J., Michie, C., Hart, S. D., & Hare, R. D. (1999). Evaluating the. Screening Version of the Hare Psychopathy Checklist–Revised (PCL:SV): An item response theory analysis. *Psychological Assessment, 11,* 3–13.

Costa, P. T., & McCrae, R. R. (1992). The five-factor model of personality and its relevance to personality disorders. *Journal of Personality Disorders, 6,* 343–359.

Costa, P. T., & Widiger, T. A. (2002). *Personality disorder and the five-factor model of personality* (2nd ed.). Washington: American Psychological Association.

Cronbach, L. J., & Meehl, P. E. (1955). Construct validity of psychological tests. *Psychological Bulletin, 52,* 281–302.

Forth, A. E., Kosson, D., & Hare, R. D. (2003). *The Hare Psychopathy Checklist: Youth Version (PCL:YV).* Toronto, Ontario, Canada: Multi-Health Systems.

Frick, P. J., & Hare, R. D. (2001). *The Antisocial Process Screening Device.* Toronto, Ontario, Canada: Multi-Health Systems.

Frick, P. J., & Marsee, M. A. (2006). Psychopathy and developmental pathways to antisocial behavior in youth. In C. J. Patrick (Ed.), *Handbook of psychopathy* (pp. 353–374). New York: Guilford Press.

Guay, J. P., Ruscio, J., Knight, R. A., & Hare, R. D. (2005, July). *The latent structure of psychopathy: When more is simply more.* Paper presented at the inaugural meeting of the Society for the Scientific Study of Psychopathy, Vancouver, British Columbia, Canada.

Hare, R. D. (1965a). Acquisition and generalization of a conditioned fear response in psychopathic and nonpsychopathic criminals. *Journal of Psychology, 59*, 367–370.

Hare, R. D. (1965b). A conflict and learning theory analysis of psychopathic behavior. *Journal of Research in Crime and Delinquency, 2*, 12–19.

Hare, R. D. (1965c). Psychopathy, fear arousal, and anticipated pain. *Psychological Reports, 16*, 499–502.

Hare, R. D. (1965d). Suppression of verbal behavior as a function of delay and schedule of severe punishment. *Journal of Verbal Learning and Verbal Behavior, 4*, 216–221.

Hare, R. D. (1980). A research scale for the assessment of psychopathy in criminal populations. *Personality and Individual Differences, 1*, 111–119.

Hare, R. D. (1986). Twenty years experience with the Cleckley psychopath. In W. H. Reid, D. Dorr, J. I. Walker, & J. W. Bonner III (Eds.), *Unmasking the psychopath* (pp. 3–27). New York: W. W. Norton.

Hare, R. D. (1991). *The Hare Psychopathy Checklist–Revised*. Toronto, Ontario, Canada: Multi-Health Systems.

Hare, R. D. (1996a). Psychopathy and antisocial personality disorder: A case of diagnostic confusion. *Psychiatric Times, 13*, 39–40.

Hare, R. D. (1996b). Psychopathy: A clinical construct whose time has come. *Criminal Justice and Behavior, 23*, 25–54.

Hare, R. D. (1997). The NATO Advanced Study Institute on psychopathy, Alvor, Portugal, 1995. *Journal of Personality Disorders, 11*, 301–303.

Hare, R. D. (1998). Psychopaths and their nature: Implications for the mental health and criminal justice systems. In T. Millon, E. Simonson, M. Burket-Smith, & R. Davis (Eds.), *Psychopathy: Antisocial, criminal, & violent behavior* (pp. 188–212). New York: Guilford Press.

Hare, R. D. (1998a). *Without conscience: The disturbing world of the psychopaths among us.* New York: Guilford Press.

Hare, R. D. (2003). *The Hare Psychopathy Checklist–Revised* (2nd ed.). Toronto, Ontario, Canada: Multi-Health Systems.

Hare, R. D., Hart, S. D., & Harpur, T. J. (1991). Psychopathy and the *DSM–IV* criteria for antisocial personality disorder. *Journal of Abnormal Psychology, 100*, 391–398.

Hare, R. D., & Hervé, H. (1999). *The Hare P-Scan: Research Version*. Toronto, Ontario, Canada: Multi-Health Systems.

Hare, R. D., & Neumann, C. S. (2005). Structural models of psychopathy. *Current Psychiatry Reports, 7*, 57–64.

Hare, R. D., & Neumann, C. S. (2006). The PCL–R assessment of psychopathy: Development, structural properties, and new directions. In C. Patrick (Ed.), *Handbook of psychopathy* (pp. 58–88). New York: Guilford Press.

Harpur, T. J., Hare, R. D., Zimmerman, M., & Corryell, W. (1990, August). *Dimensions underlying DSM-III personality disorders: Cluster 2*. Paper presented at the Annual Meeting of the American Psychological Association, Boston, MA.

Harpur, T. J., Hart, S. D., & Hare, R. D. (2002). The personality of the psychopath. In P. T. Costa & T. A. Widiger (Eds.), *Personality disorders and the five-factor model of personality* (2nd ed., pp. 299–324). Washington, DC: American Psychological Association.

Harris, G. T., & Rice, M. E. (2006). Treatment of psychopathy: A review of empirical findings. In C. Patrick (Ed.), *Handbook of psychopathy* (pp. 555–572), New York: Guilford Press.

Harris, G. T., Rice, M. E., & Quinsey, V. L. (1994). Psychopathy as a taxon: Evidence that psychopaths are a discrete class. *Journal of Consulting and Clinical Psychology, 62*, 387–397.

Hart, S. D. (1998). The role of psychopathy in assessing risk for violence: Conceptual and methodological issues. *Legal and Criminological Psychology, 3,* 121–137.

Hart, S. D., Cox, D. N., & Hare, R. D. (1995). *The Hare Psychopathy Checklist: Screening Version (PCL:SV).* Toronto, Ontario, Canada: Multi-Health Systems.

Hiatt, K. D., & Newman, J. P. (2006). Understanding psychopathy: The cognitive side. In C. J. Patrick (Ed.), *Handbook of psychopathy* (pp. 334–352). New York: Guilford Press.

Intrator, J., Hare, R., Strizke, P., Brichtswein, K., Dorfman, D., Harpur, T., Bernstein, D., et al. (1997). Brain imaging (SPECT) study of semantic and affective processing in psychopaths. *Biological Psychiatry, 2,* 96–103.

Kiehl, K. A., Bates, A. T., Laurens, K. R., Hare, R. D., & Liddle, P. F. (in press). Brain potentials implicate temporal lobe abnormalities in criminal psychopaths. *Journal of Abnormal Psychology.*

Kiehl, K. A., Hare, R. D., McDonald, J., & Brink, J. (1999). Semantic and affective processing in psychopaths: An event-related potential (ERP) study. *Psychophysiology, 36,* 765–774.

Kiehl, K. A., Liddle, P. F., Smith, A. M., Mendrek, A., Forster, B. B., & Hare, R. D. (1999). Neural pathways involved in the processing of concrete and abstract words. *Human Brain Mapping, 7,* 225–233.

Kiehl, K. A., Smith, A. M., Hare, R. D., Mendrek, A., Forster, B. B., Brink, J., & Liddle, P. F. (2001). Limbic abnormalities in affective processing by criminal psychopaths as revealed by functional magnetic resonance imaging. *Biological Psychiatry, 50,* 677–684.

Kiehl, K. A., Smith, A. M., Mendrek, A., Forster, B. B., Hare, R. D., & Liddle, P. F. (2004). Temporal lobe abnormalities in semantic processing by criminal psychopaths as revealed by functional magnetic resonance imaging. *Psychiatry Research: Neuroimaging, 130,* 27–42.

Larsson, H., Andershed, H., & Lichtenstein, P. (in press). A genetic factor explains most of the variation in the psychopathic personality. *Journal of Abnormal Psychology.*

Lilienfeld, S. O. (1990). *Development and preliminary validation of a self-report measure of psychopathic personality.* Unpublished doctoral dissertation, University of Minnesota, Minneapolis.

Lilienfeld, S. O., & Andrews, B. P. (1996). Development and preliminary validation of a self-report measure of psychopathic personality traits in noncriminal populations. *Journal of Personality Assessment, 66,* 488–524.

Lilienfeld, S. O., & Fowler, K. A. (2006). The self-report assessment of psychopathy: Problems, pitfalls, and promises. In C. J. Patrick (Ed.), *Handbook of psychopathy* (pp. 107–132). New York: Guilford Press.

Livesley, W. J., & Schroeder, M. L. (1991). Dimensions of personality disorder: The *DSM–III–R* cluster B diagnoses. *Journal of Nervous and Mental Disease, 179,* 320–328.

Lorenz, A. R., & Newman, J. P. (2002). Utilization of emotion cues in male and female offenders with antisocial personality disorder: Results from a lexical decision task. *Journal of Abnormal Psychology, 111,* 513–516.

Lykken, D. T. (1995). *The antisocial personalities.* Hillsdale, NJ: Lawrence Erlbaum Associates.

Lynam, D. R. (1997). Pursuing the psychopath: Capturing the fledgling psychopath in the nomological net. *Journal of Abnormal Psychology, 106,* 425–438.

Lynam, D. R. (1998). Early identification of the fledgling psychopath: Locating the psychopathic child in the current nomenclature. *Journal of Abnormal Psychology, 107,* 566–575.

Lynam, D. R. (2002a). Psychopathy from the perspective of the five-factor model of personality. In P. T. Costa & T. A. Widiger (Eds.), *Personality disorder and the five-factor model of personality* (2nd ed., pp. 325–348). Washington, DC: American Psychological Association.

Lynam, D. R. (2002b). Fledgling psychopathy: A view from personality theory. *Law and Human Behavior, 26,* 255–259.

Lynam, D. R. (2004, November). *Development and psychopathy.* Colloquium at the Department of Psychology, Northwestern University, Evanston, IL.

Minzenberg, M. J., & Siever, L. J. (2005). Neurochemistry and pharmacology of psychopathy and related disorders. In C. J. Patrick (Ed.). *Handbook of psychopathy* (pp. 251–277). New York: Guilford Press.

Müller, J. L., Sommer, M., Wagner, V., Lange, K., Taschler, H., Röder, C. H., et al. (2003). Abnormalities in emotion processing within cortical and subcortical regions in criminal psychopaths. Evidence from an fMRI study using pictures with emotional contents. *Biological Psychiatry, 54,* 152–162.

Neumann, C. S., Vitacco, M. J., Hare, R. D., & Wupperman, P. (2005). Re-construing the reconstruction of psychopathy: A reply to Cooke, Michie, Hart, & Clark. *Journal of Personality Disorders, 19,* 624–640.

Patrick, C. J. (Ed.). (2006). *Handbook of psychopathy.* New York: Guilford Press.

Paulhus, D., Hemphill, J., & Hare, R. D. (in press). *The SRP–III.* Toronto, Ontario, Canada: Multi-Health Systems.

Pinizzotto, A. J., & Davis, E. F. (1992). *Killed in the line of duty.* Washington, DC: U.S. Department of Justice, FBI Uniform Crime Reporting Program.

Poythress, N. G., & Skeem, J. L. (2006). Disaggregating psychopathy: Where and how to look for subtypes. In C. J. Patrick (Ed.). *Handbook of psychopathy* (pp. 172–192). New York: Guilford.

Quinsey, V. L., Harris, G. T., Rice, M. E., & Cormier, C. A. (1998). *Violent offenders: Appraising and managing risk.* Washington, DC: American Psychological Association.

Raine, A., & Yang, Y. (2006). The neuroanatomical bases of psychopathy: A review of brain imaging findings. In C. J. Patrick (Ed.). *Handbook of psychopathy* (pp. 278–295). New York: Guilford Press.

Rogers, R. D. (2006). The functional architecture of the frontal lobes: Implications for research with psychopathic offenders. In C. J. Patrick (Ed.), *Handbook of psychopathy* (pp. 313–333). New York: Guilford Press.

Rogers, R., Salekin, R. T., Sewell, K. W., & Cruise, K. R. (2000). Prototypical analysis of antisocial personality disorder: A study of inmate samples. *Criminal Justice and Behavior, 27,* 234–255.

Rutter, M. (2005). Commentary: What is the meaning and utility of the psychopathy concept? *Journal of Abnormal Child Psychology 33,* 499–503.

Schneider, F., Habel, U., Kessler, C., Posse, S., Grodd, W., & Müller-Gärtner, H. (2000). Functional imaging of conditioned aversive emotional responses in antisocial personality disorder. *Neuropsychobiology, 42,* 192–201.

Schneider, F., Weiss, U., Kessler, C., Salloum, J. B., Posse, S., Grodd, W., et al. (1998). Differential amygdala activation in schizophrenia during sadness. *Schizophrenia Research, 34,* 133–142.

Skeem, J. L., Miller, J. D., Mulvey, E., Tiemann, J., & Monahan, J. (2005). Using a five-factor lens to explore the relation between personality traits and violence in psychiatric patients. *Journal of Consulting and Clinical Psychology, 73,* 454–465.

Söderström, H., Hultin, L., Tullberg, M., Wikkelso, C., Ekholm, S., & Forsman, A. (2002). Reduced frontotemporal perfusion in psychopathic personality. *Psychiatry Research: Neuroimaging, 114,* 81–94.

Steadman, H. J., Silver, E., Monahan, J., Appelbaum, P. S., Robbins, P. C., Mulvey, E. P., et al. (2000). A classification tree approach to the development of actuarial violence risk assessment tools. *Law and Human Behavior, 24,* 83–100.

Tellegen, A. (in press). *Manual for the Multidimensional Personality Questionnaire.* Minneapolis, MN: University of Minnesota Press.

Ullrich, S., & Marneros, A. (2004). Dimensions of personality disorders in offenders. *Criminal Behaviour and Mental Health, 14,* 202–213

Veit, R., Flor, H., Erb, M., Hermann, C., Lotze, M., Grodd, W., et al. (2002). Brain circuits involved in emotional learning in antisocial behavior and social phobia in humans. *Neuroscience Letters, 328,* 233–236.

Viding, E., Blair, R. J. R., Moffitt, T. E., & Plomin, R. (2005). Evidence for substantial genetic risk for psychopathy in 7-year-olds. *Journal of Child Psychology and Psychiatry, 46,* 592–597.

Vitacco, M. J., Neumann, C. S., & Jackson, R. (2005). Testing a four-factor model of psychopathy and its association with ethnicity, gender, intelligence, and violence. *Journal of Consulting and Clinical Psychology, 73,* 466–76.

Waldman, I. D., & Rhee, S. H. (2006). Genetic and environmental influences on psychopathy and antisocial behavior. In C. J. Patrick (Ed.), *Handbook of psychopathy* (205–228). New York: Guilford Press.

Webster, C. D., Douglas, K. S., Eaves, D., & Hart, S. D. (1997). *HCR-20: Assessing risk for violence—Version 2.* Burnaby, British Columbia, Canada: Mental Health, Law and Policy Institute, Simon Fraser University.

Webster, C. D., Müller-Isberner, R., & Fransson, G. (2002). Violence risk assessment: Using structured clinical guides professionally. *International Journal of Forensic Mental Health, 1,* 43–51.

Weiler, B. L., & Widom, C. S. (1996). Psychopathy and violent behaviour in abused and neglected young adults. *Criminal Behaviour and Mental Health, 6,* 253–271.

Westen, D., & Wienberger, J. (2004). When clinical description becomes statistical prediction. *American Psychologist, 59,* 595–613.

Widiger, T. A. (2006). Psychopathy and *DSM–IV* psychopathology. In C. J. Patrick (Ed.), *Handbook of psychopathy* (pp. 156–171). New York: Guilford Press.

Widiger, T. A., Cadoret, R., Hare, R. D., Robins, L., Rutherford, M., Zanarini, M., et al. (1996). *DSM–IV* antisocial personality disorder field trial. *Journal of Abnormal Psychology, 105,* 3–16.

Widiger, T. A., & Lynam, D. R. (1998). Psychopathy from the perspective of the five-factor model of personality. In T. Millon, E. Simonson, M. Birket-Smith, & R. D. Davis. (Eds.), *Psychopathy: Antisocial, criminal, and violent behavior* (pp. 171–187). New York: Guilford Press.

Williamson, S. E., Harpur, T. J., & Hare, R. D. (1991). Abnormal processing of affective words by psychopaths. *Psychophysiology, 28,* 260–273.

Wong, S., & Hare, R. D. (2005). *Guidelines for a psychopathy treatment program.* Toronto, ON: Multi-Health Systems.

Woodworth, M., & Porter, S. (2002). In cold blood: Characteristics of criminal homicides as a function of psychopathy. *Journal of Abnormal Psychology, 111,* 436–445.

I

THE EVOLUTION OF THE CONSTRUCT

2

Psychopathy Across the Ages: A History of the Hare Psychopath

Hugues Hervé

Descriptions of psychopaths, instrumentally impulsive individuals with poor behavioral controls who callously and remorselessly bleed others for purely selfish reasons via manipulation, intimidation, and violence, are found across time and cultures. Arguably, it is their ability to easily supersede morality for personal gain and do so without remorse that made them such interesting topics of discussion throughout history. With the emergence and growth of mental health professions, their unique clinical picture—intelligent but socially deviant beings without emotional safeguards—has made them intriguing case studies. It is thus not surprising that the construct of psychopathy has a rich clinical foundation. Nonetheless, it was not until late in the 20th century, with the development of the Hare Psychopathy Scales, that psychopathy became a well-defined and accepted clinical syndrome. Before then, diagnostic confusion over the definition of psychopathy prevailed.

With the Hare psychopath in mind (Hare, 1991, 2003), in this chapter I provide a historical account of the growth of this construct, from its emergence in the psychiatric literature in the late 18th century to the development of the Hare Psychopathy Checklist in the late 20th century (Hare, 1980).[1] Although other historical accounts have been rendered, these were either conducted before an accepted definition was in place (e.g., Henderson, 1947; Werlinder, 1978) or focused more so on antisocial personality disorder (APD; e.g., Millon, Simonsen, & Birket-Smith, 1998), arguably a much broader construct, which potentially subsumes various conditions, than psychopathy per se (Cunningham & Reidy, 1998; Hart & Hare, 1996; Rogers, Duncan, Lynett, & Sewell, 1994). It is hoped that this chapter not only provides readers with a better understanding of the foundation from which the Hare psychopath evolved but also rekindles interest into important clinical features and theoretical accounts that were forgotten not because they were found invalid but because of political pressure and/or practical considerations. Furthermore, I hope to bring attention to the fact that many contemporary theories and research topics have, to one degree or another, deeper roots than suggested by the current literature.

---

[1]For a review of the history of the Hare Psychopathy Scales, please see Hare (1996a).

A HISTORY OF THE HARE PSYCHOPATH

Although psychopathic individuals have been described throughout the ages, psychopathy, as it was defined in the 20th century (Hare, 1991, 2003), only began evolving into a clinical concept in the late 1700s to early 1800s (see reviews by Henderson, 1947; Werlinder, 1978). Before that time, mental health problems were viewed as diseases of the mind or intellect (see Millon, Simonsen, & Birket-Smith, 1998; Werlinder, 1978) and, consequently, any discussion of psychopathy, which itself is best characterized as a disease of affect, was negated (e.g., Arieti, 1963; Cleckley, 1941/1988; Craft, 1966; Hare, 1996a; Karpman, 1955; McCord & McCord, 1964; also see Newman, 1998, for another view). By the late 18th century, however, psychiatric descriptions began to include problems in regulating affect and feeling as well as the mind (see McCord & McCord, 1964; Millon et al., 1998; Werlinder, 1978). These descriptions, in combination with the emerging view that antisocial actions could result from illness rather than just vice or evil forces (Rush, 1786/1972; Werlinder, 1978), laid the foundation for the development of the psychopathic construct as a real clinical entity.

THE CLINICAL TRADITION

An Emerging Construct

Pinel's manie sans delire

Although many anecdotal accounts regarding individuals with psychopathic traits were rendered, Pinel, a French psychiatrist, first designated this construct, which he termed *manie sans delire* (mania [or madness] without delirium) and later *manie/folie raisonnante* (madness-like), as a clinical syndrome (1801/1806, as cited in Henderson, 1947; also see McCord & McCord, 1964; Pichot, 1978). To Pinel, manie sans delire was diagnosed in psychiatric patients "who at no period gave evidence of any lesion of the understanding but who were under the domination of instinctive and abstract fury, as if the faculties of affect alone had sustained injury" (1801/1806, as cited in Werlinder, 1978, p. 29). Such individuals engaged in impulsive and socially unacceptable acts that had, more often than not, negative consequences for themselves and those involved. What struck Pinel the most was that these individuals, unlike those affected by other syndromes, were fully aware of the irrationality and destructive nature of their actions.

Rush's Moral Derangement

Around the same time but independent of Pinel, Rush, an American physician, described a similar condition, which he termed *moral derangement* or *anomia* (i.e., ethical derangement; 1812, as cited in Craft, 1966; Werlinder,

1978). Similar to Pinel's manie sans delire, persons who were morally deranged, although having intact intellect and reasoning abilities, engaged in socially disruptive behaviors and deception from an early age without showing remorse, guilt, or preoccupation with the negative consequences of their actions. Unlike Pinel, Rush emphasized the irresponsible and antisocial nature of such individuals and, therefore, turned a morally neutral syndrome into a socially condemned phenomenon (Millon et al., 1998), a value-laden position that has been debated ever since (i.e., Is it a disorder or a value judgment? Are they mentally ill or just bad? See Adshead, 2000; Benn, 2000; Blackburn, 1988, 1998a; Fenster, 1993; Gunn, 1998; Hare, 1996a; 1998b; Hedinbotham, 2000; Henderson, 1947; McCord & McCord, 1964; Millon et al., 1998; Schopp & Slain, 2000; Tucker, 1999; Werlinder, 1978).

Prichard's Moral Insanity

This morally loaded approach to defining psychopathy was also evident in the work of Prichard, an English physician (1835, as cited in Henderson, 1947; Berrios, 1999). Although often credited for providing the first comprehensive description of psychopathy (Henderson, 1947; Millon et al., 1998; Partridge, 1930), he, as can be seen from the preceding review, was not the first to do so. However, Prichard expanded previous conceptualizations and, unlike his predecessors, was instrumental in introducing Pinel's work and, more importantly, the concept, to the English-speaking world (Berrios, 1999; Werlinder, 1978). Like Pinel and Rush, Prichard viewed manie sans delire, or, as he termed it, *moral insanity* (later referred to as *moral imbecility* and *moral defective*, respectively), as a psychiatric state characterized by disordered affect in individuals whose understanding and intellect were nevertheless intact:

> There is likewise a form of mental derangement in which the intellectual faculties appear to have sustained little or no injury, while the disorder is manifested, principally or alone, in the state of the feelings, temper or habits. In cases of this nature, the moral and active principles of the mind are strongly perverted or depraved; the power of self-government is lost or greatly impaired and the individual is found to be incapable, not of talking or reasoning upon any subject proposed to him, but of conducting himself with decency and propriety in the business of life. (1835, as cited in Henderson, 1947, p. 11)

Like Rush, Prichard believed the morally insane to have strong criminal propensities that were immutable to punishment and, consequently, should be socially condemned (1835, as cited in Berrios, 1999; Millon et al., 1998). In contrast to Pinel's and Rush's attempts to refine the diagnostic features of this disorder, Prichard actually expanded the construct (Berrios, 1999), a decision probably based in both theory and morality. Theoretically, Prichard was interested in adding to the etiological understanding of this syndrome and, toward this aim, proposed several different pathways to the disorder. He believed that "The varieties of moral insanity are perhaps as numerous as the modifications of feelings or passions in the human mind" (1835, as cited in Werlinder, 1978, p. 40). Morally, he, like many others, was concerned with the social damage caused by (some) mentally ill individuals and, consequently, extended his nosological net to include all disorders that render those with the disorder unable to guide themselves according to social and moral norms (Karpman, 1948a; Millon et al., 1998). As a result the term *moral insanity* became a wastebasket category for emotionally disordered but intellectually intact individuals who engaged in impulsive and antisocial behaviors. It consisted of an array of disorders, including clinical syndromes (e.g., schizophrenic states, mania, hypomania, and obsessional states), personality disorders (e.g., antisocial, psychopathy, histrionic, and borderline), and organic brain syndromes (e.g., brain injuries and degenerative diseases; see Craft, 1966; Karpman, 1948a; McCord & McCord, 1964; Millon et al., 1998; Pichot, 1978; Werlinder, 1978). Unfortunately, although Prichard's widening of the syndrome exerted a great impact on the legal and psychiatric communities of both the United Kingdom and North America (Henderson, 1947; Millon et al., 1998; Pichot, 1978; Werlinder, 1978), it also resulted in a heterogeneous classification that put into question the clinical reality of psychopathy and, similarly, his notion that the condition may have various etiological pathways.

Koch's Psychopathic Inferiority

A parallel situation occurred in Germany in the latter part of the 19th century. Koch was the first to introduce the term *psychopathy*, under the rubric *psychopathic inferiority*, to the psychiatric literature (1888, as cited in Craft, 1966; Henderson, 1947; McCord & McCord, 1964; Millon et al., 1998; Partridge, 1930; Pichot, 1978; Schneider, 1950/1958). Unlike his English counterpart, Koch's depiction of psychopathy was restricted to personality pathology (i.e., disorders between mental illness and health), which he advocated was biologically rather than environmentally predetermined (Craft, 1966; Henderson, 1947; McCord & McCord, 1964; Partridge, 1930; Schneider, 1950/1958). However, in contrast to the 20th century conceptualization (Hare, 1991), his definition reflected a class of personality disorders (i.e., psychopathic inferiority referred to personality disorders in general) and was therefore overinclusive (Partridge, 1930; Werlinder, 1978). Nevertheless, his work set the stage for others, such as Kraepelin (1907/1981, 1913, 1915, as cited in Henderson, 1947) and Schneider (1950/1958), to investigate psychopathy in its current form; that is, as a personality disorder rather than some obscure clinical syndrome.

Kraepelin's Psychopathies

In the early 1900s, Kraepelin (1907/1981, 1913, 1915, as cited in Henderson, 1947; also see Millon et al., 1998; Partridge, 1930; Schneider, 1950/1958; Werlinder, 1978), influenced by both Prichard's view of the morally insane and Koch's work on personality pathology (Partridge, 1930; Schneider, 1950/1958; Werlinder, 1978), proposed several types of *psychopathies* (i.e., personality disorders), all of which had in common deficiencies in emotions and will that were not attributable to any specific clinical syndrome or disease process (Henderson, 1947; McCord & McCord, 1964; Schneider, 1950/1958; Werlinder, 1978): the *born criminal* (i.e., a morally blind individual who lacks social feelings and remorse over his antisocial and violent actions; also see Lombroso, 1887, as cited in Werlinder, 1978; Huertas, 1993; McCord & McCord, 1964), the *unstables* (i.e., individuals lacking drive to carry out tasks); the *morbid liars and swindlers* (i.e., superficial individuals who engage in deception for the intrinsic joy it brings them); the *pseudo-querulants* (i.e., self-centered and egocentric individuals with subclinical forms of paranoia); the *excitable* (i.e., individuals with very labile and dramatic emotions); the *impulsive* (i.e., individuals who exhibit impulsiveness or compulsion in their actions); and the *eccentrics* (i.e., individuals with a lack of uniformity or consistency in their mental lives).

Clearly, Kraepelin's typology included disorders other than psychopathy (see Cleckley, 1941/1988; McCord & McCord, 1964; Millon et al., 1998; Partridge, 1930; Werlinder, 1978), including hysteria (i.e., the excitable), paranoid or schizoid personality (i.e., the pseudo-querulant), hypomania (i.e., the excitable or one of the impulsive subtypes), schizotypal personality (i.e., the eccentric), and antisocial personality (i.e., the unstable). However, the characteristics of the born criminals and morbid liars and swindlers (Kraepelin, 1907/1981, 1913), as well as some subtypes of the impulsive (i.e., the spendthrift who lives a lifestyle he or she cannot afford by economically bleeding friends and society; the vagabond who lives life day-to-day, often taking off on nothing more than a whim or out of boredom; Kraepelin, 1915, as cited in Werlinder, 1978), appear to reflect, at least in part, current conceptualizations of psychopathy.

Schneider's Psychopathies

Following Kraepelin, Schneider (1950/1958) proposed a typology of psychopathic personalities of his own. Unlike Kraepelin, who used value-laden labels, Schneider was more interested in building a nosology based primarily on characterological deviations that caused the individual and/or society to suffer (Craft, 1966; Partridge, 1930; Werlinder, 1978): the *hyperthymic* (i.e., cheerful, overly optimistic, and boastful individuals with elevated moods who constantly start new projects but lack endurance in their activities); the *depressive* (i.e., pessimistic individuals characterized by predominantly depressed mood); the *insecure* (i.e., anxious individuals with high standards, inner uncertainty, and feeling of insufficiency); the *fanatic* (i.e., individuals with prevailing, or overvalued, ideas which control and confine them); the *attention-seeking* (i.e., entitled, boastful, and dramatic individuals who, in their quest to appear better then they are, are prone to manipulate and deceive those around them); the *labile* (i.e., individuals with labile and reactive emotions, especially depressive ones); the *explosive* (i.e., impulsive individuals with violent affective outbreaks to seemingly innocuous situations); the *affectionless* (i.e., callous, remorseless, deceptive, and incorrigible individuals with an emotional dullness toward others and a propensity to engage in criminal activities); the *weak-willed* (i.e., shallow, chameleon-like individuals who appear to have few motivations of their own and, consequently, are at the whim of their environment); and the *asthenic* (i.e., highly nervous and anxious individuals who are prone to psychosomatic complications). Like Prichard and Kraepelin, Schneider's typology included an array of disorders, only three of which (the attention-seeking, affectionless, and explosive psychopaths) had traits in common with the 20th century concept of psychopathy (Hare, 1991, 2003).

The Wastebasket Effect

Although influential in the development of psychopathy as a clinical construct (Hare, 1970), Pinel, Rush, Prichard, Kraepelin, and Schneider, as well as many others in the 19th and early 20th centuries, failed to arrive at any one definition of psychopathy, thereby leaving psychiatry in a state of confusion regarding the diagnostic boundaries of the disorder (Cleckley, 1941/1988; Karpman, 1941, 1946, 1948a, 1955). As a result, psychopathy became a wastebasket category that included either an array of clinical syndromes, as was seen in England, or personality disorders, as was found in Germany. Unfortunately, the lack of diagnostic specificity regarding psychopathy, coupled with the relative lack of knowledge at that time regarding the various pathways to antisocial behavior, resulted in many (antisocial) individuals being wrongly diagnosed with psychopathy based on value judgments rather than sound clinical observations (see Craft, 1966; Gunn, 1998; Hare, 1970; Henderson, 1947; Karpman, 1946, 1955; McCord & McCord, 1964; Partridge, 1930; Werlinder, 1978).

The Refinement of the Construct

Partridge's Sociopath

In contrast to the English and German traditions, Partridge (1928, 1929, 1930), an American psychologist, felt it of paramount importance to restrict the term *psychopathy* to one rather than many disorders so as to not lose sight of the construct (Cleckley, 1941/1988): a disorder characterized by antisocial and socially futile behaviors, immature values, interests and activities, emotional instability, disturbances in social emotions, irresponsibility, manipulativeness, impulsiveness, an unstable lifestyle, egocentricity, and poor judgment (Partridge, 1930). Given the nonspecific fashion in which the label of psychopathy was being applied, Partridge in fact advocated that the term itself be replaced with what he believed to be the more specific concept of *sociopathy* (1930).[2]

Based on an in-depth review of 50 psychopathic cases (i.e., individuals diagnosed as such by hospital staff), Partridge (1928) also proposed two etiological pathways to the disorder (for further details, see Hervé, chap. 17, this volume), an etiological perspective that had yet to be advocated.[3] On the one hand, he noted that delinquent and inadequate psychopaths had a relatively high rate of psychopathy in their families, suggesting that this condition was biologically predetermined. On the other hand, he felt that emotionally unstable psychopaths, who had little or no family history of the disorder, were the product of an early chaotic environment. This perspective led to the view that psychopathy had many gradations (i.e., mild to severe), some of which, however, could be so severe and immutable to any punitive techniques as to be treated as a class of their own (Partridge, 1929; 1930). It also suggested that psychopathy, in some individuals, may be more reflective of a clinical syndrome than a personality disorder (Partridge, 1930). In other words, psychopathy, according to Partridge (1929), could (in some cases) be an adaptation (i.e., adjustment) to psychosocial demands, an etiological perspective that has resurfaced in the work of contemporary theorists (e.g., Harris, Lalumière, & Rice, 1997; Mealey, 1995a, 1995b; Porter, 1996). This multi-etiology view was another reason why Partridge advocated for a change in terminology: He believed that the use of the term *sociopath* served to highlight how sociopathy can as easily be the product of environment (social factors) as of constitution (i.e., biology; Partridge, 1930).

Henderson's Psychopath

Henderson (1947) was another influential clinician to address the conceptualization of psychopathy. Like Partridge (1930), he believed that psychopathy, as a diagnostic term, should be restricted to one specific syndrome, a syndrome deserving a sophisticated and focused psychiatric approach given its serious and negative impact on society at large (Henderson, 1947). Henderson defined psychopathy as a personality disorder characterized, from an early age, by conduct of an antisocial or asocial nature, an unstable and irresponsible lifestyle, explosiveness, impulsivity, egocentricity, a sense of entitlement, a lack of social emotions, and poor judgment with no apparent intellectual defects. He viewed psychopaths as persons unable to live as social creatures, choosing instead an individualistic and egocentric lifestyle with no thought or feeling for those around them. To Henderson, the psychopath was much like a spoiled and unmanageable child, a syndrome indicating a person of intense immaturity.

---

[2]The term *sociopathy* was originally proposed by Birnbaum (1909; as cited in Millon et al., 1998).

[3]Although Prichard (1835, as cited in Werlinder, 1978) addressed this topic, his view reflected the heterogeneity of his classification rather than heterogeneity in psychopathy per se.

Consistent with early traditions, he viewed the pathology of psychopathy as a separation of the affective and moral systems from the intellect, the former being lacking in the psychopath. Etiologically, Henderson, unlike Partridge (1930), believed psychopathy to have a strong biological foundation in which psychological and sociological factors have little room to exert any influence. Indeed, he stated, "The inadequacy or deviation or failure to adjust to ordinary social life is not a mere willfulness or badness which can be threatened or thrashed out of the individual so involved, but constitutes a true illness for which we have no specific explanation" (Henderson, 1947, p. 17).

Karpman's Psychopath

Karpman (1946, 1948a, 1955, 1961), another influential clinician to broach the topic, was also pessimistic about the ability to change the psychopath's nature. Like Partridge (1930) and Henderson (1947), Karpman (1941, 1946, 1948a, 1948b, 1955) was concerned with the lack of specificity with which the diagnosis of psychopathy was being applied and, therefore, urged his peers to restrict the term to individuals who, in addition to showing an antisocial lifestyle, were characterized by a strong need for immediate gratification, a lack of anxiety, guilt or remorse over their actions, a grandiose sense of self, an entitled attitude, and callous, impulsive, and irresponsible actions, a description that mirrors contemporary views.

Karpman (1946, 1955, 1961), a psychoanalyst in the midst of a behavioral era, also made it a point to clearly describe the internal world of the psychopath and, toward this aim, wrote a great deal about the emotional experiences of such individuals. Like Henderson (1947), he described psychopaths as being emotionally superficial and immature, not unlike a child: They do not experience deep-rooted, complex social emotions (e.g., love, empathy, guilt, and remorse), emotions that, to the rest of us, convey important social messages that act as behavioral moderators (Karpman, 1961). Consequently, psychopaths are unable to learn to control their behaviors in ways analogous to nondisordered individuals. In Karpman's view, psychopaths only experience fleeting yet intense simple emotions, such as tension, worry, frustration, and elation, which have little or no future and/or social implications. These emotions are closely tied to the situation at hand and, therefore, easily oscillate between pleasure and displeasure with moment-to-moment changes in their environment. Positive emotions are evoked by primitive, instinctual needs (e.g., sex, power, greed, and lust) and, conversely, negative emotions by threats to goal attainment. Given the psychopath's need for immediate gratification and inability to effectively cope with emotional build-up (or tension), these emotions are highly motivating and can only be tolerated for a short period of time before being acted upon. This, in combination with a lack of emotional safeguards (i.e., people- and future-oriented emotions), creates an individual prone to engage in an impulsive, irresponsible, and socially damaging lifestyle.

Arieti's Psychopath

Arieti (1963, 1967) was another psychoanalyst with great insights into the internal world of the psychopath. In general, he viewed psychopathy much like Karpman and like that described today: disorder characterized from an early age by a strong need for immediate gratification, callousness, lack of anxiety or guilt over past and future events, grandiosity, irresponsibility, an inability to learn from experience, and an antisocial lifestyle.

Although acknowledging a lack of anxiety in psychopaths for past and future deeds, Arieti did not suggest that psychopaths did not experience anxiety (i.e., tension or worry not pathology) or, more generally, emotions. Indeed, he believed *emotions* to be the motivating force behind psychopathic behaviors. However, Arieti, like Karpman (1961), felt that psychopaths only experienced superficial emotions (e.g., shallow, behaviorally motivating emotions, such as tension, worry, discomfort, fear, rage, appetite, and pleasure, that dissipate quickly upon action) rather than deep-rooted ones (e.g., profound, long-lasting emotions such as love, hate, empathy, guilt, and remorse). This is in contrast to the anxiety-based emotions experienced by *neurotic* individuals (i.e., those suffering from anxiety disorders; Arieti, 1967). According to Arieti (1963, 1967) neurotic anxiety had to do with future events (i.e., fear of real or imagined dangers in the near or distant future), which he called *long-circuited* anxiety. The psychopath's anxiety, however, is *short-circuited*; that is, tension or discomfort resulting from current frustrations. In this view, the psychopath, motivated by shallow emotions and uninhibited by deeper ones, is unable to postpone gratification (i.e., pursue long-range goals) and acts solely upon the pleasure principle, doing so irrespective of whether or not his or her behavior is socially sanctioned. Moreover, given that his or her behavior alleviates unwanted tension, the behavior itself is followed by positive feelings (e.g., satisfaction) and is, therefore, reinforced.

Arieti proposed that this short-circuited mechanism is the reason that psychopaths seem incorrigible: "punishment is a possibility concerning the future, and therefore [the psychopath] does not experience the idea of it with enough emotional strength to change the course of his present actions" (Arieti, 1967, p. 248; also see Karpman, 1961, for a similar view). He also believed the psychopath's short-circuited emotional system to be the reason that he or she is unable to form strong loyalties or empathize with others (Arieti, 1963; also see Karpman, 1961, for a similar view); loyalty and empathy are based on strong, deeply felt, long-circuited emotions, which are absent in the psychopath. Finally, Arieti, like Karpman (1955, 1961), postulated that psychopaths' lack of long-circuited emotions may make them appear more reactive and impulsive than they truly are. That is, they may actually think before they act and, therefore, be more instrumental and controlled than their behavior overtly suggests, as supported by contemporary research (see Cornell et al., 1996; Woodworth & Porter, 2002):

> A person who has no anxiety can mentally scan all possible ways by which he can obtain quick gratification, and he can promptly translate them into action. For a person who experiences adequate amounts of anxiety, such scanning is not possible. The antisocial possibilities are automatically inhibited or suppressed by the anxiety. (Arieti, 1967, p. 253)

Hence, to Arieti, the immature emotional system of the psychopath (i.e., short-circuited with no long-circuited emotions) is the basis of his or her pathology and, consequently, can be used to explain his or her psychopathic lifestyle.

McCord and McCord's Psychopath

McCord and McCord (1964) also put forward a clear, specific, and influential interpretation of psychopathy, one that further delineated the psychopath's affective qualities. They described the psychopath as having a dangerously maladaptive personality characterized by a deep-rooted lack of social emotions, including empathy, love, guilt, and remorse, and an asocial, egocentric, and manipulative attitude that, in the psychopath's view, gives him or her the right to impulsively, callously, and aggressively act upon his or her selfish urges and to do so without any regard for the consequences of his or her actions to self or others. They present as very immature and childlike, living only in the moment and uninhibitedly seeking immediate gratification, reacting with frustration and aggression when their needs are not met.[4]

McCord and McCord (1964) were concerned, like many others (Cleckley, 1941/1988; Karpman, 1955; Partridge, 1930), with the lack of specificity in how the label of psychopathy was being used. They emphasized that although psychopaths are inclined to engage in severe, chronic, and varied criminal acts and are, therefore, overrepresented in criminal populations, psychopathy is nevertheless not synonymous with criminality. Antisociality is only a secondary symptom that, when taking the psychopath's personality into account, is easily understood: "The psychopath's uninhibited search for pleasure often clashes with society" (McCord & McCord, 1964, p. 11). Indeed, unlike other criminals, as well as noncriminals, they viewed psychopaths as relatively unmotivated, that is, as lacking any external motives that could explain their actions, criminal or otherwise.

McCord and McCord (1964) viewed psychopaths' profound lack of social emotions, that is, their "guiltlessness and lovelessness" as their primary pathology and, therefore, as the characteristics that best separate them from other individuals. In their view, any emotional connection is at best superficially felt and at worst parasitic in nature. This lack of emotional depth in

---

[4]Interestingly, this suggests that, for psychopaths, initially instrumentally motivated behavior can quickly take on reactive qualities.

respect to other humans results in their having no capacity for empathy and, consequently, no emotional inhibitors to their aggressive tendencies. Lacking guilt, they never internalize others' values or social norms and, therefore, never develop a conscience. However, that they do not experience social emotions does not negate the experience of other emotions. Indeed, although less clear in this regard, the McCords alluded to the fact that psychopaths *do* in fact experience intense, fleeting emotions: "The panic which any animal experiences when faced with serious frustration more often causes the psychopath to react with aggression" (McCord & McCord, 1964, p. 11). Similarly, they repeatedly noted that psychopaths characteristically react to frustration with fury, which is an emotion, albeit a primitive one. Thus, it seems that for the McCords, the emotional deficit characteristic of psychopathy is one restricted to long-circuited emotions (Arieti, 1967), therefore leaving psychopaths' primitive, socially damaging, and immature short-circuited urges intact and, more importantly, uninhibited.

The McCords discuss psychopathic anxiety in a very similar fashion, that is, psychopaths' anxiety is only short-circuited, never experienced for any period of time, as they waste little time acting upon their *anxious* state. Although prone to tension and frustration (i.e., short-circuited anxiety), psychopaths, according to the McCords, are immune to anxiety proper (i.e., long-circuited anxiety): "In fact, psychopathy is almost the antithesis of neurosis. In terms of emotional sensitivity, the neurotic is 'thin-skinned,' and the psychopath is 'thick-skinned'" (McCord & McCord, 1964, p. 47).

Etiologically, they adopted a biopsychosocial model and suggested three pathways to psychopathy, thereby expanding on Partridge's two-pathway model (1928): one resulting from severe parental rejection or neglect; one resulting from mild parental rejection or neglect in an individual with a strong biological predisposition toward impulsivity ("neural malfunction seems to be the catalyst which, in some cases, turns a rejected child into a psychopath"; McCord & McCord, 1964, p. 84); and one resulting from mild parental rejection or neglect in a socially disadvantaged environment (e.g., psychopathic parental role model, erratically harsh discipline, and absence of adult supervision). In other words, the McCords, like Partridge (1928), believed that, in a strongly biologically predisposed individual, only a mild psychosocial catalyst is required for the condition to develop and, conversely, in those weakly predisposed, a significant catalyst must occur. To the McCords, parental rejection and neglect was the psychosocial catalyst most likely to lead to psychopathy, in that such rejection would negate any possibility of the child developing strong emotional ties to others, which they viewed as the central symptom of the disorder.

Consensus Regarding the Syndrome

Viewed together, the work of Partridge, Henderson, Karpman, Arieti, and the McCords painted a portrait of the psychopath with a much clearer outline then had previously been accomplished. The label was being increasingly applied to a specific syndrome rather than being used to denote persons who were clinical enigmas with antisocial features. The syndrome itself, across various renditions, emerged consistently as a disorder of affective bluntness toward others and the future, accompanied by immature or primitive emotions and grandiose, superficial, and manipulative attitudes that, together, manifested in irresponsible, callous, impulsive, and aggressive behaviors.

Of interest, this clinical picture was also quite consistent with that provided by the forensic professionals of the era: a lack of social emotions (i.e., affectionlessness or lovelessness); a propensity to act on impulse without forethought; aggressive behavior; a lack of shame or remorse over past deeds; an inability to profit from experience or imposed sanctions; an apparent lack of drive or motivation to behave in a socially acceptable manner; callousness; lack of any psychosis or intellectual deficit that could explain the presentation; poor judgment; and an apparent lack of external motivations that could explain their criminal behaviors (Craft, 1966; McCord & McCord, 1964; McGrath, 1966).

Moreover, influenced by psychodynamic views (e.g., Arieti, 1963; Henderson, 1947; Karpman, 1955), a glimpse at the internal world of the psychopath began to emerge: an affective wasteland governed by primitive instincts that require immediate action no matter the consequences. The consistency with which psychopathy was being described across theorists, clinicians, and professionals suggested that psychopathy was not simply of academic or theoretical interest but a real entity with significant clinical implications.

The Narrowing of the Construct:
The Cleckley Psychopath

As the preceding review illustrates, the construct of psychopathy was broached by many influential theorists and clinicians. Nonetheless, it was Cleckley, in his influential book, *The Mask of Sanity* (1941/1988), who, in providing a specific and well-defined set of symptoms anchored in rich clinical case examples, exerted the most influence on how the construct would eventually be defined (Hare, 1991; Millon et al., 1998). Like Partridge, Henderson, and Karpman, Cleckley (1941/1988) was quite dissatisfied with the misuse of the term. He felt that defining psychopathy as personality pathology in general, as seen in the work of Kraepelin and Schneider, resulted in psychiatric confusion over the more specific syndrome. In addition, he noted that, even when psychopathy was used to define a specific disorder, many of his contemporaries did so inappropriately, often to define clinically enigmatic persons with antisocial features, only some of whom were in fact psychopaths. As highlighted earlier, this concern was not specific to Cleckley. For example, McCord & McCord (1964) pointed out that "much of psychology's confusion over the psychopath can be traced to a basic mistake: equating deviant behavior with the psychopathic personality" (p. 8). Cleckley attributed this diagnostic mishap largely to the lack of an explicit, agreed upon, and well-delineated definition of psychopathy (also see Karpman,

1955; McCord & McCord, 1964). Consequently, he also questioned the growing trend to discuss psychopathic subtypes (see Hervé, chap. 17, this volume), noting "before these fine distinctions can be made to any good purpose, there must first appear some recognition of the basic group that is to be further differentiated" (Cleckley, 1941/1988, p. 229). In support of this claim, Cleckley found that many of the existing psychopathic typologies had little to do with psychopathy proper (see earlier).

In an attempt to resolve this problem, Cleckley (1941/1988) set out to define the core characteristics of the disorder and did so in a much more explicit and methodical fashion than any of his predecessors. Based on years of clinical experience with such individuals in forensic and psychiatric settings, he described in detail what he believed to be the 16 most defining characteristics or traits of the disorder: superficial charm and good intelligence; absence of delusions and other signs of irrational thinking; absence of "nervousness" or psychoneurotic manifestations; unreliability; untruthfulness and insincerity; lack of remorse or shame; inadequately motivated antisocial behavior; poor judgment and failure to learn by experience; pathologic egocentricity and incapacity for love; general poverty in major affective reactions; specific loss of insight; unresponsiveness in general interpersonal relations; fantastic and uninviting behavior with drink and sometimes without; suicide rarely carried out; sex life impersonal, trivial, and poorly integrated; and failure to follow any life plan.

To Cleckley, the psychopath's general poverty in major affective reactions was central to, if not the cause of, his or her condition. Indeed, although noncommittal in respect to etiological causes, Cleckley believed that "If we grant the existence of a far-reaching and persistent blocking, absence, deficit, or dissociation of [affect], we have all that is needed, at the present level of our inquiry, to account for the psychopath" (1941/1988, p. 371). He even defined this abnormality as reflecting, at least clinically, a type of "semantic aphasia": a deep-seated semantic disorder in which the affective and semantic components of language are dissociated. According to Cleckley, this explained, among other things, why psychopaths often say one thing but do another.

That Cleckley believed psychopaths to be emotionally lacking, should not be interpreted, however, as suggesting that he viewed psychopaths as unable to experience any affect whatsoever:

> Vexation, spite, quick and labile flashes of quasi-affection, peevish resentment, shallow moods of self-pity, puerile attitudes of vanity, and absurd and showy poses of indignation are all within his emotional scale and are freely sounded as the circumstances of life play upon him. But mature, whole-hearted anger, true or consistent indignation, honest, solid grief, sustaining pride, deep joy, and genuine despair are reactions not likely to be found within this scale. (p. 348)

Similarly, his designating the "lack of any psychoneurotic manifestations" (i.e., clinically significant anxiety as seen, for example, in the anxiety disorders;

see American Psychiatric Association (APA), 1994) as a core characteristic should not be taken to mean, as many subsequent investigators have erroneously suggested (e.g., Schmitt & Newman, 1999; Skeem, Poythress, Edens, Lilienfeld, & Cale, in press), that Cleckley believed psychopaths to be free from anxiety altogether. In fact, he noted, much in the same vein as Karpman (1961) and Arieti (1963), that the type of anxiety experienced by psychopaths is simply different from that experienced by their nonpsychopathic counterparts:

> There are usually no symptoms to suggest a psychoneurosis in the clinical sense. In fact, the psychopath is nearly always free from minor reactions popularly regarded as 'neurotic' or as constituting 'nervousness.'. . . Even under concrete circumstances that would for the ordinary person cause embarrassment, confusion, acute insecurity, or visible agitation, his relative serenity is likely to be noteworthy. . . . It is true [the psychopath] may become vexed and restless when held in jails or psychiatric hospitals. This impatience seems related to his inability to realize the need or justification for his being restrained. What tension or uneasiness of this sort he may show seems provoked entirely by external circumstances, never by feelings of guilt, remorse, or intrapersonal insecurity. (Cleckley, 1941/1988, pp. 339–340)

In other words, Cleckley viewed psychopathic anxiety as reflecting mere tension and worry of an egocentric nature rather than a clinical condition. Psychopaths' anxiety, unlike that of individuals who suffer from anxiety disorders, is not self-induced, be it conscious or not, but evoked by external circumstances in which they are unable to gratify their selfish needs. Given their general poverty in affect, they are immune to socially induced anxiety; that is, anxiety over how their actions may have an impact on their future or on that of other individuals. By including "lack of any psychoneurotic manifestations" as a defining characteristic of psychopathy, Cleckley, as had been suggested by Karpman (1946, 1948a, 1955), simply hoped to restrict the diagnosis to individuals whose primary pathology was psychopathy, that is, to primary or idiopathic types (see Karpman, 1955). As noted earlier, he felt that much more knowledge about the idiopathic psychopath was needed before we turn our attention (and limited resources) to the study of other forms of the disorder.

Thus, it appears that Cleckley (1941/1988), like Karpman (1961) and Arieti (1963), believed that, although psychopaths experience short-circuited emotions (e.g., rage, frustration, lust, and elation), they are incapable of experiencing, in any significant way, long-circuited emotions (Arieti, 1963), that is, deep-rooted, complex social affective states (e.g., love, empathy, remorse, or guilt), for which they have only a superficial, intellectual, or theoretical understanding. Unfortunately, such emotions are required to control basic human impulses (Cleckley, 1941/1988), either by providing alternatives (e.g., love vs. lust) or by signaling their inappropriateness (e.g., via some empathetic response or future projection of remorse or guilt). Accordingly, lacking complex social emotions in their day-to-day activities, psychopaths are left with no alternatives other than to uninhibitedly act upon their short-circuited emotions (i.e., impulses, urges, and so forth) in whichever way they see fit. In other words, it is not that psychopaths do not experience any emotions. Rather, the emotions that they do experience are different from those of nonpsychopaths in kind, degree, and duration and in the manner in which they are elicited.

Psychopathy According to Clinical Literature

Although the construct of psychopathy began as a wastebasket category, it evolved into a clear and meaningful clinical syndrome rooted, as had originally amazed Pinel two centuries ago (1801/1806, as cited in Henderson, 1947; also see Pichot, 1978; McCord & McCord, 1964; Werlinder, 1978), in a profound affective bluntness toward the past, the future, and anything human. So meaningful is the syndrome that it has withstood the test of time, regularly reemerging in the writings of prominent clinicians from various backgrounds, all of which point to a specific psychopathic pattern of interpersonal, affective, behavioral, and lifestyle characteristics. Across these various renditions, the psychopath's portrait consistently emerged as depicting a manipulative, grandiose, and superficial parasite who, devoid of emotional connections to the world, irresponsibly and selfishly drifts through life, only stopping long enough to callously, impulsively, and aggressively satisfy the urge of the moment.

THE EMPIRICAL REVOLUTION

Having rich clinical descriptions to guide them, North American clinicians, researchers, and theorists of the mid to late 20th century now turned their attention to developing an accepted, clinically sound, and scientifically grounded operational definition of the construct, as advocated by their predecessors. Two overlapping yet distinct constructs emerged, each stemming from different philosophical and methodological approaches. The first, APD, from the *Diagnostic and Statistical Manual of Mental Disorders (DSM)*, 4th ed. (APA, 1994), emerged out of clinical necessity in the 1950s, an era following Partridge's (1929, 1930) conceptualization and in which behaviorism prevailed and mental health professionals struggled to find an accepted nomenclature for the various mental health problems of the time. The second, the Hare psychopath, emerged to satisfy research requirements in the early 1980s, an era in which the Cleckley psychopath was receiving increasing empirical attention, the study of personality traits had become accepted, and scientific rigor was a necessity. Because the APD–psychopathy debate is extensively covered in the literature (e.g., Hare, 1996b), it will only briefly be summarized in the following sections, with special attention given to how each conceptualization adhered to its clinical roots.

The *DSM* Conceptualization

As noted earlier, Partridge advocated for restricting the term *psychopathy*, or more precisely *sociopathy*, to a single clinical entity as to not lose sight of the construct. Eventually, his work led to sociopathy being adopted by the APA in their first edition of the *DSM* (APA, 1952):

> This term refers to chronically antisocial individuals who are always in trouble, profiting neither from experience nor punishment, and maintaining no real loyalties to any person, group, or code. They are frequently callous and hedonistic, showing marked emotional immaturity, with lack of responsibility, lack of judgment, and an ability to rationalize their behavior so that it appears warranted, reasonable, and justified (p. 38).

As the *DSM* underwent revisions, the term *sociopathy* was eventually replaced with the current *DSM-IV* concept of *antisocial personality disorder* (APA, 1994). At present, APD is defined by an early (i.e., before the age of 15 years) and chronic disregard for, and violation of, the rights of others as exemplified by criminal behavior, deceitfulness, impulsivity, irritability and aggressiveness, reckless disregard for the safety of self or others, consistent irresponsibility, and lack of remorse (APA, 1994).

Although it is noted in *DSM-IV* that psychopathy (as operationalized by Hare, 2003) is simply another term for APD (APA, 1994), there now exists ample evidence suggesting otherwise (for a review, see Hare, 1996b). Not only are the *DSM-IV* APD criteria heavily weighted toward the behavioral manifestations of the disorder (i.e., APD criteria include only one interpersonal [i.e., deceitfulness] and one affective [i.e., lack of remorse] characteristic), thereby deviating significantly from its origins (Partridge, 1928, 1929, 1930), but a diagnosis of APD, which only requires three of seven symptoms, could easily be rendered solely on the basis of antisocial behaviors. Yet, as noted so long ago by the McCords, "The actions of the psychopath are only outward symptoms of a sick mind. . . . [and therefore,] . . . any adequate study of the psychopath must look beyond asociality" (McCord & McCord, 1964, p. 8). Clearly, APD fails to capture the personality features that clinicians (e.g., Cleckley, 1941/1988; Karpman, 1955; McCord & McCord, 1964) and researchers (e.g., Abbott, 2001; Bolt, Hare, Vitale, & Newman, 2004; Cooke & Michie, 1997; Frick, 2000; Hare, 2003; Rogers, Duncan, Lynett, & Sewell, 1994) have noted to be most essential in discriminating psychopaths from other criminals.

As a result, the relationship between APD and psychopathy has consistently been found to be asymmetrical (Cunningham & Reidy, 1998; Hart & Hare, 1996, 1998; Lilienfeld, 1998; Rutherford, Alterman, Caccioia, & McKay, 1998; Serin, 1991): Although most individuals with psychopathy qualify for a diagnosis of APD (i.e., both display antisocial conduct), most individuals with APD are not diagnosed as psychopathic (i.e., they do not display the interpersonal and affective features of psychopathy). Moreover, although both conditions share criminal propensities, psychopathy is undoubtedly a better predictor of general, violent, and sexual recidivism, institutional maladjustment, and treatment failure than APD in forensic and civil–psychiatric settings (Cunningham & Reidy, 1998; Hare, Clark, Grann, & Thornton, 2000; Harris, Rice, & Cormier, 1991; Hemphill, Hare, & Wong, 1998; Salekin, Rogers, & Sewell, 1996), thereby further attesting to the importance of the interpersonal and affective features. As an index of psychopathy, APD, relying so heavily on behavioral anchors, therefore lacks specificity and, consequently, results in too many false-positive diagnoses (see Arieti, 1963; Blackburn, 1998b; Cleckley, 1941/1998; Prichard, 1930). Despite a psychopathy base rate of about 15%–25% in forensic settings, 50%–80% of offenders meet the criteria for APD (Cunningham & Reidy, 1998; Hare, 1996b, 2003; Lilienfeld, 1998). Given the serious implications associated with a diagnosis of psychopathy (e.g., Hare, 1996a, 1998c), such a high rate of false-positive diagnoses is simply unacceptable.

Acknowledging the lack of specificity for APD in forensic settings, it is suggested in the *DSM–IV* section on "Associated Features and Disorders" of APD that

> Lack of empathy, inflated self-appraisal, and superficial charm are features that have been commonly included in traditional concepts of psychopathy and may be particularly distinguishing of the Antisocial Personality Disorder in prison or forensic settings where criminal, delinquent, or aggressive acts are likely to be nonspecific. (APA, 1994, p. 647)

Not only is this text inclusion likely to further propel the false notion that these two disorders are one and the same (Hare, 1991, 1998a, 1998b), but it is wholly nonspecific and, therefore, of questionable utility. For example, how are these additional traits to be measured? Are they to count as one of the three items required for the diagnosis or as additional symptoms?

Several other criticisms of APD have been noted in the literature as well, including the shifting diagnostic criteria from one *DSM* version to the next (Rogers & Dion, 1991; Rogers, Salekin, Sewell, & Cruise, 2000), questionable reliability (Rogers et al., 1994), absence of symptom weighing (i.e., APD equally weighs all items although some are unquestionably more important than others in diagnosing psychopathy; Lykken, 1995; Rogers et al., 1994), and temporal instability (Cunningham & Reidy, 1998). In addition, the fact that APD can coexist with anxiety and depressive disorders (APA, 1994) further questions its validity as an indicator of psychopathy, in which such disorders are not typically seen (Stålenheim & von Knorring, 1996). Most perplexing of all, however, is the fact that the APD criteria in the *DSM-IV* were not the ones field tested (Hare 1996b). Instead, "political and non-empirical considerations appear to have overridden matters of diagnostic validity" (Rogers et al., 2000, p. 216).

Overall, the conceptualization in *DSM–IV*, which relies so heavily on behavioral anchors, resulted, despite Partridge's intentions (1929, 1930), in too heterogenous a category, a category that unfortunately reflects social value judgments rather than sound clinical insights. Indeed, there are simply too many variations in which APD symptoms can combine into a diagnosis to be of any real clinical utility (i.e., 3.2 million variations; Rogers et al., 2000), especially as an index of psychopathy (Cunningham & Reidy, 1998; Hart & Hare, 1996; Rogers et al., 1994).[5] We must recall that, "Like behavior and seemingly like personality traits may have different etiologies and motivations and, therefore, have entirely different significances and meanings" (Karpman, 1946, p. 287). With this in mind, we now turn our attention to the Hare psychopath.

The Hare Psychopath

By the mid-to-late 20th century, psychopathy began receiving an increasing amount of attention within the academic arena. As this interest grew, so did the need for a reliable and valid measure of psychopathy, one that would meet research standards and provide a common nomenclature to guide this promising area of investigation. Accordingly, relying, in large part, on the clinical accounts noted earlier and acknowledging the importance of both personality and behavioral indices, Hare and his colleagues set out to operationally define the interpersonal, affective, behavioral, and lifestyle characteristics of psychopathy in the form of a clinical rating scale: the Hare Psychopathy Checklist (PCL; Hare, 1980) and, later, the Hare Psychopathy Checklist–Revised (PCL–R: Hare, 1991, 2003).

The PCL–R contains 20 items (see Table 2–1), each of which is operationally defined and scored on a three-point scale ($0 = no$; $1 = maybe/sometimes$; and $2 = yes$), that, when summed, provide an indication of the degree to which a particular individual matches the prototypical profile of a psychopath. By definition, those individuals who meet the PCL–R criteria for psychopathy (i.e., PCL–R score ≥ 30 in North America; Hare, 2003; PCL–R score ≥ 25 in Europe; Cooke & Michie, 1999; Hare, 2003) share many common features; that is, they must possess high levels of the interpersonal, affective, behavioral, and lifestyle characteristics of the disorder (Hare, 2003). Neither set of symptoms in isolation is sufficient for a diagnosis of psychopathy, unlike suggested by the diagnostic criteria for APD in *DSM–IV*.

Early factor analytical investigations demonstrated that the PCL–R items fall into two correlated ($r = 0.5$–0.6), yet distinct, factors (see Table 2–1; Hare et al., 1990; Harpur, Hakstian, & Hare, 1988). Factor 1 (Interpersonal/Affective) consists of items that measure the affective and interpersonal features of psychopathy, such as egocentricity, manipulativeness, callousness, and lack of remorse, whereas Factor 2 (Lifestyle) consists of items that describe an impul-

---

[5]This is not to say that antisocial personality disordered individuals do not exist. Indeed, there are numerous non-psychopathic offenders with well-engrained and long-standing antisocial attitudes and values that deserve our clinical and research attention.

TABLE 2–1.
Hierarchical Model of Psychopathy

	Psychopathy			
PCL–R*	Factor 1		Factor 2	
PCL–R (2nd ed.)*	Facet 1	Facet 2	Facet 3	Facet 4
PCL:3F†	Facet 1	Facet 2	Facet 3	
	Interpersonal	Affective	Lifestyle	Antisocial
	Glib/Superficial	Shallow Affect	Gets Bored	Poor Controls
	Grandiose	Callous	Impulsive	Early Problems
	Lying	Lacks Guilt	Irresponsible	Juvenile Crime
	Conning	Not Responsible	Parasitic	Revocations
			No Realistic Goals	Versatility

*Two items (sexual promiscuity and many marital relationships), although included in these 20-item scales, do not load on any one factor or facet. Criminal versatility did not load on any one factor in the first edition of the PCL–R.

†All 13 items from the Cooke & Michie (1997, 2001) scale, the PCL: Three Factor (PCL:3F), are included.

sive, antisocial, and unstable lifestyle. Although the personality traits (i.e., Factor 1) have been found to be stable throughout the life span, it appears that the manifestation of the disorder (i.e., Factor 2) decreases with age, especially after age 40 (Harpur & Hare, 1994; Porter, Birt, & Boer, 2001), a finding that further warns against relying too heavily on behavioral indicators in the assessment of personality pathology (i.e., having less energy to act does not mean that one no longer wants to act). Further investigation also revealed each factor to have its own correlates (Dempster et al., 1996; Edens et al., Cruise, & Cauffman, 2001; Hart & Hare, 1998; Lilienfeld, 1998), again highlighting the need for a holistic approach to the assessment of psychopathy: one that takes both personality and lifestyles features into consideration.

Recent analyses, relying on more sophisticated statistical approaches that combine item response theory and factor analysis, have resulted in either a three-factor (Cooke & Michie, 1997, 2001) or four-factor (or facet) structure (Bolt et al., 2004; Hare, 2003; Parker, Sitarinios, & Hare, 2002), which differ only in degree, not kind (see Table 2–1). Interestingly, both camps have identified the affective items as having the most informative value in discriminating psychopaths from other offenders, thereby supporting the view that the psychopath's affective bluntness is his or her most salient feature (Abbot, 2001; Arieti, 1967; Cleckley, 1941/1988, Frick, 2000; Hare, 1996a, 1998a; Karpman, 1961; McCord & McCord, 1964; Patrick, 1994; Porter, 1996; also see Newman, 1998, for a different view). At present, it appears that the four-facet structure appears to be more methodologically sound and, by having an additional descriptive level, of greater clinical utility than the three-factor structure (for further details, see Bolt et al., 2004; Hare, 2003; Parker et al.,

2002; Neumann, Kosson, & Salekin, chap. 4, this volume). Nonetheless, unlike the well-validated original two-factor structure, neither of these new structures has been empirically validated; that is, the individual facets have not yet been proven to have unique and theoretically meaningful correlates.

Although debate still exists regarding the factor structure of the PCL–R, there is little confusion regarding the reliability and validity of this instrument (Cunningham & Reidy, 1998; Hare, 2003). Indeed, it has been deemed the gold standard in the assessment of psychopathy (see reviews by Fulero, 1995; Stone, 1995). As the evidence behind this statement is amply reviewed in subsequent chapters, it will not be broached here. Suffice to say, however, that the research, be it laboratory investigations of the neurocognitive, psychophysiological, and emotional functioning of psychopaths or applied research on their criminal/antisocial affinity, has consistently supported the clinical insights of the past. That is, both the internal world and outward behaviors of psychopaths differ significantly from those of nonpsychopaths and, typically, in manners that carry grave consequences for society. In other words, the Hare psychopath is a creature like no other: one who demonstrates, from an early age and across various situations, egocentricity, grandiosity, deceptiveness, shallow emotions with poor frustration tolerance, lack of empathy, guilt, or remorse, impulsivity, irresponsibility, and the ready violation of social and legal norms and expectations; a psychopath as depicted in the clinical tradition.

CONCLUSION

The construct of psychopathy has a rich clinical history, one in which the entity, as well as its consequences for society, are clearly outlined. Moreover, these past accounts, relying on clinical experience and insight, provide clues to the inner world of the psychopath and his or her actions that simply cannot be appropriately reflected by research alone. We arguably have much to learn from these archived case studies and qualitative analyses. Indeed, without these accounts, the PCL–R, the only instrument developed that adequately taps the construct, would never have been conceived, at least not in its current format. By rooting their instrument in clinical wisdom, Hare and his colleagues were able to provide a common nomenclature, as had been advocated by Cleckley.

Having this tool at their disposal, clinicians, theorists, and researchers have since been able to focus their attention on a specific clinical entity, resulting in a body of research that—true to its roots—has not only validated the clinical insights of the past but also has had an unsurpassed influence in applied settings around the world (e.g., Cunningham & Reidy, 1998; Dolan & Doyle, 2000; Hare et al., 2000; Moltó, Poy, & Torrubia, 2000). In light of its success, it has been adapted for use with civil psychiatric patients (Psychopathy Checklist: Screening Version [PCL:SV]: Hart, Cox, & Hare, 1995), adolescent offenders (Psychopathy Checklist: Youth Version [PCL:YV]: Forth, Kosson, &

Hare, 2004), and children (Antisocial Process Screening Device [APSD]: Frick & Hare, 2001). There are even new scales for use by nonmental health professionals (Hare P-Scan; Hare & Hervé, 2003) and for use in industrial settings (B-Scan 360; Babiak & Hare, in press), thereby allowing the study of psychopathy to progress into new and exciting arenas (e.g., O'Toole, chap. 11, this volume; Babiak, chap. 16, this volume). Clearly, we owe much to our predecessors.

ACKNOWLEDGMENTS

The views expressed are those of the authors, and do not necessarily reflect the position of the Forensic Psychiatric Hospital.

I acknowledge Kristin Kendrick, BA, and John Yuille, PhD, for their helpful comments.

REFERENCES

Abbott, A. (2001). Into the mind of a killer, *Nature, 410*, 296–298.

Adshead, G. (2000). Through a glass darkly: Ethical dilemmas in the treatment and management of psychopathic disorder. In C. Hedinbotham (Ed.), *Philosophy, psychiatry and psychopathy: Personal identity in mental disorder* (pp. 13–28). Aldershot, England: Ashgate.

American Psychiatric Association (1952). *Diagnostic and statistical manual of mental disorders.* Washington, DC: Author.

American Psychiatric Association (1994). *Diagnostic and statistical manual of mental disorders* (4th ed.). Washington, DC: Author.

Arieti, S. (1963). Psychopathic personality: Some views on its psychopathology and psychodynamics. *Comprehensive Psychiatry, 4*, 301–312.

Arieti, S. (1967). *The intrapsychic self: Feeling, cognition, and creativity in the health and mental illness.* New York: Basic Books.

Babiak, P., & Hare, R. D. (in press). *The B-Scan 360—Manual.* Toronto, Ontario Canada: Multi-Health Systems.

Benn, P. (2000). Freedom, resentment and the psychopath. In C. Hedinbotham (Ed.), *Philosophy, psychiatry and psychopathy: Personal identity in mental disorder* (pp. 29–46). Aldershot, England: Ashgate.

Berrios, G. E. (1999). J. C. Prichard and the concept of 'moral insanity.' *History of Psychiatry, 10*, 111–126.

Blackburn, R. (1988). On moral judgements and personality disorders: The myth of psychopathic personalities revisited. *British Journal of Psychiatry, 153*, 505–512.

Blackburn, R. (1998a). Psychopathy and personality disorder: Implications of interpersonal theory. In D. J. Cooke, A. E. Forth, & R. D. Hare (Eds.), *Psychopathy: Theory, Research, and Implications for Society* (pp. 269–301). Dordrecht, The Netherlands: Kluwer.

Blackburn, R. (1998b). Psychopathy and the contribution of personality to violence. In T. Millon, E. Simonson, M. Burket-Smith, & R. Davis (Eds.), *Psychopathy: antisocial, criminal, and violent behavior* (pp. 50–68). New York: Guilford Press.

Bolt, D. M., Hare, R. D., Vitale, J. E., & Newman, J. P. (2004). A multigroup item response theory analysis of the Psychopathy Checklist–Revised. *Psychological Assessment, 16*, 155–168.

Cleckley, H. (1988). *The mask of sanity* (5th ed.). St. Louis, MO: Mosby. (Original work published in 1941)

Cooke, D. J., & Michie, C. (1997). An item response theory analysis of the Hare Psychopathy Checklist. *Psychological Assessment, 9*, 3–13.

Cooke, D. J., & Michie, C. (1999). Psychopathy across cultures: North America and Scotland compared. *Journal of Abnormal Psychology, 108*, 58–68.

Cooke, D. J., & Michie, C. (2001). Refining the construct of psychopathy: Towards a hierarchical model. *Psychological Assessment, 13*(2), 171–188.

Cornell, D., Warren, J., Hawk, G., Stafford, E., Oram, G., & Pine, D. (1996). Psychopathy in instrumental and reactive violent offenders. *Journal of Consulting and Clinical Psychology, 64*, 783–790.

Craft, M. (1966). The meanings of the term "psychopath." In M. Craft (Ed.), *Psychopathic disorders* (pp. 1–22). Oxford, England: Pergamon Press.

Cunningham, M. D., & Reidy, T. J. (1998). Antisocial personality disorder and psychopathy: Diagnostic dilemmas in classifying patterns of antisocial behavior in sentencing evaluations. *Behavioral Sciences and the Law, 16*, 333–351.

Dempster, R. J., Lyon, D. R., Sullivan, L. E., Hart, S. D., Smiley, W. C., & Mulloy, R. (1996, August). *Psychopathy and instrumental aggression in violent offenders.* Paper presented at the 104th Annual Convention of the American Psychological Association, Toronto, Ontario, Canada.

Dolan, M., & Doyle, M. (2000). Violence risk prediction: Clinical and actuarial measures and the role of the Psychopathy Checklist. *British Journal of Psychiatry, 177*, 303–311.

Edens, J. F., Skeem, J. L., Cruise, K. R., & Cauffman, E. (2001). Assessment of "juvenile psychopathy" and its association with violence: A critical review. *Behavioral Sciences and the Law, 19*, 53–80.

Fenster, A. (1993). Social psychopathy, social distress, family breakdown, and custody disputes in the 1900s: Implications for Mental Health Professionals. *Journal of Social Distress and the Homeless, 2*, 35–59.

Forth, A. E., Kosson, D. S., & Hare, R. D. (2004). *The Psychopathy Checklist: Youth Version (PCL:YV).* Toronto, Ontario, Canada: Multi-Health Systems.

Frick, P. J. (2000). The problems of internal validation without a theoretical context: The different conceptual underpinnings of psychopathy and the disruptive behavior disorder criteria. *Psychological Assessment, 12*, 451–456.

Frick, P., & Hare, R. D. (2001). *The Antisocial Processes Screening Device: Technical manual.* Toronto, Ontario, Canada: Multi-Health Systems.

Fulero, S. M. (1995). Review of the Hare Psychopathy Checklist–Revised. In J. C. Conoley & J. C. Impara (Eds.), *Twelfth mental measurements yearbook* (pp. 453–454). Lincoln, NE: Buros Institute.

Gunn, J. (1998). Psychopathy: An elusive concept with moral overtones. In T. Millon, E. Simonson, M. Burket-Smith, & R. Davis (Eds.), *Psychopathy: antisocial, criminal, and violent behavior* (pp. 32–39). New York: Guilford Press.

Hare, R. D. (1970). *Psychopathy: Theory and research.* New York: Wiley.

Hare, R. D. (1980). A research scale for the assessment of psychopathy in criminal populations. *Personality and Individual Differences, 1*, 111–119.

Hare, R. D. (1991). *The Hare Psychopathy Checklist–Revised.* Toronto, Ontario, Canada: Multi-Health Systems.

Hare, R. D. (1996a). Psychopathy: A clinical construct whose time has come. *Criminal Justice and Behavior, 23*, 25–54.

Hare, R. D. (1996b). Psychopathy and antisocial personality disorder: A case of diagnostic confusion. *Psychiatric Times, 13*, 39–40.

Hare, R. D. (1998a). Psychopathy, affect, and behavior. In D. Cooke, A. Forth, & R. Hare (Eds.). *Psychopathy: Theory, research, and implications for society* (pp. 105–137). Dordrecht, The Netherlands: Kluwer.

Hare, R. D. (1998b). The Hare PCL–R: Some issues concerning its use and misuse. *Legal and Criminological Psychology, 3*, 99–119.

Hare, R. D. (1998c). *Without conscience: The disturbing world of the psychopaths among us*. New York: Guilford Press.

Hare, R. D. (2003). *The Hare Psychopathy Checklist–Revised* (2nd ed.). Toronto, Ontario, Canada: Multi-Health Systems.

Hare, R. D., Clark, D., Grann, M., & Thornton, D. (2000). Psychopathy and the predictive validity of the PCL–R: An international perspective. *Behavioral Sciences and the Law, 18*, 623–645.

Hare, R. D., Harpur, T. J., Hakstian, A. R., Forth, A. E., Hart, S. D., & Newman, J. P. (1990). The revised psychopathy checklist: Reliability and factor structure. *Psychological Assessment, 2*, 338–341.

Hare, R. D., & Hervé, H. (2003). *The Hare P-Scan: Research version 2*. Toronto, Ontario, Canada: Multi-Health Systems.

Harpur, T. J., Hakstian, A. R., & Hare, R. D. (1988). Factor structure of the psychopathy checklist. *Journal of Consulting and Clinical Psychology, 56*, 741–747.

Harpur, T. J., & Hare, R. D. (1994). The assessment of psychopathy as a function of age. *Journal of Abnormal Psychology, 103*, 604–609.

Harris, G. T., Lalumière, M. L., & Rice, M. E. (1997). Evidence that psychopathy is a Darwinian adaptation [Abstract]. *Canadian Psychology, 38*(2a), 2.

Harris, G. T., Rice, M. E., & Cormier, C. A. (1991). Psychopathy and violent recidivism. *Law and Human Behavior, 15*, 625–637.

Hart, S. D., Cox, D. N., & Hare, R. D. (1995). *Manual for the Psychopathy Checklist: Screening Version (PCL:SV)*. Toronto, Ontario, Canada: Multi-Health Systems.

Hart, S. D., & Hare, R. D. (1996). Psychopathy and antisocial personality disorder. *Current Opinion in Psychiatry, 9*, 129–132.

Hart, S. D., & Hare, R. D. (1998). Psychopathy: Assessment and association with criminal conduct. In D. M. Stoff, J. Breiling, & J. D. Maser (Eds.), *Handbook of Antisocial Behavior* (pp. 22–35). New York: Wiley.

Hedinbotham, C. (2000). Philosophy, psychiatry and personal identity: Clinics, concepts and philosophy of psychopathy. In C. Hedinbotham (Ed.), *Philosophy, psychiatry and psychopathy: Personal identity in mental disorder* (pp. 1–12). Aldershot, England: Ashgate.

Hemphill, J. F., Hare, R. D., & Wong, S. (1998). Psychopathy and recidivism: A review. *Legal and Criminological Psychology, 3*, 141–172.

Henderson, D. K. (1947). *Psychopathic states* (2nd ed.). New York: W. W. Norton.

Huertas, R. (1993). Madness and degeneration, III. Degeneration and criminality. *History of Psychiatry, 4*, 141–158.

Karpman, B. (1941). On the need of separating psychopathy into distinct clinical types: The symptomatic and the idiopathic. *Journal of Criminal Psychopathology, 3*, 112–137.

Karpman, B. (1946). Psychopathy in the scheme of human typology. *Journal of Nervous and Mental Disease, 103*, 276–288.

Karpman, B. (1948a). The myth of the psychopathic personality. *American Journal of Psychiatry, 104,* 523–234.

Karpman, B. (1948b). Conscience in the psychopath: Another version. *American Journal of Orthopsychiatry, 18,* 455–491.

Karpman, B. (1955). Criminal psychodynamics: A platform. *Archives of Criminal Psychodynamics, 1,* 3–100.

Karpman, B. (1961). The structure of neuroses: With special differentials between neurosis, psychosis, homosexuality, alcoholism, psychopathy and criminality. *Archives of Criminal Psychodynamics, 4,* 599–646.

Kraepelin E. (1913). Lectures on clinical psychiatry (3rd English ed., T. Johnstone, Trans.). New York: William Wood.

Kraepelin, E. (1981). Clinical psychiatry (2nd English ed., A. R. Diefendorf, Trans.). New York: Scholars' Facsimiles & Reprints. (Original work published in 1907)

Lilienfeld, S. O. (1998). Methodological advances and developments in the assessment of psychopathy. *Behavior Research and Therapy, 36,* 99–125.

Lykken, D. T. (1995). *The antisocial personalities.* Hillsdale, NJ: Erlbaum.

McCord, W., & McCord J. (1964). *The psychopath: An essay on the criminal mind.* Princeton, NJ: D. Van Nostrand.

McGrath, P. (1966). Methods of care. III. The English special hospital system. In M. Craft (Ed.), *Psychopathic disorders* (pp. 135–144). Oxford, England: Pergamon Press.

Mealey, L. (1995a). The sociobiology of sociopathy: An integrated evolutionary model. *Behavioral and Brain Sciences, 19,* 523–540.

Mealey, L. (1995b). Primary sociopathy (psychopathy) is a type, secondary is not. *Behavioral and Brain Sciences, 19,* 579–599.

Millon, T., Simonsen, E., & Birket-Smith, M. (1998). Historical conceptions of psychopathy in the United States and Europe. In T. Millon, E. Simonson, M. Burket-Smith, & R. Davis (Eds.), *Psychopathy: Antisocial, criminal, and violent behavior* (pp. 3–31). New York: Guilford Press.

Moltó, J., Poy, R., & Torrubia, R. (2000). Standardization of the Hare Psychopathy Checklist–Revised in a Spanish prison sample. *Journal of Personality Disorders, 14,* 84–96.

Newman, J. P. (1998). Psychopathic behavior: An information processing perspective. In D. Cooke, A. Forth, & R. Hare (Eds.), *Psychopathy: theory, research, and implications for society* (pp. 81–105). Dordrecht, The Netherlands: Kluwer.

Parker, J., Sitarinios, G., & Hare, R. D. (2002). *Factor structure of the PCL–R.* Manuscript in preparation.

Partridge, G. E. (1928). A study of 50 cases of psychopathic personalities. *American Journal of Psychiatry, 7,* 953–974.

Partridge, G. E. (1929). Psychopathic personality and personality investigation. *American Journal of Psychiatry, 8,* 1053–1055.

Partridge, G. E. (1930). Current conceptions of psychopathic personality. *American Journal of Psychiatry, 10,* 53–99.

Patrick, C. J. (1994). Emotion and psychopathy: Startling new insights. *Psychophysiology, 31,* 319–330.

Pichot, P. (1978). Psychopathic behaviour: A historical overview. In R. Hare & D. Schalling (Eds.), *Psychopathic behaviour: Approaches to research* (pp. 55–70). New York: Wiley.

Porter, S. (1996). Without conscience or without active conscience? The etiology of psychopathy revisited. *Aggression and Violent Behavior 1,* 1–11.

Porter, S., Birt, A. R., & Boer, D. P. (2001). Investigation of the criminal and conditional release profiles of Canadian federal offenders as a function of psychopathy. *Law and Human Behavior, 25,* 647–661.

Rogers, R., & Dion, K. (1991). Re-thinking the DSM-III-R diagnosis of antisocial personality disorder. *Bulletin of the American Academy of Psychiatry and Law, 19,* 21–31.

Rogers, R., Duncan, J. C., Lynett, E., & Sewell, K. W. (1994). Prototypical analysis of antisocial personality disorder. *Law and Human Behavior, 18,* 471–484.

Rogers, R., Salekin, R. T., Sewell, K. W., & Cruise, K. R. (2000). Prototypical analysis of antisocial personality disorder: A study of inmate samples. *Criminal Justice and Behavior, 27,* 234–255.

Rush, B. (1972). An enquiry into the influence of physical causes upon the moral faculty. In Rush B., *Two essays of the mind* (pp. 1–40). New York: Brunner/Mazel. (Original work published in 1786)

Rutherford, M. J., Alterman, A. I., Cacciola, J. S., & McKay, J. R. (1998). Gender differences in the relationship of antisocial personality disorder criteria to Psychopathy Checklist–Revised scores. *Journal of Personality Disorders, 12,* 69–76.

Salekin, R. T., Rogers, R., & Sewell, K. W. (1996). A review and meta-analysis of the Psychopathy Checklist and Psychopathy Checklist–Revised: Predictive validity of dangerousness. *Clinical Psychology: Science and Practice, 3,* 203–215.

Schmitt, W. A., & Newman, J. P. (1999). Are all psychopathic individuals low-anxious? *Journal of Abnormal Psychology, 108,* 353–358.

Schneider, K. (1958). *Psychopathic personalities* (9th ed., M. Hamilton, Trans.). London, England: Cassell. (Original work published in 1950)

Schopp, R. F., & Slain, A. J. (2000). Psychopathy, criminal responsibility, and civil commitment as a sexual offender. *Behavioral Sciences and the Law, 18,* 247–274.

Serin, R. C. (1991). Psychopathy and violence in criminals. *Journal of Interpersonal Violence, 6,* 423–431.

Skeem, J. L., Poythress, N., Edens, J. F., Lilienfeld, S. O., & Cale, E. M. (in press). Psychopathic personality or personalities? Exploring potential variants of psychopathy and their implications for risk assessment. *Aggression and Violent Behaviour.*

Stålenheim, E. G., & von Knorring, L. (1996). Psychopathy and Axis I and Axis II psychiatric disorders in a forensic psychiatric population in Sweden. *Acta Psychiatrica Scandinavica, 94,* 217–223.

Stone, G. L. (1995). Review of the Hare Psychopathy Checklist–Revised. In J. C. Conoley & J. C. Impara (Eds.), *Twelfth mental measurements yearbook* (pp. 454–455). Lincoln, NE: Buros Institute.

Tucker, W. (1999). The "mad" vs. the "bad" revisited: Managing predatory behavior. *Psychiatry Quarterly, 70,* 221–230.

Werlinder, H. (1978). *Psychopathy: A history of the concepts. Analysis of the origin and development of a family of concepts in psychopath*ology. Stockholm, Sweden: Almqvist & Wiksell.

Woodworth, M., & Porter, S. (2002). In cold blood: Characteristics of criminal homicides as a function of psychopathy. *Journal of Abnormal Psychology, 111,* 436–445.

3

Psychopathy Research at Oak Ridge: Skepticism Overcome

Grant T. Harris and Marnie E. Rice

This chapter is the story of a program of research that began a quarter century ago and of the collaboration on which it was founded. The collaboration started when we began working together at the Oak Ridge maximum security division of the Mental Health Centre, Penetanguishene, Ontario (a provincial psychiatric hospital). For years beforehand, our institution was the home of a radical and world famous therapeutic community (the Social Therapy Unit [STU]) for the treatment of offenders with mental disorders. Despite its fame and many testimonials, the program had never received an empirically sound evaluation. Because of a power struggle between the program's clinical leadership and the security-oriented nursing staff, the program's integrity was suddenly destroyed in 1978. From the outset, our collaboration featured conversations in which we decried the abolition of the program before anything was learned about its effectiveness. We had many talks about how such an evaluation could be achieved. Because the program's clinical leaders had been especially optimistic about its benefits for psychopaths, these talks also concentrated on the nature of psychopathy, whether it truly existed, and how it could be measured. In 1985, we finally submitted a research proposal to evaluate the effects of the STU and to do so separately for those patients who were psychopaths. To measure psychopathy, we proposed the use of a promising new assessment device known as the Psychopathy Checklist. We obtained funding from the Ontario Mental Health Foundation and a mimeographed manual for the Psychopathy Checklist–Revised (PCL–R) from Vancouver and began our work.

An important element of almost all the research described in this chapter was the care and attention taken by Oak Ridge case historians in compiling detailed histories of most patients admitted to our institution. Long before our first arrival in the mid-1970s, administrative assistant Marjory Buck, supported by superintendent Barry Boyd, began a practice of thoroughly describing each newly admitted patient's past life, current circumstances, and the details of the offenses that had resulted in his or her admission. This history-taking exercise never focused exclusively on psychiatric symptoms and prevalent psychiatric theories. Instead, case historians compiled as unbi-

ased an account of the patient's life as possible, covering topics such as pregnancy, early childhood, school experiences, academic and vocational adjustment, friends and hobbies, sexual behavior, criminal behavior, adult adjustment, and so on. The historians did not rely exclusively on what offenders
said about themselves; they developed questionnaires to be completed by
patients' families, especially parents. Whenever possible, family members
were also interviewed. In addition, records from schools, other clinicians, and
correctional institutions were also sought. At the time, this history-gather-
ing work was greatly valued by the psychiatrists in charge of Oak Ridge and
the historians were accorded considerable status on the clinical teams.

In addition to their great value in making disposition decisions and
in planning treatment, these case histories proved to be a rich lode for
researchers. The quality of the histories and the fact that they had been compiled for almost all patients for such a long time meant that we could conduct
credible research on patients who had long since left our institution. Rather
than begin accumulating cases slowly over time, we were able to use the historical material to study the hundreds of patients who had come and gone
before our arrivals. Most notably, this material allowed us to use measures
that had not even existed when the histories were compiled; for example,
we were able to show that we could score the PCL–R with reliability, concurrent validity, predictive accuracy, internal consistency, and factor structure equal to or better than those that had been reported for its administration
on "live" subjects that included extensive structured interviews.

At the outset, we were skeptical about the value of the psychopathy concept. Because we were more familiar with the MMPI Pd scale than with the
PCL–R, it seemed to us that psychopathy was probably nothing more than a
pseudonym for having an extensive criminal history and really had little to
offer to an understanding of the psychology of antisocial behavior. Nevertheless, intrigued by the work of Robert Hare (and encouraged by our colleague and department head, Vern Quinsey), we decided to measure the construct so that we could try to falsify our expectation. Our first investigation
brought us a surprise and throughout the years that followed, we were surprised several times at the signal importance of the psychopathy construct.

PSYCHOPATHY IS NOTHING MORE
THAN CRIMINAL HISTORY

Our first study of psychopaths in Oak Ridge exemplified aspects of our
research common to all of the research described in this chapter. First, the
subjects of the research had all been patients in a maximum security psychiatric hospital, but most did not have what has now come to be called *serious
mental illness* (psychotic or serious affective disorder). The institution's clinicians had also recruited young men who appeared to have serious personality disorders, either by transferring convicted offenders from prison for treatment, or by testifying that offenders had such serious disorders of personality
that they qualified for a defense of insanity. Clearly, this was done to permit

men who might otherwise not be able to participate to benefit from an intensive treatment regimen. We think it is important to appreciate that the subjects of our research (27% of whom were schizophrenic) more closely resembled convicted violent offenders (as many as 25% of whom are psychotic; Hodgins & Coté, 1990) than typical psychiatric patients. Elsewhere, we have provided other data to support our belief that our subjects fairly represent serious convicted offenders (Harris, Rice, Quinsey, Chaplin, & Earls, 1992).

Our first study in this program of research (Harris, Rice, & Cormier, 1991b) examined 176 graduates of the therapeutic community mentioned earlier. Of approximately 50 separate variables reflecting childhood history, adult adjustment, offense characteristics, assessment results, and institutional progress, the score on the PCL–R yielded the largest association with violent recidivism (and this has become quite a general finding in the literature). We wanted, however, to evaluate the hypothesis that an appropriate collection of criminal history variables could do just as good a job as the PCL–R. Based on multiple regression analyses, we ascertained that the four criminal history variables that provided the largest independent contribution to the prediction of violent recidivism were whether the subject had a violent offense prior to the index offense, the number of admissions to correctional institutions prior to the index offense, the number of previous criminal convictions, and a score reflecting the frequency and severity of previous criminal convictions (appendix E; Quinsey, Harris, Rice, & Cormier, 2006). Together, these four criminal history variables accounted for a significant and large amount of variance in violent recidivism, $R = .31$, but the addition of PCL–R score significantly improved prediction, $R = .45$. Clearly, in the prediction of violence, at least, PCL–R did something more than just capture adult criminal history.

Another interesting observation came from a study of a smaller group of men, all of whom qualified for a diagnosis of schizophrenia (Rice & Harris, 1992). In that sample of 96 male insanity acquittees (for previous violent offenses), the score on the PCL–R was again the largest single predictor of violent recidivism, even though almost none of them would have qualified as psychopaths by even the most liberal criteria. The PCL–R outperformed a 55-item risk-needs inventory (the Level of Supervision Inventory; Andrews, 1982), which included many items reflecting criminal history. Measures of the severity of schizophrenic psychopathology were unrelated to violent recidivism. Clearly, for the prediction of violence, the PCL–R's measure of psychopathic traits afforded considerably more in the way of predictive validity than that achieved by antisocial history or even the severity of the schizophrenic symptoms almost anyone would have assumed caused the index violent offense in the first place (Rice & Harris, 1992).

These early results persuaded us of several things: First, there must be something to this concept of psychopathy, and psychopathic offenders are different in important ways from other offenders. This difference was not best captured by the offense that brought the offender to our institution (what we called the *index offense*). Second, the offender's adult record of criminal behavior, even though much worse among psychopaths, also did not capture all of the difference between psychopaths and others. Third, even among severely mentally ill offenders, psychopathic characteristics were much more informative about the risk of violent recidivism than were the patient's specific disorder or the severity of his or her symptoms.[1] Indeed, among clinicians, the idea that the risk posed by a patient is indicated by the severity of his or her symptoms is received wisdom; every clinician (and layperson) knows it as fact. That this clinical "fact" appeared to be generally false (see also Bonta, Law, & Hanson, 1998) caused us to doubt strongly that clinical intuition, guided clinical judgment, or structured clinical decision-making would ever be the optimal way to assess risk (Quinsey et al., 1998; Quinsey et al., 2006).

VIOLENT RECIDIVISM IS TOO RARE TO PREDICT

When we began our careers, it was understood by the academically informed that it was pointless to try to predict whether an offender or forensic patient would engage in subsequent violent conduct after release. Studies had shown judgments about who was likely to be violent upon release were twice as likely to be wrong than right (Monahan, 1981). Men judged to be dangerous who managed to escape committed no more violent offenses than those released as safe (Pasewark, Bieber, Bosten, Kiser, & Steadman, 1982). More important, the rates of violence were so low that it was clear that it would be pointless to try to predict who would be violent. The classic Baxstrom study (Steadman & Cocozza, 1974) followed (for an average opportunity to reoffend of 2.5 years) a cohort of men who had been certified by experts as dangerous, but were released anyway in response to a legal challenge. Almost none of them committed another violent offense. Studies conducted at our own institution (Quinsey & Boyd, 1977; Quinsey, Pruesse, & Fernley, 1975; Quinsey, Warneford, Pruesse, & Link, 1975) also revealed very low rates of violent recidivism, although, as was the case with the Baxstrom study, the follow-up time was relatively short, and the men were all quite old at the time of their release.

Later studies of men released from our institution, however, began to show that rates of violent recidivism were much higher[2] than had been pre-

---

[1]Subsequent research has confirmed this interesting finding. Even among nonforensic psychiatric patients, PCL scores predicted violence much better than did the severity of psychotic symptoms, many of which were inversely related to violent outcome (Harris, Rice, & Camilleri, 2004; Monahan et al., 2001). Similarly, among forensic psychiatric patients, fluctuations in psychopathic and antisocial characteristics predicted changes in the probability of violence, whereas psychotic symptoms did not (Quinsey, Coleman, Jones, & Altrows, 1997; Quinsey et al., 2006).

[2]Although there are assertions that recidivism base rates are quite low (e.g., Wollert, 2001), it is empirically clear that if all serious offenders were followed for long periods after release, base rates of violent recidivism would often exceed 50% (e.g., Hanson, Steffy, & Gauthier, 1993; Harris et al., 2003; Prentky, Knight, & Lee, 1997).

viously reported. In a study of 253 insanity acquittees (almost all of whom had a previous violent offense), 20% committed another violent offense after a mean opportunity to reoffend of 6 years (Rice, Harris, Lang, & Bell, 1990). Of 136 child molesters studied in our Sexual Behaviour Laboratory, 43% committed a violent recidivistic offense after a mean opportunity to reoffend of 6 years (Rice, Quinsey, & Harris, 1991). Among 87 rapists seen in the same laboratory (followed for an average of <4 years), 43% met our criteria for violent recidivism (Rice, Harris, & Quinsey, 1990). Finally, in the study of the STU graduates a 40% rate of violent recidivism was obtained (Harris et al., 1991b) when they were followed for an average of 10 years.

Clearly, these base rates had important implications. They were high enough to have clinical and social significance. There was every reason (Quinsey, 1980) to suppose that these rates could be better; that taxpayers, if they knew about them, would demand that they be better; and that tackling the problem of prediction could help achieve improvement. In our studies, the score on the PCL–R was usually the most powerful predictor of violent recidivism. Base rates as high as these were good statistical news (although certainly bad news for the victims) in that base rates between 40% and 60% give the best chance for detecting valid predictors. How should we proceed? Should we convene a panel of expert clinicians to develop a risk assessment scheme? Should we survey the opinions of forensic experts as to the appropriate indicators of violence risk? Should we provide a list of risk factors and encourage users to then exercise clinical intuition? Should we create a system that matched our own hypotheses about the ways forensic decision-makers think?

Although we realized that surrendering to some of these temptations might make whatever system we developed more popular among those we hoped would use it, we were swayed by the arguments of scholars such as Dawes, Faust, and Meehl (and the example of such researchers as Hare) who favored an empirical approach to questions tackled by psychologists. Accordingly, we assembled the largest data set we could (Harris, Rice, & Quinsey, 1993), in which we had promising predictor variables (especially the PCL–R) and independently coded outcome (especially violent recidivism). We included among the set of possible predictors variables that were supported by the available empirical literature as well as variables nominated as promising by experienced clinicians. The subjects comprised 618 men, all of whom already had a history of serious criminal offending, more than half had been convicted of their index offense, and about 20% qualified for a diagnosis of schizophrenia. We believed and subsequent analyses substantiated our belief that they were representative of serious offenders in general. We employed additional tactics to ensure that the system that resulted would perform well on cross-validation: Although we used multiple regression to select predictor variables, weights were determined using a much simpler and more robust approach described by Nuffield (1982), and we subdivided our sample in various ways and retained only those predictors that worked in all (Harris et al., 1993).

The result was the *Violence Risk Appraisal Guide* (VRAG), whose story is most fully described elsewhere (Quinsey et al., 1998, 2006). We demonstrated that the VRAG had excellent psychometric properties (Harris et al., 1993), that its predictive accuracy corresponded to a large and pragmatically useful effect under a wide variety of conditions (Rice & Harris, 1995a), and that its accuracy was replicated in a sample of offenders not used in its construction (Rice & Harris, 1997). There have by now been approximately three dozen independent replications of the ability of the VRAG to predict violence in many different offender populations and jurisdictions in North America and Europe (www.mhcp-research.com/ragreps.htm), and most of these studies have been conducted by other researchers not affiliated with us. For present purposes, however, the important thing about the VRAG is the fact that PCL–R score is the most heavily weighted of its 12 items. In a typical data set, the correlation of the PCL–R with violent recidivism is approximately .30, whereas the correlation achieved with the entire VRAG is .45 or so. Looked at the other way, the correlation achieved with the 11 non-PCL–R items is about .40, but it appears that improvement beyond that cannot be accomplished without a direct measure of psychopathy. Thus, despite earlier skepticism about the validity of psychopathy as a psychological construct and the value in trying to predict violent recidivism, we now believed that psychopathy was real, that it was not just another term for lengthy criminal history, and that its power in predicting violence was evidence of its importance to the criminal justice system and to the field of psychology.

TREATMENT FOR PSYCHOPATHS PRESENTS PROBLEMS NO DIFFERENT THAN THOSE FOR OTHER OFFENDERS

As we described in the Introduction, our early collaboration featured many conversations about the STU program. Because the program had been destroyed so suddenly, we regretted that it had never been evaluated empirically. It is interesting to note that the program had been extolled by prominent authorities including Maxwell Jones (the originator of the therapeutic community concept) and by a "blue ribbon" panel of experts in a report to the Ontario Ombudsman that had also been entered in testimony presented in a Canadian Parliamentary Subcommittee (Harris, Rice, & Cormier, 1994; Weisman, 1995). Subsequent proof of the invalidity of this expert clinical opinion probably contributed to our general skepticism as to the value of clinical judgment in general. In any case, our early conversations also inevitably addressed our hunches as to whether the program had done any good. Even though we were both firmly entrenched behaviorists, we agreed that if an insight-oriented, emotionally evocative, psychodynamic therapy could ever reduce criminal behavior, this was the therapy that would succeed.

Two developments finally got us past the conversation stage. First, enough research material had accumulated that we felt confident that we could achieve a convincing quasi-experimental design by matching treated and untreated subjects. During the years the STU program operated, many offenders were sent to our institution only for psychiatric assessment. Matching treated patients to offenders sent for assessment on age at the time of the index offense, year of the index offense, nature of the index offense, and offenders' criminal history for each of violent and nonviolent crimes meant that we could argue that the groups were equivalent with respect to risk at the outset. The second development was acquiring an early copy of the PCL–R, which convinced us that we could retrospectively determine, in a scientifically defensible fashion, which patients had been psychopaths. Although we did not match our comparison cases on PCL–R score, it turned out that the groups were identical anyway. The matched comparison subjects were men who had served prison sentences that were about as long on average as the treatment regimen for the participants in the therapeutic community.

The results with respect to violent recidivism were probably the biggest surprise we have ever had from data. There was little evidence of any overall benefit to the program, even though patients had participated for an average of 5 years (Rice, Harris, & Cormier, 1992). The program was associated with a statistically significant reduction in violent recidivism among the nonpsychopaths, but a significant corresponding increase in violence among the psychopaths. We had to double and triple check these results before we could believe them. These are the most striking data showing a differential effect of psychological treatment that we have ever seen. The program had been seen as especially beneficial for psychopaths—how could it actually have made them worse? Perhaps the STU program had no effect on violent recidivism, but prison actually had a differential effect by increasing recidivism among nonpsychopaths and decreasing it among psychopaths. That prison might have an especially deleterious effect on nonpsychopaths has been suggested by many others. Although it is implausible that prison could decrease recidivism among psychopaths, we cannot rule out this possibility.

More plausible to us was the idea that the STU program actually made changes in the psychopathic clients, whereas prison had little effect. Perhaps the therapy raised self-esteem and taught its participants how to use interpersonal influence, to take the perspective of others, to understand how others feel, and to delay gratification. Such skills might aid nonpsychopaths in remaining free of committing violent crime but would simultaneously make psychopaths into bolder, more dangerous criminals.

A thorough knowledge of the literature on offender treatment shows that our findings might not be quite as surprising as we first thought. Other researchers (Andrews, Bonta, & Hoge, 1990) reviewed the literature on offender treatment and concluded that variations in the severity of criminal sanction have no effect on recidivism and that insight-oriented, psychodynamic therapy has, at best, no positive effect on subsequent criminal conduct. They elucidated the principles of risk, needs, and responsivity for offender treatment, and the STU program, developed long before these principles had been described, clearly violated at least the latter two of these. That is, the program targeted few things empirically related to criminal behavior, and a skills teaching or cognitive–behavioral approach was actively avoided.

For several years, ours was the only study that reported on the violent outcome of psychopaths after treatment. More recently, however, Hare, Clark, Grann, and Thornton (2000) have reported essentially identical findings after participation in several cognitive–behavioral offender treatment programs (apparently conforming to the risk, need, and responsivity principles)— treatment was associated with increased recidivism for offenders high in psychopathy. Perhaps the principles for effective offender treatment are valid only for nonpsychopaths; to the extent that adult offender samples contain large numbers of psychopaths, treatment effects will not be obtained, even if the principles of risk, need, and responsivity are followed. Of course, these results would never have been obtained and this prediction never entertained without Hare's description and operationalization of the psychopathy construct. We think the data are now clear: Because of the risk of harm, unstructured, insight-oriented, psychodynamic treatment should not be provided for psychopaths[3] (and are not the treatments of choice for any offenders). Yet, at least partly because they prefer it, psychopaths continue to receive this form of treatment in several places. We are now sometimes surprised to hear the claim that designing correctional rehabilitation is an enterprise that need not be concerned with the issue of psychopathy.

PSYCHOPATHY HAS NO SPECIAL RELEVANCE IN FORENSIC ASSESSMENT

As implied in the last sentence, a theme of some of our work on psychopathy is that our skepticism about the construct and the research results generated by it has been outstripped by the skepticism we have encountered in trying to get clinicians and other decision-makers to pay attention. Those involved in clinical practice with respect to risk assessment, especially as it pertains to psychopaths,[4] have sometimes stubbornly refused to change much. For example, although VRAG scores have been available for several years for all Oak Ridge patients, there is recent evidence (Hilton & Simmons, 2001) that the release decisions made by the Ontario Review Board (the government tribunal

---

[3]It is beyond our scope here to review all the research on the treatment of psychopathy, but we have provided such a review elsewhere (Harris & Rice, 2006). In that more complete review, we address a meta-analysis (Salekin, 2002) of treatments for psychopathy (many of which were psychodynamic) and another study (Skeem, Monahan, & Mulvey, 2001) of mental health therapy-as-usual to demonstrate why we believe the positive conclusions of those articles were unwarranted.

[4]There are several empirical studies (e.g., Elbogen, 2002; Elbogen, Mercado, Scalora, & Tomkins, 2002; Elbogen, Tomkins, Pothuloori, & Scalora, 2003; Mercado, Elbogen, Scalora, & Tomkins, 2001) showing that forensic clinicians fail to rely on valid predictors of violence risk such as measures of psychopathy.

charged with overseeing insanity acquittees in our province), have been unrelated to actuarially determined risk. The data supported the conclusion that this occurred because the Review Board relied entirely on the testimony of hospital psychiatrists whose opinions were not influenced by actuarial scores. Hilton and Simmons showed that VRAG scores were significantly correlated (.42) with recidivism whereas psychiatrists' testimony was not.

The consequences of ignoring VRAG scores have also become apparent in some of our recent research characterizing the entire forensic population of Ontario. In earlier research (Rice & Harris, 1988), we studied the clinical characteristics of forensic patients and reported that there was a significant subpopulation of mentally disordered offenders who exhibited few signs of psychological distress and few traditional psychiatric symptoms while in the hospital. Many such patients met the criteria for a diagnosis of psychopathy (or antisocial personality). Such patients often exhibited problem behaviors (lying, manipulation, rule breaking, insolence, and so on) that, although not usually thought of as symptoms, represented threats to the safety of others and to the integrity of therapeutic efforts (Rice & Harris, 1988; Rice, Harris, & Quinsey, 1996; Rice, Harris, Quinsey, & Cyr, 1990). Interestingly, such behaviors often appear to be overlooked, and such patients often succeeded in obtaining discharge even though their in-hospital conduct was poor (Rice et al., 1992; see also Harris, Rice, & Cormier, 1991a). In addition, of course, other psychopathic patients, although representing a high risk of violence if released, are actually very well behaved while in the hospital. In a study that included a cluster analysis of forensic patients, we called this group of patients "dangerous model patients" (Rice et al., 1996). We showed that many high-risk forensic patients are released, not because they are seen to be low risk, but because forensic clinicians know of nothing they can do for them. Indeed, we demonstrated that, as far as can be measured using actuarial risk scores, forensic hospitals sometimes release more dangerous patients than they retain (Rice et al., 2004). We regard this to be a problem largely caused by the puzzle of psychopaths—dangerous patients who appear to have no traditional mental health or clinical needs.

In a recent validation of the VRAG, we showed that its ability to predict violent recidivism was replicated (with the same effect size as in construction) in a large sample of offenders with mental disorders, none of whom were used in its construction (or any other subsequent testing). This study (Harris, Rice, & Cormier, 2002) was a prospective cross-validation in that we scored the VRAG for a cohort of insanity acquittees in the early 1990s before most had the opportunity to commit new offenses. Over the ensuing years, most of these men were given the opportunity through release to a minimum security hospital or to the community. The group of dangerous model patients referred to in the preceding paragraph, for example, exhibited a very high rate of release (74%) and a predictably high rate of violent recidivism (46%). Even though all the required evidence and information was available, forensic decision-makers failed to use it, with the result that violent offenses occurred that could have been prevented. We believe the problem lies in the ways clinicians have been trained (or not trained), especially about psychopathy. In our view, a thorough grounding in the research on psychopathy and the PCL–R should be mandatory before any mental health professional may work in a forensic or criminal justice setting.

PSYCHOPATHY MUST BE PART OF THE ORDINARY CONTINUUM OF HUMAN PERSONALITY

As we mentioned earlier, the interaction between psychopathy and treatment in violent recidivism was one of the most striking differential effects of treatment we had ever seen: One treatment appeared to have the opposite effect on psychopaths compared with nonpsychopaths. This immediately caused us to consider the possibility that we had been wrong about the nature of psychopathy and how fundamental a phenomenon it might be. In fact, several times in our research we have obtained similar interactions involving psychopathy.

Among nonpsychopaths, we observed an expected decline in the likelihood of violent recidivism as a function of age, but, among psychopaths, violence risk did not decline with age and even seemed to increase (Harris et al., 1991b). We regarded these findings as only very tentative because we had only very small numbers of older released psychopaths, but some support for our conclusions also came from a study by Porter, Birt, and Bohr (2001). In another study of sex offenders (Rice & Harris, 1997), psychopathy interacted with sexual deviance in the prediction of sexual recidivism. That is, nonpsychopaths and sexually nondeviant psychopaths exhibited similar rates of sexual recidivism, but sexually deviant psychopaths were at extremely high risk—more than half recidivated violently in less than 3 years. It seemed to us that if the legally defined idea of a sexually violent predator had any scientific meaning, these sexually deviant psychopaths came close.[5] Finally, we examined the independent contribution of a history of alcohol abuse in the prediction of violent recidivism of offenders with mental disorders (Rice & Harris, 1995b). Interestingly, psychopaths had, on average, much worse histories of alcohol abuse than did nonpsychopaths, and, of course, alcohol abuse history was related to the likelihood of violent recidivism overall. But this effect was confined to the nonpsychopaths; alcohol abuse did not seem to be a risk factor among psychopaths even though they were much more likely to have a history of alcohol abuse. Perhaps, we thought, contrary to conventional wisdom, reducing alcohol abuse among psychopaths would not actually lower recidivism even though such an intervention would work for nonpsychopaths.

---

[5]This multiplicative interaction between measures of psychopathy and indicators of sexual deviance has more recently been replicated by others (Gretton, McBride, Hare, O'Shaughnessy, & Kumka, 2001; Harris et al., 2003; Hildebrand, de Ruiter, & de Vogel, 2004; Serin, Mailloux, & Malcolm, 2001; Seto, Harris, Rice, & Barbaree, 2004).

In that same study (Rice & Harris, 1995b), we also reported another intriguing interaction involving psychopathy: Psychopathy and schizophrenia were not independent. An offender who met the criteria for one diagnosis was especially unlikely to meet the (independently scored) criteria for the other. Both diagnoses appear to be underlain, at least in part, by some anomaly in the neurotransmitters (dopamine and serotonin in the case of schizophrenia and serotonin in the case of psychopathy; Harris, Skilling, & Rice, 2001) regulated by the enzyme monoamine oxidase type A. We hypothesized that perhaps psychopathy is a phenomenon like schizophrenia in that it is a heritable neurological condition but with a completely different substrate. And of course, we were again struck by the data suggesting how fundamentally different psychopaths are from other offenders.

This idea of a fundamental difference led us to the work of Paul Meehl and colleagues on taxometrics—mathematical techniques intended to discover qualitative differences among individuals within a population. That is, Meehl and colleagues have worked on distinguishing phenomena that can be considered part of a continuum from those that are best thought of as disjunctions in nature (Meehl, 1992, 1995, 1996; Meehl & Golden, 1982). Golden and Meehl (1997) reported that schizotypy is a taxon, a fundamental discontinuity. People at risk for schizophrenia (i.e., those with schizotypy) do not merely form part of the ordinary continuum of human personality; rather, they differ qualitatively from those who are not. Investigators have reported that other psychological phenomena give evidence of being taxa, for example, some kinds of autism and dementia (Golden, 1982; Waterhouse et al., 1996), whereas other conditions such as depression and bulimia do not (Gleaves, Lowe, Green, Corove, & Williams, 2000; Ruscio & Ruscio, 2000).

Meehl and his colleagues have also developed the statistical techniques to evaluate the hypothesis of taxonicity for a phenomenon. Fully grasping the descriptions of these methods can be a challenge (it has been for us anyway), but the basic logic is quite simple. The idea is that if a fundamental disjunction exists, indicators of the phenomenon would not covary in a pure sample of taxon members or in a pure sample containing no taxon members. Only when groups were mixed would the indicators actually covary. On the other hand, a continuous, nontaxonic entity would not show this pattern of results. A home-spun example might help.

Imagine that a one wished to detect a sex taxon among 4-year-olds, but knew only a few indirectly informative things about each child, for example, hair length, favorite toy, commonly worn color, favorite game, and so on. If the taxon exists, then among a group of only girls, toy choice, hair length, and wearing pink should not covary (or should show low covariation). In a group of only boys, similar low covariation would be expected. However, in a group composed equally of boys and girls, hair length, toy choice, and clothing color would covary much more highly because they are effects of (or are correlated with) a common cause, the sex taxon. Without that curvilinear relationship between covariance among indicators as a function of the proportion of boys (or girls) in the group, there would be no evidence that sex is underlain by a natural disjunction, class, or type.

Several statistical taxometric methods are all based, one way or another, on this basic idea. We showed in a large sample of offenders that measures of psychopathy gave evidence of a discrete natural class (Harris, Rice, & Quinsey, 1994). Evidence came most strongly from PCL–R items and non-PCL–R variables reflecting antisocial and aggressive childhood conduct. As well, measures of adult criminal history, by contrast, did not give evidence of a taxon. Recently, we and our colleagues have shown that the *DSM* criteria for antisocial personality disorder (APD) support the existence of an underlying taxon (Skilling, Harris, Rice, & Quinsey, 2001; also see Ayers, 2000; Haslam, 2001; cf., Marcus, John, & Edens, 2004), although probably not as strongly as some of the PCL–R items and the variables reflecting antisocial and aggressive childhood conduct. This study also showed that when the APD criteria were scored in the same manner as the PCL–R items (i.e., 0, 1, or 2), there is a strong association between the PCL–R and APD scale scores. The Spearman rank order correlations in two samples were approximately .85. Also, if these correlations were recomputed after correcting for the attenuation caused by unreliable measurement, they would approach unity. We also used the taxometric methods to classify the subjects into the taxon underlying PCL–R scores and the taxon underlying APD scale scores and compared the correspondence of the two classifications. This resulted in a kappa of .82, which we demonstrated would also approach unity after disattenuation for unreliable measurement. We concluded that the phenomenon that the *DSM* manuals attempt to identify as APD is the same phenomenon known as psychopathy and is probably somewhat better measured by the PCL–R.

These results caused us to reconsider the interactions we had found in data we reported earlier in this chapter. If psychopaths comprised a distinct type or class of offender, it was perhaps not quite so surprising that treatment had the differential effects we found. Furthermore, the interactions between psychopathy and each of the following—alcohol abuse, history, age, schizophrenia, and sexual deviance—in the prediction of recidivism impressed us as very unusual in psychological research. Is there, we wondered, another psychological (or physical) measure that produces so many statistical interactions with a theoretically relevant variable? We could not think of even one such interaction, for example, involving IQ, probably psychology's most thoroughly studied construct. In the space of less than a decade we had changed from believing that psychopathy was merely a proxy for having a history of criminal behavior to the hypothesis that psychopaths comprised a natural, biological type, so different from other humans that drugs and therapy had effects on them quite opposite to their effects on other people.

PSYCHOPATHY MUST BE AN EXTREME DISORDER

There is strong indirect evidence that psychopathy is substantially heritable. First, the widely accepted dimensions of human personality and temperament have all demonstrated substantial heritability. Second, there is a significant heritable component to criminal behavior. Third, psychopathy appears to be a sex-linked condition. Fourth, antisocial personality and its childhood precursor, conduct disorder, have been shown to be substantially heritable. Fifth, psychopathic traits measured with assessments other than the PCL–R have been shown to be substantially heritable. Although behavior genetic studies using the PCL–R have yet to be done, we firmly anticipate that psychopathy will be shown to be heritable (Harris, Skilling, et al., 2001). Parenthetically, we note that this does not mean we think there is no environmentally based variability in the expression of psychopathy. For example, nothing about a heritable component to psychopathy (and antisocial personality) is incompatible with data showing that the prevalence of antisocial personality is associated with extreme prenatal malnutrition (Neugebauer, Hoek, & Susser, 1999).

If psychopathy is a fairly rare (<5% of the male population), heritable condition, what kind of a heritable condition is it? For example, it seemed to us that psychopathy was unlikely to be a disorder due to the deleterious combination of recessive alleles of a single gene (similar to Huntington's disease and cystic fibrosis, for example) because psychopaths exhibited no observable neurophysiological malfunctions or lesions. In fact, although psychopaths showed differences (compared with nonpsychopaths) in many neurocognitive tasks, neurophysiological recordings, and neurotransmitter assays (Harris, Skilling, et al., 2001; Intrator et al., 1997), no one had demonstrated that any of these neurophysiological and neurocognitive differences were associated with real-world deficits. It seemed to us that it was possible to arrange laboratory conditions in which the neurocognitive differences characteristic of psychopathy led to poorer scores (and to better scores), but these told us little about whether such neurocognitive differences constituted any real handicap (in terms of reproductive success, for example) for psychopaths in the natural world.

This thinking about psychopathy in the natural world quickly got us wondering about the world in which humans (and their personalities) must have evolved. It seemed possible to us that in the ancestral environment, psychopathic traits might have represented a reproductively viable approach to life. We had begun to apply selectionist ideas (often called evolutionary psychology) in other areas of our research (e.g., Hilton, Harris, & Rice, 2000) and the phenomenon of psychopathy also seemed relevant. A seminal paper by Mealey (1995) also sharpened our interest in the possibility that psychopathy was a distinct heritable condition that owed its existence in the human population to the fact that it had led (and probably still does lead) to successful reproduction, especially, as Mealey hypothesized, when its prevalence was low.

As intriguing as such a hypothesis seemed, everyone knows that evolutionary explanations for human characteristics cannot be tested scientifically because the explanation says that everything happened in the past. Of course, what everyone knows to be true (as in the geocentrality of the universe) sometimes turns out to be false. We believe we have been able to test this selectionist notion about the ultimate basis of psychopathy. For example, pregnancy difficulties and perinatal problems have been shown to be related to severe mental disorders such as schizophrenia and mental retardation. The idea that psychopathy is also a severe mental disorder leads directly to a similar expectation. Instead, however, we found that psychopaths actually have significantly fewer such problems in their backgrounds than do other offenders, even when schizophrenic offenders are excluded (Lalumière, Harris, & Rice, 2001). Furthermore, although such neurodevelopmental insults are associated with some violent behavior, they are unrelated to psychopathy, which itself is a much more important cause of criminal violence (Harris, Rice, & Lalumière, 2001).

As a second example, we and many others have shown that fluctuating bilateral asymmetry is a good measure of the degree to which development has been perturbed by a wide variety of environmental (and some genetic) stressors (Lalumière, Harris, & Rice, 1999). If psychopathy were a neurodevelopmental disorder (as are schizophrenia and mental retardation), one would expect psychopaths to be less symmetrical than other people. On the contrary, however, we found that psychopaths were more symmetrical than other forensic patients, and those offenders who received the highest scores on the PCL–R were indistinguishable (in symmetry) from healthy nonpatient volunteers (Lalumière et al., 2001). If psychopathy is a severe mental disorder, it is a truly odd disorder[6]—one that shows no evidence of the neurodevelopmental problems characteristic of other mental disorders.

We also tested the idea that psychopathy represents a viable reproductive life strategy more directly in a sample of sex offenders whose recidivism we had reported earlier (Rice & Harris, 1997). Of 274 sex offenders for whom we had PCL–R scores and complete information about the age and sex of their victims, about half had confined their sexual offending to children (people with whom sexual activity could have no reproductive outcome), and the others had included adult women (reproductively viable persons for a male offender) among their victims. Offenders against children had much lower PCL–R scores than the others (Harris, Rice, Hilton, Quinsey & Lalumière, 2004, 2005). In other words, psychopaths were much more likely to include reproductively viable persons in their choice of victims than were other sex offenders.

Using a completely different sample of sex offenders (Harris, Rice, Hilton, et al., 2004), we examined these expectations again. We found that PCL–R score was significantly inversely correlated with the number of prepubescent victims and positively correlated with the number of adult female victims. As well, PCL–R score was associated with whether the sex offenders included genital–genital contact in their offenses (Harris, Rice, Hilton, et al., 2004, 2005). We concluded that psychopaths were more likely than other sex

---

[6]By at least one definition of *disorder* (Wakefield, 1992), this selectionist account of psychopathy says that it is not actually a disorder because a disorder is defined as a harmful dysfunction, the harmful failure of a mechanism to perform as designed by natural selection.

offenders to target reproductively viable victims and to engage in reproductive behavior in their offenses. As far as we can see, no theoretical account of psychopathy, other than our selectionist hypothesis, has a ready explanation for all of these findings.

WHERE TO BE WRONG NEXT?

Everything about our selectionist account leads one to expect large and persistent neurocognitive differences between psychopaths and others, exactly the kinds of differences identified by Newman et al. (chap. 7, this volume) and Patrick (chap. 8, this volume), for example. In addition, of course, in our account we anticipate that the psychopathy taxon might be identifiable at very young ages, something already reported (Skilling, Quinsey, & Craig, 2001) and that core aspects of the psychopathic temperament measured in childhood would predict life course aggression and antisociality, something also already reported (Frick, chap. 13, this volume). In our current research, we are trying to extend our ideas further.

For example, in a preliminary study we have already reported that PCL–R scores predict recidivism among wife batterers (Hilton, Harris, & Rice, 2001). In a much larger study of men much more representative of wife batterers in general, we are testing the idea that psychopathy is an important cause of wife assault. That is, although sexual proprietariness is an important cause of men's violence against women (Wilson & Daly, 1993), no one knows how important psychopathy might be in the expression of sexual proprietariness. Also motivated by our selectionist hypotheses, we are examining the roles of psychopathy, mating effort, general antisociality, and sexual deviance as causes of male sexual aggression against women. Finally, we are examining the sexuality of psychopaths. On theoretical grounds, high mating effort and sexual dominance are expected to be an inherent aspect of the reproductively viable psychopathic life strategy (Harris, Skilling, et al., 2001; Lalumière, Harris, Quinsey, & Rice, 2005). It has always been puzzling to us that the sexual behavior items (promiscuity and many marital relationships) have not been seen as central to the psychopathic construct. Recent analyses of data on sex offenders (Harris, Rice, Hilton, et al., 2004, 2005) suggest that, rather than high mating effort, per se, the most diagnostic aspects of psychopathic sexuality are sexual behavior at a very young age and the willingness to use sexual coercion or domination. We are also attempting to examine these expectations in phallometric studies.

It is certainly possible that empirical research will show our predictions and theories to be wrong; it appears to us that almost every scientist is eventually shown to be wrong about almost everything (Porter, 1997). Nevertheless, we owe a debt to Robert Hare for stimulating our thinking about violent offenders, for providing us with a superb psychological measure, and for giving us the model of a scholar for whom empirical results are the evidentiary standard.

ACKNOWLEDGMENTS

The research described in this chapter was supported by the Ontario Ministry of Health, the Ontario Mental Health Foundation, and the Social Sciences and Humanities Research Council of Canada. We gratefully acknowledge the invaluable contributions of many collaborators: Vern Quinsey, Valerie Bell, Catherine Cormier, Terry Chaplin, Sonja Dey, Zoe Hilton, Martin Lalumière, Carol Lang, Caroline Ostrowski, Michael Seto, and Tracey Skilling.

REFERENCES

Andrews, D. A. (1982). *The Level of Supervision Inventory (LSI)*. Toronto, Ontario, Canada: Ministry of Correctional Services.

Andrews, D. A., Bonta, J., & Hoge, R. D. (1990). Classification for effective rehabilitation: Rediscovering psychology. *Criminal Justice and Behavior, 17*, 19–52.

Ayers, W. A. (2000). Taxometric analysis of borderline and antisocial personality disorders in a drug and alcohol dependent population. *Dissertation Abstracts International: Section B: The Sciences & Engineering, 61*(3-B), 1684.

Bonta, J., Law, M., & Hanson, K. (1998). The prediction of criminal and violent recidivism among mentally disordered offenders: A meta-analysis. *Psychological Bulletin, 123*, 123–142.

Elbogen, E. B. (2002). The process of violence risk assessment: A review of descriptive research. *Aggression and Violent Behavior, 7*, 591–604.

Elbogen, E. B., Mercado, C., Scalora, M. J., & Tomkins, A. J. (2002). Perceived relevance of factors for violence risk assessment: A survey of clinicians. *International Journal of Forensic Mental Health, 1*, 37–47.

Elbogen, E. B., Tomkins, A. J., Pothuloori, A. P., & Scalora, M. J. (2003). Documentation of violence risk information in psychiatric hospital patient charts: An empirical examination. *Journal of the American Academy of Psychiatry and the Law, 31*, 58–64.

Gleaves, D. H., Lowe, M. R., Green, B. A., Corove, M. B., & Williams, T. L. (2000). Do anorexia and bulimia nervosa occur on a continuum? A taxometric analysis. *Behavior Therapy, 31*, 195–219.

Golden, R. R. (1982). A taxometric model for the detection of a conjectured latent taxon. *Multivariate Behavioral Research, 17*, 389–416.

Golden, R. R., & Meehl, P. E. (1979). Detection of the schizoid taxon with MMPI indicators. *Journal of Abnormal Psychology, 88*, 217–233.

Gretton, H. M., McBride, M., Hare, R. D., O'Shaughnessy, R., & Kumka, G. (2001). Psychopathy and recidivism in adolescent sex offenders. *Criminal Justice and Behavior, 28*, 427–449.

Hanson, R. K., Steffy, R. A., & Gauthier, R. Long-term recidivism of child molesters. *Journal of Consulting and Clinical Psychology, 61*, 646–652.

Hare, R. D., Clark, D., Grann, M., & Thornton, D. (2000). Psychopathy and the predictive validity of the PCL–R: An international perspective. *Behavioral Sciences and the Law, 18*, 623–645.

Harris, G. T., & Rice, M. E. (2005). Treatment of psychopathy: A review of empirical findings. In C. Patrick (Ed.) *The handbook of psychopathy*. New York: Guilford.

Harris, G. T., Rice, M. E., & Camilleri, J. A. (2004). Applying a forensic actuarial assessment (the Violence Risk Appraisal Guide) to nonforensic patients. *Journal of Interpersonal Violence, 19,* 1063–1074.

Harris, G. T., Rice, M. E., & Cormier, C. A. (1991a). Length of detention in matched groups of insanity acquittees and convicted offenders. *International Journal of Law and Psychiatry, 14,* 223–236.

Harris, G. T., Rice, M. E., & Cormier, C. (1991b). Psychopathy and violent recidivism. *Law and Human Behavior, 15,* 625–637.

Harris, G. T., Rice, M. E., & Cormier, C. (1994). Psychopaths: Is a "therapeutic community" therapeutic? *Therapeutic Communities, 15,* 283–300.

Harris, G. T., Rice, M. E., & Cormier, C. A. (2002). Prospective replication of the Violence Risk Appraisal Guide in predicting violent recidivism among forensic patients. *Law and Human Behavior, 26,* 377–394.

Harris, G. T., Rice, M. E., Hilton, N. Z., Quinsey, V. L., & Lalumière, M. L. (2004, October). *Psychopathic sexuality: Implications for the assessment and understanding of psychopathy.* Paper presented at the annual conference of the Association for the Treatment of Sexual Abusers, Albuquerque, NM.

Harris, G. T., Rice, M. E., Hilton, N. Z., Quinsey, V. L. & Lalumière, M. L. (2005, March). *Psychopathic sexuality: Implications for the assessment and understanding of psychopathy.* Paper presented at the conference of the American Psychology Law Society. La Jolla, CA.

Harris, G. T., Rice, M. E., & Lalumière, M. (2001). Criminal violence: The roles of psychopathy, neurodevelopmental insults and antisocial parenting. *Criminal Justice and Behavior, 28,* 402–426.

Harris, G. T., Rice, M. E., & Quinsey, V. L. (1993). Violent recidivism of mentally disordered offenders: The development of a statistical prediction instrument. *Criminal Justice and Behavior, 20,* 315–335.

Harris, G. T., Rice, M. E., & Quinsey, V. L. (1994). Psychopathy as a taxon: Evidence that psychopaths are a discrete class. *Journal of Consulting and Clinical Psychology, 62,* 387–397.

Harris, G. T., Rice, M. E., Quinsey, V. L., Chaplin, T. C., & Earls, C. (1992). Maximizing the discriminant validity of phallometric assessment. *Psychological Assessment, 4,* 502–511.

Harris, G. T., Rice, M. E., Quinsey, V. L., Lalumière, M. L., Boer, D., & Lang, C. (2003). A multi-site comparison of actuarial risk instruments for sex offenders. *Psychological Assessment, 15,* 413–425

Harris, G. T., Skilling, T. A., & Rice, M. E. (2001). The construct of psychopathy. In M. Tonry & N. Morris (Eds.), *Crime and justice: An annual review of research.* Chicago: University of Chicago Press.

Haslam, N. (2003). The dimensional view of personality disorders: A review of the taxometric evidence. *Clinical Psychology Review, 23,* 75–93.

Hildebrand, M., de Ruiter, C., & de Vogel, V. (2004). Psychopathy and sexual deviance in treated rapists: Association with sexual and nonsexual recidivism. *Sexual Abuse, 16,* 1–24.

Hilton, N. Z., Harris, G. T., & Rice, M. E. (2000). The functions of aggression by male teenagers. *Journal of Personality and Social Psychology, 79,* 988–994.

Hilton, N. Z., Harris, G. T., & Rice, M. E. (2001). Predicting violent recidivism by serious wife assaulters. *Journal of Interpersonal Violence, 16,* 408–423.

Hilton, N. Z., & Simmons, J. L. (2001). Actuarial and clinical risk assessment in decisions to release mentally disordered offenders from maximum security. *Law and Human Behavior, 25*, 393–408.

Hodgins, S., & Coté, G. (1990). Prevalence of mental health disorders among penitentiary inmates in Quebec. *Canada's Mental Health, 38*, 1–4.

Intrator, J., Hare, R., Stritzke, P., Brichtswein, K., Dorfman, D., Harpur, T., et al. (1997). A brain imaging (single photon emission computerized tomography) study of semantic and affective processing in psychopaths. *Biological Psychiatry, 42*, 96–103.

Lalumière, M. L., Harris, G. T., Quinsey, V. L., & Rice, M. E., (2005). *The causes of rape: Understanding individual differences in the male propensity for sexual aggression.* Washington, DC: American Psychological Association.

Lalumière, M. L., Harris, G. T., & Rice, M. E. (2001). Psychopathy and developmental instability. *Evolution and Human Behavior, 22*, 75–92.

Lalumière, M., Harris, G. T., & Rice, M. E. (1999). Birth order and fluctuating asymmetry. *Proceedings of the Royal Society of London B, 266*, 2351–2354.

Marcus, D. K., John, S. L., & Edens, J. (2004). A taxometric analysis of psychopathic personality. *Journal of Abnormal Psychology, 113*, 626–635.

Mealey, L. (1995). The sociobiology of sociopathy: An integrated evolutionary model. *Brain and Behavioral Sciences, 18*, 523–599.

Meehl, P. E. (1992). Factors and taxa, traits and types, differences of degree and differences in kind. *Journal of Personality, 60*, 117–174.

Meehl, P. E. (1995). Bootstraps taxometrics: Solving the classification problem in psychopathology. *American Psychologist, 50*, 266–275.

Meehl, P. E. (1996). Bootstraps taxometrics. *American Psychologist, 50*, 266–275.

Meehl, P. E., & Golden, R. R. (1982). Taxometric methods. In J. N. Butcher and P. C. Kendall (Eds.), *The handbook of research methods in clinical psychology* (pp. 127–181). New York: Wiley.

Mercado, C. C., Elbogen, E. B., Scalora, M., & Tomkins, A. (2001). Judgements of dangerousness: Are sex offenders assessed differently than civil psychiatric patients? *Psychiatry, Psychology & Law, 8*, 146–153.

Monahan, J. (1981). *Predicting violent behavior: An assessment of clinical techniques.* Beverly Hills, CA: Sage.

Monahan, J., Steadman, H. J., Silver, E., Appelbaum, P. S., Clark Robbins, P., Mulvey, E. P., et al. (2001). *Rethinking risk assessment.* New York: Oxford University Press.

Neugebauer, R., Hoek, H. W., & Susser, E. (1999). Prenatal exposure to wartime famine and development of antisocial personality disorder in early adulthood. *Journal of the American Medical Association, 282*, 455–462.

Nuffield, J. (1982). *Parole decision-making in Canada: Research towards decision guidelines.* Ottawa, Ontario, Canada: Supply and Services Canada.

Pasewark, R. A., Bieber, S., Bosten, K. J., Kiser, M., & Steadman, H. J. (1982). Criminal recidivism among insanity acquittees. *International Journal of Law and Psychiatry, 5*, 365–374.

Porter, R. (1997). *The greatest benefit to mankind: A medical history of humanity.* New York: HarperCollins.

Porter, S., Birt, A., & Boer, D. P. (2001). Investigation of the criminal and conditional release profiles of Canadian federal offenders as a function of psychopathy and age. *Law and Human Behavior, 25*, 647–661.

Prentky, R. A., Knight, R. A. & Lee, A. F. S. (1997). Risk factors associated with recidivism among extrafamilial child molesters. *Journal of Consulting and Clinical Psychology, 65*, 141–149.

Quinsey, V. L. (1980). The baserate problem and the prediction of dangerousness: A reappraisal. *Journal of Psychiatry and Law, 8*, 329–340.

Quinsey, V. L., & Boyd, B. A. (1977). An assessment of the characteristics and dangerousness of patients held on Warrants of the Lieutenant Governor. *Crime and Justice, 4*, 268–274.

Quinsey, V. L., Coleman, G., Jones, B., & Altrows, I. (1997). Proximal antecedents of eloping and reoffending among mentally disordered offenders. *Journal of Interpersonal Violence, 12*, 794–813.

Quinsey, V. L., Harris, G. T., Rice, M. E., & Cormier, C. A. (1998). *Violent offenders: Appraising and managing risk.* Washington, DC: American Psychological Association.

Quinsey, V. L., Harris, G. T., Rice, M. E., & Cormier, C. A. (2005). *Violent offenders: Appraising and managing risk* (2nd. ed.). Washington, DC: American Psychological Association.

Quinsey, V. L., Pruesse, M., & Fernley, R. (1975). A follow-up of patients found "unfit to stand trial" or "not guilty" because of insanity. *Canadian Psychiatric Association Journal, 20*, 461–467.

Quinsey, V. L., Warneford, A., Pruesse, M., & Link, N. (1975). Released Oak Ridge patients: A follow-up of review board discharges. *British Journal of Criminology, 15*, 264–270.

Rice, M. E., & Harris, G. T. (1988). An empirical approach to the classification and treatment of maximum security psychiatric patients. *Behavioral Sciences and the Law, 6*, 497–514.

Rice, M. E., & Harris, G. T. (1992). A comparison of criminal recidivism among schizophrenic and nonschizophrenic offenders. *International Journal of Law and Psychiatry, 15*, 397–408.

Rice, M. E., & Harris, G. T. (1995a). Violent recidivism: Assessing predictive validity. *Journal of Consulting and Clinical Psychology, 63*, 737–748.

Rice, M. E., & Harris, G. T. (1995b). Psychopathy, schizophrenia, alcohol abuse and violent recidivism among mentally disordered offenders. *International Journal of Law and Psychiatry, 18*, 333–342.

Rice, M. E., & Harris, G. T. (1997). Cross validation and extension of the Violence Risk Appraisal Guide for child molesters and rapists. *Law and Human Behavior, 21*, 231–241.

Rice, M. E., Harris, G. T., & Cormier, C. (1992). Evaluation of a maximum security therapeutic community for psychopaths and other mentally disordered offenders. *Law and Human Behavior, 16*, 399–412.

Rice, M. E., Harris, G. T., Cormier, C. A., Lang, C., Coleman, G., & Smith Krans, T. (2004). An evidence-based approach to planning services for forensic psychiatric patients. *Issues in Forensic Psychology, 5*, 13–49.

Rice, M. E., Harris, G. T., Lang, C., & Bell, V. (1990). Recidivism among male insanity acquittees. *Journal of Psychiatry and Law, 18*, 379–403.

Rice, M. E., Harris, G. T., & Quinsey, V. L. (1990). A followup of rapists assessed in a maximum security psychiatric facility. *Journal of Interpersonal Violence, 5*, 435–448.

Rice, M. E., Harris, G. T., & Quinsey, V. L. (1996). Treatment for forensic patients. In B. Sales & S. Shah (Eds.), *Mental health and law: Research, policy and services* (pp. 141–189). New York: Carolina Academic Press.

Rice, M. E., Harris, G. T., Quinsey, V. L., & Cyr, M. (1990). Planning treatment programs in secure psychiatric facilities. In D. Weisstub (Ed.), *Law and mental health: International perspectives* (pp. 162–230). New York: Pergamon.

Rice, M. E., Quinsey, V. L., & Harris, G. T. (1991). Sexual recidivism among child molesters released from a maximum security psychiatric institution. *Journal of Consulting and Clinical Psychology, 59,* 381–386.

Ruscio, J., & Ruscio, M. A. (2000). Informing the continuity controversy: A taxometric analysis of depression. *Journal of Abnormal Psychology, 109,* 473–487.

Salekin, R. T. (2002). Psychopathy and therapeutic pessimism: Clinical lore or clinical reality? *Clinical Psychology Review, 22,* 79–112.

Serin, R. C., Mailloux, D. L., & Malcolm, P. B. (2001). Psychopathy, deviant sexual arousal and recidivism among sexual offenders: A psycho-culturally determined group offense. *Journal of Interpersonal Violence, 16,* 234–246.

Seto, M. C., Harris, G. T., Rice, M. E., & Barbaree, H. E. (2004). The Screening Scale for Pedophilic Interests and recidivism among adult sex offenders with child victims. *Archives of Sexual Behavior, 33,* 455–466.

Skeem, J. L., Monahan, J., & Mulvey, E. P. (2002). Psychopathy, treatment involvement, and subsequent violence among civil psychiatric patients. *Law and Human Behavior, 26,* 577–603.

Skilling, T. A., Harris, G. T., Rice, M. E., & Quinsey, V. L. (2002). Identifying persistently antisocial offenders using the Hare Psychopathy Checklist and DSM antisocial personality disorder criteria. *Psychological Assessment, 14,* 27–38.

Skilling, T., Quinsey, V. L., & Craig, W. A. (2001). Evidence of a taxon underlying serious antisocial behavior in boys. *Criminal Justice and Behavior, 28,* 450–470.

Steadman, H. J., & Cocozza, J. J. (1974). *Careers of the criminally insane: Excessive social control of deviance.* Toronto, Ontario, Canada: Lexington Books.

Wakefield, J. C. (1992). The concept of mental disorder: On the boundary between biological facts and social values. *American Psychologist, 47,* 373–388.

Waterhouse, L., Robin, M., Allen, D., Dunn, M., Fein, D., Feinstein, C., et al. (1996). Diagnosis and classification in autism. *Journal of Autism and Developmental Disorders, 26,* 59–86.

Weisman, R. (1995). Reflections on the Oak Ridge experiment with mentally disordered offenders, 1965–1968. *International Journal of Law and Psychiatry, 18,* 255–290.

Wilson, M., & Daly, M. (1993). An evolutionary psychological perspective on male sexual proprietariness and violence against wives. *Violence and Victims, 8,* 271–294.

Wollert, R. (2001). An analysis of the argument that clinicians under-predict sexual violence in civil commitment cases: Commentary. *Behavioral Sciences & the Law, 19,* 171–184.

II

METHODOLOGICAL AND MEASUREMENT ISSUES

4

Exploratory and Confirmatory Factor Analysis of the Psychopathy Construct: Methodological and Conceptual Issues

Craig S. Neumann, David S. Kosson, and Randy T. Salekin

In 2004, factor analysis became 100 years old. Charles Spearman's (1904) seminal article, "General Intelligence: Objectively Determined and Measured," was fundamental in establishing the theory and methodology of factor analysis (www.fa100.info). No doubt, the long history of this statistical tool in social science research is, in part, testament to its utility. In this chapter we examine the use of exploratory and confirmatory factor analysis as tools for research focused on elucidating the dimensions of the psychopathy construct. It is not intended to be a technical discussion of how to conduct such analyses or the mathematical underpinnings of these statistical tools. The goals of the current chapter are to (a) provide a brief overview of previous exploratory factor analytic research on the Psychopathy Checklist (PCL) and Psychopathy Checklist–Revised (PCL–R); (b) present conceptual and methodological issues that pertain to the application of exploratory and confirmatory factor analysis for research on psychopathy; and (c) discuss the recent three-factor (Cooke & Michie, 2001) and four-factor (Hare, 2003) models of psychopathy. To assist in illustrating some of the issues raised in this chapter, a large sample ($N =$ 4,865) of North American PCL–R data, provided by Dr. Robert Hare, is used to test contemporary factor models of psychopathy.

EXPLORATORY FACTOR ANALYSIS OF THE PCL AND PCL–R

Traditionally, psychopathy has been referred to as a construct underpinned by two stable factors or dimensions. However, despite widespread acceptance of the two-factor model, our review of many factor analytic studies indicates that there have been a variety of factor solutions for adults based on use of the PCL and the PCL–R; see Table 4–1 for a summary of factor analysis research on the PCL–R). Initial development and factor analysis of the PCL was conducted by Hare (1980). Prior to his factor analysis of the 22 PCL

TABLE 4–1.
Exploratory Factor Analysis Solutions for the PCL/PCL–R Across Studies (Adults)

VAF/Type of Factor Analysis	Factor Label						
	Factor 1	Factor 2	Factor 3	Factor 4	Factor 5	Factor 6	Factor 7
Hare (1980): 64.0% PCA	Lack of empathy, callous (29.3%)	Transient unstable lifestyle (12.0%)	Rejects responsibility for antisocial lifestyle (8.3%)	Absence of intellectual, psychiatric problems (7.1%)	Poor behavioral controls (6.6%)		
Hare (1980): 61% PCA	Impulsive, unstable lifestyle (27.3%)	Lack of empathy, callous (13.0%)	Superficial relationships with others (8.0%)	Early antisocial behavior (6.9%)	Impulsive, poorly motivated criminal acts (5.7%)		
Raine (1985): 65.0% PCA	Impulsivity (25%)	Emotional detachment (10.5%)	Egocentricity/ duplicity (7.6%)	Superficial relationships (6.5%)	Unclear (5.4%)	Early anti-sociality (5.2%)	Unclear (4.8%)
Harpur, Hakstian, & Hare (1988): NR PCA/PAF	Selfish, callous	Antisocial lifestyle					
Hare, Harpur, Hakstian, Forth, Hart, & Newman (1990): NR PCA?	Selfish, callous remorseless use of others	Chronically unstable, antisocial, socially deviant					

(continued)

TABLE 4-1.
(Continued)

VAF/Type of Factor Analysis	Factor Label						
	Factor 1	Factor 2	Factor 3	Factor 4	Factor 5	Factor 6	Factor 7
Salekin et al. (1997): 41.3% PAF	Lack of empathy or guilt/ interpersonal deception/ sensation seeking (34.0%)	Behavioral problems/ antisocial behavior/ sexual promiscuity (7.3%)					
Hobson & Shine (1998): 59.1% PCA	Antisocial lifestyle (24.4%)	Interpersonal characteristics (14.2%)	Unspecified (7.9%)	Unspecified (6.8%)	Unspecified (5.8%)		
Cooke & Michie (2001): NR PAF?	Interpersonal/ affective characteristics	Early behavior problems	Promiscuous, many short-term relations	Impulsive, irresponsible lifestyle	Revocation of release, criminal versatility		

Note. Percentages of variance accounted for (VAF) by the two-factor solution obtained by Harpur et al. (1988) and Hare et al. (1990) were not reported (NR), nor were such results for Cooke and Michie (2001).

81

items, Hare (1980) conducted a principal components factor analysis (PCA) of the 16 criteria of psychopathy outlined by Cleckley (1976). Using PCA with varimax rotation, Hare found that five factors resulted, which accounted for 64% of the variance of the Cleckley criteria. The first factor, *callous, lack of empathy*, accounted for 29.3%, and the second factor, *unstable, transient lifestyle* accounted for 12% of the variance. The third factor, *rejects responsibility for antisocial behavior*, accounted for 8.3% of the variance. The fourth factor, *absence of intellectual or psychiatric problems*, accounted for 7.1%. The fifth factor was difficult to interpret but appeared to reflect poor behavioral controls and accounted for an additional 6.6% of the variance.

Following his analysis of Cleckley's 16 criteria, Hare (1980) conducted a second factor analysis, this time utilizing the initial 22 PCL items he had developed. Hare again relied upon PCA with varimax rotation and found a five-factor solution that accounted for 61% of the variance. The first factor, *impulsive, unstable lifestyle* accounted for 27.3% of the variance. The second factor, *callous, lack of empathy*, accounted for 13.0% of the variance. The third factor, *superficial relationships with others*, accounted for 8.0% of the variance. The fourth factor, *early antisocial behavior*, accounted for 6.9% of the variance. The fifth factor, *impulsive, poorly motivated criminal acts*, accounted for 5.7% of the variance. Interestingly, this early factor solution has some similarities to a four-factor model currently being proposed for both adolescents (Forth, Kosson, & Hare, 2003; Kosson, Neumann, Forth, and Hare, 2004) and adults (Hare, 2003; Hill, Neumann, & Rogers, 2004; Vitacco, Neumann, & Jackson, 2005; Vitacco, Rogers, Neumann, Harrison, & Vincent, 2005), which is discussed in detail in the following.

Raine (1985) conducted a factor analysis of the PCL to determine whether the PCL could be used with forensic populations in England. He found a seven-factor solution for the PCL that accounted for 65.0% of the variance. The seven factors were labeled (a) *impulsivity* (25% variance accounted for), (b) *emotional detachment* (10.5%), (c) *egocentricity/duplicity* (7.6%), (d) *superficial relationships* (6.5%), (e) "unclear" (5.4%), (f) *early antisociality* (5.2%), and (g) "unclear" (4.8%). Although Raine's factor analysis produced seven factors, he compared his factor structure directly to Hare's (1980) earlier analyses and concluded that there was a high degree of concordance.

In the late 1980s, Hare and colleagues conducted additional independent factor analyses of the PCL and PCL–R, and in these studies a two-factor model was selected as the best representation of the dimensions that underlie the psychopathy construct. The first of these studies was conducted by Harpur, Hakstian, and Hare (1988). Contrary to the previous factor analyses of the 22-item PCL, the authors determined that a two-factor solution for the PCL was suitable. Factor 1 was labeled *selfish, callous, and remorseless use of others*, and Factor 2 was labeled *chronically unstable and antisocial lifestyle*. Unfortunately, the authors did not provide the overall variance accounted for by each factor.

The study by Harpur et al. (1988) was indeed an exceptional effort to try and determine the proper number of factors that underpinned PCL ratings. In their search for a single invariant factor pattern, the investigators relied upon independent samples so that they could conduct split-half cross-validation (via Samples 1, 2, and 3) to derive comparability coefficients (i.e., correlations between two sets of factor scores) and compared congruence coefficients among Samples 1–5. They also used both PCA and principal axis factoring (PAF; also known as common factor analysis). Of particular interest, Harpur et al. reported that three components were reliable for two of the larger samples. Similarly, in a follow-up PAF of Sample 1, three factors were again indicated. Nonetheless, relying upon the congruence coefficient results ($\geq.85$), the authors concluded that a two-factor solution was best.

Following the procedures of Harpur et al. (1988), Hare et al. (1990) conducted an independent factor analysis of the PCL–R, because they argued that the PCL–R differed slightly from the PCL and that it was important for the continuity of research to demonstrate empirically that the revised version did not differ substantially from the original. This latter study helped to demonstrate that the changes introduced with the PCL–R did not alter its psychometric properties, and, thus, the body of research accumulated using the PCL could be generalized to the PCL–R. Hare et al. conducted factor analyses on five of eight samples and reported a two-factor solution similar to that reported by Harpur et al. Notably, of the five samples, only four were used to obtain the pooled two-factor solution, because analysis of Sample 2 did not result in a two-factor solution. Hare et al. concluded again that the two factors reflected *selfish, callous, and remorseless use of others* and *chronically unstable, antisocial, and socially deviant lifestyle*. Taken together, the Harpur et al. and Hare et al. studies helped to establish that at least two factors were needed to understand the construct of psychopathy.

Using a British sample as opposed to the primarily North American samples in the Hare studies, Hobson and Shine (1998) conducted PCA with oblique rotation and identified five factors for the PCL–R. However, to be consistent with earlier factor analysis of the PCL–R, the authors decided on a two-factor model and reported the following results. The first factor was similar to the *antisocial lifestyle* factor described in the studies by Hare and colleagues. Ten items loaded at .4 or greater on this factor. Unlike the Hare studies, Item 20 (criminal versatility) loaded highly in their sample. The second factor was reported to be similar to Hare's factor measuring the *interpersonal characteristics* of psychopathy. Nine items loaded at .40 or greater on this factor, with eight being identical to the items reported by Hare (1991). The only difference noted by these authors was that Item 11 (promiscuous sexual behavior) loaded at .50 in their factor analysis but is not included in the items for either factor in the Hare model. For Hare et al. (1990), the loading for promiscuity was .35 and in Harpur et al. (1988), it was .32.

Salekin, Rogers, and Sewell (1997) conducted an exploratory factor analysis (EFA) on a sample of 103 female participants to see if the factor structure in a female sample was similar to that found in male samples. The authors reported two factors that appeared to be somewhat similar to the factors reported by Harpur et al. (1988), one being marked by interpersonal traits and the other by socially deviant behaviors; however, several of the individual

PCL–R items did not load on these factors in the same way as they did in male samples. Three of the items (poor behavioral controls, impulsivity, and lack of realistic long-term goals) cross-loaded (i.e., loaded on both factors), and three of the items (failure to accept responsibility, many short-term marital relationships, and revocation of conditional release) failed to load over .40 on any factor.

Recently, Cooke and Michie (2001) have called into question the adequacy of the two-factor solution. These authors reanalyzed PCL–R data sets from North America, and their EFA results indicated that five factors could be extracted from the data. Two of the factors resembled those for the two-factor model (Hare, 1991), one factor comprised Items 11 and 17 and the remaining two factors reflected juvenile and adult antisocial behavior, respectively.

In sum, the EFA studies indicated that at least two factors are required to represent the construct of psychopathy. However, they also suggested that its possible to model this construct with additional and perhaps more refined factors. Cooke and Michie (2001) argued that rigorous statistical tests of the PCL instruments do not offer strong support for a two-factor model of psychopathy. Using confirmatory factor analysis (CFA), these authors developed and tested a three-factor hierarchical model in which the Factor 1 dimension originally defined by Hare (1991) was reconceptualized as two distinct factors, named *arrogant and deceitful interpersonal style* (PCL–R Items 1, 2, 4, and 5) and *deficient affective experience* (Items 6, 7, 8, and 16). Cooke and Michie also suggested that modifications could be made to Factor 2 (Hare, 1991) by deleting various behavioral items such as "poor behavioral controls," "early behavioral problems," "juvenile delinquency," and "revocation of conditional release." Cooke and Michie's (2001) third factor was termed *impulsive and irresponsible behavioral style* (Items 3, 9, 13, 14, and 15), because they explicitly excluded antisocial behavior items (Items 10, 12, 18, 19, and 20; see later in the chapter for more on this decision).

Although Cooke and Michie's (2001) use of CFA may have helped in furthering research on the underlying dimensions of the psychopathy construct, their conclusion that a three-factor model was the best representation of the construct may have been premature. Subsequent confirmatory factor analytic studies have found support for a four-factor model of psychopathy when all, or nearly all, of the items are used from the PCL–R (Hare, 2003; Vitacco et al., 2005), the Psychopathy Checklist: Screening Version (PCL:SV) (Hill et al., 2004; Vitacco, Neumann, & Jackson, 2005), or the Psychopathy Checklist: Youth Version (PCL:YV) (Forth et al., 2003; Kosson et al., 2004; Salekin, Neumann, Leistico, & Zalot, 2004). In these studies, the three factors identified by Cooke and Michie (2001) were modeled in conjunction with a fourth factor that involved the items Cooke and Michie excluded. Thus, the four-factor model of psychopathy includes a dimension of antisocial behavior. The inclusion of antisocial behavior in a model of psychopathy is certainly consonant with many of the EFA studies reviewed earlier. However, before turning to a critique of the recent three- and four-factor models, a discussion of factor analysis and related methodological issues follows.

EFA VERSUS CFA

As is well known, EFA is a statistical tool for identifying a small number of factors (or latent variables) that summarize or explain the correlations among a larger set of items (or scales). No doubt, EFA is especially helpful when the underlying dimensionality of a measure or a set of measures is unclear (Everitt & Dunn, 2001). Based on recent research (Reise, Waller, & Comrey, 2000), it has been recommended that investigators consider the EFA method of PAF, instead of PCA. The recommendation stems from the fact that PAF solutions are based on the common variance shared among the items of a specific measure or the scales of several different measures (Gorsuch, 1983). Variance that is unique to some of the items (specific and error variance) is not part of the factor solution. In contrast, the PCA method attempts to explain all of the variance of the observed variables and does not distinguish between common versus unique variance (Everitt & Dunn, 2001). Thus, PAF can be used to explain the variance in common among a large set of observed variables via underlying (latent) factors, whereas PCA is simply used to create summaries of the observed variables (Reise et al., 2000). As such, the EFA studies discussed previously, which relied upon a PCA approach, are limited to the extent that the factor solutions may have been influenced, in part, by measurement error.

Although factor solutions that emerge from EFA provide a means for understanding of the pattern of correlations among large sets of variables, a number of issues affect the veracity of EFA solutions (Everitt & Dunn, 2001; Reise et al., 2000; Velicer & Fava, 1998). First, because no single index is definitive, investigators rely on a variety of different criteria; however, different criteria often yield different answers regarding the number of factors to retain. The eigenvalue and Scree test criteria have been commonly used, although each has notable problems in determining a viable factor solution (Everitt & Dunn, 2001; Reise et al., 2000). Pattern analysis has recently emerged as a useful method for determining factor solutions, although with an unambiguous solution cannot be guaranteed (Reise et al., 2000). For instance, Templeman and Wong (1994) used nine different criteria to try to identify the proper number of factors to extract from the PCL. These authors concluded that six to eight factors could be extracted using more upward biased criteria, but that the true factor solution lay somewhere between two and five factors. Although this study is not included in our review of PCL/PCL–R EFA studies because it was based solely on file review, it demonstrates a critical problem of EFA in determining the number of factors to retain.

The interpretability of a solution is, of course, critical for all EFA results. Interpretability refers to the subjective determination that the factors identified are theoretically meaningful. A factor solution is interpretable if the items (e.g., nervousness, variable mood, and loneliness) that load onto a factor appear to reflect an underlying dimension or factor (e.g., neuroticism). Thus, interpretable factors are helpful in "explaining" the covariance among the items (Everitt & Dunn, 2001). If the EFA results suggest that more than one factor can be extracted from the data, then the items that load onto each factor should manifest at least some conceptual distinction from the factors on which other items load.

Thus, the extent to which a solution provides a simple structure is also important. A solution yields a simple structure to the extent that particular items load highly on one and only one factor (i.e., items manifest little cross-loading onto other factors), and there are few items that fail to load on any of the factors. However, there are no objective guidelines for factor interpretation or determining how clean a factor solution is (Everitt & Dunn, 2001). Thus, the inherent subjectivity of EFA is one of its primary disadvantages. For example, in the Harpur et al. (1988) analyses Item 8 cross-loaded at greater than .40 on both Factors 1 and 2 for two of five independent samples, although this was not considered to be an interpretive problem.

It is also possible to estimate the amount of variance that a factor solution accounts for in the data, although, unfortunately, investigators often fail to provide such information. To the extent that a factor solution accounts for a substantial proportion (e.g., >50%) of the common variance, it provides a satisfactory solution for explaining the pattern of intercorrelations among the variables (Gorsuch, 1983). A different but related index is the extent to which a solution is able to reproduce the correlation matrix for a set of items. The reproduced correlation matrix (based on the factor solution) is subtracted from the observed correlation matrix, and the proportion of residual correlations exceeding a particular magnitude (e.g., .05) can be assessed to determine how well the factor solution reproduces the observed data. To the extent that there are few discrepancies between observed and reproduced correlation matrices, a factor solution is said to provide an accurate representation of the intercorrelations among the variables. However, both proportion of variance explained and the proportion of substantial residual correlations can be enhanced by simply extracting additional factors; therefore, interpretability of EFA is essential.

Finally, investigators also have the problem of determining the factor invariance of their solutions across EFA studies. Whereas congruence coefficients were once regularly derived to compare the similarity of factor solutions, this approach has come under considerable criticism (see Cooke & Michie, 2001, for a discussion of this issue). Moreover, congruence coefficients stemming from EFA that relies on PCA are likely to be based upon biased factor loadings because error of measurement is not taken into account. As discussed later, there is a stringent statistical method for comparing factor solutions across samples using CFA.

Although the subjective nature and uncertainty of EFA solutions is problematic, early studies depended upon this bottom-up approach for delineating the dimensions of psychopathy because it was one of the most sophisticated statistical approaches available. With advances in latent variable modeling and statistical software (Bentler, 1995; MacCallum & Austin, 2000), more recent researchers have been able to use a top-down or theory-driven approach to the study of psychopathy. This research is based, in part, on model-based measurement theory (Embretson, 1996; Embretson & Hershberger, 1999).

CFA is a relatively new and powerful statistical method for modeling theoretical constructs and the relations among constructs (Bentler, 1980; Dunn, Everett, & Pickels, 1993; Hoyle, 1995; MacCallum & Austin, 2000). This multivariate approach allows investigators to examine whether a set of observed or manifest variables (MVs) are valid indicators of specific hypothetical constructs or latent variables (LVs). A specific LV (e.g., deficient affective experience) is hypothesized to be responsible for generating the correlations among a specific set of MVs (e.g., PCL–R items 6, 7, 8, and 16). The value of LV CFA models is that they represent the common factor variance in a set of MVs separately from their unique/error variance (Bentler, 1980, 1995). In contrast, MV models are less reliable because the correlation between MVs is strongly influenced by the level of measurement error for each MV (and the same can be said of the PCA approach to EFA). Because LV models represent the common variance among two or more MVs, such models can be used to evaluate the cross-set correlations between factors (e.g., dimensions of psychopathy) in a less biased manner, because the factor correlations have been freed from the unique variance (Hoyle, 1995). As such, CFA provides precise parameter estimates adjusted for measurement error (Bentler, 1995). With the current PCL–R data as an example, the correlation between F1 and F2 at the MV level is .47 but at the LV level is .59.

Another advantage of a CFA approach is that hypothesized models can be directly tested for their statistical goodness of fit to the observed data. In conducting CFA, investigators must explicitly specify the number of factors, the variable-to-factor relations, and the factor variances and covariances within a model and then statistically test the adequacy of the model in terms of standard model fit criteria (MacCallum, 1995). In the structural equation modeling (SEM) literature (Bentler, 1980; Hoyle, 1995), CFA refers to the measurement model component of SEM (variable-to-factor relations), whereas the regression of factors onto other factors involves the structural component (factors-to-factors) of SEM.

When CFA is used to test a factor (or LV) model, investigators use several indices of model fit. Because each fit index captures different information about model fit, researchers are encouraged to report multiple fit indices (Hu & Bentler, 1999). A distinction is made between absolute and incremental (or relative) indices of fit (Hu & Bentler, 1995). Generally, absolute fit indices examine the discrepancy between the observed sample covariances and the model-generated covariances, whereas incremental fit indices compare the improvement of fit of the hypothesized model over a null (or independence) model, which assumes little or no clear factor structure in explaining the covariance among items (Hu & Bentler, 1995). Research by Hu and Bentler (1999) has shown that the standardized root-mean-square (SRMR) index and the comparative fit index (CFI), respectively, are preferred indices for assessing absolute and relative model fit. Good fit is evident when the SRMR value is .08 or less and the CFI value is at least .90 or greater (with >.94 providing evidence of excellent fit). One other absolute index, the root-mean-square error of approximation (RMSEA), measures how well a model fits the data in the population, given the number of free parameters (Steiger, 1990) and is a good measure of a model's parsimony. A RMSEA value of approximately .06–.08 or less is indicative of good fit. A second relative fit index is the non-normed fit index (NNFI), which quantifies the degree to which a hypothesized model provides improvement over the null model (Chou & Bentler, 1995). In contrast, the CFI index quantifies the reduction in the amount of misfit of the hypothesized model (because no model can perfectly explain the data) compared to the null model.

Finally, it is possible to conduct multiple group (or sample) CFA to determine whether a particular model is invariant among two or more groups. In multiple group CFA, the variable-to-factor loadings and factor relations are constrained to be equal across groups, and the model fit indices indicate the adequacy of such constraints (Bentler, 1995). Follow-up analyses indicate which constraints, if any, could be released to improve model fit. Thus, as opposed to congruence coefficients in EFA, multiple group CFA allows investigators to determine precisely where a model is not invariant or if the groups (samples) can be constrained to the same pattern of factor loadings and factor correlations.

In sum, the CFA approach has some advantages relative to EFA. In EFA there are no definitive criteria for ensuring the appropriate number of factors to extract (Gorsuch, 1983; Reise et al., 2000). In CFA, the adequacy of a model specifying a specific number of factors and variable-to-factor relationships is tested directly. Also, although factor solutions in which each variable loads primarily onto one factor are desired, investigators often report EFA models in which variables cross-load onto multiple factors (Dunn et al., 1993; Reise et al., 2000), and this result makes interpretation of factor solutions and corresponding factor correlations difficult (Comrey, 1988). It could be argued that CFA is too restrictive in that variables are often set to load on only one factor, and, thus, CFA models may not reflect the complexity of some constructs (Reise et al., 2000). However, it is entirely possible to test CFA models with hypothesized cross-loadings. Moreover, because of the necessary precise model specifications in conducting CFA, such models are often more meaningful and interpretable than EFA solutions.

Also, EFA models are data driven, whereas models tested with CFA are specified a priori via a theoretical model. As a consequence of this limitation, EFA-generated models often fit poorly in CFA follow-up studies (van Prooijen & van der Kloot, 2001), and this has sometimes been the case when the EFA-generated two-factor model of psychopathy has been tested using CFA (Kosson et al., 2004; Vitacco et al., 2005), although there are some exceptions (Hill et al., 2004). Nevertheless, when the underlying factor structure of a particular measure is unknown, investigators may have little choice but to begin to explore their data with EFA and then use CFA for follow-up analyses to confirm or reject EFA solutions. Fortunately, research on the psychopathy construct (Cooke & Michie, 2001; Hare, 2003) has provided theoretical models that may be tested with CFA. These models will be discussed in detail later in this chapter; however, the point for now is that CFA provides a comprehensive statistical approach for testing hypotheses about relations among observed and latent variables (Hoyle, 1995). Thus, CFA, more so than EFA, allows investigators to pursue explicit tests of their theoretical constructs. Next, we turn to a discussion of the data used for conducting EFA and CFA.

Data Subjected to Factor Analysis

A critical issue in conducting either EFA or CFA pertains to the nature of the data (i.e., items or scales) that are subjected to such analyses. Maximum likelihood (ML) is the most relied upon statistical method for estimating the parameters (e.g., factor loadings) in a factor analysis model (Everitt & Dunn, 2001). However, the ML method is based upon the assumption of multivariate normality and to the extent that the data depart from such a distribution, the parameter estimates from the factor analysis will be biased (Dunn et al., 1993). As is often the case when one is studying clinical phenomena, the data are most definitely not normal.

There are several potential remedies to help deal with non-normal data, but each has implications for model testing. First, investigators will often transform their raw data (e.g., square root or natural logarithm) and then analyze the transformed data. This is certainly a viable option but is problematic if both means and covariances are being modeled and the transformation results in nonlinearity of the model-generated means (Dunn et al., 1993). Also, transforming the data creates interpretive problems if it results in a departure from an original scale metric, which has practical significance (e.g., PCL–R ratings).

Second, investigators have the option to exclude cases that play a prominent role in creating the non-normality. The EQS modeling program (Bentler, 1995) has several excellent features that identify cases that make large contributions to multivariate kurtosis or parameter variance. Deletion of such extreme cases may result in a significant drop in kurtosis and improvements in model fit. However, investigators must seriously consider whether such extreme cases represent outliers and, thus, data points that could bias model fit and parameter estimates or whether they represent the more severe expression of psychopathology. In the latter case, deleting such cases may reduce the accuracy of the model as a representation of the phenomenon of interest.

Third, and perhaps the best approach for dealing with non-normal clinical data, is to estimate the model using the raw data, but then obtain model fit indices and parameter estimates via robust methods that are designed to correct for non-normality. The EQS program (Bentler, 1995) provides a scaled chi-square statistic, robust standard errors, and a robust CFI fit statistic, all of which are corrected for the degree of kurtosis in the variables and thus provide more precise fit and parameter estimates under conditions of multivariate non-normality (Chou & Bentler, 1995). Similarly, the Mplus modeling program (Muthen & Muthen, 2001) uses a robust weighted least squares procedure for parameter estimation and model fit and is designed for modeling categorical (as well as continuous) data. The EQS program's robust features have been helpful for modeling psychopathy in adolescent data that are highly skewed and kurtotic (Kosson et al., 2004), and the Mplus program has also worked well for modeling psychopathy in both adjudicated adolescent (Salekin, Neumann, Lestico, & Zalot, 2004) and adult psychiatric samples (Vitacco, Neumann, & Jackson, 2005).

A related issue concerns the availability of samples in which participants manifest the full range of possible scores on the items subjected to analysis. Such samples aid in the accurate estimation of the population item intercorrelations and in the identification of replicable factor solutions (Reise et al., 2000). When data from specialized samples are subjected to factor analyses, there may be a restriction in some item scores, leading to skewed and kurtotic data, which may result in sample-dependent solutions that are not replicated in independent samples. Thus, the use of larger, more heterogeneous, samples tends to yield more reliable factor solutions than do more restricted samples (Reise et al., 2000). At a minimum, investigators need to report both the univariate and multivariate skew and kurtosis of their sample data to assist in the interpretation of their model results.

Finally, one of the most under-recognized problems in applied factor analytic research concerns the nature of the items used to assess various constructs. In many areas of psychology and psychiatry, individuals are assessed with instruments using symptom or trait ratings that are based on an ordinal rather than an interval scale. For example, psychopathy ratings usually involve a determination of whether a trait is absent (0), present but below a clinical threshold (1), or present at a clinically significant level (2). In such cases, there is no clear interval scale between the ordered ratings. Of course, it may be that each trait being rated is continuously distributed in the population, and, thus, ratings are not conceptualized as categorical variables. Instead, such ordinal ratings arise from thresholding an underlying continuous variable (Everitt & Dunn, 2001). Nevertheless, such ordinal variables are not ideally suited to factor analysis, which relies on the maximum likelihood procedure (Everitt & Dunn, 2001; West, Finch, & Curran, 1995). Attenuation of parameter estimates can occur when few ordinal categories are used (fewer than five), and such variables are skewed (West et al., 1995). In particular, factor loadings and factor correlations will be underestimated to the extent that the ordinal variables are skewed (Everitt & Dunn, 2001; West et al., 1995). Of note is the fact that error variance parameters may be severely biased, and spurious correlations may occur between variables whose error variances reflect a similar degree of skewness (West et al., 1995). As a consequence, attenuation of parameters and spurious correlations will probably contribute to model mis-specification and adversely affect model fit.

To illustrate the results of not accounting for the ordinal nature of the PCL–R items, a model was tested using Mplus (Muthen & Muthen, 2001) in which the PCL–R items were treated as continuous variables and the ML procedure for estimating parameters was used. Then, the same model was retested, but the PCL–R items were treated as ordinal variables and a robust weighted least squares (RWLS) procedure was used for parameter estimation. The model tested for this illustration was the four-factor model (Hare, 2003), because it is featured below in a discussion on models of psychopathy and because the Cooke and Michie (2001) three-factor model is contained within the four-factor model. To test the model, the North American PCL–R data of male offenders was used; only those cases that had values for all 20 PCL–R items ($N = 4,865$) were included. The items showed differential skew (range $= 0.10$ to 0.31 versus -0.03 to -0.77), but were uniformly platykurtic (range $= -0.61$ to -1.63). Mardia's multivariate kurtosis estimate was 5.74, and the normalized estimate was 7.47. Fit for the four-factor model using the ML procedure was SRMR $= .05$, RMSEA $= .06$, NNFI $= .85$, and CFI $= .90$. Model fit for the four-factor-model using RWLS was SRMR $= .05$, RMSEA $= .07$, NNFI $= .94$, and CFI $= .90$.

As can be seen, the model results using ML resulted in underestimation of relative fit compared with the model tested using RWLS. However, more salient differences between these two model runs occurred at the level of factor loadings. Standardized parameters are presented for the four-factor model of psychopathy tested via ML (see Fig. 4–1) versus RWLS (see Fig. 4–2). On average, the ML procedure underestimated factor loadings by approximately .08. This is not a trivial difference. Because factor loadings

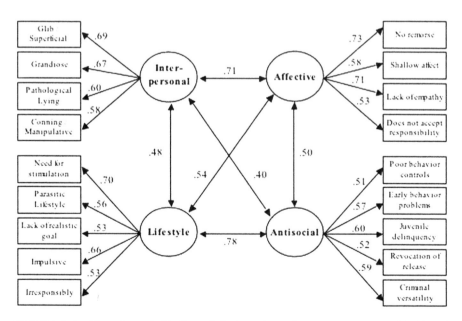

FIGURE 4–1. Four-factor PCL–R model of psychopathy using maximum likelihood estimation.

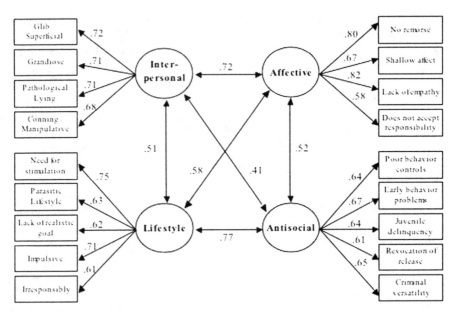

FIGURE 4–2.   Four-factor PCL–R model of psychopathy using robust weighted least squares.

are equivalent to item discrimination parameters in item response theory (Reise, 1999), the ML-based loadings provide biased estimates of how well each PCL–R item discriminates those low versus high on the respective psychopathy factors. For example, the interpersonal factor explained less than 50% of the variance in the "glib/superficial" item in the ML results (i.e., $.69^2 = .47$). The RWLS results indicated that the interpersonal factor accounted for the majority of the variance of this item (i.e., $.72^2 = .52$), showing that the item performs well in discriminating individuals on this psychopathy dimension. Of note is the fact that in other psychopathy research in which the PCL items were treated as ordinal versus continuous, we have found more pronounced differences in model fit and factor loadings using smaller sample sizes (Salekin, Neumann, Leistico, & DiCicco, 2004; Vitacco et al., 2005).

An additional advantage of Mplus is that it generates item threshold values when the items are treated as binary or ordinal variables. These parameters provide information on the difficulty or extremity of each item (Reise, 1999). In terms of the PCL instruments, item threshold parameters allow investigators to identify which items tend to be endorsed at high levels of the psychopathy latent trait. For instance, in this large sample of male offenders the PCL–R interpersonal (Items 1, 2, and 4) and affective (Item 7) items tended to have large (b2) threshold parameters, suggesting that these characteristics were expressed (i.e., item ratings of 2) at relatively high levels of the psychopathy latent trait. Not surprisingly, given the composition of the sample, certain antisocial items (Items 18 and 20) had low threshold parameters and thus were expressed at low levels of the psychopathy trait. However, it should be noted that other behavioral (Item 9) and antisocial (Item 12) items had relatively high threshold values as well.

Items versus Parcels versus Testlets

Depending on one's approach, binary or ordinal variables may not pose a problem (Reise, 1999), and as shown in the preceding section, the Mplus program (Muthen & Muthen, 2001) is well suited for analysis of such variables. However, one other solution proposed by West et al. (1995) for dealing with ordinal variables is to re-express the items to form item composites (or "parcels"). This approach involves summing or taking the mean of several items that measure the same construct (or dimension) to obtain variables that more closely approximate a normal distribution than the original items (Bagozzi & Heatherton, 1994; Little, Cunningham, Shahar, & Widaman, 2002). The use of item-based (or scale-based) parcels rather than all single items (scales) as indicators for LVs has been established in applications of structural equation modeling (Byrne, 1988; Greenbaum & Dedrick, 1998; Marsh, 1994; Marsh & O'Neill, 1984; Marsh, Smith, & Barnes, 1985). Moreover, the use of parcels may be particularly important for modeling clinical variables, which tend to come from small samples that often have skewed and kurtotic distributions.

The use of parcels, versus single items, as indicators for the LVs (latent variables or factors) is advantageous because parcels are more reliable and valid indicators of LVs, have higher communalities, provide more efficient (low variability) parameter estimates, and reduce the number of parameters that have to be estimated, thus improving the ratio of the number of subjects relative to the number of estimated parameters (Bagozzi & Heatherton, 1994; Little et al., 2002; Marsh, 1994; West et al., 1995). In addition, parcels are more normally distributed than individual items, given that items tend to have fewer, larger, and less equal intervals between scale points compared with parcels (Little et al., 2002).

Several key issues must be addressed before using parcels (Little et al., 2002). First, investigators must understand the dimensionality of their constructs and the measures used to assess them. Both constructs and measures can be either unidimensional or multidimensional. Therefore, it is important to initially model data at the item level to ensure that the items that will be used to make up a parcel reflect a single dimension (Bandalos & Finney, 2001). Otherwise, parceling could mask cross-loadings of items (Bandalos, 1997), which may or may not be a source of model mis-specification (Little et al., 2002). Second, constructs vary in terms of their level of explicitness, and highly explicit constructs (e.g., autonomic responsivity) are more easily represented in terms of specific variables or *items* (e.g., heart rate or skin conductance). Conversely, other constructs (e.g., fearlessness) can be determined by a broader domain of variables and, thus, may be best represented by aggregating many representative items into parcels (Little et al., 2002).

Finally, measures vary in terms of unwanted sources of systematic error variance (e.g., rating bias or social desirability). To the extent that a measure's items contain such variance, the modeling results will be jeopardized (e.g., spurious factors). However, parcels have been shown to cancel out random and systematic error variance by aggregating across such errors (Little et al., 2002).

Recently, Neumann and colleagues have found the parcel approach to be effective for modeling psychopathy in adolescents (Forth et al., 2003; Kosson et al., 2004) as well as for modeling psychopathy and other related constructs involved in juvenile transfer to adult court (Salekin, Yiff, Neumann, Leistico, & Zalot, 2002), psychopathy and intelligence (Salekin, Neumann, Leistico, & DiCicco), and malingering (Rogers & Neumann, 2003).

To illustrate the viability of the parcel approach with the PCL–R data, a four-factor parcel model of psychopathy was tested, based on the same North American PCL–R data used earlier. Creation of unidimensional parcels was guided by Cooke and Michie's (2001) item response theory research with the PCL–R. These authors found that pairs or triplets of items could be represented by unidimensional first-order factors (which they referred to as *testlets*). This research provides evidence that single dimensions underlie specific pairs or triplets of items and thus can be safely converted into item composites (i.e., parcels).[1]

Eight parcels were derived by computing the mean of the following item pairs or triplets: (a) 1 and 2, (b) 4 and 5, (c) 7 and 8, (d) 6 and 16, (e) 3, 14, and 15, (f) 9 and 13, (g) 10 and 12, and finally, (h) 18, 19, and 20. Each item correlated, on average, .82 with its respective parcel. Next, two parcels each were designated indicators for their respective interpersonal (a and b), affective (c and d), behavioral (e and f), or antisocial (g and h) factor (see Fig. 4–3). As recommend by Little et al. (2002), the loadings for each parcel that loaded onto a specific factor were constrained to be equal. Model fit for the four-factor par-

---

[1]Note that parcels (i.e., sums or means of item groupings) are quite different from teslets (i.e., items set to load on particular first-order factors), even though each may have similar purposes (e.g., controlling for systematic specific or error variance). The most obvious difference is that parceling items results in a different covariance matrix to be modeled, compared to the same item set that is not parceled. For example, suppose someone wanted to test a two-factor model based on a measure that has 20 items. To create a two-factor parcel model, one could take pairs of items from the 20 items to form 10 parcels and then load 5 parcels onto one (first-order) common factor and the remaining 5 parcels set to load onto the second (first-order) common factor. This 10 "item" parcel model has 55 data points to be modeled (i.e., variances/covariances = $10 \times 11/2 = 55$), is estimating 21 free parameters (10 factor loadings, 10 error variances, and 1 factor correlation), and, thus, has 34 df. Conversely, a 20-item testlet model could be created that uses 10 testlets (with 2 items each serving as indicators for one of the respective testlets—i.e., first-order factors) and then have 5 testlets loading onto one (second-order) common factor, and the remaining 5 testlets set to load onto the second (second-order) common factor. This 20-item testlet model has 210 data points to be modeled ($20 \times 21/2$), is estimating 41 free parameters (10 first-order factor loadings [given that 1 loading/testlet must be set to unity], 20 error variances, 10 second-order factor loadings, and 1 second-order factor correlation), and, thus, has 169 df. Conceptually, each model may be similar, but statistically they are completely different.

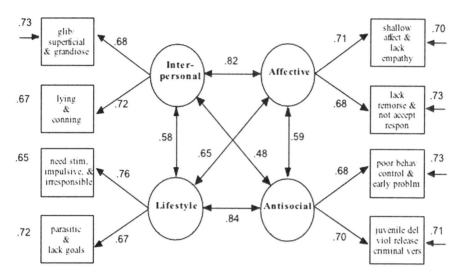

FIGURE 4–3.   Four-factor parcel model of psychopathy.

cel model was excellent, SRMR = .04, RMSEA = .07, NNFI = .92, and CFI = .95, and closely approximated the RWLS fit results presented above.

Noteworthy is the good convergence between parcel-based and item-based four-factor model parameters, particularly the results based on ordinal items and RWLS parameter estimation. As expected, the parcels generally had communalities equal to or greater than the items in the item-based models, while also reducing skew (range = 0.00 to 0.25; −0.06 to −0.65) and kurtosis (range = −0.55 to −1.12). Mardia's multivariate kurtosis estimate was −2.65 (normalized estimate = −7.30) for the parcel model. The factor correlations were higher in the parcel model compared with the item-based models. However, as discussed earlier, this may be due to spurious correlations between individual items that tend to be less reliable and valid than parcels and, thus, will reduce correlations between factors. In fact, the use of parcel (vs. item) models reduces the probability of spurious correlations (Little et al., 2002). Because CFA involves modeling covariance structures, this source of bias is a serious concern. For instance, the four-factor 18-item-based PCL–R model has, by chance alone (α = .05, Type 1 error = 1/20), the possibility of having approximately eight spurious correlations ([18 × 17]/2 = 153 unique correlations, and 153/20 = 7.65). In contrast, the four-factor parcel model will by chance have only about one spurious correlation in its eight-item correlation matrix.

An alternative to the parceling approach is the identification of group factors or testlets. Instead of aggregating across items, the testlet approach is a factor analytic method of accounting for specific variance as part of an overall hierarchical model (see Footnote 1). In this approach, smaller groups of items may share specific variance with each other (separate from their common variance with a larger set of items), representing a narrowly defined but legitimate group factor (Reise et al., 2000). Cooke and Michie (2001) believed the testlet level was important for obtaining improved fit because of "local dependence" among specific items.

However, it is also possible that testlets may reflect what has been referred to as difficulty factors. As discussed by West et al. (1995, p. 64), "When there are only a small number of categories (e.g., two), the degree of skewness is determined by the percentage of subjects in the study agreeing with (or pass-ing) the item. Thus, a set of items with similar agreement rates (e.g., 15% to 20%) can give rise to a spurious factor (so-called difficulty factor) reflecting only the common degree of skewness among the items." To the extent that the testlets identified by Cooke and Michie (2001) represent difficulty factors, they may reflect distributional tendencies of the PCL–R items rather than aspects of the psychopathy construct.

A larger concern with the Cooke and Michie (2001) testlet model is that it appears to result in overfactoring of the data. That is, in their hierarchical PCL–R model 10 factors are used to explain the covariances of 13 items. Not surprisingly, for this nearly saturated model some of the residual error para-meters are reported to be zero (see Cooke & Michie, 2001, Fig. 2, p. 177). Is it feasible that certain factors were able to provide perfect errorless measure-ment? Realistically, it is unlikely that the residual parameters were estimated to be zero; rather the computations carried out by EQS most likely resulted in lower bound errors (e.g., negative error variance), which causes EQS to set specific parameters at zero value (see Bentler, 1995, for an extended discus-sion of this issue). In other modeling research (Kosson, Cyterski, Steuerwald, Neumann, & Walker-Matthews, 2002; Salekin, Neumann, Leistico, & DiCicco, 2004) testlets were not required to fit the three-factor model, but including the testlets resulted in lower bound error model mis-specifications.

DO TWO, THREE, OR FOUR DIMENSIONS UNDERLIE THE PSYCHOPATHY CONSTRUCT?

It is essential that investigators understand the dimensionality of their con-struct(s). In other words, CFA researchers must understand how many latent variables are influencing the items used to measure each construct. Not only is this important for interpreting scores on a measure, but also the different dimensions of a construct may correlate differentially with critical external variables (Reise, 1999).

Typically, statistical comparisons of two or more theory-based CFA mod-els involve use of the same items or scales within each model (Hoyle, 1995). In this way, a model (e.g., two correlated factors) can be nested within another model (e.g., four correlated factors) by setting the parameters in one model to be a subset of the free parameters of the other model (Mulaik &

James, 1995). Differences between the fit of such models can be determined via a chi-square difference test (Bentler, 1995). Using the PCL–R data again, it is straightforward to show that the four-factor model provides better fit than the version of the two-factor model $[\chi^2(5)_{\text{diff}} = 1{,}180]$ in the revised PCL–R manual (Hare, 2003). A four-factor model that excludes item 20 still provides better fit than the traditional two-factor model $[\chi^2(5)_{\text{diff}} = 1{,}044]$.

Direct comparison of the three- and four-factor models, however, is no easy task. The decision by Cooke and Michie (2001) to exclude items from the three-factor model resulted in a fundamental change in the item set that had regularly been used by investigators in the study of psychopathy. Because the three-factor model is based on a different covariance matrix compared with the two- and four-factor models, direct statistical comparison between the three- and four-factor models is not possible. Thus, assessment of the verisimilitude (Meehl, 2002) of each model must be based on other criteria (Mulaik, 2002).

A full discussion of the consequences stemming from Cooke and Michie's (2001) decision to delete PCL items from their model and the difficulty it poses for comparison with other models of psychopathy is outside the scope of the current chapter. Moreover, Neumann and colleagues have attempted to address these issues at length elsewhere (see Vitacco, Neumann, & Jackson, 2005). Briefly, we have suggested that the three- and four-factor models can be compared in terms of different aspects of validity: substantive, structural, and external. The first is the theoretical basis upon which certain symptom or trait ratings are included in or excluded from the model. The second involves whether a model's factor structure accurately represents the processes underlying the construct of interest. Finally, the third suggests that models can be evaluated with respect to the network of inter-relations they have with external correlates.

Of course, the community of scholars will have to determine whether Cooke and Michie's (2001) claim that antisocial behavior is not a core feature of psychopathy is substantively valid. Some investigators do and others do not include antisocial behavior as part of the psychopathy construct (Berrios, 1996; Cleckley, 1941; Coid, 1993; Hare, 2003; Pinel, 1801). Certainly, psychopathic traits (e.g., callousness and impulsivity) are predictors of future antisocial behavior (Frick, Cornell, Barry, Bodin, & Dane, 2003; Vitacco, Neumann, Robertson, & Durrant, 2002). However, it is also important to highlight the fact that prior antisocial behavior is associated with higher levels of callousness and other psychopathic traits (Brandt, Kennedy, Patrick, & Curtin, 1997; Dowson, Sussams, Grounds, & Taylor, 2001; Frick et al., 2003; Lynam, 1998). Such findings are consistent with the fact that repeated exposure to antisocial acts desensitizes individuals' negative emotional responses to such behavior (Anderson et al., 2003), suggesting that antisocial behavior can precede callousness or other psychopathy traits. For instance, Knight and Sims-Knight (2003) found good fit for an SEM hypothesizing that physical/verbal abuse produced callousness/lack of emotionality.

In contrast, other researchers suggest that adults' retrospective reports of their childhood conduct problems primarily predict their ratings on PCL:YV F2 (Abramowitz, Kosson, and Seidenberg, 2004). Similarly, Sullivan, Bagley, and Kosson (2004) found that adolescents early externalizing/antisocial behaviors were unrelated to PCL:YV F1 scores but were significantly correlated with PCL:YV F2 scores. Clearly, longitudinal studies will be helpful in furthering our understanding of the link between antisocial behavior and other psychopathic traits.

In terms of structural validity, the three-factor model is associated with good fit (Cooke & Michie, 2001), whether it is modeled as a hierarchical model with testlets (which may result in a mis-specified model), or the testlets are eliminated and the PCL–R items load directly onto three correlated factors (i.e., a modified three-factor model, see Kosson et al., 2002, 2004). As shown earlier, the four-factor model also results in good fit. A critical difference between the three- and four-factor models is that the former is a less parsimonious model from a mathematical modeling perspective. That is, the 13 items in the Cooke and Michie (PCL–R) testlet model has only 91 data points (variances and covariances) to be modeled, but requires 35 free parameters to achieve good fit ($df = 56$). However, the four-factor model (18 items) is a less saturated model ($df = 129$) because it explains 171 data points while using only 42 free parameters to do so. Thus, despite having more factors, the four-factor model explains more data points with fewer parameters: data points. The same point holds when a modified (i.e., without testlets) three-factor model (29:91) is compared with the four-factor model (42:171).

Mulaik (2002) and MacCallum (1995) provided excellent discussions on the link between degrees of freedom and model disconfirmability. Specifically, a model's degrees of freedom can be used as a measure of its disconfirmability because they reflect the number of dimensions in which the data are free to differ from the model-generated data. Models with more degrees of freedom have greater verisimilitude when they acceptably fit the data (Mulaik, 2002). Thus, the four-factor model's structural validity is enhanced to the degree that it survives a riskier test of disconfirmation compared with the three-factor model. As expected the parsimony-driven RMSEA index is higher for the (modified) three-factor model (.07) than for the four-factor model (.06), indicating that the former results in slightly less parsimonious fit.

Finally, in research with the PCL:SV, Neumann and colleagues have found that the four-factor model, compared with the three-factor, accounts for greater variance in maximum security patients' aggression at a 6-month follow up (Hill et. al., 2004) and in psychiatric patients' community violence at a 10-week follow-up (Vitacco et al., 2005). Each study showed that, in addition to the antisocial factor, other psychopathy factors were also critical predictors. In terms of research with the PCL–R, Walsh, Swogger, and Kosson (2003) found that the antisocial factor of the PCL–R contributed uniquely to postdicting blind ratings of the instrumentality of violence. Thus, current findings suggest that the four-factor model has incremental validity over the three-factor in predicting important external correlates of psychopathy.

First-Order versus Higher-Order Latent Variable Models

In the same way that a set of intercorrelated manifest variables can be represented by a higher-order latent variable, the strong correlations between the factors in the current PCL–R models reveal that they are indicators for a second-order latent variable (or second-order latent variables, see Hare, 2003). Indeed, it would be a simple task to remove the correlations between the first-order factors and set them to load onto a superordinate psychopathy factor. However, if the four factors have differential associations with external correlates, then it would be unwise to use a superordinate model to seek out such differential associations. For example, using SEM, we recently reported that the PCL:SV interpersonal factor positively predicted verbal intelligence (IQ), whereas the affective and behavioral factors negatively predicted verbal IQ (Vitacco et al., 2005). The negative relation between behavioral impulsivity and verbal IQ is consistent with previous research (Harris et al., 2001; Loeber et al., 2001). However, the fact that the interpersonal factor positively predicted IQ is consistent with Cleckley's assertion that some aspects of psychopathy are associated with good intelligence, which Salekin, Neumann, Leistico, & Zalot et al. (2004) have previously demonstrated as well. Taken together, the findings that verbal IQ is differentially related to the dimensions of psychopathy helps to explain previous inconsistent findings regarding IQ and psychopathy (Hare, 2003).

Several additional studies have also shown that the psychopathy dimensions are differentially related to key external correlates. Using the PCL:SV, Dolan and Anderson (2003) found that the interpersonal factor was positively related to serotonergic functioning but that an impulsivity–antisocial behavior factor was inversely associated with serotonin. These investigators found no correlation between serotonin and PCL:SV total score.

With respect to the PCL–R, Sullivan (2003) reported that the interpersonal and affective factors were differentially related to measures of interpersonal behavior. Further, Walsh et al. (2003) reported that the interpersonal and antisocial factors positively postdicted ratings of the instrumentality of violent crime per se, whereas the affective factor was inversely related to instrumentality of violence. More recently, Walsh, Allen, Sullivan, and Kosson (2004) reported that the PCL–R factors were uniquely associated with abuse of and dependence on different psychoactive substances. Whereas lifestyle scores were generally predictive of abuse of or dependence on most psychoactive substances, antisocial scores were uniquely predictive of alcohol abuse or dependence, and interpersonal scores were uniquely predictive of cocaine abuse or dependence. Finally, Swogger, Walsh, and Kosson (2004) have shown that, among offenders with three or more features of antisocial personality disorder, PCL–R affective scores positively postdicted charges for domestic battery, whereas lifestyle scores *negatively* postdicted charges for domestic battery, and interpersonal scores were not significantly related to charges for such offenses. In sum, these differential relations between the psychopathy factors and a variety of important criteria would not have been identified if a superordinate model (or total PCL scores) had been used. Thus, we recommend using first-order models with correlated factors in future research.

FUTURE DIRECTIONS

It may turn out that there is no single best model of psychopathy; rather it may be that certain models have greater utility in certain contexts or depend upon one's research goals. Moreover, we realize that only a great deal of additional research will help resolve the role that antisocial behavior should play in future conceptualizations of psychopathy. As such, in conducting further research on latent variable models of psychopathy, we believe there are several avenues that are worth pursuing. First, the four-factor model appears to be a viable model for representing the dimensions of psychopathy, particularly because it allows one to test whether the interpersonal, affective, or behavior factors exhibit incremental validity, above and beyond the antisocial factor, in predicting external correlates. The four-factor parcel model may be useful in such research, because it has a good subject-to-parameter ratio and, thus, additional factors for testing more complex models can be easily incorporated (see Salekin, Neumann, Leistico, & Zalot, 2004). Second, the four-factor model tested longitudinally would allow investigators to determine whether antisocial behavior predicts the other psychopathy factors, or if the reverse is true. On the other hand, the relations between the four-factors may be reciprocal, as is the case for substance abuse and antisocial traits (Neumann, Vitacco, Robertson, & Sewell, 2003, Rohde, Lewinsohn, P., Kahler, C. W., Seeley J. R., Brown, 2001). For instance, the longitudinal cross-lag associations between the affective and antisocial factors may be of similar magnitude. Finally, there are a host of other latent variable approaches (e.g., multilevel, linear growth, multiple indicator-multiple cause [MIMC], mixture models) that can be used to address other issues in psychopathy such as treatment outcome, growth in psychopathic traits over time, the effects of background variables (e.g., socioeconomic status or school quality) on the expression of psychopathy and latent profile analysis. Indeed, other latent variable approaches will allow investigators to test comprehensive theories of the causes and consequences of psychopathy.

ACKNOWLEDGMENT

The authors are indebted to Dr. Robert D. Hare and Multi-Health Systems Inc. for allowing use of the North American PCL–R data of male offenders.

REFERENCES

Abramowitz, C. S., Kosson, D. S., & Seidenberg, M. (2004). The relationship between childhood attention deficit hyperactivity disorder, conduct problems and adult psychopathy. *Personality and Individual Differences, 36*, 1031–1037.

Anderson, C. A., Berkowitz, L., Donnerstein, E., Huesmann, L. R., Johnson, J. D., Linz, D., et al. (2003). The influence of media violence on youth. *Psychological Science in the Public Interest, 4(3)*, 81–110.

Bagozzi, R. P., & Heatherton, T. F. (1994). A general approach to representing multi-faceted personality constructs: Application to state self-esteem. *Structural Equation Modeling, 1*, 35–67.

Bandalos, D. L. (1997). Assessing sources of error in structural equation models: The effects of sample size, reliability, and model misspecification. *Structural Equation Modeling, 4*, 177–192.

Bandalos, D. L., & Finney, S. J. (2001). Item parceling issues in structural equation modeling. In G. A. Marcoulides and R. E. Schumacker (Eds.), *New developments and techniques in structural equation modeling* (pp. 269–296). Mahwah, NJ: Lawrence Erlbaum Associates.

Bentler, P. M. (1980). Multivariate analysis with latent variables: Causal modeling. *Annual Review of Psychology, 31*, 419–456.

Bentler, P. M. (1995). *EQS structural equations program manual*. Encino, CA: Multivariate Software.

Berrios, G. E. (1996). *The history of mental symptoms: Descriptive psychopathology since the nineteenth century*. Cambridge, England: Cambridge University Press.

Brandt, J. R., Kennedy, W. A., Patrick, C. J., & Curtin, J. J. (1997). Assessment of psychopathy in a population of incarcerated adolescent offenders. *Psychological Assessment, 9*, 429–435.

Byrne, B. M. (1998). Measuring adolescent self-concept: Factorial validity and equivalency of the SDQ III across gender. *Multivariate Behavioral Research, 23*, 361–375.

Chou, C. P., & Bentler, P. M. (1995). Estimates and tests in structural equation modeling. In Hoyle, R. H. (Ed.). *Structural equation modeling: Concepts, issues and applications* (pp. 37–55). Thousand Oaks: Sage.

Cleckley, H. (1941). *The mask of sanity*. St. Louis, MO: Mosby.

Cleckley, H. (1976). *The mask of sanity* (5th ed.). St. Louis, MO: Mosby.

Comrey, A. L. (1998). Factor-analytic methods of scale development in personality and clinical psychology. *Journal of Consulting and Clinical Psychology, 56*, 754–761.

Coid, J. (1993). Current concepts and classifications of psychopathic disorder. In P. Tyrer & G. Stein (Eds.), *Personality disorder reviewed* (pp. 113–164). London: Royal College of Psychiatrists Gaskell Press.

Cooke, D. J., & Michie, C. (2001). Refining the construct of psychopathy: Towards a hierarchical model. *Psychological Assessment, 13*, 171–188.

Dolan M. C., & Anderson, I. M. (2003). The relationship between serotonergic function and the Psychopathy Checklist: Screening Version. *Journal of Psychopharmacology 17*, 216–222.

Dowson, J. H., Sussams, P., Grounds, A. T., & Taylor, J. C. (2001). Associations of past conduct disorder with personality disorders in 'non-psychotic' psychiatric patients. *European Journal of Psychiatry, 16*, 49–56.

Dunn, G., Everitt, B., & Pickels, A. (1993). *Modeling covariance structures using EQS*. New York: Chapman & Hall.

Embretson, S. E. (1996). The new rules of measurement. *Psychological Assessment, 8*, 341–349.

Embretson, S. E., & Hershberger, S. L. (1999). *The new rules of measurement: What every psychologist and educator should know*. Mahwah, NJ: Lawrence Erlbaum Associates.

Everitt, B., & Dunn, G. (2001). *Applied multivariate data analysis*. New York: Oxford University Press.

Forth, A. E., Kosson, D. S., & Hare, R. D. (2003). *The Psychopathy Checklist: Youth Version manual*. Toronto, Ontario, Canada: Multi-Health Systems.

Frick, P. J., Cornell, A. H., Barry, C. T., Bodin, S. D., & Dane, H. E. (2003). Callous–unemotional traits and conduct problems in the prediction of conduct problem severity, aggression, and self-reported delinquency. *Journal of Abnormal Child Psychology, 31*, 474–470.

Gorsuch, R. L. (1983). *Factor analysis* (2nd ed.). Hillsdale, NJ: Lawrence Erlbaum Associates.

Greenbaum, P. E., & Dedrick, R. F. (1998). Hierarchical confirmatory factor analysis of the Child Behavior Checklist/4–18. *Psychological Assessment, 10*, 149–155.

Hare, R. D. (1980). A research scale for the assessment of psychopathy in criminal populations. *Personality and Individual Differences, 1*, 111–119.

Hare, R. D. (1991). *The Hare Psychopathy Checklist–Revised*. Toronto, Ontario, Canada: Multi-Health Systems.

Hare, R. D. (2003). *The Hare Psychopathy Checklist–Revised* (2nd ed.). Toronto, Ontario, Canada: Multi-Health Systems.

Hare, R. D., Harpur, T. J., Hakstian, R., Forth, A. E., & Hart, S. D. (1990). The Revised Psychopathy Checklist: Reliability and factor structure. *Psychological Assessment, 2*, 338–341.

Harpur, T. J., Hakstian, R., & Hare, R. D. (1988). Factor structure of the Psychopathy Checklist. *Journal of Consulting and Clinical Psychology, 56*, 741–747.

Harris, G. T., Rice, M. E., & Lalumière, M. (2001). Criminal violence: The roles of psychopathy, neurodevelopmental insults and antisocial parenting. *Criminal Justice and Behavior, 28*, 402–426.

Hill, C., Neumann, C. S., & Rogers, R. (2004). Confirmatory factor analysis of the Psychopathy Checklist: Screening Version (PCL: SV) in offenders with Axis I disorders. *Psychological Assessment, 16*, 90–95.

Hobson, J., & Shine, J. (1998). Measurement of psychopathy in a UK prison population referred for long-term psychotherapy. *British Journal of Criminology, 38*, 504–515.

Hoyle, R. H. (1995). *Structural equation modeling: Concepts, issues and applications*. Thousand Oaks, CA: Sage.

Hu, L., & Bentler, P. M. (1995). Evaluating model fit. In R. H. Hoyle (Ed.), *Structural equation modeling: Issues, concepts, and applications* (pp. 76–99). Newbury Park, CA: Sage.

Hu, L., & Bentler, P. M. (1999). Cut-score criteria for fit indexes in covariance structure analysis: Conventional criteria versus new alternatives. *Structural Equation Modeling, 6*, 1–55.

Knight, R. A., & Sims-Knight, J.E. (2003). The developmental antecedents of sexual coercion against women: Testing alternative hypotheses with structural equation modeling. *Annuals of the New York Academy of Sciences, 989*, 72–85.

Kosson, D. S., Cyterski, T. D., Steuerwald, B. L., Neumann, C. S., & Walker-Matthews, S. (2002). The reliability and validity of the Psychopathy Checklist: Youth Version in non-incarcerated adolescent males. *Psychological Assessment, 14*, 97–109.

Little, T. D., Cunningham, W. A., Shahar, G., & Widaman, K. F. (2002). To parcel or not to parcel: Exploring the questions, weighting the merits. *Structural Equation Modeling, 9*, 151–173.

Lynam, D. R. (1998). Early identification of the fledgling psychopathy: Locating the psychopathic child in the current nomenclature. *Journal of Abnormal Psychology, 107*, 566–575.

MacCallum, R. C. (1995). Model specification: Procedures, strategies, and related issues. In Hoyle, R. H. (Ed.), *Structural equation modeling: Concepts, issues and applications* (pp. 16–36). Thousand Oaks, CA: Sage.

MacCallum, R. C., & Austin, J. (2000). Applications of structural equation modeling in psychological research. *Annual Review of Psychology, 51*, 201–226.

Marsh, H. W. (1994). Using the National Longitudinal Study of 1988 to evaluate theoretical models of self-concept: The Self Description Questionnaire. *Journal of Educational Psychology, 86*, 439–456.

Marsh, H. W., & O'Neill, R. (1984). Self-Description Questionnaire III (SDQ-III): The construct validity of multidimensional self-concept ratings by late-adolescents. *Journal of Educational Measurement, 21*, 153–174.

Marsh, H. W., Smith, I. D., & Barnes, J. (1985). Multidimensional self-concepts: Relationships with sex and academic ability. *Journal of Educational Psychology, 77*, 581–596.

Meehl, P. E. (2002). Cliometric methatheory: II. Criteria scientists use in theory appraisal and why it is rational to do so. *Psychological Reports, 91*, 339–404.

Mulaik, S. A. (2002). Commentary on Meehl and Waller's (2002) path analysis and verisimilitude. *Psychological Methods, 7*, 316–322.

Mulaik, S. A., & James, L. R. (1995). Objectivity and reasoning in science and structural equation modeling. In Hoyle, R. H. (Ed.), *Structural equation modeling: Concepts, issues and applications* (pp. 118–137). Thousand Oaks, CA: Sage.

Muthen, L. K., & Muthen, B. O. (2001). *Mplus User's Guide* (2nd ed). Los Angeles, CA: Muthen & Muthen.

Neumann, C. S., Vitacco, M. J., Robertson, A., & Sewell, K. (2003). Longitudinal assessment of callous/impulsive traits, substance abuse, and symptoms of depression in adolescents: A latent variable approach. *Annals of the New York Academy of Sciences, 1008*, 276–280.

Neumann, C. S., Kosson, D., & Salekin, R. (2006). Exploratory and confirmatory factor analysis of the psychopathy construct: Methodological and conceptual issues. In H. Herve and J. Yuille (eds.). *The Psychopath: Theory, Research, and Practice*. New York: Lawrence Erlbaum.

Neumann, C. S., Kosson, D. S., Forth, A. E., & Hare, R. D. (in press). Factor structure of the Hare Psychopathy Checklist: Youth Version (PCL:YV) in incarcerated adolescents. *Psychological Assessment*.

Pinel, P. (1801). *Traite medico-philosophique sur l'alientation mentale*. Paris: Caille et Ravier.

Raine, A. (1985). A psychometric assessment of Hare's checklist for psychopathy on an English prison population. *British Journal of Clinical Psychology, 24*, 247–258.

Reise, S. P. (1998). Personality measurement issues viewed through the eyes of IRT. In S. E. Embretson and S. L. Hershberger (Eds.), *The new rules of measurement* (pp. 219–242). Mahwah, NJ: Lawrence Erlbaum Associates.

Reise, S. P., Waller, N. G., & Comrey, A. L. (2000). Factor analysis and scale revision. *Psychological Assessment, 12*, 287–297.

Rohde, P., Lewinsohn, P., Kahler, C. W., Seeley, J. R., & Brown, R. A.. (2001). Natural course of alcohol use disorders from adolescence to young adulthood. *Journal of the American Academy of Child and Adolescent Psychiatry, 40*, 83–90.

Salekin, R. T., Neumann, C. S., Leistico, A. M., & DiCicco, T. M. (2004a). Psychopathy and comorbidity in a youth offender sample: Taking a closer look at psychopathy's potential importance over disruptive behavior disorders. *Journal of Abnormal Psychology, 113*, 416–427.

Salekin, R. T., Neumann, C. S., Leistico, A. R., & Zalot, A. A. (2004b). Psychopathy in youth and intelligence: An investigation of Cleckley's hypothesis. *Journal of Clinical Child and Adolescent Psychology, 33*, 731–42.

Salekin, R. T., Rogers, R., & Sewell, K. W. (1996). A review and meta-analysis of the Psychopathy Checklist and Psychopathy Checklist–Revised: Predictive validity of dangerousness. *Clinical Psychology: Science and Practice, 3*, 203–215.

Salekin, R. T., Yiff, R., Neumann, C. S., Leistico, A-M., & Zalot, A. A. (2002). Juvenile transfer to adult courts: A look at the prototypes for dangerousness, sophistication-maturity, and amenability to treatment through a legal lens. *Psychology, Public Policy, and Law, 8*(4), 373–410.

Steiger, J. H. (1990). Structural equation model evaluation and modification: An interval estimation approach. *Multivariate Behavioral Research, 25*, 173–180.

Sullivan, E. A. (2003). A statistical comparison of the construct validity of the two-factor and hierarchical three-factor models of psychopathy. Unpublished master's thesis, Rosalind Franklin University of Medicine and Science, North Chicago, IL.

Sullivan, E. A., Bagley, A., & Kosson, D. S. (2004, March). *Early problem behavior predictors of adolescent psychopathy*. Paper presented at the annual meeting of the American Psychology-Law Society, Scottsdale, AZ.

Swogger, M. T., Walsh, Z., & Kosson, D. S. (2004). *Domestic violence and psychopathic traits in antisocial offenders*. Manuscript in preparation.

Templeman, R., & Wong, S. (1994). Determining the factor structure of the Psychopathy Checklist: A converging approach. *Multivariate Experimental Clinical Research, 10*, 157–166.

van Prooijen, J.-W., & van der Kloot, W. A. (2001). Confirmatory analysis of exploratively obtained factor structure. *Educational and Psychological Measurement, 61*, 777–792.

Velicer, W. F., & Fava, J. L. (1998). Effects of variable and subject sampling on factor pattern recovery. *Psychological Methods, 3*, 231–251.

Vitacco, M., Neumann, C. S., Robertson, A., & Durrant, S. (2002). Contributions of impulsivity and callousness in the assessment of adjudicated adolescent males: A prospective study. *Journal of Personality Assessment, 78*, 87–103.

Vitacco, M. J., Neumann, C. S., & Jackson, R. (2005a). Testing a four-factor model of psychopathy and its association with ethnicity, gender, intelligence, and violence. *Journal of Consulting and Clinical Psychology, 73*, 466–476.

Vitacco, M. J., Rogers, R., Neumann, C. S., Harrison, K., & Vincent, G. (2005b). A comparison of factor models on the PCL–R with mentally disordered offenders: The development of a four-factor model. *Criminal Justice and Behavior, 32*, 526–545.

Walsh, Z., Allen, L. C., Sullivan, E. A., & Kosson, D. S. (2004, June). *Beyond social deviance: Substance-specific relationships with PCL–R facets*. Poster presented at the annual meeting of the American Psychological Society, Chicago, IL.

Walsh, Z. T., Swogger, M. T., & Kosson, D. S. (2003, October). *The nature of violence in psychopathic and nonpsychopathic offenders: Instrumentality and related constructs*. Poster presented at the meeting of the Society for Research in Psychopathology, Toronto, Ontario, Canada.

West, S. G., Finch, J. F., & Curran, P. J. (1995). Structural equation modeling with nonnormal variables: Problems and remedies. In R. H. Hoyle (Ed.), *Structural equation modeling: Concepts, issues and applications* (pp. 56–75). Thousand Oaks, CA: Sage.

5

Analyzing the Psychopathy Checklist–Revised Using Factor Analysis and Item Response Theory

Daniel M. Bolt

Building from Cleckley's (1976) conceptualization of the construct of psychopathy, Hare developed the Psychopathy Checklist–Revised (PCL–R; Hare, 1991) as a diagnostic rating scale instrument for measuring psychopathic personality disorder. The PCL–R consists of 20 affective, personality, and behavioral characteristics that function as items on the instrument. Examples of PCL–R items include "Grandiose sense of self-worth," "Impulsivity," and "Failure to accept responsibility."

Much validation evidence has been gathered for the PCL–R, particularly within prison populations. The clinical utility of the PCL–R has been supported by its successful prediction of violent behavior and recidivism, revocations of parole, and poor participation and response to therapeutic treatments, among other outcomes (see, e.g., Hare & McPherson, 1984; Hart, 1998; Hemphill, Templeman, Wong, & Hare, 1998; Salekin, Rogers, & Sewell, 1996). Laboratory studies have successfully linked PCL–R scores to various psychophysiological differences associated with psychopathy (e.g., Hare, Cooke, & Hart, 1999; Newman & Wallace, 1993). The PCL–R has also demonstrated a generalizable factor structure across populations of varying nationality, race, and gender, including nonprison populations (Alterman, Cacciola, & Rutherford, 1993; Hart & Hare, 1989; McDermott et al., 2000; Salekin, Rogers, & Sewell, 1997; Windle & Dumenci, 1999). Such findings, combined with the other attractive psychometric properties of the instrument (e.g., high interrater reliability, test–retest reliability, and convergent and discriminant validity), have helped make the PCL–R the psychopathy measure of choice in both clinical and research settings.

Because of its prominence in measuring psychopathy, it is not surprising that the PCL–R has also been the focus of attempts to build a structural model for the construct (e.g., Cooke & Michie, 2001). Test structure can be investigated "internally" by fitting a *latent variable model* to test item scores. In a latent variable model, statistical dependencies (e.g., correlations) among items are explained by their measurement of a smaller number of unobserved attribute(s), referred to as *common factors* or *latent traits*, that underlie the assessment. Besides helping to communicate what a test measures, latent variables also provide a standard against which the measurement characteristics of test items—such as their reliability, discrimination, and difficulty—can be assessed.

In this chapter I provide an overview of two types of latent variable models that have proven useful in psychometric studies of the PCL–R: (a) factor analysis, based on the common factor model (Spearman, 1904), and (b) item response theory (IRT; Lord, 1980). As will be demonstrated, both methods are based on similar statistical models that can be used to investigate many of the same psychometric properties of tests and test items. However, fundamental differences also exist. Perhaps most important, IRT models assume a nonlinear relationship between the latent trait and item score, whereas factor analysis assumes a linear relationship. The nonlinearity of IRT allows item discrimination and, consequently, the standard error of measurement of a test to vary across trait levels (Embretson, 1996). By contrast, factor analysis assumes that item discrimination and standard errors of measurement are constant. Two other important differences between the methods are (a) the assumption of unidimensionality, which is made by IRT but not factor analytic models and (b) the modeling of mean (or expected) item scores in factor analysis, as opposed to the individual item score categories in IRT.

Some of the most useful applications of factor analysis and IRT with the PCL–R have occurred in measurement invariance studies (e.g., Cooke, Kosson, & Michie, 2001; Cooke & Michie, 1999; Windle & Dumenci, 1999). Measurement invariance studies address whether the same underlying construct is measured by the PCL–R in the same way across different populations of respondents. Most PCL–R research has been done for Caucasian male prison inmates. As a result, measurement invariance studies can help validate use of the instrument within other groups, such as African American populations. Measurement invariance is also needed before PCL–R score comparisons across populations can be regarded as psychologically meaningful. For example, mean differences in PCL–R scores across race can only be assumed to represent differences in the underlying construct provided it can be shown that PCL–R scores represent the same levels of the construct within each race. In this chapter, both factor analytic and IRT-based strategies for studying measurement invariance are illustrated.

FACTOR ANALYSIS

Factor analysis is a statistical method for investigating patterns in correlation or covariance matrices. Using the *common factor model*, Spearman (1904) and later Thurstone (1947) showed how correlations among tests of cognitive ability could be explained by their common measurement of a small number of underlying "intelligence" factors. When used to study correlations among items from a single test, the model is written as

$$X_i = \tau_i + \lambda_{i1}f_1 + \lambda_{i2}f_2 + \ldots + \lambda_{iM}f_M + e_i, \tag{1}$$

where X_i is the score on item i, the M factors—$f_1, \ldots, f_M$—function as predictor variables, and e_i is a random error or uniqueness variable, which is assumed to be uncorrelated with the error variables of other items as well as the factors.

Although the model contains many parameters, a simple distinction can be made between parameters that characterize the item/factor relationships and those that characterize the distributions of the factors in a population. Three types of parameters describe the relationships between the factors and items:

the *factor loadings*, λ_{im}, represent the causal influences of the factors on the items,

the *item intercepts*, τ_i, represent the expected (mean) scores on the items when the levels of the factors are 0 (typically the factor means), and

the *error variances*, ψ_i^2, represent unique variance in the item scores that is not explained by the common factors, that is, the variance of e_i.

Two types of parameters characterize the factor distributions in a population:

the *factor means*, denoted $\kappa_1, \kappa_2, \ldots, \kappa_M$ and

the *factor variances/covariances*, denoted φ_{mn} for factors m and n (with factor variances thus denoted $\varphi_{mm}, \varphi_{nn}$).

Because of the arbitrary scaling and orientation of the factor axes, the factor means and covariances are often set at 0 and factor variances at 1.

Although the common factor model is similar in appearance to an ordinary linear regression model, the predictor variables (i.e., factors) are not observed. Thus, its parameters cannot be estimated as in regression analysis. Because of the various independence assumptions of the model (see Kim & Mueller, 1978), however, the λs and ψ^2s can be directly related to the observed covariances (or correlations) between items. Specifically, the covariance of any pair of items i and j is the inner product of their factor loadings, that is,

$$\sigma_{X_iX_j} = \sum_{m=1}^{M} \lambda_{im}\lambda_{jm},$$

whereas the variance of an item (the item's covariance with itself) is the sum of its squared factor loadings and error variance, that is,

$$\sigma^2_{X_i} = \sum_{m=1}^{M} \ddot{e}^2_{im} + \varnothing^2_i.$$

In factor analysis, estimates for the λs and ψ^2s, denoted $\hat{\lambda}_{im}$ and $\hat{\psi}^2_i$, that reproduce covariances that resemble as closely as possible the sample covariances computed from the data are determined. The goodness of fit of the factor model is determined by the accuracy of this approximation. For this reason, the factor model is sometimes referred to as a model of the *covariance structure* of the test items. (It should be noted that the item intercepts, τ_i, and factor means, κ_m become irrelevant in such applications, as they have no influence on the interitem covariances).

Exploratory Factor Analysis

The common factor model (Equation 1) can be used to perform both *exploratory* and *confirmatory factor analyses* of test structure. Exploratory factor analysis (EFA) is used when a test is hypothesized to measure a small number of common factors, but the nature of the factors is unknown. EFA has been frequently used to study the structure of the PCL–R (e.g., Hare et al., 1990; Harpur, Hakstian, & Hare, 1988; Kosson, Smith, & Newman, 1990; McDermott et al., 2000).

A first consideration in EFA is the number of factors (M) to include in the model. Various criteria have been proposed (see Zwick & Velicer, 1986); many are based on the eigenvalues of the interitem correlation matrix. Eigenvalues represent the variances of principal components of the correlation matrix. It is common to extract only as many factors as have eigenvalues greater than 1 (the *Kaiser–Guttman criterion*), as these correspond to components that account for some amount of shared variance among items. However, in actual practice, eigenvalues are frequently greater than 1 because of random sampling error, especially when the number of test items is large (Cliff, 1988). An alternative number-of-factors criterion that addresses this problem is the scree test (Cattell, 1966). In a scree test, the eigenvalues of each component are plotted in order from largest to smallest, and factors are extracted up to where a visual elbow occurs in the plot, suggesting that subsequent factors account for negligible amounts of variance. Still other criteria include *parallel analysis* (Horn, 1965), *minimum average partial correlation* (Zwick & Velicer, 1986), and a *likelihood ratio test*. Unfortunately, as a collection these criteria can be quite inconsistent in the number of factors they suggest (Harpur et al., 1988) and are known to be differentially affected by variables such as sample size and test length.

To illustrate an EFA of the PCL–R, item score data from 3,282 North American prison inmates are analyzed. The dataset comprises 14 samples, including 7 from Hare's original 1991 sample (Ns = 313, 103, 369, 78, 87, 101, and 60), 2 collected from minimum security prisons in Wisconsin (total N = 1,190), and 3 from Hare's 2001 PCL–R second edition (Ns = 60, 238, and 376). The racial composition for these samples was 55.7% Caucasian, 25.8% African American, 1.1% Native American, and 0.7% Asian, Middle Eastern, East Indian, or Hispanic; 16.7% had no race reported. All participants were scored by a trained rater based on information obtained through an interview with the inmate and file review. Each item is scored 0 (*definitely not present*), 1 (*possibly present*), or 2 (*definitely present*). Only inmates with complete item score vectors were analyzed.

Figure 5–1 illustrates the scree plot for these data. The large first eigenvalue, combined with the substantial drop from the first to second eigenvalues, suggests the presence of a strong single factor, that is, a general psychopathy trait. However, because the scree test relies to a large degree on subjective judgment, it is not always clear exactly how many factors to extract. Either two or three factors would appear to be possibilities here. Further complicating matters, the other number-of-factors criteria lead to different conclusions, with the Kaiser–Guttman criterion suggesting five factors and the likelihood ratio test nine factors. Thus, the "number of factors problem," which is frequently a limitation in EFA analyses, also appears to be a problem in studying the PCL–R (see also Harpur et al., 1988).

The primary goal of EFA is interpretation of the factors. Usually this is based on inspection of the factor loadings of the items. However, in EFA the

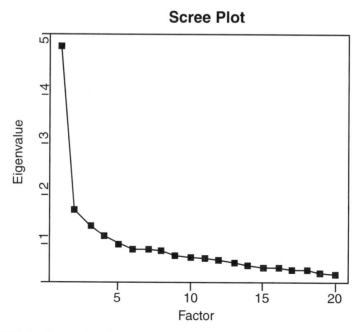

FIGURE 5–1. Scree plot of eigenvalues from PCL–R interitem correlation matrix.

factor loadings are not unique, as any rotation of the factor axes produces a
new factor solution that has an equivalent statistical fit. This rotational inde-
terminacy permits application of various factor rotation methods, which
attempt to define factor axes that can be easily interpreted (McDonald, 1999).
Table 5–1 displays the factor loading matrix for a two-factor EFA solution following a Promax rotation (Hendrickson & White, 1964), a rotation method
that produces oblique (correlated) factors. The loadings in bold identify the
correspondence between items and factors according to the traditional two-
factor model that has been observed in previous factor analyses of the PCL–R
(Hare, 1991; Harpur et al., 1988; Harpur, Hare, & Hakstian, 1989; Kosson
et al., 1990; Windle & Dumenci, 1999). Three items—items 11 "Promiscuous
sexual behavior," 17 "Many short-term marital relationships," and 20 "Crim-

TABLE 5–1.
Exploratory Two-Factor Solution, Psychopathy Checklist–Revised (PCL–R)

| Item Number and Stem | Two-Factor Solution* | | | Models of PCL–R Structure | |
	$\hat{\lambda}_1$	$\hat{\lambda}_2$	$1 - \hat{\varphi}^2$	Two-Factor	Three-Factor
1. Glibness/superficial charm	**.76**	−.19	.44	1	1
2. Grandiose sense of self-worth	**.74**	−.16	.44	1	1
3. Need for stimulation/proneness to boredom	.05	**.57**	.36	2	3
4. Pathological lying	**.53**	.04	.31	1	1
5. Conning/manipulative	**.43**	.21	.33	1	1
6. Lack of remorse or guilt	**.53**	.13	.38	1	2
7. Shallow affect	**.41**	.18	.28	1	2
8. Callous/lack of empathy	**.41**	.32	.42	1	2
9. Parasitic lifestyle	.04	**.43**	.21	2	3
10. Poor behavioral controls	.13	**.40**	.24	2	
11. Promiscuous sexual behavior	.22	.23	.16		
12. Early behavior problems	−.06	**.58**	.30	2	
13. Lack of realistic, long-term goals	.15	**.33**	.19	2	3
14. Impulsivity	−.06	**.61**	.33	2	3
15. Irresponsibility	.09	**.43**	.24	2	3
16. Failure to accept responsibility	**.54**	−.06	.26	1	2
17. Many short-term marital relationships	.11	.23	.07		
18. Juvenile delinquency	−.18	**.60**	.27	2	
19. Revocation of conditional release	−.06	**.41**	.14	2	
20. Criminal versatility	.02	.41	.18		

*Following Promax rotation, correlation between factors = .59.

inal versatility"—are generally excluded from this model and thus have no bold loadings.

Table 5–1 also provides an estimate of the *communality* of each item. The communality is the proportion of item score variance that is explained by the common factors and thus is also the complement of $\hat{\psi}_i^2$. Items with high communalities represent items that are good indicators of the factors. Items 11 "Promiscuous sexual behavior," 17 "Many short-term marital relationships," 19 "Revocation of conditional release," and 20 "Criminal versatility" all have low communality estimates—.16, .07, .14, and .18, respectively—implying that they measure neither of the two factors very well.

On the basis of the factor loading pattern in Table 5–1, there would appear to be support for the traditional two-factor model. At the same time, the results make apparent the frequent difficulty in clearly discerning PCL–R structure using only EFA, as all items load to some extent on both factors. A more suitable way of testing a hypothesized factor structure, such as the two-factor model, is through *confirmatory factor analysis* (CFA).

Confirmatory Factor Analysis

Lawley (1940) provided estimation procedures that allow the common factor model to test hypothesized factor structures. By constraining certain factor loadings to zero (implying no direct association between the factor and item), a confirmatory factor model can be specified in which factors are defined by the items selected to have nonzero loadings. Ideally, each item has a nonzero loading on only one factor, in which case the factor model is said to possess *simple structure*.

The rightmost columns in Table 5–1 show the correspondence between items and factors according to two simple structure models that have been proposed for the PCL–R. In the previously mentioned two-factor model, Factors 1 and 2 are labeled as "Personality" and "Behavioral" factors of psychopathy, respectively. Cooke and Michie (2001) also proposed a three-factor structure for 13 PCL–R items. In the three-factor model Factor 1 of the two-factor model is regarded as two distinct factors (now denoted Factors 1 and 2) and four items from Factor 2 of the two-factor model (now denoted Factor 3) are excluded. Factors 1, 2, and 3 have been labeled as "Arrogant and Deceitful Interpersonal Style," "Deficient Affective Experience," and "Impulsive and Irresponsible Behavioral Style," respectively (Cooke & Michie, 2001). The items measuring each factor also possess a testlet structure (Steinberg & Thissen, 1986), which can account for the higher levels of statistical dependence between different groups of items measuring a common factor. In effect, the three-factor model is a second-order factor model in which each item loads on one of six testlet factors, and the six testlet factors load on three second-order factors—Factors 1, 2, and 3 of primary interest. For additional details and alternative specifications of this model, see Cooke and Michie (2001).

In CFA, a χ^2 test can be performed to test whether the proposed model fits. However, this test is very sensitive to sample size and will reject for even negligible amounts of misfit whenever sample size is large. Thus, various goodness-of-fit indices, which quantify the degree of model fit, are frequently also used. Four common indices are the root-mean-square error of approximation (RMSEA; Steiger & Lind, 1980), the comparative fit index (CFI; Bentler, 1990), the Tucker–Lewis index (TLI; Tucker & Lewis, 1973), and the goodness-of-fit index (GFI; Jöreskog & Sörbom, 1981). RMSEA values of .05 and lower are indicative of a well-fitting model; for CFI and TLI, values greater than .90, and for GFI, values greater than .95, are considered well-fitting models.

Empirical Illustration of CFA using PCL–R Data

The two- and three-factor models were fit using the same data analyzed using EFA. To allow for model respecification, the dataset was first randomly divided into calibration and cross-validation datasets, each containing the score patterns of 1,641 inmates. An interitem covariance matrix was computed for each dataset. For the calibration data, the two-factor model fit rather poorly ($\chi^2 = 1271.80$, $df = 118$, $p = .000$; RMSEA $= .081$; CFI $= .82$; TLI $= .80$; GFI $= .91$). The lack of fit could be attributed to a small number of item pairs that had larger covariances than implied by the two-factor model. A common strategy for addressing this problem is to allow the error variables of these item pairs to covary (Byrne, 1998). With the use of LISREL-supplied modification indices (Jöreskog & Sörbom, 1996), the two-factor model was respecified so as to allow six pairs of items to have covarying measurement errors—Items 1 and 2, 3 and 14, 4 and 5, 6 and 16, 8 and 10, and 12 and 18. The fit of this respecified model was then evaluated using the cross-validation dataset. Results of the χ^2 test and fit indices are reported in Table 5–2, suggesting a close fit. The standardized parameter estimates for the respecified two-factor model and its associated path diagram are shown in Figure 5–2. Factor loading estimates ($\hat{\lambda}$s) are reported on the arrows from the factors to the items, error variable variance estimates ($\hat{\psi}_i^2$ s) are reported beside the arrows to the right of the items, and error variable covariance estimates are reported along the bidirectional arrows connecting the ψ^2 s. The correlation between factors, .80, is along the bidirectional arrow between factors; its large magnitude points to a single influential higher-order factor underlying all of the items, a finding consistent with the EFA analysis (see also Hare, 1991).

TABLE 5–2.
Goodness of Fit for the Two- and Three-Factor PCL–R Models,
Cross-Validation Dataset ($N = 1,641$)

Model	χ^2	df	RMSEA	CFI	TLI	GFI
Two-factor	535.97	112	.049	.93	.91	.96
Three-factor	260.17	56	.047	.98	.94	.96

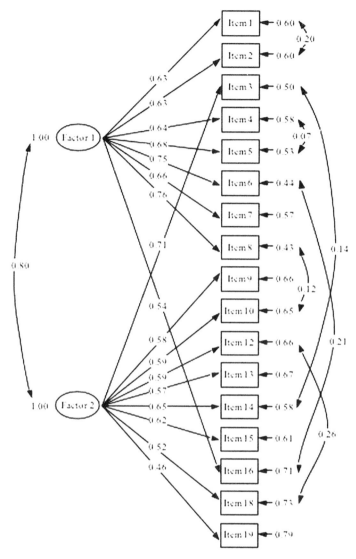

FIGURE 5–2. Standardized confirmatory factor solution for the two-factor PCL–R model.

Based on the factor loading estimates, Items 6 "Lack of remorse or guilt" ($\hat{\lambda}_1 = .75$) and 8 "Callous/lack of empathy" ($\hat{\lambda}_1 = .76$) would appear to be among the best Personality characteristics; Items 3 "Need for stimulation/proneness to boredom" ($\hat{\lambda}_2 = .71$) and 14 "Impulsivity" ($\hat{\lambda}_2 = .65$) would appear to be among the best Behavioral characteristics.

The three-factor model provided a good fit to the calibration dataset without any additional respecification ($\chi^2 = 279.64$, $df = 56$, $p = .000$; RMSEA = .05; CFI = .96; TLI = .94; GFI = .97). Its path diagram and standardized parameter estimates are reported in Figure 5–3, and its χ^2 and goodness-of-fit indices using the cross-validation dataset are reported in Table 5–2. A primary difference between the two- and three-factor models is the distinction made between Factors 1 and 2 in the three-factor model. Thus, a χ^2 test was performed to determine whether factors 1 and 2 of the model were statistically distinct. The test was significant ($\chi^2 = 214.09$, $df = 2$, $p < .00$), suggesting that the two factors are distinct. This result is consistent with the finding of Cooke and Michie (2001), who obtained a slightly lower correlation, .71, between factors 1 and 2. The estimated loadings of each item onto the higher-order factors can be derived by multiplying the item loadings by the testlet loadings. Thus, Item 5 "Conning/manipulative" would appear to be the best indicator of Factor 1 ($\hat{\lambda}_1 = .75 \times .97 = .73$), Item 8 "Callous/lack of empa-

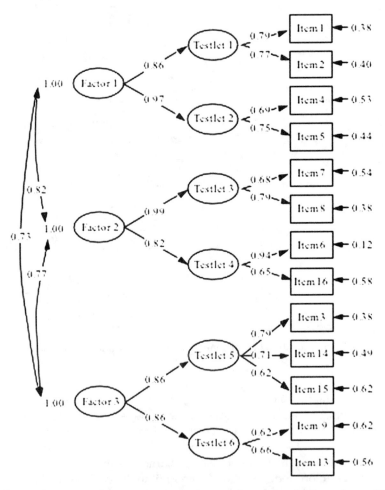

FIGURE 5–3.   Standardized confirmatory factor solution for the three-factor PCL–R model.

thy" ($\hat{\lambda}_2 = .79 \times .99 = .78$) the best for Factor 2, and Item 3 "Need for stimulation/proneness to boredom" ($\hat{\lambda}_3 = .79 \times .86 = .68$) the best for Factor 3.

Both the two- and three-factor models appear to fit the data well; unfortunately, their relative fit cannot be compared statistically owing to their analysis of different subsets of PCL–R items. Determining the most appropriate model for the PCL–R thus relies on substantive, as well as statistical, considerations. The omission of PCL–R items from both models naturally raises questions about the completeness of either model and the possibility of underrepresentation of the psychopathy construct. For example, Items 10 "Poor behavioral controls," 12 "Early behavior problems," and 18 "Juvenile delinquency" have moderate standardized loadings on Factor 2 in both the exploratory and confirmatory two-factor models (suggesting that they may be useful behavioral characteristics of psychopathy) and moderate communalities in the EFA analysis but are among the seven PCL–R items excluded from the three-factor model. If such items are theoretically regarded as important components of psychopathy, the comprehensiveness of the three-factor model could be debated. On the other hand, including PCL–R items that are less central to the construct can also be detrimental, as all items contribute equally to evaluating the fit of a CFA model. For a discussion of these and related issues in support of the three-factor model, see Cooke and Michie (2001).

Using CFA Models to Assess Measurement Invariance

Once a hypothesized factor structure—such as the two-factor or three-factor models—has been confirmed, the structure can be tested for equivalence across different populations for which PCL–R data have been obtained (e.g., males and females, Caucasians and African Americans, and prison inmates and substance abusers). According to the common factor model, measurement invariance exists when (a) the same underlying factor(s) are measured within each group and (b) the factor and test score metrics are equivalent across groups, implying that test scores represent the same factor levels (Drasgow, 1984, Meredith, 1993; Steenkamp & Baumgartner, 1998; Widaman & Reise, 1997).

Measurement invariance can be assessed using *multigroup factor analysis* (Jöreskog, 1971). Essentially a multigroup factor analysis is a simultaneous factor analysis of data from more than one group. The existence of measurement invariance is evaluated by statistically testing whether the factor structure and common factor model parameters can be assumed to be equivalent across groups.

Although CFA is usually performed on a covariance (or possibly correlation) matrix, when one is studying measurement invariance, it is also informative to model the item means. In a *mean and covariance structure analysis* (Sörbom, 1974), an augmented covariance matrix, consisting of both an interitem covariance matrix and a vector of item means, is analyzed. Thus, in addition to the parameters used to model the interitem covariance structure (i.e., factor loadings, λs; error variances/covariances, ψ^2s; and factor variances/covariances, φs), the means of the common factors, $\kappa_1, \kappa_2, \ldots \kappa_M,$ and item intercepts, $\tau_i,$ are estimated to account for the item mean structure. In this respect, in addition to generalizing the common factor model to account for multiple groups, a measurement invariance analysis also generalizes the model to fit both the interitem covariances and item means in each group. For an example of how this strategy has been used to study measurement invariance in the PCL–R, see Windle & Dumenci (1999).

Measurement invariance is principally concerned with the relationships between factors and item scores, not the distributions of the factors, when groups are compared. For this reason, the equivalence of the λs, ψ^2s, and τs across groups are of primary interest. The κs and φs, which characterize the distributions of the factors, need not be equivalent for measurement invariance to exist.

Distinguishing Different Forms of Measurement Invariance

Different forms of measurement invariance can be distinguished according to which aspects of the common factor model are equivalent across groups (see Meredith, 1993; Steenkamp & Baumgartner, 1998; Widaman & Reise, 1997). Each form of measurement invariance carries different implications for the meaningfulness of PCL–R scores and score comparisons within and across groups. We consider several forms of measurement invariance in the following.

The least restrictive form of measurement invariance, *configural invariance*, exists when the same pattern of fixed (to zero) and freed (nonzero) factor loadings apply for each group (Steenkamp & Baumgartner, 1998). Configural invariance indicates that the same factor loading pattern applies for each group and thus that the underlying factors have similar interpretations. It is a necessary requirement before one tests any other forms of invariance. Because all of the nonzero factor loadings are allowed to vary across groups, a configural invariance model imposes equivalence constraints only on factor loadings fixed to 0, not the nonzero loadings. For this reason, it is common to refer to configural invariance as a nonmetric form of factorial invariance (Widaman & Reise, 1997).

A second form of invariance, *metric invariance*, exists when both the zero and nonzero factor loadings are equivalent (Meredith, 1993). In addition to configural invariance, metric invariance implies that the item/factor covariances are equivalent across groups. Because factor loadings are regression coefficients in the common factor model, their equivalence implies that any unit change in the underlying factor(s) produces the same change in expected item scores for each group. In this sense, the factor score metrics are said to be equivalent.

If metric invariance holds, the equivalence of the error variable variances (ψ_i^2 s) and covariances (ψ_{ij}^2 s) can be tested. Windle & Dumenci (1999) refer to this condition as *tau-equivalence*. Tau-equivalence implies that the items have the same reliabilities and thus are equally good indicators of the underlying factors across groups. Because the reliability of the overall test is a function of the item reliabilities, tau-equivalence also implies that the test scores contain equivalent amounts of measurement error in each population.

Finally, provided tau-equivalence holds, the equivalence of the item intercepts (τ_is) can be assessed. Because the item intercepts relate to the mean levels of the item scores, equivalent intercepts imply that at the same factor level each group is expected to receive the same scores on the items. If the factor loadings, error variances/covariances, and item intercepts can all be shown to be equivalent, the test is said to possess *strict invariance* (Meredith, 1993). Failure to find equivalent item intercepts implies the existence of item bias and raises the question of whether overall test scores represent consistent levels of the factors across groups.

The fit of any multigroup invariance model can be evaluated using the same criteria that were applied to evaluate single-group CFA models. However, the equivalence of individual parameters or parameter types (i.e., λs, ψ^2s, or τs) can also be statistically tested by comparing nested models. Specifically, a test of equivalence for any set of parameters can be performed based on the difference in the χ^2 fit of two multigroup models: one in which the studied parameters are constrained to be equal across groups (i.e., a *compact model*) and one in which they are allowed to vary (i.e., a *comparison model*). The χ^2 difference between these models is itself χ^2 distributed under a null hypothesis of no difference in fit, with degrees of freedom equal to the number of parameters being tested. As before, this χ^2 test is also sensitive to sample size; thus, it is also useful to compare the goodness-of-fit indices for the models.

Measurement Invariance in the PCL–R: Comparing Caucasian and African American Inmates

With the same dataset considered in the EFA and CFA analyses, separate augmented covariance matrices were computed for 1,828 Caucasian and 847 African American male inmates. The multigroup measurement invariance models described in the previous section (configural, metric, tau-equivalence, and strict invariance) were investigated for both the two- and three-factor models. Goodness-of-fit results for each model are reported in Table 5–3 (Panels A and B, respectively). Because of the hierarchical relationships of the models, the configural invariance model can serve as a comparison model for testing metric invariance, the metric invariance model as a comparison model for testing tau-equivalence, and the tau-equivalence model as a comparison model for testing strict invariance.

Based on their overall fit statistics, the configural invariance models fit well for both the two- and three-factor models, implying that similar PCL–R factor structures apply for each race. Similarly, the metric invariance[1] and tau

---

[1]For the three-factor model, the metric invariance model constrains both the testlet loadings and item loadings to be equivalent across groups.

TABLE 5–3.
Goodness of Fit for Measurement Invariance Models Comparing
Caucasians and African Americans

	χ^2	df	RMSEA	CFI	TLI	GFI	χ^2_{diff}	df_{diff}	p
Two-factor model									
Configural invariance	1082.44	224	.054	.92	.90	.95	—	—	—
Metric invariance	1116.81	239	.053	.92	.90	.95	34.37	15	.00
Tau equivalence	1263.06	262	.054	.90	.90	.94	146.25	23	.00
Strict invariance	1710.09	277	.064	.86	.86	.93	447.03	15	.00
Three-factor model									
Configural invariance	466.39	112	.049	.96	.94	.97	—	—	—
Metric invariance	533.31	131	.048	.95	.94	.96	66.92	19	.00
Tau equivalence	613.67	144	.051	.94	.94	.95	80.36	13	.00
Strict invariance	944.33	154	.063	.90	.90	.95	330.66	10	.00

equivalence models provide a close fit based on their goodness-of-fit indices, despite significant χ^2 differences relative to their comparison models. However, strict invariance does not appear to be supported for either the two- or three-factor models. Constraining the item intercepts to be equivalent produced not only a large reduction in model fit according to the goodness-of-fit indices but also a substantial χ^2 increase relative to the tau-equivalence model, implying that at least some PCL–R items appear to have different intercepts across groups.

In short, based on results for both the two- and three-factor models, it appears that configural invariance, metric invariance, and tau-equivalence are reasonably well satisfied; however, strict invariance does not hold, implying that certain PCL–R items perform differentially across race.

Implications of Measurement Invariance Analysis

Each measurement invariance model carries different implications for the types of PCL–R score comparisons that can be conducted within and across races. These implications are best realized by recalling how each of the parameters tested for equivalence function in the common factor model. The most critical form of invariance—configural invariance—implies that the factors measured by the PCL–R are similar. In particular, the distinctions between factors defined by the two- and three-factor models appear to apply for each race. Finding that configural invariance holds also provides evidence that PCL–R scores order the members within each race with respect to similar underlying psychopathy trait(s). However, it implies nothing about the comparability of scores across populations.

Finding that metric invariance holds implies an even greater degree of cross-racial similarity among factors, in that the factors and items covary in a similar fashion. Consequently, the items that are most and least representative of the underlying factor levels would appear to be the same for each race. A primary objective of measurement invariance analysis is to determine which types of test score comparisons are meaningful across groups. When metric invariance holds, the factor metrics are the same, and thus the correlations of the PCL–R factor(s) (but not test scores) with external criterion variables can be meaningfully compared across race.

Establishment of tau-equivalence carries the further implication that the individual items, and thus total PCL–R scores, contain equal amounts of measurement error. Thus, besides measuring the same construct, PCL–R scores appear to provide equally precise measures of that construct in each race. Such a finding makes correlations between PCL–R scores and external criterion variables comparable across race.

The failure to find invariance in the item intercepts, however, implies that the levels of the latent construct at which PCL–R items become manifest varies across race. That is, for fixed levels of the latent construct, certain psychopathy characteristics would appear to be more prevalent in one race than the other. Such findings are not surprising, given the likely association between many of the PCL–R characteristics and non-psychopathy-related race differences. However, the existence of such differences raises the possibility that total PCL–R scores may not be representing the same *levels* of latent psychopathy across races. The failure to find strict invariance thus makes comparisons of mean PCL–R score across race questionable.

Unfortunately, latent variable models are in many respects limited in their capacity to address this question once a lack of strict invariance is found. One possible strategy is to search for a model of *partial invariance* in which some of the item intercepts can be constrained to equivalence across groups, whereas others are freed to vary (Steenkamp & Baumgartner, 1998).

A Model of Partial Invariance

Although a model of strict invariance was not supported by the data, it is possible that only a small number of the items have race-varying intercepts. A model of *partial invariance* can allow some intercept parameters to be different across groups while holding others (i.e., marker items) equivalent, representing a compromise between the tau-equivalence and strict invariance models. Searching for a model of partial invariance can help in understanding which items perform differentially across race. To find such a model for the current dataset, a strategy advocated by Steenkamp and Baumgartner (1998) is followed (for purposes of illustration, this procedure is applied here only to the two-factor model). Modification indices calculated for the strict invariance model are used to identify which intercept parameters should be freed to significantly improve model fit. An iterative procedure is carried out in which the intercept with the largest modification index is freed to vary across groups, whereas all of the remaining intercepts are kept equivalent. If the resulting model fits, the iterative procedure stops and a partial invariance model has been attained; if not, the process is repeated by identifying the item with the next largest modification index.

In the current analysis, the intercepts for five items—Items 7, 8, 9, 10, and 13—were freed before the measurement invariance model provided a reasonable fit. Table 5–4 displays the parameter estimates of the model, and Table 5–5 displays its goodness of fit. $\hat{\tau}_C$ and $\hat{\tau}_{AA}$ denote the intercept estimates for Caucasians and African Americans, respectively, with bold values representing intercepts that were allowed to differ. Higher intercepts indicate higher expected scores. Thus, the partial invariance model suggests that at the same factor level, Caucasians receive higher scores on items 7 "Shallow affect" and 8 "Callous/lack of empathy," whereas African Americans receive higher scores on Items 9 "Parasitic lifestyle," 10 "Poor behavioral controls,"

TABLE 5–4.
Parameter Estimates, Two-Factor Partial Invariance Model
Comparing Caucasians and African-Americans

Item Number and Stem	Model Parameter Estimates				
	$\hat{\lambda}_1^*$	$\hat{\lambda}_2^*$	φ^{2^*}	$\hat{\tau}_C$	$\hat{\tau}_{AA}$
1. Glibness/superficial charm	.50		.75	0.83	0.83
2. Grandiose sense of self-worth	.51		.74	0.89	0.89
3. Need for stimulation/proneness to boredom		.63	.60	1.36	1.36
4. Pathological lying	.54		.71	0.98	0.98
5. Conning/manipulative	.54		.71	1.01	1.01
6. Lack of remorse or guilt	.61		.62	1.43	1.43
7. Shallow affect	.59		.66	**1.00**	**0.78**
8. Callous/lack of empathy	.69		.53	**1.18**	**1.03**
9. Parasitic lifestyle		.49	.76	**1.03**	**1.39**
10. Poor behavioral controls		.45	.79	**1.20**	**1.47**
12. Early behavior problems		.45	.80	1.02	1.02
13. Lack of realistic, long-term goals		.48	.77	**1.17**	**1.47**
14. Impulsivity		.59	.66	1.37	1.37
15. Irresponsibility		.49	.76	1.43	1.43
16. Failure to accept responsibility	.43		.82	1.29	1.29
18. Juvenile delinquency		.35	.88	1.25	1.25
19. Revocation of conditional release		.32	.89	1.54	1.54

*Equal estimates apply for Caucasians and African Americans.

TABLE 5–5.
Goodness-of-Fit Statistics for the Two-Factor Partial Invariance Model and Equated
Factor Distribution Models Comparing Caucasians and African Americans

Model	χ^2	df	RMSEA	CFI	TLI	GFI	χ^2_{diff}	df_{diff}	p
Partial invariance	1347.88	272	.058	.90	.90	.94	—	—	—
Equal factor means	1668.40	274	.063	.87	.87	.93	320.52	2	.00
Equal factor covariances	1367.73	275	.055	.89	.90	.94	19.85	3	.00

and 13 "Lack of realistic, long-term goals." The magnitude of the intercept differences can be directly translated to the expected differences in item scores conditional on factor level. For example, for item 9 "Parasitic lifestyle," an African American having the same underlying level on Factor 2 as a Caucasian can expect to receive on average a score that is .36 higher.

Once a model of partial invariance is found, it also becomes possible to test for differences in the factor distributions across groups (Steenkamp & Baumgartner, 1998). Table 5–5 shows goodness-of-fit results for two compact models that were used to test for factor distribution differences. In the first model, the κs are equated across race; in the second model, the φs are equated. Because both of these models are constrained versions of the partial invariance model, their relative fit can be compared to determine whether the equality constraints significantly decrease fit. For these data, the equated φs model still fits, implying no significant differences in factor covariances across race. By contrast, the equated κs model results in a much poorer fit, implying that the factor means across races are different. Inspection of the estimated factor means for the partial invariance model shows that Caucasians have higher levels on Factor 2 than African Americans ($\hat{\kappa}_{2,C} = 0.0$, $\hat{\kappa}_{2,AA} = -0.31$), but have slightly lower levels on Factor 1 ($\hat{\kappa}_{1,C} = 0.0$, $\hat{\kappa}_{1,AA} = 0.07$).

Although useful in gaining some sense as to how the test items perform differentially, results from partial invariance models should be interpreted with a large degree of caution, especially when found in an exploratory fashion (as was the case here). Ideally, the researcher will be aware of certain "marker" items that for theoretical reasons can be assumed to be equivalent across groups, thus equating the factor metrics so that the remaining items can be tested for racial differences.

IRT

Although the common factor model has been a popular tool for analyzing educational and psychological measures, the model is not always appropriate for items scored using a small number of categories, as on the PCL–R. First, because the underlying scales of the factors extend in both directions to infinity, the linearity of the common factor model implies that item scores should also be unbounded. It is well-known among psychometricians that when items are scored using few categories, interitem covariances can be affected by differences in item means, resulting in biased factor loading estimates and the extraction of spurious factors in factor analysis (Lord & Novick, 1968). The second questionable assumption relates to the interval-level meaning given to item scores. Specifically, the factor model assumes that the differences between item score categories (0 to 1 and 1 to 2 on the PCL–R) correspond to equal distances in the underlying factor metric. This assumption follows from the linear relationship assumed between the factors and item scores.

IRT provides an alternative way of modeling PCL–R item scores that addresses both of these limitations. In IRT (also referred to as *latent trait theory*), a nonlinear relationship is assumed between the factor (more commonly referred to as a *latent trait*) and item score. The nonlinearity of IRT models no longer requires that the item score metric be unbounded. By associating distinct parameters with each item score category, IRT models can account for item scores that may have only ordinal-level meaning.

Although generally regarded as a more appropriate modeling strategy for categorical items, IRT makes an additional assumption not made in factor analysis, namely test *unidimensionality*. Unidimensionality implies that the test measures only one latent trait. Given the multifactor structure of the PCL–R found in factor analysis, it might be questioned whether this assumption is tenable. Previous authors (Cooke et al., 2001; Cooke & Michie, 1997) have noted that because the PCL–R factors are highly correlated, a single dominant dimension can be assumed to underlie the PCL–R (a result also supported by the factor analyses in this chapter), and thus IRT models can be used. However, this issue merits further research attention, as it is not always clear what amount of multidimensionality will have a practical effect on IRT models. Although many applications of IRT models are robust to violations of unidimensionality, others, such as differential item functioning analyses, are not (Mazor, Hambleton, & Clauser, 1998).

IRT models were originally developed for items scored using two score categories (e.g., correct or incorrect; Embretson & Reise, 2000), as occur frequently on educational tests. An example of an IRT model is the two-parameter logistic model (2PL; Birenbaum, 1968). In the 2PL, the probability of a correct response to an item i, that is, $X_i = 1$, is modeled as

$$P(X_i = 1 | \theta) = \exp[a_i(\theta - b_i)] / \{1 + \exp[a_i(\theta - b_i)]\} \qquad (2)$$

where θ is the trait level (e.g., ability) of the respondent and the parameters a_i and b_i characterize the discrimination and difficulty levels, respectively, of the item. Although the scale for θ is arbitrary, it (like the factors in a common factor model) is often arbitrarily assigned a mean of 0 and variance of 1. Items with large positive a estimates (e.g., >1) are highly discriminating, as a large a implies that θ has a large influence on item score. The b parameters assume both positive and negative values, with higher *b*s reflecting more difficult items.

When applied to items scored using more than two score categories, the 2PL can be generalized to model each score category probability. Cooke and Michie (1997, 1999) used the graded response model (GRM; Samejima, 1969) to analyze the PCL–R. The GRM uses the 2PL to model the *cumulative score probability functions* for an item, which indicate the probability of scoring in or higher than a given score category. Because the probability of scoring 0 or higher is always 1, there exist two such functions to be estimated for each PCL–R item—the probability of scoring 1 or higher and the probability of scoring 2 or higher. The probability of an item score (0, 1, or 2) can be computed from the difference between the cumulative score probability functions:

$$P(X_i = 0|\theta) = 1 - \exp[a_i(\theta - b_{i1})]/\{1 + \exp[a_i(\theta - b_{i1})]\}$$

$$P(X_i = 1|\theta) = \exp[a_i(\theta - b_{i1})]/\{1 + \exp[a_i(\theta - b_{i1})]\} - \exp[a_i(\theta - b_{i2})]/\{1 + \exp[a_i(\theta - b_{i2})]\}$$

$$P(X_i = 2|\theta) = \exp[a_i(\theta - b_{i2})]/\{1 + \exp[a_i(\theta - b_{i2})]\}$$

where b_{i1} and b_{i2} represent threshold parameters for the 2PL cumulative score probability functions. Because the probability of scoring 1 or higher is always greater than the probability of scoring 2 or higher, b_{i1} is always less than b_{i2}. As will be illustrated shortly, a graphical illustration of $P(X_i = k|\theta)$, called an *item category characteristic curve* (ICCC), frequently helps in interpreting GRM parameters.

Fitting the GRM to the PCL–R

Using the same data studied in the factor analysis section, GRM estimates ($\hat{a}_i$, $\hat{b}_{i1}$, and $\hat{b}_{i2}$) for all 20 PCL–R items were obtained using the computer program MULTILOG (Thissen, 1991) and are reported in Table 5–6. As for the 2PL, the *a* parameter in the GRM reflects the discriminating power of the item. Thus, Items 17, 18, 19, and 20, all having low *a* estimates, appear to be poorer indicators of the latent trait than the remaining 16 items. The b_1 and b_2 parameters reflect the levels of θ at which the ICCCs for successive score categories (0 and 1 and 1 and 2) cross and thus indicate where along the θ scale the psychopathy characteristics occur. The higher the $\hat{b}_{i1}$s and $\hat{b}_{i2}$s, the higher the latent psychopathy levels needed before the PCL–R characteristic becomes manifest. For example, item 19 "Revocation of conditional release" would be a characteristic that is present even at low levels of psychopathy ($\hat{b}_1 = -2.70$, $\hat{b}_2 = -1.27$), whereas higher levels are needed before item 17 "Many short-term marital relationships" is likely to be present ($\hat{b}_1 = 0.00$, $\hat{b}_2 = 2.00$).

For comparison purposes, estimates are reported in Table 5–6 for a one-factor model, hereafter referred to as the single common factor model (SCFM). In addition to the estimated factor loading ($\hat{\lambda}_1$) and error variance ($\hat{\psi}^2$) for each item, the intercept ($\hat{\tau}$) is also reported. When fit simultaneously

TABLE 5–6.
GRM and SCFM Parameter Estimates

Item	GRM			SCFM		
	$\hat{a}$	$\hat{b}_1$	$\hat{b}_2$	$\hat{\lambda}_1$	$\hat{\psi}^2$	$\hat{\tau}$
1	1.08	−0.75	1.67	0.34	0.36	0.86
2	1.14	−0.89	1.27	0.36	0.38	0.94
3	1.17	−1.80	0.31	0.38	0.36	1.28
4	1.14	−1.24	1.24	0.36	0.37	1.01
5	1.28	−1.06	0.76	0.42	0.40	1.06
6	1.56	−2.01	−0.21	0.41	0.28	1.45
7	1.18	−0.98	1.17	0.39	0.38	0.98
8	1.76	−1.33	0.46	0.47	0.30	1.19
9	0.87	−1.95	1.33	0.29	0.36	1.06
10	0.99	−1.61	0.34	0.37	0.44	1.23
11	0.83	−1.49	0.45	0.33	0.52	1.17
12	0.95	−0.73	0.89	0.40	0.54	0.96
13	0.86	−1.93	0.65	0.32	0.43	1.19
14	1.05	−2.21	0.29	0.33	0.34	1.31
15	0.98	−2.53	0.18	0.31	0.35	1.36
16	0.89	−2.35	0.18	0.30	0.40	1.32
17	0.57	0.00	2.00	0.25	0.62	0.75
18	0.72	−1.49	0.12	0.33	0.59	1.20
19	0.59	−2.70	−1.27	0.26	0.53	1.49
20	0.73	−1.98	0.14	0.33	0.51	1.29

to the covariance and mean structure of the items, the SCFM behaves similarly to an item response model. The λ_1s function similarly to the as, whereas the τs, which relate to the mean item scores, are closely related to the b_1s and b_2s. Items with larger $\hat{a}$s also tend to have higher $\hat{\lambda}$s, whereas items with larger $\hat{\tau}$s tend to have lower $\hat{b}_1$s and $\hat{b}_2$s.

Figure 5–4 provides a graphical illustration of two PCL–R items—Item 5 "Conning/manipulative," and Item 6 "Lack of remorse or guilt" based on their GRM and SCFM estimates. Figure 5–4, A and B, illustrates the GRM-based ICCCs for these items. Characteristic of the GRM, the ICCCs for score 0 strictly decrease as θ increases, and the ICCC for score 2 strictly increases as θ increases. Item 6, which has lower $\hat{b}_1$ and $\hat{b}_2$, is more likely than Item 5 to receive scores of 1or 2 at lower levels of θ. Thus, a "Lack of remorse or guilt" would appear to be a more common characteristic of individuals with low psychopathy levels than being "Conning/manipulative." Also displayed is each item's *expected response function* (ERF; Fig. 5–4, C and D, respectively), which is the expected item score at each level of θ. The ERF is a weighted sum of the item score categories in which the probabilities of each score serve as weights. The steeper the slope of the ERF, the more effective the item score is in distinguishing the trait levels of individuals and thus the more discrim-

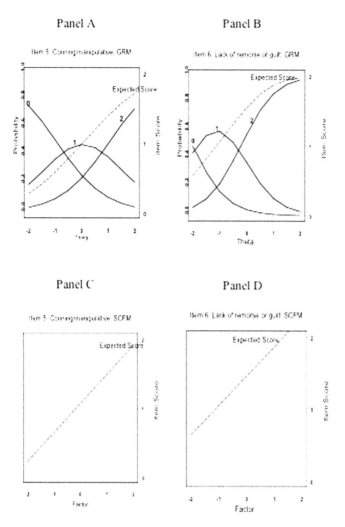

FIGURE 5–4.   GRM-based item category characteristic curves and expected response function and SCFM-based expected response function for Item 5 "Conning/manipulative" (A and C, respectively) and for Item 6 "Lack of remorse or guilt" (B and D, respectively).

inating the item. Items 5 and 6 are both items that provide high levels of discrimination, as suggested by the high âs for these items ($â_5 = 1.28$, $â_6 = 1.56$) and the steepness of their ERFs. The ERF can also help in evaluating the difficulty of the item, as items having higher ERFs across θ levels are easier than those with lower ERFs.

Several differences between the GRM and SCFM are apparent from these graphs. First, in the SCFM only the ERF is modeled, not the ICCCs. The SCFM-based ERFs for Items 5 and 6 are shown in Fig. 5–4, C and D, respectively. The second difference is that the ERFs are always linear when fitting the SCFM, having slopes $\hat{\lambda}_1$, and intercepts $\hat{\tau}$. In the GRM, the ERF can be nonlinear, as is most evident for Item 6. A third difference, also due to the linearity of the SCFM, is that the SCFM ERFs can assume values outside the range of item scores when factor levels become very high or very low. Notice in Fig. 5–4D that the ERF for Item 6 moves above 2 for factor levels above 1.3. This result highlights the problem mentioned earlier in applying the common factor model to categorical items, namely, that expected item scores can go outside the actual item score range. This does not occur for IRT models, which always produce ERFs having values between the highest and lowest item score categories.

Item and Test Information Using the GRM

The nonlinear ERF for a GRM item implies that varying amounts of discrimination are provided by the item across different levels of the latent trait. As a result, a GRM item can be more useful in estimating the trait levels of respondents at certain θ levels than others. A primary advantage of IRT relative to factor analysis is its ability to represent where along the latent trait scale an item is most useful.

For this reason, *item information functions* are a core feature of IRT. An information function describes the contribution of the item to trait estimation at each level of the latent trait and is equal to the inverse of the trait estimation error based on the item score. Statistically, each item score category contributes to an item's information. A score category information is computed as

$$I_{ik}(\theta) = [P'_{ik}(\theta)]^2 / P_{ik}(\theta) - P''_{ik}(\theta)$$

where $P_{ik}(\theta) = P(X_i = k|\theta)$, and $P'_{ik}(\theta)$, $P''_{ik}(\theta)$ represent the first and second derivatives, respectively, of the ICCC at θ. The item information function weights the amount of information provided by each score category by the probability of obtaining that score:

$$I_i(\theta) = \sum_{k=1}^{K} I_{ik}(\theta) P_{ik}(\theta).$$

An attractive feature of item information functions is that they are additive. A test information function can be computed as the sum of the item information functions:

$$T(\theta) = \sum_i I_i(\theta),$$

and represents the precision with which θ can be estimated using all item scores. In this respect, the test information function is inversely related to the standard error of estimate of the latent trait: $T(\theta) = 1/SE(\hat{\theta})$.

The concept of test information is of much practical use in test construction. Once an item's GRM estimates are obtained, the contribution of the item to trait estimation can be determined even before the item is administered as part of an intact test. Thus, the items chosen for a test can be deliberately selected to provide more precise estimation at levels of the trait at which greater precision is needed, as might correspond to a diagnostic cut-score, for example. Alternatively, if equal amounts of precision are desired across all trait levels, items can be chosen to produce a test information function that is flat across trait levels.

With the GRM estimates in Table 5–6, Fig 5–5A provides illustrations of item information functions for four PCL–R items: Item 5 "Conning/manipulative," Item 6 "Lack of remorse or guilt," Item 10 "Poor behavioral controls," and Item 20 "Criminal versatility." As seen in these examples, GRM items can vary not only according to how much information they provide but also by where along the θ scale they provide information. For example, Item 6, while providing much information at low levels of θ, provides very little information at high levels of θ. Item 5 "Conning/manipulative" becomes more important than Item 6 "Lack of remorse or guilt" at higher levels of θ and thus would be more useful in distinguishing individuals having higher levels of psychopathy. This is consistent with the previous observation that the characteristic "Lack of remorse or guilt" is more common at lower levels of θ than being "Conning/manipulative."

Figure 5–5B provides an illustration of the overall test information function for the 20-item PCL–R, as well as the *test characteristic curve* (TCC), which illustrates the expected total PCL–R scores at different levels of θ. The TCC is computed as the sum across items of the ERFs and can aid in interpreting the θ scale. For example, from the TCC it can be seen that a θ level of 0 corresponds to a PCL–R score of approximately 20, whereas a θ level of 2 corresponds to a score of approximately 32. The test information function suggests that the PCL–R is most informative (and thus provides its most accurate trait estimation) at approximately $\theta = -.5$, or for persons expected to receive PCL–R scores a little less than 20. Nevertheless, it would appear that trait estimation is still quite good at higher levels of θ. For example, at $\theta = 2.0$, $SE(\hat{\theta}) = 1/\sqrt{4.0} = .5$.

Information functions can also be used to compare the relative amount of information provided by different test items or different tests. In recalling the two- and three-factor models, it might be questioned whether the items of either factor type provide similar amounts of information across the latent trait scale. Aside from differences in the amount of information provided, however, the shape of each factor curve is approximately the same. Each factor tends to be maximally informative at approximately $\theta = -.5$ and becomes gradually less informative for θ levels above 0. In general, it appears that the relative contribution of each of the factors to estimation of the trait

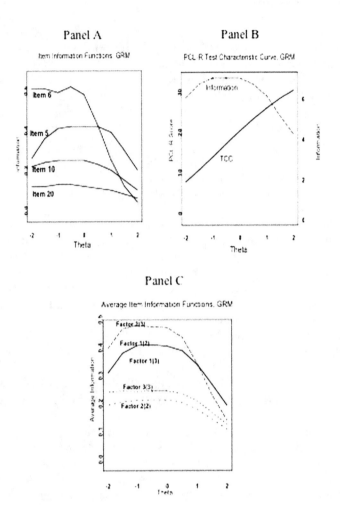

FIGURE 5–5.   GRM-based item information functions for four PCL–R items (A), GRM-based test information function and characteristic curve (B), and GRM-based average item information functions for items measuring different factors (C).

is approximately the same across θ levels. One exception occurs for the three-factor model, in which items categorized as Factor 2 items tend to be more informative than Factor 1 items at lower levels of θ, but Factor 1 items become more informative when θ > 1.

Item and Test Information Using the Common Factor Model

Information can also be investigated using the SCFM. Plots similar to those in Fig. 5–5 are displayed for the SCFM in Fig. 5–6 based on the estimates in Table 5–6. Figure 5–6A shows item information functions for Items 5, 6, 10,

Panel A   Panel B

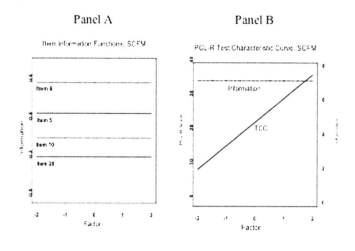

Panel C

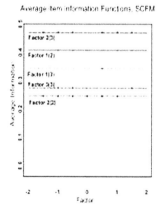

FIGURE 5–6.   SCFM-based item information functions for four PCL–R items (A), SCFM-based test information function and characteristic curve (B), and SCFM-based average item information functions for items measuring different factors (C).

and 20. Consistent with the constant slopes of their ERFs, the information functions are constant across all levels of the common factor, as each item is assumed to be equally informative across trait levels. The constant amount of information for each SCFM item is equal to $\hat{\lambda}_1 / \hat{\varphi}^2$ (McDonald, 1999). Intuitively, the items providing the most information will be those having large factor loadings and small error variance estimates.

For the four items considered here, the GRM and SCFM are generally in agreement as to the relative amounts of information provided by each item at lower levels of θ; however, the SCFM is not able to account for how the information provided by these items reduces at higher trait levels. In Fig. 5–6, B and C, the effects of the linear model on the TCC, as well as the test information and average factor information functions is apparent. The TCC, which is the sum of the ERFs across items, is also linear for the SCFM, having slope equal to the sum of the factor loadings across items ($\sum_j \hat{\lambda}_{j1} = 6.95$). The test information function, like the item information functions, is thus also constant, implying that trait estimation is equally precise across all trait levels. Lastly, the relative ordering of the factor information functions is generally consistent with that observed for the GRM, with Factor 1 items of the two-factor model, and Factor 2 items of the three-factor model, providing the most information.

Using IRT Models to Study Measurement Invariance:
Differential Item Functioning Analysis

IRT models can also be used to investigate measurement invariance. In IRT, *differential item functioning* (DIF) is said to occur when the relationship between θ and item score is different across two or more studied populations. Because GRM items model an ICCC for each score category, there is technically more than one way to define DIF (Chang & Mazzeo, 1994; Cohen, Kim, & Baker, 1993). One definition implies that DIF occurs when any of an item's ICCCs are different across groups. Following this definition, the conditional probabilities of every score category must be the same. Alternatively DIF is defined as occurring only when the ERFs for the item differ. According to this latter definition, the conditional probability of each score category need not be the same, as long as the expected score for the item is the same. This definition is consistent with how differentially performing items (i.e., items having different intercepts) were identified in the common factor model, which only models the ERFs. Many IRT methods exist to statistically test for DIF with respect to either of these two definitions (see Millsap & Everson, 1993).

A multigroup GRM can be used to test for DIF according to the first definition. The multigroup GRM strategy starts by the assumption that the GRM parameters for all items are the same across groups and iteratively "frees up" the parameters of items found to perform differentially, similar to the factor analytic approach used to find a model of partial invariance. The basis for identifying differentially performing items is a likelihood ratio test (Thissen, Steinberg, & Gerrard, 1986). The likelihood ratio test is a test of the difference in log-likelihoods between a comparison model in which the studied item is allowed to have different parameters across groups and a constrained model in which the studied item parameters are constrained to be equivalent. The difference in the log-likelihoods of these two models follows a chi-square distribution under a null hypothesis of no DIF. A significant chi-square difference implies the item parameters are different. This process is repeated until a core set of items (i.e., anchor items) are found that have the same parameters across groups. Similar to marking items in partial invariance models, these items serve to equate the factor metrics across groups in testing the remaining suspect items for DIF. Cooke and Michie (1997) and Cooke et al. (2001) used this general procedure in testing for DIF among PCL–R items.

When anchor items are searched for in an exploratory fashion, the same caution applied in searching for factor analytic partial invariance models is relevant here. Ideally, anchor items can be selected based on substantive, as well as statistical, considerations.

A second IRT-based DIF detection method, Poly-SIBTEST (Chang, Mazzeo, & Roussos, 1996), follows the second DIF definition and is sensitive only to differences in the ERFs across groups. For each studied item, Poly-SIBTEST estimates for each group a nonparametric regression of the studied item score onto the total score from the anchor items. Because scores on the anchor items are a close approximation to θ, these regression functions closely approximate the ERFs for each group. A DIF index β_{UNI} is computed as the average vertical difference between the ERFs. The statistic can be shown to follow an approximately normal distribution under conditions of no DIF and thus can be tested for statistical significance. In effect, β_{UNI} represents the expected score difference between groups on the studied item, conditional on trait level.

A common explanation for the occurrence of DIF is that an item measures some nuisance dimension unrelated to the dimension intended to be measured by the test that favors either of the two groups being compared for DIF. For example, on a test of mathematics ability, an item presented in the context of baseball batting averages may display DIF in favor of North American males due to their greater familiarity with the sport. This interpretation makes use of IRT methods problematic in studying DIF in tests that are intentionally multidimensional (see Embretson & Reise, 2000, p. 262), as DIF can occur because of measurement of secondary dimensions actually intended to be measured by the test.

For this reason, in the current DIF analysis Factor 1 items were analyzed separately from Factor 2 items. Tables 5–7 and 5–8 display the results. In this

TABLE 5–7.
Differential Item Functioning Analysis Comparing Caucasians and African Americans, Factor 1 Items

Item Number and Stem	GRM Estimates					Poly-SIBTEST	
	$\hat{a}^*$	$\hat{b}_{1,C}$	$\hat{b}_{2,C}$	$\hat{b}_{1,AA}$	$\hat{b}_{2,AA}$	β_{UNI}	p
1. Glibness/superficial charm	1.42	−0.80	1.32	−0.80	1.32		
2. Grandiose sense of self-worth	1.47	−0.89	1.05	−0.89	1.05		
4. Pathological lying	1.34	−1.27	0.99	−1.27	0.99		
5. Conning/manipulative	1.16	−1.15	0.72	−1.15	0.72		
6. Lack of remorse or guilt	1.93	−1.89	−0.30	−1.89	−0.30		
7. Shallow affect	1.20	**−1.19**	**0.88**	**−0.71**	**1.42**	.199	.00
8. Callous/lack of empathy	1.63	**−1.55**	**0.34**	**−1.15**	**0.64**	.150	.00
16. Failure to accept responsibility	1.16	−1.97	0.07	−1.97	0.07		

*Equal estimates apply for Caucasians and African Americans.

TABLE 5–8.
Differential Item Functioning Analysis Comparing Caucasians and African
Americans, Factor 2 Items

Item Number and Stem	$\hat{a}^*$	$\hat{b}_{1,C}$	$\hat{b}_{2,C}$	$\hat{b}_{1,AA}$	$\hat{b}_{2,AA}$	β_{UNI}	p
			GRM Estimates			Poly-SIBTEST	
3. Need for stimulation/ proneness to boredom	1.87	−0.92	0.73	−0.92	0.73		
9. Parasitic lifestyle	1.08	−0.77	**1.98**	**−1.92**	**0.92**	−0.329	.00
10. Poor behavioral controls	0.88	−1.05	**1.10**	**−1.64**	**0.31**	−0.235	.00
12. Early behavior problems	1.07	−0.13	1.35	−0.13	1.35		
13. Lack of realistic, long-term goals	1.01	−0.96	**1.27**	**−1.80**	**0.48**	−0.234	.00
14. Impulsivity	1.64	−1.24	0.77	−1.24	0.77		
15. Irresponsibility	1.05	−1.85	0.60	−1.85	0.60		
18. Juvenile delinquency	0.84	−0.73	0.59	−0.73	0.59		
19. Revocation of conditional release	0.71	−1.75	−0.67	−1.75	−0.67		

*Equal estimates apply for Caucasians and African Americans.

analysis DIF was only investigated with respect to the threshold (i.e., b_1 and b_2) parameters of each item. After a subset of anchor items was found, the GRM likelihood ratio test was performed to test each of the nonanchor items for DIF. For both the Factor 1 and Factor 2 items, the multigroup GRM procedure led to the same general results observed in the partial invariance factor analytic model. Among Factor 1 items, Items 7 and 8 have lower thresholds for Caucasians than for African Americans, suggesting higher scores, conditional on trait level, for Caucasians. For Factor 2 items, lower thresholds are observed for African Americans on Items 9, 10, and 13, implying higher scores for African Americans, conditional on trait level.

Tables 5–7 and 5–8 also show results for a Poly-SIBTEST analysis of these items. In this analysis, positive β_{UNI}s imply higher average expected scores on the item (conditional on trait level) for Caucasians; negative β_{UNI}s imply higher scores for African Americans. Consequently, the β_{UNI} estimate of .199 on item 7 implies that, conditional on trait level (as approximated by the sum score for the anchor items), Caucasians on average receive a score .199 higher on the item. The largest amount of DIF occurs for Item 9 "Parasitic lifestyle," which results in an expected score differential of .329, with African-Americans receiving higher scores. Recall that the partial invariance model likewise suggested that Item 9 contained the most DIF, but estimated the expected score difference as .36 (i.e., $\hat{\tau}_{AA} - \hat{\tau}_C = 1.39 - 1.03$).

Interpretation of DIF can also be facilitated by a graphical inspection of the ERFs in each group. Figure 5–7 illustrates the ERFs for Item 9 "Parasitic

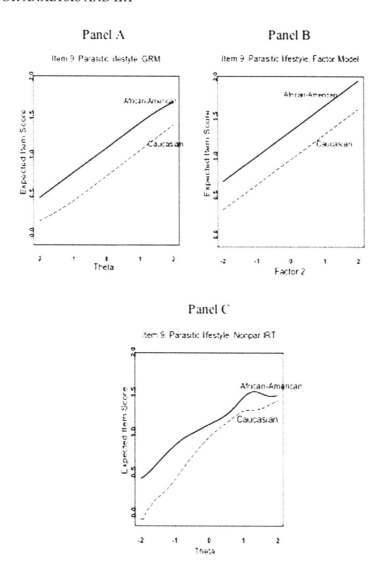

FIGURE 5–7.   GRM-based expected response functions (A), common factor model-based expected response functions, and nonparametrically estimated expected response functions (C) for Caucasians and African Americans, Item 9 "Parasitic lifestyle."

lifestyle" as defined by the common factor model (Fig. 5–7A), the GRM (Fig. 5–7B), and nonparametrically estimated ERFs (Fig. 5–7C), as used in Poly-SIBTEST. Each model shows that African Americans consistently receive higher scores on the item than Caucasians across all trait levels. Both the β_{UNI} statistic and the difference in τs according to the common factor model represent estimates of the average vertical distance between ERFs.

CONCLUSION

The purpose of this chapter was to provide an overview of factor analysis and item response theory as methods for studying psychometric properties of the PCL–R. By studying a common dataset using each modeling framework, it is hoped that the reader might gain a deeper appreciation for how both often provide similar insights into the same measurement issues, while also recognizing some of their fundamental differences.

Relative to IRT, factor analysis is better suited for (a) investigating and confirming multifactor latent structures and (b) evaluating the factorial invariance of tests across groups. Indeed, factor analysis can be a useful first step in evaluating whether the unidimensionality is sufficiently satisfied to apply IRT models. IRT models are attractive because of their nonlinearity, a property that not only makes them statistically more appropriate for categorical data but also permits inspection of the varying amounts of information provided by items and tests across latent trait levels. By modeling the probability of each score category outcome as opposed to the expected score, IRT models also provide a higher degree of specificity in modeling item/trait relationships.

Compared with factor analysis, IRT is a relatively new methodology, and its usefulness with psychological measures has only recently been appreciated. As a result, several aspects of this methodology are not as developed as for factor analysis. For example, relatively little has been done in proposing goodness-of-fit and/or model comparison criteria in IRT.

Model selection decisions are also more complex in IRT. Up to this point, only the GRM has been considered with the PCL–R. Various other IRT models (see Van der Linden & Hambleton, 1997, for many examples) could also be fit. The rating scale model (Andrich, 1978) provides an attractive alternative because of its assumption of a common rating scale metric across items. Nonparametric IRT models, which have recently received attention in psychological measurement (Santor & Ramsay, 1998; Santor, Ramsay, & Zuroff, 1994), are also appealing ways to study test items because of their fewer modeling assumptions and greater flexibility in characterizing item/trait relationships. Finally, multidimensional IRT (MIRT) models also exist and are receiving growing attention in the measurement literature. MIRT models incorporate several θs into modeling item scores and can be used for both confirmatory and exploratory analyses of test structure just as in factor analysis (Ackerman, 1994; Muraki & Carlson, 1995). Although traditional IRT applications (e.g., differential item functioning and test equating) are not as easily conducted with such models (or at least have yet to be implemented), MIRT models may have important applications in future studies of PCL–R dimensional structure.

One application of IRT modeling that has yet to be investigated with the PCL–R is *appropriateness measurement*. When an IRT model such as the GRM is fit to a test, the model parameter estimates can be used to evaluate the validity of each individual's item score pattern (Drasgow, Levine, & Williams,

1985). Appropriateness measures quantify the degree to which a response pattern is typical, or expected, based on the estimated item parameters; in the context of the PCL–R, such measures can assist in identifying individuals that may possess unique constellations of psychopathy traits. Such individuals are important to identify because they may be receiving higher scores on items for reasons other than their latent psychopathy levels and probably merit special attention when one interprets their scores.

A common limitation of both factor analysis and item response theory with the PCL–R is their failure to account for rater effects. Although the PCL–R has demonstrated high interrater reliability at the test score level, it is not always clear whether this rater consistency extends to scores at the item level nor whether item-level rater differences could be affecting factor analysis or IRT solutions. It is plausible that rater effects may account for some of the inconsistencies found across studies regarding the factor structure of the PCL–R and/or DIF analyses. Psychometric models that incorporate rater influence are receiving growing attention in psychometrics (e.g., Patz & Junker, 1999; Engelhard, 1994), and their future use with the PCL–R may help in evaluating the significance of this problem.

It should be recalled that in the current analyses only a subset of the 20 PCL–R items was analyzed. By only considering items that could be clearly associated with a common latent dimension, the interpretation given to the psychometric properties of items and their equivalence across groups is clearest. However, the results speak less directly to the equivalence of the instrument as a whole because of the omission of some items. In this regard, models that can include more items (such as a recent four-factor model considered by Hare, 2003) may be particularly useful.

Finally, it should be noted that both of the modeling frameworks considered in this chapter are best suited for conditions in which the latent construct of psychopathy is regarded as continuous. To the contrary, in many cases it has been found more useful to regard psychopathy as a taxon (Harris, Rice, & Quinsey, 1994). For example, laboratory evidence has demonstrated that psychopaths frequently display neuropsychological deficits of a discrete nature when compared with nonpsychopaths (Brinkley, 2001; Newman, 1998). Statistical analyses have also supported a taxon interpretation of PCL–R scores. For example, Harris et al. (1994) applied taxometric procedures to show that a PCL–R score distribution may be more appropriately regarded as a mixture of score distributions representing psychopath and nonpsychopath populations. For such conditions, methods such as latent class analysis (Lazarsfeld & Henry, 1968) or latent variable mixture models (Titterington, Smith, & Makov, 1985) may be more suitable methods.

ACKNOWLEDGMENT

The author thanks Robert Hare and Joseph Newman for the data used to perform the analyses in this chapter.

REFERENCES

Ackerman, T. A. (1994). Using multidimensional item response theory to understand what items and tests are measuring. *Applied Measurement in Education, 7*, 255–278.

Alterman, A. I., Cacciola, J. S., & Rutherford, M. J. (1993). Reliability of the Revised Psychopathy Checklist in substance abuse patients. *Psychological Assessment, 5*, 442–448.

Andrich, D. (1978). A rating formulation for ordered response categories. *Psychometrika, 43*, 561–573.

Bentler, P. M. (1990). Comparative fit indexes in structural models. *Psychological Bulletin, 107*, 238–246.

Birenbaum, A. (1968). Some latent trait models and their use in inferring an examinee's ability. In F. M. Lord & M. R. Novick (Eds.), *Statistical theories of mental test scores*. Reading, MA: Addison-Wesley.

Brinkley, C. (2001). *Challenges associated with studying neuropsychological versus behavioral correlates of the psychopathy construct*. Unpublished manuscript.

Byrne, B. M. (1998). *Structural equation modeling with LISREL, PRELIS, and SIMPLIS*. Mahwah, NJ: Lawrence Erlbaum Associates.

Cattell, R. B. (1966). The meaning and strategic use of factor analysis. In R. B. Cattell (Ed.), *Handbook of multivariate experimental psychology*, Chicago: Rand McNally.

Chang, H. H., & Mazzeo, J. (1994). The unique correspondence of the item response function and item category response functions in polychotomously scored item response models. *Psychometrika, 59*, 391–404.

Chang, H. H., Mazzeo, J., & Roussos, L. (1996). Detecting DIF for polychotomously scored items: An adaptation of the SIBTEST procedure. *Journal of Educational Measurement, 33*, 333–353.

Cleckley, H. (1976). *The mask of sanity* (5th ed.). St. Louis: Mosby.

Cliff, N. (1988). The eigenvalue-greater than one criterion and the reliability of components. *Psychological Bulletin, 103*, 276–279.

Cohen, A. S., Kim, S.-H., & Baker, F. B. (1993). Detection of differential item functioning in the graded response model. *Applied Psychological Measurement, 17*, 335–350.

Cooke, D. J., Kosson, D. S., & Michie, C. (2001). Psychopathy and ethnicity: Structural, item and test generalizability of the Psychopathy Checklist–Revised (PCL–R) in Caucasian and African-American participants. *Psychological Assessment, 13*, 531–542.

Cooke, D. J., & Michie, C. (1997). An item response theory analysis of the Hare Psychopathy Checklist–Revised. *Psychological Assessment, 9*, 3–14.

Cooke, D. J., & Michie, C. (1999). Psychopathy across cultures: North America and Scotland compared. *Journal of Abnormal Psychology, 108*, 55–68.

Cooke, D. J., & Michie, C. (2001). Refining the construct of psychopathy: Towards a hierarchical model. *Psychological Assessment, 13*, 171–188.

Drasgow, F. (1984). Scrutinizing psychological tests: Measurement equivalence and equivalent relations with external variables are central issues. *Psychological Bulletin, 95*, 134–135.

Drasgow, F., Levine, M. V., & Williams, E. A. (1985). Appropriateness measurement with polychotomous item response patterns and standardized indices. *British Journal of Mathematical and Statistical Psychology, 38*, 67–86.

Embretson, S. E. (1996). The new rules of measurement. *Psychological Assessment, 8*, 341–349.

Embretson, S. E., & Reise, S. P. (2000). *Item response theory for psychologists.* Mahwah, NJ: Lawrence Erlbaum Associates.

Engelhard, G. J. (1994). Examining rater errors in the assessment of written composition with a many-faceted Rasch model. *Journal of Educational Measurement, 31,* 93–112.

Hare, R. D. (1991). *Manual for the Revised Psychopathy Checklist* (1st ed.). Toronto, Ontario, Canada: Multi-Health Systems.

Hare, R. D. (2003). *Manual for the Revised Psychopathy Checklist* (2nd ed.). Toronto, Ontario, Canada: Multi-Health Systems.

Hare, R. D., Cooke, D. J., & Hart, S. D. (1999). Psychopathy and sadistic personality disorder. In T. Millon & P. H. Blaney (Eds.), *Oxford textbook of psychopathology.* Oxford, England: Oxford University Press.

Hare, R. D., Harpur, T. J., Hakstian, A. R., Forth, A. E., Hart, S. D., & Newman, J. P. (1990). The revised psychopathy checklist: Reliability and factor structure. *Psychological Assessment, 2,* 338–341.

Hare, R. D., & McPherson, L. M. (1984). Violent and aggressive behavior by criminal psychopaths. *International Journal of Law and Psychiatry, 7,* 35–50.

Harpur, T. J., Hakstian, A. R., & Hare, R. D. (1988). Factor structure of the psychopathy checklist. *Journal of Consulting and Clinical Psychology, 56,* 741–747.

Harpur, T. J., Hare, R. D., & Hakstian, A. R. (1989). Two-factor conceptualization of psychopathy: Construct validity and assessment implications. *Psychological Assessment: A Journal of Consulting and Clinical Psychology, 1,* 6–17.

Harris, G. T., Rice, M. E., & Quinsey, V. L. (1994). Psychopathy as a taxon: Evidence that psychopaths are a discrete class. *Journal of Consulting and Clinical Psychology, 62,* 387–397.

Hart, S. D. (1998). Psychopathy and risk for violence. In D. J. Cooke, A. E. Forth, & R. D. Hare (Eds.), *Psychopathy: Theory, research, and implications for society* (pp. 355–373). London: Kluwer Academic.

Hart, S. D., & Hare, R. D. (1989). The discriminant validity of the Psychopathy Checklist in a forensic psychiatric population. *Psychological Assessment, 1,* 211–218.

Hemphill, J. F., Templeman, R., Wong, S., & Hare, R. D. (1998). Psychopathy and crime: Recidivism and criminal careers. *Psychopathy: Theory, research, and implications for society* (pp. 375–399). London: Kluwer Academic.

Hendrickson, A. E., & White, P. O. (1964). Promax: A quick method for rotation to simple structure. *British Journal of Statistical Psychology, 17,* 65–70.

Horn, J. L. (1965). A rationale and test for the number of factors in factor analysis. *Psychometrika, 30,* 179–186.

Jöreskog, K. G. (1971). Simultaneous factor analysis in several populations. *Psychometrika, 36,* 409–426.

Jöreskog, K. G., & Sörbom, D. (1981). *Analysis of linear structural relationships by maximum likelihood and least squares methods* (Research Report 81-8). Uppsala, Sweden: University of Uppsala.

Jöreskog, K. G., & Sörbom, D. (1996). *LISREL 8: User's reference guide.* Chicago: Scientific Software.

Kim, J.-O., & Mueller, C. W. (1978). *Introduction to factor analysis.* Newbury Park, CA: Sage.

Kosson, D. S., Smith, S. S., & Newman, J. P. (1990). Evaluating the construct of validity in psychopathy in black and white male inmates: Three preliminary studies. *Journal of Abnormal Psychology, 99,* 250–259.

Lawley, D. N. (1940). The estimation of factor loadings by the method of maximum likelihood. *Proceedings of the Royal Society of Edinburgh, 60,* 64–82.

Lazarsfeld, P. A., & Henry, N. W. (1968). *Latent structure analysis.* Boston: Houghton Mifflin.

Lord, F. M. (1980). *Applications of item response theory to practical testing problems.* Hillsdale, NJ: Lawrence Erlbaum Associates.

Lord, F. M., & Novick, M. R. (1968). *Statistical theories of mental test scores.* Reading, MA: Addison-Wesley.

Mazor, K. M., Hambleton, R. K., & Clauser, B. E. (1998). Multidimensional DIF analyses: The effects of matching on unidimensional subtest scores. *Applied Psychological Measurement, 22,* 357–367.

McDermott, P. A., Alterman, A. I., Cacciola, J. S., Rutherford, M. J., Newman, J. P., & Mulholland, E. M. (2000). Generality of Psychopathy Checklist–Revised factors over prisoners and substance-dependent patients. *Journal of Consulting and Clinical Psychology, 68,* 181–186.

McDonald, R. P. (1999). *Test theory: A unified treatment.* Mahwah, NJ: Lawrence Erlbaum Associates.

Meredith, W. (1993). Measurement invariance, factor analysis and factorial invariance. *Psychometrika, 58,* 525–543.

Millsap, R. E., & Everson, H. T. (1993). Methodology review: Statistical approaches for assessing measurement bias. *Applied Psychological Measurement, 17,* 297–334.

Muraki, E., & Carlson, J. E. (1995). Full-information factor analysis for polytomous item responses. *Applied Psychological Measurement, 19,* 73–90.

Newman, J. P. (1998). Psychopathy: An information processing perspective. In D. J. Cooke, A. E. Forth, & R. D. Hare (Eds.), *Psychopathy: Theory, research, and implications for society* (pp. 81–104). London: Kluwer Academic.

Newman, J. P., & Wallace, J. F. (1993). Psychopathy and cognition. In P. Kendell & K. Dobson (Eds.), *Psychopathology and cognition* (pp. 293–349). New York: Academic Press.

Patz, R. J., & Junker, B. W. (1999). Applications and extensions of MCMC in IRT: Multiple item types, missing data, and rated responses. *Journal of Educational and Behavioral Statistics, 24,* 342–366.

Salekin, R. T., Rogers, R., & Sewell, K. W. (1996). A review and meta-analysis of the Psychopathy Checklist and the Psychopathy Checklist–Revised: Predictive validity of dangerousness. *Clinical Psychology: Science and Practice, 3,* 203–215.

Salekin, R. T., Rogers, R., & Sewell, K. W. (1997). Construct validity of psychopathy in a female offender sample: A multitrait-multimethod evaluation. *Journal of Abnormal Psychology, 106,* 576–585.

Samejima, F. (1969). *Estimation of latent ability using a pattern of graded scores.* Psychometrika Monograph, No. 17.

Santor, D. A., & Ramsay, J. O. (1998). Progress in the technology of measurement: Applications of item response models. *Psychological Assessment, 10,* 345–359.

Santor, D. A., Ramsay, J. O., & Zuroff, D. C. (1994). Nonparametric item analyses of the Beck Depression Inventory: Evaluating gender item bias and response option weights. *Psychological Assessment, 6,* 255–270.

Sörbom, D. (1974). A general method for studying differences in factor means and factor structures between groups. *British Journal of Mathematical and Statistical Psychology, 27,* 229–239.

Spearman, C. (1904). General intelligence, objectively determined and measured. *American Journal of Psychology, 15,* 201–293.

Steenkamp, J. E. M., & Baumgartner, H. (1998). Assessing measurement invariance in cross-national consumer research. *Journal of Consumer Research, 25,* 78–90.

Steiger, J. H., & Lind, J. C. (1980, May). *Statistically based tests for the number of common factors.* Paper presented at the annual meeting of the Psychometric Society, Iowa City, IA.

Steinberg, L., & Thissen, D. (1996). Uses of item response theory and the testlet concept in the measurement of psychopathology. *Psychological Methods, 1,* 81–97.

Thissen, D. (1991). *MULTILOG user's guide: Multiple categorical item analysis and test scoring using item response theory.* Chicago: Scientific Software.

Thissen, D., Steinberg, L., & Gerrard, M. (1986). Beyond group-mean differences: The concept of item bias. *Psychological Bulletin, 99,* 118–128.

Thurstone, L. L. (1947). Multiple factor analysis. Chicago: University of Chicago Press.

Titterington, D. M., Smith, A. F. M, & Makov, U. E. (1985). *Statistical analysis of finite mixture distributions.* New York: Wiley.

Tucker, L. R., & Lewis, C. (1973). A reliability coefficient for maximum likelihood factor analysis. *Psychometrika, 38,* 1–10.

Van der Linden, W. J., & Hambleton, R. K. (1997). *Handbook of modern item response theory.* New York: Springer-Verlag.

Widaman, K. F., & Reise, S. P. (1997). Exploring the measurement invariance of psychological instruments: Applications in the substance use domain. In K. J. Bryant, M. Windle, & S. G. West (Eds.), *The science of prevention: Methodological advances from alcohol and substance abuse research* (pp. 281–324). Washington, DC: American Psychological Association.

Windle, M., & Dumenci, L. (1999). The factorial structure and construct validity of the Psychopathy Checklist–Revised among alcoholic inpatients. *Structural Equation Modeling, 6,* 372–393.

Zwick, W. R., & Velicer, W. F. (1986). Comparison of five rules for determining the number of components to retain. *Psychological Bulletin, 99,* 432–442.

6

The Hare Psychopathy Checklist and Recidivism: Methodological Issues and Guidelines for Critically Evaluating Empirical Evidence

James F. Hemphill

The broad purpose of this chapter is to familiarize readers with statistical and methodological issues that influence the interpretation of research findings involving the Psychopathy Checklist and recidivism. Results from quantitative reviews involving the Psychopathy Checklist and recidivism are briefly summarized, and then methodological and statistical factors that influence the quality of research evidence are discussed. The basic research design for risk assessment studies is presented, assumptions of this design are identified, and factors that investigators might consider to critically evaluate the quality of research evidence are discussed. Questions that investigators might consider when evaluating results from individual studies and from literature reviews are summarized in the Appendix. Examples of criticisms that some investigators have leveled against the Psychopathy Checklist are presented to illustrate the implications of the previously discussed methodological and statistical issues on clinical practice.

PSYCHOPATHY AND RECIDIVISM

The Psychopathy Checklist (PCL) is a popular instrument among forensic clinicians. Boothby and Clements (2000) surveyed 830 correctional psychologists in the United States, and these clinicians reported using the PCL at a rate higher than those for other instruments designed primarily for use in forensic contexts.[1] The number of publications involving the PCL and recidivism has increased exponentially across time. To get a crude index of this

---

[1]Eleven percent of correctional psychologists reported using the PCL. This would almost certainly be an underestimate of its use in forensic contexts today given the rapidly expanding body of research literature and familiarity with the PCL among clinicians.

increase, the terms *psychopathy checklist* and *recidivism* were entered into PsycINFO. These terms appeared together only once before 1989, 10 times from 1990 to 1994, 26 times from 1995 to 1999, and 57 times from 2000 to 2004. The greatest number of entries in a single year was 18 for 2004, followed by 14 in 2003. These findings suggest that the body of research literature is expanding rapidly and that investigators need to constantly keep up to date with recent developments and the applicability of the instrument to their population(s) of interest.

Psychopaths engage in persistently antisocial and criminal behaviors beginning at an early age, and they lack characteristics important for inhibiting antisocial and aggressive behaviors (Miller & Eisenberg, 1988). These defining features presumably place psychopaths at high risk for future criminal and violent behavior. The most widely validated measure of psychopathy is the PCL (Hare, 1980) and its derivatives, which include the Psychopathy Checklist–Revised (PCL–R; Hare, 1991, 2003), the Psychopathy Checklist: Screening Version (PCL:SV; Hart, Cox, & Hare, 1995), and the Psychopathy Checklist: Youth Version (PCL:YV; Forth, Kosson, & Hare, 2003). Unless otherwise indicated, the term *PCL* will be used throughout this chapter to refer to the PCL and related measures.

The PCL has been subjected to a considerable amount of psychometric analyses, and several factors and facets have been identified (see Hare, 2003, for a review). Virtually all researchers who have conducted analyses between PCL factors and recidivism have focused on the two-factor structure initially identified by Harpur and colleagues (Hare, 2003; Harpur, Hakstian, & Hare, 1988; Harpur, Hare, & Hakstian, 1989; Hare et al., 1990). PCL Factor 1 describes a constellation of interpersonal and affective traits commonly considered fundamental to most clinical descriptions of the psychopath, whereas PCL Factor 2 describes a chronically unstable, antisocial, and socially deviant lifestyle.

Four sets of meta-analytic reviews have been conducted in which the association between the PCL and recidivism was systematically examined (Gendreau, Goggin, & Smith, 2002, 2003; Hemphill & Hare, 1996; Hemphill, Hare, & Wong, 1998; Salekin, Rogers, & Sewell, 1996; Walters, 2003a, 2003b; also, see Dolan & Doyle, 2000, and narrative reviews by Edens, Skeem, Cruise, & Cauffman, 2001; Hare, 2003; Hare, Clark, Grann, & Thornton, 2000). Meta-analysis is a set of procedures that attempt to integrate and quantify statistical results across related studies. Several general conclusions can be reached from the meta-analytic reviews. The three most recent meta-analyses (i.e., Gendreau et al., 2002, 2003; Hemphill, Hare, et al., 1998; Walters, 2003a, 2003b) showed significant heterogeneity among effect sizes that were combined in each respective set of meta-analyses (but, see Salekin et al., 1996). This finding means that effect sizes involving the PCL and indices of recidivism vary considerably in magnitude across studies. There was remarkable consistency across meta-analyses in terms of the magnitudes of mean correlation coefficients between the PCL and indices of general recidivism (see Table 6–1). In their review, Salekin et al. (1996) produced mean correlation

TABLE 6–1.
Mean Correlation Coefficients Between Hare PCL Scores and Indices of Recidivism for Four Sets of Meta-Analyses

	Salekin, Rogers, & Sewell (1996)[a]		Hemphill, Hare, & Wong (1998)		Gendreau, Goggin, & Smith (2002)		Walters (2003a, 2003b)[b]	
	ks	rs (ds)[c]	ks and ns	rs	ks and ns	rs	ks and ns	rs
General recidivism								
PCL Total score	11 effect sizes	.27 (d = .55)	7 studies, 1,275 subjects	.25	30 studies, 4,365 subjects	.23	35 effect sizes, 4,870 subjects	.27
PCL Factor 1 score	—	—	5 studies, 1,072 subjects	.13	14 studies	.10	33 effect sizes, 4,360 subjects	.14
PCL Factor 2 score	—	—	5 studies, 1,072 subjects	.31	14 studies	.24	33 effect sizes, 4,360 subjects	.26
Violent recidivism								
PCL Total score	15 effect sizes	.37 (d = .79)	6 studies, 1,374 subjects	.21	26 studies, 4,823 subjects	.21	40 effect sizes, 6,506 subjects	.24
PCL Factor 1 score	—	—	3 studies, 370 subjects	.13	13 studies	.13	41 effect sizes, 6,356 subjects	.16
PCL Factor 2 score	—	—	3 studies, 370 subjects	.18	13 studies	.19	41 effect sizes, 6,356 subjects	.25
Sexual recidivism								
PCL Total score	3 effect sizes	.29[d] (d = .61[d])	1 study, 178 subjects	.23	—	—	5 effect sizes, 726 subjects	.06
PCL Factor 1 score	1 effect size	.21[d] (d = .42[d])	—	—	—	—	5 effect sizes, 726 subjects	.04
PCL Factor 2 score	1 effect size	.34[d] (d = .73[d])	—	—	—	—	5 effect sizes, 726 subjects	.06

Note: Effect sizes (rs, ds) unweighted by sample sizes were smaller in magnitude than were effect sizes weighted by sample sizes. Unweighted values are presented here because these values are conservative. Dashed lines indicate that the authors did not report these values. k = number of effect sizes or studies; r = correlation coefficient; d = effect size d (Rosenthal, 1991); n = number of participants.

[a]Some samples overlapped and contributed more than one effect size per set of analyses. [b]Walters provided results for values that were not available from published analyses. Values include both institutional misbehaviors and recidivism in the community, and some samples contributed more than one effect size per set of analyses. [c]Formula 2.2.6 in Cohen (1988, p. 23) was used to convert ds to rs. [d]Salekin et al. (1996) included studies involving "deviant sexual arousal and sexual sadism" (p. 210), which is broader in scope than behaviorally based indices of sexual recidivism.

143

coefficients for violent recidivism that were larger than those from the other three sets of meta-analyses, in part because Salekin et al. included studies that did not have behavioral indices of misbehavior, were not predictive, and had several (nonindependent) effect sizes per study.[2] For general recidivism, PCL total and PCL Factor 2 each correlated approximately .25 with recidivism, and PCL Factor 1 correlated in the .10 to .15 range. For violent recidivism, PCL Total and PCL Factor 2 each correlated in the .20 to .25 range with recidivism, and PCL Factor 1 correlated approximately .15. These findings indicate that the PCL is correlated to a similar degree with general recidivism and with violent recidivism. Results across studies were less clear for indices of sexual recidivism because there was considerable variability among studies and relatively few studies are available (see Table 6–1). Mean effect sizes for general and violent recidivism are in the moderate range for psychological assessment in general.[3] Taken together, these findings support the clinical use of the PCL for assessing risk for future antisocial and criminal behavior across diverse settings.

METHODOLOGICAL AND STATISTICAL CONSIDERATIONS

In this part of the chapter I focus on conceptual and methodological issues with respect to conducting risk assessment research. The purpose of this discussion is to provide readers with a framework for evaluating the methodological quality of research studies involving the PCL and indices of recidivism. By understanding how risk assessment research is conducted and by being able to identify the strengths and weaknesses of individual research studies, I hope that investigators will be able to critically evaluate the research literature and determine the strength of empirical evidence upon which conclusions are based. It is incumbent upon clinicians to evaluate the strength of empirical evidence because ultimately clinicians determine how much weight to assign to individual studies or quantitative reviews given their particular purposes, clinical demands, settings, and groups with whom they work. Although this discussion broadly applies to risk assessment research in general, the discussion will focus on research involving the PCL. A process for identifying the methodological rigor of meta-analytic and quantitative reviews follows a discussion of how to critically examine the methodological rigor of individual risk assessment studies.

---

[2]Results weighted by sample size tended to provide effect sizes that were slightly larger; the former results were presented here because these values are the most conservative.

[3]Meyer et al. (2001) examined the magnitude of validity coefficients in psychological research, and research involving the PCL and prediction of violence appears as the 61st largest entry of 144 meta-analyses.

Single Study Designs

Research Methodology

Research studies vary considerably in terms of quality. This is important to recognize because one methodologically strong study with a solid research design can yield conclusions that are far stronger and more persuasive than can scores of methodologically weak studies. Critical discussions of empirical approaches to conducting risk assessment studies have been discussed elsewhere (e.g., Hart, 1998a, 1998b; Monahan, 1981/1995; Monahan & Steadman, 1994; see also Quinsey, Harris, Rice, & Cormier, 1998), and readers are encouraged to review these publications for more details. As such, the following discussion concerning research methodology for single risk assessment studies will be brief. The standard research design for risk assessment studies involves five key elements: the sample studied, the predictor variable, the criterion variable, the length of follow-up, and one or more statistical indices to examine the association between predictor and criterion variables.

Researchers must identify a sample to study and obtain research participants from this group. Studies vary widely in terms of types of clinical settings and groups studied, procedures used to select participants, attrition rates during the study, number of participants ultimately involved, and so forth. Many of these factors can have important implications for the interpretation of research findings that are produced.

The predictor variable in studies reviewed at the beginning of this chapter is the PCL, and it can be a reliable and valid measure of psychopathy if used in the manner outlined in the PCL manual (Hare, 1991, 2003). This proviso is essential because the PCL is a complex instrument that requires considerable experience and training to use properly. Hare (1998) has provided evidence that some investigators have misused the PCL and have used flawed PCL ratings to make important clinical decisions that can have life-altering implications for both the community and individuals assessed.

The criterion variable in risk assessment studies is the measure of recidivism. Researchers frequently use the term *recidivism* (or *failure* or *outcome*) to refer to measures of antisocial and/or criminal behavior that take place during the follow-up period. Researchers have overwhelmingly used officially recorded indices of recidivism, which include institutional infractions, antisocial behaviors in the community, and rehospitalizations among psychiatric patients. Some researchers have expanded this measure to incorporate information from collateral informants and self-reports from study participants. Researchers frequently code multiple indices of recidivism per study, and the most common indices are general, violent, and sexual recidivism. What specific offenses fall into each of these groupings is often inconsistent from study to study. Researchers compute the time that has elapsed between the date of the PCL rating and the date that data were obtained for coding the index of

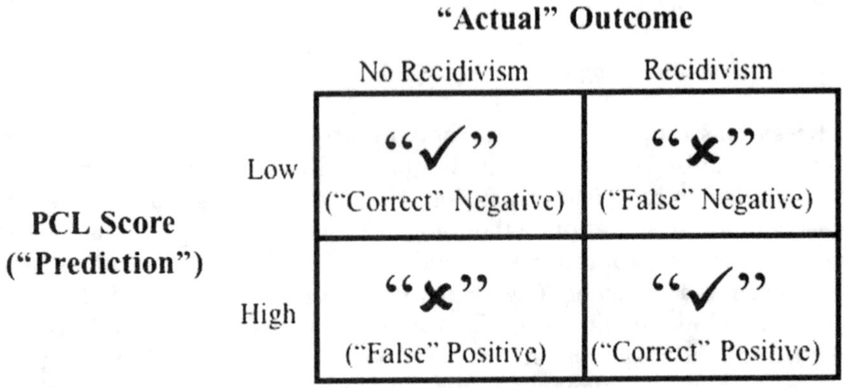

"Actual" Outcome

		No Recidivism	Recidivism
	Low	"✓" ("Correct" Negative)	"✗" ("False" Negative)
PCL Score ("Prediction")	High	"✗" ("False" Positive)	"✓" ("Correct" Positive)

FIGURE 6–1.   Outcomes for a standard 2 × 2 risk assessment research design involving the Hare Psychopathy Checklist and an index of recidivism.

recidivism. This is done for each study participant, and the average value across participants is referred to as the "follow-up" period. Mean follow-up lengths commonly range in duration from several months to decades.

One or more statistical indices are computed per study to quantify the degree of association between the PCL and an index of recidivism. As Hart (1998b) succinctly put it, "most studies cleave the risk factor and outcome into simplistic dichotomies" (p. 128). For example, PCL–R total scores that range from 0 to 40 are simply recoded to 0 ("nonpsychopath" or low PCL group) or 1 ("psychopath" or high PCL group). Similarly, frequency rates for indices of recidivism are recoded to 0 (no evidence of recidivism) or 1 (1 or more incidents of recidivism). Once the PCL scores and index of recidivism have been recoded, a variety of statistical indices can be computed. Conceptually, the basic form that the data take is a 2 × 2 table with four possible outcomes—two "correct" predictions (denoted by tick marks in Fig. 6–1) and two "incorrect" predictions (denoted by Xs in Figure 6–1).[4] The two "correct" predictions involve the cell in the upper left corner, where study participants with low PCL scores have no evidence of recidivism during the follow-up period, and the cell in the lower right corner, where participants with high PCL scores have evidence of recidivism. The two "incorrect" predictions involve the cell in the upper right corner, where participants with low PCL scores have evidence of recidivism during the follow-up, and the lower left corner, where participants with high PCL scores have no evidence of recidivism.

---

[4]Although Hart (1998b, p. 128) denoted "correct" predictions by happy faces and "incorrect" predictions by sad faces, check marks and Xs are used here. The latter symbols are more explicitly tied to the process of prediction, whereas the former symbols can be conceptually confusing if happy or sad faces are thought to reflect the desirability of the outcomes rather than the "accuracy" of the clinical predictions.

Assumptions of 2 × 2 Research Designs

Many key statistics in risk assessment research are conceptually based on this 2 × 2 research design. Coefficients that have predictor and criterion variables each measured on dichotomous scales (e.g., phi and tetrachoric correlation coefficients) are clearly computed from this 2 × 2 design. Perhaps less obvious is the fact that area under the curve analyses incorporate statistics derived from a series of 2 × 2 designs that are computed at each cutoff on the predictor variable and that survival analyses incorporate statistics derived from 2 × 2 designs estimated at points across time.

Key assumptions of 2 × 2 research designs are briefly outlined and critically evaluated here because investigators who conduct risk assessment research virtually never explicate these assumptions and because these assumptions have important implications for how risk assessment research is conducted and interpreted (see also Hart, 1998a, 1998b).

Assumption 1: The 2 × 2 research design is appropriate for risk assessment research. The 2 × 2 research design does not reflect the complexity of risk assessment research very well. The design simplifies complex processes into two variables (or two sets of variables) and neglects many other key elements including length of follow-up and methodological rigor.

Assumption 2: Investigators are primarily interested in passively predicting recidivism rather than actively lowering risk. Of course, clinicians who can accurately identify individuals or groups who are at high risk actively oversee or set into place plans to monitor, manage, and lower risk. This action necessarily results in statistically lower effect sizes for prediction purposes but increased continuity of services, better client care, and safer communities. Indeed, in many clinical contexts there is little reason to engage in comprehensive risk assessments if no actions are taken to lower risk.

Assumption 3: The PCL is the only predictor variable of interest. The implicit assumption when the PCL is entered by itself into a 2 × 2 table as the predictor variable of interest (see Fig. 6–1) is that the PCL is the sole variable of interest for assessing risk. Yet, the PCL is not and was never intended to be a comprehensive risk assessment instrument (Hemphill & Hare, 2004). Investigators should not expect a simple linear association between PCL score and risk level, particularly for individuals with low PCL scores who nonetheless may pose considerable risk (Hemphill & Hart, 2003). The importance of not using the PCL by itself is outlined in the PCL–R manual, which states that "the PCL–R should not be the sole criterion for making decisions. . . . Interpretation of the PCL–R should be made in conjunction with information obtained from other sources" (Hare, 2003, p. 16).

Assumption 4: Traditional cutoffs are firmly established for assessing risk using the PCL. Figure 6–1 illustrates that low- and high-risk groups need to be formed on the basis of particular scores to compute statistics from 2 × 2 tables. Researchers consequently need to identify cutoff scores when using the PCL for assessing risk in this context. Even though the second edition of the PCL manual provides some guidance on this point (e.g., Hare, 2003, pp.

30–31), firm cutoffs and selection ratios have not been established for using the PCL in the context of risk assessment. Indeed, different research groups have used widely varying cutoffs, and some investigators have even proposed that different cutoffs be used in different clinical contexts (e.g., Harris, Rice, & Quinsey, 1994, p. 395). That PCL scores coded from files alone yield consistently lower scores than scores coded from interview and file information might suggest to some investigators that cutoffs several points lower than those listed in the PCL manual be used for file-only PCL ratings.

Assumption 5: Estimates of recidivism are reasonably accurate measures of the criterion. The terms *true positives* and *true negatives* (i.e., *correct* decisions) and *false positives* and *false negatives* (i.e., *incorrect* decisions), which are used to classify individuals into one of four groups based on recidivism status (see Fig. 6–1), suggest that researchers know with reasonable or perfect accuracy whether or not each individual has failed or not during the follow-up period. These terms make little sense if the criterion (i.e., index of recidivism or outcome) is viewed as a fallible and insensitive measure of the criterion. The position that many commonly used indices are insensitive measures of recidivism is discussed later in this chapter. Although researchers strive to accurately measure and estimate recidivism rates, in actuality they never really know how close they have gotten to this laudable goal.

Assumption 6: Effect sizes (e.g., correlation coefficients and area under the curve statistics) provide important estimates of the associations between PCL scores and indices of recidivism. Effect sizes appear to provide objective, quantitative estimates that have an air of precision about them. In fact, the level of precision suggested by these quantitative indices is to a large extent artificial. The magnitude of a single effect size is linked to a particular research design, study methodology, scale(s) of measurement (e.g., ordinal, interval, and ratio) used, and index of effect size. It is important to recognize that different effect sizes do not produce results that are necessarily interchangeable. The magnitude of effect size cannot even be generalized across time within a single study because longer follow-up periods increase observed base rates, which in turn influence magnitudes of effect sizes. Further, it is important to keep in mind that effect sizes quantify associations between variables that are *measured*. Variables that provide questionable or insensitive measures of complex concepts (e.g., convictions as an index of recidivism) will necessarily yield effect sizes that are themselves questionable and difficult to interpret. Measures of recidivism that ignore dimensions of severity (e.g., use of weapons or victim injury) will concomitantly yield effect sizes whose magnitudes also ignore dimensions of severity. Many investigators who conduct recidivism research seem to implicitly assume that larger effect sizes indicate greater clinical utility. In some instances, small effect sizes are desirable and may indicate efficacious clinical practice. For example, small effect sizes can be desirable when high-risk cases have been accurately identified within a larger group of participants and clinical interventions or management strategies have successfully mitigated risk during the follow-up period or when a criterion variable is a poor or indirect measure of the concept. Interpreting the magnitudes of effect sizes clearly is a complex process and not as deceptively straightforward as it would initially appear.

Critical Evaluation of Research Methodology

Researchers endeavor to empirically study issues in a systematic and transparent manner that closely approximates "reality." The research domain of risk assessment is complex and difficult to study, and researchers have been creative and made many important strides in advancing clinical knowledge during the past 25 years. Nonetheless, the standard research design described earlier has many limitations that have an impact on the results derived from this methodology and interpretations that can be offered. Research designs generate results that depart considerably from "reality" in many key respects. Rarely have these limitations been raised or critically evaluated and the corollary implications on clinical practice been made explicit. Put candidly—even though research findings appear clear, crisp, and unambiguous in published form—research methodologies in the area of risk assessment are at present very crude.

In this section, issues that investigators should consider when determining the quality and relevance of research evidence are presented. Concrete questions that stem from this discussion are delineated in the Appendix. Note that this is not meant to be an exhaustive list of issues to consider but rather a framework for evaluating research evidence and its utility for using the PCL to assist with the process of conducting risk assessments.

1. Is the Study Relevant for Your Purposes?

The first issue to consider when evaluating findings from a research study is whether or not the study is of relevance for your purposes. There are many different procedures for assessing psychopathy and, in general, these are not interchangeable (Hare, 1985). Therefore, a central question to ask is whether the study involved the PCL or one of its derivatives. If the study did not, then research findings may be limited in terms of informing the clinical use of the PCL. Investigators cannot assume that research done using the PCL will generalize to other measures of psychopathy or vice versa. Relevance of any particular study depends on the particular purpose of the assessment (American Educational Research Association, American Psychological Association, & National Council on Measurement in Education, 1999). Studies that involve behavioral measures of misbehaviors are of greater relevance to the domain of risk assessment than are studies that use other indices. For example, studies with measures of criminal charges and/or convictions, rehospitalizations, and violations of institutional infractions generally provide stronger evidence for informing risk assessments than do measures of perceptions, affect, and psychophysiological responding unaccompanied by behavioral indices of misbehaviors. Investigators cannot assume that physiological arousal in the context of an experimental situation will, by itself, necessarily translate into misbehaviors of concern to clinicians who conduct risk assessments. Clinicians involved in risk assessment generally place more weight on study designs that are prospective rather than retrospective in nature. Prospective research designs involve coding recidivism from information that temporally occurs after PCL ratings are conducted, whereas retrospective research designs involve coding misbehaviors from information that occurs up to and including the time of the PCL ratings. In general, the closer the match between clinical practice and the published literature (e.g., training of PCL raters, detail and quality of collateral information), the better the research findings are expected to generalize to clinical settings. Put another way, studies that do not closely mimic clinical practice may have only limited utility for informing clinical practice.

2. Is the Research Study Methodologically Strong?

Although there is no clear set of criteria that indicate whether a study is methodologically strong, such studies tend to be based on large samples of participants who are representative of the population from which they were drawn, measure variables in a reliable manner, include PCL scores that are scored according to the procedures recommended in the PCL manual, and use behavioral indices of recidivism that are sensitive to detecting antisocial behaviors.

Sample Size.   Studies based on large sample sizes produce findings that are more statistically reliable and that can be reproduced by other investigators, whereas small sample sizes may produce statistically spurious findings that are not easily replicated. A basic rule of thumb for deciding upon the adequacy of sample size is difficult to establish and depends to some extent on the purpose of the PCL assessment. As previously mentioned, the average correlation coefficient between the PCL and indices of recidivism is approximately $r = .25$. Coefficients of this magnitude require approximately 50 participants to achieve statistical significance (at $p < .05$, one-tailed test). This means that studies with fewer than 50 participants would be expected to yield less statistically robust findings than would studies with more participants. Studies conducted on samples with particular characteristics (e.g., adolescents who have committed homicide) generally have fewer participants than other studies, but these studies nonetheless may be relevant and important for clinicians who work with similar groups.

Sample Representativeness.   It is particularly helpful for researchers to examine and report the extent to which the sample that is studied is actually representative of the larger group(s) from which participants were drawn. Research that has samples of participants who are representative of the larger groups from which they were drawn produce results that investigators can be more confident will generalize from a particular sample to other similar samples. Unfortunately, researchers often neglect either to report or to conduct these analyses. Two sets of analyses are relevant with respect to representativeness. The first set of analyses has to do with whether or not the pool of participants who form the sample are similar in many key respects to the population from which the sample was drawn. Researchers who use volunteers or other nonrandom procedures for selecting participants run the risk of producing results that may not generalize to individuals in the researchers' *own* research setting; results are even less likely to generalize to other settings. Many researchers do not systematically report on issues of sample representativeness, and it is not always clear what criminal history, demographic, clinical, and other variables might be important to consider when characteristics of samples and populations are contrasted. The second set of analyses has to do with whether or not participants included in key analyses (e.g., analyses examining associations between PCL scores and indices of recidivism) are representative of the initial sample. The sample that is actually studied may differ in composition from the initial sample because of attrition during the study period. Attrition is not necessarily a significant concern in interpreting research findings as long as attrition is random and few subjects are excluded. Unfortunately, attrition rarely seems to be random in risk assessment research.

It is perhaps not surprising that individuals with more extensive index offenses are kept incarcerated for longer periods of time and at higher rates than those with less extensive index offenses (e.g., Quinsey et al., 1998). Put another way, individuals who have committed "serious" offenses are not released during the study period and are not available to study in the community, which means that results from such studies tend to generalize better to "lower-risk" and "moderate-risk" individuals than to "high-risk" individuals. In contrast, we might expect official databases to include a disproportionately large number of recidivists when follow-up periods approaching decades are used (e.g., Hemphill, 1998). This is because recidivists who continue to receive official sanctions are maintained in databases, whereas those who do not may be purged for administrative or other reasons. Results from such studies are expected to generalize better to recidivists than to nonrecidivists. Taken together, these findings illustrate the complexity of sample representativeness and potential impact of differential attrition on interpreting research findings.

PCL Scores. Much recidivism research has been conducted with the PCL, PCL–R, PCL:SV, and PCL:YV, and by and large these measures have been completed using rating procedures outlined in rating booklets and technical manuals. This means that researchers and clinicians who depart substantially from standard rating procedures (e.g., Hare, 1998) will have difficulties drawing from published and other empirical findings to support their particular use (or misuse) of the PCL and its derivatives. Revalidation of these nonstandard procedures and consistent replication are required to persuasively demonstrate the clinical utility of alternative scoring methods. The PCL rating booklets and technical manuals recommend that raters code the PCL from both interview and collateral information.

At a minimum, raters should have the requisite training and experience to adequately score the PCL in a reliable manner (e.g., different clinicians using the same information should arrive at similar PCL scores), systematically consider all relevant evidence for each PCL item and, when appropriate, weigh evidence across the lifespan both for and against a high PCL score, and carefully score PCL items according to published PCL criteria. Hare (www.hare .org) recommended additional criteria for investigators using the PCL in clinical settings (see also Hare, 2003, pp. 15–17). Adequate training and experience in the use of the PCL is important because the scoring of many PCL criteria involves considerable clinical judgment. A corollary of this position is that researchers can help readers evaluate the reliability of PCL ratings by providing one or more quantitative indices of reliability. Interrater reliability indices include those that examine relative rankings of participants (e.g., product–moment correlations) and classification of participants into groups (e.g., kappa coefficients). Investigators should be aware that many indices of reliability emphasize relative rankings of participants and high reliability coefficients can be achieved even if absolute scores differ substantially. This means that one rater could consistently score everyone higher on the PCL than another rater would, thereby identifying proportionately more individuals as "psychopaths" when standard cutoffs are used. Just as reliability coefficients that are low in magnitude are not desirable, so too are reliability coefficients that are too large. This is because many PCL criteria involve the consideration of a multitude of behaviors across the entire lifespan, integrating and differentially weighting diverse and sometimes contrary information, and incorporating both clinical observations and collateral materials into a single score. This clinical discretion necessarily means that PCL scores should not be perfectly reliable. As Hare (1998) put it, some "investigators report interrater reliabilities for their PCL–R assessments that are unbelievably high (e.g., .95 or higher) . . . [this] usually occurs when the PCL–R assessments are based entirely on file information, a procedure that, if improperly used, places too much weight on specific entries made by other individuals" (p. 107).

Raters who score the PCL should not know scores on the index of recidivism for the files they code and vice versa. Use of this procedure avoids potentially inflating statistical associations between measures of psychopathy and recidivism and reduces biases that could complicate the interpretation of research findings.

Collateral information must be sufficient to adequately score the PCL. Thus, information should come from a variety of sources, be sufficiently lengthy and detailed, and contain reliable data of good quality. PCL scores cannot be completed without adequate collateral information, and the importance of solid collateral information cannot be understated. Indeed, the PCL–R technical manual (Hare, 2003) states that "**PCL–R ratings should not be made in the absence of adequate collateral information**" (p. 19, emphasis in original), and the PCL:YV technical manual (Forth et al., 2003) admonishes that "If no chart or collateral information is available, the PCL:YV rating should be delayed until such information becomes available" (p. 19).

Recidivism Measures.   There are two broad types of *recidivism* studies. The first set involves antisocial and/or criminal behaviors that occur in the community (e.g., convictions following release from a correctional facility or rehospitalizations following release from a psychiatric institution), and the second set involves behaviors that occur while an individual is institutionalized (e.g., infractions while in the institution or aggression coded from progress notes). Researchers rarely conduct studies that incorporate both institutional and community measures into a single index, although this could be done from a conceptual standpoint.

It is important to recognize that recidivism, like all constructs, is a theoretical concept that cannot be readily operationalized or measured. It is generally desirable to include many sources of information when complex constructs such as recidivism are evaluated (e.g., Achenbach, Krukowski, Dumenci, & Ivanova, 2005). This is rarely done in applied research on recidivism. Investigators routinely acknowledge that indices of recidivism provide underestimates of recidivism and appropriately caution readers about the limitations of their outcome measures. Despite these cautions, many investigators refer to recidivism and reconvictions (or similar measures) as if they were one and the same. They are not. Empirical studies indicate that official sources of information greatly underestimate the criterion (e.g., Elliott, Dunford, and Huizinga, 1987; Mulvey, Shaw, & Lidz, 1994; Steadman et al., 1998; Swanson, Borum, Swartz, & Hiday, 1999). For example, investigators from the MacArthur Violence Risk Assessment Study (Monahan et al., 2001) estimated *violent recidivism* from three sources of information: collateral informants, patient self-reports, and official records. The percentages of individuals who would have been identified as violent from each of these sources alone were, respectively, 12.7%, 22.4%, and 4.5%, and from all three sources combined was 27.5%. If these three combined indices provide valid estimates of violence, then official records underestimated violence by a factor of 6 (i.e., 27.5%/4.5% = 6.11). Put another way, at least six times as many individuals in this study would have been identified as violent using three measures of violent recidivism versus the single index based on official sources. Estimates of violent recidivism would have been even larger if longer follow-up periods were used. Many researchers use official indices of antisocial and criminal behaviors for practical and not theoretical reasons. Consequently, data that rely exclusively on these measures must be interpreted cautiously.

Indices of recidivism coded from closely monitored behaviors and diligently recorded observations in institutional settings are expected to provide more sensitive measures of recidivism than are indices coded solely from databases in which official institutional sanctions or criminal violations are recorded. Similarly, databases that contain information of misconduct across broad jurisdictional boundaries are expected to yield more sensitive measures of recidivism than are databases that contain information within geographically small jurisdictional boundaries. This result is due, in large part, to the mobile nature of many persistent criminal offenders (e.g., Hunter, Hemphill, Hare, & Anderson, 2003). Misbehaviors might go undetected and unrecorded if individuals continue to commit antisocial acts outside juris-dictional boundaries that do not form part of the official database that is used to code recidivism. Statistics computed from insensitive measures of recidi-vism generally can be expected to yield underestimates of the magnitudes of effect sizes, and these underestimates may be large.

Many diverse indices of recidivism have been used across the years to validate the clinical use of the PCL. Some indices of recidivism will be of greater relevance to investigators than others, depending in large part on the purpose(s) of the assessments. Investigators interested in using the PCL to assist in assessing risk posed to staff in institutional settings, for example, should generally place greater weight on studies in which the validity of the PCL in similar or related contexts has been examined. It is important to rec-ognize that recidivism categories (i.e., general, violent, and sexual) may not closely match legislative or clinical requirements, and investigators must be vigilant as to the operational definitions that researchers have used. In Canada, for example, there is a requirement that individuals considered for "Dangerous Offender" designations commit a "serious personal injury offence [sic]." This definition involves certain types of sexual offenses, or "the use or attempted use of violence against another person, or conduct . . . likely to endanger the life or safety of another person or . . . likely to inflict severe psychological damage on another person, and for which the offender may be sentenced to imprisonment for ten years or more" (see Part XXIV of the Criminal Code of Canada). Studies in which recidivism is defined in a man-ner that closely matches the definition of a serious personal injury offense will be of greater relevance to clinicians conducting Dangerous Offender assessments than will studies in which broad indices of physical violence or antisocial and criminal behavior in general have been largely examined.

Criminal and other official records often provide rich information regard-ing dates and locations, types and numbers of transgressions, institutional-ization lengths, and so forth. This rich set of information is frequently recoded to a dichotomous variable (yes or no) for each index of recidivism. As such, recidivism studies often provide little or no direct information regarding degree of victim injury, imminence or timing of antisocial behav-ior, escalating patterns of reoffending, and other issues that are of direct clin-ical relevance. All of these factors must be taken into account when the use-fulness of empirical information for particular clinical tasks is weighed.

The manner in which indices of recidivism have been operationalized and coded in research has differed widely. For example, some researchers code robberies and/or threats as violent offenses whereas others do not; some researchers operationalize violence using several (e.g., broad or narrow) overlapping categories. Although the process of coding official data seems like it would be relatively straightforward, in fact considerable judgment is often required. In addition to making research decisions about which anti-social behaviors count as recidivism, how to temporally distinguish differ-ent sets of transgressions from each other, and so forth, dates and times some-times need to be estimated from databases that were created for administrative and not research purposes. Researchers rarely present interrater reliability statistics for indices of recidivism despite the considerable subjectivity inherent in coding information from official databases. Measures of recidivism should be reliable when reliability statistics are presented.

Statistical Indices. Many different statistical indices are commonly computed in recidivism research. Although statistical computations are by and large "objective," researchers make a series of decisions that make the field of applied research complex and not completely objective. Researchers decide on what research questions they will focus on when analyzing data sets that are often large and can address a potentially infinite number of research questions, how they will approach the analyses, which statistical analyses they will conduct, whether continuous or group scores will be emphasized, what interpretation(s) will be made of findings that can be legitimately interpreted many different ways, and so forth. Researchers rarely publish results from all of their statistical analyses because of space limitations. That applied social science research is not completely objective is illustrated by the following quote. Rosenthal (1991) wrote that

> . . . the conclusion drawn by the investigator . . . is often only vaguely related to the actual results. The metamorphosis that sometimes occurs between the results section and the discussion section is itself a topic worthy of detailed consideration . . . a fairly ambiguous result often becomes quite smooth and rounded in the discussion section, so that reviewers who dwell too much on the discussion and too little on the results can be quite misled as to what actually was found. (p. 13)

Each set of statistical analyses provides slightly different types of information to investigators. A correlation coefficient used to examine the association between PCL scores and an index of recidivism tells us the approximate magnitude of the association at one point using a particular research methodology. Time is incorporated into survival analyses so investigators can estimate recidivism rates across follow-up periods. The impact of other variables on the results can be statistically removed from analyses involving covariates to potentially clarify statistical relationships. Hierarchical regression analyses can be used to examine the incremental validity of adding additional predictor variables into statistical equations. Receiver operator characteristic analyses and area under the curve statistics are related to false-positive and true-positive rates and help investigators identify "optimal" cutoff points on predictor variables across the continuous range of scores. Because different sets of statistical analyses provide somewhat different but related information, investigators frequently conduct and report several sets of statistical analyses. Unfortunately, research findings are not always consistent across different statistical analyses—or even within statistical methods (e.g., standard multiple regression, hierarchical regression, or stepwise regression)—and different conclusions can be reached, depending on what sets of analyses are emphasized (e.g., Hemphill, Templeman, Wong, & Hare, 1998). For example, Hemphill (1992) found that a group with high PCL scores was reconvicted at a rate almost twice that of a group with low PCL scores when survival analyses were conducted, but there was only a weak association ($r = .10$) between PCL scores and reconvictions when a point–biserial analysis was conducted (see Hemphill, Hare, et al., 1998, pp. 165–166 for a discussion). Investigators who want to conclude that the PCL is useful for assessing future risk for recidivism might emphasize the former results, whereas those who want to argue the opposite position might emphasize the latter results.

Much has been written about base rates and their potential impact on statistical indices. It is common for recidivism researchers to comment that base rates were too low to permit a meaningful or large association between predictor and criterion variables. In fact, it is not the base rate per se that limits the association. Rather, it is the mismatch between the selection ratio (i.e., the percentage of individuals identified as high risk from the predictor variable[s]) and the base rate (i.e., the percentage of individuals observed to have committed the antisocial act during the follow-up period) that is the relevant issue. A low statistical magnitude will emerge whenever there is a considerable mismatch between the selection ratio and the base rate. If both the selection ratio and the base rate are low, or, conversely, if both are high, then statistical indices have the potential to be relatively large in magnitude.

Analyses that are purported to statistically examine the relative and incremental contributions of several predictor variables are particularly tricky to interpret. These types of statistical analyses are not always statistically robust, and results can be influenced a great deal by how the analyses were approached. Researchers must make decisions about which set of predictor variables will be statistically compared. Obviously, predictor variables that are not included in the analyses in the first place cannot be statistically compared and contrasted. This means that excluded predictor variables cannot emerge as important predictors of the criterion. Similarly, there are many different ways a single variable can be measured, and it may be that, intentionally or not, the measure included in the published article is the one that best supports the a priori position of the researcher(s). Decisions regarding how to enter predictor variables into statistical equations and establishing the order of entry are often important because results may not replicate across different but related statistical procedures. All of these issues highlight the fact that conducting statistical analyses is not a straightforward and objective process. Even though results and conclusions do not always converge when different statistical indices are computed, investigators can be more confident in reaching solid conclusions if a variety of statistical methods and procedures arrive at converging findings across studies.

Quantitative Literature Reviews

Investigators are appropriately cautioned against overinterpreting findings from a single study because the findings may not be robust and reproducible.

For this reason, many investigators examine the consistency of empirical findings across studies and place considerable weight on the overall patterns of results. Meta-analytic techniques provide an important method for conducting quantitative reviews of the research literature. Despite the many advantages of meta-analytic approaches, there are several important limitations. Significant limitations of meta-analyses can be easily overlooked by investigators unfamiliar with these statistical approaches. In part, this is because the studies comprising each meta-analysis are several steps removed from the original studies, which can obscure the methodological and statistical limitations of studies upon which the units of analyses are based.

Although meta-analytic reviews appear to be more objective than traditional reviews, in many respects both approaches have similar limitations (Mintz, 1983; Strube & Hartmann, 1983; Wilson & Rachman, 1983). Researchers who conduct meta-analyses make important decisions. This complex process involves selecting studies to include and exclude from reviews, choosing the index of effect size (e.g., *r* or *d*), computing effect sizes from raw data, selecting one or more effect sizes from the many available within a single study, integrating results into a single statistical index for each meta-analysis, choosing to differentially weight individual studies that comprise the overall index or to simply average indices together, computing indices of heterogeneity and then deciding whether to include or exclude heterogeneous effect sizes, deciding on what set of results to focus on, and so forth. These decisions are important because contradictory results and conclusions can be derived by different sets of investigators who are ostensibly reviewing the same topic (Wilson & Rachman, 1983).

Meta-analytic approaches have been criticized for lumping together studies that vary considerably in terms of quality. Reviewers who have assembled studies involving the PCL and recidivism openly acknowledge that these studies have "diverged widely in methodology" (Walters, 2003b, p. 543). Discussions earlier in this chapter highlight the complexities inherent in defining study quality and the lack of consensus that exists among researchers. This complexity is a key reason why investigators must be familiar with the process of how to critically evaluate the strength of evidence upon which conclusions are based. This is true regardless of whether the evidence comes from individual studies or meta-analytic reviews. Understanding how to interpret the quality of research findings is essential because authors ultimately put their own "spin" on research findings when interpreting results.

Researchers who conduct meta-analyses often use a set of statistical techniques specific to this type of quantitative review. They may evaluate the degree of heterogeneity among effect sizes, compute fail-safe estimates and common language effect size indicators, and examine the potential influence of varying base rates and publication status (yes or no) on results. Some investigators become intimidated by statistical terms with which they are unfamiliar. It is important to recognize that statistical techniques cannot improve research designs with significant flaws. Statistics are simply a research tool. Investigators should interpret statistical results cautiously and be vigilant of statistical results that are overinterpreted. This caution is particularly important because statistics have an air of precision and sophistication about them.

Heterogeneity among effect sizes is important from a clinical perspective because it indicates that some studies find the PCL to be a stronger predictor than do other studies. Unless investigators have conducted extensive research in their particular setting and consistently find similar patterns across studies, it is not always clear when results will be expected to generalize to their setting and not another. Nonetheless, effect sizes found in meta-analytic reviews generally indicate that the PCL is an important predictor of general and violent recidivism, and this applies to total PCL scores and PCL factor scores. However, future research may reveal that the PCL has greater applicability among certain subgroups of participants, and research findings may not generalize to all samples. Future meta-analyses in which moderator variables are incorporated into statistical analyses may allow investigators to more clearly delineate when it is appropriate to clinically use the PCL. For example, the PCL may have greater applicability among sex offenders who also score high on measures of sexual deviance than among sex offenders in general (e.g., Hare, 2003).

RESEARCH EXAMPLES CRITICIZING THE PCL

The PCL is among the most widely validated psychological instruments available for any purpose. It has broad applicability and conceptual relevance to a wide range of clinical contexts. Results derived from the PCL are robust and have been cross-validated using a variety of methodological and statistical approaches. In the most recent version of the PCL–R manual, Hare (2003) summarizes a large, diverse, and impressive empirical database. However, with such success come detractors.

In recent years, a small but vocal group of investigators have criticized research involving the PCL and recidivism. On the one hand, keen critical discussions have the potential to raise awareness of important clinical issues that can ultimately improve clinical practice. On the other hand, inaccurate or misdirected critical discussions can take the focus away from key clinical issues, lead to erroneous conclusions, and harm clinical practice. In this section concrete examples of criticisms directed toward the PCL are discussed to illustrate some of the methodological and statistical issues raised previously.

Freedman (2001)

One of the first comprehensive attempts to criticize research involving the PCL and recidivism was by Freedman (2001). Freedman concluded that the PCL is "the strongest in a field of weaklings" when it comes to assessing risk for violence, is "by no means reliable and valid in the prediction of future dangerousness" (p. 94), and is "surprisingly weak" (p. 93). Much of Freedman's "evidence" was based on arguments that reflect only a basic understanding of applied research, statistics, and research design. The following critical examination of key evidence that Freedman considered when reaching his conclusions is discussed here to illustrate some of the methodological issues discussed throughout this chapter. (See also Hemphill & Hare, 2004, for further discussions regarding criticisms directed toward the PCL, and methodological and statistical factors that investigators should consider when using the PCL for assessing risk for future antisocial behavior.)

Misunderstanding the Meaning of Effect Sizes

An effect size "quantifies the strength of association between a predictor test scale and a relevant criterion variable" (Meyer et al., 2001, p. 129). The fifth edition of the *Publication Manual of the American Psychological Association* states that "it is almost always necessary to include some index of effect size or strength of relationship . . . [f]or the reader to fully understand the importance of your findings" (American Psychological Association, 2001, p. 25). There are many indices of effect sizes, and the correlation coefficient is among the most popular (Rosenthal, 1991).

Many investigators implicitly or explicitly seem to assume that psychological studies yield results that are statistically inferior to those obtained from other disciplines. Freedman (2001) made his views explicit by asserting that "psychological research . . . generally permits lower coefficients than other types of scientific research" (p. 93). Freedman offered no empirical evidence to support this claim. A large-scale review of the assessment literature in both psychology and medicine was conducted that bears directly on this issue. The authors of the review concluded that "psychological tests often generate substantial effect sizes" from an applied research perspective and that "validity coefficients for many psychological tests are indistinguishable from those observed for many medical tests" (Meyer et al., 2001, p. 135, and Footnote 8 on p. 135). The average effect size for psychological research in general is approximately $r = .25$ (Hemphill, 2003). This magnitude is in line with mean associations found between PCL scores and various indices of recidivism and is larger than effect sizes typically found in criminological research (Gendreau, Little, & Goggin, 1996).

Conducting Unbalanced Reviews

It is commonplace for effect sizes to be distributed across a range of scores, which necessarily means that some effect sizes will be smaller (or larger) than others. Investigators must be aware of conclusions based on unbalanced reviews of empirical evidence. The large body of PCL research allows researchers who wish to make extreme arguments to selectively pick and choose studies at either end of the distribution of effect sizes. This selective procedure, whether intentional or not, can make discussions appear as if they are grounded in the empirical literature, even though biased reviews produce spurious conclusions that do not accurately reflect the range of studies available.

At times, Freedman (2001) engaged in selective and unbalanced discussions that resulted in erroneous conclusions. For example, Freedman wrote that "There is no evidence currently available to suggest that the PCL–R is reliable or valid as a predictor of risk for violence during incarceration in prison" (p. 94). (This conclusion is inconsistent with research findings, including the recent meta-analyses by Walters, 2003a, 2003b, whose reviews were based on large numbers of studies.) Freedman made this assertion after selectively reviewing only five (predictive and postdictive) studies. Of these five, two (Edens, Poythress, & Lilienfeld, 1999; Serin, 1991; see also Hicks, Rogers, & Cashel, 2000) showed mixed findings, and another one (Hare & McPherson, 1984) had results contrary to what Freedman reported. In addition to one study that indicated an inverse relationship between PCL scores and institutional aggression (Rasmussen & Levander, 1996) and one that did not show a significant association (Kosson, Steuerwald, Forth, & Kirkhart, 1997), at least 12 other studies were available that did.[5] Readers who uncritically accepted Freedman's assertions at face value would be misled into believing that the empirical literature did not support the clinical use of the PCL for assessing risk for institutional misbehavior.

Another key conclusion Freedman (2001) arrived at was that "When the prediction is narrowed to behaviors of real concern, violence and aggression, the PCL–R fares much worse than when measuring vague and ill-defined failures" (p. 91). This conclusion is inconsistent with the finding by Hemphill, Hare, et al. (1998), who found that PCL scores were correlated to a similar extent with indices of general recidivism and violent recidivism. Indices of recidivism in these studies represented behaviors serious enough to culminate in convictions and/or psychiatric hospitalizations while research participants were residing in the community. Freedman's conclusions also do not appear to be consistent with the evidence regarding institutional misconduct that was available at the time his review was published. Results for institutional misconduct that included indices of both threatening/disruptive behavior and physical aggression were reported in at least eight studies. The average correlations between the PCL and threatening/disruptive behavior, and between the PCL and physically aggressive

---

[5]PCL scores correlated .28 with institutional disciplinary infractions for physical or verbal aggression (Edens et al., 1999), .31 with prison misconduct (Hare et al., 2000, p. 635), .30 with physical or verbal aggression coded from patient charts during the first 2 months of institutionalization (Heilbrun et al., 1998; behavior 2 months before discharge was not significantly correlated with PCL scores), .30 with treatment noncompliance (Hill, Rogers, & Bickford, 1996), .44 with disruptive behavior on an institutional wing (Hobson, Shine, & Roberts, 2000), −.62 with overall clinical change in an institution (Hughes, Hogue, Hollin, & Champion, 1997), .63 with institutional convictions (Loucks & Zamble, 2000), .36 with institutional infringements per year imprisoned (Moltó, Carmona, Poy, Avila, & Torrubia, 1996), −.29 with days spent in institutional treatment (Ogloff, Wong, & Greenwood, 1990), .39 with noncompliance rated by correctional officers (Rogers, Salekin, Hill, Sewell, Murdock, & Neumann, 2000), .18 with noncompliance in an institution (Salekin et al., 1997), and −.16 with positive treatment behavior coded from institutional files (Seto & Barbaree, 1999).

behavior, are virtually indistinguishable (see Table 6–2). These results provide consistent support for the view that the PCL is associated to a similar extent with both threatening/disruptive behavior and physical aggression in institutional settings. Freedman's contention that the PCL is not associated with criterion variables of real concern appears to be incorrect for both prospective recidivism studies and for studies involving institutional misconduct and is largely the result of an unbalanced and unsystematic review of the empirical literature.

Overinterpreting Research Findings From 2 × 2 Designs

Much criticism directed toward the PCL in the context of risk assessment is based on the assumption that the study methodology and associated 2 × 2 research design represent valid, accurate, and appropriate procedures for conducting risk assessment research. Much of this criticism evaporates if this assumption is invalid.

Several investigators have argued that the PCL falsely identifies individuals as high risk who actually are not (i.e., false-positive results). Freedman (2001) took this argument further and attempted to quantify the false-positive rates by arguing that the PCL produces "excessive false-positive rates [that are] . . . above 50 percent" (pp. 92–93), which results in decisions that are "worse than a coin toss" (p. 91). Investigators who advance these arguments are implicitly

TABLE 6–2.
Correlations Between Hare PCL Scores and Aggression in Institutional Settings

		Institutional Misbehavior	
Study	n	Threatening/ Disruptive	Physically Aggressive
Edens, Poythress, & Lilienfeld (1999)	50	.18	.18
Hare, Clark, Grann, & Thornton (2000)	652	.18	.24
Heilbrun et al. (1998)	218	.24	.14
Hicks, Rogers, and Cashel (2000)	<58[a]	.51	.57
Loucks and Zamble (2000)	≤100	.63	.38
Moltó, Carmona, Poy, Avila, & Torrubia (1996)	117	.30	.38
Rogers et al. (2000)	103	.38	.37
Salekin, Rogers, & Sewell (1997)	103	.13	.20
Average correlations			
Unweighted		.33	.31
Weighted by $n - 3$ df		.26	.27

Note: Average correlations were computed by converting each correlation coefficient to Fisher z_rs, averaging these values within a column, and converting each resulting average z_r to r.

[a]Analyses were based on a subsample of offenders. Hicks et al. (2000) reported results separately for three ethnic groups, and results from the largest group (i.e., African Americans) is reported here.

accepting the assumption that indices of recidivism in research studies are definitive and accurate estimates of the criterion when they are not.

In reality, "actual" false-positive rates are unknown and largely unknowable. What is clear is that indices of recidivism based largely upon official sources of information yield insensitive and conservative estimates of recidivism. Contemporary investigators openly acknowledge that procedures currently available for estimating recidivism are poor (see Edens & Douglas, 2005). Researchers able to incorporate more comprehensive and sensitive measures of recidivism and longer follow-up periods would almost certainly find that false-positive rates would shrink dramatically (Monahan et al., 2001). Simply put, many false-positive rates estimated from research studies are probably not.

Because we do not know the "actual" base rates of recidivism and because estimates of base rates vary according to the definitions of recidivism, measures, and research methodologies used, lengths of follow-up, and so forth, we cannot know how many individuals have been "misclassified" into false-positive, false-negative, correct-positive, and correct-negative groups. The situation is further complicated when we recognize that the percentage of individuals identified as high risk according to the PCL (i.e., the selection ratio) can vary according to clinical decisions being made and characteristics of the sample (e.g., Hare, 2003, pp. 30–31), that measurement error and unreliability occur whenever the PCL or any other instrument is scored, that there are no simple and direct associations between PCL scores and risk posed, that different statistical indices may produce different effect sizes, that results can be legitimately interpreted many ways, and so forth. Taken together, these individual and collective findings from research studies clearly are crude and should not be overinterpreted.

Gendreau, Goggin, and Smith (2002, 2003)

Gendreau et al. (2002) published a reasonably comprehensive set of meta-analyses that purported to statistically compare the magnitudes of predictive validity coefficients among the Level of Service Inventory–Revised (LSI–R; Andrews & Bonta, 1995) and the PCL–R. These investigators conducted analyses using advanced statistical techniques and research methodologies. Despite the appearance of objectivity and sophistication, meta-analytic techniques and statistical analyses are not completely objective, and subtle biases can enter the meta-analytic process and potentially distort interpretations that are made from empirical reviews. Researchers who have allegiances to particular points of view or preconceived notions with respect to what they will find are particularly likely to influence the "objectivity" of reviews. Indeed, Hemphill and Hare (2004) concluded "that virtually all the choices, inconsistencies, clerical errors, and so on, that we discovered favored the central thesis of Gendreau et al. [2002] concerning the predictive superiority of the LSI–R [over the PCL]" (p. 218).

Applying Statistics in a Biased Manner

Gendreau et al. (2003) published a reanalysis of their original data in an Erratum. The publication appears to further develop the position that the LSI–R demonstrates greater predictive validity than does the PCL. Gendreau et al. stated that "A mistake was made . . . in the original publication . . . the distribution of effect sizes was not homogeneous as had been originally reported . . . removal of the outliers tended to improve the predictive validity of the LSI–R relative to that of the PCL–R" (p. 722). Hemphill and Hare (2004, see Footnote 8) compared the reanalyses with the original analyses and determined that Gendreau et al. had defined 64% and 55% of participants as "outliers" in analyses involving the LSI–R and the PCL, respectively. Hemphill and Hare (2004) observed that "This hardly seems consistent with the purpose of testing for heterogeneity and removing a reasonably small set of statistical outliers that unduly influence the magnitude of effect sizes. Eliminating the majority of participants gives new meaning to the term outlier and raises the question as to whether some results in the erratum are best conceptualized as recomputations on data that represent outliers rather than pooled samples of 'inliers'" (p. 238). Clearly, although statistical analyses are by and large objective, the decisions regarding when and how to apply statistical techniques are not.

Failing to Use Caution When Interpreting Statistics

Gendreau et al. (2002) conducted a series of statistical analyses involving "fail-safe estimates" that appear to offer definitive conclusions regarding the robustness of statistical findings. Based largely on these analyses, Gendreau et al. concluded that "Given the present pattern of results, it will be virtually impossible for the PCL–R to achieve parity with the LSI–R . . . catching up will be hard to do" (Gendreau et al., 2002, p. 411). Several points are worth mentioning here. First, if results weighted by sample sizes are considered, then few large-scale studies are needed to "overturn" these conclusions (see Hemphill & Hare, 2004, Footnote 8). The single study involving 22,533 offenders (Washington State Institute for Public Policy, 2003), which showed a correlation of $r = .12$ between the LSI–R and violent recidivism, would seem to suffice. Second, when the magnitudes of predictive validities among instruments used to assess risk are directly compared, it is essential that comparisons be made within studies (see Hemphill & Hare, 2004, for a detailed discussion). These comparisons are important because they allow study characteristics and methodological issues to be ruled out as plausible interpretations of statistical findings. Indeed, when Gendreau et al. (2002) conducted within-study analyses, they concluded that "In predicting violent recidivism, the results indicated a tendency for the two measures [the PCL and LSI–R] to perform at parity" (p. 409). Third, virtually all studies measured recidivism on a dichotomous (yes or no) scale. We do not know whether or not the PCL and LSI–R are differentially associated with important offense characteristics such as severity, frequency, and timing of recidivism after release.

CONCLUSIONS

PCL researchers have contributed a broad and robust body of literature of considerable relevance to the field of risk assessment. The purpose of this chapter was to familiarize readers with statistical and methodological issues that influence the interpretation of research findings involving the PCL and recidivism. By understanding how risk assessment research is conducted, the limitations of 2×2 research designs, and procedures for identifying the strengths and weaknesses of the empirical literature, it is hoped that investigators will be able to critically evaluate research findings and the strength of the empirical evidence. This is essential because ultimately it is up to clinicians to determine the relevance of the literature given their particular purposes, clinical demands, settings, and groups with which they work and to determine how much weight to assign individual studies or quantitative reviews.

ACKNOWLEDGMENTS

The author thanks Glenn Walters for providing results that were not available from published sources.

The views and conclusions of the author do not necessarily reflect those of the Ministry of Children and Family Development or the government of British Columbia.

APPENDIX

Considerations in the Evaluation of the Relevance and Methodological Strength of Research Studies

Note: Refer to the body of the chapter to put the following questions into context.

Evaluating Individual Studies

Relevance.   Was the PCL (or one of its derivatives) used as the measure of psychopathy? Did the study involve a behavioral index of recidivism or antisocial behavior? Was the sample similar in composition (e.g., age, gender, and ethnicity) to groups you work with? Was the study related in important ways to your particular purpose, clinical demands, and setting?

Sample Size and Representativeness.   Did the study include a reasonably large number of participants (e.g., in most cases this will be at least 50, and preferably 100 or more)? Were participants selected randomly? If not, was the sample representative of the population from which it was drawn? Were analyses conducted to compare the sample and population on PCL scores, measures of recidivism, and key demographic, criminal history, clinical, and other variables? If yes, did the sample and population differ on any of these variables? What might be the potential impact of these findings on the interpretation of the research findings? Were attrition rates reported? Was attrition of participants random? If not, what might be the potential impact of these findings on the interpretation of the research findings?

PCL Scores.   Were PCL scores rated according to standard procedures outlined in the appropriate rating booklets and technical manuals? Was both interview and collateral information used for scoring? Were collateral sources adequate in terms of variety of sources, length, detail, content, and quality? Did raters have adequate training and experience in the use of the PCL? Did raters carefully consider evidence both for and against a high score on each PCL item and across the lifespan, when appropriate? Were standard cutoffs used to define PCL groups (e.g., ratings made from both file and collateral information: low PCL-R group = <20, medium = between 20 and 30, high = ≥30)? Were one or more quantitative indices of reliability provided (e.g., correlation coefficient for continuous PCL scores or kappa coefficient for PCL groups)? If yes, were these values in an appropriate range (e.g., *r*s between .80 and .90)? Were measures of psychopathy and recidivism coded by independent raters who were unaware of scores on the other measure?

Recidivism Measures.   Were indices of recidivism or antisocial behavior coded prospectively or retrospectively with respect to PCL ratings? Did definitions of recidivism closely match clinical or legislative requirements? Was the index of "recidivism" a reasonably sensitive measure of the criterion (e.g., included information from closely monitored institutional behaviors or from collateral informants and/or participants' self-reports)? What scale of measurement (e.g., ordinal, interval, or ratio) was used for the index of recidivism? Did the measure of recidivism incorporate relevant dimensions such as degree of victim injury, timing of antisocial behavior, escalating patterns of offending, frequency of offending, and other issues of direct clinical relevance? Was a measure of reliability computed? If yes, was the measure of recidivism reliable (e.g., *r* = .80 or greater)? Were several indices of recidivism (e.g., general, violent, or sexual; and broad and narrow definitions) examined? Why or why not? Did the database used to code the index of recidivism contain behaviors that occurred across broad (e.g., national) or narrow (e.g., within a single state, county, province, or municipality) jurisdictional and geographical boundaries? Were follow-up lengths long (e.g., 5 or 10 years) for studies involving indices of violent or sexual recidivism coded exclusively from official sources? Was the base rate extreme (i.e., either large or small) in magnitude? If yes, what impact might this have had on the magnitude of the effect size? Was the magnitude of the effect size consistent with that typically found in PCL and psychological research (e.g., $r = .25$)?

Statistical Indices.   Did researchers report results from several basic statistical indices (e.g., correlation coefficient between PCL scores and recidivism or recidivism rates for each PCL group)? Were statistical indices appropriate for the purposes to which the PCL will be put (e.g., survival analyses for estimating timing of reconvictions or hierarchical analyses to examine incremental validity among predictor variables)? Was an intervention (e.g., treatment or management) introduced that might be expected to influence recidivism rates? If yes, what might be the possible impact of this intervention on the magnitude of the effect size? Was there a considerable mismatch (e.g., more than 25% absolute difference) between the magnitude of the selection ratio and base rate that could have lowered the magnitude of the effect size? Were results and conclusions consistent across different sets of analyses?

Evaluating Quantitative Reviews

Did researchers attempt to locate all published and unpublished studies? How were studies selected for inclusion or exclusion in the review? Was this process biased? Were samples that contributed to the analyses independent of each other? How did researchers select one or more effect sizes from the many available within a single study? Were effect sizes heterogeneous across studies? If yes, where would you expect your sample to fall on the distribution of effect sizes? Did researchers choose to include or exclude studies that were identified as outliers? Did this make a difference to the conclusions reached? Did researchers compute results separately for samples weighted and unweighted by sample sizes? If yes, were results consistent across sets of analyses? Did researchers systematically test whether or not conclusions varied according to the methodological quality of the studies? Was the predictive validity of the PCL compared with other predictor variables or scales? If yes, were each set of comparisons done within studies?

REFERENCES

Achenbach, T. M., Krukowski, R. A., Dumenci, L., & Ivanova, M. Y. (2005). Assessment of adult psychopathology: Meta-analyses and implications for cross-informant correlations. *Psychological Bulletin, 131*, 361–382.

American Educational Research Association, American Psychological Association, and National Council on Measurement in Education (1999). *Standards for educational and psychological testing.* Washington, DC: American Educational Research Association.

American Psychological Association (2001). *Publication manual of the American Psychological Association* (5th ed.). Washington, DC: Author.

Andrews, D. A., & Bonta, J. L. (1995). *The Level of Service Inventory–Revised (LSI–R): User's manual.* Toronto, Ontario, Canada: Multi-Health Systems.

Boothby, J. L., & Clements, C. B. (2000). A national survey of correctional psychologists. *Criminal Justice and Behavior, 27*, 716–732.

Cohen, J. (1988). *Statistical power analysis for the behavioral sciences* (2nd ed.). Hillsdale, NJ: Lawrence Erlbaum Associates.

Dolan, M., & Doyle, M. (2000). Violence risk prediction: Clinical and actuarial measures and the role of the Psychopathy Checklist. *British Journal of Psychiatry, 177*, 303–311.

Edens, J. F., & Douglas, K. S. (2005). Call for papers. *Assessment, 12*, 118.

Edens, J. F., Poythress, N. G., & Lilienfeld, S. O. (1999). Identifying inmates at risk for disciplinary infractions: A comparison of two measures of psychopathy. *Behavioral Sciences and the Law, 17*, 435–443.

Edens, J. F., Skeem, J. L., Cruise, K. R., & Cauffman, E. (2001). Assessment of "juvenile psychopathy" and its association with violence: A critical review. *Behavioral Sciences and the Law, 19*, 53–80.

Elliott, D. S., Dunford, F. W., & Huizinga, D. (1987). The identification and prediction of career offenders utilizing self-reported and official data. In J. D. Burchard & S. Burchard (Eds.), *Prevention of delinquent behavior: Vermont conference on the primary prevention of psychopathology* (Vol. 10, pp. 90–121). Beverly Hills, CA: Sage.

Forth, A. E., Kosson, D. S., & Hare, R. D. (2003). *Hare Psychopathy Checklist: Youth Version (PCL:YV)*. Toronto, Ontario, Canada: Multi-Heath Systems.

Freedman, D. (2001). False prediction of future dangerousness: Error rates and Psychopathy Checklist—Revised. *Journal of the American Academy of Psychiatry and the Law, 29*, 89–95.

Gendreau, P., Goggin, C., & Smith, P. (2002). Is the PCL-R really the "unparalleled" measure of offender risk? A lesson in knowledge cumulation. *Criminal Justice and Behavior, 29*, 397–426.

Gendreau, P., Goggin, C., & Smith, P. (2003). Erratum. *Criminal Justice and Behavior, 30*, 722–724.

Gendreau, P., Little, T., & Goggin, C. (1996). A meta-analysis of the predictors of adult offender recidivism: What works? *Criminology, 34*, 575–607.

Hare, R. D. (1980). A research scale for the assessment of psychopathy in criminal populations. *Personality and Individual Differences, 1*, 111–117.

Hare, R. D. (1985). Comparison of procedures for the assessment of psychopathy. *Journal of Consulting and Clinical Psychology, 53*, 7–16.

Hare, R. D. (1991). *Hare Psychopathy Checklist–Revised manual.* Toronto, Ontario, Canada: Multi-Health Systems.

Hare, R. D. (1998). The Hare PCL-R: Some issues concerning its use and misuse. *Legal and Criminological Psychology, 3*, 99–119.

Hare, R. D. (2003). *The Hare Psychopathy Checklist–Revised* (2nd ed.). Toronto, Ontario, Canada: Multi-Health Systems.

Hare, R. D., Clark, D., Grann, M., & Thornton, D. (2000). Psychopathy and the predictive validity of the PCL-R: An international perspective. *Behavioral Sciences and the Law, 18*, 623–645.

Hare, R. D., Harpur, T. J., Hakstian, A. R., Forth, A. E., Hart, S. D., & Newman, J. P. (1990). The Revised Psychopathy Checklist: Reliability and factor structure. *Psychological Assessment, 2*, 338–341.

Hare, R. D., & McPherson, L. M. (1984). Violent and aggressive behavior by criminal psychopaths. *International Journal of Law and Psychiatry, 7*, 35–50.

Harpur, T. J., Hakstian, A. R., & Hare, R. D. (1988). Factor structure of the Psychopathy Checklist. *Journal of Consulting and Clinical Psychology, 56*, 741–747.

Harpur, T. J., Hare, R. D., & Hakstian, A. R. (1989). Two-factor conceptualization of psychopathy: Construct validity and assessment implications. *Psychological Assessment: A Journal of Consulting and Clinical Psychology, 1*, 6–17.

Harris, G. T., Rice, M. E., & Quinsey, V. L. (1994). Psychopathy as a taxon: Evidence that psychopaths are a discrete class. *Journal of Consulting and Clinical Psychology, 62*, 387–397.

Hart, S. D. (1998a). Psychopathy and risk for violence. In D. J. Cooke, A. E. Forth, & R. D. Hare (Eds.), *Psychopathy: Theory, research, and implications for society* (pp. 355–373). Dordrecht, The Netherlands: Kluwer.

Hart, S. D. (1998b). The role of psychopathy in assessing risk for violence: Conceptual and methodological issues. *Legal and Criminological Psychology, 3*, 121–137.

Hart, S. D., Cox, D. N., & Hare, R. D. (1995). *The Hare Psychopathy Checklist: Screening Version (PCL:SV)*. Toronto, Ontario, Canada: Multi-Health Systems.

Heilbrun, K., Hart, S. D., Hare, R. D., Gustafson, D., Nunez, C., & White, A. J. (1998). Inpatient and postdischarge aggression in mentally disordered offenders: The role of psychopathy. *Journal of Interpersonal Violence, 13*, 514–527.

Hemphill, J. F. (1992). *Recidivism of criminal psychopaths after therapeutic community treatment*. Unpublished master's thesis, University of Saskatchewan, Saskatoon, Saskatchewan, Canada.

Hemphill, J. F. (1998). *Psychopathy, criminal history, and recidivism*. Unpublished doctoral dissertation, The University of British Columbia, Vancouver, British Columbia, Canada.

Hemphill, J. F. (2003). Interpreting the magnitudes of correlation coefficients. *American Psychologist, 58*, 78–79.

Hemphill, J. F., & Hare, R. D. (1996). Psychopathy Checklist factor scores and recidivism. In D. J. Cooke, A. E. Forth, J. Newman, & R. D. Hare (Eds.), *International perspectives on psychopathy* (pp. 68–73). Leicester, England: The British Psychological Society.

Hemphill, J. F., & Hare, R. D. (2004). Some misconceptions about the Hare PCL-R and risk assessment: A reply to Gendreau, Goggin, and Smith. *Criminal Justice and Behavior, 31*, 203–243.

Hemphill, J. F., Hare, R. D., & Wong, S. (1998). Psychopathy and recidivism: A review. *Legal and Criminological Psychology, 3*, 139–170.

Hemphill, J. F., & Hart, S. D. (2003). Forensic and clinical issues in the assessment of psychopathy. In I. B. Weiner (Series Ed.) & A. M. Goldstein (Vol. Ed.), *Handbook of psychology: Vol. 11. Forensic psychology* (pp. 87–107). New York: Wiley.

Hemphill, J. F., Templeman, R., Wong, S., & Hare, R. D. (1998). Psychopathy and crime: Recidivism and criminal careers. In D. J. Cooke, A. E. Forth, & R. D. Hare (Eds.), *Psychopathy: Theory, research, and implications for society* (pp. 375–399). Dordrecht, The Netherlands: Kluwer.

Hicks, M. M., Rogers, R., & Cashel, M. (2000). Predictions of violent and total infractions among institutionalized male juvenile offenders. *Journal of the American Academy of Psychiatry and the Law, 28*, 183–190.

Hill, C. D., Rogers, R., & Bickford, M. E. (1996). Predicting aggressive and socially disruptive behavior in a maximum security forensic psychiatric hospital. *Journal of Forensic Sciences, 41*, 56–59.

Hobson, J., Shine, J., & Roberts, R. (2000). How do psychopaths behave in a prison therapeutic community? *Psychology, Crime, and Law, 6*, 139–154.

Hughes, G., Hogue, T., Hollin, C., & Champion, H. (1997). First-stage evaluation of a treatment programme for personality disordered offenders. *The Journal of Forensic Psychiatry, 8*, 515–527.

Hunter, S. M., Hemphill, J. F., Hare, R. D., & Anderson, G. (2003, February). *Psychopathy and geographic mobility.* Paper presented at the 30th Annual Conference of the Western Society of Criminology, Vancouver, British Columbia, Canada.

Kosson, D. S., Steuerwald, B. L., Forth, A. E., & Kirkhart, K. J. (1997). A new method for assessing the interpersonal behavior of psychopathic individuals: Preliminary validation studies. *Psychological Assessment, 9,* 89–101.

Loucks, A. D., & Zamble, E. (2000). Predictors of criminal behavior and prison misconduct in serious female offenders. *Empirical and Applied Criminal Justice Research Journal, 1,* 1–47.

Meyer, G. J., Finn, S. E., Eyde, L. D., Kay, G. G., Moreland, K. L., Dies, R. R., et al. (2001). Psychological testing and psychological assessment: A review of evidence and issues. *American Psychologist, 56,* 128–165.

Miller, P. A., & Eisenberg, N. (1988). The relation of empathy to aggressive and externalizing/antisocial behavior. *Psychological Bulletin, 103,* 324–344.

Mintz, J. (1983). Integrating research evidence: A commentary on meta-analysis. *Journal of Consulting and Clinical Psychology, 51,* 71–75.

Moltó, J., Carmona, E., Poy, R., Avila, C., & Torrubia, R. (1996). Psychopathy Checklist–Revised in Spanish prison populations: Some data on reliability and validity. In D. J. Cooke, A. E. Forth, J. Newman, & R. D. Hare (Eds.), *Issues in criminological and legal psychology: No. 24. International perspectives on psychopathy* (pp. 109–114). Leicester, England: British Psychological Society.

Monahan, J. (1995). *The clinical prediction of violent behavior.* Northvale, NJ: Jason Aronson. (Original work published in 1981.)

Monahan, J., & Steadman, H. J. (1994). *Violence and mental disorder: Developments in risk assessment.* Chicago: The University of Chicago Press.

Monahan, J., Steadman, H. J., Silver, E., Appelbaum, P. S., Robbins, P. C., Mulvey, E. P., et al. (2001). *Rethinking risk assessment: The MacArthur study of mental disorder and violence.* New York: Oxford University Press.

Mulvey, E. P., Shaw, E., & Lidz, C. W. (1994). Why use multiple sources in research on patient violence in the community? *Criminal Behavior and Mental Health, 4,* 253–258.

Ogloff, J. R. P., Wong, S., & Greenwood, A. (1990). Treating criminal psychopaths in a therapeutic community program. *Behavioral Sciences and the Law, 8,* 181–190.

Quinsey, V. L., Harris, G. T., Rice, M. E., & Cormier, C. A. (1998). *Violent offenders: Appraising and managing risk.* Washington, DC: American Psychological Association.

Rasmussen, K., & Levander, S. (1996). Individual rather than situational characteristics predict violence in a maximum security hospital. *Journal of Interpersonal Violence, 11,* 376–389.

Rogers, R., Salekin, R. T., Hill, C., Sewell, K. W., Murdock, M. E., & Neumann, C. S. (2000). The Psychopathy Checklist–Screening Version: An examination of criteria and subcriteria in three forensic samples. *Assessment, 7,* 1–15.

Rosenthal, R. (1991). *Meta-analytic procedures for social research* (Rev. ed.). Newbury Park, CA: Sage.

Salekin, R. T., Rogers, R., & Sewell, K. W. (1996). A review and meta-analysis of the Psychopathy Checklist and Psychopathy Checklist–Revised: Predictive validity of dangerousness. *Clinical Psychology: Science and Practice, 3,* 203–215.

Salekin, R. T., Rogers, R., & Sewell, K. W. (1997). Construct validity of psychopathy in a female offender sample: A multitrait-multimethod evaluation. *Journal of Abnormal Psychology, 106,* 576–585.

Serin, R. C. (1991). Psychopathy and violence in criminals. *Journal of Interpersonal Violence, 6,* 423–431.

Seto, M. C., & Barbaree, H. E. (1999). Psychopathy, treatment behavior, and sex offender recidivism. *Journal of Interpersonal Violence, 14,* 1235–1248.

Steadman, H. J., Mulvey, E. P., Monahan, J., Robbins, P. C., Appelbaum, P. S., Grisso, T., Roth, L. H., & Silver, E. (1998). Violence by people discharged from acute psychiatric inpatient facilities and by others in the same neighborhoods. *Archives of General Psychiatry, 55,* 393–401.

Strube, M. J., & Hartmann, D. P. (1983). Meta-analysis: Techniques, applications, and functions. *Journal of Consulting and Clinical Psychology, 51,* 14–27.

Swanson, J., Borum, R., Swartz, M., & Hiday, V. (1999). Violent behavior preceding hospitalization among persons with severe mental illness. *Law and Human Behavior, 23,* 185–204.

Walters, G. D. (2003a). Predicting criminal justice outcomes with the Psychopathy Checklist and Lifestyle Criminality Screening Form: A meta-analytic comparison. *Behavioral Sciences and the Law, 21,* 89–102.

Walters, G. D. (2003b). Predicting institutional adjustment and recidivism with the Psychopathy Checklist factor scores: A meta-analysis. *Law and Human Behavior, 27,* 541–558.

Washington State Institute for Public Policy (2003, December). *Washington's Offender Accountability Act: An analysis of the Department of Corrections' risk assessment* (Document No. 03-12-1202). Olympia, WA: Author.

Wilson, G. T., & Rachman, S. J. (1983). Meta-analysis and the evaluation of psychotherapy outcome: Limitations and liabilities. *Journal of Consulting and Clinical Psychology, 51,* 54–64.

III

ETIOLOGY

7

Psychopathy as Psychopathology: Beyond the Clinical Utility of the Psychopathy Checklist–Revised

Joseph P. Newman, Chad A. Brinkley, Amanda R. Lorenz,
Kristina D. Hiatt, and Donal G. MacCoon

In an article entitled "Psychopathy: A Clinical Construct Whose Time Has Come," Hare (1996) demonstrated that psychopathy is a construct with broad relevance for both the criminal justice system and clinical psychology. More specifically, he argued that the availability of a reliable method for identifying the construct has enabled researchers to (a) establish psychopathy's association with clinically significant behaviors such as violent and nonviolent crimes, substance abuse, and criminal recidivism and (b) document its association with etiologically relevant processes that include relatively specific physiological, learning, cognitive, emotional, and language anomalies.

Most investigators credit Cleckley with setting out the modern construct of psychopathy owing to his brilliant description and insightful hypotheses. However, it is not possible to study a clinical phenomenon such as psychopathy or advance the field without a reliable and valid measure of the construct. In this regard, Hare's development of the Psychopathy Checklist (PCL) and the revised version (PCL–R; Hare, 1980, 1991, 2003) enabled the construct of psychopathy to "arrive" (i.e., reach its current level of significance). There has, in fact, been an explosion of interest in the psychopathy construct since the publication of Hare's PCL–R, and the literature is rich with examples demonstrating the reliability and clinical utility of this measure.

Echoing the sentiments of numerous investigators who have examined the evidence, Harris, Skilling, and Rice (2001) recently concluded that "Hare's Psychopathy Checklist–Revised is the best available assessment" of psychopathy. Moreover, they wrote "psychopathy is the most important psychological construct for policy and practice in the criminal justice field" (p. 197). However, in contrast to their strong praise for the clinical utility of the psychopathy construct, Harris et al.'s evaluation of its etiological validity was less flattering. They wrote "although psychopaths might exhibit very subtle neurological, psychological, and cognitive differences compared to other people, it is unclear whether these differences constitute defective brain function or the execution of a viable life strategy." An important implication of Harris et al.'s proposal is that psychopathy reflects a strategy as opposed to an affective or inhibitory deficit (Cleckley, 1976) is that it calls to question psychopathy's status as a form of psychopathology.

Harris et al.'s (2001) comments highlight the distinction between predictive and etiological validity. This distinction has important implications for the use of the PCL–R and the psychopathy construct more generally. Although the PCL–R was designed to tap the psychopathy construct as defined by Cleckley (1976), it is possible for the instrument to outperform other predictors of criminal conduct without necessarily capturing the psychobiological dysfunction described by Cleckley (see Brinkley, Newman, Widiger, & Lynam, 2004). Individuals who earn high scores on the PCL–R are characterized by a "callous remorseless use of others" and "antisocial lifestyle" (Harpur et al., 1989) and such attributes may be expected to predict chronic antisocial behavior regardless of the origins of these traits. Whereas some individuals meeting this profile may be chronic offenders because environmental and/or developmental factors have fostered extremely antisocial attitudes and beliefs, the same characteristics may relate more strongly to a psychobiological predisposition in others. Criminologists, for instance, have traditionally distinguished among subcultural, neurotic/inadequate, and psychopathic offenders (Quay, 1986). To the extent that all three processes contribute to a person's risk for chronic offending, then a risk assessment instrument may be successful regardless of its ability to distinguish among these offender subtypes. Identifying reliable etiologically relevant correlates of offenders, on the other hand, demands that such distinctions be operationalized and utilized.

To the extent that a person is interested in using PCL–R psychopathy to evaluate risk, the evidence supporting the predictive validity of the PCL–R provides a strong justification for using this construct regardless of its etiological validity (Hare, Clark, Grann, & Thornton, 2000). On the other hand, using the PCL–R to draw inferences about *causal processes* contributing to an individual's behavior problems for the purposes of designing theoretically guided interventions relies on the evidence supporting the etiological validity of the PCL–R (see Brinkley et al., 2004). In our view, the challenges associated with identifying etiologically relevant correlates of psychopathy are substantially greater than those related to establishing the predictive validity of a measure owing to the increased demands for homogeneity. When one takes into account the challenges inherent in establishing the etiological validity of a disorder, it is fair to say that impressive strides have been made.

In this chapter, we attempt to illustrate the progress that has been made in clarifying the etiologically relevant, psychobiological processes associated with psychopathy by comparing two independent programs of research.[1] In particular, we review the extent to which research in our labo-

---

[1]The original purpose of this chapter was to address Robert Hare's remarkable contributions to the field of psychopathy for a Festschrift honoring his retirement. For this reason, the literature reviewed in the chapter focuses on Hare's applied, theoretical, and empirical contri-

ratory complements the theoretical and empircal contributions of the Hare laboratory. Despite the fact that these research programs reflect different theoretical perspectives, use widely different methodologies, and involve psychopathic offenders from different countries, the research appears to yield a relatively consistent and well-defined picture of the psychopath's cognitive–affective deficit.

PSYCHOPATHY AS PSYCHOPATHOLOGY: CLECKLEY'S PERSPECTIVE

In his classic book *The Mask of Sanity*, Cleckley (1976) describes psychopathy as a grave form of psychopathology that rivals schizophrenia in depth of impairment. When discussing the severity of this disorder, Cleckley does not refer to the psychopathic individual's violent or criminal behavior but to a "very serious disability" (p. 367) that gives ready expression to virtually any response inclination.

> Of course I am aware of the fact that many persons showing the characteristics of those here described do commit major crimes and sometimes crimes of maximal violence. There are so many, however, who do not, that such tendencies should be regarded as the exception rather than the rule, perhaps, as a pathologic trait independent, to a considerable degree, of the other manifestations which we regard as fundamental. It is, of course, granted that when serious criminal tendencies do emerge in the psychopath, they gain ready expression. (p. 262)

Although their propensity for violence may be the most salient aspect of psychopathic individuals, Cleckley did not view specific response inclinations (e.g., for violence, sex, money, and so forth) to be fundamental. Nevertheless, to the extent that psychopathy is responsible for the unusually high risk for antisocial behavior demonstrated by some individuals, reducing this risk is likely to require understanding the root cause or etiology of their problem. Although the current strategy of incapacitation through incarceration does not require such understanding, it is fair to say that progress in treating and preventing the disorder will.

In addition to his insightful and widely endorsed characterization of psychopathy, Cleckley (1976) offered a number of important insights regarding the psychopath's core dysfunction. He wrote that psychopaths have "a serious and subtle abnormality or defect at deep levels disturbing the integration and normal appreciation of experience" (p. 388). According to Cleckley, this

butions to psychopathy and the extent to which the efforts of the researchers in our laboratory in these domains support his contributions. Despite the selective nature of this review, we have opted to retain the organization and primary points of the chapter rather than write a more general review as we have done in other chapters (see Hiatt & Newman, 2004; Newman & Lorenz, 2003; Newman & Wallace, 1993).

integrative deficit interferes with the psychopath's ability to understand and use affective, inhibitory, and other important cues that normally govern the behavior of others. Indeed, nearly all of the psychopath's core characteristics (Cleckley, 1976) may be understood as a failure to accommodate the meaning of potentially relevant cues (Newman & Wallace, 1993). The meaningful associations elicited by such cues normally (a) mediate classical conditioning and facilitate learning from experience (e.g., passive avoidance), (b) give rise to appropriate and sustained emotions, and (c) enable a person to recognize and appreciate the emotional experience of others. Arguably, then, a deficit in utilizing such associations could explain the behavioral, affective, and interpersonal symptoms of psychopathy (see Hare, 1996).

THE RESPONSE-MODULATING FUNCTION
OF THE LIMBIC SYSTEM

Hare's 1970 book, *Psychopathy: Theory and Research* contains many important facts and theoretical speculations about the nature of psychopathy. During his brief discussion of the electroencephalographic abnormalities associated with psychopathy, Hare focused on McCleary's (1966) chapter on the "Response Modulating Functions of the Limbic System." He wrote: "A more general effect of these lesions may be to produce *perseveration* of the most dominant response in a given situation. . . . According to McCleary's concept of response perseveration, the result would be that the most dominant response in any given situation would tend to occur regardless of its consequences" (pp. 33–34). Pursuing this intriguing association between psychopathy and limbic system dysfunction, Gorenstein and Newman (1980) proposed a physiological, animal model of psychopathy involving the septohippocampal-orbital frontal (SHF) system. Although their proposal has occasionally been misunderstood (e.g., Lykken, 1995), the authors did not propose that psychopathy was associated with a brain lesion or damage to this system. Rather, based on existing similarities between the laboratory correlates of psychopathy and those observed in animals with SHF dysfunction, Gorenstein and Newman proposed that the more extensive literature on SHF dysfunction could be used as a model for generating hypotheses about the psychological (e.g., perceptual, motivational, and learning) correlates of psychopathy. These early proposals regarding the SHF system have given rise to the response modulation hypothesis, which guides our laboratory's etiological investigations of psychopathy.

The response modulation hypothesis provides a cogent explanation for the integrative deficit described by Cleckley (1976). As noted by McCleary (1966), poor response modulation is associated with perseveration of dominant responses and a failure to make use of nondominant (i.e., incidental) information that contraindicates the dominant response. Such deficits may well underlie the psychopath's failure to inhibit punished responses (i.e., poor passive avoidance learning) and, by extension, their recidivistic antisocial behavior. Although perseveration involves a tendency to carry out or enact dominant responses despite environmental feedback (i.e., information) indicating that a dominant response is no longer appropriate, most research on SHF lesions involves laboratory rats and, thus, focuses on the consequences of SHF lesions for ongoing behavior as opposed to potential information processing deficits.

The response modulation hypothesis has evolved considerably during the past 20 years. Although our laboratory's early investigations focused on response perseveration (Newman, Patterson, & Kosson, 1987), more recent investigations place greater emphasis on psychopaths' failure to use peripheral information with implications for their ongoing behavior. In general, the response modulation hypothesis holds that psychopathic individuals meeting Cleckley's criteria for the disorder have a deficit in *response modulation* that underlies their failure to integrate incidental information with their deliberate goal-directed behavior. Response modulation is defined as a brief and relatively automatic (nondeliberate) shift of attention to accommodate the meaning of incidental or peripheral information. Such information may involve, among other things, response feedback, acquired or conditioned associations, implicit rules of conduct, past experience in similar circumstances, and the meaning of others' nonverbal communication (Patterson & Newman, 1993; Wallace, Vitale, & Newman, 1999), as well as the affective connotations of words, pictures, and other events (Newman & Lorenz, 2003).

CONDITIONED FEAR STIMULI AND POOR PASSIVE AVOIDANCE LEARNING

Physiological models of psychopathology have become increasingly common during the past decade, which has been dubbed the "Decade of the Brain" (Sabshin & Weissman, 1996). Because it is easy to be misled by superficial similarities between psychopathology and the function of physiological systems, Newman (1997) suggested that investigators distinguish between the applicability and the utility of physiological models. Applicability concerns the extent to which existing evidence may be interpreted as consistent with a particular physiological dysfunction. Applicability establishes the potential relevance of a proposed model but does not necessarily deepen our understanding of behavior problems. Utility is demonstrated when a model advances our understanding of psychopathology by generating new and valid hypotheses about the etiologically relevant, psychological, and physiological processes associated with the disorder.

As noted by Hare (1970) and elaborated on by Gorenstein and Newman (1980), the SHF model is compelling (i.e., applicable) because animals with SHF lesions demonstrate poor fear conditioning, passive avoidance learning, and behavioral inhibition like psychopathic individuals. To demonstrate the utility of the model, however, it is important to generate and test novel hypotheses regarding psychopathy. Toward this end, Gorenstein and Newman reviewed the literature on psychopathy to identify the most promising research developments and the implications of the SHF model for advancing these developments.

Inspection of the laboratory evidence on psychopathy indicated that Lykken's (1957) and Hare's (1965) research relating psychopaths' weak anticipatory fear responses to their poor passive avoidance learning was most promising. In addition to the theoretical and methodological rigor of the work, the research suggested a powerful hypothesis regarding psychopaths' antisocial behavior, namely that their inadequate fear conditioning undermines their passive avoidance learning and, consequently, disrupts normal socialization (see Lykken, 1995, Mednick, 1977; Trasler, 1978, for discussions of the link between passive avoidance and socialization). In agreement with the low-fear hypothesis, the SHF model holds that psychopaths are deficient in using conditioned punishment stimuli to inhibit behavior. However, the SHF model predicts that the performance deficits of psychopathic individuals will be both more specific (i.e., occur in only some avoidance contexts) and more general (i.e., appear in nonthreat contexts) than would be expected on the basis of a simple low-fear or insensitivity to punishment model. In contrast to their difficulty using punishment cues to inhibit dominant approach responses, rats with septal lesions appear at least as sensitive as control rats when sensitivity to punishment is measured using active rather than inhibitory indices. For instance, they perform at least as well as controls on active avoidance tasks and escape as quickly as controls from experimental chambers that have been associated with omission of expected rewards (i.e., a form of punishment). In addition, rats with septal lesions are relatively deficient at delaying gratification and otherwise inhibiting responses when anticipating reward.

Although Hare's research did more than anyone else's to advance the low-fear model of psychopathy, he was also among the first to document the specificity of psychopaths' insensitivity to punishment. Using the same laboratory paradigm that had demonstrated psychopaths' weak electrodermal activity in anticipation of aversive events, he showed that their electrodermal deficit was not paralleled by weak cardiovascular conditioning to threat cues. In his own words, "psychopaths showed poor electrodermal, but good cardiovascular, conditionability" (Hare, 1986, p. 9). Moreover, this combination of electrodermal and cardiovascular data led Hare to propose that psychopaths are adept at "tuning out" or ignoring aversive stimuli. In summarizing his extensive research in the area, Hare concluded that: "there is ample evidence that psychopaths are quite capable of giving normal electrodermal (and other autonomic) responses under appropriate conditions (i.e., they are capable of "feeling" fear but tune it out; see Hare, 1968, 1978). Anomalies in the autonomic responses of psychopaths are more likely a reflection of the particular motivational and cognitive demands placed on them, than an autonomic nervous system that does not function properly" (Hare, 1986, p. 13).

In addition to highlighting the specificity of psychopaths' insensitivity to threat cues, Hare and colleagues also demonstrated that their information-processing deficit is more general than would be expected on the basis of the low-fear hypothesis alone. Underscoring the potential importance of a more general information-processing deficit, Jutai and Hare (1983) found that psychopaths were hyporeactive to affectively neutral stimuli as well as to punishment cues once their attention was allocated elsewhere. This and other findings led Hare (1986) to propose that "psychopaths may have difficulty in allocating their attentional and processing resources between competing demands of two tasks. It appears that rather than distributing resources between tasks they focus attention on the one that is most interesting to them" (p. 13).

Whereas in his laboratory, Hare and his colleagues demonstrated the specificity and generality of psychopath's information processing deficits using psychophysiological measures, in our laboratory we have used performance measures to demonstrate the specificity and generality of their self-regulatory deficits. This difference not withstanding, our findings are highly consistent with those of Hare and colleagues. According to the response modulation hypothesis, psychopaths are less likely than nonpsychopaths to interrupt a dominant response set to accommodate incidental information that would normally modulate ongoing behavior. According to this hypothesis, then, psychopaths' failure to inhibit punished responses (i.e., poor passive avoidance) will be specific to conditions in which punishment cues are peripheral to their dominant response set. Conversely, they should regulate punished responses as well as control participants when doing so is part of their dominant response set or deliberate focus of attention.

To examine the specificity of psychopaths' passive avoidance deficit, Newman and Kosson (1986) used a go/no-go discrimination task with four "go" and four "no-go" stimuli. The stimuli were two-digit numbers (e.g., 27, 86, 32, and 73) and were presented one at a time for approximately 2 s on a computer monitor. The set of eight numbers was repeated eight times in quasi-randomized orders. In one condition, participants earned 10 cents each time they responded to a go stimulus and lost 10 cents each time they responded to a no-go stimulus. A second group of participants performed the same task under punishment-only conditions. Specifically, participants began the task with a cash stake of $8 and lost 10 cents each time that they responded to a no-go cue or failed to respond to a go cue (see Fig. 7–1). Participants were told that they would see numbers appear one at a time and that their task was to learn, by trial and error, when to respond and when not to respond to maximize their earnings.

Based on the response modulation hypothesis, the authors predicted that psychopaths would commit more passive avoidance errors than control participants in the reward–punishment task but perform both punishment contingencies as well as control participants in the punishment-only task. In other words, they predicted that psychopaths' avoidance deficit would be specific to the condition that required them to alter a dominant response set for reward. As shown in Fig. 7–2, this prediction was supported. Although participants found the punishment-only condition significantly more difficult than the reward–punishment condition, the group difference was specific to the reward–punishment condition. Similar findings have been reported by

CONDITION

STIMULUS	RESPONSE	REW PUN	PUN ONLY
S+	YES	WIN	---
	NO	---	LOSE
S-	YES	LOSE	LOSE
	NO	---	---

FIGURE 7–1.   Reward plus punishment and punishment-only conditions of the go/no-go passive avoidance task. Responses to S− stimuli constitute passive avoidance errors. Not responding to an S+ stimulus constitutes an omission error.

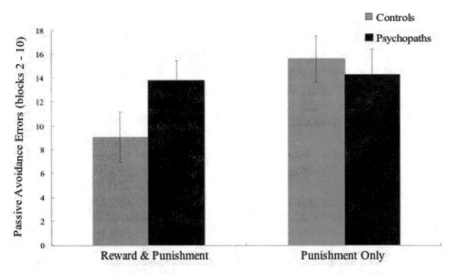

FIGURE 7–2.   Number of passive avoidance errors committed by psychopathic and nonpsychopathic offenders in the reward plus punishment and punishment-only conditions of the passive avoidance study reported by Newman and Kosson (1986).

other researchers (e.g., Hartung, Milich, Lynam, & Martin, 2002; Milich, Hartung, Martin, & Haigler, 1994; Moses, Ratliff, & Ratliff, 1979; Newman, Patterson, Howland, & Nichols, 1990; Newman & Schmitt, 1998; Thornquist & Zuckerman, 1995; cf. Scerbo et al., 1990).

If psychopaths' insensitivity to punishment cues reflects a problem shifting sets to process incidental information, they should be less likely to display avoidance deficits when the need to attend to punishment cues is made highly salient, when their dominant response set is interrupted by task procedures, and when they are provided with ample time to attend to all aspects of the task. Consistent with this assertion, psychopaths performed as well as control participants on a reward–punishment task like those described earlier when it was modified to ensure that participants attended to both reward and punishment cues from the outset of the task (Newman et al., 1990, Experiment 3). In addition, psychopaths inhibited punished responses as well as control participants on a card-playing task in a condition when a 5-s pause was used to encourage participants to process the response feedback even though they perseverated reward seeking on the same task when they were allowed to play at their own pace (Newman et al., 1987). Also, psychopaths performed the go/no-go passive avoidance task as well as control participants when the requirement for effective response modulation was reduced by providing participants with a long (variable interval, 10 s) intertrial interval (Arnett, Howland, Smith, & Newman, 1993).

Regarding psychopaths' response to conditioned threat stimuli and passive avoidance learning, our findings complement those of Hare and colleagues in showing that the psychopath's laboratory anomalies are more specific than would be expected if a general incapacity for fear or insensitivity to punishment was responsible for the psychopath's passive avoidance deficit. Rather than displaying consistent insensitivity to punishment, this deficit appears to be moderated by the focus of their deliberate or dominant response set and the amount of time available to alter it.

Like Hare and colleagues, we have also examined psychopaths' responsivity to affectively neutral cues that are peripheral to their dominant response set. More specifically, we have used a variety of Stroop-like paradigms in which participants are instructed to focus attention on one aspect of a display and ignore other aspects. Nevertheless, such tasks are designed so that the to-be-ignored stimuli interfere with primary task performance by automatically engendering an incompatible (i.e., incongruent) response. In general, such incongruent stimuli are distracting because they require allocation of effortful processing to adjudicate the response conflict. Based on the response modulation hypothesis, Newman, Schmitt, and Voss (1997) predicted that psychopaths would be less distractible on such tasks because they are less likely to process and integrate the meaning of peripheral cues.

Newman et al. (1997) used a computerized, picture–word task developed by Gernsbacher and Faust (1991) to examine this hypothesis in psychopathic and nonpsychopathic offenders. Briefly, in this task participants are shown a "context display" for 700 ms, which always consists of a word and a superimposed picture. Following the context display by 50 or 1000 ms, participants are shown a "test display," which is either a word or a picture. Before each trial, participants are shown a "ready stimulus" that is a "–P–" if it is a picture trial or a "–W–" if it is a word trial. On picture trials, participants are supposed to indicate by pressing one of two buttons whether the pictures in the context and test displays are conceptually related while ignoring the word on the context display. On word trials, participants are supposed to focus on the words and ignore the picture. Of importance for engendering Stroop-like interference, on a subset of trials, the to-be-attended-to stimulus and the test display are unrelated but the to-be-ignored stimulus is related to the test display. For example, in a word trial, the word MONTH may appear with a picture of a broom superimposed as the context display and the word SWEEP as the test display. The corresponding comparison trial might involve the word MONTH with a picture of a sandwich superimposed and the same test display. In both cases, the correct answer is "unrelated," but in the first case the incongruent inputs produce response conflict because the peripheral, to-be-ignored stimulus primes a "related" response that conflicts with the unrelated response primed by the deliberate processing of the to-be-attended-to stimulus. Research by Gernsbacher and Faust indicates that such trials produce reliable interference at the 50-ms interstimulus interval even though most individuals can overcome or suppress this interference when the test display is delayed by 1000 ms (see Fig. 7–3).

Resembling the performance of healthy control participants, nonpsychopathic prisoners responded significantly more slowly when the to-be-ignored contextual cues were conceptually related to the test display, and this effect disappeared when test displays were delayed by 1000 ms. However, as predicted by the response modulation hypothesis, incongruent contextual cues had virtually no effect on psychopathic offenders regardless of the interstimulus interval (see Fig. 7–4). Thus, paralleling their insensitivity to secondary punishment cues, psychopaths were less affected than control participants by emotionally neutral information that was peripheral to their dominant response set (primary focus of attention). In contrast to the evidence on psychopaths' passive avoidance deficits, however, which is open to a variety of interpretations, these findings provide more direct evidence of a fundamental deficit concerning the automatic accommodation of peripheral cues.

Schmitt and colleagues reported two conceptual replications of this finding. In the first task a simple 8.5 × 11-inch card that was divided into 30 rectangles was used. Each rectangle contained a simple line drawing (e.g., dog or hat) with a superimposed word (e.g., pig or shoe) that was incongruous with the picture. Another card contained the same pictures presented in a different order with superimposed nonwords (e.g., gip or seoh). By subtracting the time to name all of the pictures on the nonword card from the time taken to name the pictures on the incongruent word card, it is possible to compute a measure of interference. Replicating the findings from the computerized picture–word task, psychopathic offenders displayed significantly less interference than nonpsychopathic control participants (Hiatt, Schmitt, &

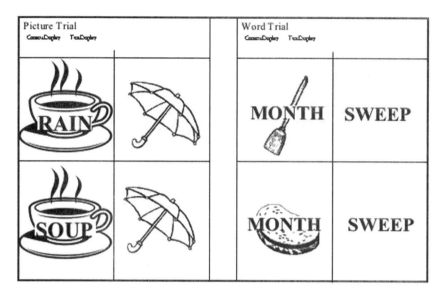

FIGURE 7–3.   Examples of experimental and comparison word and picture trials used in the picture-word task. *Note.* From Gernsbacher, M. A., & Faust, M. E. (1991). From "The Mechanism of Suppression: A Component of General Comprehension Skill," by M. A. Gernsbacher and M. W. Faust, 1991, *Journal of Experimental Psychology: Learning, Memory, and Cognition, 17*, pp. 245–262. Copyright 1991 by the American Psychological Association. Adapted with permission.

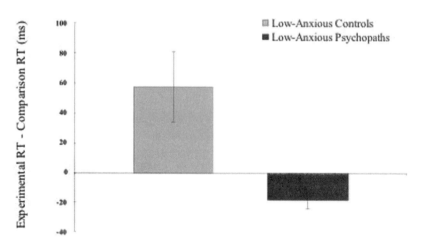

FIGURE 7–4.   Amount of interference displayed by low-anxious psychopaths and controls on the picture–word task. *Note.* From "The Impact of Motivationally Neutral Cues on Psychopathic Individuals: Assessing the Generality of the Response Modulation Hypothesis," by J. P. Newman, W. A. Schmitt, & W. Voss, 1997, *Journal of Abnormal Psychology, 106*, pp. 563–575. Copyright 1997 by the American Psychological Association. Adapted with permission.

Newman, 2004). The second task involved discrete trials that were presented on a computer monitor. In each trial a large rectangle in red, green, yellow, or blue with a word in the center was presented. Interference was computed by subtracting participants' response times to name the box color when non-words versus incongruent color words appeared in the center. Here, too, psychopathic offenders displayed significantly less interference than nonpsychopathic control participants (Hiatt et al., 2004; see Fig. 7–5).

When findings from both the Hare and Newman laboratories are considered, there is good evidence that psychopaths' *insensitivity to potentially important cues* in their environment is not limited to threat cues. Thus, in addition to being more specific than expected, psychopaths' information-processing deficiencies appear to be *more general* than one would expect if a general incapacity for fear or insensitivity to punishment were responsible for their information-processing deficiencies.

EMOTION AND LANGUAGE PROCESSING ANOMALIES

Passive avoidance learning has special significance in psychopathy research because of psychopaths' legendary failure to inhibit punished behavior outside of the laboratory. However, their deficient passive avoidance is most

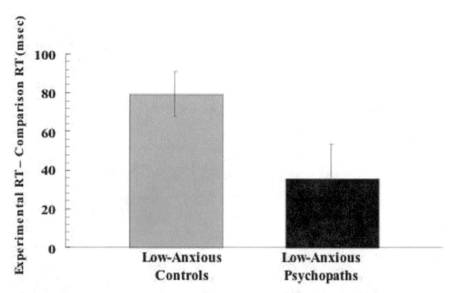

FIGURE 7–5.   Amount of interference displayed by low-anxious psychopaths and controls on the spatially separated (i.e., box) version of the color–word Stroop task. From "Stroop Tasks Reveal Abnormal Selective Attention in Psychopathic Offenders," K. D. Hiatt, W. A. Schmitt, & J. P. Newman, 2004, *Neuropsychology, 18*, pp. 50–59. Copyright 2004 by the American Psychological Association. Reprinted with permission.

accurately regarded as one manifestation of a more pervasive biopsycholog-ical dysfunction. In this regard, R. D. Hare (personal communication, June 11, 1987) once argued that our early focus on impulsivity and passive avoid-ance learning was interesting but that we failed to address the core features of Cleckley's psychopathy construct. Indeed, a careful reading of Cleckley's (1976) book shows that his view of the psychopath's deficit is both more sub-tle and more profound than is generally understood. He wrote, "In attempt-ing to account for the abnormal behavior observed in the psychopath, we have found useful the hypothesis that he has a serious and subtle abnormal-ity or defect at deep levels disturbing the integration and normal apprecia-tion of experience and resulting in a pathology that might, in analogy with Henry Head's classification of the aphasias, be described as semantic" (p. 388). To the extent that Cleckley's writings capture the essence of the disorder, an accurate understanding of psychopaths' affective and self-regulatory deficits may require clarifying their more general difficulty appreciating the signifi-cance of events.

Hare and his colleagues used a variety of methods to study the psy-chopath's semantic deficit (see Hare, 1998; Hare, Williamson, & Harpur, 1988). In one of the most widely cited studies, the extent to which psy-chopaths and nonpsychopaths were influenced by the affective components of linguistic stimuli was examined (Williamson, Harpur, & Hare, 1991). Per-forming a lexical decision task with emotional and nonemotional words, par-ticipants pressed a button to indicate, as quickly as possible, whether a briefly presented letter-string was a word or nonword. Half of the strings were words and half of the words were emotional. A word's "emotionality" was determined by its ratings on indices of arousal and affective valence (Rubin & Friendly, 1986). Emotional words were either positive or negative in valence and relatively high in arousal (e.g., sunrise and devil) whereas neu-tral words were neither positive nor negative and were low in arousal (e.g., table and bowl). Resembling the performance of nonincarcerated individ-uals, nonpsychopathic offenders identified emotional words more quickly than neutral words. That is, they displayed emotion facilitation. Psycho-paths, however, displayed significantly less emotion facilitation than con-trol participants regardless of affective valence. Williamson et al. (1991) also recorded event-related potentials (ERP) during the lexical decision task. Whereas the ERP data for control participants revealed the expected differ-ence between emotional and nonemotional words, the ERP for psychopaths did not. Such evidence is consistent with Cleckley's (1976) proposal that psy-chopaths are relatively unaffected by the meaning of words.

Using a modified version of this lexical decision task that allowed the investigators to take brain scans during the task, Intrator et al. (1997) reported a different pattern of results. Surprisingly, psychopaths displayed greater dif-ferentiation between emotional and neutral slides than control participants did. Interpreting these results, Hare (1998) proposed that the use of affective information was more automatic in control participants than in psychopaths. "In normal individuals the neurophysiological processes involved in decoding the affective information contained in words no doubt are so overlearned and efficient that metabolic requirements are minimal. However, it is as if emotion is a second language for psychopaths, a language that requires a considerable amount of mental transformation and cognitive effort on their part" (p. 115).

Investigations of emotional facilitation using lexical decision tasks provide compelling evidence that psychopaths do not accommodate a word's affective connotations as readily as nonpsychopathic control participants. Psychopaths' anomalous processing of linguistic stimuli, however, is not specific to emotional meaning. Such findings raise the possibility that psychopaths' insensitivity to the emotion connotations of words is best conceptualized as a subset of a more general problem in processing word meaning. For instance, Kiehl, Hare, McDonald, and Brink (1999) used lexical decision and word identification tasks to examine semantic and affective information processing in psychopaths and control participants. Relative to control participants, psychopaths committed more errors identifying abstract words than concrete words. Although group differences in ERP were observed for each of the tasks, psychopaths and control participants displayed comparable performance on the affective processing tasks.

Group differences in ERPs to nonemotional speech stimuli were also observed by Jutai, Hare, and Connolly (1987). Specifically, participants were instructed to discriminate between speech phonemes either alone (i.e., single-task condition) or while playing an engaging video game (dual-task condition). Although psychopaths and control participants displayed comparable ERPs during the single-task condition, significant differences were observed in their dual-task condition. Relative to control participants, psychopaths displayed a positive slow wave that overlapped their P300 response, suggesting less efficient processing of the speech stimuli and greater response uncertainty. According to the authors, the results suggest that "the demands of the Dual-Task used in the present study may have strained relatively limited left-hemisphere resources available to Group P" (p. 183).

Kiehl, Hare, Liddle, and McDonald (1999) examined ERPs during a visual oddball task that also emphasized nonemotional stimuli. In this task, participants were instructed to "respond as quickly and accurately as possible, by pressing a designated button on a computer keyboard whenever a small square (the target) appeared, but not to respond when a large square (nontarget) appeared" (p. 1501). Targets appeared on 25% of the trials. Although there were no significant group differences in performance, analysis of the ERP data revealed a number of significant group differences. A significant Group × Target Condition interaction revealed that group differences were specific to the target (vs. nontarget) condition. Whereas nonpsychopaths displayed significantly larger P300 to target stimuli than to nontarget stimuli, this effect was not significant in psychopaths whose P300 to target stimuli was significantly smaller than that of nonpsychopaths. Kiehl et al. also found a significant Group × Hemisphere interaction, which indicated that, relative to psychopaths and similar to normal control participants, P300 was more lateralized to the right hemisphere in nonpsychopaths. In this respect, the data for nonpsychopaths, but not for psychopaths, resembled those for nonincarcerated participants. Finally, psychopaths displayed a larger N550 than nonpsychopaths, which was inversely correlated with P300. According to the authors, their results "support the hypothesis that psychopathy is associated with difficulties in the effective modulation and allocation of attentional resources" (p. 1505). Moreover, their results "provide further confirmation that psychopaths exhibit an abnormal late centrofrontal negativity in a task . . . that places no explicit demands on linguistic processing" (p. 1505).

Research results from our laboratory are consistent with the findings published by Hare and colleagues and with Cleckley's speculation regarding the integration of words and meaning. Using a modified version of the lexical decision task used by Williamson et al. (1991), Lorenz and Newman (2002) predicted and found that psychopaths display significantly less emotion facilitation than control participants (see Fig. 7–6). Moreover, in parallel with results from the Williamson et al, study, psychopaths demonstrated less emotion facilitation than control participants regardless of affective (i.e., positive or negative) valence (i.e., the Group × Valence interaction was not significant).

Beyond examining the speed and accuracy with which psychopaths process the meaning of verbal stimuli, Hare and colleagues also examined

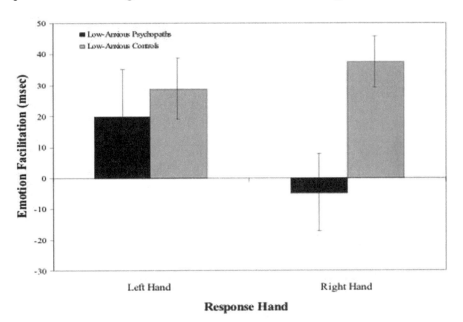

Response Hand

FIGURE 7–6.   Emotion facilitation (RT to neutral words minus RT to emotion words) displayed by low-anxious psychpaths and controls on a lexical decision task as a function of respoonse hand. From "Deficient response modulation and emotion processing in low-anxious Caucasian psychopathic offenders: Results from a lexical decision task," A. R. Lorenz & J.P. Newman 2002. *Emotion*, 2, pp.. 91–104. Copyright 2002 by the American Psychological Association. Reprinted with permission.

language production in psychopaths. Here too, significant differences have been found. For instance, Gillstrom and Hare (1988) found that psychopaths used more hand gestures that were unrelated to the content of their speech than did control participants. Using voice analysis, Louth, Williamson, Alpert, Pouget, and Hare (1998) demonstrated that psychopaths display less differentiation of affective and neutral words relative to control participants. Williamson (1991) analyzed the quality of speech produced by psychopathic and nonpsychopathic offenders using an established coding system and recorded speech segments. Her results indicated that psychopaths use fewer cohesive ties in their speech and are less likely to resolve plots (i.e., tie up loose ends) when telling stories. Moreover, there was some evidence that psychopaths' speech anomalies were most apparent when describing emotional or personal events.

Following Williamson (1991), Brinkley, Newman, Harpur, and Johnson (1999) scored emotion-related speech segments produced by psychopathic and nonpsychopathic offenders. Consistent with her findings, the speech of psychopathic offenders consisted of smaller speech units (i.e., was choppy) and was characterized by fewer cohesive ties. In a separate study, Brinkley, Bernstein, and Newman (1999) instructed participants to tell a story using a series of plot elements (i.e., general story framework) that were listed on a printed card. Half of the participants were allowed to keep the card as they related the story whereas the other half had to remember the list of story elements. Consistent with Williamson's earlier findings, the stories provided by psychopathic inmates were less coherent. That is, psychopaths were less likely than control participants to resolve plot units while telling their stories. However, contrary to prediction, psychopaths' stories were especially incoherent when they were allowed to retain the list to assist them in story telling. Although the list was intended to make story telling easier for psychopaths because they would be able to focus on the story content without also attending to the story structure, the results indicated otherwise. In fact, the list of elements appeared to dominate the attention of psychopathic offenders and interfered with their story elaboration and coherence.

Although the studies are limited, it seems clear that psychopaths do, indeed, manifest a number of language-related (i.e., semantic) deficits. In particular, the performance of psychopathic offenders suggests that they have greater difficulty integrating the affective connotations of words, processing the abstract meaning of words, and remaining coherent while linking words with meaning in the process of speaking. Such findings are consistent with Cleckley's proposal that the core deficit in psychopathy involves a failure to appreciate the affective, and more general significance, of events.

In light of such evidence, researchers from our laboratory set out to test the semantic deficit hypothesis more directly. In one study the extent to which psychopaths and control participants could use the meaning of a word to prime and thus facilitate the processing of a second word was compared. Each trial consisted of a 140-ms presentation of a word (prime) that was set off by two asterisks followed by a letter string (target) that was a word on 50% of the trials and a pronounceable nonword on the remaining trials. For one-half of the target words, the prime was semantically and associatively related to the target word (e.g., Doctor–Nurse) whereas the prime and target were unrelated (e.g., Knife–Cotton) in the remaining trials. Contrary to prediction, both psychopaths and control participants demonstrated significant and comparable priming (see Brinkley, Schmitt, & Newman, 2005). That is, both groups identified words more quickly when they were preceded by a related word.

In a second study the extent to which incongruent semantic associations interfered with color naming using a modified Stroop procedure was examined. Specifically, Brinkley et al. (2005) used a computerized Stroop task in which participants were instructed to name the color of stimulus words while ignoring their meaning. Adopting a procedure used by Klein (1964), these authors examined interference using words with semantically incongruent meanings (e.g., the word *lemon* appearing in green) as well as the usual incongruent color words (e.g., the word *green* appearing in red). To the extent that psychopaths are deficient in semantic processing, they may be expected to display less interference than control participants on trials involving the color-related words. Contrary to hypothesis, however, psychopaths and control participants displayed comparable interference on incongruent color-related word trials as well as incongruent color-word trials. Although both groups demonstrated less interference on trials involving incongruent color-related words than on trials involving incongruent color words, this difference was comparable for both groups. In other words, the greater semantic processing required by the color-related words did not differentiate psychopaths and nonpsychopathic offenders.

One interpretation of this inconsistent evidence regarding semantic processing is that psychopaths' deficient processing of semantic information, like their processing of fear stimuli, is situation specific. That is, whether or not psychopaths and control participants differ in the processing of word meanings may relate to as yet unspecified aspects of the experimental tasks. In this regard, there is growing evidence that semantically related interference in psychopaths is more dependent on the location of incongruent stimuli than on their specific content. Using a variety of Stroop-like procedures, researchers from our laboratory showed that psychopaths demonstrate normal interference when the color to be named appears in the same space as the incongruent word but that psychopaths demonstrate significantly less interference than control participants when the color and word are spatially separated. For instance, consistent with the aforementioned study, psychopaths and control participants show comparable performance on standard color–word Stroop tasks (Hiatt et al., 2004; Smith, Arnett, & Newman, 1992) and on emotion Stroop tasks in which threat-related and other emotion-related words appear in diverse colors (Lorenz, Newman, & Lilienfeld, 2001). However, psychopaths demonstrate significantly less interference than control participants while naming the color of rectangles that surround incongruent words and while naming pictures that appear in conjunction with incongruent words (Hiatt et al., 2004; Newman et al., 1997).

Regarding the situation specificity of psychopaths' emotional and more general semantic processing deficits, it appears that psychopaths display anomalous processing of semantic information that is incidental, as in the lexical decision assessments of emotion facilitation (Lorenz & Newman, 2002; Williamson et al., 1991), or presented in a different spatial location, as in the Stroop-like procedures described earlier (e.g., Newman et al., 1997). These conditions resemble those identified when the situational specificity of psychopaths' passive avoidance deficit is described. Recall that psychopaths are relatively insensitive to threat cues when they are engaged in reward seeking but were equally responsive to the threat cues when their primary focus was avoidance learning. Across these paradigms, psychopaths appear to process the meaning of stimuli as well as control participants when they are part of their primary focus or dominant response set, but they often appear insensitive to the same stimuli when they are secondary or peripheral to their dominant response set.

CEREBRAL ASYMMETRIES

An extraordinary aspect of Hare's investigations of psychopathy is his commitment to integrating research on the biological, psychological, and sociolegal correlates of psychopathy. For decades, Hare has been using a variety of techniques to study the physiological correlates of psychopathy and clarify their implications for psychopathic behavior. As already described, Hare and colleagues have used psychophysiological measures (e.g., skin conductance and heart rate) to elucidate psychopaths' restricted anticipation of aversive events, ERPs to document their anomalous information processing under conditions of distraction, and a combination of ERPs and brain imaging techniques to characterize psychopaths' inefficient and impoverished emotion processing (see Hare, 1998). Another particularly promising and long-standing area of investigation that illustrates Hare's attempts to integrate neurological and psychological explanations for psychopathy concerns his research on the abnormal cerebral asymmetries demonstrated by psychopathic individuals.

In his first investigation of cerebral asymmetries in psychopathy, Hare (1979) used a tachistoscopic recognition task "to test the hypothesis that psychopathy is associated with dysfunction of the dominant hemisphere" (p. 605). Three-letter words were presented, in a vertical orientation, to the left or right of a central fixation point. Contrary to prediction, both psychopaths and control participants identified words presented in the right visual field more accurately than those presented in the left visual field. That is, despite observing a highly significant laterality effect, this main effect was equally apparent in psychopathic and nonpsychopathic offenders. In discussing the results, Hare noted the possibility that differences between psychopaths and others may be found "with tasks that require a greater degree of semantic process-ing, place greater demands on the more anterior parts of the brain, or tap storage and retrieval processes" (p. 609).

Following up this early investigation, Hare and McPherson (1984) used a verbal dichotic listening task with a greater memory load to investigate lin-guistic processing in psychopaths and control participants. On each trial, two sets of three, one-syllable words were presented simultaneously to each ear using stereo headphones. After each trial, participants reported aloud all of the words that they could recall from that trial. Because language is processed preferentially by the left hemisphere, right-handed individuals tend to display superior processing when verbal stimuli are presented to their right ear as opposed to their left ear. Consistent with the performance of normal control participants, nonpsychopathic inmates displayed a strong right-ear advantage for verbal stimuli. However, psychopathic inmates dis-played a significantly smaller right-ear advantage (i.e., less lateralized per-formance) than control participants. Of note, psychopaths' overall perfor-mance was comparable to that of control inmates. In fact, psychopaths performed significantly better than control participants at recalling words presented to the left ear/right hemisphere.

Hare and Jutai (1988) used a divided-field methodology to examine semantic processing in psychopathic and nonpsychopathic offenders. On each trial, a concrete noun was presented tachistoscopically to the right or left visual field. In one condition, participants were required to decide whether the noun was the same as another word (i.e., identity match). In two other conditions, participants decided whether or not the noun was an exemplar of a specific or abstract category, respectively. Psychopaths and control partici-pants did not differ in the identity match or specific category conditions. However, when the task required participants to classify nouns according to an abstract category, the groups displayed an opposite pattern of results. Whereas nonpsychopaths showed a right visual field/left hemisphere advantage as in the other two conditions, psychopaths performed the abstract categorization task more accurately when responding to nouns pre-sented in the left as opposed to the right visual field.

Of relevance to the interpretation of these findings, Kiehl et al. (2001) examined the neural pathways associated with processing (i.e., making lexi-cal decisions regarding) concrete and abstract words using functional mag-netic resonance imaging. According to the authors, "a direct comparison between the abstract and concrete stimuli epochs yielded a significant area of activation in the right anterior temporal cortex" (p. 225) and provided "sup-port for a right hemisphere neural pathway in the processing of abstract word representations" (p. 225). Consistent with past research, the authors reported that concrete words were identified more quickly than abstract words. These findings suggested that right hemisphere resources are recruited to assist with the more complex processing requirements associated with identifying abstract words. Combined with the Hare and Jutai results, these findings may indicate that, relative to control participants, psychopaths are less able to benefit from right hemisphere resources while processing words presented to the right visual field/left hemisphere.

As in the other research domains, our assessment of cerebral asymmetries associated with psychopathy serve to replicate and extend the work of Hare and colleagues. In one study, Howland, Kosson, Patterson, and Newman (1993) used a version of Posner's cueing paradigm to examine behavioral inhibition and attentional switching in psychopathic and nonpsychopathic offenders. On each trial, participants were presented with a warning stimulus or cue that predicted with 80% validity the location of the target stimulus that followed. That is, if the warning stimulus appeared on the left or right side of the computer monitor, the target appeared in the same location on 80% of the trials. Participants were instructed to respond as quickly and accurately as possible to indicate whether the target stimuli appeared on the left or right side of the monitor using their left and right index fingers, respectively. Participants were also informed that the location of the warning stimuli would be the best predictor of target location. Such cuing establishes a dominant response set so that participants respond to right-sided targets more quickly when they are preceded by right-sided cuing stimuli and visa versa. By comparing participants' response times to targets presented in the expected and unexpected locations (relative to neutral trials), it is possible to examine a person's ability to alter a dominant response set (i.e., switch attention).

The results of this study yielded only partial support for our hypothesis that psychopaths would be deficient in altering a dominant response set. Of relevance to the current focus on cerebral asymmetries, support for this hypothesis was moderated by the location of the cuing stimuli. When participants were presented with a right-sided cue followed by a left-sided target, psychopaths committed significantly more errors than nonpsychopaths even though they performed as well as control participants when the left-sided cues were followed by right-sided targets.

Based on this finding and related results from the Hare laboratory, Kosson (1998) proposed that psychopaths' information processing deficiencies may involve "momentary over-arousal of left hemisphere resources" (p. 375). Consistent with this speculation, Kosson (1998, see also 1996) found that "psychopaths misclassified more secondary task and marginally more primary task targets than nonpsychopaths" (p. 373) under conditions involving differential activation of the left hemisphere.

As already described, Lorenz and Newman (2002) found that psychopaths demonstrated significantly less facilitation than control participants while identifying emotional and high-frequency words. Although not described earlier, another goal of this study was to evaluate Kosson's (1996, 1998) proposal regarding differential activation of the left hemisphere. Toward this end, Lorenz and Newman used alternating blocks of trials that were performed with the right or left hand to activate the left and right hemispheres respectively. Consistent with earlier findings and speculation by Kosson (1998), the authors found a significant psychopathy by response hand interaction with psychopaths demonstrating normal emotion facilitation in the left hand/right hemisphere blocks (M = 20.0 ms, SE = 9.4 and M = 28.9 ms, SE 11.0, for psychopaths and control participants, respectively) while showing no emotion facilitation in the right hand/left hemisphere condition (M = −4.6 ms, SE = 10.6, and M = 37.7 ms, SE 8.5, for psychopaths and control participants, respectively). The same interaction was also found in the word frequency analyses. Paralleling our laboratory's findings with the Posner paradigm, these results suggest that psychopaths' deficient processing of secondary unexpected cues is specific to conditions involving differential activation of the left hemisphere.

As noted by Hare and McPherson (1984), it is difficult to determine whether the weaker cerebral asymmetries demonstrated by psychopaths reflect an usual distribution of language and emotional processing resources in the brain or some less specific problem related to left hemisphere arousal or interhemispheric integration. For this reason, it is important to examine whether psychopaths' unusual perceptual asymmetries apply only to the emotional and abstract connotations of words or whether they are also found on tasks involving other types of secondary information. This question was examined by Bernstein, Newman, Wallace, and Luh (2000) using a recall task developed by Hockey and Hamilton (1970). Participants were told that they were going to see a series of eight words, presented one at a time, and that their task was to recall as many words as possible in their proper order. Participants were given a sheet of paper with eight lines that were numbered 1 through 8. Although not mentioned in the instructions, the eight words appeared in different spatial locations with two words appearing in each corner of the visual display. After giving participants a minute to write down all of the words they could remember, the experimenter noted that the words appeared in different locations and asked participants to recall the spatial locations of the words. This was done by having them draw a box next to each line and place an "X" in the corner where the word appeared.

The results of the Bernstein et al. (2000) study parallel other findings in this area. As in the Hare (1979) study, both psychopaths and control participants displayed a strong right visual field advantage for the verbal stimuli. That is, both groups recalled significantly more words from the right visual field than from the left visual field. However, paralleling results from more complex tasks involving abstract words, memory for multiple words, and emotional connotations, there was a significant Group × Side interaction for location recall. As in prior research, control participants demonstrated better processing of the secondary/incidental information (i.e., recall of locations) than psychopaths when stimuli were presented to the right visual field/left hemisphere whereas psychopaths tended to outperform control participants when stimuli were presented in the left visual field/right hemisphere (see Fig. 7.7). The authors proposed that psychopaths are less adept at processing secondary cues under conditions that differentially activate the left hemisphere. Moreover, the authors speculated that the psychopath's difficulty in accessing secondary information relates to the coordination of left and right

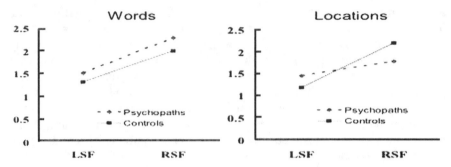

FIGURE 7–7.   Number of words and word locations correctly recalled by low-anxious psychopaths and control participants on the memory task used by Bernstein, Newman, Wallace, and Luh (2000). A total of four words/locations appeared in the left spatial field (LSF) and right spatial field (RSF), respectively.

hemisphere resources as opposed to deficits in emotional or semantic processing per se (see also, Kiehl, Liddle, et al., 1999).

Hiatt, Lorenz, & Newman (2002) examined perceptual asymmetries using a dichotic listening task developed by Bryden and MacRae (1988). The stimuli consist of four words (*dower, bower, tower,* and *power*) spoken in four affective tones of voice (*sad, angry, fearful,* and *neutral*). In one condition, participants were instructed to listen for a particular word, whereas in a second condition, participants were instructed to listen for a particular affect. Right-handed participants typically identify more target words when they are presented to the right ear/left hemisphere and they identify more target affects when they are presented to the left ear/right hemisphere. The authors reported mixed support for their hypothesis that psychopaths would display weaker asymmetries than control participants in both conditions. Contrary to expectation, both psychopaths and control participants demonstrated significantly greater and comparable accuracy for target words presented to the right ear/left hemisphere. Although psychopaths demonstrated a weaker asymmetry in the emotion condition as predicted, inspection of the group means indicated that psychopaths displayed better accuracy than control participants for right ear targets and comparable accuracy for targets presented to the left ear.

According to Hiatt et al. (2002), the results from the word condition are consistent with those of Hare (1979) and support his contention that psychopaths and control participants display comparable asymmetries when performing relatively simple word identification tasks. On the other hand, the reduced asymmetry demonstrated by psychopaths in the affect identification condition suggests that their emotion processing may be more distributed. That is, psychopaths' difficulty accommodating information from the right hemisphere when making right-handed or verbal responses may have resulted in greater distribution of emotion processing functions across cerebral hemispheres. Alternatively, if psychopaths use deliberate cognitive strategies to process affective stimuli as proposed by Hare (1998) and others (e.g., Kiehl et al., 2001), then their emotion processing might be less dependent upon right hemisphere processing resources.

As in other research domains, investigations of cerebral asymmetries in psychopathy commonly reveal significant group differences, but these differences appear to be situation specific. Specifically, psychopaths and control participants appear to display comparable cerebral asymmetries when performing simple tasks, but psychopaths typically display weaker asymmetries than control participants when performing relatively complex tasks or when processing secondary aspects of experimental stimuli. Furthermore, psychopaths are relatively deficient in the ability to access a word's emotional connotations, abstract meaning, and spatial location while responding with their right hand or processing information from the right visual field. Yet, they perform the same tasks as well as control participants when responding with their left hand or when incidental information is presented to their right hemisphere via the left visual field or left ear. Such findings serve to link psychopaths' emotion, language, and other information processing limitations and, moreover, raise the possibility that a dysfunction in interhemispheric integration underlies these diverse information processing anomalies.

INTEGRATION OF RESEARCH EVIDENCE

Owing to the range of specific hypotheses tested and paradigms used, it is easy to be overwhelmed by the apparent hodgepodge of laboratory findings on psychopathy. However, close examination of the existing literature reveals that there is impressive consistency and an emerging clarity with regard to the psychopathic deficit. Once psychopaths focus attention, they are unlikely to accommodate other (i.e., nondominant or incidental) information that modulates the ongoing behavior of others. We have referred to this problem as a response modulation deficit and demonstrated its effects by measuring psychopaths' sensitivity to (a) secondary threat cues in passive avoidance tasks (Newman & Kosson, 1986), (b) changes in environmental contingencies using a modified extinction paradigm (Newman et al, 1987), (c) incongruent contextual cues using modified Stroop procedures (Newman et al., 1997), and (d) the affective connotations of words using a lexical decision task (Lorenz & Newman, 2002). In a recent summary of his work, Hare (1998) wrote that his findings and interpretation of the evidence were "consistent with the view that psychopaths exhibit information processing deficits that result in poor self-regulation, difficulties in linking current actions and stimuli to past experiences, and decoding of the significance of cognitive and affective contextual cues" (p. 122).

Regarding the underpinnings of their information processing deficits, Hare (1998) wrote that the "neurobiological basis for the difficulties psychopaths appear to have with affective and deep semantic processes are unknown but may involve anomalies in the integration of activities within and between hemispheres" (p. 124). In this section, we attempt to clarify the association between psychopaths' anomalous cerebral asymmetries and their situation-specific information processing deficits. To foreshadow our conclusion, we propose that the anomalous cerebral asymmetries demonstrated by psychopaths indicate that their left and right hemisphere processing resources are difficult to integrate, whereas the more typical cerebral asymmetries demonstrated by nonpsychopaths indicate that the processing resources of their left and right hemisphere are more readily coordinated. In addition, we propose that the functional dissociation of left and right hemisphere processing resources in psychopaths favors selective attention over the automatic integration of peripheral information whereas the greater interhemispheric cooperation of nonpsychopaths enhances response flexibility at the expense of distractibility.

Despite years of investigation, the differential functions of the cerebral hemispheres are still a matter of debate, as are the factors governing interhemispheric interactions (Banich & Nicholas, 1998; Beaumont, 1997). For the present purposes, we assume that the left and right hemispheres are capable of operating as separate information processors and that, with few exceptions related to particular language functions, both hemispheres are able to process the same information (Banich & Belger, 1990; Banich & Shenker, 1994). Following Chiarello, Burgess, Richards, and Pollock (1990), we also assume that the left hemisphere is especially adept at selective attention (i.e., focusing narrowly on information that is directly relevant to one's goal or dominant response set) whereas the right hemisphere is relatively unselective. Furthermore, because the focus of right hemisphere processing is less selective, we assume that it routinely processes information that is beyond the focus of the left hemisphere. Although the hemispheres are capable of acting in a relatively independent manner, they are especially likely to coordinate processing resources as task complexity increases (Weissman & Banich, 2000). Under such conditions, we assume that a person's right hemisphere processing resources normally follow and enhance their left hemisphere-mediated focus of attention. However, as already noted, we believe that psychopaths are relatively unable to accommodate the products of right hemisphere processing to supplement the more specific left hemisphere focus that mediates goal-directed behavior (Davidson, 1992; Harmon-Jones & Allen, 1998; Sutton & Davidson, 1997).

Although this proposal is speculative, we, like Hare (1998), believe that it offers a useful means of integrating psychopaths' emotional, semantic, and language processing anomalies and is generally consistent with the laboratory evidence on psychopathy. Given a relatively simple processing task, both psychopaths and control participants perform the task using left hemisphere processing resources primarily. This contention is consistent with the fact that both psychopaths and control participants display a left hemisphere (i.e., right ear and right visual field) bias when performing simple tasks (e.g., Hare, 1979; Hiatt et al., 2002). It is also consistent with the fact that psychopaths perform as well as control participants on relatively simple or unidimensional tasks.

As demands for information processing increase, however, people are more likely to perform tasks using a combination of left and right hemisphere resources because the enhanced processing capacity associated with interhemispheric integration begins to outweigh the costs associated with integrating information across hemispheres (Belger & Banich, 1998). Furthermore, when bilateral processing is called for, in most cases the person's right hemisphere resources will be used to augment their specific goal-directed behavior as determined by the left hemisphere. Consistent with this latter statement, nonpsychopathic control participants display a left hemisphere processing bias for most tasks and, thus, display a right ear and visual field advantage regardless of complexity. In contrast to control participants, the relatively weak interhemispheric cooperation associated with psychopathy works against a clear left hemisphere advantage. Thus, psychopaths will tend to favor the left or right hemisphere processing resources depending upon the nature of the task. Whereas the superior selective attention associated with the left hemisphere enhances processing of expected targets presented to their right ear and right visual field, the more holistic processing of the right hemisphere facilitates their multidimensional processing of more complex stimuli. Thus, relative to control participants, psychopaths have more difficulty processing complex stimuli or performing complex analysis of stimuli presented to the right ear or right visual field. Conversely, the fact that psychopaths perform as well as or better than control participants when such stimuli are presented to the left ear or visual field probably indicates that their right hemisphere resources are more available to process such stimuli because, relative to those of control participants, they are less likely to be co-opted by the attentional bias of the left hemisphere.

This speculation concerning the relative independence of psychopaths' left and right hemisphere processing is consistent with recent findings reported by Bernstein et al. (2000). Although both psychopaths and control participants showed superior processing of words (i.e., the deliberate task) presented to the right spatial field/left hemisphere, only control participants displayed this advantage for the incidental, location cues. Whereas the incidental recall of control participants paralleled their primary focus, psychopaths' recall of incidental cues was comparable across the two spatial fields (i.e., was independent of their left hemisphere-mediated attentional bias). Thus, as task complexity increases, we assume that controls use a combination of left and right hemisphere processing resources to process the multiple dimensions of task stimuli but, because they also continue to show a right visual field advantage, we also assume that their left hemisphere has remained dominant. We assume that psychopaths are more likely to use a combination of left and right hemisphere processing resources as task complexity increases. However, in contrast with control participants, this dual activation of the hemispheres works against the standard asymmetry because the increasing activation of the right hemisphere equalizes their attentional bias as opposed to strengthening the right visual field/left hemisphere bias.

Although psychopaths in the Bernstein et al. (2000) study recalled fewer incidental cues than control participants from the right spatial field, they recalled more incidental cues from the left spatial field and, thus, performed as well as control participants overall. The Bernstein et al. study illustrates the fact that psychopaths display weaker cerebral asymmetries as task complexity increases, but it does not necessarily clarify the association between psychopaths' anomalous cerebral asymmetries and their response modulation and self-regulatory deficits. Indeed, the processing of secondary location cues in this study was essentially irrelevant for participants' primary task performance (i.e., word recall).

Of greater relevance to psychopaths' response modulation and self-regulatory deficits is the investigation of emotion facilitation conducted by Lorenz and Newman (2002). This is because performance on the primary task (i.e., recognizing stimulus words) is influenced by a word's affective connotations that, although secondary to the primary task, serve to facilitate word recognition. In this regard, the lexical decision task resembles the incidental use of emotion cues to modulate dominant responses and, thus, has immediate relevance for self-regulation (see Newman & Lorenz, 2003). Notably, the psychopath's failure to use emotion cues to facilitate lexical decisions was specific to the right-hand condition. Assuming that the left hemisphere was more likely to be controlling task performance in the right-hand condition than in the left-hand condition, the results are consistent with our proposal that the selective attention of psychopathic individuals is less likely to be augmented by right hemisphere processing of secondary cues. Although we assume that the right hemisphere is processing the affective connotations of words in psychopaths as well as in control participants, we have proposed that psychopaths are relatively unable to coordinate this information with their left hemisphere processing.

It seems clear that the information processing of psychopathic offenders is better suited to primary task performance than it is to response flexibility and elaborative processing. It is, however, often difficult to specify what information is secondary and, thus, what information will or will not influence the psychopath's behavior. We believe that the literature on cerebral asymmetries and interhemispheric communication is particularly useful in this regard. When participants are motivated by a specific goal, we assume that the left hemisphere focuses narrowly on aspects of the situation that are deemed directly relevant to achieving their goal. We also assume that the right hemisphere is less selective and thus processes more information. Furthermore, to the extent that the incidental information processed by the right hemisphere has relevance for the dominant response set, it will normally gain salience, perceived significance, and merit selective attention by the left hemisphere. By contrast, the right hemisphere processing of psychopathic individuals is relatively unlikely to influence their dominant response set.

This integration of response modulation and cerebral asymmetries may clarify why spatial separation appears to moderate Stroop interference in psychopathic individuals. In three separate studies, we have found that incongruent pictures and words engender significantly less interference in psychopaths than in control participants when the incongruent stimuli are spatially separated from the target stimuli (Hiatt et al., 2004; Newman et al., 1997). In three other studies, we observed comparable Stroop interference in psychopaths and control participants when the incongruent and target stimuli were spatially coincident (Brinkley et al, 2005; Hiatt et al., 2004; Smith et al., 1992). Assuming that the left hemisphere focuses primarily on the target stimuli and that the focus of the right hemisphere includes surrounding stimuli, then a deficit in interhemispheric integration would be more likely to reduce response conflict/interference when incongruent information is spatially separated as opposed to coincident.

To the extent that negative affect and behavioral withdrawal are processed preferentially by the right hemisphere as proposed by Davidson and colleagues (e.g., Davidson, 1992), the current proposal is also consistent with research and clinical observations regarding psychopaths' insensitivity to punishment stimuli. If, as proposed, psychopaths' dysfunction involves accommodating right hemisphere processing once a dominant response set has been adopted by the left hemisphere, it follows that they would be relatively insensitive to punishment cues and prone to behavioral disinhibition. This assertion is consistent with the fact that psychopaths commit excessive passive avoidance errors while responding for reward but perform as well as control participants when avoiding punishment is their dominant response set (Newman & Kosson, 1986).

It is also worth noting that although language processing is typically associated with the left hemisphere, there is growing evidence that the right hemisphere plays an important role in supporting left hemisphere-mediated language production and reception (Beeman & Chiarello, 1998). Indeed, the right hemisphere appears to be especially important for the type of abstract, semantic, and elaborative processing described in this chapter (e.g., Chiarello et al., 1990; Kiehl, Liddle, et al., 1999). Thus, the current integration is highly consistent with Hare's (1998) focus on psychopaths' semantic, language, and emotion deficits.

In light of the fact that psychopaths' performance deficits are largely consistent with the proposal that they have difficulty integrating the products of right hemisphere processing, it is reasonable to speculate that a deficit in interhemispheric transfer gives rise to their information processing deficiencies. What remains unclear, however, is whether their failure to accommodate incidental information reflects a problem in interhemispheric transfer per se or some other problem that hampers interhemispheric integration. For example, psychopaths' difficulty with integrating information from the right hemisphere could also reflect an exaggeration of their left hemisphere-mediated selective attention or a dysfunction in the neurological circuitry that mediates the automatic direction of selective attention to potentially important information.

SUMMARY AND IMPLICATIONS

In comparison to other areas of psychopathology, there has been relatively little research using laboratory paradigms to identify the psychobiological underpinnings of psychopathy. Despite the dearth of research, there is good evidence that psychopaths manifest an array of performance anomalies that are consistent with regarding psychopathy as a manifestation of psychopathology as opposed to an alternative lifestyle. For instance, relative to control participants, psychopaths display (a) less electrodermal activity in anticipation of punishment or in response to conditioned threat cues, (b) weaker inhibition of punished responses, (c) smaller evoked potential to affectively neutral stimuli that are peripheral to their primary focus of attention, (d) less interference of primary task performance by incongruent peripheral cues, (e) less utilization of emotional connotations to distinguish words from nonwords, (f) a lack of verbal fluency and coherence especially while telling stories or describing past events, and (g) poor processing of emotion cues, abstract meaning, location cues, and recall of simple words while left hemisphere resources are being taxed.

Historically, interpretation of these and other correlates of psychopathy has been relatively specific. For instance, psychopaths' weak electrodermal activity to threat cues and poor passive avoidance have been attributed to a fear deficit (Lykken, 1995). Other investigators have posited specific deficits in processing negative affect (Patrick, 1994), general emotion processing (Hare, 1998), deficient behavioral inhibition (Fowles, 1980), a dysfunctional violence inhibition mechanism (Blair, 2001; Fisher & Blair, 1998), and language and semantic processing deficits (Hare, 1998; Hare et al., 1988). Although experimental research provides support for each of these proposals, there are good reasons to contemplate the associations among these explanations.

First, proposing numerous deficits for one disorder lacks parsimony. Although there is no guarantee that psychopaths' weaker processing of emotional and affectively neutral contextual cues are related, the philosophy of science teaches us that a unitary explanation is preferable to multiple explanations even if it is simpler to interpret each set of results using separate theories. Second, positing separate deficits for each research domain revealing group differences reduces the likelihood that researchers will identify abstract principles that cut across the diverse domains. Third, the inconsistent findings observed in each research domain reviewed in this chapter are difficult to reconcile with content-specific processing deficits. There is substantial evidence that psychopaths do not manifest fear deficits, emotion processing deficits, cognitive deficits, language reception or production deficits, or anomalous cerebral asymmetries under all experimental circumstances.

Once the convenient, but questionable, strategy of postulating multiple deficits is questioned, a variety of new questions and implications become apparent. Most important is the possibility that the diverse laboratory correlates of psychopathy reflect a common vulnerability or processing deficit. Another implication is that it may be possible to identify particular task requirements that expose the psychopathic deficits across diverse research domains. A further implication concerns the search for neurological substrates of psychopathy. Whereas consideration of content-specific deficits such as fearlessness may lead investigators to focus on particular anatomical substrates such as the amygdala, psychopaths' language processing deficits and insensitivity to affectively neutral peripheral cues implicate other neurological substrates.

Overall, research suggests that psychopaths typically process information as well or better than control participants by attending selectively to the primary demands of a situation. Although this strategy enables them to achieve their explicit goals in a relatively efficient manner, psychopaths are less likely to process a range of incidental information that normally provides perspective on behavior. Failure to accommodate such information hampers self-regulation because it renders the individual relatively insensitive to unexpected feedback that signals potential punishment, unexpected changes in environmental contingencies which indicate that current behavior is no longer adaptive, incidental affective cues that normally guide interpersonal interactions, and a range of other incidental cues that would otherwise accentuate alternative response strategies (e.g., delay of gratification).

Cleckley (1976) wrote about a "selective defect or elimination which prevents important components of normal experience from being integrated into the whole human reaction" (p. 374), a process with obvious resemblance to the attentional deficit characterized earlier. In reference to this defect, he argued that "if we grant the existence of a far-reaching and persistent blocking, absence, deficit, or dissociation of this sort, we have all that is needed, at the present level of our inquiry, to account for the psychopath" (p. 371).

Owing, in large part to Hare's (1991) PCL–R, psychopathy has become "the most important psychological construct for policy and practice in the criminal justice field" (Harris et al., 2001, p. 197). The basis for this statement concerns the superior predictive validity of the PCL–R. However, psychopathy is also a grave form of psychopathology and, as such, has substantial significance for the fields of clinical psychology and psychiatry as well as for the criminal justice system (Cleckley, 1976). The potential significance of the construct in this domain is that it may identify etiological processes that result in personally and socially devastating consequences. To treat and, more importantly, prevent this disorder, it is essential to characterize these etiologically relevant processes and the factors that moderate their expression. Although we have provided only a superficial summary of his work in this area, it seems clear that Hare's program of research and writings have provided clinicians and researchers alike with an invaluable foundation for conceptualizing psychopaths' dysfunction. In our view, it is this aspect of Hare's contribution that is most essential to the ultimate goals of early identification, clinical management, and primary prevention of psychopathy.

ACKNOWLEDGMENT

The authors acknowledge financial support from the National Institute of Mental Health (Grants MH53041 and MH57150), which has enabled the writing of this chapter as well as the authors' research with psychopathic offenders. We also thank the staff and inmates at the Oakhill and Columbia Correctional Institutions and the Wisconsin Department of Corrections for making this research possible.

REFERENCES

Arnett, P. A., Howland, E. W., Smith, S. S., & Newman, J. P. (1993). Autonomic responsivity during passive avoidance in incarcerated psychopaths. *Personality and Individual Differences, 14,* 173–185.

Banich, M. T., & Belger, A. (1990). Interhemispheric interaction: How do the hemispheres divide and conquer a task? *Cortex, 26*(1), 77–94.

Banich, M. T., & Nicholas, C. D. (1998). Integration of processing between the hemispheres in word recognition. In M. Beeman & C. Chiarello (Eds.), *Right hemisphere language comprehension: Perspectives from cognitive neuroscience.* Matwah, NJ: Lawrence Erlbaum Associates.

Banich, M. T., & Shenker, J. I. (1994). Investigations of interhemispheric processing: Methodological considerations. *Neuropsychology, 8,* 263–277.

Beaumont, J. G. (1997). Future research directions in laterality. *Neuropsychology Review, 7,* 107–126.

Beeman, M., & Chiarello, C. (1998). *Right hemisphere language comprehension: Perspectives from cognitive neuroscience.* Matwah, NJ: Lawrence Erlbaum Associates.

Belger, A., & Banich, M. T. (1998). Costs and benefits of integrating information between the cerebral hemispheres: A computational perspective. *Neuropsychology, 12,* 380–398.

Bernstein, A., Newman, J. P., Wallace, J. F., & Luh, K. E. (2000). Left-hemisphere activation and deficient response modulation in psychopaths. *Psychological Science, 11,* 414–418.

Blair, R. J. R. (2001). Neurocognitive models of aggression, the antisocial personality disorders, and psychopathy. *Journal of Neurology, Neurosurgery & Psychiatry, 71,* 727–731.

Brinkley, C. A., Bernstein, A., & Newman, J. P. (1999). Coherence in the narratives of psychopathic and nonpsychopathic criminal offenders. *Personality and Individual Differences, 27,* 519–530.

Brinkley, C. A., Newman, J. P., Harpur, T. J., & Johnson, M. M. (1999). Cohesion in the texts of psychopathic and nonpsychopathic criminal inmates. *Personality and Individual Differences, 26,* 873–885.

Brinkley, C. A., Newman, J. P., Widiger, T. A., & Lynam, D. R. (2004). Two approaches to parsing the heterogeneity of psychopathy. *Clinical Psychology: Science and Practice, 11,* 69–94.

Brinkley, C. A., Schmitt, W. A., & Newman, J. P. (2005). Semantic processing in psychopathic offenders. *Personality and Individual Differences, 38,* 1047–1056..

Bryden, M. P., & MacRae, L. (1988). Dichotic laterality effects obtained with emotional words. *Neuropsychiatry, Neuropsychology, and Behavioral Neurology, 1,* 171–176.

Chiarello, C., Burgess, C., Richards, L., & Pollock, A. (1990). Semantic and associative priming in the cerebral hemispheres: Some words do, some words don't . . . sometimes, some places. *Brain and Language, 38*, 75–104.

Cleckley, H. (1976). *The mask of sanity* (5th ed.). St. Louis, MO: Mosby.

Davidson, R. J. (1992). Emotion and affective style: Hemispheric substrates. *Psychological Science, 3*, 39–43.

Fisher, L., & Blair, R. J. R. (1998). Cognitive impairment and its relationship to psychopathic tendencies in children with emotional and behavioral difficulties. *Journal of Abnormal Child Psychology, 26*, 511–519.

Fowles, D. C. (1980). The three arousal model: Implications of Gray's two-factor learning theory for heart rate, electrodermal activity, and psychopathy. *Psychophysiology, 17*, 87–104.

Gernsbacher, M. A., & Faust, M. E. (1991). The mechanism of suppression: A component of general comprehension skill. *Journal of Experimental Psychology: Learning, Memory, and Cognition, 17*, 245–262.

Gillstrom, B. J., & Hare, R. D. (1988). Language-related hand gestures in psychopaths. *Journal of Personality Disorders, 2*, 21–27.

Gorenstein, E. E., & Newman, J. P. (1980). Disinhibitory psychopathology: A new perspective and a model for research. *Psychological Review, 87*, 301–315.

Hare, R. D. (1965). Temporal gradient of fear arousal in psychopaths. *Journal of Abnormal Psychology, 70*, 442–445.

Hare, R. D. (1970). *Psychopathy: Theory and research.* New York: Wiley.

Hare, R. D. (1979). Psychopathy and laterality of cerebral function. *Journal of Abnormal Psychology, 88*, 605–610.

Hare, R. D. (1980). A research scale for the assessment of psychopathy in criminal populations. *Personality and Individual Differences, 1*, 111–119.

Hare, R. D. (1986). Twenty years of experience with the Cleckley psychopath. In W. H. Reid, D. Dorr, J. I. Walker, & J. W. Bonner, III (Eds.), *Unmasking the psychopath: Antisocial personality and related syndromes* (pp. 3–27). New York: W. W. Norton.

Hare, R. D. (1991). *The Hare Psychopathy Checklist–Revised.* Toronto, Ontario, Canada: Multi-Health Systems.

Hare, R. D. (1996). Psychopathy: A clinical construct whose time has come. *Criminal Justice and Behavior, 23*, 25–54.

Hare, R. D. (1998). Psychopathy, affect and behavior. In D. J. Cooke, R. D. Hare, & A. Forth (Eds.), *Psychopathy: Theory, research and implications for society* (pp. 105–137). Dordrecht, The Netherlands: Kluwer Academic.

Hare, R. D. (2003). *The Hare Psychopathy Checklist–Revised* (2nd ed.). Toronto, Ontario, Canada: Multi-Health Systems.

Hare, R. D., Clark, D., Grann, M., & Thornton, D. (2000). Psychopathy and the predictive validity of the PCL-R: An international perspective. *Behavioral Sciences & the Law, 18*, 623–645.

Hare, R. D., & Jutai, J. W. (1988). Psychopathy and cerebral asymmetry in semantic processing. *Personality and Individual Differences, 9*, 329–337.

Hare, R. D., & McPherson, L. M. (1984). Psychopathy and perceptual asymmetry during verbal dichotic listening. *Journal of Abnormal Psychology, 93*, 141–149.

Hare, R. D., Williamson, S. E., & Harpur, T. J. (1988). Psychopathy and Language. In T. E. Moffitt and S. A. Mednick (Eds.), *Biological contributions to crime causation.* Dordrecht, The Netherlands: Nijhoff Martinus.

Harmon-Jones, E., & Allen, J. J. B. (1998). Anger and frontal brain activity: EEG asymmetry consistent with approach motivation despite negative affective valence. *Journal of Personality & Social Psychology, 74*, 1310–1316.

Harpur, T. J., Hare, R. D., & Hakstian, A. R. (1989). Two-factor conceptualization of psychopathy: Construct validity and assessment implications. *Psychological Assessment: A Journal of Consulting and Clinical Psychology, 1*, 6–17.

Harris, G. T., Skilling, T. A., & Rice, M. E. (2001). The construct of psychopathy. In M. Tonry & N. Morris (Eds.), *Crime and justice: An annual review of research* (Vol. 28, pp. 197–264). Chicago: University of Chicago Press.

Hartung, C. M., Milich, R., Lynam, D. R., & Martin, C. A. (2002). Understanding the relations among gender, disinhibition, and disruptive behavior in adolescents. *Journal of Abnormal Pscyhology, 111(4)*, 659–665.

Hemphill, J. F., Newman, J. P., & Hare, R. D. *Psychopathy and recidivism among black and white adult male offenders.* Unpublished manuscript.

Hiatt, K. D., Lorenz, A. R., & Newman, J. P. (2002). Assessment of emotion and language processing in psychopathic offenders: Results from a dichotic listening task. *Personality and Individual Differences, 32*, 1255–1268.

Hiatt, K. D., & Newman, J. P. (2004). Understanding psychopathy: The cognitive side. In C. J. Patrick (Ed.), *Handbook of Psychopathy*. New York: Guilford Press.

Hiatt, K. D., Schmitt, W. A., & Newman, J. P. (2004). Stroop tasks reveal abnormal selective attention in psychopathic offenders. *Neuropsychology, 18*, 50–59.

Hockey, G. R. J., & Hamilton, P. (1970). Arousal and information selection in short-term memory. *Nature, 226*, 866–868.

Howland, E. W., Kosson, D. S., Patterson, C. M., & Newman, J. P. (1993). Altering a dominant response: Performance of psychopaths and low socialization college students on a cued reaction time task. *Journal of Abnormal Psychology, 102*, 379–387.

Intrator, J., Hare, R., Stritzke, P., Brichtswein, K., Dorfman, D., Harpur, T. J., et al. (1997). A brain imaging (single photon emission computerized tomography) study of semantic and affective processing in psychopaths. *Biological Psychiatry, 42*, 96–103.

Jutai, J. W., & Hare, R. D. (1983). Psychopathy and selective attention during performance of a complex perceptual–motor task. *Psychophysiology, 20*, 146–151.

Jutai, J. W., Hare, R. D., & Connolly, J. F. (1987). Psychopathy and event-related brain potentials (ERPs) associated with attention to speech stimuli. *Personality and Individual Differences, 8*, 175–184.

Kiehl, K. A., Hare, R. D., Liddle, P. F., & McDonald, J. J. (1999). Reduced P300 responses in criminal psychopaths during a visual oddball task. *Biological Psychiatry, 45*, 1498–1507.

Kiehl, K. A., Hare, R. D., McDonald, J. J., & Brink, J. (1999) Semantic and affective processing in psychopaths: An event-related potential (ERP) study. *Psychophysiology, 36*, 765–774.

Kiehl, K. A., Liddle, P. F., Smith, A. M., Mendrek, A., Forster, B. B., & Hare, R. D. (1999). Neural pathways involved in the processing of concrete and abstract words. *Human Brain Mapping, 7*, 225–233.

Kiehl, K. A., Smith, A. M., Hare, R. D., Mendrek, A., Forster, B.B., Brink, J., et al. (2001). Limbic abnormalities in affective processing by criminal psychopaths as revealed by functional magnetic resonance imaging. *Biological Psychiatry, 50*, 677–684.

Klein, G. S. (1964). Semantic power measured through the interference of words with color-naming. *American Journal of Psychology, 77*, 576–588.

Kosson, D. S. (1996). Psychopathy and dual-task performance under focusing conditions. *Journal of Abnormal Psychology, 105*, 391–400.

Kosson, D. S. (1998). Divided visual attention in psychopathic and nonpsychopathic offenders. *Personality and Individual Differences, 24*, 373–391.

Lorenz, A. R., & Newman, J. P. (2002). Deficient response modulation and emotion processing in low-anxious Caucasian psychopathic offenders: Results from a lexical decision task, *Emotion 2*, 91–104.

Louth, S. M., Williamson, S., Alpert, M., Pouget, E. R., & Hare, R. D. (1998). Acoustic distinctions in the speech of male psychopaths. *Journal of Psycholinguistic Research, 27*, 375–384.

Lykken, D. T. (1957). A study of anxiety in the sociopathic personality. *Journal of Abnormal and Social Psychology, 55*, 6–10.

Lykken, D. T. (1995). *The antisocial personalities*. Hillsdale, NJ: Lawrence Erlbaum Associates.

McCleary, R. A. (1966). Response-modulating function of the limbic system: Initiation and suppression. In E. Stellar & J. M. Sprague (Eds.), *Progress in physiological psychology* (Vol. 1, pp. 209–271). New York: Plenum.

Mednick, S. A. (1977). A biosocial theory of the learning of law-abiding behavior. In S. A. Mednick and K. O. Christiansen (Eds), *Biosocial bases of criminal behavior*, (pp. 1–8). New York: Gardner Press.

Milich, R., Hartung, C. M., Martin, C. A., & Haigler, E. D. (1994). Behavioral disinhibition and underlying processes in adolescents with disruptive behavior disorders. In D. K. Routh (Ed.), *Disruptive behavior disorders in childhood* (pp. 109–138). New York: Plenum.

Moses, J. A., Ratliff, R. G., & Ratliff, A. R. (1979). Discrimination learning of delinquent boys as a function of reinforcement contingency and delinquent subtype. *Journal of Abnormal Child Psychology, 7*, 443–453.

Newman, J. P. (1997). Conceptual models of the nervous system: Implications for antisocial behavior. In D. M. Stoff, J. Breiling, & J. D. Maser (Eds.), *Handbook of antisocial behavior* (pp. 324–335). New York: Wiley.

Newman, J. P., & Kosson, D. S. (1986). Passive avoidance learning in psychopathic and nonpsychopathic offenders. *Journal of Abnormal Psychology, 95*, 257–263.

Newman, J. P., & Lorenz, A. R. (2003). Response modulation and emotion processing: Implications for psychopathy and other dysregulatory psychopathology. In R. J. Davidson, K. Scherer, & H. H. Goldsmith (Eds.), *Handbook of affective sciences* (pp. 1043–1067). New York: Oxford University Press.

Newman, J. P., Patterson, C. M., Howland, E. W., & Nichols, S. L. (1990). Passive avoidance in psychopaths: The effects of reward. *Personality and Individual Differences, 11*, 1101–1114.

Newman, J. P., Patterson, C. M., & Kosson, D. S. (1987). Response perseveration in psychopaths. *Journal of Abnormal Psychology, 96*, 145–148.

Newman, J. P., & Schmitt, W. A. (1998). Passive avoidance in psychopathic offenders: A replication and extension. *Journal of Abnormal Psychology, 107*, 527–532.

Newman, J. P., Schmitt, W. A., & Voss, W. (1997). The impact of motivationally neutral cues on psychopathic individuals: Assessing the generality of the response modulation hypothesis. *Journal of Abnormal Psychology, 106*, 563–575.

Newman, J. P., & Wallace, J. F. (1993). Psychopathy and cognition. In P. C. Kendall & K. S. Dobson (Eds.), *Psychopathology and Cognition* (pp. 293–349). New York: Academic Press.

Patrick, C. J. (1994). Emotion and psychopathy: Startling new insights. *Psychophysiology, 31*, 319–330.

Patterson, C. M., & Newman, J. P. (1993). Reflectivity and learning from aversive events: Toward a psychological mechanism for the syndromes of disinhibition. *Psychological Review, 100*, 716–736.

Quay, H. C. (1986). Classification. In H. C. Quay & J. S. Werry (Eds.), *Psychopathological disorders of childhood* (3rd ed., pp. 1–42), New York: Wiley.

Rubin, D. C., & Friendly, M. (1986). Predicting which words get recalled: Measures of free recall, availability, goodness, emotionality, and pronounceability for 925 nouns. *Memory and Cognition, 14*, 79–94.

Sabshin, M., & Weissman, S. H. (1996). Forces and choices shaping American psychiatry in the 20th century. *American Psychiatric Press Review of Psychiatry, 15*, 507–525.

Scerbo, A., Raine, A., O'Brien, M., Chan, C., Rhee, C., & Smiley, N. (1990). Reward dominance and passive avoidance learning in adolescent psychopaths. *Journal of Abnormal Child Psychology, 18*, 451–463.

Smith, S. S., Arnett, P. A., & Newman, J. P. (1992). Neuropsychological differentiation of psychopathic and nonpsychopathic criminal offenders. *Personality and Individual Differences, 13*, 1233–1245.

Sutton, S. K., & Davidson, R. J. (1997). Prefrontal brain asymmetry: A biological substrate of the behavioral approach and inhibition systems. *Psychological Science, 8*, 204–210.

Thornquist, M. H., & Zuckerman, M. (1995). Psychopathy, passive-avoidance learning and basic dimensions of personality. *Personality and Individual Differences, 19*, 525–534.

Trasler, G. (1978). Relations between psychopathy and persistent criminality—Methodological and theoretical issues. In R. D. Hare & D. Schalling (Eds.), *Psychopathic behaviour: Approaches to research* (pp. 273–298). New York: Wiley.

Wallace, J. F., Vitale, J. E., & Newman, J. P. (1999). Response modulation deficits: Implications for the diagnosis and treatment of psychopathy. *Journal of Cognitive Psychotherapy, 13*, 55–70.

Weissman, D. H., & Banich, M. T. (2000). The cerebral hemispheres cooperate to perform complex but not simple tasks. *Neuropsychology, 14*, 41–59.

Williamson, S. E. (1991). *Cohesion and coherence in the speech of psychopathic criminals.* Unpublished doctoral dissertation, University of British Columbia, Vancouver, British Columbia, Canada.

Williamson, S. E., Harpur, T. J., & Hare, R. D. (1991). Abnormal processing of affective words by psychopaths. *Psychophysiology, 28*, 260–273.

8

Getting to the Heart of Psychopathy

Christopher J. Patrick

In this chapter I focus on the nature and bases of emotional deviation in psychopathy and describe how new concepts and methods in the field of emotion science have been used to extend understanding of different facets of the psychopathy construct. A *dual-process* model of psychopathy is proposed in which the core affective–interpersonal symptoms of psychopathy, emphasized by Cleckley (1941, 1976) in his classic treatise, are posited to reflect an underlying etiologic mechanism distinct from that associated with chronic antisocial deviance ("externalizing").

The chapter begins with a brief review of early psychophysiological research on psychopathy and fear and of the Psychopathy Checklist–Revised (PCL–R) and its factors. This is followed by a review of recent developments in the field of emotion science, centering around two themes: (a) that emotion is differentiated at a basic functional level, into appetitive and defensive drive states, and (b) that affective processing is hierarchical, involving interactions between basic subcortical systems and higher cortical–cognitive systems. The startle probe paradigm is described as a methodology for investigating basic emotional processes. Evidence is reviewed concerning the relationship between emotional states and temperament traits. The remainder of the chapter is a review of research in which these concepts and techniques have been applied to the study of psychopathy and behavioral disinhibition. On the basis of these findings, it is proposed that the two facets of psychopathy reflected in Hare's PCL–R reflect fundamentally different deviations in emotional processing. The chapter closes with a discussion of alternative mechanisms of disinhibition from the standpoint of a hierarchical conceptualization of affect.

PSYCHOPATHY AND FEAR: EARLY RESEARCH

Early psychophysiological investigations of emotional reactivity in psychopaths, by Hare and colleagues, were inspired by two keynote works. One was Cleckley's (1941, 1976) monograph, *The Mask of Sanity*, in which he described the psychopath in vivid detail. Cleckley's clinical conception of psychopathy emphasized absence of remorse and deficient affect as central to the disorder. In particular, he theorized that the behavioral symptoms of the disorder were the product of a deep-rooted emotional deficit that he termed *semantic dementia* (Cleckley, 1941) or *semantic aphasia*, (Cleckley, 1976), involving a disconnection between cognitive–linguistic processing and emotional "experience." In this regard, Cleckley drew a sharp distinction between the psychopath and the common criminal offender.

A second influence on this early work was an empirical study by Lykken (1957), who used laboratory methods to test the hypothesis that psychopathy ("sociopathy") involves a deficit in the capacity to experience anxiety. Drawing on Lykken's findings and on concepts from the learning literature (Miller, 1959; Mowrer, 1960), Hare (1965a) advanced the theory that psychopathy is characterized by an abnormally steep gradient of fear arousal: That is, punishments that are remote in time fail to inhibit the behavior of psychopaths because distal threat cues do not evoke normal anticipatory fear. Hare proceeded to test this hypothesis in a series of now classic laboratory studies of incarcerated offenders (e.g., Hare, 1965b, 1965c), in which diagnoses reflected clinical judgments of the degree to which participants met Cleckley's criteria for psychopathy, and fear was operationalized by increases in electrodermal activity (*galvanic skin response*). In one of these early experiments, Hare (1965b) introduced the "countdown" anticipatory paradigm (i.e., measurement of physiological reactivity during anticipation of a stressor, signaled by a designated number in a sequential display), which became a cornerstone of theorizing in the psychopathy area (e.g., Fowles, 1980; Hare, 1978; Lykken, 1995; Patrick, 1994).

In addition to this early work by Hare, my own research in this area has been influenced by two significant developments. One was the publication of Hare's (1991, 2003) PCL–R, which established a standard for the assessment of the syndrome in research studies and highlighted the existence of different facets of psychopathy. The other consisted of advances in the conceptualization and measurement of emotion that created opportunities to study and theorize about psychopathology in new ways. These developments are considered in turn in the next two sections.

HARE'S PCL–R

The syndrome of psychopathy is distinguishable from antisocial deviance or persistent criminality. Psychopaths exhibit a distinctive emotional and interpersonal style, marked by callous exploitation of others (*guiltlessness*) and an absence of close affectional ties (*lovelessness*). Unbounded by moral imperatives, abiding loyalties, or genuine intimacies, the psychopath operates as a social strategist or predator, fulfilling immediate selfish aims without regard for broader consequences. The term *primary* (or *true*) psychopath has been used to refer to individuals of this type.

Cleckley (1976) characterized psychopathy as a "mask of sanity" in which pervasive emotional deficits are hidden behind a veneer of overtly' normal cognitive and linguistic behavior. The psychopath presents as normal on first impression but upon closer inspection is found to be profoundly lacking in the ability to connect or to empathize with other people. In this regard, Cleckley's classic criteria for psychopathy included absence of nervousness, lack of remorse or shame, egocentricity, incapacity for love, and general poverty in major affective reactions, as well as reckless and irresponsible behavior. He viewed the underlying emotional deviation in psychopathy as a constitutional weakness that manifested itself in varying degrees and in contrasting ways in different people. Thus, his case histories included examples of roguish professionals and scholars as well as amoral criminal types.

Hare (1980) devised the Psychopathy Checklist (PCL) as an instrument for identifying Cleckley psychopaths in prison settings. The revised version of the Checklist (PCL–R; Hare, 1991, 2003) comprises 20 items, each rated on a 0–2 scale (absent, equivocal, or present) on the basis of information obtained from a semistructured interview and from prison files. The constituent item scores are summed to provide an overall score, with totals of 30 or more leading to a diagnosis of psychopathy. Factor analyses of Hare's Checklist (Hare et al., 1990; Harpur, Hakstian, & Hare, 1988; Harpur, Hare, & Hakstian, 1989) have revealed two correlated factors, labeled *emotional detachment* and *antisocial behavior* by Patrick, Bradley, and Lang (1993). Factor 1 is marked by items reflecting the core affective and interpersonal symptoms of psychopathy that Cleckley emphasized. Factor 2 is marked by items describing a chronic antisocial lifestyle, including child behavior problems, impulsiveness, irresponsibility, and absence of long-term goals.

The two PCL factors show divergent relationships with independent indices of personality and behavior, particularly when their overlap (covariance) is controlled for. Scores on Factor 1 tend to be negatively correlated with self-report anxiety scales and positively related to measures of social dominance, narcissistic personality, and Machiavellianism (Hare, 1991, 2003; Harpur et al., 1989; Verona, Patrick, & Joiner, 2001; but see Schmitt & Newman, 1999), reflecting traits of shallow affectivity and self-serving exploitation of others. Ratings on Factor 2 are positively correlated with impulsivity, sensation seeking, and frequency of criminal offending (Hare, 1991; Harpur et al, 1989), and also substance abuse (Smith & Newman, 1990).

The *Diagnostic and Statistical Manual of Mental Disorders*, 4th ed. construct of antisocial personality disorder (APD; American Psychiatric Association [APA], 1994) is closely related to the behavioral but not the emotional factor of the PCL. This is because the criteria for APD consist primarily of behavioral signs and symptoms (e.g., rule-breaking, recklessness, and aggression in childhood and in adulthood). In prison settings, the prevalence of APD (70%–80%) is much higher than that of PCL-defined psychopathy (25%–30%).

CONTEMPORARY EMOTION SCIENCE:
CONCEPTS AND METHODS

Affective Response is Nonunitary: Motive Systems and Emotion Dispositions

The Unitary Activation Model

During the 1950s and 1960s, psychological theories of emotion and affiliated measurement strategies were dominated by a unitary activation perspective. Following the discovery of the general arousal function of the brainstem reticular formation (Moruzzi & Magoun, 1949), Lindsley (1951) formulated an activation theory of emotion that emphasized level of cortical arousal as the primary determinant of motivational drive. Sympathetic activation and emotional intensity were presumed to increase in direct proportion to cortical arousal, and autonomic (electrodermal, cardiovascular) and electroencephalographic activity were taken as indicants of the overall drive state.

A weakness of this unitary activation model was that it failed to account for qualitative differences in affective states and reactions. To address this issue, Hebb (1955) advanced a two-factor theory that characterized emotions as involving a directional as well as an arousal element. The direction of expression of an activated state was believed to be modulated by environmental cues that dictated a particular course of action (e.g., flight vs. attack). In a social–psychological extension of this theory, Schachter (1964) posited that the diversity of emotional experience and expression is determined by the cognitive interpretation or label attached to an undifferentiated state of arousal, as a function of the situational context of elicitation. Schachter and colleagues (Schachter & Singer, 1962; Shachter & Wheeler, 1962) demonstrated, for example, that surreptitious administration of epinephrine prompted reactions indicative of either joy or anger, depending upon whether participants were accompanied by playful or hostile confederates.

Dual-Motive Systems

In contrast to the unitary activation perspective, contemporary theories of emotion assume that affective states are differentiated at a basic functional level. Through natural selection, distinct brain systems have evolved to subserve different broad classes of self-preservative behavior. Input to these basic systems results in the priming of adaptive action dispositions, and these preparatory states are considered the essence of emotion (Izard, 1993; P. J. Lang, 1995; Plutchik, 1984): Just as the word *motive* connotes both motion- and goal-directedness, the motivated organism is one that is mobilized for strategic action (Lang, Bradley, & Cuthbert, 1990).

Furthermore, it has been theorized that the basic underlying structure of emotion is bidimensional, reflecting the operation of two brain motive systems: an aversive system governing defensive reactions, and an appetitive system governing approach and consummatory behaviors (Gray, 1987; P. J. Lang, 1995). Evidence for this position comes from several quarters. On the basis of ethological studies, Schneirla (1959) concluded that approach and withdrawal represent the basic dimensions of motivated behavior in all animal species, from the simplest to the most complex. Relatedly, Konorski (1967) concluded that exteroceptive reflexes in mammals fall into two basic categories, appetitive and aversive, mediated by reciprocally interacting motivational systems. MacLean (1958) proposed, following Papez (1937), that the core emotion centers in the brain are phylogenetically primitive subcortical structures that mediate basic defensive and appetitive behaviors.

Consistent with this dual-motive perspective, factor analyses of language descriptors of mood and emotion in humans have revealed two major dimensions, corresponding either to pleasure and arousal (Russell & Mehrabian, 1977) or positive affect (PA) and negative affect (NA; Watson & Tellegen, 1985), depending upon the rotational model. The PA/NA framework differs from the valence–arousal model in that it implies two independent arousal systems, a pleasurable activation system and an aversive activation system (cf. Tellegen, 1985). The structure of emotion ratings for discrete emotional stimuli coincides more closely with the PA/NA model: When affective and neutral pictures of diverse content (cf. Lang, Bradley, & Cuthbert, 1999) are rated using either valence/arousal descriptors (Lang, Greenwald, Bradley, & Hamm, 1993) or PA/NA descriptors (Patrick & Lavoro, 1997), the locations of pictures within the two-dimensional affect rating space follow a PA/NA alignment (i.e., rated arousal increases monotonically with either increasing picture pleasantness or increasing picture aversiveness). A similar structure has been reported for affective sounds (Bradley, Cuthbert, & Lang, 2000). The implication is that emotional reactions to phasic stimuli are driven by two separate motivational systems.

A substantial body of evidence likewise indicates that physiological reactions to affective stimuli are nonunitary. Skin conductance (electrodermal) activity, for example, increases during either pleasurable or aversive stimulation and may be regarded as an index of undifferentiated sympathetic arousal (Greenwald, Cook, & Lang, 1989; Lang et al., 1993; Venables & Christie, 1973). On the other hand, facial muscle reactions are differentially responsive to pleasant and unpleasant stimuli: Activity of the corrugator supercilli (*frown*) muscle increases selectively during aversive stimulus processing, whereas activity of the zygomaticus major (*smile*) muscle increases selectively during pleasurable stimulus processing (Cacioppo, Petty, Losch, & Kim, 1986; Fridlund, Schwartz, & Fowler, 1984; Greenwald et al., 1989; Lang et al., 1993; Schwartz, Brown, & Ahern, 1980). The startle-probe reflex (discussed more extensively below) is modulated in opposing directions by pleasurable and aversive foreground stimulation, showing inhibition and potentiation, respectively (Lang et al., 1990). These findings are again consistent with the notion of separate systems for positive and negative emotional reactivity.[1]

Emotion and Behavioral Inhibition

The PA/NA structural model, which is based on analyses of ad hoc mood ratings, posits two orthogonal affective dimensions. An implication of this model is that appetitive and defensive dispositions have the potential to coexist and to interact synergistically (Zillmann, 1983). However, other evidence indicates that appetitive and defensive drives act in opposition to one another (Konorski, 1967). A synthesis of these competing positions is that appetitive motivational tendencies can persist up to a certain level or threshold of defensive activation, beyond which the aversive system predominates (cf. Miller, 1959; Lang, Bradley, & Cuthbert, 1997).

This automatic transition from a state of appetitive engagement to one of defensive withdrawal, prompted by the detection of cues signaling danger or pain, represents an essential mechanism for interrupting and redirecting behavior in the natural environment (see Fig. 8–1). It reflects an adaptive tradeoff between two core survival tendencies, one concerned with sustenance and generativity and the other with immediate self-preservation. From this perspective, trait variations in fearfulness reflect differences in the threshold for this transition (i.e., for the interruption of ongoing behavior by signals of threat). Variations of this kind presumably arise through natural selection because priorities for exploration and goal-seeking versus self-protection differ as a function of environmental resources. From this standpoint, naturally fearless individuals (e.g., psychopaths; Hare, 1965a; Lykken, 1995), although not impervious to immediate danger or pain, should be less readily moved toward avoidance or withdrawal from states of appetitive approach or engagement.

Affective Processing is Nonunitary: Cognitive–Emotion Interactions

Hierarchical Conceptualization of Emotion

A second key point arising from recent biobehavioral research on emotion is that there are different pathways by which stimulus information can reach the core motivational systems and therefore varying levels or modes

---

[1]Cardiovascular responses to emotional stimuli can covary with either affective valence or arousal, depending upon the eliciting circumstances (Lang et al., 1990; Miller, Patrick, & Levenston, 2002). Covariation between electrocortical activity and emotional response is similarly complex. For example, the amplitude of phasic (event-related potentials) reactions to pictures appears to covary primarily with stimulus arousal (Cuthbert, Schupp, Bradley, Birbaumer, & Lang, 2000), whereas frontal electroencephalographic asymmetry (i.e., relative right versus left hemispheric activation) during affective film viewing appears to differ as a function of emotional valence (cf. Davidson, 1992).

Behavioral Inhibition:

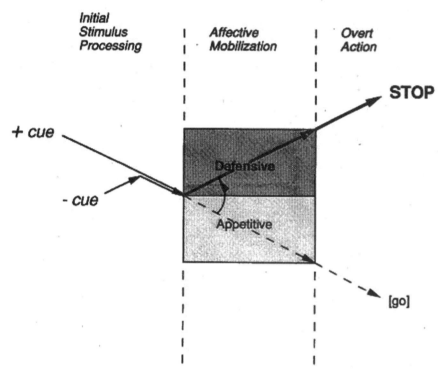

FIGURE 8–1.   Schematic representation of the mechanism by which behavior in the natural environment is interrupted by signals of threat. In the figure, the detection of a threat activates the defensive motivational ("stop") system, leading to inhibition of the ongoing appetitive ("go") response.

of emotional processing. Affective reactions can be elicited by cues ranging from simple sensory events to complex semantic/linguistic information. For example, negative affect can be instigated by an unconditioned stimulus such as a shock or pinprick or by a threat cue that is immediate and explicit, for example, by the physical presence of an assailant or an aimed weapon. Negative emotional reactions can also be evoked by cues or events that are remote or indirect: a film depicting the pursuit of an unsuspecting victim; a lurid verbal description of a physical injury; the wail of a siren as one exceeds the speed limit; the scent of diesel fuel attached to memories of war; or fleeting thoughts or images of incapacitation or failure.

In this regard, P. J. Lang (1979) hypothesized some time ago that associative memory networks might include emotion "nodes" (i.e., links to affective response systems) in addition to iconic and conceptual representations, so that mere remembrance of a traumatic or exhilarating experience can

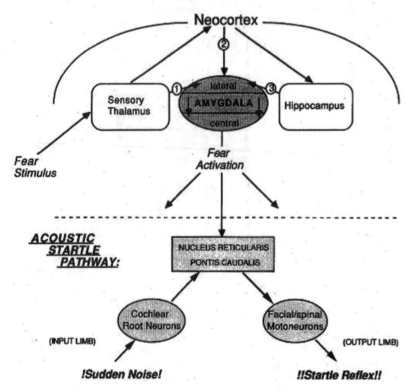

FIGURE 8–2.   See caption on next page.

prompt a relevant emotional set. In the intervening years, neuroscience researchers have generated insights into the mechanisms by which cues of varying complexity can trigger emotional reactions. The present discussion focuses on mechanisms and levels of fear processing because the emotion of fear has been of particular interest to psychopathy researchers and because a well-developed neural model of fear processing now exists.

Substantial evidence indicates that the subcortical amygdaloid complex is the heart of the defensive (fear) system (see Davis, 1992; Fanselow, 1994; LeDoux, 1995). The motor output system of the amygdala is the central nucleus, which projects to other brain structures that directly mediate fear expression and behavior (e.g., central grey and lateral hypothalamus). When the central nucleus of the amygdala is activated, defensive mobilization occurs. However, sensory information reaches the amygdala via its lateral and basolateral nuclei, which in turn project to the central nucleus. The

FIGURE 8–2.   The upper part of this figure, adapted from LeDoux (1995), depicts some of the neural pathways by which sensory stimulation is believed to elicit fear activation. The lateral nucleus of the amygdala receives processed stimulus input from "higher" brain regions including the sensory association cortex, perirhinal cortex, and hippocampus, as well as direct input from extralemniscal areas of the sensory thalamus. The direct thalamic–amygdaloid pathway [1] is sufficient to mediate explicit fear conditioning involving a simple conditioned stimulus (CS)–unconditioned stimulus (US) pairing (Romanski & LeDoux, 1992); sensory cortical regions and presumably thalamic–cortical-amygdaloid pathways [2], are needed for differential conditioning involving dual (paired and unpaired) CSs (Jarrell, Gentile, Romanski, McCabe, & Schneiderman, 1987); the hippocampal formation and by inference the hippocampal–amygdaloid pathway [3], appears to be necessary for contextual fear learning (Kim, Rison, & Fanselow, 1993; Phillips & LeDoux, 1992; Selden, Everitt, Jarrard, & Robbins, 1991). The central nucleus of the amygdala projects to various behavioral systems involved in fear expression, including the central gray (freezing and active defense; Fanselow, 1994), lateral hypothalamus (sympathetic autonomic reactions; Iwata, Chida, & LeDoux, 1987), and pontine reticular formation (startle reflex potentiation; Davis, 1996). The lower part of the figure depicts the trisynaptic circuit believed to underlie the primary acoustic startle reflex (cf. Davis, 1996). The mechanism for fear-potentiated startle is a modulatory pathway from the central nucleus of the amygdala to the nucleus reticularis pontis caudalis. This model is based on pharmacological and lesion studies conducted by Davis and colleagues (e.g., Boulis & Davis, 1989; Hitchcock & Davis, 1986; Lee, Lopez, Meloni, & Davis, 1996; Rosen, Hitchcock, Sananes, Miserendino, & Davis, 1991).

lateral–basolateral complex is thus considered the input substation of the amygdala. Focusing on the lateral nucleus, LeDoux (1995) noted that this structure receives inputs from the sensory thalamus and from perceptual processing regions of the neocortex.[2] Additionally, the lateral nucleus receives projections from higher representational systems, including the hippocampal formation (see Fig. 8–2, upper part). The hippocampus is a cornerstone of complex cognitive functions, including declarative memory (Squire, 1992) and related spatial, contextual, and associative functions (e.g., Nadel & Willner, 1980; Rudy & Sutherland, 1992). Connections between the hippocampus and the amygdala thereby provide one mechanism by which higher-order cognitive activities can instigate or moderate affective reactions, in a "top-down" fashion (LeDoux, 1995).

Relevant to this conceptualization, animal neuroscience studies have revealed striking dissociations between different fear-learning capabilities following surgical lesioning of the hippocampus. Specifically, hippocampal lesions produce selective impairment of contextual fear conditioning without affecting explicit fear conditioning (Kim et al., 1993; Phillips & LeDoux, 1992). Control rats, after being placed in a distinctive new environment and receiving shock in the presence of a tone conditioned stimulus (CS), display a fear reac-

---

[2]LeDoux's work deals primarily with auditory conditioned fear (i.e., pairing of shock with a tone CS). The basolateral region of the amygdala may be more important for conditioning in other modalities (e.g., visual; Davis & Lee, 1998).

tion not only to the explicit CS but also to the learning context, as evidenced by freezing behavior upon being returned to the training environment in which shock was administered. In contrast, rats with hippocampal lesions exhibit freezing to the tone CS, but not to the context itself. These data are consistent with the neuroanatomic model described earlier in that projections from the thalamus and auditory cortex to the amygdala can be viewed as sufficient to mediate fear conditioning to a simple tone cue, whereas associations between more complex environmental information and fear reactivity appear to depend upon the integrity of hippocampal–amygdaloid connections (LeDoux, 1995).[3]

Neuroscience findings such as these encourage a hierarchical conceptualization of emotional processing in which higher brain regions interact with subcortical motive systems. Moreover, the work of LeDoux (1995) suggested that fear can be elicited in diverse ways: On one hand, by simple sensory cues that activate the amygdala through direct thalamoamygdaloid pathways and, on the other hand, by more complex cues (including contexts, linguistic cues, memories, and images) that operate through "top-down" neural pathways. It has been hypothesized that parallel cortical–subcortical circuits underlie positive emotional processing (P. J. Lang, 1994), but substantial work remains to be done in this area (LeDoux, 1995). A central subcortical system, analogous to the amygdaloid fear system, may exist for appetitive motivation. Alternatively, the appetitive system may be fundamentally variegated, with distinct subsystems mediating different appetites (e.g., hunger, thirst, sex, affiliation, and so forth). A third, integrative possibility is that distinct appetitive subsystems exist, but their deployment is regulated by a broader system that governs attention–allocation and goal-seeking (cf. Berridge & Robinson, 1998; Gray, 1987; Lang et al., 1997).

Levels of Emotional Processing

This conceptualization encourages a differentiated perspective on affective processing: Different brain systems participate in the detection and analysis of emotional cues as a function of stimulus modality and complexity and the context of emotion evocation. For example, physiological activation during imagery of text descriptions of emotional events (e.g., Lang, Levin, Miller, & Kozak, 1983; Miller et al., 1987) can be attributed to top-down activation of subcortical motive systems by declarative memory structures (P. J. Lang, 1994). Mood state-dependent memory effects (Blaney, 1986; Bower, 1981;

---

[3]It should be noted that other emotion centers in addition to the amygdala may be involved in mediating contextual fear. Davis and Lee (1998) have presented evidence that the bed nucleus of the stria terminalis, a structure that, like the amygdala, projects to output systems involved in negative affective expression and receives input from the hippocampus, plays a role in anxiety reactions not linked to simple, explicit cues. Although this research has focused on separate phenomena (i.e., light-enhanced startle; CRH-enhanced startle), it is conceivable that this "anxiety" system plays an important role in contextual aversive conditioning.

Eich, 1995) can be conceptualized similarly: Because cognitive systems are interconnected with emotion systems, the elicitation of a distinct mood state can serve as a "prime" for declarative memories acquired under parallel mood conditions.

The hierarchical perspective thus accommodates the idea that cognitive factors, including learning history, ongoing information processing, and perceptions of the eliciting context can influence emotional state. However, in contrast to traditional appraisal theories of emotion (e.g., Lazarus, 1982; Schachter, 1964), the hierarchical model presumes that cognitive operations shape the expression of differentiated motive tendencies, as opposed to undifferentiated arousal. From this perspective, discrete affective states (Ekman, 1992; Izard, 1993) are viewed as context-molded variants of the core *strategic* (appetitive, defensive) action dispositions (Lang et al., 1990). Furthermore, the current conceptualization does not assume the "primacy" of either cognition or affect (Lazarus, 1984; Zajonc, 1984). Affect can precede and modulate information processing (P. J. Lang, 1994; LeDoux, 1995; Öhman, 1993; Zajonc, 1980), as well as the reverse.

The hierarchical conceptualization also provides a framework for thinking about automatic affective processing and "bottom-up" effects of emotional priming on cognition. For example, Öhman and Soares (1993, 1994) demonstrated that pictorial images of snakes evoke measurable physiological reactions in phobic humans even when presented under conditions (i.e., rapid, masked exposure) that preclude accurate recognition. The existence of direct pathways from perceptual processing centers to the amygdala provides a mechanism whereby sensory cues might trigger a defensive reaction in the absence of conscious awareness (Öhman, 1993). LeDoux (1995) argued that the capacity for "automatic" fear processing of this kind is adaptive because it permits the organism to prepare rapidly for evasive action at the first sign of threat; at the same time, however, this capacity may play a significant role in pathological anxiety conditions in which defensive reactions arise unpredictably and uncontrollably.

This conceptual framework suggests that different types of emotional processing deviations, associated with different neural systems, can contribute to disinhibitory psychopathology. Evidence to be reviewed in the following sections suggests, for example, that the two correlated factors of psychopathy assessed by Hare's PCL–R may reflect distinctly different anomalies in affective processing.

Measuring Affective Valence: The Startle Modulation Paradigm

Startle Potentiation as an Index of Defensive (Fear) Activation

The foregoing neural model of fear has its origins in aversive conditioning experiments with animals. However, important links have been made to the human literature. One point of intersection is the phenomenon of fear-potentiated startle (Davis, 1989, 1996). Animal work has shown that the reflexive startle reaction to a sudden, intense event (e.g., an abrupt noise) increases during exposure to threatening or aversive stimuli. Brown, Kalish, and Farber (1951) reported that startle reactions to sudden noise stimuli in rats were larger during presentation of a cue for shock (CS+) than during exposure to a neutral cue (CS−), and this effect has been consistently replicated in subsequent studies (cf. Davis, 1989, 1996).

Vrana, Spence, and Lang (1988) investigated the eyeblink component of the startle reflex as an index of affective responding in humans. Emotional states were manipulated by presenting pleasant, neutral, and unpleasant slides to participants; acoustic startle probes (i.e., sudden noise bursts) were delivered during some of the slide-viewing periods to elicit reflexive blink reactions. Consistent with animal findings, blink reactions were found to be potentiated during exposure to unpleasant slides (e.g., snakes, mutilations, or aimed guns) compared with neutral slides. Furthermore, blink magnitude was attenuated during exposure to pleasant slides (e.g., smiling babies or nudes), indicating a bidirectional effect of foreground stimulus pleasantness on the startle reflex. This finding has been replicated in many subsequent studies (cf. P. J. Lang, 1995; Lang et al., 1990, 1997).

Valence-related modulation of the startle probe response was first observed in human participants viewing affective pictures, but this effect has since been demonstrated using evocative film clips (Jansen & Frijda, 1994) as well as pleasant and unpleasant odors (Miltner, Matjak, Braun, Diekmann, & Brody, 1994). Startle reflex potentiation has also been demonstrated during mental imagery of frightening events (Vrana & Lang, 1990) and during anticipation of electric shock (Hamm, Greenwald, Bradley, & Lang, 1993; Grillon, Ameli, Woods, Merikangas, & Davis, 1991).

The fact that the protective startle reflex is potentiated during aversive emotional processing can be understood from the *behavioral* perspective of fear as defensive action readiness. Lang et al. (1990) theorized that emotionally evocative stimuli (e.g., pleasant or unpleasant pictures) prime one or the other motivational system, resulting in approach or withdrawal mobilization. Depending upon the direction of the activated response tendency, the protective reflex response to a sudden, startling noise is increased or attenuated. Unpleasant pictures instigate a defensive action state that is synchronous with the reaction to the noxious noise probe, resulting in reflex potentiation. In this regard, Lang et al. (1990) likened the fear-activated organism to a cocked pistol. Conversely, pleasant stimuli trigger an approach tendency that is antagonistic to the defensive probe reflex, resulting in startle reflex inhibition.

This response match–mismatch interpretation is readily reconciled with the *neurobiological* circuitry underlying fear-potentiated startle, which has been precisely mapped in animals. Davis and his colleagues (e.g., Boulis & Davis, 1989; Hitchcock & Davis, 1986; Lee et al., 1996; Rosen et al., 1991) established that two interacting neural circuits mediate fear-potentiated acoustic startle in rats (see Fig. 8–2, lower part). The primary brainstem startle circuit involves transmission of input from the auditory receptors to spinal and facial muscle effectors via the nucleus reticularis pontis caudalis. Lesioning or blocking of this primary pathway results in overall suppression of the startle reflex. Potentiation of the primary reflex by fear, however, is achieved via a modulatory pathway consisting of monosynaptic projections from the central nucleus of the amygdala to the pontine reticular nucleus; through this route, fear-relevant stimuli that activate the amygdala prime the startle response. Lesions of this pathway selectively abolish fear-potentiated startle, leaving the primary reflex intact.

If startle potentiation during unpleasant slide viewing in humans and fear-potentiated startle in animals is mediated by a common defensive state, this potentiation effect should be attenuated or eliminated by drugs that are known to reduce fear or anxiety. Consistent with this hypothesis, Patrick, Berthot, and Moore (1996) found that diazepam (Valium), a commonly prescribed anxiolytic, blocked the effect: Participants administered a placebo pill exhibited robust startle potentiation during exposure to unpleasant slides compared with neutral slides, but this effect was small and unreliable in individuals administered 10 mg of diazepam and completely absent in a 15-mg drug group. This finding replicates, in humans, prior research by Davis (1979) showing that diazepam blocks fear-potentiated startle in animals.

As an index of fear reactivity, the phenomenon of potentiated startle has unique practical and conceptual value. Because a precise neurobiological model exists for this effect, it permits specific inferences about brain mechanisms. Furthermore, unlike autonomic or facial responses, which are elicited by the emotional stimulus itself (e.g., slide), the probe reflex is a separate reaction to an intervening event. Its potentiation or inhibition reveals something about the ongoing motivational process in time. Because the reflex is immediate and because probe stimuli can be introduced at any point, the startle probe response can be used to precisely track a developing affective process from its onset to its completion (cf. Bradley, Cuthbert, & Lang, 1993; Levenston & Patrick, 1995). Furthermore, as an automatic response to an unwarned probe, the startle reflex is potentially less susceptible than facial electromyographic indices of emotional valence to the biasing effects of experimental demand (Fridlund, Ekman, & Oster, 1986) and deliberate faking (Craig, Hyde, & Patrick, 1991).

Startle Inhibition as an Index of Appetitive
Activation and Orienting

Lang et al. (1990) proposed that the attenuation of startle that reliably occurs during viewing of pleasant pictures reflects appetitive system activation: Pleasant pictures elicit a state of appetitive–approach that is antagonistic to the defensive startle reaction, resulting in reflex inhibition. Subsequently, Lang et al. (1997) theorized that foreground attentional engagement (perceptual orienting) may also be important to this inhibition effect. This position is supported by at least three lines of evidence. The first is that startle reflex inhibition occurs most reliably during *perceptual* processing of positive valence stimuli. Imaginal processing of pleasant scenes, even scenes that are highly arousing (Witvliet & Vrana, 1995) or personally relevant (Miller, Patrick, & Levenston, 2002), does not lead to inhibition of startle.

A second pertinent finding is that normal individuals show attenuated startle reactivity for *both* pleasurable and aversive pictures early in the viewing interval. During the first few hundred milliseconds after a picture is presented, there is a general inhibition of the acoustic probe reflex. This early *prepulse effect* (described by Graham, 1975 as a gating-out of new input to protect processing of the preceding stimulus) subsequently gives way to startle facilitation for stimuli that are aversive. As a demonstration of this facilitation, Bradley et al. (1993) assessed blink responses to noise probes occurring 300, 800, 1,300, and 3,800 ms after picture onset. Probe reactions were generally smaller at 300 and 800 ms, implying enhanced processing protection early in the viewing interval. Furthermore, at 300 ms, startle reactions were smaller for both pleasant and unpleasant pictures than for neutral pictures, indicating rapid discrimination and enhanced processing protection for motivationally relevant stimuli (Lang et al., 1997). By 800 ms, startle reflex potentiation was evident for unpleasant pictures, signifying an ascendance of defensive priming—an effect that became more robust at later probe times (1,300 and 3,800 ms).

Other relevant evidence comes from a study by Cuthbert, Bradley, and Lang (1996) in which skin conductance and startle–probe reactions were both assessed during viewing of pleasant and unpleasant pictures that varied in rated arousal. For both picture types, skin conductance response (a nonspecific index of activation; Greenwald et al., 1989) increased monotonically with picture intensity. For pleasant pictures, startle magnitude *decreased* monotonically with increasing stimulus arousal. For unpleasant pictures, startle decreased up to an intermediate level of picture intensity, but at higher arousal levels aversive pictures produced increasing startle *potentiation*. The interpretation was that less intense aversive scenes engage attention and compete with noise probe processing (Anthony & Graham, 1985) but that defensive priming overrides the modulatory effect of attention as scenes become more potent.

Based on these and other data, Lang et al. (1997) proposed that attention is more readily engaged by environmental cues that are motivationally meaningful, whether pleasant or aversive, than by routine or neutral stimuli. For aversive cues, however, attentional orienting gives way automatically to defense, as the cues become increasingly intense. Citing Fanselow's (1994) predator imminence model of defensive behavior, Lang et al. theorized that this transition occurs in stages, with orienting and defensive dispositions coexisting at intermediate levels of cue intensity, but shifting to pure defense (active fight or flight) when danger is imminent. This staged transition is presumed to reflect an adaptive tradeoff between two core survival tendencies, appetitive approach and defensive withdrawal or attack. A central hypothesis, developed below, is that the threshold of transition from orienting to defense is higher in individuals with traits of psychopathy than in normal individuals.

Affective Traits: Emotion, Temperament, and Personality

Another important development in the field of emotion science has been the delineation of connections between affective states and personality traits. Tellegen (1985) proposed that the affective dimensions of PA and NA have their counterparts in two broad temperament dimensions that he termed *positive emotionality* (PEM) and *negative emotionality* (NEM). PEM was conceptualized as reward sensitivity and proneness to states of pleasurable engagement, whereas NEM was conceptualized as sensitivity to stress and proneness to negative emotion. Tellegen showed that questionnaire scores on PEM and NEM reliably predict the frequency of positive and negative mood states assessed via self-report. Other research (e.g., Larsen & Ketelaar, 1991) has shown that the closely related trait dimensions of extraversion and neuroticism predict individuals' sensitivity to the impact of manipulations of positive and negative affective state. From the perspective of emotional states as action dispositions mediated by core brain systems, this work suggests the possibility of referencing personality traits to underlying biological systems and processes.

Tellegen (1982, in press) developed the Multidimensional Personality Questionnaire (MPQ) to assess personality traits in the emotion–temperament domain. The MPQ comprises 11 primary trait scales that coalesce around three higher order factors (see Table 8–1): the PEM and NEM dimensions mentioned above, and a third Constraint (CON) factor, reflecting behavioral restraint as opposed to impulsivity and disinhibition. An alternative, four-factor structure of the MPQ has also been reported (Tellegen & Waller, 1992), in which PEM bifurcates into two distinct interpersonal facets: Agentic PEM, reflecting a disposition to seek fulfillment via dominance and status (i.e., Achievement, Social Potency, and Wellbeing scales load on this factor), and Communal PEM, reflecting a disposition to seek fulfillment through affiliation and connectedness with others (i.e., loadings of Social Closeness and Wellbeing scales).

Consistent with the notion that the MPQ scales index basic temperament constructs, human behavior genetic studies have revealed the various traits and factors assessed by the MPQ to be substantially heritable. For example, in a study of monozygotic and dizygotic twins, Tellegen, Lykken, Bouchard, Wilcox, Segal, and Rich (1988) reported significant genetic variance components for all MPQ primary traits (range = .39−.55), as well as for the three higher-order MPQ factors (range = .40−.58). More recently, Krueger (2000) reported close correspondence between the phenotypic, three-factor structure of the MPQ and the structure of the genetic variance of the individual trait scales, extracted via Cholesky decomposition (Neale & Cardon, 1992). Correlations between phenotypic PEM, NEM, and CON factor scores and scores on the corresponding genotypic factors were .97, .96, and .98, respectively.

It should be noted that the structural model of personality represented by Tellegen's MPQ is complementary to that of the well-known five-factor model, represented by Costa and McCrae's (1985) NEO Personality Inventory. In a joint factor analysis of the two inventories, Church (1994) showed

TABLE 8–1.
Multidimensional Personality Questionnaire (Tellegen, 1982, in press):
Scale Descriptions

MPQ Scale	Description of a High Scorer
[Positive Emotionality:]	
Wellbeing	Happy, cheerful; likes self; optimistic
Social Potency	Forceful, persuasive; enjoys leadership
Achievement	Ambitious, works hard; seeks challenge
Social Closeness	Sociable, affiliative; seeks consolation
[Negative Emotionality:]	
Stress Reaction	Nervous, sensitive; prone to worry
Alienation	Feels mistreated, victimized, betrayed
Aggression	Vengeful; hurts others for own gain
[Constraint:]	
Control	Cautious, planful, reflective
Harm Avoidance	Avoids danger; prefers safety to excitement
Traditionalism	Conventional, conservative, moralistic
Absorption	Imaginative; engaged by sights/sounds

Note. Trait scales are grouped according to the higher order factor (in brackets) on which they principally load. Absorption does not load primarily on any one factor; it shows moderate loadings on both PEM and NEM. From "Brief Manual for the Multidimensional Personality Questionnaire" by A. Tellgen, Unpublished manuscript, University of Minnesota.

that NEM encompasses Neuroticism and Agreeableness (reversed), PEM involves Extraversion and achieving/surgent aspects of Conscientiousness, and CON encompasses impulse-control aspects of Conscientiousness along with elements of Openness to Experience (reversed). In our own work we use the MPQ because we are interested in psychopathy from the standpoint of emotion and temperament, and these constructs serve as benchmarks for the MPQ structural model. In this regard, empirical studies (reviewed later) have revealed patterns of relationships between the two factors of Hare's (1991, 2003) PCL–R and the MPQ that coincide with relationships observed for indices of emotional reactivity.

PSYCHOPATHY AND EMOTIONAL REACTIVITY

Theoretical Perspectives

Cleckley (1976) maintained that the true ("primary") psychopath is incapable of genuine emotional reactions, either positive or negative. As noted earlier, Hare (1965a) hypothesized that psychopathy involves a specific deficiency in fear, a position also maintained by Lykken (1957, 1995). Relatedly, Fowles

(1980) postulated that psychopaths have a deficient behavioral inhibition (punishment) system (Gray, 1987) but a normal behavioral activation (reward) system. Much of the empirical research on affective reactivity in psychopaths has been directed to evaluating this low fear hypothesis, and a good deal of supportive evidence has accumulated. The most consistent findings have been that psychopathic offenders show attenuated skin conductance reactions to anticipatory cues or conditioned stimuli signaling shock or aversive noise and poor passive avoidance learning (see reviews by Hare, 1970, 1978, 1986; Lykken, 1957, 1995; Siddle & Trasler, 1981).

The finding of diminished electrodermal response to threat cues in psychopaths can be interpreted in varying ways, however. As noted earlier, skin conductance is a nonspecific index of sympathetic arousal that reflects negative affect only indirectly. Neuroimaging research indicates that cortical systems play a direct role in the regulation of electrodermal activity (Tranel & Damasio, 1994), and psychophysiological studies have suggested that awareness of the CS-unconditioned stimulus contingency is necessary for electrodermal fear conditioning (Dawson & Schell, 1985) but not for conditioned startle potentiation (Hamm & Vaitl, 1996). Thus, an alternative to the low-fear interpretation of reduced skin conductance reactivity in psychopaths is that it reflects an absence of normal cognitive and attentional processing during anticipation of an affectively potent event (Miller, Curtin, & Patrick, 1999).

The finding of impaired passive avoidance learning in psychopaths is also subject to varying interpretation. The passive avoidance learning task is inherently a conflict paradigm, in that the participant must learn to suppress a previously rewarded behavior in the face of cues for punishment. Consequently, a deficiency in passive avoidance learning could reflect either heightened appetitive reactivity or reduced punishment sensitivity (Newman & Kosson, 1986; Newman, Widom, & Nathan, 1985; Patterson & Newman, 1993). Furthermore, because passive avoidance is a complex form of learning involving concurrent processing of competing cues, deficits in this task might well reflect impairments in higher analytic capacities rather than excesses or deficits in core motive systems (LeDoux, 1995; see Alcohol and Fear Reduction section).

There are also indications that these effects are not confined to individuals manifesting the classic Cleckley profile. Raine (1993), reviewing the literature on electrodermal fear conditioning in varied criminal offender groups (including nonincarcerated juvenile delinquents and unselected adult offenders as well as incarcerated psychopaths), concluded that "poor conditioning is related to the general development of antisocial behavior" (p. 220). Similarly, passive avoidance learning deficits have been reported in juvenile offenders selected for high scores on antisociality questionnaires (e.g., Minnesota Multiphasic Personality Inventory Pd scale; Newman et al., 1985) and in nonpsychopathic adult criminals classified as *secondary sociopaths* (Lykken, 1957). These findings suggest some complexities in the relationships of these experimental procedures to fear response and to psychopathy.

Another body of empirical research has focused on cognitive and attentional disturbances in psychopathy. One hypothesis has been that psychopaths are generally less able to process peripheral events when attending to stimuli of immediate interest (Jutai & Hare, 1983; Kosson & Newman, 1986). However, the evidence for this simple "overfocusing" hypothesis has been mixed (Kosson & Harpur, 1997; Newman & Wallace, 1993). A more refined perspective is that psychopathy involves a diminished ability to process peripheral features of stimuli in divided-attention tasks involving prioritization of attention to specified dimensions of a compound cue; Kosson (1996, 1998) presented evidence in support of this position. Relatedly, Newman, Schmitt, and Voss (1997) reported that psychopaths failed to show a normal response delay in matching a target stimulus to a prime when interfering contextual information was presented concurrently with the prime.

Other work suggests that affective and attentional deviations in psychopathy could be interrelated. Christianson et al. (1996) reported that nonpsychopathic prisoners and normal participants showed poorer recall for a peripheral detail of an accident photo than for a central detail, whereas psychopaths showed no such memory difference. The implication was that the attentional processing of psychopaths was not constrained by affective, elaborative processing of the central accident image. Williamson, Harpur, and Hare. (1991) reported that psychopaths discriminated pleasant, neutral, and unpleasant words from nonwords as quickly and accurately as nonpsychopaths, but they did not differentiate between neutral and emotional words in either reaction time or event-related potentials (P240 and P600), implying a deficiency in early "motivated attention" (Lang et al., 1997).

Explicit Emotional Stimuli and Startle Reflex Modulation

Affective Picture Processing

Research with the startle probe reflex as an index of defensive activation has helped to clarify relations between psychopathy and fear reactivity. Patrick et al. (1993) examined eyeblink startle reactions to unwarned noise probes during viewing of pleasant, neutral, and unpleasant slides in criminal offender groups classified using Hare's (1991) PCL–R. Groups comprised equal numbers of psychopathic (PCL–R ≥ 30), nonpsychopathic (PCL–R <20), and "mixed" (i.e., moderately psychopathic) adult male sex offenders ($N = 54$). The stimuli were 27 color slides (9 of each valence) selected from the International Affective Picture System (Lang et al., 1999). Slides were presented for 6 s each, with varying (10–20 s) intertrial intervals. Acoustic probes were 50-ms, 95 dB(A) bursts of white noise, delivered binaurally through headphones at intervals of either 3.5, 4.5, or 5.5 s following slide onset. Blink responses to the noise probes were recorded from the orbicularis muscle beneath the left eye.

The groups did not differ in overall startle blink magnitude. To ensure that participants contributed equally to group patterns, startle modulation effects were analyzed using scores that were standardized across trials within participants. Statistical analyses revealed a normal, linear pattern of startle modulation in both the nonpsychopathic and mixed groups, with blink reactions being larger during unpleasant slides and smaller during pleasant slides, relative to neutral slides. In contrast, psychopaths showed an abnormal quadratic startle pattern, with blink responses attenuated during both pleasant and unpleasant slides compared with neutral slides.

In light of the animal and human data linking startle reflex potentiation to fear, the absence of this effect in psychopaths during unpleasant picture processing (a finding also reported by Mejia, Vanman, Dawson, Raine, & Lencz, 1997) suggests a weakness in the capacity of an aversive stimulus to prime defensive actions—in this context, to intensify a protective reflex, but perhaps more broadly to interrupt goal-seeking and to promote avoidance of danger. Regarding positive (appetitive) emotional reactivity, psychopaths in this study did not differ from nonpsychopaths or mixed participants in their reactions to pleasant slides: All groups showed normal startle inhibition during pleasant compared with neutral slide viewing. Thus, the findings of this experiment as a whole were consistent with the hypothesis that "primary" psychopathy is characterized by weak defensive responsivity but at least normal reactivity to appetitive stimuli (cf. Fowles, 1980; Hare, 1965a, 1978; Lykken, 1995).

However, an intriguing question was why psychopaths showed relative *inhibition* of startle during aversive picture viewing, a pattern that might be interpreted as evidence of appetitive activation (Lang et al., 1990). Subsequent research on the parameters of affect-modulated startle suggests that this pattern may instead have reflected a predominance of foreground attention over defensive reactivity. In normal individuals, the startle probe reflex is inhibited for both pleasant and aversive pictures during the earliest stages of picture processing, reflecting immediate prioritization of attention to stimuli of motivational significance (Bradley et al., 1993). As processing continues, pictures with aversive connotations prime the defensive system, producing startle potentiation (Cuthbert et al., 1996). This later-processing potentiation is maximal for potent, directly threatening pictures (Balaban & Taussig, 1994; Levenston & Patrick, 1995).

These findings indicate that the startle reflex is sensitive to the dynamic interplay of attention and emotion during picture viewing. Viewed in this light, blink inhibition during aversive picture viewing in psychopaths could reflect a predominance of attentional modulation in the absence of the defensive activation that normally emerges across time and with increasing picture intensity. Pertinent to this hypothesis are data from a study by Levenston, Patrick, Bradley, and Lang (2000) that examined startle responses in male prisoners during viewing of neutral pictures and discrete categories of aversive and pleasant pictures. The aversive picture categories included depictions of direct threat (aimed weapons and menacing attackers) and victimization (assaults on others and injured people). The pleasant categories were erotic pictures (nudes and intimate couples) and risky adventure ("thrill") pictures (e.g., roller coasters and cliff diving). Noise probes occurred both

early (300 and 800 ms; cf. Bradley et al., 1993) and late in the viewing interval (1,800, 3,000, and 4,500 ms).

Replicating the results of Patrick et al (1993), contrasting startle modulation
patterns were observed for high versus low PCL–R scorers: Nonpsychopathic
prisoners showed blink potentiation for unpleasant pictures beginning at 800
ms, but psychopaths showed reflex inhibition for both pleasant and unpleasant pictures compared with neutral pictures. For specific contents, nonpsychopaths showed moderate potentiation for victim scenes, strong potentiation
for threat, and inhibition only for erotic pictures (with modest potentiation for
thrill scenes). For psychopaths, startle was *inhibited* during victim scenes and
only weakly potentiated during threat (see Fig. 8–3). Psychopaths also showed
reliable reflex inhibition for both erotic and thrill scenes.

These group differences were interpreted with reference to the normal
directional shift that occurs in startle modulation—from inhibition to potentiation, reflecting an ascendance of defensive reflex priming over attentional

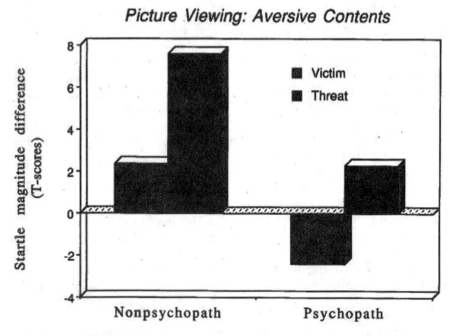

FIGURE 8–3.   Mean startle response magnitude to noise probes presented during
victim and threat pictures, depicted as the difference from the mean during neutral
pictures. Victim pictures include scenes of injury/mutilation and physical assaults on
other people; threat pictures include scenes of aimed weapons and looming attackers;
neutral pictures include scenes of inactive people, household objects, and plants.
Results are for two groups of male prisoners, psychopaths and nonpsychopaths ($n =$
18 per group). Blink magnitude is expressed in T-score units, computed by standard-
izing raw magnitude scores across trials within participants (for details, see Levenston, Patrick, Bradley, & Lang, 2000).

modulation—as aversive foregrounds become increasingly intense (Cuthbert et al., 1996). In normal individuals, "victim" scenes are nearer the threshold of transition than "threat" pictures: They engage more attention (Sarlo, Palomba, Angrilli, and Stegagno, 1998) and yield weaker startle potentiation (Balaban & Taussig, 1994; Lang, 1995). That psychopaths showed startle inhibition during victim scenes implies that attentive engagement (orienting) was the predominant reaction of these individuals to these less potent scenes. The weak potentiation for threat pictures indicates that in psychopaths, defensive reactivity only began to supersede orienting at a level of aversive cue intensity at which nonpsychopaths (and normal individuals; e.g., Levenston & Patrick, 1995) showed predominantly defensive mobilization.

Group effects for erotic and thrill contents were interpreted similarly: For purely pleasurable erotic pictures, both groups showed attentional inhibition; for adventure scenes entailing excitement and risk, psychopaths showed attentional inhibition, whereas nonpsychopaths showed modest defensive potentiation. From a "motivated attention" standpoint (Lang et al., 1997), the implication is that psychopaths have a higher threshold of transition from orienting to defense, such that aversive cues must be more intense to prime a defensive disposition (see Fig. 8–4).

However, an interesting twist on this interpretation was suggested by a group difference at the earliest (300 ms) probe time. Nonpsychopaths showed enhanced reflex inhibition for affective pictures (both pleasant and unpleasant) compared with neutral pictures at this early probe time. This result, which is the expected normal pattern (Bradley et al., 1993), reflects rapid discrimination and enhanced processing protection for motivationally relevant stimuli (Lang et al., 1997). In contrast to nonpsychopaths and normal participants, psychopaths did not show evidence of this effect until the next later probe time (800 ms), implying a delay in "recognition" of the motivational significance of these stimuli (Lang et al., 1997, 1998).

In view of other work indicating that psychopaths process affective stimuli in a superficial, undifferentiated fashion (Christianson et al., 1996; Williamson et al., 1991), the early probe results reported by Levenston et al. (2000) could signify a deficit in the early, automatic detection of affect-relevant stimuli (i.e., motivated attention; Lang et al., 1997). The abnormal attentional startle pattern shown by psychopaths late in the viewing interval might in turn arise from this early processing deficit (i.e., reflecting more a ratiocinative than an affective evaluation of content). This interpretation is compatible with the low-fear hypothesis, but it is also potentially broader, in that it could encompass appetitive as well as defensive response representations (cf. Cleckley, 1976). This hypothesis could be directly tested by assessing early brain potential responses to affective slides in psychopathic individuals (cf. Cuthbert, Schupp, Bradley, Birbaumer, & Lang, 2000; Williamson et al., 1991).

It should be noted that the Levenston et al. (2000) study focused on psychopathic individuals who scored high on both factors of the PCL–R. Evidence reviewed in the next section indicates that late-interval startle modulation

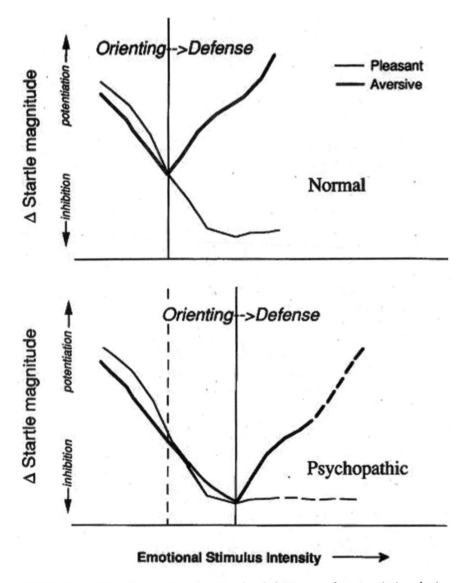

FIGURE 8–4. Hypothesized mechanism for deficient startle potentiation during aversive picture processing in psychopathic individuals. According to the model, psychopaths have a higher-than-normal threshold for shifting from attentional orienting to defense (Levenston et al., 2000).

effects are related specifically to Factor 1 of the PCL–R ("emotional detachment"). This raises the possibility that different facets of psychopathy could have accounted for different group effects in the Levenston et al. study. For example, it is conceivable that deficient late startle potentiation for aversive scenes was associated mainly with high emotional detachment, whereas separate traits associated with overall psychopathy or with the antisocial factor accounted for the early attentional differences. Further research using groups selected for elevations on one or the other PCL–R factor will be needed to resolve this issue.

Diagnostic Features of Psychopathy Associated With Deviant Startle Modulation

A post hoc dissection of groups in the Patrick et al. (1993) study revealed that abnormal startle modulation was especially marked among individuals who scored highest on Factor 1 of the PCL–R. When participants with high "antisocial behavior" scores (i.e., at least two thirds of the possible maximum on PCL–R Factor 2) were subdivided into those low and high on Factor 1 (emotional detachment), only the "detached-antisocial" group showed a deviant pattern of startle modulation. Offenders with high scores on the behavioral factor of psychopathy only ("simple antisocial" group, most of whom, like the detached-antisocial group, met the diagnostic criteria for antisocial personality disorder) showed normal startle potentiation during aversive slide viewing (see Fig. 8–5).

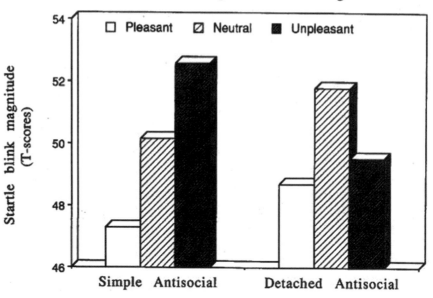

FIGURE 8–5. Mean startle reflex magnitude during viewing of pleasant, neutral, and unpleasant slides among prisoners high on PCL–R Factor 2 only (simple antisocial; $n = 18$), and prisoners high on both factors of the PCL–R (detached antisocial; $n = 17$). Blink response magnitude is expressed in standard (T-score) units. The data are from: "Emotion in the Criminal Psychopath: Startle Reflex Modulation," by C. J. Patrick, M. M. Bradley, & P. J. Lang, 1993, *Journal of Abnormal Psychology*, *102*, pp. 82–92.

A follow-up study (Patrick, 1994) replicated and extended these findings within a new experimental paradigm, using diagnostic groups selected a priori on the basis of PCL–R factor scores. Participants were 58 male inmate residents of a federal prison selected from a larger sample assessed for psychopathy using the PCL–R and antisocial personality using *Diagnostic and Statistical Manual of Mental Disorders, 3rd ed., revised (DSM–III–R)* (APA, 1987) criteria. Four groups were formed: (a) *nonpsychopaths*, rated low on both psychopathy factors ($n = 18$); (b) *detached* offenders, with high ratings on PCL–R Factor 1 but low scores on Factor 2 ($n = 14$); (c) *antisocial* offenders, with high Factor 2 scores only ($n = 8$); and (d) *psychopaths*, with high ratings on both factors ($n = 18$). The startle responses of these four study groups were assessed in an aversive anticipation procedure.

The experiment consisted of two phases. In the first (baseline), participants viewed a monitor on which a simple cue (i.e., a string of asterisks) was presented intermittently for 6 s at a time. At varying times, a white noise probe (50 ms, 95-dB) was introduced to elicit a startle blink reaction. Startle probes occurred during 3 of the 6 cue presentations, and during 3 of the intertrial intervals. In the second (anticipation) phase, the procedure was identical, except that a loud noxious noise blast (110 dB[A]) was delivered following the offset of the visual cue; startle probes were presented during 9 of 14 warning cue intervals, and during 3 of the 6 intertrial intervals.

No group differences in overall startle reactivity were found, and in the baseline phase, startle blink magnitude during cue intervals did not differ from startle magnitude during intertrial intervals in any of the groups. As in nonincarcerated control individuals (Patrick & Berthot, 1995), startle reactions to cue probes generally exceeded reactions to intertrial probes during the anticipation phase, when the cue signaled an upcoming aversive event. However, the psychopathic and the detached groups both showed reduced startle potentiation during noise anticipation compared with the nonpsychopathic and antisocial groups. Furthermore, this group difference was evident from the beginning of the anticipation procedure, indicating that the effect was not simply attributable to faster habituation to the threat of noise.

These results further indicated that psychopathy is associated with diminished fear reactivity and that this fear deficit is linked specifically to the classic emotional and interpersonal features of the disorder. Of note, and in contrast with Patrick et al. (1993) and Levenston et al. (2000), psychopaths in the noise anticipation study did not show inhibited startle reactivity during aversive (warning cue) periods relative to neutral (intertrial) intervals. A plausible explanation, consistent with findings reviewed in the preceding section, is that the aversive foreground in the noise anticipation procedure was not inherently interesting: The warning cue engaged attention only because it signaled an imminent noxious event. Thus, while lesser blink potentiation was observed in psychopaths compared to nonpsychopaths, reflecting diminished defensive reactivity, attentional inhibition of startle did not occur. A similar group difference was reported by Levenston et al. (2000) for pictorial depictions of direct threat stimuli (see Fig. 8–3).

Language Cuing and Visceral Reactivity:
Fear Image Processing

Aversive pictures and threat cues are explicit stimuli whose impact is not reliant upon abstract, verbal mediation. Diminished fear reactivity to cues of this type appears to characterize individuals who score high on the core affective–interpersonal features of psychopathy. However, other data indicate that deficits in emotional reactivity to language cues may be associated with antisociality more broadly. Patrick, Cuthbert, and Lang (1994) investigated physiological responses (heart rate, skin conductance, and corrugator electromyographic activity) during a text-processing task in which participants recalled and imagined descriptions of neutral and fearful situations when prompted by cue tones. Nonemotional scenarios included descriptions of reading and relaxing; fearful scenes included descriptions of a home invasion, dental examination, speech, injection, car accident, and bedtime spider encounter. The study sample comprised the same sample of criminal offenders who participated in the Patrick et al. (1993) study, classified into nonpsychopathic, simple antisocial, and detached-antisocial subgroups on the basis of scores on the two PCL–R factors. Most participants in the two antisocial groups met *DSM–III–R* criteria for APD (72% and 88%, respectively), compared with a minority of the nonpsychopathic participants (11%). In addition, the two antisocial groups scored higher on a self-report index of sensation seeking and lower on a questionnaire measure of socialization.

The principal finding of this study was that *both* antisocial groups showed lesser heart rate and skin conductance reactivity compared with nonpsychopaths during processing of fearful material (see Fig. 8–6), whereas their verbal reports of distress did not differ. The fact that group response patterns matched in all other respects (including configuration and timing of physiological reactions, and artifact frequency; Patrick et al., 1994) points to a selective deficiency in the reactions of antisocial offenders to fear-related scripts, not easily attributable to inattention or noncompliance. In normal individuals, language cues that match with representations in an emotional memory network activate the network as whole, including associated affect–action tendencies, prompting measurable bodily responses (P. J. Lang, 1979, 1984). The relative absence of physiological activation during fear image processing in antisocial offenders implies a deficit in the normal links between language cues and the action mobilization that is the essence of emotion (Izard, 1993; P. J. Lang, 1979; Plutchik, 1984).

The aforementioned physiological experiments reveal a dissociation between the reactions of simple antisocial offenders in a processing task involving emotional language cuing vis-à-vis procedures involving exposure to explicit threat cues. Only in the former instance, in which emotional response was prompted by semantic, linguistic processing, was there evidence of attenuated fear reactivity. In terms of the hierarchical conceptualization of emotion described earlier, this implies a dysfunction in the normal interplay between higher neurocognitive systems and the subcortical motive

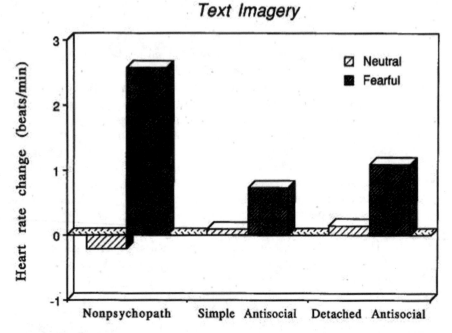

FIGURE 8–6.   Mean heart rate change during imaginal processing of fearful and non-fearful sentences in three criminal offender groups: (a) offenders low on both Factor 1 and Factor 2 of the PCL–R (nonpsychopath; $n = 18$); (b) offenders high on PCL–R Factor 2 only (simple antisocial; $n = 18$); and (c) prisoners high on both PCL–R factors (detached antisocial; $n = 17$). Heart rate change is for a 6-s image-processing period deviated from a 6-s preprocessing baseline. The findings are from "Emotion in the Criminal Psychopath: Fear Image Processing," by C. J., Patrick, B. N. Cuthbert, & P. J. Lang, 1994, *Journal of Abnormal Psychology, 103*, pp. 523–534.

systems that prime behavior (P. J. Lang, 1994; LeDoux, 1995). Findings to be reviewed in a subsequent section provide compelling evidence that dysfunctions of this type account for the putative stress-dampening effects of alcohol and that the ethanol challenge paradigm offers a useful model for investigating cognitive–emotional mechanisms in disinhibitory psychopathology.

TEMPERAMENT CORRELATES OF THE PCL–R FACTORS

The aforementioned research on physiological responses to phasic affective stimuli suggests that different affective processing deviations may underlie the two facets of the PCL–R. Consistent with this dual-process model, the two PCL–R factors show diverging relationships with affect and temperament traits assessed via self-report. Patrick (1994) reported relationships among

PCL–R total and factor scores and the following individual difference measures for a sample of 80 male prisoners, including participants in the noise anticipation study described earlier: (a) the trait form of the Positive and Negative Affect Schedule (PANAS; Watson, Clark, & Tellegen, 1988) and (b) Buss and Plomin's (1975, 1984) temperament inventory. Because the two PCL–R factors were moderately correlated (cf. Hare, 1991, 2003), partial correlations were used to assess relationships for each factor, controlling for the influence of the other. Scores on Factor 1 of the PCL–R (emotional detachment) were correlated negatively with the PANAS NA scale and the Fear and Distress scales of the Buss–Plomin inventory and positively with PANAS PA. Factor 2 (antisocial behavior), on the other hand, was positively related to PANAS NA and to Buss and Plomin's Impulsivity and Anger scales. Overall scores on the PCL–R, reflecting the common variance between the two factors, were correlated only with the Impulsivity and Anger scales of the Buss–Plomin inventory.

Other researchers (Patrick, 1995; Verona et al., 2001) have examined relationships between the PCL–R and lower- and higher-order traits assessed by Tellegen's (1982, in press) MPQ. Table 8–2 depicts these relationships for a sample of 219 incarcerated male offenders. Overall PCL–R scores are related negatively to the higher-order MPQ dimension of CON and its constituent traits of Control and Harm Avoidance, and positively to the higher-

TABLE 8–2.
Correlations Between MPQ Trait Scales and Factors and PCL–R Scores ($N = 219$)

| MPQ Scores | PCL–R Scores | | |
	Factor 1[a]	Factor 2[a]	Total
Trait scales			
Wellbeing	.12	−.19*	−.06
Social Potency	.31**	−.09	.20**
Achievement	.24**	−.27**	−.04
Social Closeness	−.07	−.10	−.16*
Stress Reaction	−.24**	.33**	.11
Alienation	−.03	.16*	.14
Aggression	−.02	.35**	.33**
Control	.13	−.29**	−.16*
Harm Avoidance	−.02	−.16*	−.19**
Traditionalism	−.08	−.06	−.13
Absorption	.08	.00	.08
Factors			
PEM–Agentic	.30**	−.27**	.03
PEM–Communal	.05	−.12	−.06
NEM	−.06	.27**	.22**
CON	.02	−.27**	−.24**

[a]Coefficients for each of the PCL–R factors are partial correlations, controlling for the influence of the other factor. *$p <. 05$; **$p < .005$

order NEM dimension and its Aggression subscale. Additionally, total psychopathy scores are related positively to the trait of Social Potency (dominance) and negatively to Social Closeness (affiliation). PCL–R Factor 1, controlling for Factor 2, is related positively to the higher-order factor of Agentic PEM and its Social Potency and Achievement facets and negatively to Stress Reaction (trait anxiety). PCL–R Factor 2 is correlated negatively with Agentic PEM and its Wellbeing and Achievement facets, positively with NEM and all its constituent traits, and negatively with CON and its facets of Control and Harm Avoidance.

In summary, converging results are evident for these various trait measures of emotional reactivity and temperament. Overall scores on the PCL–R are related to impulsivity/low CON and anger/aggression. The unique variance in PCL–R Factor 1 is associated with diminished negative affect (i.e., low anxiety, distress, and fear), and heightened positive affectivity in connection with the pursuit of dominance and status (Agentic PEM). Unique variance in PCL–R Factor 2 was associated with impulsivity/low CON, high scores on NEM and all its facets (anxiety/distress, alienation, and anger/aggression), and diminished well-being and achievement. The findings for PCL–R Factor 1 are consistent with the hypothesis, arising from the aforementioned research using the affect-modulated startle paradigm, that the affective-interpersonal features of psychopathy reflect a heightened threshold for the transition from orienting to defense. Behaviorally, this disposition would be reflected by an increased tolerance for risk and a persistence of goal-directed behavior in the presence of explicit cues signaling the possibility of punishment.

On the other hand, the affect and temperament findings for PCL–R factor 2 suggest that the disinhibition associated with this facet of psychopathy is not attributable to a core weakness in defensive reactivity. From the perspective of the hierarchical conceptualization of emotion described earlier, the findings of the fear imagery study by Patrick et al. (1994) raise the possibility that this component of psychopathy might instead reflect dysfunction of higher brain systems important for processing affective stimuli that are subtle or symbolic, as opposed to explicit. In the next section I describe evidence for a connection between PCL–R factor 2 and an "externalizing" spectrum of psychopathology for which evidence of neurocognitive anomalies has been reported. This is followed by a discussion of the alcohol challenge paradigm as a model for understanding how impairments in cognitive processing can affect emotional processing and behavioral inhibition.

PCL–R FACTOR 2 AND THE
EXTERNALIZING SPECTRUM

The temperament dimensions of NEM and impulsivity/constraint, which correlate significantly with PCL–R Factor 2, have been discussed in relation to a range of disinihibitory syndromes and behaviors—including APD, alcohol and drug abuse, reactive violence, and impulsive suicide (Krueger, 1999a; Krueger, Caspi, Moffitt, Silva, & McGee, 1996; Verona & Patrick, 2000). Relationships between Factor 2 of the PCL–R and these various disinhibitory syndromes have also been established in empirical studies. PCL–R Factor 2 is related to *DSM* APD diagnoses and symptoms (Hare, 1991, 2003); controlling for Factor 2, PCL–R Factor 1 is unrelated to APD (Verona et al., 2001). Factor 2, but not Factor 1, is positively related to alcohol and drug abuse or dependence (Smith & Newman, 1990). PCL–R Factor 2 is also related preferentially to indices of impulsive, reactive violence (including fights, assaults, and partner abuse; Patrick, Zempolich, & Levenston, 1997), and to history of suicidal attempts (Verona et al., 2001).

This pattern of relationships points to the possibility of a link between PCL–R Factor 2 and a latent psychopathology dimension identified via structural analysis of the covariance among mental disorders within *DSM–III–R*. Utilizing diagnostic data from the National Comorbidity Survey, Kessler et al. (1994) and Krueger (1999b) reported evidence for two broad factors underlying the most common Axis I disorders: an "externalizing" factor encompassing APD, alcohol dependence, and drug dependence, and an "internalizing" dimension encapsulating the mood and anxiety disorders (see also Krueger, Caspi, Moffitt, & Silva, 1998). In an independent dataset, Krueger (1999a) showed that scores on the personality dimension of NEM at age 18 predicted the development of symptoms of both internalizing and externalizing disorders at age 21, but that scores on the constraint dimension uniquely predicted externalizing disorder symptoms. These findings are consistent with the idea that "core psychopathological processes" (Krueger, 1999b; Krueger et al., 1998), associated with extremes of temperament, account for the comorbidity among disorders within the internalizing and externalizing spectra.

With regard to the etiological basis of the externalizing spectrum, evidence has emerged for overlapping neurocognitive processing deviations in disorders of this type. It has been known for some time that the P300 component of the event-related brain potential, a positive deflection elicited by infrequent target events within a stimulus sequence, is diminished in alcoholic individuals and their biological relatives (cf. Polich, Pollock, & Bloom, 1994). P300 is theorized to reflect the updating of information in working memory (Donchin, 1981; Donchin & Coles, 1988) and therefore a reduction in P300 amplitude implies a deviation in higher cognitive functioning. Iacono, Carlson, Taylor, Elkins, and McGue (1999) reported findings from a large epidemiological sample, indicating reduced P300 in a range of externalizing disorders: In comparison with control participants, reduced P300 was evident in male adolescents meeting *DSM–III–R* criteria for attention deficit hyperactivity disorder, conduct disorder, oppositional defiant disorder, nicotine dependence, alcohol abuse or dependence, and drug abuse or dependence. Moreover, unaffected individuals at risk for such disorders by virtue of a paternal diagnosis of alcoholism, drug abuse or dependence, conduct disorder, or adult antisocial behavior also showed reduced P300. Other studies have indicated parallel results for individual disorders within this spectrum (e.g., Bauer & Hesselbrock, 1999; Johnstone & Barry, 1996; Klorman, 1991).

The findings of studies on psychopathy and P300 response have been mixed (cf. Raine, 1989), but these studies have used widely varying task procedures, some markedly different from the standard "oddball" paradigm used in the aforementioned work, and the two facets of psychopathy assessed by the PCL–R have not been considered separately in analyses. An investigation by Bauer, O'Connor, and Hesselbrock (1994) that used a visual oddball task reported clear evidence for reduced P300 in nonalcoholic men who met DSM–III–R criteria for antisocial personality disorder. A parallel divergence arises in the literature on neuropsychological test performance in psychopathic and antisocial individuals: Whereas individuals defined as psychopathic on the basis of overall scores on Hare's PCL appear not to differ on standardized indices of frontal lobe function (Hare, 1984; Hart, Forth, & Hare, 1990), a meta-analysis by Morgan and Lilienfeld (2000) revealed clear evidence of differences among individuals defined more broadly as antisocial.

To summarize, the available data suggest a relationship between the construct assessed by PCL–R Factor 2 and a variety of externalizing behaviors and syndromes. The overlap among these syndromes has been conceptualized in terms of a "core psychopathological process" (Krueger et al., 1998) that has been linked to anomalies in higher cognitive functions (cf. Iacono et al., 1999). It seems reasonable therefore to suppose that the chronic antisocial behavior associated with extreme scores on Factor 2 of the PCL–R might reflect a similar etiology. Consistent with this, Patrick, Hicks, Krueger, and Lang (2005) directly examined the association between PCL–R Factor 2 and the broad externalizing factor of general psychopathology and found a close association between the two. A question that remains, however, is how impairments in cognitive processing might give rise to the impulsivity, risk-taking, and aggressiveness characteristic of the extreme antisocial individual. In the next section I consider the phenomenon of acute alcohol intoxication as a model for this type of individual.

ALCOHOL AND FEAR REDUCTION

As with the disinhibitory behavioral features of psychopathy, alcohol-related disinhibition has often been attributed to a direct suppression of emotional response capacity. "Tension reduction" and "stress-response dampening" have been dominant themes in the alcohol literature for many years (see Conger, 1956, for the seminal theoretical statement). Pihl and colleagues (Pihl & Peterson, 1993; Pihl, Peterson, & Lau, 1993) have argued that a major contributor to alcohol-related aggression (see Bushman & Cooper, 1990, for a review) is "fearlessness." From this viewpoint, the anxiolytic effect of alcohol is thought to attenuate the inhibitory impact of fear on the expression of behavior associated with past punishment or threat exposure. Similar hypotheses have been put forth to account for relationships between drinking and other behaviors, such as sexual expression, believed to be under inhibitory control (see A. R. Lang, 1985, for a review).

However, of the many analytic reviews of the relevant literature that have been conducted (e.g., Cappell & Greeley, 1987; Sher, 1987), none has provided firm support for the premise that alcohol consistently reduces tension, anxiety, or fear, except perhaps in conflict situations. Part of the reason for this state of affairs is that, until recently, direct and unequivocal indices of negative emotional reactivity were not available. Another reason is that stress-reduction theories of drinking have failed to consider the possibility that inconsistencies in the observed effects of alcohol might be due to variability in the processing demands of task paradigms used to assess emotional reactivity.

My and my colleagues' experiments have provided new insights into the mechanisms by which alcohol attenuates stress reactivity and disinhibits behavior in humans. In the first of this series of studies, Stritzke, Patrick, and Lang (1995) examined startle reflex modulation during viewing of pleasant, neutral, and unpleasant pictures in participants administered either a moderate dose of alcohol (mean peak blood alcohol level = 0.071) or no alcohol. Intoxication produced a decrease in the *overall* magnitude of startle reactions to noise probes (cf. Pohorecky, Cagan, Brick, & Jaffe, 1976), but *affective modulation* of startle was not affected by alcohol: Intoxicated participants and control participants showed equivalent reflex potentiation during aversive slides and reflex inhibition during pleasant slides. These results contrast with evidence, cited earlier, that the anxiolytic drug diazepam (Valium) blocks fear-potentiated startle in a dose-related fashion without suppressing general startle reactivity. The strong implication is that diazepam directly suppresses defensive reactivity, whereas alcohol does not.

An alternative to the direct stress-dampening hypothesis is that alcohol affects emotional reactivity indirectly, by impairing higher cognitive capacities required to detect and process stimuli under complex cuing conditions (Stritzke, Lang, & Patrick, 1996). In particular, the ability to allocate attention may be compromised (Steele & Josephs, 1988, 1990), along with associative memory processes involved in processing complex situations, anticipating consequences, and selecting appropriate responses (Sayette, 1993). In a test of this hypothesis, Curtin, Lang, Patrick, and Stritzke (1998) presented sober or moderately intoxicated (*M* peak blood alcohol level = 0.075) individuals with a series of 2-min light cues signaling either the possibility that an electric shock could be delivered at any moment (red light = "threat") or that no shock would be delivered (green light = "safe"; cf. Grillon et al., 1991). During half of the threat and half of the safe periods, 6-s pleasant slides were presented intermittently as distracters. Acoustic startle probes were delivered at varying unpredictable points within the threat and safe intervals, either during viewing of slides or during intervals between slides.

Replicating the results of Stritzke et al. (1995), alcohol produced an overall reduction in startle reflex magnitude across the experiment. Also consistent with that initial study, there was no effect of alcohol on fear-potentiated startle in the simple cuing condition (i.e., threat cue vs. safe cue alone). However, startle reflex potentiation *was* blocked by alcohol in the condition in which a pleasant foreground distracter (slide) appeared simultaneously with the threat cue (see Fig. 8–7). This, of course, is the condition in which the greatest cognitive demands were placed on participants, particularly in terms of dual allocation of attention or processing of competing stimuli. These results, obtained using a more potent and direct stress manipulation (i.e., threat of shock), coincided with those of Stritzke et al. (1995) in suggesting that alcohol's anxiolytic effects may be limited to complex stimulus-processing contexts.

However, conclusions regarding the mechanisms of alcohol's effects in the Curtin et al. (1998) study were constrained by the fact that attention was not assessed directly. To address these issues and to examine the effects of alcohol on response inhibition, a third study (Curtin, Patrick, Lang, Cacioppo, &

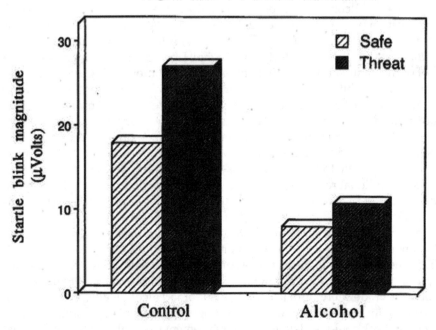

FIGURE 8–7. Mean startle reflex magnitude for alcohol-intoxicated and nonintoxicated student participants during "safe" and threat intervals, under conditions of concurrent distraction (i.e., viewing of engaging, pleasant pictures). Shock intervals were designated by a red light signifying that an electric shock could be presented at any time; safe intervals were signaled by a green light, indicating that shock would not be administered. Results are from "Alcohol and Fear-Potentiated Startle: The Role of Distraction in the Stress-Reducing Effects of Intoxication," by J. J. Curtin, A. R., Lang, C. J., Patrick, & W. G. K. Stritzke, 1998, *Journal of Abnormal Psychology*, *107*, pp. 545–555.

Birbaumer, 2001) was conducted in which measures of fear, attention, and behavioral response were assessed concurrently. In this study, the impact of alcohol on emotional reactivity to a cue signaling the delivery of an aversive stimulus was compared under two conditions: (a) a *threat focus*, in which the warning cue was presented in isolation, and (b) *divided attention*, in which the threat cue was presented as an incidental feature of S1 in a two-stimulus (S1–S2) go/no-go task. Fear response to the threat cue was indexed by fear–potentiated startle, attentional processing of the cue was assessed using the P3 component of the cortical event-related potential, and response inhibition was assessed via reaction time on the go/no go task.

Consistent with the findings of Curtin et al. (1998), the alcohol group showed a reduction in fear-potentiated startle in the divided attention condition, in which the threat cue appeared as a nonattended feature of S1, but not when the threat cue was presented on its own. Paralleling the startle measure, attentional processing of the threat cue as indexed by brain potential (P300) response was reduced in the alcohol group during the divided-attention task, but not when the threat cue was presented in isolation. The implication is that alcohol reduced fear only under competing stimulus conditions, in which a division of attentional resources was required to process the incidental fear cue. Furthermore, as a function of their reduced fear response to the threat cue on "go" trials in the divided attention condition, intoxicated participants showed lesser slowing of reaction time (i.e., lesser response inhibition) to the S2 when the threat cue appeared as a facet of S1. This finding coincides with substantial anecdotal and empirical evidence indicating that the power of threat or punishment cues to inhibit behavior is reduced under conditions of intoxication.

In summary, our research in this area demonstrates that acute intoxication can serve as a model of how deficits in cognitive functioning can interfere with fear processing and behavioral inhibition in complex or competing stimulus contexts. In three separate investigations (Curtin et al., 1998, 2001; Stritzke et al., 1995), we found no evidence that alcohol decreased reactivity to simple, explicit aversive stimuli. However, in two of these studies we found that alcohol did block fear-potentiated startle when a potent distracter was presented simultaneously with the threat cue, and in the most recent of these we obtained direct evidence of a mediating effect of reduced cognitive–attentional capacity. In terms of the hierarchical emotion perspective advanced earlier, these findings suggest that alcohol diminishes sensitivity to fear cues not by directly suppressing the subcortical defensive system but rather by disrupting higher brain systems that mediate emotional reactivity in complex cuing contexts (cf. Stritzke et al., 1996). This interpretation is supported by animal work demonstrating deleterious effects of ethanol on the acquisition of contextual but not explicit fear (Melia, Corodimas, Ryabinin, Wilson, & LeDoux, 1994).

The broader behavioral implications of these effects of alcohol on cognitive–emotional processing are illustrated by findings from two aggression studies reported by Zeichner and Pihl (1979, 1980). In the first of these, nonintoxicated participants modulated their behavior in response to subtle feed-back indicating a quid pro quo relationship between the intensity of shocks that they delivered and those received from a supposed competitor. How-ever, alcohol-intoxicated participants were insensitive to the feedback: They persisted in delivering high-intensity shocks despite the adverse conse-quences for themselves. Parallel results were obtained in the second experi-ment: Unlike sober participants, intoxicated individuals did not reduce the levels of shock they delivered to an opponent when advised that the latter had no control (versus complete control) over the shock intensities adminis-tered to the participant.

These findings underscore the impairments in reflectivity and planning associated with intoxication and the affiliated insensitivity to threat or pun-ishment cues. Alcohol-intoxicated individuals seemed willing to risk per-sonal harm to react to the immediate situation with the most dominant and immediately gratifying response. Behavior of this kind is also typical of highly antisocial individuals and may reflect parallel underlying cognitive–emotional disturbances.

CONCLUSIONS: EMOTION, PSYCHOPATHY, AND DISINHIBITION

In this review, I have outlined an integrated, hierarchical conceptualization of emotion that emphasizes differentiated motive systems and varying levels of cognitive–emotional processing. This perspective encourages considera-tion of variables not traditionally attended to in psychopathology research: the valence and intensity of emotion-eliciting cues, the context of affective stimulation, the brain systems required to detect and analyze cues of vary-ing complexity, and the functional significance of different physiological measures in relation to these other parameters.

In theorizing about disinhibitory clinical syndromes, it is important to con-sider the possibility that varying types of emotional processing deficits exist, involving distinct neural pathways and systems, and that the performance of different behavioral tasks (e.g., explicit–cue conditioning, contextual condi-tioning, and passive avoidance learning) may draw upon different process-ing capacities. Through further systematic research, it should be possible to develop a taxonomy of affect-processing paradigms capable of detecting dif-ferent deviations in emotional and cognitive–emotional processing. Bio-behavioral measurement strategies such as the startle-probe technique, which can be used in parallel with animals and humans and which permit inferences about underlying neural pathways, provide a valuable means to this end.

The clinical studies reviewed here suggest that different affective pro-cessing deviations are associated with the two facets of psychopathy assessed by Hare's PCL–R. Factor 1 is associated with diminished defen-sive reactivity to explicit aversive cues and a temperament profile involv-ing agency and stress resistance. Factor 2, on the other hand, is linked to a

Disinhibition I: Weak Defense RESPONSE

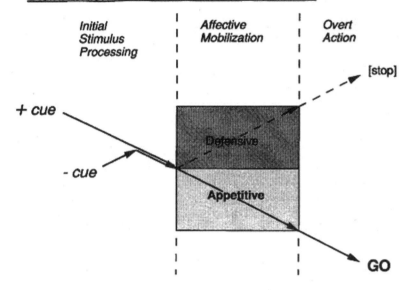

Disinhibition II: Impaired STIMULUS Processing

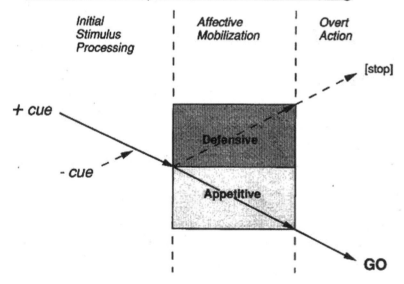

FIGURE 8–8. Depiction of two alternative mechanisms for behavioral disinhibition. Upper panel: In this case, the presence of a threat cue fails to interrupt ongoing appetitive behavior because the defense system itself is weak (i.e., the threshold for activation of a defensive state is high). The aversive cue is detected, but the defense system is not activated, and therefore no interruption of ongoing behavior occurs. Lower panel: Here, the core defensive system is normal, but the intervening threat cue is not detected because of impaired stimulus processing. Consequently, the defense system is not activated, and appetitive behavior persists.

range of externalizing syndromes that are marked by traits of low constraint and heightened NEM. Evidence for neurocognitive abnormalities in antisocial individuals (Morgan & Lilienfeld, 2000; Raine, 1993) and in externalizing syndromes more generally (Iacono et al., 1999) suggests that this dimension of deviance may reflect deficits in higher processing systems that interact with primary motive centers, but that are anatomically and functionally distinct (LeDoux, 1995).

Following from the hierarchical concepualization of emotion and the model of response inhibition presented earlier in Fig. 8–1, Fig. 8–8 depicts two alternative mechanisms for defective behavioral inhibition. The first of these (upper panel) depicts a situation in which the defensive system itself is weak (i.e., the threshold for instigation of a defensive reaction is higher); in this case, the aversive cue is processed, but the defense system is not activated, and no interruption of appetitive behavior occurs. It is proposed that high scores on Factor 1 of the PCL–R are associated with disinhibition of this kind (cf. Levenston et al., 2000). The second illustration (Fig. 8.8, lower panel) depicts a case in which the core defensive system is normal, but there is an impairment in the ability to process complex environmental cues. In this case, an absence of defensive activation (and consequent persistence of appetitive behavior) is attributable to a failure to process the aversive cue. It is proposed that disinhibition associated with acute alcohol intoxication (cf. Stritzke et al., 1996), and by extension chronic externalizing behavior (cf. Patrick & Lang, 1999), reflects a mechanism of this type.

In conclusion, progress in understanding clinical disorders is likely to benefit from a differentiated, hierarchical perspective on emotional processing. The dual-process model proposed here represents an effort to bring this conceptualization to bear on the syndrome of psychopathy. Further research along these lines should help to elucidate the etiologic factors that underlie this important, but perplexing, phenomenon.

ACKNOWLEDGMENT

Preparation of this chapter was supported by Grants MH48657, MH52384, MH072850, and MH65137 from the National Institute of Mental Health, Grant R01 AA12164 from the National Institute on Alcohol Abuse and Alcoholism, and funds from the Hathaway endowment at the University of Minnesota.

REFERENCES

American Psychiatric Association. (1987). *Diagnostic and statistical manual of mental disorders* (3rd ed., revised). Washington, DC: Author.
American Psychiatric Association. (1994). *Diagnostic and statistical manual of mental disorders* (4th ed.). Washington, DC: Author.

Anthony, B. J., & Graham, F. K. (1985). Blink reflex modification by selective attention: Evidence for the modulation of "automatic" processing. *Biological Psychology, 21*, 43–59.

Balaban, M. T., & Taussig, H. N. (1994). Salience of fear/threat in the affective modulation of the human startle blink. *Biological Psychology, 38*, 117–131.

Bauer, L. O., & Hesselbrock, V. M. (1999). P300 decrements in teenagers with conduct problems: Implications for substance abuse risk and brain development. *Biological Psychiatry, 46*, 263–272.

Bauer, L. O., O'Connor, S., & Hesselbrock, V. M. (1994). Frontal P300 decrements in antisocial personality disorder. *Alcoholism: Clinical and Experimental Research, 18*, 1300–1305.

Berridge, K. C., & Robinson, T. E. (1998). What is the role of dopamine in reward: Hedonic impact, reward learning, or incentive salience? *Brain Research Reviews, 28*, 309–369.

Blaney, P. H. (1986). Affect and memory: A review. *Psychological Bulletin, 99*, 229–246.

Boulis, N. M., & Davis, M. (1989). Footshock induced sensitization of electrically elicited startle reflexes. *Behavioral Neuroscience, 103*, 504–508.

Bower, G. H. (1981). Mood and memory. *American Psychologist, 36*, 129–148.

Bradley, M. M., Cuthbert, B. N., & Lang, P. J. (1993). Pictures as prepulse: Attention and emotion in startle modification. *Psychophysiology, 30*, 541–545.

Bradley, M. M., Cuthbert, B. N., & Lang, P. J. (2000). Affective reactions to acoustic stimuli. *Psychophysiology, 37*, 204–215.

Brown, J. S., Kalish, H. I., & Farber, I. E. (1951). Conditioned fear as revealed by magnitude of startle response to an auditory stimulus. *Journal of Experimental Psychology, 41*, 317–328.

Bushman, B. J., & Cooper, H. M. (1990). Effects of alcohol on human aggression: An integrative research review. *Psychological Bulletin, 107*, 341–354.

Buss, A. H., & Plomin, R. (1975). *A temperament theory of personality development.* New York: Wiley.

Buss, A. H., & Plomin, R. (1984). *Temperament: Early developing personality traits.* Hillsdale, NJ: Lawrence Erlbaum Associates.

Cacioppo, J. T., Petty, R. E., Losch, M. E., & Kim, H. S. (1986). Electromyographic activity over facial muscle regions can differentiate the valence and intensity of affective reactions. *Journal of Personality and Social Psychology, 50*, 260–268.

Cappell, H., & Greeley, J. (1987). Alcohol and tension reduction: An update on research and theory. In H. Blane & K. Leonard (Eds.), *Psychological theories of alcoholism* (pp. 15–54). New York: Guilford.

Christianson, S.-Å., Forth, A. E., Hare, R. D., Strachan, C., Lidberg, L., & Thorell, L-H. (1996). Remembering details of emotional events: A comparison between psychopathic and nonpsychopathic offenders. *Personality and Individual Differences, 20*, 437–443.

Church, A. T. (1994). Relating the Tellegen and the five-factor models of personality structure. *Journal of Personality and Social Psychology, 67*, 898–909.

Cleckley, H. (1941). *The mask of sanity* (1st ed.). St. Louis, MO: Mosby.

Cleckley, H. (1976). *The mask of sanity* (4th ed.). St. Louis, MO: Mosby.

Conger, J. (1956). Reinforcement theory and the dynamics of alcoholism. *Quarterly Journal of Studies on Alcohol, 17*, 296–305.

Costa, P. T., Jr., & McCrae, R. R. (1985). *The NEO Personality Inventory Manual Form S and Form R.* Odessa, FL: Psychological Assessment Resources.

Craig, K. D., Hyde, S. A., & Patrick, C. J. (1991). Genuine, suppressed, and faked facial behavior during exacerbation of chronic low back pain. *Pain, 46*, 161–171.

Curtin, J. J., Lang, A. R., Patrick, C. J., & Stritzke, W. G. K. (1998). Alcohol and fear-potentiated startle: The role of distraction in the stress-reducing effects of intoxication. *Journal of Abnormal Psychology, 107*, 545–555.

Curtin, J. J., Patrick, C. J., Lang, A. R., Cacioppo, J. T., & Birbaumer, N. (2001). Alcohol affects emotion through cognition. *Psychological Science, 12*, 527–531.

Cuthbert, B. N., Bradley, M. M., & Lang, P. J. (1996). Probing picture perception: Activation and emotion. *Psychophysiology, 33*, 103–111.

Cuthbert, B. N., Schupp, H., Bradley, M. M., Birbaumer, N., & Lang, P. J. (2000). Brain potentials in affective picture processing: Covariation with autonomic arousal and affective report. *Biological Psychology, 52*, 95–111.

Davidson, R. J. (1992). Emotion and affective style: Hemispheric substrates. *Psychological Science, 3*, 39–43.

Davis, M. (1979). Diazepam and flurazepam: Effects on conditioned fear as measured with the potentiated startle paradigm. *Psychopharmacology, 62*, 1–7.

Davis, M. (1989). Neural systems involved in fear-potentiated startle. In M. Davis, B. L. Jacobs, & R. I. Schoenfeld (Eds.), *Annals of the New York Academy of Sciences: Vol. 563. Modulation of defined neural vertebrate circuits* (pp. 165–183). New York: Author.

Davis, M. (1992). The role of the amygdala in conditioned fear. In J. Aggleton (Ed.), *The amygdala: Neurobiological aspects of emotion, memory and mental dysfunction* (pp. 255–305). New York: Wiley.

Davis, M. (1996). Differential roles of the amygdala and bed nucleus of the stria terminalis in conditioned fear and startle enhanced by corticotrophin-releasing hormone. In T. Ono, B. L. McNaughton, S. Molotchnikoff, E. T. Rolls, & H. Nishijo (Eds.), *Perception, memory, and emotion: Frontiers in neuroscience* (pp. 525–548). Oxford, England: Elsevier.

Davis, M., & Lee, Y. (1998). Fear and anxiety: Possible roles of the amygdala and bed nucleus of the stria terminalis. *Cognition and Emotion, 12*, 277–305.

Dawson, M. E., & Schell, A. M. (1985). Information processing and human autonomic classical conditioning. In P. K. Ackles, J. R. Jennings, & M. G. H. Coles (Eds.), *Advances in psychophysiology* (Vol. 1, pp. 89–165). Greenwich, CT: JAI.

Donchin, E. (1981). Surprise! . . . Surprise? *Psychophysiology, 18*, 493–513.

Donchin E., & Coles, M. G. H. (1988). Is the P300 component a manifestation of context updating? *Behavioral and Brain Sciences, 11*, 357–374.

Eich, E. (1995). Searching for mood dependent memory. *Psychological Science, 6*, 67–75.

Ekman, P. (1992). An argument for basic emotions. *Cognition and Emotion, 6*, 169–200.

Fanselow, M. S. (1994). Neural organization of the defensive behavior system responsible for fear. *Psychonomic Bulletin and Review, 1*, 429–438.

Fowles, D. C. (1980). The three arousal model: Implications of Gray's two-factor learning theory for heart rate, electrodermal activity, and psychopathy. *Psychophysiology, 17*, 87–104.

Fridlund, A. J., Ekman, P., & Oster, H. (1986). Facial expressions of emotion. In A. Siegman, & S. Feldstein (Eds.), *Nonverbal behavior and communication* (pp. 143–223). Hillsdale, NJ: Lawrence Erlbaum Associates.

Fridlund, A. J., Schwartz, G. E., & Fowler, S. C. (1984). Pattern recognition of self-reported emotional state from multiple-site facial EMG activity during affective imagery. *Psychophysiology, 21*, 622–637.

Graham, F. K. (1975). The more or less startling effects of weak prestimulation. *Psychophysiology, 2*, 238–247.

Gray, J. A. (1987). *The psychology of fear and stress* (2nd ed.). Cambridge, England: University of Cambridge Press.

Greenwald, M. K., Cook, E. W., & Lang, P. J. (1989). Affective judgment and psychophysiological response: Dimensional covariation in the evaluation of pictorial stimuli. *Journal of Psychophysiology, 3,* 51–64.

Grillon, C., Ameli, R., Woods, S. W., Merikangas, K., & Davis, M. (1991). Fear-potentiated startle in humans: Effects of anticipatory anxiety on the acoustic blink reflex. *Psychophysiology, 28,* 588–595.

Hamm, A. O., Greenwald, M. K., Bradley, M. M., & Lang, P. J. (1993). Emotional learning, hedonic change, and the startle probe. *Journal of Abnormal Psychology, 102,* 453–465.

Hamm, A. O., & Vaitl, D. (1996). Affective learning: Awareness and aversion. *Psychophysiology, 33,* 698–710.

Hare, R. D. (1965a). A conflict learning theory analysis of psychopathic behavior. *Journal of Research in Crime and Delinquency, 2,* 12–19.

Hare, R. D. (1965b). Temporal gradient of fear arousal in psychopaths. *Journal of Abnormal Psychology, 70,* 442–445.

Hare, R. D. (1965c). Acquisition and generalization of a conditioned fear response in psychopathic and nonpsychopathic criminals. *Journal of Psychology, 59,* 367–370.

Hare, R. D. (1970). *Psychopathy: Theory and research.* New York: Wiley.

Hare, R. D. (1978). Electrodermal and cardiovascular correlates of psychopathy. In R. D. Hare & D. Schalling (Eds.), *Psychopathic behavior: Approaches to research* (pp. 107–143). Chichester, England: Wiley.

Hare, R. D. (1980). A research scale for the assessment of psychopathy in criminal populations. *Personality and Individual Differences, 1,* 111–119.

Hare, R. D. (1984). Performance of psychopaths on cognitive tasks related to frontal lobe function. *Journal of Abnormal Psychology, 93,* 133–140.

Hare, R. D. (1986). Twenty years of experience with the Cleckley psychopath. In W. H. Reid, D. Dorr, J. I. Walker, & J. W. Bonner (Eds.), *Unmasking the psychopath* (pp. 3–27). New York: W. W. Norton.

Hare, R. D. (1991). *The Hare Psychopathy Checklist–Revised.* Toronto, Ontario, Canada: Multi-Health Systems.

Hare, R. D. (2003). *The Hare Psychopathy Checklist–Revised: 2nd Edition.* Toronto, Ontario: Multi-Health Systems.

Hare, R. D., Harpur, T. J., Hakstian, A. R., Forth, A. E., Hart, S. D., & Newman, J. P. (1990). The Revised Psychopathy Checklist: Reliability and factor structure. *Psychological Assessment, 2,* 338–341.

Harpur, T. J., Hakstian, A. R., & Hare, R. D. (1988). Factor structure of the psychopathy checklist. *Journal of Consulting and Clinical Psychology, 56,* 741–747.

Harpur, T. J., Hare, R. D., & Hakstian, A. R. (1989). Two-factor conceptualization of psychopathy: Construct validity and assessment implications. *Psychological Assessment: A Journal of Consulting and Clinical Psychology, 1,* 6–17.

Hart, S. D., Forth, A. E., & Hare, R. D. (1990). Performance of criminal psychopaths on selected neuropsychological tests. *Journal of Abnormal Psychology, 99,* 374–379.

Hebb, D. O. (1955). Drives and the C.N.S. (conceptual nervous system). *Psychological Review, 62,* 243–254.

Hitchcock, J., & Davis, M. (1986). Lesions of the amygdala, but not of the cerebellum or red nucleus, block conditioned fear as measured with the potentiated startle paradigm. *Behavioral Neuroscience, 100,* 11–22.

Iacono, W. G., Carlson, S. R., Taylor, J., Elkins, I. J., & McGue, M. (1999). Behavioral disinhibition and the development of substance-use disorders: Findings from the Minnesota Twin Family Study. *Development and Psychopathology, 11,* 869–900.

Iwata, J., Chida, K., LeDoux, J. E. (1987). Cardiovascular responses elicited by stimulation of neurons in the central amygdaloid nucleus in the central amygdaloid nucleus in awake but not anesthetized rats resemble conditioned emotional responses. *Brain Research, 383,* 195–214.

Izard, C. E. (1993). Four systems for emotion activation: Cognitive and noncognitive processes. *Psychological Review, 100,* 68–90.

Jansen, D. M., & Fridja, N. (1994). Modulation of acoustic startle response by film-induced fear and sexual arousal. *Psychophysiology, 31,* 565–571.

Jarrell, T. W., Gentile, C. G., Romanski, L. M., McCabe, P. M., & Schneiderman, N. (1987). Involvement of cortical and thalamic auditory regions in retention of differential bradycardia conditioning to acoustic conditioned stimuli in rabbits. *Brain Research, 412,* 285–294.

Johnstone, S. J., & Barry, R. J. (1996). Auditory event-related potentials to a two-tone discrimination paradigm in attention deficit hyperactivity disorder. *Psychiatry Research, 64,* 179–192

Jutai, J. W., & Hare, R. D. (1983). Psychopathy and selective attention during performance of a complex perceptual-motor task. *Psychophysiology, 20,* 146–151.

Kessler, R. C., McGonagle, K. A., Zhao, S., Nelson, C. B., Hughes, M., Eshleman, S., et al. (1994). Lifetime and 12-month prevalence of DSM-III-R psychiatric disorders in the United States: Results from the National Comorbidity Survey. *Archives of General Psychiatry, 51,* 8–19.

Kim, J. J., Rison, R. A., & Fanselow, M. S. (1993). Effects of amygdala, hippocampus, and peri-aqueductal gray lesions on short- and long-term contextual fear. *Behavioral Neuroscience, 107,* 1093–1098.

Klorman, R. (1991). Cognitive event-related potentials in attention deficit disorder. *Journal of Learning Disabilities, 24,* 130–140.

Konorski, J. (1967). *Integrative activity of the brain: An interdisciplinary approach.* Chicago: University of Chicago Press.

Kosson, D. S. (1996). Psychopathy and dual-task performance under focusing conditions. *Journal of Abnormal Psychology, 105,* 391–400.

Kosson, D. S. (1998). Divided visual attention in psychopathic and nonpsychopathic offenders. *Personality and Individual Differences, 24,* 373–391.

Kosson, D. S., & Harpur, T. J. (1997). Attention functioning and psychopathic individuals: Current evidence and developmental implications. In J. A. Burack & J. T. Enns (Eds.), *Attention, development, and psychopathology* (pp. 379–402). New York: Guilford Press.

Kosson, D. S., & Newman, J. P. (1986). Psychopathy and allocation of attentional capacity in a divided-attention situation. *Journal of Abnormal Psychology, 95,* 257–263.

Krueger, R. F. (1999a). Personality traits in late adolescence predict mental disorders in early adulthood: A prospective-epidemiological study. *Journal of Personality, 67,* 39–65.

Krueger, R. F. (1999b). The structure of common mental disorders. *Archives of General Psychiatry, 56,* 921–926.

Krueger, R. F. (2000). Phenotypic, genetic, and nonshared environmental parallels in the structure of personality: A view from the Multidimensional Personality Questionnaire. *Journal of Personality and Social Psychology, 79,* 1057–1067.

Krueger, R. F., Caspi, A., Moffitt, T. E., & Silva, P. A. (1998). The structure and stability of common mental disorders (DSM-III–R): A longitudinal-epidemiological study. *Journal of Abnormal Psychology, 107*, 216–227.

Krueger, R. F., Caspi, A., Moffitt, T. E., Silva, P. A., & McGee, R. (1996). Personality traits are differentially linked to mental disorders: A multi-trait, multi-diagnosis study of an adolescent birth cohort. *Journal of Abnormal Psychology, 105*, 299–312.

Lang, A. R. (1985). The social psychology of drinking and human sexuality. *Journal of Drug Issues, 15*, 273–289.

Lang, P. J. (1979). A bio-informational theory of emotional imagery. *Psychophysiology, 16*, 495–512.

Lang, P. J. (1984). Cognition in emotion: Concept and action. In C. E. Izard, J. Kagan, & R. B. Zajonc (Eds.), *Emotions, cognition, and behavior* (pp. 192–226). New York: Cambridge University Press.

Lang, P. J. (1994). The motivational organization of emotion: Affect-reflex connections. In S. Van Goozen, N. E. Van de Poll, & J. A. Sergeant (Eds.), *The emotions: Essays on emotion theory* (pp. 61–93). Hillsdale, NJ: Lawrence Erlbaum Associates.

Lang, P. J. (1995). The emotion probe: Studies of motivation and attention. *American Psychologist, 50*, 372–385.

Lang, P. J., Bradley, M. M., & Cuthbert, B. N. (1990). Emotion, attention, and the startle reflex. *Psychological Review, 97*, 377–398.

Lang, P. J., Bradley, M. M., & Cuthbert, B. N. (1997). Motivated attention: Affect, activation, and action. In P. J. Lang, R. F. Simons, & M. T. Balaban (Eds.), *Attention and orienting: Sensory and motivational processes* (pp. 97–135). Hillsdale, NJ: Lawrence Erlbaum Associates.

Lang, P. J., Bradley, M. M., & Cuthbert, B. N. (1999). *The international affective picture system (IAPS): Technical manual and affective ratings*. Gainesville, FL: Center for Research in Psychophysiology, University of Florida.

Lang, P. J., Bradley, M. M., Fitzsimmons, J. R., Cuthbert, B. N., Scott, J. D., Moulder, B., et al. (1998). Emotional arousal and activation of the visual cortex: An fMRI analysis. *Psychophysiology, 35*, 199–210.

Lang, P. J., Greenwald, M. K., Bradley, M. M., & Hamm, A. O. (1993). Looking at pictures: Affective, facial, visceral, and behavioral reactions. *Psychophysiology, 30*, 261–273.

Lang, P. J., Levin, D. N., Miller, G. A., & Kozak, M. J. (1983). Fear behavior, fear imagery, and the psychophysiology of emotion: The problem of affective response integration. *Journal of Abnormal Psychology, 92*, 276–306.

Larsen, R. J., & Ketelaar, T. (1991). Personality and susceptibility to positive and negative emotional states. *Journal of Personality and Social Psychology, 61*, 132–140.

Lazarus, R. (1982). Thoughts on the relations between emotion and cognition. *American Psychologist, 37*, 1019–1024.

Lazarus, R. (1984). On the primacy of cognition. *American Psychologist, 39*, 124–129.

LeDoux, J. E. (1995). Emotion: Clues from the brain. *Annual Review of Psychology, 46*, 209–235.

Lee, Y., Lopez, D., Meloni, E., & Davis, M. (1996). A primary acoustic startle pathway: Obligatory role of cochlear root neurons and the nucleus reticularis pontis caudalis. *Journal of Neuroscience, 16*, 3775–3789.

Levenston, G. K., & Patrick, C. J. (1995). Probing the time course of picture processing: Emotional valence and stimulus content. *Psychophysiology, 32*, S55.

Levenston, G. K., Patrick, C. J., Bradley, M. M., & Lang, P. J. (2000). The psychopath as observer: Emotion and attention in picture processing. *Journal of Abnormal Psychology, 109*, 373–385.

Lindsley, D. B. (1951). Emotions. In S. S. Stevens (Ed.), *Handbook of experimental psychology* (pp. 473–516). New York: Wiley.

Lykken, D. T. (1957). A study of anxiety in the sociopathic personality. *Journal of Abnormal and Clinical Psychology, 55*, 6–10.

Lykken, D. T. (1995). *The antisocial personalities.* Hillsdale, NJ: Lawrence Erlbaum Associates.

MacLean, P. D. (1958). Contrasting functions of limbic and neocortical systems of the brain and their relevance to psychophysiological aspects of medicine. *American Journal of Medicine, 25*, 611–626.

Mejia, V. Y., Vanman, E. J., Dawson, M. E., Raine, A., & Lencz, T. (1997). An examination of affective modulation, psychopathy, and negative schizotypy in a non-incarcerated sample. *Psychophysiology, 34*, S63.

Melia, K., Corodimas, K., Ryabinin, A., Wilson, M., & LeDoux, J. (1994). Ethanol (ETOH) pre-treatment selectively impairs classical conditioning of contextual cues: Possible involvement of the hippocampus. *Society for Neuroscience Abstracts, 24*, 1007.

Miller, G. A., Levin, D. N., Kozak, M. J., Cook, E. W., McLean, A., & Lang, P. J. (1987). Individual differences in emotional imagery. *Cognition and Emotion, 1*, 367–390.

Miller, M. W., Curtin, J. J., & Patrick, C. J. (1999). A startle-probe methodology for investigating the effects of active avoidance on stress reactivity. *Biological Psychology, 50*, 235–257.

Miller, M. W., Patrick, C. J., & Levenston, G. K. (2002). Startle responding during text-prompted imagery: Probing specific emotions, personal experiences, and mechanisms of modulation. *Psychophysiology, 39*, 519–529.

Miller, N. E. (1959). Liberalization of basic S–R concepts: Extensions to conflict behavior, motivation and social learning. In S. Koch (Ed.), *Psychology: A study of a science* (Vol. 2, pp. 196–292). New York: McGraw-Hill.

Miltner, W., Matjak, M., Braun, C., Diekmann, H., & Brody, S. (1994). Emotional qualities of odors and their influence on the startle reflex in humans. *Psychophysiology, 31*, 107–110.

Morgan, A. B., & Lilienfeld, S. O. (2000). A meta-analytic review of the relation between antisocial behavior and neuropsychological measures of executive function. *Clinical Psychology Review, 20*, 113–136.

Moruzzi, G., & Magoun, H. W. (1949). Brain stem reticular formation and activation of the EEG. *Electroencephalography and Clinical Neurophysiology, 1*, 455–473.

Mowrer, O. H. (1960). *Learning theory and behavior.* New York: Wiley.

Nadel, L., & Willner, J. (1980). Context and conditioning: A place for space. *Physiological Psychology, 8*, 218–228.

Neale, M. C., & Cardon, L. R. (1992). *Methodology for genetic studies of twins and families.* Dordrecht, The Netherlands: Kluwer Academic.

Newman, J. P., & Kosson, D. S. (1986). Passive avoidance learning in psychopathic and nonpsychopathic offenders. *Journal of Abnormal Psychology, 95*, 252–256.

Newman, J. P., Schmitt, W. A., & Voss, W. D. (1997). The impact of motivationally neutral cues on psychopathic individuals: Assessing the generality of the response modulation hypothesis. *Journal of Abnormal Psychology, 106*, 563–575.

Newman, J. P., & Wallace, J. F. (1993). Psychopathy and cognition. In K. S. Dobson & P. C. Kendall (Eds.), *Psychopathology and cognition* (pp. 293–349). Academic Press.

Newman, J. P., Widom, C. S., & Nathan, S. (1985). Passive avoidance in syndromes of disinhibition: Psychopathy and extraversion. *Journal of Personality and Social Psychology, 48,* 1316–1327.

Öhman, A. (1993). Fear and anxiety as emotional phenomena: Clinical phenomenology, evolutionary perspectives, and information processing mechanisms. In M. Lewis & J. M. Haviland (Eds.), *Handbook of emotions* (pp. 511–536). New York: Guilford.

Öhman, A., & Soares, J. J. F. (1993). On the automatic nature of phobic fear: Conditioned electrodermal responses to masked fear-relevant stimuli. *Journal of Abnormal Psychology, 102,* 121–132.

Öhman, A., & Soares, J. J. F. (1994). "Unconscious anxiety": Phobic responses to masked stimuli. *Journal of Abnormal Psychology, 103,* 231–240.

Papez, J. W. (1937). A proposed mechanism of emotion. *Archives of Neurology and Psychiatry, 38,* 725–743.

Patrick, C. J. (1994). Emotion and psychopathy: Startling new insights. *Psychophysiology, 31,* 319–330.

Patrick, C. J. (1995, Fall). Emotion and temperament in psychopathy. *Clinical Science,* 5–8.

Patrick, C. J. (1997). Deconstructing psychopathy. *Psychological Inquiry, 8,* 244–251.

Patrick, C. J., & Berthot, B. D. (1995). Startle potentiation during anticipation of a noxious stimulus: Active versus passive response sets. *Psychophysiology, 32,* 72–80.

Patrick, C. J., Berthot, B., & Moore, J. D. (1996). Diazepam blocks fear-potentiated startle in humans. *Journal of Abnormal Psychology, 105,* 89–96.

Patrick, C. J., Bradley, M. M., & Lang, P. J. (1993). Emotion in the criminal psychopath: Startle reflex modulation. *Journal of Abnormal Psychology, 102,* 82–92.

Patrick, C. J., Cuthbert, B. N., & Lang, P. J. (1994) Emotion in the criminal psychopath: Fear image processing. *Journal of Abnormal Psychology, 103,* 523–534.

Patrick, C. J., Hicks, B. M., Krueger, R. F., & Lang, A. R. (2005). Relations between psychopathy facets and externalizing in a criminal offender sample. *Journal of Personality Disorders, 19,* 339–356.

Patrick, C. J., & Lang, A. R. (1999). Psychopathic traits and intoxicated states: Affective concomitants and conceptual links. In M. E. Dawson, A. M. Schell, & A. H. Boehmelt (Eds.), *Startle modification: Implications for clinical science, cognitive science, and neuroscience* (pp. 209–230). New York: Cambridge University Press.

Patrick, C. J., & Lavoro, S. A. (1997). Ratings of emotional response to pictorial stimuli: Positive and negative affect dimensions. *Motivation and Emotion, 21,* 297–321.

Patrick, C. J., Zempolich, K. A., & Levenston, G. K. (1997). Emotionality and violent behavior in psychopaths: A biosocial analysis. In A. Raine, D. Farrington, P. Brennan, & S. A. Mednick (Eds.), *The biosocial bases of violence* (pp. 145–161). New York: Plenum.

Patterson, C. M., & Newman, J. P. (1993). Reflectivity and learning from aversive events: Toward a psychological mechanism for the syndromes of disinhibition. *Psychological Review, 100,* 716–736.

Phillips, R. G., & LeDoux, J. E. (1992). Differential contribution of amygdala and hippocampus to cued and contextual fear conditioning. *Behavioral Neuroscience, 106,* 274–285.

Pihl, R. O., & Peterson, J. B. (1993). Alcohol and aggression: Three potential mechanisms of the drug effect. In S. Martin (Ed.), *Alcohol and interpersonal violence: Fostering interdisciplinary perspectives* (NIAAA Research Monograph No. 24, pp. 149–159). Washington, DC: U.S. Department of Health and Human Services.

Pihl, R. O., Peterson, J. B., & Lau, M. (1993). A biosocial model of the alcohol-aggression relationship. *Journal of Studies on Alcohol,* Suppl. 11, 128–139.

Plutchik, R. (1984). Emotions: A general psychoevolutionary theory. In K. Scherer & P. Ekman (Eds.), *Approaches to emotion* (pp. 197–219). Hillsdale, NJ: Lawrence Erlbaum Associates.

Pohorecky, L. A., Cagan, M., Brick, J., & Jaffe, L. S. (1976). The startle response in rats: Effects of ethanol. *Pharmacology: Biochemistry and Behavior, 4,* 311–316.

Polich, J., Pollock, V. E., & Bloom, F. E. (1994). Meta-analysis of P300 amplitude from males at risk for alcoholism. *Psychological Bulletin, 115,* 55–73.

Raine, A. (1989). Evoked potentials and psychopathy. *International Journal of Psychophysiology, 8,* 1–16.

Raine, A. (1993). *The psychopathology of crime.* San Diego, CA: Academic Press.

Romanski, L. M., & LeDoux, J. E. (1992). Equipotentiality of thalamo-amygdala and thalamo-cortico-amygdala projections as auditory conditioned stimulus pathways. *Journal of Neuroscience, 12,* 4501–4509.

Rosen, J. B., Hitchcock, J. M., Sananes, C. B., Miserendino, M. J. D., & Davis, M. (1991). A direct projection from the central nucleus of the amygdala to the acoustic startle pathway: Anterograde and retrograde tracing studies. *Behavioral Neuroscience, 102,* 817–825.

Rudy, J. W., & Sutherland, R. J. (1992). Configural and elemental associations and the memory coherence problem. *Journal of Cognitive Neuroscience, 4,* 208–216.

Russell, J. A., & Mehrabian, A. (1977). Evidence for a three-factor theory of emotions. *Journal of Research in Personality, 11,* 273–294.

Sarlo, M., Palomba, D., Angrilli, A., & Stegagno, L. (1998). Autonomic and attentional correlates of affective processing [Abstract]. *Psychophysiology, 35,* S71.

Sayette, M. A. (1993). An appraisal-disruption model of alcohol's effects on stress response in social drinkers. *Psychological Bulletin, 114,* 459–476.

Schachter, S. (1964). The interaction of cognitive and physiological determinants of emotional state. In L. Berkowitz (Ed.), *Advances in experimental social psychology* (Vol. 1, pp. 49–80). New York: Academic Press.

Schachter, S., & Singer, J. E. (1962). Cognitive, social, and physiological determinants of emotional state. *Psychological Review, 69,* 379–399.

Schachter, S., & Wheeler, L. (1962). Epinephrine, chlorpromazine, and amusement. *Journal of Abnormal and Social Psychology, 65,* 121–128.

Schmitt, W. A., & Newman, J. P. (1999). Are all psychopathic individuals low anxious? *Journal of Abnormal Psychology, 108,* 353–358.

Schneirla, T. C. (1959). An evolutionary and developmental theory of biphasic processes underlying approach and withdrawal. In *Nebraska Symposium on Motivation: 1959* (pp. 1–42). Lincoln: University of Nebraska Press.

Schwartz, G. E., Brown, G., & Ahern, G. (1980). Facial muscle patterning and subjective experience during affective imagery: Sex differences. *Psychophysiology, 17,* 75–82.

Selden, N. R. W., Everitt, B. J., Jarrard, L. E., & Robbins, T. W. (1991). Complementary roles for the amygdala and hippocampus in aversive conditioning to explicit and contextual cues. *Neuroscience, 42,* 335–350.

Sher, K. (1987). Stress-response dampening. In H. Blane & K. Leonard (Eds.), *Psychological theories of alcoholism* (pp. 227–271). New York: Guilford.

Siddle, D. A. T., & Trasler, G. B. (1981). The psychophysiology of psychopathic behavior. In M. J. Christie & P. G. Mellett (Eds.), *Foundations of psychosomatics* (pp. 283–303). New York: Wiley.

Smith, S. S., & Newman, J. P. (1990). Alcohol and drug abuse-dependence disorders in psychopathic and nonpsychopathic criminal offenders. *Journal of Abnormal Psychology, 99*, 430–439.

Squire, L. R. (1992). Memory and the hippocampus: A synthesis from findings with rats, monkeys, and humans. *Psychological Review, 99*, 195–231.

Steele, C. M., & Josephs, R. A. (1988). Drinking your troubles away. II: An attention-allocation model of alcohol's effect on psychological stress. *Journal of Abnormal Psychology, 97*, 196–205.

Steele, C. M., & Josephs, R. A. (1990). Alcohol myopia: Its prized and dangerous effects. *American Psychologist, 45*, 921–933.

Stritzke, W. G. K., Lang, A. R., & Patrick, C. J. (1996). Beyond stress and arousal: A reconceptualization of alcohol-emotion relations with special reference to psychophysiological methods. *Psychological Bulletin, 120*, 376–395.

Stritzke, W. G. K., Patrick, C. J., & Lang, A. R. (1995). Alcohol and human emotion: A multidimensional analysis incorporating startle-probe methodology. *Journal of Abnormal Psychology, 104*, 114–122.

Tellegen, A. (1982). *Brief Manual for the Multidimensional Personality Questionnaire.* Unpublished manuscript, University of Minnesota.

Tellegen, A. (1985). Structures of mood and personality and their relevance to assessing anxiety, with an emphasis on self-report. In A. H. Tuma & J. D. Maser (Eds.), *Anxiety and the anxiety disorders* (pp. 681–706). Hillsdale, NJ: Lawrence Erlbaum Associates.

Tellegen, A. (in press). *Manual for the Multidimensional Personality Questionnaire.* Minneapolis, MN: University of Minnesota Press.

Tellegen, A., Lykken, D. T., Bouchard, T. S., Wilcox, K. J., Segal, N. L., & Rich, S. (1988). Personality similarity in twins reared apart and together. *Journal of Personality and Social Psychology, 54*, 1031–1039.

Tellegen, A., & Waller, N. G. (1992). Exploring personality through test construction: Development of the Multidimensional Personality Questionnaire. Unpublished manuscript, University of Minnesota.

Tranel, D., & Damasio, H. (1994). Neuroanatomical correlates of electrodermal skin conductance responses. *Psychophysiology, 31*, 427–438.

Venables, P. H., & Christie, M. J. (1973). Mechanisms, instrumentation, scoring techniques, and quantification of responses. In W. F. Prokasy & D. C. Raskin (Eds.), *Electrodermal activity in psychological research* (pp. 1–124). New York: Wiley.

Verona, E., & Patrick, C. J. (2000). Suicide risk in externalizing syndromes: Temperamental and neurobiological underpinnings. In T. E. Joiner (Ed.), *Suicide science: Expanding the boundaries*, pp. 137–173. Boston: Kluwer Academic.

Verona, E., Patrick, C. J., & Joiner, T. T. (2001). Psychopathy, antisocial personality, and suicide risk. *Journal of Abnormal Psychology, 110*, 462–470.

Vrana, S. R., & Lang, P. J. (1990). Fear imagery and the startle probe reflex. *Journal of Abnormal Psychology, 99*, 181–189.

Vrana, S. R., Spence, E. L., & Lang, P. J. (1988). The startle probe response: A new measure of emotion? *Journal of Abnormal Psychology, 97*, 487–491.

Watson, D., Clark, L. A., & Tellegen, A. (1988). Development and validation of brief measures of positive and negative affect: The PANAS scales. *Journal of Personality & Social Psychology, 54*, 1063–1070.

Watson, D., & Tellegen, A. (1985). Toward a consensual structure of mood. *Psychological Bulletin, 98*, 219–235.

Williamson, S., Harpur, T. J., & Hare, R. D. (1991). Abnormal processing of affective words by psychopaths. *Psychophysiology, 28*, 260–273.

Witvliet, C. V., & Vrana, S. R. (1995). Psychophysiological responses as indices of affective dimensions. *Psychophysiology, 32*, 436–443.

Zajonc, R. B. (1980). Feeling and thinking: Preferences need no inferences. *American Psychologist, 35*, 151–175.

Zajonc, R. B. (1984). On the primacy of affect. *American Psychologist, 39*, 117–123.

Zeichner, A., & Pihl, R. O. (1979). Effects of alcohol and behavior contingencies on human aggression. *Journal of Abnormal Psychology, 88*, 153–160.

Zeichner, A., & Pihl, R. O. (1980). Effects of alcohol and instigator intent on human aggression. *Journal of Studies on Alcohol, 41*, 265–276.

Zillmann, D. (1983). Transfer of excitation in emotional behavior. In J. T. Cacioppo & R. E. Petty (Eds.), *Social psychophysiology* (pp. 215–240). New York: Guilford.

9

The Neurobiology of Psychopathy: A Focus on Emotion Processing

Catherine M. Herba, Sheilagh Hodgins, Nigel Blackwood, Veena Kumari, Kris H. Naudts, and Mary Phillips

The ability to identify emotionally salient cues in the environment (including signals of reward and danger) and to respond appropriately is a core component of human social cognition (Darwin, 1872; Ekman, 2003; Phillips, Drevets, Rauch, & Lane, 2003a). Developmental deficits in social cognition are risk factors for maladjustment and psychiatric disorders across the life span (Izard, 1977; Green, Kern, Robertson, Sergi, & Kee, 2000; for reviews, see Blair, 2003; Phillips, Drevets, Rauch, & Lane, 2003b). In this chapter we focus on the developmental deficit in emotion processing observed in men with psychopathy: the factor known as *Deficient Affective Experience* from the Psychopathy Checklist–Revised (PCL–R; Hare, 1991) and from the screening version (PCL:SV; Hart, Cox, & Hare, 1995). The correlates of this emotional dysfunction observed in children are described. Next, the abnormalities in autonomic and cognitive functioning displayed by adults with psychopathy indicative of deficient emotion processing are reviewed. The structural and functional neurobiology of deficient affective processing among adults with psychopathy is described in detail and discussed in light of explanatory models arising from Damasio's (1995) somatic marker hypothesis and Blair's (1995) violence inhibition hypothesis. The chapter concludes with a discussion of the utility of brain imaging for identifying the neural deficits associated with psychopathy and a proposal for future research, with a specific focus on the development of deficient affective processing in men with psychopathy.

DEFICIENT AFFECTIVE EXPERIENCE IN MEN WITH PSYCHOPATHY

Factor analytic studies suggest that the syndrome of psychopathy, as diagnosed in adulthood, is composed of three factors[1] (Cooke & Michie, 2001): an

---

[1]Although a four-factor model was suggested in some recent studies, our work is based on the older three-factor mode. Deficient affective experience from the three-factor model is iden-

Impulsive Behavioral Style resulting in persistent antisocial behavior from a young age; an *Arrogant and Deceitful Interpersonal Style*; and *Deficient Affective Experience*. The first factor is not specific to psychopathy. It describes individuals similar to those who meet the *Diagnostic and Statistical Manual of Mental Disorders*, 4th ed. *(DSM–IV)* (American Psychiatric Association, 1994) criteria for antisocial personality disorder (APD), who by definition had conduct disorder (CD) as children. Within this population of persons who display persistent antisocial behavior from a young age, those characterized by arrogant and deceitful interpersonal behavior and deficient affective experience constitute a subgroup labeled *psychopaths*. Deficient Affective Experience is a profound emotional dysfunction. Four items of the PCL–R load onto this factor: lack of remorse or guilt, shallow affect, callous/lack of empathy, and failure to take responsibility for one's own actions. This trait has been found to be the most important factor for identifying individuals who meet the diagnostic criteria for psychopathy (Cooke & Michie, 2001), even in samples drawn from different cultures (Cooke & Michie, 1999).

Callous and Unemotional Children:
A Developmental Perspective

The proposal that adults with psychopathy constitute a subgroup of individuals within a larger population of persons who all display persistent antisocial behavior across the life span is supported by the results of studies of children and adolescents. Prospective longitudinal investigations of birth cohorts conducted in different countries (Hodgins, 1994; Moffitt & Caspi, 2001) have consistently identified approximately 4% to 5% of males and less than 1% of females who show persistent antisocial behavior across the lifespan. As children, such individuals would meet *DSM–IV* criteria for CD with onset before age 10. Studies of clinical samples of children referred for behavior problems have found that whereas most display antisocial behavior and poor impulse control, a small subgroup show, in addition to conduct problems, callous–unemotional traits (Frick, O'Brien, Wootton, McBurnett, 1994; O'Brien & Frick, 1996). The children characterized by callous–unemotional traits are distinguished from other children with CD in that they have a greater number and variety of conduct problems, more instrumental aggression, more police contacts, higher IQ scores, and a higher prevalence rate of APD among their parents (Caputo, Frick, & Brodsky, 1999; Christian, Frick, Hill, Tyler, & Frazer, 1997; Frick, Cornell, Barry, Bodin, & Dane, 2003). Further, this subgroup of children defined by callous–unemotional traits has been found to be unresponsive to parenting practices that positively influence the behavior of other children with CD (Wootten, Frick, Shelton, & Silverthorn, 1997). Similarly, among a sample of incarcerated adolescent delin-

---

tical to that in the four-factor model and describes the emotional dysfunction that we hypothesize denotes the core of psychopathy. As reviewed in the chapter, there is evidence that this factor is related to brain abnormalities and that it is inherited.

quents, cluster analysis again revealed a small subgroup characterized not only by persistent antisocial behavior since a young age but also callous–unemotional traits (Vincent, Vitacco, Grisso, & Corrado, 2003). After release, this subgroup had significantly higher rates of reconviction for violent offenses and shorter times in the community free of conviction than the other groups of delinquents.

Studies focused specifically on children with psychopathic tendencies as indexed by the presence of callous–unemotional traits have identified deficits in emotion recognition (Stevens, Charman, & Blair, 2001; for review, see Blair, 2003) and in cognitive and emotional empathy (Pardini, Lochman, & Frick, 2003). Blair, Colledge, Murray, and Mitchell (2001) examined facial expression recognition in boys with emotional and behavioral problems, split into two groups based on the presence or absence of psychopathic tendencies, as assessed by teachers using the Antisocial Process Screening Device (APSD; Frick & Hare, 2001). Children with psychopathic tendencies made more errors in detecting fearful expressions (i.e., misclassifying them to another emotion category) and were also less sensitive in detecting sad expressions (i.e., requiring a significantly higher intensity of facial expression before correctly identifying sadness) compared with the comparison group. Consistent with these findings, Stevens et al. (2001) reported similar selective impairments in boys with psychopathic tendencies in recognizing sad and fearful faces and sad vocal tone. They did not differ from boys without psychopathic tendencies in their ability to recognize happy and angry faces and happy, angry, and fearful tones. These studies provide evidence for a deficit in emotion recognition that is specific to fear and sadness among children with psychopathic tendencies and early-onset antisocial behavior.

Pardini et al. (2003) studied social cognition and callous–unemotional traits in a sample of adjudicated youths. Callous–unemotional traits (assessed by the APSD) were associated with deficits in cognitive and emotional empathy, whereas the impulsivity/conduct problems were linked to self-reported deficits in behavioral regulation. Higher levels of callous–unemotional traits were associated with increased expectations of positive consequences and decreased expectations of punishment for aggressive behavior. These findings, together with evidence of lower levels of fearfulness in these children, suggest a dampened sensitivity to punishment (Frick, Lilienfeld, Ellis, Loney, & Silverthorn, 1999; Pardini et al., 2003). Children with early-onset CD in addition to callous–unemotional traits fail to learn in passive avoidance paradigms and fail to learn from punishment (Fisher & Blair, 1998), which is consistent with findings in psychopathic male adults (see Newman, 1998). Intact emotion processing of sadness and fear may be important components in learning empathy from a young age, through the ability to experience emotional distress when punished or when viewing others experiencing emotional distress (Blair, Morris, Frith, Perrett, & Dolan, 1999, Pardini et al., 2003).

In addition to the emotional deficits observed among children with callous–unemotional traits, there are also cognitive abnormalities similar to those observed among adult men with psychopathy. Children with these

traits expect rewards for aggressive behavior, focus on the positive consequences of aggression (Pardini et al., 2003), and show a preference for more
risky decision making in the gambling task (Bechara, Damasio, Damasio, &
Anderson, 1994; Bechara, Damasio, Damasio, & Lee, 1999; Blair, Colledge, &
Mitchell, 2001). Unlike men with psychopathy (LaPierre, Braun, & Hodgins,
1995; Mitchell, Colledge, Leonard, & Blair, 2002), however, children with
callous–unemotional traits do not appear to show impairment on response
reversal (i.e., learning to reverse previously rewarded behavior when it is
no longer associated with reward) (Blair et al., 2001; see the section on *A
Contrast of the Theories* later in the chapter for possible implications of this
observation).

The studies reviewed suggest that the core symptoms of psychopathy
emerge at a young age. This suggestion is further supported by recent findings from twin studies: one in adults (Blonigen, Carlson, Krueger, & Patrick,
2003), two in adolescents (Larsson, Andershed, & Lichtenstein, in press; Taylor, Loney, Bobadilla, Iacono, & McGue, 2003), and one in 7-year-old twins
(Viding, Blair, Moffitt, & Plomin, 2005). All four studies indicate that hereditary factors contribute to callous–unemotional traits. In addition, in a recent
meta-analysis of twin and family studies, the genetic contribution to early-
onset persistent antisocial behavior was estimated to be ~41% (Rhee & Waldman, 2002). Interestingly, the Swedish twin study (Larsson et al., in press) in
which hereditary factors were examined in relation to the three-factor model
of psychopathy showed no evidence for an impact of genes on Arrogant and
Deceitful Interpersonal Behavior.

A Hypothesis

We and others (Hare, 1998; Blair, 2003) hypothesize that deficient affective
processing represents the core deficit of psychopathy. We postulate that it
emerges at a very young age and contributes to the development of the other
aspects of the syndrome of psychopathy. If an inability to experience emotions as others do and to empathize with the emotions experienced by others were present early in childhood, it would limit learning requiring an emotional response or the recognition of emotional responses. Such a deficit could
in turn contribute to the development of an arrogant and deceitful interpersonal style. Four items define this latter factor derived from the PCL–R:
glibness and superficial charm, grandiose sense of self-worth, pathological
lying, and conning/manipulative behavior. A child characterized by shallow
affect and callousness could easily feel superior toward others who are constantly constrained and limited by their emotions. Such experiences could
generalize so that the child comes to believe that he or she is not responsible
for the consequences of his or her own actions. Together the childhood variants of Deficient Affective Experience and Arrogant and Deceitful Interpersonal Style would contribute to the development of persistent antisocial
behavior. Pain inflicted on others as a consequence of lies or manipulation

would not be recognized. Harm to others would not be constrained by the recognition of distress in the victims, learning in passive avoidance paradigms would not occur, and negative reinforcement and punishment would not be associated with appropriate behavior because the perpetrator would fail to take responsibility for his or her own actions. This hypothesized developmental trajectory is presented in Fig. 9–1.

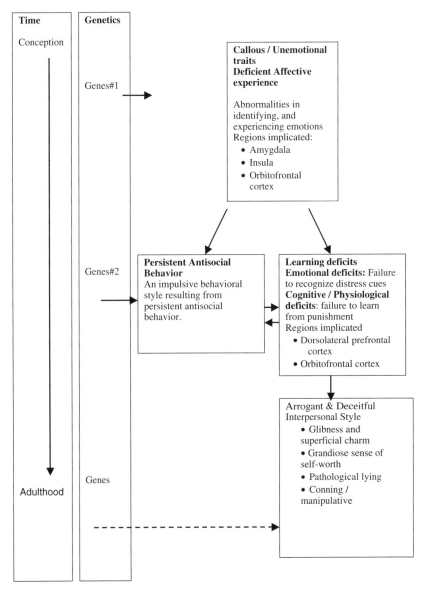

FIGURE 9–1.   Hypothesized pathways to psychopathy: neurobiological correlates.

Deficient Affective Experience in Adults With Psychopathy: Physiological and Neuropsychological Studies

Autonomic Nervous System Deficits

Men with psychopathy display attenuated autonomic responses (see Hare, 1998). Studies assessing autonomic responses in adults with psychopathy and without psychopathy have tended to use basic learning paradigms, incorporating conditions of reward and punishment (Newman & Kosson, 1986, for review, see Newman, 1998), together with physiological measures, such as heart rate[2] (HR), skin conductance response[3] (SCR), and electroencephalography.[4] There is evidence that men diagnosed with psychopathy have difficulty in acquiring a conditioned fear response as assessed by SCR (Lykken, 1957), consistently demonstrating smaller increases in SCR and larger increases in HR compared with male offenders without psychopathy (Hare, 1998). SCR is an index of arousal, whereas HR varies with the metabolic processing requirements of a task and secondarily with the emotional significance of stimuli (Flor, Birbaumer, Hermann, Ziegler, & Patrick, 2002). Hare (1998) proposed that healthy adults, unlike those with psychopathy, elicit a defensive response (i.e., increased SCR and HR) to an anticipated aversive stimulus. This ability to block an anticipatory fear response in individuals with psychopathy might limit the emotional or psychological impact of cues associated with pain or punishment.

There is evidence that the startle reflex is altered in response to viewing emotional stimuli such that presentation of pleasant stimuli attenuates and

---

[2]The HR response is controlled by both the sympathetic and parasympathetic systems of the autonomic nervous system and may rapidly increase or decrease (Hare, 1998).

[3]The SCR reflects a change in secretion of the sweat glands, associated with a concomitant decrease in electrical resistance (see Hare, 1998), and increases are based on sympathetic system arousal. The response usually begins after a few seconds of stimulus presentation and remains for a few seconds.

[4]The electrochemical output of neural activity when large numbers of neurons working together produce electrical potentials that can be measured by electrodes placed on the scalp. A change in voltage from the signal between a recording and reference electrode can be measured, and has been referred to as an electroencephalogram. The electroencephalogram yields a continuous recording of overall brain activity and owing to well-established electroencephalographic patterns, electroencephalogram recordings can help to detect abnormalities in brain activity. The ERP assesses brain activity in response to a particular task. In ERPs, electroencephalographic traces for specific events (i.e., the onset of a stimulus or a response in a particular task) are averaged together. These *average* traces will highlight the neural activity specifically related to the event of interest (i.e., sensory, motor, or cognitive response). One advantage of the ERP relates to a good temporal recording of neural activity and associated changes as information is being processed in the brain. Compared with functional magnetic resonance imaging (MRI) that assesses brain activity indirectly (i.e., blood flow), ERPs yield a direct assessment of neuronal activity. From a practical point of view, measurement of ERPs is much less expensive than MRI and the equipment is much more mobile. This is a particular advantage for a prison population where it is not easy to remove people from the prison for testing.

unpleasant stimuli potentiates the response compared with presentation of neutral material (Vrana, Spence, & Lang, 1988). Individuals with psychopathy fail to show the potentiation of startle while viewing unpleasant stimuli (Patrick, Bradley, & Lang, 1993) and show abnormal physiological responses to positive and negative emotional sounds (Verona, Patrick, Curtin, Bradley, & Lang, 2004). It has been suggested that these abnormalities are mediated by the affective component of psychopathy rather than by the behavioral or antisocial aspects (Patrick, 1994; Patrick et al., 1993). Patrick (1994) further linked deficient startle response in individuals with psychopathy to deficits in responding to fearful stimuli.

Flor et al. (2002) examined passive avoidance learning in nonincarcerated men with psychopathy, using unpleasant odor as the unconditioned stimulus (US) and neutral faces as the conditioned stimulus (CS). Startle reflex and SCR were assessed. There was evidence of a specific deficit in acquiring conditioned aversive responses (which related to aversive conditioning in general and not just fear conditioning). The authors concluded that emotional learning subserved by the orbitofrontal cortex may be deficient in both APD and psychopathy.

Low-anxious offenders with psychopathy have also been shown to respond more quickly and demonstrate greater HR responses to reward rather than to punishment, whereas incarcerated men without psychopathy demonstrated greater HR responses to punishment than to reward (Arnett, Howland, Smith, & Newman, 1993). Offenders with psychopathy also showed lower SCR following punishment. Nevertheless, physiological differences in responses to reward and punishment exist among men with psychopathy.

In summary, the available evidence indicates that autonomic responses to emotional stimuli, particularly in aversive conditioning paradigms, may be deficient among men with psychopathy. Autonomic reactivity to social stimuli is a core component of the somatic marker hypothesis (Damasio, 1995, 1996): Optimal decision making in incompletely specified circumstances depends on the generation and interpretation of signals from the autonomic nervous system. The areas involved in processing such autonomic nervous system-generated cues include the amygdala and orbitofrontal cortex. Intriguingly, patients with orbitofrontal cortex damage and/or amygdalar damage show abnormalities in autonomic reactivity to emotional stimuli similar to those of psychopathic individuals (Mitchell et al., 2002).

Brain Processing Deficits Measured by ERPs

Studies using ERPs to examine language processing in psychopathy have indicated that compared with nonpsychopathic inmates, psychopathic inmates showed less behavioral and electrocortical differentiation between emotional and neutral words (Williamson, Harpur, & Hare, 1991) and less differentiation between concrete and abstract words, with the strongest effect at frontotemporal sites (Kiehl, Hare, McDonald, & Brink, 1999b). This suggests that men with psychopathy do not make appropriate use of the emotional components of language. There is further evidence that incarcerated inmates with and without psychopathy differ from one another in processing even simple cognitive tasks with inhibitory demands, such as the "visual oddball task" (Kiehl, Hare, Liddle, & McDonald, 1999a).

Cognitive Functioning

Men with psychopathy do not display a general cognitive or IQ deficit but rather more specific deficits in executive functioning (Pham, Vanderstukken, Philippot, & Vanderlinden, 2003), autonomic processing of contextual cues during goal-directed behavior, and selective attention (Pham et al., 2003; for review see Hallé, Hodgins, & Roussy, 2000). The response modulation hypothesis, proposed to partially explain the deficient emotional experience of persons with psychopathy, suggests that individuals with psychopathy are less influenced by affective stimuli that are secondary to their goal-directed behavior (Newman, 1998) because they fail to understand the potential significance of contextual cues when processing relies on automatically shifting attention (Newman, 1998). Smith, Arnett, and Newman (1992) examined neuropsychological test performance of male inmates with and without psychopathy and distinguished between inmates with high and low anxiety. No global deficits in performance were observed. However, low-anxious psychopathic inmates performed significantly more poorly on an executive functioning test (the Trail-Making test), and the Block-Design subtest of the IQ test compared with the low-anxious nonpsychopathic inmates. The authors concluded that the low-anxious psychopathic inmates might have difficulty completing cognitively demanding tasks that involve integrating cognitive perceptual and motor processes. In another study, psychopathic individuals with low anxiety showed less interference to motivationally neutral stimuli compared with low-anxious nonpsychopathic individuals indicating, perhaps, a difficulty in automatic processing of contextual cues during goal-directed behavior (Newman, Schmitt, & Voss, 1997). Overall, studies have demonstrated greater deficits among low-anxiety psychopaths relative to high-anxiety nonpsychopaths than among high-anxiety psychopaths.

Executive Functioning

Executive functions[5] may also have an impact on emotion processing. In addition, these self-regulatory functions have been linked with social functioning, such as social sensitivity, social awareness, and empathy, and with the self-regulation of emotions and motivation (Barkley, 1997; Benton, 1991; Pennington & Ozonoff, 1996; Temple, 1997; Wiers, Gunning, & Sergeant,

---

[5]*Executive functioning* is an umbrella term for the coordinated operation of various complex cognitive processes and subprocesses required to accomplish a particular goal in a flexible manner (e.g., solving novel problems, modifying behavior in light of recent information, generating strategies, and sequencing actions) (Elliott, 2003).

1998). The prefrontal cortex is important for higher-order cognitive processes and has been closely linked with executive functions (Roberts & Pennington, 1996; Shallice & Burgess, 1998; Welsh, Pennington, & Groisser, 1991). Damage to the frontal lobes leads to the disruption of executive skills and to impulsive behavior, poor insight, lack of planning ability and good judgment, inflexible thinking, defective affect, attentional problems, and disinhibitory problems (Giancola & Zeichner, 1994; Teichner & Golden, 2000).

Mitchell et al. (2002) noted the behavioral similarities of persons with orbitofrontal cortex lesions and those diagnosed with psychopathy, cautioning, however, that those with orbitofrontal lesions engage in reactive aggression, whereas those with psychopathy engage in instrumental aggression. Although most individuals with persistent antisocial behavior engage in reactive or emotionally charged aggressive behavior, those who meet the criteria for psychopathy use aggressive behavior, as a tool or instrument, to achieve specific ends (Cornell et al., 1996). Mitchell et al. (2002) examined functions thought to depend on orbitofrontal structures, comparing men with and without psychopathy on the gambling task and intradimensional/extradimensional shift task. It was hypothesized that if psychopathic individuals have orbitofrontal deficits, they would show impairment on the gambling task and response-reversal difficulties on the intradimensional/extradimensional shift task. Consistent with the hypothesis, the psychopathic men continued to select from the high-risk deck of cards on the gambling task (whereas the nonpsychopathic men took less risk over time) and showed a deficit in response reversal compared with nonpsychopathic men. They performed similarly to nonpsychopathic men on the attentional, set-shifting, and learning components of the intradimensional/extradimensional shift task. The response-reversal deficits observed among men with psychopathy suggest a failure to take account of relevant peripheral information. Because a key component of the somatic marker hypothesis is that individuals with orbitofrontal cortex lesions demonstrate dampened autonomic responding to emotional stimuli and because boys and men with psychopathy show a specific deficit in recognizing sad and angry expressions but intact responding to other emotions, Mitchell et al. (2002) noted that their findings more strongly supported the response modulation hypothesis than the somatic marker hypothesis. Alternatively, the results can be interpreted as suggesting that a deficit originates in the amygdala and later affects connections necessary to identify the motivational value of a stimulus.

Selective attention, or the ability to ignore irrelevant cues to focus on a current task, may be particularly efficient among men with psychopathy (Hallé et al., 2000). However, Pham et al. (2003) reported contradictory findings in a study of executive functioning and selective attention in psychopathic and nonpsychopathic male inmates. A number of tests assessing executive functioning and selective attention were administered. The results indicated deficits in selective attention but no global deficits in planning ability among inmates with psychopathy. Results also suggested that the performance of men with psychopathy was more affected by distractibility than perseverative responding.

In summary, neuropsychological tests used to investigate cognition among male inmates with psychopathy have highlighted the role of attention. The response modulation hypothesis posits that individuals with psychopathy do not pay attention to affective cues when these stimuli are secondary to their goal-directed behavior. Men with psychopathy fail to attend to peripheral stimuli and have difficulty effectively modulating attention. Selective attention may be particularly evident when reward is involved. Individuals diagnosed with psychopathy may be unlikely to respond emotionally to cues of punishment as indicated by increases in skin conductance responses to affective stimuli if they are focused on a task that is likely to be rewarded.

THE NEURAL CIRCUITRY UNDERLYING EMOTION PROCESSING

Neural Systems That Process Emotions

The brain mechanisms involved in the various processes of emotion perception are not well understood. A recent critical review of animal and human studies proposed that three processes are important for emotion perception: (a) identification and appraisal of the emotional stimulus; (b) production of an affective state or behavior in response to the stimulus; and (c) regulation of the affective state and emotional behavior, which potentially involves the inhibition or modulation of processes (a) and (b) (Phillips et al., 2003a, 2003b). Two neural systems were proposed to underlie emotion processing: a ventral and dorsal system. The ventral system, which includes the amygdala, insula, ventral striatum, and the ventral regions of the anterior cingulate gyrus and prefrontal cortex, is proposed to be important for the identification of emotional stimuli and the production of affective states. The dorsal system, which includes the hippocampus and the dorsal regions of the anterior cingulate gyrus and prefrontal cortex, where cognitive processes may be integrated, is proposed to be important for the effortful regulation of affective states.

A meta-analysis of positron emission tomography (PET)[6] and functional magnetic resonance imaging MRI[7] studies exploring neural regions activated

---

[6]Functional imaging enables the assessment of neural activity during a particular task. Changes in brain activity in response to the task in the regions involved relates to changes in blood flow and metabolism. PET and SPECT are methods of functional neuroimaging and are based on detection of photons emitted by radioactive substances injected into the body. In PET, assessments of local variation in cerebral blood flow associated with mental activity are conducted by introducing a tracer (i.e., radioactive element) into the bloodstream. A higher level of blood flow is evident through increased radiation in that region. To assess the specific effect of the task, radiation measured during the control condition is subtracted from that measured during the experimental condition.

[7]MRI is based on the principle that atoms within the body possess a magnetic charge, which is exaggerated when immersed in a strong magnetic field. In such a magnetic field, the atoms

by various types of emotional stimuli (i.e., faces, voices, and smells) indicated that no specific brain region was consistently activated by all emotional tasks (Phan, Wager, Taylor, & Liberzon, 2002). The medial prefrontal cortex (located within the ventromedial prefrontal cortex), however, was activated by a number of different emotional stimuli, suggesting that it may play a role in emotion processing. The anterior cingulate cortex may contribute to focusing attention on emotionally relevant stimuli and in regulating emotion (see Phan et al., 2002; Phillips et al., 2003a). Other functional imaging studies have consistently shown that the amygdala and the ventral striatum (ventral putamen and caudate nucleus) play a critical role in ascribing emotional significance to stimuli, particularly in the recognition of fearful facial expressions, whereas the insula may play a specific role in the recognition of disgusted facial expressions (Breiter et al., 1996; Calder, Lawrence, & Young, 2001; Killgore, Oki, & Yurgelun-Todd, 2001; Killgore & Yurgelun-Todd, 2001; Morris et al., 1996; Phillips et al., 1997, 1998; Wright et al., 2001). Other studies provide evidence for the role of the amygdala in response to sad and happy facial expressions (Blair et al. 1999; Breiter et al., 1996; Schneider et al., 1997). These neural regions may be differentially activated depending on the emotional stimuli presented, and whether the task involves emotional identification, emotional regulation, or experiencing the emotion.

Very little research has been conducted on the development of these brain structures, and the impact of brain development on emotion processing abilities. There is evidence to suggest, however, that the structures that mediate emotion processing in adults may differ from those used by children (Karmiloff-Smith, 1997; McClure, 2000; for review see Herba & Phillips, 2004).

The Somatic Marker Hypothesis

One way of conceptualizing the affective processing deficits central to psychopathy is within the framework of the somatic marker hypothesis (Damasio, 1995, 1996; Bechara, Damasio, & Damasio, 2000, 2003). *Somatic markers* are

---

resonate at a particular radiofrequency. The radiowaves that are released as the atom returns to its normal state can be detected, and this information is generated into an image via a computer using physics and mathematical functions. There are two types of MRI: structural and functional. Structural MRI provides good spatial resolution and distinguishes between gray and white matter in the brain, allowing for the examination of neuroanatomical structures across different planes in the brain. It allows for the investigation of any abnormalities in brain structure. Functional MRI (fMRI) assesses neural activity indirectly by assessing changes in blood flow associated with a particular task. When a brain area is activated by a task, more oxygen and glucose are made available to neurons by increased blood flow. Assessing brain function during a particular cognitive task allows examination of those brain regions important in performing the task and also the study functional anatomy. An advantage of fMRI over structural MRI is the ability to examine more subtle functional differences between groups relating to information processing.

thought to be responsible for linking an event with a particular feeling. Somatic states, feelings, and emotions are induced from *primary inducers* (stimuli that either innately or by learning lead to pleasurable or aversive feelings). *Secondary inducers* are generated by recalling an emotional event and thereby re-experiencing the emotion associated with the event (e.g., a woman who cries while recalling the death of her son 10 years earlier). The *somatic marker hypothesis* highlights the importance of early normal amygdalar development and subsequent links with the orbitofrontal cortex. Studies of patients with specific lesions suggested that the amygdala is crucial to the primary inducer networks (Bechara et al., 2003). The amygdala has been implicated in classical appetitive and/or aversive conditioning (Buchel, Morris, Dolan, & Friston, 1998), and amygdalar lesions have been shown to impede autonomic reactions to aversive stimuli such as a loud noise. Processing the primary inducer, an emotional stimulus, generates an internal representation of this inducer, and it is this internal representation that now serves as the secondary inducer. Bechara et al. proposed that the ventromedial prefrontal cortex (composed of the orbitofrontal and medial frontal cortex) triggers somatic states in response to secondary inducers by linking an event in memory with the structures that induce somatic responses and with the neural substrates involved in feeling.

The Violence Inhibition Mechanism and Developmental Psychopathy

Blair (1995) proposed the *violence inhibition mechanism* (VIM) to explain the failure of adults with psychopathy to develop morality. This hypothesis is based on evidence from animal research showing that distress cues of a victim play a central role in limiting aggressive behavior by an attacker. Blair suggested that viewing distress cues in others (i.e., US) triggers the VIM (unconditioned response), which leads to empathy with the plight of the victim. Through classical conditioning, representations of the victim's plight are paired with the activation of the VIM (i.e., US). In the case of psychopathy, Blair proposed that there is a disruption to this system, such that the distress cues of the victim do not trigger the VIM (see Blair, 2001). Persons with psychopathy may fail to learn the conditioned emotional response reflecting role-taking or empathy to the cues of distress from the victim. This is consistent with studies indicating an inability on the part of adult men with psychopathy and children with callous–unemotional traits to learn in aversive conditioning paradigms. Evidence for Blair's proposed VIM comes from studies of adult inmates with psychopathy and children with psychopathic tendencies who both demonstrate a selective deficit in emotion processing. These studies, outlined earlier, provide evidence for a specific deficit in recognizing cues of sadness or fear, but no deficits in recognizing happy, angry, or disgust stimuli (Blair et al., 2001; Stevens et al., 2001).

A Contrast of the Theories

The aforementioned theories will be used to guide our examination of the evidence for a disruption in the emotion processing of individuals with psychopathy and associated neurobiological underpinnings. Damasio's (1995, 1996) somatic marker hypothesis has gained support from studies of patients with brain lesions, some of whom have sustained damage, leading to what is called *acquired sociopathy*. The amygdala is proposed to be the primary structure necessary for experiencing emotional stimuli, whereas the ventromedial prefrontal cortex is a key structure in retrieving memories of emotional events or stimulating an emotional response when one is thinking of a hypothetical situation. Blair's (1995) theory is more specific to psychopathy and focuses on emotion processing as a precursor to *moral development* and the ability to empathize with another's distress. It postulates that the amygdala is central to the selective deficits in emotion processing that are observed among men with psychopathy and also highlights the role of the orbitofrontal cortex. The amygdala is thought to be involved in basic learning paradigms, which Blair links to the ability to learn "morality" through conditioning of a learned response between the unconditioned stimuli (distress cues) and conditioned response (i.e., taking the role of the victim, empathizing with the victim, and responding emotionally). The orbitofrontal cortex is highlighted as being important for the response-reversal learning that has been shown to be impaired in adult men with psychopathy but not among children with callous–unemotional traits. Blair's theory focuses on the distinction between the neurobiology of reactive (i.e., involvement of the orbitofrontal cortex) and instrumental aggression (i.e., greater amygdalar involvement). This distinction in type of aggression may be particularly relevant for understanding the neurobiology of psychopathy, because psychopathy is the only syndrome characterized by persistent instrumental aggression (Cornell et al, 1996; Woodworth & Porter, 2002).

NEUROBIOLOGY OF EMOTION PROCESSING

Studies of Patients With Brain Damage

The results of the studies of patients with brain lesions[8] support the somatic marker hypothesis and suggest that the amygdala is necessary for learning

---

[8]Early investigators of brain function and dysfunction relied on lesion studies. In animals, the aim of this research has been to examine the contribution of a particular structure by lesioning or damaging it and then examining the impact of the removal of this structure on subsequent functioning or behavior. Experimental lesioning is impossible in humans; however the effect of brain damage sustained through accident or disease on subsequent behavioral or cognitive functioning has been examined. It proved to be a valuable method before more advanced methodology was available. A disadvantage of lesion studies is that the dysfunction of one brain region may

an emotional response and for making social judgments based on visual, but not necessarily verbal, information (Adolphs, Tranel, Damasio, & Damasio, 1994, 1995; Adolphs, Tranel, & Damasio, 1998). The amygdala and hippocampus may also play different roles in emotional conditioning, with the hippocampus being important for learning the association between a CS and an US and the amygdala being involved with generating a SCR to a CS (Bechara et al., 1995). Further evidence indicates that damage sustained early in life leads to the most severe outcomes. Early damage to the orbitofrontal regions has been associated with more severe disruption to social functioning and behavior than with similar lesions acquired in adulthood (Anderson, Bechara, Damasio, Tranel, & Damasio, 1999; Damasio, Tranel, & Damasio, 1990). Amygdalar damage that occurred later in life was not associated with the same degree of impairment in judging emotional expressions as amygdalar damage early in development (Hamann et al., 1996). Bechara et al. (2003) suggested that the amygdala is a crucial precursor to the normal development of the orbitofrontal system in triggering somatic states. If an individual sustained amygdalar damage early in life, emotion expression recognition was severely impaired. The amygdala has extensive connections with the ventromedial prefrontal cortex. If, early in development, the amygdala was damaged or was abnormal, feed-forward connections and the ventromedial prefrontal cortex would be compromised, leading to a reduced ability to respond to secondary inducers. If, however, the amygdala was damaged later in life, after the connections with the orbitofrontal cortex and appropriate responding to secondary inducers were established, significantly less impairment in judging emotional expressions would be evident. Nonetheless, normal amygdalar development may be necessary for later appropriate functioning of the orbitofrontal cortex.

In summary, the results of studies of patients with brain lesions and of neuroimaging studies of healthy adults concur in identifying the amygdala as being important for ascribing social significance to emotional stimuli, the recognition of fearful expressions, and aversive conditioning. However, the results from studies of patients with brain lesions should be interpreted with caution, principally because brain damage is rarely limited to only one structure and because patients with similar damage are rare.

BRAIN IMAGING STUDIES OF MEN
WITH PSYCHOPATHY

We hypothesize that, consistent with the somatic marker hypothesis, psychopathy can be characterized by an early amygdalar abnormality that is

---

alter the normal functioning of other brain regions as the brain attempts to compensate for the damage. Furthermore, lesion studies are often not very specific; because the brain is highly interconnected, damage in one area may have extensive consequences for a range of areas (for review, see Gazzaniga, 1998).

exacerbated during development as pathways to frontal regions fail to develop appropriately. This hypothesis is based on the notion that the core component of psychopathy is a deficient affective experience and on the robust body of literature in which the role of the amygdala and ventromedial prefrontal cortex in emotion processing in healthy adults is delineated. Disruptions to the amygdala–ventromedial prefrontal cortex circuit may lead to deficits in emotional learning that have been consistently observed in behavioral studies of men with psychopathy (see Newman, 1998). Furthermore, based on Phillips et al.'s (2003a) neurobiological model of emotion processing, the deficient affective experience of the psychopath may depend to a greater extent on the subcortical and ventral frontal cortical regions necessary for identifying and generating emotional states, whereas the impulsive behavioral component of psychopathy may relate to the second system involved in the regulation of subsequent behavior.

Before we review the available neuroimaging literature on psychopathy, it is essential to note that our understanding of psychopathy is limited by the characteristics of the sample groups who have been studied. Almost all research on psychopathy has been undertaken with adults. Consequently, identifying a core deficit is difficult. A primary deficit in emotion processing, we hypothesize, emerges very early in life. It is well known that children learn to compensate for deficits just as the brain compensates by reorganizing and using alternate structures when specific areas are damaged. The abnormalities that may characterize the adult diagnosed with psychopathy may represent the ways in which the brain reorganized after an early insult or they may reflect the ways in which the individual learned to cope in a world that was hard to understand, for example, due to his or her inability to recognize emotions. Abnormalities observed in adult psychopaths could also result from abuse of alcohol and/or drugs or have been exacerbated by repeated intoxication. Our understanding is further limited by the fact that almost all of the relevant studies have been undertaken with men. A final limitation is that available evidence derives from studies of offenders. Given that persons with psychopathy are characterized by reduced emotionality, they may be affected in different ways than nonpsychopathic offenders by lengthy periods of incarceration; yet, personality traits change little over the life span (Harpur & Hare, 1994). A deficient affective experience is present in adults with psychopathy, and we aim to review studies in an effort to understand the neurobiological underpinnings of this emotional deficit.

Methodological advances in neuroimaging techniques have expanded the possibilities for examining the neurobiology underlying psychopathy. Structural and fMRI, PET, and single-photon emission computed tomography (SPECT) techniques have made it possible to examine brain structures and functions while subjects engage in cognitive or affective processing tasks (see Bassarath, 2001, for explanation of techniques and applications to antisocial behavior).

Studies of Brain Structures

Prefrontal Cortex[9]

Raine, Lencz, Bihrle, LaCasse, and Colletti (2000), using structural MRI, reported a significant reduction in prefrontal gray matter volume in men with APD compared with control men. It is not presently known whether men who meet criteria for psychopathy on the PCL–R are characterized by similar reductions in volume, although the sample of men with APD had an average PCL–R score of 28. This study did not specifically examine orbito-frontal cortex volumes.

Laakso et al. (2002) examined prefrontal volume loss in men with APD and Cloninger Type 2 alcoholism,[10] who had been convicted of a serious crime compared with hospital staff and relatives with no history of substance abuse who were similar in age. Regions of interest (ROIs)[11] were generated for different regions of the frontal lobe and covered the dorsolateral pre-frontal cortex, the orbitofrontal cortex, the medial frontal gyrus, and the pre-frontal white matter. There were no significant correlations between the volumes of the different regions and PCL–R scores in the antisocial group. Volumes of the dorsolateral prefrontal cortex, orbitofrontal cortex, and medial frontal gyrus were significantly smaller in the group with APD, but differences disappeared after controlling for duration of alcohol abuse and education. No comparison group of nonpsychopathic offenders was included, thereby limiting the interpretations of the findings.

Hippocampus[12]

Laakso et al. (2001) examined the association between the volume of the hippocampus and PCL–R scores in violent male offenders with Type 2

---

[9]The prefrontal cortex is important for higher-order cognitive processes, executive functions, and coordinating and integrating cognitive and perceptual processes across time and space (Roberts & Pennington, 1996; Shallice & Burgess, 1996; Welsh, Pennington, & Groisser, 1991).

[10]Cloninger Type 2 alcoholism is a subtype of alcoholism associated with novelty seeking, harm avoidance and reward dependence, and antisocial behavior (Johnson, Waid, & Anton, 1997; Laakso et al., 2002).

[11]A ROI can be defined around particular brain areas of interest, allowing for the examination of activity within that region during a cognitive task with functional MRI or structural differences in that area. ROIs can be defined anatomically or functionally; for anatomical ROIs, the boundaries of the region are delineated based on anatomical landmarks and for functional ROIs the region is defined based on the extent of the activated cluster. Functional ROI allows for more detailed hypothesis-driven examination of function and structure rather than activation changes over the whole brain.

[12]The hippocampus, situated close to the amygdala in the temporal lobe, plays a critical role in memory (Rolls & Treves, 1999) and in emotion processing (Lange et al., 2003; Phillips et al., 2003a) and may play a role as a comparator, computing the degree to which a stimulus matches a template based upon previous experience (Gray, 1982; Gray & McNaughton, 2000). The hip-

Cloninger alcoholism (mean PCL–R = 31.2; range 21–38; mean age = 30 years). Unfortunately no comparison group was included. Posterior hippocampal volume was negatively correlated with PCL Factor 1 scores (indexing deficient affective experience and arrogant and deceitful interpersonal style) but not with Factor 2 scores that index antisocial and criminal behavior. The posterior hippocampus may identify stimuli with behavioral relevance and may also be involved in associative learning (i.e., combining both emotion and memory), which may be important in understanding the well-documented aversive conditioning deficits observed among men with psychopathy (Flor et al., 2002; Veit et al., 2002). Given that prefrontal volume reductions in men with psychopathy were related to alcohol abuse rather than the PCL–R score (Laakso et al., 2002), it would be interesting to know how previous duration of alcohol abuse might have affected the reported association between PCL–R scores and posterior hippocampal volume.

Raine et al. (2004) used structural MRI to compare hippocampal volumes of "unsuccessful" men with psychopathy (i.e., a criminal record; mean PCL–R = 27.7), "successful" men with psychopathy (i.e., no criminal record; mean PCL–R = 31.5), and men with low PCL–R scores and no criminal record (mean PCL–R = 10.9) recruited from temporary employment agencies. All subjects showed laterality of increased right versus left hippocampal volumes, although this was particularly pronounced in the anterior hippocampus for unsuccessful psychopathic offenders, whereas successful men with psychopathy did not differ from control men. However, the mean total PCL–R rating of the unsuccessful compared with the successful psychopathic offenders was slightly higher with a wider range of scores. It would be interesting to know whether the two psychopathy groups differed significantly in scores for Arrogant and Deceitful Interpersonal Style, Deficient Affective Experience, and Impulsive and Irresponsible Behavioral Style. For instance, men scoring higher on items relating to Impulsive and Irresponsible Behavioral Style may be more easily arrested for their offenses than less impulsive men who obtained higher scores for Deficient Affective Experience. Furthermore, the nonpsychopathic men were significantly younger than the unsuccessful psychopathic offenders; age may be an important factor when examining the links between psychopathy and volumes of brain structures (Laakso et al., 2001). The most marked differences in structure were evident among the unsuccessful psychopathic offenders. As the greater right to left asymmetry decreases with age in normally developing children, the pronounced asymmetry observed in unsuccessful psychopathic offenders may result from a disruption early in the course of development. Such a disruption in the symmetry of the anterior hippocampus might emerge from disrupted frontal subcortical neural activity.

---

pocampus is important for learning the relationship between two stimuli (Bechara et al., 1995) and therefore may play a role in aversive conditioning, which is deficient in individuals with psychopathy.

Amygdala

Despite the key role of the amygdala in emotion processing, to date there is no direct neuroimaging study support for any amygdalar abnormalities among men diagnosed with psychopathy. Indirect evidence is available from studies indicating psychophysiological abnormalities among male inmates with psychopathy (i.e., startle reflex abnormalities, Patrick, 1994; selective deficits in fear processing, Blair et al., 2001). Clearly, further research is needed to specifically examine the role of the amygdala in psychopathy.

Corpus Callosum[13]

Raine et al. (2003) argued that the interconnectivity of brain structures may be important for normal affect regulation and that structural abnormalities in the corpus callosum could contribute to the reduced asymmetry indexed by performance on psychophysiological (e.g., autonomic and emotion deficits) and neuropsychological tasks (e.g., poor spatial ability) previously reported among offenders with psychopathy. Raine et al. compared men who met the DSM–IV criteria for APD and had high PCL–R scores (mean PCL–R = 30.3) with men who did not (mean PCL–R = 10.8). Word identification and letter-matching tasks were used to assess the degree of interhemispheric connectivity. Men with high PCL–R scores displayed significantly increased volumes of callosal white matter, whole-brain volumes, increased callosal length, and reduced callosal thickness compared with low PCL–R scorers, and, in addition, significantly increased functional connectivity between the two hemispheres. Increased callosal volume was significantly associated with a number of interpersonal correlates of psychopathy, including a lack of close friends, a lack of social closeness, reduced SCR and heart rate activity, and reduced spatial ability. Scores for Deficient Affective Experience were positively correlated ($r = 0.46$, $p < 0.001$) with an overall "callosal factor" score. More specifically, the length of the corpus callosum correlated with scores for Deficient Affective Experience ($r = 0.22$, $p < 0.05$). The greater callosal volume and thinner and longer callosi among men with psychopathy may suggest disruption to the developing brain early in life. These abnormalities could result from attenuated axonal pruning or disruption in myelination during childhood, caused by neurodevelopmental or genetic factors (see Raine et al., 2003).

Although these structural neuroimaging findings suggest abnormalities in regions important for emotion processing in adult males with psychopathy, the extent to which these are associated with functional neurological and behavioral abnormalities remains unclear. It is therefore important to also consider data from studies measuring functional neural abnormalities in individuals with psychopathy.

---

[13]The corpus callosum, the largest interhemispheric commissure connecting the two hemispheres, is responsible for transferring information between the hemispheres (for review of function and lesion studies, see Devinsky & Laff, 2003).

Functional Brain Imaging Studies

Intrator et al. (1997) used SPECT to conduct the first study of functional brain imaging comparing men with psychopathy recruited from a substance abuse program and healthy men. The behavioral results for the psychopathic and nonpsychopathic men were similar. However, psychopathic men showed greater activation in a number of brain regions (assessed through relative blood flow) when they processed negatively valenced emotional words compared with neutral words. The authors noted that this counterintuitive finding could suggest that individuals with psychopathy require additional resources for an emotional task.

Söderström et al. (2002) used SPECT and MRI to examine functional abnormalities among persons with psychopathy who had been charged with a serious crime. Subjects were assessed using DSM–IV and the PCL–R, and several participants also met the criteria for Axis I or Axis II disorder. Relative cerebral blood flow, assessed in a number of ROIs in the frontal and temporal lobes, was not significantly correlated with total PCL–R scores. However, traditional Factor 1 scores (from the 1991 PCL–R manual) were negatively correlated with frontal and temporal activity.

Schneider et al. (2000) used fMRI to examine aversive conditioning in men with high scores on the PCL–R (mean score of 28.6), and healthy men. A neutral face (CS) was paired with a pleasant or unpleasant smell (US). All participants rated the neutral face paired with the unpleasant smell negatively, whereas the neutral face paired with the neutral smell maintained its neutral rating. For the fMRI analyses, there was evidence of additional effort required by the psychopathic men to perform the aversive conditioning task, through their greater brain activity in the amygdala and dorsolateral prefrontal cortex compared with healthy men. Unfortunately, activation in the insula, which responds to disgust stimuli and has been linked to empathy, was not examined.

Veit et al. (2002) used fMRI to examine the functional neuroanatomy subserving aversive conditioning in healthy men, men with social phobia, and men with psychopathy (mean PCL–R = 25.3). Data from the nondisordered men confirmed the theory that aversive conditioning involves the anterior cingulate, insula, and orbitofrontal cortex. Reduced activation in these regions was reported for men with psychopathy. Furthermore, men diagnosed with psychopathy did not respond differentially to the CS+ and CS−. The authors concluded that the lack of conditioned emotional responding among men with psychopathy was related to insufficient activation of the orbitofrontal area rather than insufficient amygdala activation. Men with psychopathy failed to show SCRs in anticipation of the aversive stimuli. This finding concurs with much previous research (see, e.g., Hare, 1998) and is consistent with the somatic marker hypothesis, such that increases in skin conductance provide feedback that is essential for emotional responding. However, given the small sample, caution in interpreting these results is necessary until they are replicated.

Kiehl and colleagues conducted two fMRI studies assessing lexical decision-making among men with psychopathy. In the first study (Kiehl et al., 2001), they compared male offenders with psychopathy (mean PCL–R = 32.8), offenders without psychopathy (mean PCL–R = 16.6), and nonoffenders without psychopathy. The neural systems involved in emotion processing during an affective memory task (involving the processing of neutral and affectively negative words) were examined. There were no group differences in accuracy, but there was a suggestion that men with psychopathy better recalled affective compared with neutral words ($p < 0.067$). There were no group differences in processing neutral stimuli compared with the resting baseline. However, psychopathic offenders showed less affect-related activity associated with emotion processing than either comparison group in the limbic and cortical areas. Furthermore, psychopathic offenders demonstrated greater activation than nonpsychopathic offenders and healthy men for affective compared with neutral stimuli in brain regions outside the limbic system (i.e., superior temporal gyrus or inferior frontal gyrus). The authors concluded that the neural systems associated with attentional processing of affective stimuli at the limbic and paralimbic level are abnormal in men with psychopathy.

Kiehl et al. (2004) compared processing of abstract and concrete words and nonwords (i.e., one letter was changed so it was no longer a real word) using fMRI. Following from research demonstrating that the right hemisphere, particularly the right superior frontal gyrus, may be involved in processing abstract representations of language, it was hypothesized that male offenders with psychopathy would be slower and less accurate in processing abstract compared with concrete words and would demonstrate reduced neural differentiation between concrete and abstract words in the right anterior superior temporal gyrus. Healthy men with no criminal record were compared with eight male psychopathic offenders (PCL–R > 28). Psychopathic offenders were slower than healthy men in processing both concrete and abstract words. Imaging data demonstrated that men with psychopathy showed similar activation to non-psychopathic men for the concrete word versus baseline comparisons. As predicted, psychopathic offenders did not show the expected activation in the anterior superior temporal gyrus for abstract words that was evident among the nonpsychopathic men. There was also evidence for abnormalities in the right superior temporal gyrus and associated surrounding cortex among men with psychopathy. Results suggested that the psychopathic offenders demonstrate a specific deficit in processing abstract stimuli.

Müller et al. (2003) examined emotional processing abnormalities among male psychopathic offenders (PCL–R ≥ 30) and healthy men (PCL–R < 10) similar in age who had no substance abuse in the past 6 months. Participants were presented with neutral, positive, and negative pictures and were instructed to "feel the emotions the pictures suggest." In response to negative pictures, offenders with psychopathy showed increased activation, compared with nonpsychopathic men, of the right prefrontal regions, anterior cingulate, and amygdala, and reduced activation in the right subgenual cingulate and right medial temporal gyrus and the left lobulus paracentralis, left dorsal cingulate, and left parahippocampal gyrus. These findings are consistent with those of Intrator et al. (1997) indicating overactivity of the fronto-temporal regions among men with high PCL–R scores. Because the amygdala responds to emotional stimuli, particularly facial expressions of fear (for review, see Phan et al., 2002; Phillips et al., 2003a), the observed increased blood flow in the amygdala among men with psychopathy for negative emotional pictures could indicate that more effort was necessary to perform the task. The small number of participants limits the reliability and generalizability of findings. Furthermore, there was no criminal nonpsychopathic group matched to the psychopathic inmates for effects of institutionalization and substance abuse. The effects of emotional pictures on brain activation were investigated by comparing pictures of positive and negative valence; however, these stimuli may not be sufficiently specific to identify the hypothesized emotion processing deficit in individuals with psychopathy (i.e., poor recognition of facial expressions of sadness; Blair et al., 2001; Stevens et al., 2001). These findings do not concur with those of Kiehl et al. (2001), who observed a reduction in limbic, hippocampal, and amygdalar activation among men with psychopathy during a neutral and negatively valenced lexical decision-making task. This could, however, be due to the different types of stimuli used in the two studies (i.e., pictures versus words).

Summary of Functional Brain Imaging Studies

Only a small number of studies using functional neuroimaging have been performed for persons with psychopathy. There is nevertheless preliminary evidence of amygdalar abnormalities and abnormalities in frontal and temporal regions among men with psychopathy when processing emotional stimuli (Kiehl et al., 2001, 2004; Müller et al., 2003).

CONCLUSION

We have attempted to bring together the literature on the neurobiological underpinnings of emotion processing and how these might be linked to psychopathy. Figure 9–1 shows a proposed framework within which to explore the neurobiology of psychopathy, based on the available evidence, examined from a developmental perspective. Evidence suggests that an emotional deficit emerges early in childhood and is reflected in the callous–unemotional traits observed in a subset of children with early-onset CD, who present with similar cognitive and psychophysiological profiles to adults with psychopathy.

We began by outlining the somatic marker hypothesis (Damasio, 1995), which highlights the role of the amygdala in emotion processing early in life, followed by the development of the orbitofrontal cortex that takes over, to some extent, from the amygdalae in adulthood. Studies of patients with early amygdalar damage demonstrated a failure to activate secondary inducers (i.e., a conditioned response, or memory of an emotional event) and an inability to accurately judge the facial affect of others. It is interesting, in light of Bechara et al.'s (2003) suggestion of the developmental progression of primary and secondary inducers (i.e., development of the amygdala leading to the subsequent development of the ventromedial prefrontal cortex), that no deficits have been observed in response reversal among children with psychopathic tendencies (Blair et al., 2001), even though such deficits have been reported in adults with psychopathy (Mitchell et al., 2002). If, as Bechara et al. (2003) proposed, the amygdala is necessary for normal functioning of the orbitofrontal cortex, then it is surprising that performance on a gambling task (i.e., assessing amygdala dysfunction) is not associated with impaired performance on the response-reversal tasks (assessing orbitofrontal functioning). If the amygdala is necessary for the subsequent development of the orbitofrontal cortex, then one would predict that early amygdala dysfunction would impede performance on tasks assessing orbitofrontal functioning. Blair et al.'s VIM provides a framework to examine the more selective impairments in emotion processing among adults with psychopathy and children with psychopathic tendencies and highlights the crucial role of the amygdala. Neuroimaging studies indicate amygdalar dysfunction; however, this clearly needs further examination.

The role of the insula in emotion processing and psychopathy has been relatively unexamined. The insula may play an important role in empathy. Carr, Iacoboni, Dubeau, Mazziottaa, and Lenzi (2003) examined the neural mechanisms associated with empathy and highlighted the role of the amygdala and insula in imitating facial expressions of emotion. They further highlighted the role of the insula in connecting action representation networks and limbic areas, potentially key factors for the generation of empathy.

The role of the anterior cingulate gyrus has also been highlighted by Phillips et al. (2003a) as an important neural correlate of both the ventral and dorsal systems underlying emotion perception, and it is implicated in attention to emotional stimuli. Behavioral and neuropsychological studies of persons with psychopathy have suggested that attention to emotional stimuli may be particularly dampened in light of competing rewards. A paradigm within which participants are required to judge emotional expressions in both the presence and absence of reward conditions would help to clarify the role of the anterior cingulate gyrus in emotion processing among persons with psychopathy.

Intriguing associations have been reported between brain structure and PCL–R factor scores. Most notably, the score for Deficient Affective Experience was correlated with both the volume of the hippocampus and the length of the corpus callosum. A similar approach, focusing on PCL–R factor scores and associations with brain function, may be a valuable strategy for understanding specific impairments in emotion perception among persons with psychopathy.

Studies of autonomic reactivity demonstrate that persons with psychopathy have a dampened response to emotional stimuli, which is particularly evident for conditioned and learned responses and not apparent to unconditioned emotional stimuli. Damasio's (1995) somatic marker hypothesis and Blair's (1995) violence inhibition mechanism are both attempts to explain this deficit in classical conditioning. The underlying mechanisms of these failure-to-learn associations between behavior and future consequences remain unclear.

Blair (2003) highlighted the importance of taking account of the psychopathic person's lifestyle when studying the neural correlates of psychopathy, particularly in relation to substance misuse and how this might affect brain function. Many studies have not sufficiently dealt with the confound of substance abuse, which must be an important consideration for future work, particularly in view of the importance of orbitofrontal cortical abnormalities in the pathogenesis of substance abuse (for review, see Lawrence & Stein, 2003).

Although most individuals with psychopathy meet the criteria for APD, many also meet criteria for other Axis II disorders, in particular, paranoid, narcissistic, and borderline personality disorder (Dolan, 2002). Similarly, Söderström et al. (2002) reported that a large number of their sample of individuals diagnosed with psychopathy using the PCL–R also met criteria for other *DSM–IV* disorders. It may be helpful to take into account these comorbid conditions when one is assessing the underlying neural correlates of psychopathy.

Finally, it is very difficult to study the development of psychopathy, which may be the key to understanding the underlying neurobiology. First, psychopathy is very rare in the general population. To examine developmental processes, longitudinal prospective studies are needed that include large numbers of children and adolescents. It may be helpful to target children with conduct disorder, distinguishing those with and without a capacity to empathize with others, and follow them over time. Early abnormalities in brain structures may alter the development of connections between cortical and subcortical structures, which may be further affected by factors such as substance abuse (see Blair, 2003). If we believe that psychopathy develops from an early abnormality in the brain function or structures specific to emotion processing, for example, an early amygdalar abnormality, it is likely that the brain reorganizes during the course of development to compensate for this abnormality. Such reorganization of brain function could potentially compromise our understanding of the functional neuroanatomy of psychopathy, such that structures observed to subserve specific functions in healthy adults may differ from the structures mediating the same processes within the brain of a person with psychopathy. Evidence for this brain reorganization comes from studies of language in persons with psychopathy (see Hare, 1998) and from one functional study (Kiehl, et al., 2001) and could be interpreted as consistent with findings of corpus callosal abnormalities (Raine et al., 2004).

To examine the more subtle functional deficits that are likely to character-ize psychopathy, future studies may need to identify stimuli that selectively activate particular brain regions important in emotion processing. Future studies may benefit from the use of more ecologically valid assessments of emotion processing in psychopathy. Rather than focusing solely on the valence of emotion of stimuli, it is important to consider how different emo-tions might be abnormally processed among persons with psychopathy. Given that psychopathy is associated with reward dominance, it would be particularly interesting to try to manipulate rewards to examine whether spe-cific impairments persist once participants are rewarded for accurate perfor-mance. These studies should also include an assessment of *passive* and *active* emotional processing (Lange et al., 2003).

In summary, we hypothesize that an emotion processing deficit, linked to the abnormal development of the amygdala and its projections to other sub-cortical and cortical areas, occurs early in childhood and contributes to the development of the other aspects of psychopathy. This hypothesis is largely speculative, but like all hypotheses, it is generated to orient future research by presenting a specific, empirically testable set of propositions. To test this hypothesis requires prospectively collected data using a number of experi-mental modalities including structural and functional neuroimaging on a sample of young children. However, given the low prevalence of psychopa-thy in the general population, a very large number of children would have to be studied to include some who would develop psychopathy as adults. If, as we propose, the emotion processing deficit precedes the onset of antisocial behavior, a study of a sample of children with conduct problems would fail to test the hypothesis. Yet, as noted earlier, callousness and a lack of empathy in a subgroup of children with CD have been identified in a small number of studies. Follow-up studies of such children are needed to determine the proportion who develop the syndrome of psychopathy.

REFERENCES

Adolphs, R., Tranel, D., & Damasio, A. R. (1998). The human amygdala in social judg-ment. *Nature, 393*, 470–474.

Adolphs, R., Tranel, D., Damasio, H., & Damasio, A. (1994). Impaired recognition of emotion in facial expressions following bilateral damage to the human amygdala. *Nature, 372*, 669–672.

Adophs, R., Tranel, D., Damasio, H., & Damasio, A. (1995). Fear and the human amyg-dala. *Journal of Neuroscience, 15*, 5879–5891.

American Psychiatric Association (1994). *Diagnostic and statistical manual of mental disorders* (4th ed.). Washington, DC: Author.

Anderson, S. W., Bechara, A., Damasio, H., Tranel, D., & Damasio, A. R. (1999). Impairment of social and moral behavior related to early damage in human pre-frontal cortex. *Nature Neuroscience, 2*, 1032–1037.

Arnett, P. A., Howland, E. W., Smith, S. S., & Newman, J. P. (1993). Autonomic responsivity during passive avoidance in incarcerated psychopaths. *Personality and Individual Differences, 14*, 173–184.

Barkley, R. A. (1997). Behavioral inhibition, sustained attention, and executive functions: Constructing a unified theory of ADHD. *Psychological Bulletin, 121,* 65–94.

Bassarath, L. (2001). Review paper: Neuroimaging studies of antisocial behaviour. *Canadian Journal of Psychiatry, 46,* 728–732.

Bechara, A., Damasio, H., & Damasio, A. R. (2000). Emotion, decision making and the orbitofrontal cortex. *Cerebral Cortex, 10,* 295–307.

Bechara, A., Damasio, H., & Damasio, A. R. (2003). Role of the amygdala in decision-making. *Annals of the New York Academy of Science, 985,* 356–369.

Bechara, A., Damasio, A. R, Damasio, H., & Anderson, S. W. (1994). Insensitivity to future consequences following damage to human prefrontal cortex. *Cognition, 50,* 7–15.

Bechara, A., Damasio, A. R., Damasio, H., & Lee, G. P. (1999). Different contributions of the human amygdala and ventromedial prefrontal cortex to decision-making. *Journal of Neuroscience, 19,* 5473–5481.

Bechara, A., Tranel, D., Damasio, H., Adolphs, R., Rockland, C., & Damasio, A. R. (1995). Double dissociation of conditioning and declarative knowledge relative to the amygdala and hippocampus in humans. *Science, 269,* 1115–1118.

Benton, A. L. (1991). The prefrontal region: Its early history. In: H. S. Levin, H. M. Eisenberg, & A. L. Benton (Eds.), *Frontal lobe function and dysfunction.* Oxford, England: Oxford University Press.

Blair, R. J. R. (1995). A cognitive developmental approach to morality: investigating the psychopath. *Cognition, 57,* 1–29.

Blair, R. J. R. (2001). Neurocognitive models of aggression, the antisocial personality disorders, and psychopathy. *Journal of Neurology, Neurosurgery, and Psychiatry, 71,* 727–731.

Blair, R. J. R. (2003). Neurobiological basis of psychopathy. *British Journal of Psychiatry, 182,* 5–7.

Blair, R. J. R., Colledge, E., & Mitchell, D. G. V. (2001). Somatic markers and response reversal: Is there orbitofrontal cortex dysfunction in boys with psychopathic tendencies? *Journal of Abnormal Child Psychology, 29,* 499–511.

Blair, R. J. R., Colledge, E., Murray, L., & Mitchell, D. G. V. (2001). A selective impairment in the processing of sad and fearful expressions in children with psychopathic tendencies. *Journal of Abnormal Child Psychology, 29,* 491–498.

Blair, R. J., Morris, J. S., Frith, C. D., Perrett, D. I., & Dolan, R. J. (1999). Dissociable neural responses to facial expressions of sadness and anger. *Brain, 122,* 883–893.

Blonigen, D. M., Carlson, S. R., Krueger, R. F., & Patrick, C. J. (2003). A twin study of self-reported psychopathic personality traits. *Personality and Individual Differences, 35,* 179–197.

Breiter, H. C., Etcoff, N. L., Whalen, P. J., Kennedy, W. A., Rauch, S. L., Buckner, R. L., et al. (1996). Response and habituation of the human amygdala during visual processing of facial expression. *Neuron, 17,* 875–887.

Buchel, C., Morris, J., Dolan, R. J., & Friston, K. J. (1998). Brain systems mediating aversive conditioning: An event-related fMRI study. *Neuron, 20,* 947–957.

Calder, A. J., Lawrence, A. D., & Young, A. W. (2001). Neuropsychology of fear and loathing. *Nature Reviews Neuroscience, 2,* 352–363.

Caputo, A. A., Frick, P. J., & Brodsky, S. L. (1999). Family violence and juvenile sex offending: Potential mediating roles of psychopathic traits and negative attitudes toward women. *Criminal Justice and Behavior, 26,* 338–356.

Carr, L., Iacoboni, M., Dubeau, M. C., Mazziotta, J. C., & Lenzi, G. L. (2003). Neural systems of empathy in humans: A relay from neural systems for imitation to limbic areas. *Proceedings of the National Academy of Sciences of the United States of America, 100,* 5497–5502.

Christian, R. E., Frick, P. J., Hill, N. L., Tyler, L., & Frazer, D. R. (1997). Psychopathy and conduct problems in children. II: Implications for subtyping children with conduct problems. *Journal of the American Academy of Child and Adolescent Psychiatry, 36,* 233–241.

Cooke, D. J., & Michie, C. (1999). Psychopathy across cultures: North America and Scotland compared. *Journal of Abnormal Psychology, 108,* 58–68.

Cooke, D. J., & Michie, C. (2001). Refining the construct of psychopathy: Towards a hierarchical model. *Psychological Assessment, 13,* 171–188.

Cornell, D. G., Warren, J., Hawk, G., Stafford, E., Oram, G., & Pine, D. (1996). Psychopathy in instrumental and reactive violent offenders. *Journal of Consulting and Clinical Psychology, 64,* 783–790.

Damasio, A. R. (1995). On some functions of the human prefrontal cortex. *Annals of the New York Academy of Science, 769,* 241–251.

Damasio, A. R. (1996). The somatic marker hypothesis and the possible functions of the prefrontal cortex. *Philosophical Transactions of the Royal Society London, B Series, 351,* 1413–1420.

Damasio, A. R., Tranel, D., & Damasio, H. (1990). Individuals with sociopathic behavior caused by frontal damage fail to respond autonomically to social stimuli. *Behavioural Brain Research, 41,* 81–94.

Darwin, C. (1872). *The expression of the emotions in man and animals.* London: Albermarle.

Devinsky, O., & Laff, R. (2003). Review: Callosal lesions and behavior: history and modern concepts. *Epilepsy and Behavior, 4,* 607–617.

Dolan, M. (2002). What neuroimaging tells us about psychopathic disorders. *Hospital Medicine, 63,* 337–340.

Ekman, P. (2003). Emotions inside out: 130 years after Darwin's "The Expression of the Emotions in Man and Animal." *Annals of the New York Academy of Sciences, 1000,* 1–6.

Elliott, R. (2003). Executive functions and their disorders. *British Medical Bulletin, 65,* 49–59.

Fisher, L., & Blair, R. J. (1998). Cognitive impairment and its relationship to psychopathic tendencies in children with emotional and behavioural difficulties. *Journal of Abnormal Child Psychology, 26,* 511–519.

Flor, H., Birbaumer, N., Hermann, C., Ziegler, S., & Patrick, C. J. (2002). Aversive Pavlovian conditioning in psychopaths: Peripheral and central correlates. *Psychophysiology, 39,* 505–518.

Frick, P. J., Cornell, A. H., Barry, C. T., Bodin, S. D., & Dane, H. E. (2003). Callous-unemotional traits and conduct problems in the prediction of conduct problem severity, aggression, and self-report of delinquency. *Journal of Abnormal Child Psychology, 31,* 457–470.

Frick, P. J., & Hare, R. D. (2001). *The Antisocial Process Screening Device (APSD).* Toronto, Ontario, Canada: Multi-Health Systems.

Frick, P. J., Lilienfeld, S. O., Ellis, M., Loney, B., & Silverthorn, P. (1999). The association between anxiety and psychopathy dimensions in children. *Journal of Abnormal Child Psychology, 27,* 383–392.

Frick, P. J., O'Brien, B. S., Wootton, J. M., & McBurnett, K. (1994). Psychopathy and conduct problems in children. *Journal of Abnormal Psychology, 103,* 700–707.

Gazzaniga, M. S. (Ed.). (1998). *Cognitive neuroscience: The biology of the mind.* New York: W. W. Norton.

Giancola, P. R., & Zeichner, A. (1994). Neuropsychological performance on tests of frontal-lobe functioning and aggressive behavior in men. *Journal of Abnormal Psychology, 103,* 832–835.

Gray, J. A. (1982). *The neuropsychology of anxiety.* New York: Oxford University Press.

Gray, J. A., & McNaughton, N. (2000). *The neuropsychology of anxiety* (2nd ed.). New York: Oxford University Press.

Green, M. F., Kern, R. S., Robertson, M. J., Sergi, M. J., & Kee, K. S. (2000). Relevance of neurocognitive deficits for functional outcome in schizophrenia. In T. Sharma & P. Harvey (Eds.), *Cognition in schizophrenia: Impairments, importance, and treatment strategies* (pp. 178–192). New York: Oxford University Press.

Hallé, P., Hodgins, S., & Roussy, S. (2000). Revue critique des études expérimentales auprès de détenus adultes: Précision du syndrome de la psychopathie. In T. H. Pham & G. Côté (Eds.), *Psychopathie: Théorie et recherche* (pp. 145–182). Lille: Presses universitaires du Septentrion.

Hamann, S. B., Stefanacci, L., Squire, L. R., Adolphs, R., Tranel, D., Damasio, H., & Damasio, A. (1996). Recognising facial emotion. *Nature, 379,* 497.

Hare, R. D. (1991). *The Hare Psychopathy Checklist–Revised Manual.* Toronto, Ontario, Canada: Multi-Health Systems.

Hare, R. D. (1998). Psychopathy, affect and behavior. In D. J. Cook, A. Forth, & R. D. Hare (Eds.). *Psychopathy: Theory, research, and implications for society,* (pp. 105–137). Dordrecht, The Netherlands: Kluwer Academic.

Harpur, T. J., & Hare, R. D. (1994). Assessment of psychopathy as a function of age. *Journal of Abnormal Psychology, 103,* 604–609.

Hart, S. D., Cox, D. N., & Hare, R. D. (1995). *The Hare Psychopathy Checklist: Screening Version (PCL:SV).* Toronto, Ontario, Canada: Multi-Health Systems Inc.

Herba, C. M., & Phillips, M. (2004). Annotation: Development of facial expression recognition from childhood to adolescence: Behavioural and neurological perspectives. *Journal of Child Psychology and Psychiatry and Allied Disciplines, 45,* 1185–1198.

Hodgins, S. (1994). Status at age 30 of children with conduct problems. *Studies of Crime and Crime Prevention, 3,* 41–62.

Intrator, J., Hare, R., Stritzke, P., Brichtswein, K., Dorfman, D., Harpur, T., et al. (1997). A brain imaging (single photon emission computerized tomography) study of semantic and affective processing in psychopaths. *Biological Psychiatry, 42,* 96–103.

Izard, C. E. (1977). *Human emotions.* New York; Plenum Press.

Johnson, D. E., Waid, L. R., & Anton, R. F. (1997). Childhood hyperactivity, gender, and Cloninger's personality dimensions in alcoholics. *Addictive Behaviors, 22,* 649–653.

Karmiloff-Smith, A. (1997). Crucial differences between developmental cognitive neuroscience and adult neuropsychology. *Developmental Neuropsychology, 13,* 513–524.

Kiehl, K. A., Hare, R. D., Liddle, P. F., & McDonald, J. J. (1999a). Reduced P300 responses in criminal psychopaths during a visual oddball task. *Biological Psychiatry, 45,* 1498–1507.

Kiehl, K. A., Hare, R. D., McDonald, J. J., & Brink, J. (1999b). Semantic and affective processing in psychopaths: An event-related potential (ERP) study. *Psychophysiology, 36,* 765–774.

Kiehl, K. A., Smith, A. M., Hare, R. D., Mendrek, A., Forster, B. B., Brink, J., et al. (2001). Limbic abnormalities in affective processing by criminal psychopaths as revealed by functional magnetic resonance imaging. *Biological Psychiatry, 50,* 677–684.

Kiehl, K. A., Smith, A. M., Mendrek, A., Forster, B. B., Hare, R. D., & Liddle, P. F. (2004). Temporal lobe abnormalities in semantic processing by criminal psychopaths as revealed by functional magnetic resonance imaging. *Psychiatry Research, 130,* 27–42.

Killgore, W. D. S., Oki, M., & Yurgelun-Todd, D. A. (2001). Sex-specific developmental changes in amygdala responses to affective faces. *NeuroReport, 12,* 427–433.

Killgore, W. D., & Yurgelun-Todd, D. A. (2001). Sex differences in amygdala activation during the perception of facial affect. *NeuroReport, 12,* 2543–2547.

Laakso, M. P., Gunning-Dixon, F., Vaurio, O., Repo-Tiihonen, E., Soininen, H., & Tiihonen, J. (2002). Prefrontal volumes in habitually violent subjects with antisocial personality disorder and type 2 alcoholism. *Psychiatry Research, 114,* 95–102.

Laakso, M. P., Vaurio, O., Koivisto, E., Savolainen, L., Eronen, M., Aronen, H. J., et al. (2001). Psychopathy and the posterior hippocampus. *Behavioral Brain Research, 118,* 187–193.

Lange, K., Williams, L. M., Young, A. W., Bullmore, E. T., Brammer, M. J., Gray, J. A., et al. (2003). Task instructions modulate neural responses to fearful facial expressions. *Biological Psychiatry, 53,* 226–232.

LaPierre, D., Braun, C. M., & Hodgins, S. (1995). Ventral frontal deficits in psychopathy: neuropsychological test findings. *Neuropsychologia, 33,* 139–151.

Larsson, H., Andershed, H., & Lichtenstein, P. (in press). A genetic factor explains most of the variation in the psychopathic personality. *Journal of Abnormal Psychology.*

Lawrence, N. S., & Stein, E. S. (2003). Neuroimaging studies of human drug addiction. In C. H. Y. Fu, C. Senior, T. A. Russell, D. Weinberger, & R. Murray (Eds.), *Neuroimaging in Psychiatry* (pp. 101–129). London: Martin Dunitz.

Lykken, D. T. (1957). A study of anxiety in the sociopathic personality. *Journal of Abnormal and Social Psychology, 55,* 6–10.

McClure, E. B. (2000). A meta-analytic review of sex differences in facial expression processing and their development in infants, children, and adolescents. *Psychological Bulletin, 126,* 424–453.

Mitchell, D. G., Colledge, E., Leonard, A., & Blair, R. J. (2002). Risky decisions and response reversal: is there evidence of orbitofrontal cortex dysfunction in psychopathic individuals? *Neuropsychologia, 40,* 2013–2022.

Moffitt, T. E., & Caspi, A. (2001). Childhood predictors differentiate life-course persistent and adolescence-limited antisocial pathways among males and females. *Developmental Psychopathology, 13,* 355–375.

Morris, J., Frith, C. D., Perrett, D. I., Rowland, D., Young, A. W., Calder, A. J., & Dolan, R. J. (1996). A differential neural response in the human amygdala to fearful and happy facial expressions. *Nature, 383,* 812–815.

Müller, J. L., Sommer, M., Wagner, V., Lange, K., Taschler, H., Roder, C. H., et al. (2003). Abnormalities in emotion processing within cortical and subcortical regions in criminal psychopaths: Evidence from a functional magnetic resonance imaging study using pictures with emotional content. *Biological Psychiatry, 54,* 152–162.

Newman, J. P. (1998). Psychopathic behavior: An information processing perspective. In D. J. Cook, A. Forth, & R. D. Hare (Eds.). *Psychopathy: Theory, research, and implications for society* (pp. 81–104). Dordrecht, The Netherlands: Kluwer Academic.

Newman, J. P., & Kosson, D. S. (1986). Passive avoidance learning in psychopathic and nonpsychopathic offenders. *Journal of Abnormal Psychology, 95,* 252–256.

Newman, J. P., Schmitt, W. A., & Voss, W. D. (1997). The impact of motivationally neutral cues on psychopathic individuals: Assessing generality of the response modulation hypothesis. *Journal of Abnormal Psychology, 106*, 563–575.

O'Brien, B. S., & Frick, P. J. (1996). Reward dominance: associations with anxiety, conduct problems, and psychopathy in children. *Journal of Abnormal Child Psychology, 24*, 223–240.

Pardini, D. A., Lochman, J. E., & Frick, P. J. (2003). Callous/unemotional traits and social-cognitive processes in adjudicated youths. *Journal of the American Academy of Child and Adolescent Psychiatry, 42*, 364–371.

Patrick. C. J. (1994). Emotion and psychopathy: Startling new insights. *Psychophysiology, 31*, 319–330.

Patrick, C. J., Bradley, M. M., & Lang, P. J. (1993). Emotion in the criminal psychopath: Startle reflex modulation. *Journal of Abnormal Psychology, 102*, 82–92.

Pennington, B., & Ozonoff, S. (1996). Executive functions and developmental psychopathology. *Journal of Child Psychology and Psychiatry, 37*, 51–87.

Pham, T. H., Vanderstukken, O., Philippot, P., & Vanderlinden, M. (2003). Selective attention and executive function deficits among criminal psychopaths. *Aggressive Behavior, 29*, 393–405.

Phan, K. K., Wager, T., Taylor, S. F., & Liberzon, I. (2002). Review: Functional neuroanatomy of emotion: A meta-analysis of emotion activation studies in PET and fMRI. *Neuroimage, 16*, 331–348.

Phillips, M. L., Drevets, W. C., Rauch, S. L., & Lane, R. (2003a). Neurobiology of emotion perception. I: The neural basis of normal emotion perception. *Biological Psychiatry, 54*, 504–514.

Phillips, M. L., Drevets, W. C., Rauch, S. L., & Lane, R. (2003b). Neurobiology of emotion perception. II: Implications for major psychiatric disorders. *Biological Psychiatry, 54*, 515–528.

Phillips, M. L., Young, A. W., Scott, S. K., Calder, A. J., Andrew, C., Giampietro, V., et al. (1998). Neural responses to facial and vocal expressions of fear and disgust. *Proceedings of the Royal Society of London Series B: Biological Sciences, 265*, 1809–1817.

Phillips, M. L., Young, A. W., Senior, C., Brammer, M., Andrew, C., Calder, A. J., et al. (1997). A specific neural substrate for perception of facial expressions of disgust. *Nature, 389*, 495–498.

Raine, A., Lencz, T., Bihrle, S., LaCasse, L., & Colletti, P. (2000). Reduced prefrontal gray matter volume and reduced autonomic activity in antisocial personality disorder. *Archives of General Psychiatry, 57*, 119–129.

Raine, A., Ishikawa, S. S., Arce, E., Lencz, T., Knuth, K. H., Bihrle, S., et al. (2004). Hippocampal structural asymmetry in unsuccessful psychopaths. *Biological Psychiatry, 55*, 185–191.

Raine, A., Lencz, T., Taylor, K., Hellige, J., Bihrle, S., Lacasse, L., et al. (2003). Corpus callosum abnormalities in psychopathic antisocial individuals. *Archives of General Psychiatry, 60*, 1134–1142.

Rhee, S., & Waldman, I. D. (2002). Genetic and environmental influences on antisocial behavior: A meta-analysis of twin and adoption studies. *Psychological Bulletin, 29*, 490–529.

Roberts, R. J., & Pennington, B. F. (1996). An interactive framework for examining prefrontal cognitive processes. *Developmental Neuropsychology, 12*, 105–126.

Rolls, E. T., & Treves, A. (1999). *Neural networks and brain function*. Oxford, England: Oxford University Press.

Schneider, F., Grodd, W., Weiss, U., Klose, U., Mayer, K. R, Nagele, T., et al. (1997). Functional MRI reveals left amygdala activation during emotion. *Psychiatry Research: Neuroimaging, 76*, 75–82.

Schneider, F., Habel, U., Kessler, C., Posse, S., Grodd, W., & Muller-Gartner, H. W. (2000). Functional imaging of conditioned aversive emotional responses in antisocial personality disorder. *Neuropsychobiology, 42*, 192–201.

Shallice, T., & Burgess, P. (1996). The domain of supervisory processes and temporal organization of behavior. *Philosophical Transactions of the Royal Society of London Series B: Biological Sciences, 351*, 1405–1411.

Smith, S. S., Arnett, P. A., & Newman, J. P. (1992). Neuropsychological differentiation of psychopathic and nonpsychopathic criminal offenders. *Personality and Individual Differences, 13*, 1233–1243.

Soderström, H., Hultin, L., Tullberg, M., Wikkelso, C., Ekholm, S., & Forsman, A. (2002). Reduced frontotemporal perfusion in psychopathic personality. *Psychiatry Research, 114*, 81–94.

Stevens, D., Charman, T., & Blair, R. J. R. (2001). Recognition of emotion in facial expression and vocal tones in children with psychopathic tendencies. *Journal of Genetic Psychology, 162*, 201–211.

Taylor, J., Loney, B. R., Bobadilla, L., Iacono, W. G., & McGue, M. (2003). Genetic and environmental influences on psychopathic trait dimensions in a community sample of male twins. *Journal of Abnormal Child Psychology, 31*, 633–645.

Teichner, G., & Golden, C. J. (2000). The relationship of neuropsychological impairment to conduct disorder in adolescence: A conceptual review. *Aggression and Violent Behavior, 5*, 509–528.

Temple, C. M. (1997). Executive disorders. In *Developmental cognitive neuropsychology* (pp. 287–316). Hove, East Sussex: Psychology Press.

Veit, R., Flor, H., Erb, M., Hermann, C., Lotze, M., Grodd, W., et al. (2002). Brain circuits involved in emotional learning in antisocial behavior and social phobia in humans. *Neuroscience Letters, 328*, 233–236.

Verona, E., Patrick, C. J., Curtin, J. J., Bradley, M. M., & Lang, P. J. (2004). Psychopathy and physiological responses to emotionally evocative sounds. *Journal of Abnormal Psychology, 113*, 99–108.

Viding, E., Blair, R. J., Moffitt, T. E., & Plomin, R. (2005). Evidence for substantial genetic risk for psychopathy in 7-year-olds. *Journal of Child Psychology and Psychiatry, 46*, 592–597.

Vincent, G. M., Vitacco, M. J., Grisso, T., & Corrado, R. R. (2003). Subtypes of adolescent offenders: affective traits and antisocial behavior patterns. *Behavioral Sciences & the Law, 21*(6), 695–712.

Vrana, S. R., Spence, E. L., & Lang, P. J. (1988). The startle probe response: A new measure of emotion? *Journal of Abnormal Psychology, 97*, 487–491.

Welsh, M. C., Pennington, B. F., & Groisser, D. B. (1991). A normative-developmental study of executive function: A window on prefrontal function in children. *Developmental Neuropsychology, 7*, 131–149.

Wiers, R. W., Gunning, W. B., & Sergeant, J. A. (1998). Is a mild deficit in executive functions in boys related to childhood ADHD or to parental multigenerational alcoholism? *Journal of Abnormal Child Psychology, 26*, 415–430.

Williamson, S., Harpur, T. J., & Hare, R. D. (1991). Abnormal processing of affective words by psychopaths. *Psychophysiology, 28*, 260–273.

Woodworth, M., & Porter, S. (2002). In cold blood: characteristics of criminal homicides as a function of psychopathy. *Journal of Abnormal Psychology, 111*, 436–445.

Wootton, J. M., Frick, P. J., Shelton, K. K., & Silverthorn, P. (1997). Ineffective parenting and childhood conduct problems: The moderating role of callous-unemotional traits. *Journal of Consulting and Clinical Psychology, 65*, 301–308.

Wright, C. I., Fischer, H., Whalen, P. J., McInerney, S. C., Shin, L. M., & Rauch, S. L. (2001). Differential prefrontal cortex and amygdala habituation to repeatedly presented emotional stimuli. *NeuroReport, 12*, 379–383..

IV

Characteristic Behaviors and Problems

10

Psychopathy and Violent Crime

Stephen Porter and Sasha Porter

In 2001, the first author was asked to conduct a psychological evaluation focused on "Glen's" risk for violent behavior and to testify in his Dangerous Offender hearing in British Columbia. During this hearing, I was asked to outline Glen's major risk factors for the court, to which I responded that the major relevant characteristics included sadism, psychopathy, and a serious anger management problem. The lawyer then asked for an opinion on the severity of his anger problem relative to other offenders I had assessed. As I was giving the opinion that Glen's anger management problem was "the worst I had come across in all the offenders I have assessed, Glen attempted to bound out of the prisoner's dock screaming that he did not have a "f---ing anger management problem!"

Glen is a serial rapist who had experienced an apparently positive upbringing in a well-to-do family. File information based on interviews with family members indicates that he was a likable child, but that he constantly "lied to everyone" and was "like Jekyll and Hyde," changing from being friendly to aggressive in an instant. Later, he was described as being charming, engaging, and popular with women, the latter being facilitated by his job as a musician in a rock band. His pattern of violence was complex, perhaps even paradoxical; some of his violent acts were highly premeditated (five rapes, an attempted murder, and a robbery), whereas many others were seemingly unplanned and spontaneous (two aggravated assaults including one that put his "friend" in a wheelchair). In other words, Glen was a psychopath who engaged in both instrumental and reactive violence against diverse victims.

As Glen's actions exemplify, violence constitutes a highly heterogeneous set of behaviors. Violent actions are associated with many different motives and diverse psychological characteristics among perpetrators. Some violent acts are well planned and the external goal, such as money or sex (as in the case of many robberies or serial killings, respectively), is clear, whereas others seem to be emotional *crimes of passion* (such as an unplanned assault with an improvised weapon). This chapter is focused on the contribution of psychopathy toward improving our understanding of violence, in particular its more severe manifestations such as homicide. Because the definition and features of psychopathy have been thoroughly examined in previous chapters, it is not necessary to reiterate them here. Suffice it to say that many of the major characteristics of psychopathy described earlier are conducive to aggression and violent crime. Psychopaths are among the most dangerous individuals in society, as reflected by a consistently higher rate of criminal behavior than that of other offenders throughout adulthood (e.g., Harpur & Hare, 1994; Porter, Birt, & Boer, 2001).

In this chapter, we examine the link between psychopathy and violent behavior both quantitatively and qualitatively. First, we briefly review the role of psychopathic traits in estimating whether, and the degree to which, someone is likely to engage in violent behavior. Next, we look at a newly emerging body of research comparing the features of violent actions by psychopathic and nonpsychopathic offenders. In particular, recent studies addressing instrumental versus reactive violence, sadistic violence, and institutional violence are reviewed. We conclude by briefly discussing risks correctional staff face in dealing with psychopathic inmates.

A QUANTITATIVE ANALYSIS OF PSYCHOPATHY AND VIOLENCE

Much evidence points to a positive association between the presence of psychopathic traits and the likelihood and degree to which one will engage in violent actions. Offenders such as Glen can be expected to show a persistent pattern of perpetrating more, and more severe, aggression and violence than others from a young age. The association between psychopathy and violence is witnessed in antisocial children and adolescents, adult offenders, and psychiatric patients.

Although most research on psychopathy has focused on adults, there is growing attention on psychopathy and its association with aggression in childhood and adolescence. Nonetheless, the appropriateness of diagnosing psychopathy at younger ages has been hotly debated because of a lack of longitudinal research on psychopathy, the overlap of psychopathy with common developmental characteristics of adolescence and concerns over the stability of personality in youths (e.g., Campbell, Green, Santor, & Porter, 2004; Edens, Skeem, Cruise, & Cauffman, 2001; Frick, 2002; Seagrave & Grisso, 2002). Some authors have concluded that it is more appropriate to consider the presence of psychopathic traits at younger ages, rather than the diagnosis of the disorder per se (Forth, Kosson, & Hare, 2003). There is increasing evidence that psychopathic characteristics are manifested in early childhood as *callous–unemotional"* traits (e.g., Frick & Ellis, 1999; Frick, Bodin, & Barry, 2000; Lynam, 2002; Waschbusch et al., 2004), such as shallow emotion and a lack of concern or empathy for others. Children with elevated callous/unemotional features exhibit a greater severity and variety of conduct problems, have lower levels of anxiety, and have a reward-dominant response style (Frick & Ellis, 1999). Further, they engage in a pattern of serious aggressive actions against others that can signal persistent violent behavior in the future (e.g., Dodge, 1991; Frick, 1998; Frick, O'Brien, Wooton, & McBurnett, 1994; Lynam, 2002; Waschbusch et al., 2004). During adolescence, psychopathic traits are associated with convictions for violent offenses (e.g., Campbell, Porter, & Santor, 2004; Forth, Hart, & Hare, 1990; Forth & Mailloux, 2000; Gretton, McBride, Hare, O'Shaughnessey, & Kumka, 2001), and a high rate of violent recidivism (Brandt, Kennedy, Patrick, & Curtain, 1997; Gretton et al., 2001). For example, Campbell et al. (2004) examined patterns of aggression in 212 incarcerated young offenders. Relative to nonpsychopathic young offenders, psychopathic youths had engaged in more peer-directed aggression, more gang aggression and had more frequently used weapons and caused physical injuries to their victims.

A robust relationship exists between psychopathy and violent behavior in adult offenders, established in numerous studies (e.g., see Hart & Hare, 1997; Porter & Woodworth, 2006). An early study found that adult psychopaths had perpetrated about twice as many violent crimes as nonpsychopathic offenders (Hare & Jutai, 1983). Porter, Birt, and Boer (2001) found that psychopaths had perpetrated a mean of 7.32 violent crimes compared with a mean of 4.52 by nonpsychopathic offenders in a federal offender sample. Psychopathy is one of the most important considerations in predicting whether an offender will perpetrate future violent actions (e.g., Hemphill, Hare, & Wong, 1998; Rice & Harris, 1997; Salekin, Rogers, & Sewell, 1996). This pattern holds true for civil psychiatric patients. For example, Skeem and Mulvey (2001) found that psychopathy scores in a large sample of psychiatric patients were highly predictive of serious violence in a 1-year follow-up period, despite a low base rate of psychopathy. Overall, psychopathic characteristics are related to a relatively high level of aggression in youth, adult, and psychiatric patient samples.

A QUALITATIVE ANALYSIS OF PSYCHOPATHY AND VIOLENCE

Reactive and Proactive Aspects of Violent Crime

As evidenced from an analysis of Glen's actions, aggressive behavior by psychopaths is not unidimensional. Some of his violent acts were clearly premeditated or proactive, whereas others appeared to lack forethought or even clear motive. From a young age, psychopaths such as Glen plan aggressive actions to attain positive rewards (e.g., Pardini, Lochman, & Frick, 2003), and, later, are more likely than other offenders to perpetrate serious instrumental violence such as armed robberies and hostage takings (e.g., Hervé, Mitchell, Cooper, Spidel, & Hare, 2004). In addition to this proactive, instrumental aggression, psychopaths sometimes show a violent temper and react explosively to a seemingly minor provocation.

These qualities of instrumentality and reactivity in the violent acts of psychopaths and nonpsychopaths have been examined in a small number of studies. Williamson, Hare, and Wong (1987) determined that violent actions by psychopaths were about three times more likely to have been motivated by a clear external goal (e.g., money) than those of nonpsychopaths. Nonetheless, in more than half of all cases the violence by psychopaths was not associated with premeditation or an external goal. This research established not only that psychopaths perpetrate a disproportionate number of instrumental violent crimes (and such acts were rare in other offenders) but also that psychopaths engage in even more reactive than instrumental violence. In a second study, Cornell et al. (1996) found that psychopaths were more likely to have perpetrated at least one instrumental violent crime than were nonpsychopaths. Woodworth and Porter (2002) chose to examine, in particular, the characteristics of homicidal violence as a function of psychopathy in 125 male murderers. They hypothesized that the murders committed by psychopathic offenders would be mainly instrumental (associated with premeditation, motivated by an external goal, and not preceded by a potent emotional reaction), whereas murders committed by nonpsychopaths would typically be crimes of passion associated with a high level of reactivity and emotionality. Further, it was expected that if the results obtained by Williamson et al. (1987) and Cornell et al. (1996) for violence in general extended to murder, psychopaths would be expected to perpetrate both forms of murder unlike nonpsychopaths. The main source of information was the detailed file description of the crime, known as the Criminal Profile Report, based on police, forensic and autopsy, and court information. The results only partially confirmed the authors' predictions. Murders committed by psychopathic offenders were indeed more likely to have been instrumental than those committed by nonpsychopathic offenders. However, unlike the previous findings concerning violence in general (that psychopaths commit more reactive than instrumental violence), nearly *all* (93.3%) of the murders perpetrated by psychopaths were instrumental in nature, as were nearly half (48.4%) of those by nonpsychopaths. The instrumental murders had been perpetrated for a host of reasons, including (in order of frequency) retribution (e.g., a gang "hit"), monetary gain, sex, access to a female by killing the competition, and obtaining of drugs.

Why were psychopaths so inclined to commit instrumental as opposed to reactive murder? Such behavior is certainly consistent with their callousness and lack of empathy toward others, and they would have few affective inhibitions against planning a killing for personal gain. Further, previous work had indicated that a failure to anticipate remorse for one's violent actions may facilitate the use of proactive, instrumental aggression (e.g. Guerra, Nucci, & Huesmann, 1994). More difficult to reconcile with past research and theory was the disinclination of psychopaths to perpetrate reactive murders. According to the traditional view, psychopaths are impulsive and often fail to inhibit or modify actions that result in negative consequences (e.g., Newman & Schmitt, 1998). However, our results bring into question the assumption that the apparently impulsive criminal actions of psychopaths are beyond volition (Porter & Woodworth, 2006; Woodworth & Porter, 2002).

That is, psychopaths may be less willing to act on their impulses specifically for an offense such as murder, which entails severe negative consequences. We think that other seemingly impulsive behavior may have less to do with a *lack* of control than with a conscious decision after an expeditious consideration of the consequences. In the case of murder, psychopaths are more likely to carefully plan their actions because the stakes are high. On the flip side, they may be more able than other offenders to inhibit an impulse to kill during a conflict or perhaps less likely to experience powerful emotions in the first place.

Psychopathy and Sadistic Interests

By examining the level of premeditation, emotional context, and external goals associated with violent actions, it was determined that psychopaths engage in both reactive and instrumental aggression. However, this knowledge does not tell the whole story of psychopaths' motivations for perpetrating violence. Recent evidence suggests that thrill-seeking and sadistic interests may drive some of the violent acts by psychopaths.

Psychopaths are notorious thrill-seekers, and this attribute may extend to crime (e.g., Hare, 1993), especially sexual violence. "Mr. C," a middle-aged psychopathic offender incarcerated in a Canadian federal prison, exemplifies this motivation (Porter et al., 2000). When his psychological assessment was conducted in 1999, he had been most recently convicted of numerous sexual assaults of three teenage girls over a 1-year period. Mr. C. had initiated and maintained a *master/slave* relationship with these victims. In the past, Mr. C. had perpetrated sexual violence against almost every conceivable type of victim (the serial rapes of adults, child sexual assaults, institutional assaults on other men, and even bestiality). In the assessment interview, he candidly reported that he would change his preferred victim type when he became "bored." In addition to being considered a "heavy" who sexually abused other inmates, Mr. C. behaved very inappropriately with female staff members to the extent that he once forwarded an envelope containing obscene material to a female National Parole Board member. There was no evidence that Mr. C had either a sexual paraphilia or difficulties controlling his anger, characteristics that are often associated with sexual offenders. Rather, it seemed that his violent actions were inspired by sensation-seeking and a proneness to boredom. This thrill-seeking drive may also extend to nonsexual crime and reflect a wide array of violent and nonviolent antisocial acts. Well-known sexual murderers who appeared to share these characteristics include Ted Bundy and Albert DeSalvo, both of whom targeted a large number of victims within a wide age range and spectrum of physical characteristics. The traditional classification dichotomy of child molesters and rapists does not take into account such offenders, who victimize both children and adults. It turns out that the majority of such offenders are psychopathic. Porter et al. (2000) found a much higher base rate of psychopathy (64%) among sexual offenders who had targeted both child and adult victims than among those who "specialized," such as child molesters. In their meta-analysis, Hanson and Bussière (1998) found that one of the strongest predictors of sexual recidivism was a history of diverse sexual offenses. Rice and Harris (1997) found that sex offenders whose targets included multiple types of victims were the most dangerous, as indexed by their faster rate of violent recidivism.

Glen seemed to take great pleasure in bringing his female victims to the brink of suffocation by choking them as he raped them and denigrated them verbally. After allowing them to breathe again for a few minutes, he repeated the process. Accordingly, there is growing evidence for an element of sadism in the violence perpetrated by psychopaths. Holt, Meloy, and Strack (1999) found that sadistic personality traits were more common in psychopaths who had committed violence than in violent nonpsychopaths. In addition, a small number of studies suggested a link between psychopathy and deviant sexual arousal (Barbaree, Seto, Serin, Amos, & Preston, 1994; Quinsey, Rice, & Harris, 1995; Serin, Malcolm, Khanna, & Barbaree, 1994). As illuminated earlier in our consideration of instrumental violence, an examination of the crime of murder, in particular, may contribute to our understanding of sadistic motivations in psychopaths. A sexual homicide is one that includes sexual activity before, during, and/or after the actual commission of the homicide. Sexual homicides are rare acts of violence; they comprise only about 1% of all murders in the United States (Meloy, 2000). In Canada, between 1974 and 1986, sexual homicides were estimated to account for 4% of all homicides (Roberts & Grossman, 1993). In an attempt to better understand this little researched crime, some researchers have focused on the role of psychopathy. Firestone, Bradford, Greenberg, and Larose (1998) found that 48 sexual murderers assessed between 1982 and 1992 scored higher on both Factors 1 and 2 of the Psychopathy Checklist–Revised (PCL–R) than a comparison sample of incest offenders. Further, Meloy (2000) found that approximately two thirds of the sexual murderers in his sample had elevated PCL–R scores. Stone (1998) analyzed the biographies of 77 serial sexual murderers and found that 96% of them met his criterion for psychopathy (cutoff score of ≥25 on the PCL–R). Further, adolescents who have perpetrated a sexual murder show a high base rate of psychopathic traits (Myers & Blashfield, 1997).

To gain a more refined understanding of the link between psychopathy and sexual murder, research examining the qualities of violence exhibited in the context of the crime was necessary. In their study of 125 murderers described earlier, Woodworth and Porter (2002) found that psychopaths were more likely to have sexually assaulted their victims either before, during, or after they were murdered. In most cases, the weapon of choice for psychopathic offenders was a "hands-on" weapon, such as a knife, rather than a gun, which was the most commonly used weapon by other offenders. The crime scenes also were coded for evidence of gratuitous violence, defined as violence that exceeded the level necessary to kill the victim (e.g., torture, beating, mutilation, and the use of multiple weapons from the crime scene). Results indicated that psychopaths were more likely to have engaged in such violence. Porter, Woodworth, Earle, Drugge, and Boer (2003) followed up this research by focusing on sadistic violence in a subsample of 38 sexual murderers. Sadistic violence was indicated by evidence that the offender obtained enjoyment from the violent acts. To avoid potential circularity in PCL–R scoring, a subsample of cases was coded by coders who had not read the descriptions of the violent crimes (i.e., perhaps a more heinous offense would result in higher scores). Similarly, an individual who was unaware of the PCL–R score or other file information coded crime scene descriptions. Results indicated that murders by psychopaths showed a significantly higher level of sadistic violence than murders by nonpsychopaths. Both Total and Factor 1 PCL–R scores were positively associated with sadistic violence scores (correlations of .35 and .34, respectively). In considering the data dichotomously, 82.4% of psychopaths had engaged in sadistic violence compared with 52.6% of nonpsychopaths. It appeared that psychopaths attempted to maximize the amount of harm inflicted upon the victim in the absence of emotional inhibitions relating to empathy or remorse, combined with possible sadistic interests.

According to another view, psychopaths perpetrate instrumental and sadistic violence because of an inability to correctly interpret the emotional distress cues of others and because they do not view violence in a negative way (Blair, 2001; Nestor, Kimble, Berman, & Haycock, 2002). For example, Gray, Macculloch, Smith, Mossis, and Snowden (2003) examined the "implicit" beliefs about murder held by psychopathic and nonpsychopathic murderers and offenders who had committed other types of crime. While completing an Implicit Association Test, offenders were presented with a word and categorized it as either "unpleasant" or "pleasant" and "peaceful" or "violent." Unlike most participants, psychopathic murderers did not display the same impairment in response time as nonpsychopaths with an incongruent word presentation (pleasant and violent words). Their responses indicated that they did not associate violence with unpleasant words and they showed diminished negative reactions to violence.

Taken together, results of qualitative research examining the features of violence as a function of psychopathy indicate that although the presence of an external, instrumental goal may provide their primary motivation, psychopaths seem to enjoy inflicting harm on others during their crimes. Psychopaths may view violence as a practical tool to achieve a selfish goal, little different from other instrumental behaviors, but take advantage of the violence context to satisfy sadistic or thrill-seeking interests. Such callousness regarding their violence extends well beyond the time of the specific violent act. For example, recent research indicates that psychopaths use deception and minimize the brutality of their violence, even in the context of a confidential research interview years after the murder. Porter and Woodworth (2006) interviewed 50 incarcerated murderers about their violent crime, comparing the offender's version with the official file version in terms of the instrumentality or reactivity of the offense. First, the findings replicated those of their original study (Woodworth & Porter, 2002): Psychopaths were more likely than their counterparts to have perpetrated an instrumental murder (88.9% vs. 42.1%, respectively). Again, based on the official Criminal Profile Reports, homicides by psychopaths were rated as more instrumental than those by nonpsychopaths. However, when the self-report narratives were coded, murders by psychopaths were rated at the same level of reactivity as those described by nonpsychopaths. In other words, psychopaths were more likely than nonpsychopaths to exaggerate the reactivity of the crime in a self-exculpating manner. In addition, it was found that psychopaths omitted important crime details. Recently, studies have indicated a similar tendency among adolescent offenders with psychopathic traits; they are more likely than other young offenders to view their aggression as having been provoked (Campbell et al., 2004; Stafford & Cornell, 2003).

THE ROLE OF INTELLIGENCE IN THE PSYCHOPATHY–VIOLENCE ASSOCIATION

Not all psychopaths resort to instrumental or reactive violence. For example, "white-collar" psychopaths operating in the corporate or business world (see Babiak, 2000) seem to rarely rely on physical aggression during their criminal behavior. The difference between violent and nonviolent psychopaths could lie in the specific crimes these offenders wish to perpetrate or in an inherent difference in the psychological characteristics of the two groups. An important psychological moderator of the relationship between psychopathy and violence may be intelligence. That is, more intelligent psychopaths may be less inclined to use violence because they can use their cognitive resources to devise nonviolent ways of getting what they want (such as by conning and manipulating others). Less intelligent psychopaths may develop aggressive tendencies to compensate for their lesser abilities to manipulate others through verbal means. Heilbrun (1982) found the first evidence for this theory. In a sample of 168 male inmates, he found that less intelligent psychopaths were more likely to have a history of impulsive violence than those with greater intellect (and less intelligent nonpsychopaths). Next, in a sample of 225 offenders, Heilbrun (1985) found that the most violent offenders were characterized as being psychopathic and with low IQ and social withdrawal. Although these early studies offered correlational support for intelligence as a moderator of psychopathy and violence, an important methodological limitation must be noted. Specifically, less intelligent psychopaths may be more likely to end up in prison and be represented disproportionately in research, whereas their more intelligent counterparts may succeed in corporate or political circles and/or use violence less frequently. Therefore, a low base rate of intelligent psychopaths in prison makes them difficult to study. Another possibility is that psychopaths with higher cognitive functioning are as likely to commit violence as are other psychopaths but are less likely to be caught for such acts. Ishikawa, Raine, Lencz, Bihrle, and Lacasse (2001) examined a community sample of 13 "successful" and 16 "unsuccessful" psychopaths (grouped by their PCL–R score and whether they had received criminal convictions) on measures of autonomic stress reactivity and executive functioning (referring to the capacity for initiation, planning, abstraction, and decision-making). According to self-report, each group had engaged in a similar amount of criminal behavior, including violence. Successful psychopaths exhibited greater autonomic reactivity to emotional stresses and stronger executive functioning than did unsuccessful psychopaths. This suggested that successful psychopaths may differ from unsuccessful psychopaths in their ability to better plan their actions. They also could exhibit superior decision-making during the commission or concealment of violent criminal acts. And even if more intelligent white-collar psychopaths are less likely to use physical aggression, their sadistic interests could still be reflected in enjoyment they derive from the exploitation of others through various crimes such as theft, fraud, and embezzlement.

Institutional Aggression and Psychopathy

While some psychopaths may be such successful criminals that they never find themselves incarcerated, many or most probably end up in the correctional system at some point. Psychopaths may adapt to institutional life in a manner that poses a more serious challenge or danger to staff and other inmates than nonpsychopaths. As demonstrated anecdotally by Mr. C. (who sexually abused his fellow inmates), research indicates that psychopaths continue to commit a higher level of violence than others during incarceration in prison. For example, Hare, Clark, Grann, & Thornton (2000) found that the PCL–R scores of 652 inmates were significantly correlated with the number of reports for prison misconduct, assaults on staff, and assaults on other inmates. The mean PCL-R scores for offenders with an institutional assault on their record was 21, whereas those with no reported assaults had a mean of only 13.6. Of those offenders with a PCL–R score of at least 30 (suggesting the presence of the disorder), 42% had perpetrated at least one assault compared with 16.2% of their counterparts. Shine and Hobson (2000) found that the number of institutional infractions of 104 male offenders housed in a British prison was significantly correlated with their PCL–R total scores and Factor 2 scores (but not with Factor 1 scores). Dolan and Millington (2002) found that Factor 1 scores predicted complaints against staff by patients in a British forensic hospital. In summary, there is much evidence that psychopaths pose a serious management problem for correctional staff.

Although the general dangerousness of psychopaths (and the importance of being aware of the PCL–R score) may now be widely recognized among correctional staff, there is evidence that they can be fooled on an individual level. Seto and Barbaree (1999) focused on the treatment ratings and subsequent behavior of 216 sampled offenders enrolled in the standardized Correctional Service of Canada sex offender treatment program (in Ontario). They found that although psychopaths received the most positive evaluations pertaining to treatment gains, they showed the highest recidivism rates for violence after their release. These findings suggested that the treatment facilitators were fooled by a convincing acting performance during therapy. Likewise, Hobson, Shine, and Roberts (2000) showed that during group therapy sessions, psychopaths were more likely to play "head games" with staff and other inmates, test boundaries, and display no true interest in changing their criminal attitudes or behavior. However, staff members still reported that considerable progress had been made. In addition to contributing to false-positive conditional release decisions, such erroneous evaluations can lead to institutional jobs or privileges that could aid in opportunities for violent behavior.

SUMMARY

A large body of research has established that psychopathy is an important contributor to crime and violence (see Porter & Woodworth, 2006). Psychopathy is characterized by a profound affective deficit, a lack of respect for the rights of other people, and egocentricity. Accordingly, psychopaths are highly dangerous offenders who victimize others in diverse ways (e.g., Hart & Hare, 1997). They begin their criminal careers at an earlier age (Vitelli, 1999), have long-term criminal careers (e.g., Harpur & Hare, 1994), engage in more versatile and extensive criminal behavior (Simourd, 1997), and violate conditional releases much sooner than nonpsychopathic offenders (e.g., Hart, Kropp, & Hare, 1988). The assessment of psychopathy clearly is a critical component of adult risk assessment and violence prediction (e.g., Salekin et al., 1996). Only recently, however, have researchers begun to examine the nature (not just quantity) of psychopathic violence. It has become clear that violence by psychopaths is multidimensional. Psychopaths such as Glen and Mr. C. often perpetrate explosive, reactive violence such as aggravated assaults. In fact, the majority of violent crimes by psychopaths appear to be reactive. On the other hand, for high-stakes crimes such as murder, psychopaths almost always show a high level of premeditation and have a clear external goal. Psychopaths also seem to derive pleasure from inflicting pain on their victims, as reflected, for example, by the gratuitous and sadistic violence they inflict on victims in the context of a sexual murder. Some psychopaths, such as those operating in corporate or business circles, seem to rarely commit physical violence but still cause an enormous amount of suffering in their victims. Although it is quite possible that psychopaths derive pleasure from nonviolent crime, more research is needed to examine this hypothesis.

Given that psychopaths probably commit more nonsanctioned violence than anybody else in society, an important task for researchers is to gain a better understanding of how and why they commit violence. This goal can only be accomplished through the collective efforts of behavioral, neuroscientific, and developmental researchers.

ACKNOWLEDGMENT

The writing of this chapter was supported by grants from the Social Science and Humanities Research Council of Canada, the Natural Sciences and Engineering Research Council of Canada, and the National Judicial Institute.

REFERENCES

Babiak, P. (2000). Psychopathic manipulation at work. In C. B. Gacono (Ed.), *The clinical and forensic assessment of psychopathy: A practitioner's guide* (pp. 287–311). Mahwah, NJ: Erlbaum.

Barbaree, H., Seto, M., Serin, R., Amos, N., & Preston, D. (1994). Comparisons between sexual and non-sexual rapist sub-types. *Criminal Justice & Behavior, 21,* 95–114.

Blair, R. J. R. (2001). Neurocognitive models of aggression, the antisocial personality disorders, and psychopathy. *Journal of Neurology, Neurosurgery, & Psychiatry, 71,* 727–731.

Brandt. J. R., Kennedy, W. A., Patrick, C. J., & Curtain, J. J. (1997). Assessment of psychopathy in a population of incarcerated adolescent offenders. *Psychological Assessment, 9,* 429–435.

Campbell, M. A., Porter, S., & Santor, D. (2004, June). *Aggressive behavior patterns in adolescent offenders as a function of psychopathy.* Paper presented at the 65th annual conference of the Canadian Psychological Association, St. John's, Newfoundland.

Campbell, M. A., Porter, S., & Santor, D. (2004). Psychopathic traits in adolescent offenders: An evaluation of criminal history, clinical, and psychosocial correlates. *Behavioral Sciences and the Law, 22,* 23–47.

Cornell, D. G., Warren, J., Hawk, G., Stafford, E., Oram, G., & Pine, D. (1996). Psychopathy in instrumental and reactive violent offenders. *Journal of Consulting and Clinical Psychology, 64,* 783–790.

Dodge, K. A. (1991). The structure and function of reactive and proactive aggression. In D. J. Pepler & K. H. Rubin (Eds.), *The development and treatment of childhood aggression* (pp. 1–18). Hillsdale, NJ: Lawrence Erlbaum Associates.

Dolan, M., & Millington, J. (2002). The influence of personality traits such as psychopathy on detailed patients using the NHS complaints procedure in forensic settings. *Personality and Individual Differences, 33,* 955–965.

Edens, J. F., Skeem, J. L., Cruise, K. R., & Cauffman, E. (2001). Assessment of "juvenile psychopathy" and its association with violence: A critical review. *Behavioral Sciences and the Law, 19,* 53–80.

Firestone, P., Bradford, J. M., Greenberg, D. M., and Larose, M. R. (1998). Homicidal sex offenders: Psychological, phallometric, and diagnostic features. *Journal of the American Academy of Psychiatry and the Law, 26,* 537–552.

Forth, A. E., Hart, S. D., & Hare, R. D. (1990). Assessment of psychopathy in male young offenders. *Psychological Assessment, 2,* 342–344.

Forth, A. E., Kosson, D., & Hare, R. D. (2003). *Manual for the youth version of the Hare Psychopathy Checklist–Revised (PCLYV).* Toronto, Ontario, Canada: Multi-Health Systems.

Forth, A. E., & Mailloux, D. L. (2000). Psychopathy in youth: What do we know? In C. B. Gacono (Ed.), *The clinical and forensic assessment of psychopathy: A practitioner's guide* (pp. 25–54). Mahwah, NJ: Lawrence Erlbaum Associates.

Frick, P. J. (1998). *Conduct disorders and severe antisocial behavior.* New York: Plenum.

Frick, P. J. (2002). Juvenile psychopathy from a developmental perspective: Implications for construct development and use in forensic assessments. *Law and Human Behavior, 26,* 247–253.

Frick, P. J., Bodin, S. D., & Barry, C. T. (2000). Psychopathic traits and conduct problems in community and clinic-referred samples of children: Further development of the Psychopathy Screening Device. *Psychological Assessment, 12,* 382–393.

Frick, P. J., & Ellis, M. (1999). Callous-unemotional traits and subtypes of conduct disorder. *Clinical Child and Family Psychology Review, 2,* 149–168.

Frick, P. J., O'Brien, B. S., Wooton, J. M., & McBurnett, K. (1994). Psychopathy and conduct problems in children. *Journal of Abnormal Psychology, 103,* 700–707.

Gray, N. S., Macculloch, M. J., Smith, J., Mossis, M., & Snowden, R. J. (2003). Forensic psychology: Violence viewed by psychopathic murderers. *Nature, 423,* 497–498.

Gretton, H. M., McBride, H. L., Hare, R. D., O'Shaughnessy, R., & Kumka, G. (2001). Psychopathy and recidivism in adolescent sex offenders. *Criminal Justice and Behavior, 28,* 427–449.

Guerra, N. G., Nucci, L., & Huesmann, L. R. (1994). Moral cognition and childhood aggression. In L. R Huesmann (Ed.), *Aggressive behavior: Current perspectives* (pp. 13–33). New York: Plenum.

Hanson, R. K., & Bussière, M. T. (1998) Predicting relapse: A meta-analysis of sexual offender recidivism. *Journal of Consulting and Clinical Psychology, 66,* 348–362.

Hare, R. D. (1993). *Without conscience: The disturbing world of the psychopaths among us.* New York: Simon & Schuster.

Hare, R. D., Clark, D., Grann, M., & Thornton, D. (2000). Psychopathy and the predictive validity of the PCL–R: An international perspective. *Behavioral Sciences and the Law, 18,* 623–645.

Hare, R. D., & Jutai, J. (1983). Criminal history of the male psychopath: Some preliminary data. In K. T. Van Dusen & S. A. Mednick (Eds.), *Prospective studies of crime and delinquency* (pp. 225–236). Boston: Kluwer-Nijhoff.

Harpur, T. J., & Hare, R. D. (1994). Assessment of psychopathy as a function of age. *Journal of Abnormal Psychology, 103,* 604–609.

Hart, S. D., & Hare, R. D. (1997). Psychopathy: Assessment and association with criminal behavior. In D. Stoff, J. Breiling, & J. D. Maser (Eds). *Handbook of antisocial behavior* (pp. 22–35). New York: Wiley.

Hart, S. D., Kropp, R. P. R., & Hare, R. D. (1988). Performance of psychopaths following conditional release from prison. *Journal of Consulting and Clinical Psychology, 56,* 227–232.

Heilbrun, K. (1982). Cognitive models of criminal violence based on intelligence and psychopathy levels. *Journal of Consulting and Clinical Psychology, 50,* 546–557.

Heilbrun, M. (1985). Psychopathy and dangerousness: Comparison, integration, and extension of two psychopathic typologies. *British Journal of Clinical Psychology, 24,* 181–195.

Hemphill, J. F., Hare, R. D., & Wong, S. (1998). Psychopathy and recidivism: A review. *Legal and Criminological Psychology, 3,* 139–170.

Hervé, H. M., Mitchell, D., Cooper, B. S., Spidel, A., & Hare, R. D. (2004). Psychopathy and unlawful confinement: An examination of perpetrator and event characteristics. *Canadian Journal of Behavioural Science, 36,* 137–145.

Hobson, J., Shine, J., & Roberts, R. (2000). How do psychopaths behave in a prison therapeutic community? *Psychology, Crime, and Law, 6,* 139–154.

Holt, S. E., Meloy, J. R., & Stack, S. (1999). Sadism and psychopathy in violent and sexually violent offenders. *Journal of the American Academy of Psychiatry and the Law, 27,* 23–32.

Ishikawa, S. S., Raine, A., Lencz, T., Bihrle, S., & Lacasse, L. (2001). Autonomic stress reactivity and executive functions in successful and unsuccessful criminal psychopaths from the community. *Journal of Abnormal Psychology, 110,* 423–432.

Lynam, D. R. (2002). Fledgling psychopathy: A view from personality theory. *Law and Human Behavior, 26,* 255–259.

Meloy, J. R. (2000). The nature and dynamics of sexual murder: An integrative review. *Aggression and Violent Behavior, 5,* 1–22.

Myers, W. C., & Blashfield, R. (1997). Psychopathology and personality in juvenile sexual murder offenders. *Journal of the American Academy of Psychiatry and the Law, 25,* 497–508.

Nestor, P. G., Kimble, M., Berman, I., & Haycock, J. (2002). Psychosis, psychopathy, and murder: A preliminary neuropsychological inquiry. *American Journal of Psychiatry, 159,* 138–140.

Newman, J. P., & Schmitt, W. A. (1998). Passive avoidance in psychopathic offenders: A replication and extension. *Journal of Abnormal Psychology, 107,* 527–532.

Pardini, D. A., Lochman, J. E., & Frick, P. J. (2003). Callous/unemotional traits and social-cognitive processes in adjudicated youths. *Journal of the American Academy of Child and Adolescent Psychiatry, 42,* 364–371.

Porter, S., & Woodworth, M. (2004). A comparison of self-reported and file descriptions of violent crimes as a function of psychopathy. Manuscript in preparation.

Porter, S., & Woodworth, M. (2006). Patterns of violent behaviour in the criminal psychopath. In C. Patrick (Ed.), *Handbook of psychopathy* (pp. 481–494). New York: Guilford Press.

Porter, S., Birt, A. R., & Boer, D. P. (2001). Investigation of the criminal and conditional release histories of Canadian federal offenders as a function of psychopathy and age. *Law and Human Behavior, 25,* 647–661.

Porter, S., Fairweather, D., Drugge, J., Hervé, H., Birt, A. R., & Boer, D. P. (2000). Profiles of psychopathy in incarcerated sexual offenders. *Criminal Justice & Behavior, 27,* 216–233.

Porter, S., Woodworth, M., Earle, J., Drugge, J., & Boer, D. P. (2003). Characteristics of violent behavior exhibited during sexual murders by psychopathic and nonpsychopathic murderers. *Law and Human Behavior, 27,* 459–470.

Quinsey, V. L., Rice, M. E., & Harris, G. T. (1995). Actuarial prediction of sexual recidivism. *Journal of Interpersonal Violence, 10,* 85–105.

Rice, M. E., & Harris, G. T. (1997). Cross-validation and extension of the Violence Risk Appraisal Guide for child molesters and rapists. *Law and Human Behavior, 21,* 231–241.

Roberts, J. V., & Grossman, M. G. (1993). Sexual homicide in Canada: A descriptive analysis. *Annals of Sex Research, 6,* 5–25.

Salekin, R. T., Rogers, R., & Sewell, K. W. (1996). A review and meta-analysis of the Psychopathy Checklist–Revised: Predictive validity of dangerousness. *Clinical Psychology: Science and Practice, 3,* 203–215.

Seagrave, D., & Grisso, T. (2002). Adolescent development and the measurement of juvenile psychopathy. *Law and Human Behavior, 26,* 219–239.

Serin, R. C., Malcolm, P. B., Khanna, A., & Barbaree, H. E. (1994). Psychopathy and deviant arousal in incarcerated sex offenders. *Journal of Interpersonal Violence, 9*, 3–11.

Seto, M. C., & Barbaree, H. E. (1999). Psychopathy, treatment behavior, and sex offenders recidivism. *Journal of Interpersonal Violence, 14*, 1235–1248.

Shine, J. H., & Hobson, J. A. (2000). Institutional behaviour and time in treatment among psychopaths admitted to a prison-based therapeutic community. *Medicine, Science, and the Law, 40*, 327–335.

Simourd, D. J. (1997). The Criminal Sentiments Scale–Modified and Pride in Delinquency scale: Psychometric properties and construct validity of two measures of criminal attitude. *Criminal Justice and Behavior, 24*, 52–70.

Skeem, J. L., & Mulvey, E. P. (2001). Psychopathy and community violence among civil psychiatric patients: Results from the MacArthur violence risk assessment study. *Journal of Consulting and Clinical Psychology, 69*, 358–374.

Stafford, E., & Cornell, D. G. (2003). Psychopathy scores predict adolescent inpatient aggression. *Assessment, 10*, 102–112.

Stone, M. H. (1998). The personalities of murderers: The importance of psychopathy and sadism. In A. Skodol (Ed.), *Psychopathology and violent crime* (pp. 29–52). Washington, DC: American Psychiatric Press.

Vitelli, R. (1999). Childhood disruptive behavior disorders and adult psychopathy. *American Journal of Forensic Psychology, 16*, 29–37.

Waschbusch, D., Porter, S., Carrey, N., Kazmi, O., Roach, K., & D'Amico, D. (2004). Investigation of the heterogeneity of disruptive behaviour in elementary-age children. *Canadian Journal of Behavioural Science, 36*, 97–112.

Williamson, S. E., Hare, R. D., & Wong, S. (1987). Violence: Criminal psychopaths and their victims. *Canadian Journal of Behavioral Science, 19*, 454–462.

Woodworth, M., & Porter, S. (2002). In cold blood: Characteristics of criminal murders as a function of psychopathy. *Journal of Abnormal Psychology, 111*, 436–445.

11

Psychopathy as a Behavior Classification System for Violent and Serial Crime Scenes

Mary Ellen O'Toole

It was close to Easter 2002, and 11-year-old Sally (name changed) was playing outside with her little girlfriend. They were in a small picnic area in the front of the trailer park where Sally lived with her family. The picnic area was adjacent to a well-traveled road, and it could be seen from both directions. It was midmorning on this pleasant spring-like day, and the girls were having fun. There were other people in the area at the time, going about their normal business. It was a small community, more rural than urban, where people knew each other and were friendly to strangers. A child abduction–murder was the last thing people thought would occur in their town on that day or on any day.

Billy (name changed) initially drove past the girls and, according to witnesses, turned around on a side road where he stopped very briefly, as though he were considering what to do next. He was driving a commercial truck and his company's logo was clearly marked on the back. He then drove back to the picnic area, got out of the truck, and walked up to Sally and her friend. They just stood there. Billy mentioned something about a lost puppy and, at the same time, he reached out and grabbed Sally, threw her in the front seat, and drove away. Her friend watched. Sally was found the next day in a rural section of a nearby county.

What happened to Sally that day was sickening and repugnant, but these descriptors and others like them, although sensational and disturbing, are not helpful to law enforcement because they do not define what really happened. They explain little, if anything, about the crime scene and give us no insight into Billy's personality. Law enforcement professionals must look at what happened through a different filter. Billy's behavior was very high risk and impulsive. He abducted Sally in the middle of the day, on a well-traveled road, with people in the area and a surviving witness. He drove a vehicle that could be easily identified and remembered by witnesses. He stopped briefly, sat in his truck, and then drove back to where Sally and her friend were playing. After abducting her, Billy sexually assaulted Sally and then transported her to a location where he shot her in the back of the head, killing her. He left her small body in a gully. This case received extensive media coverage, which Billy followed closely with his unwitting wife and natural children. Within several days, Billy phoned the command center of the task force as well as the local media and admitted to the crime. He gave his location and said he intended to commit suicide later that night.

Violent crime scenes always tell a story—a story written by the offender, the victim, and the unique circumstances of their interaction. That story makes crime scenes dynamic events that will vary in complexity, and, like any narrative, will have a beginning, middle, and end. Of the many possible criminal narratives, those that involve psychopaths have a distinct tone and intent, set apart the way science fiction stands out from other literature.

A crime is like a play. We do not understand everything that is going on until we see all of the scenes. The denouement is the synergistic effect of the characters, their roles, the plots, theatrical techniques, and even the reaction of the audience. So it is in a violent crime: As events evolve we learn more and more about the offender and his[1] interaction with the victim(s). Within this evolution, the dynamics change, and victim–offender behaviors reflect these changes. When the crime comes to its conclusion, the final scene or scenes behaviorally and forensically reflect the victim–offender interaction and the reason(s) the crime occurred and provide a much better look at the offender's psyche.

During his crime, the offender behaves a certain way as a result of many factors including personality, motivation(s), affective state, existing mental conditions, background, prior criminal experience, the influence of drugs and/or alcohol, and the unique circumstances of the crime, including the victim's response (Douglas, Burgess, Burgess & Ressler, 1992; O'Toole, 1999). Correctly interpreting the complex dynamics, inferred from crime scene behaviors, can reveal critical information about how and why the crime occurred and what were the behavior patterns and trends of the offender as well as gain insight into his unique personality (Douglas et al., 1992; O'Toole, 1999). This information can include the amount of planning that went into a crime; the importance of control to the offender; the escalation of emotion during the crime; the offender's affective state; the amount of risk the offender took to commit the crime; the offender's desire for thrill and excitement; the offender's emotional maturity; the motivation(s) for the crime, aspects of the offender's lifestyle; the offender's sexual fantasies and practices; the victim selection process; the offender's feelings of remorse or empathy; the offender's ability to relate and communicate with others; the offender's criminal experience, sophistication, and versatility; and the offender's pre- and postoffense behavior (O'Toole, 1999; Ressler, Burgess, & Douglas, 1988).

---

[1]To promote reading ease, male pronouns are used to refer to psychopaths in this chapter because (a) the vast majority of serial killers are men and (b) much of what we know about psychopathy comes from research with men.

The purpose of this chapter is to blend together psychopathy, violence, and crime scene analysis. The psychopathic personality construct is operationalized in terms of behaviors observed at a violent crime scene that can be indicative of psychopathy. The four-facet model of psychopathy is discussed in relation to how the unique personality traits and behaviors of persons with psychopathy might be manifested at a violent crime scene. This information is not intended to train law enforcement professionals to become mental health experts qualified in the clinical assessment of psychopathy. Rather, this information is designed to be used as an investigative tool to provide law enforcement professionals with a better understanding of both the psychopathic offender, as well as his violent crime scene(s).

PSYCHOPATHY AND LAW ENFORCEMENT

Psychopathy has emerged as one of the most important clinical constructs in the mental health and criminal justice fields (Hare, 1993/1998, 1998a, 1998b, 1999, 2002; Hare, Cooke, & Hart, 1999; Hare & Neumann, 2005; Porter et al., 2000). The most reliable, valid, and widely used tools for the assessment of psychopathy are the Hare Psychopathy Checklist–Revised (PCL–R; Hare, 1991, 2003) and its derivatives, the Psychopathy Checklist: Screening Version (PCL:SV; Hart, Cox, & Hare, 1995) and the Psychopathy Checklist: Youth Version (PCL:YV; Forth, Kosson, & Hare, 2003). The PCL–R defines psychopathy as a unique constellation of four clusters of traits, characteristics, and behaviors: affective, interpersonal, lifestyle, and antisocial. The four clusters, or factors, measured by the PCL–R are listed in Table 11–1.

TABLE 11–1.
The PCL–R Factors and the Items That Define Them

Interpersonal	*Affective*	*Lifestyle*	*Antisocial*
Glib, superficial charm	Lack of remorse-guilt	Stimulation seeking	Poor behavior controls
Grandiose sense of self-worth	Shallow affect	Impulsivity	Early behavior problems
Pathological lying	Callous, lack of empathy	Irresponsible	Juvenile delinquency[a]
Conning and manipulative	Failure to accept responsibility	Parasitic orientation	Revocation of conditional release[a]
		Lack of realistic goals	Criminal versatility[a]

Note. Two items, Many Marital Relationships and Promiscuous Sexual Behavior contribute to the assessment of psychopathy but do not fall into any of the four factors. From *The Hare Psychopathy Checklist–Revised* (2nd ed.), by R. D. Hare, 2003, Toronto, Ontario, Canada: Multi-Health Systems. Copyright 2003 by Multi-Health Systems. Reprinted with permission.

[a]These items define a pattern of early, persistent, serious, and generalized rule-breaking.

Although not every psychopath will have contact with the criminal justice system, the traits associated with this personality disorder place psychopaths at risk for committing crime and acting out violently. Hare explains that because of their hallmark lack of conscience and ability to exploit situations, it is understandable how psychopaths can become enmeshed in criminal behavior. Personality traits and characteristics, such as empathy for others, feelings of guilt and remorse, and fear of punishment help to inhibit antisocial and violent behavior in most people but are lacking in psychopaths (Hare, 1993/1998, 1998a, 1998b, 1999; Hare et al., 1999; Porter et al., 2000).

The term *psychopath* is frequently used interchangeably with terms such as *sociopath, antisocial personality disorder, psychotic,* and *crazy.* These terms are not interchangeable, and these disorders or implied mental states are not synonymous with psychopathy. Psychopaths are a breed apart, and those who investigate their crimes, interview them, prosecute them, and supervise their incarceration should understand their distinctive natures.

Empirical research has long supported the notion that psychopathy and criminal behavior are intertwined in a distinctly unique way (Porter & Woodworth, 2005). Compared with other criminals, psychopaths are more dangerous, their victimization of others is more varied, their criminal careers begin earlier, and they commit a broader range of crimes over their lifetime. They recidivate quickly, especially if they are sexual psychopaths, and they readily violate the conditions of their parole. Overall, psychopaths tend to be more violent in their crimes and continue to offend for a longer period of time than do other offenders (Hare, 1998b, 1999, 2002; Harris, Rice, & Cormier, 1991; Porter et al., 2000; Porter & Woodworth, 2005).

There are many preconceived ideas of what a psychopath is and how he or she looks and acts. We see psychopaths portrayed on television and in the movies, but the accuracy of these portrayals is often mendacious. Hollywood's psychopath is often glamorized, demonized, made to appear "mad" or brilliantly diabolical. Sometimes they are characterized as not even human and therefore easily distinguishable. But psychopaths *are* human, and they *are not* distinguishable by their physical appearance. They are not out of touch with reality, and they know the difference between right and wrong. In other words, at first blush, a psychopath can appear like us, and this can be an unsettling fact. Psychopaths can be either male or female and are found in all races and cultures. Psychopaths are not necessarily intellectually superior to us although their ability to use, manipulate, and con people may cause them to appear smarter (Cooke, 1998; Hare, 1993/1998; Hare et al., 1999; Meloy, 1988). Some psychopaths are well educated and others are not. Some are physically attractive and others less so. Some have homes, families, and jobs and positions of trust in their community. Others live a much more transient and obviously parasitic lifestyle. Because of education and upbringing, one psychopath can possess superior verbal skills and seem particularly charming. Another psychopath, having few if any social skills, can present very harshly. Psychopaths are not all alike, and we should expect to see variations in how they present (Hare & Neumann, 2005; Hervé, chap. 17, this volume).

It is a common belief, even in some law enforcement circles, that people who commit violent, incomprehensible crimes must be crazy or psychotic or that they "just snapped." This conception of violence and the violent offender is frequently reinforced in the media. Some people even believe there is a correlation or a relationship between the degree of violence observed at a crime scene and the physical appearance of the offender. Some people are more comfortable attributing violent, bizarre, seemingly motiveless crimes to that notorious, straggly haired stranger who roams, unbridled, from town to town throughout the world, than to the man next door, or worse yet, the son, daughter, or husband down the hall. How many times have we heard expressions of shock when a community learns the identity of a serial killer? "Joe couldn't be the serial killer. He's worked at the same company for nearly 30 years." Or, "He's my next door neighbor. He says hello to me every morning when he walks his dog. He couldn't be the serial killer. I would have noticed something different or strange about him." Unfortunately, society's litmus test for assessing evil or its potential is remarkably ineffective.

"It is unnerving to realize someone capable of violence, particularly murder, can live and work among us under such a facade of normalcy. Such morally incomprehensible behavior, exhibited by a seemingly normal person, leaves us feeling bewildered and helpless" (Hare, 1993/1998, p. 5). In his classic work, *The Mask of Sanity*, Dr. Hervey Cleckley described the psychopath as someone who "more often than not . . . will seem particularly agreeable and make a distinctly positive impression when he is first encountered. Alert and friendly in his attitude, he is easy to talk with and seems to have a good many genuine interests. There is nothing at all odd or queer about him, and in every respect he tends to embody the concept of a well-adjusted happy person" (Cleckley, 1976, p. 338).

The psychopath can be described as one of law enforcement's greatest challenges. Law enforcement professionals are likely to encounter psychopaths on a more regular basis than any other group of professionals. Therefore, understanding the psychopathic construct is particularly important for people in this profession. Many psychopaths are involved in criminal activity, and a much smaller but virulent group is responsible for very violent crimes, including both single and serial homicides, acts of terrorism, kidnappings, extortions, sexual assaults, and child abductions. In every policing department in every city in the world, law enforcement officers interact with criminal psychopaths every day and yet, all too often, do not understand this personality disorder and its significance to their work.

Courses designed to study psychopathy are not a traditional part of the curriculum offered in many basic law enforcement academies. The study of violent offenders and their behavior is often lumped together under one umbrella, which, by implication, suggests that criminals are from the same basic mold. This opinion could not be further from the truth.

One or two behaviors from a violent crime scene will not be absolute indicators of psychopathy. However, given what we know about psychopathy and crime scene analysis, the development of a behavior classification system based on the psychopathic construct is very important. Research in this area could reveal the fact that psychopathic traits are distinguishable at violent crime scenes and that the identification of a particular type of psychopath will become apparent from the specificity of these behaviors.

CRIMINAL INVESTIGATIVE ANALYSIS

The Federal Bureau of Investigation's (FBI) Behavioral Analysis Unit (BAU), part of the National Center for the Analysis of Violent Crime, is located at the FBI Academy in Quantico, Virginia. Since the mid-1970s, the analysts in the BAU, which evolved out of the Behavioral Sciences Unit and is commonly referred to as the Profiling Unit, have studied some of the most violent and bizarre crimes in the world and the types of people who commit these crimes. The BAU's highly trained and experienced analysts consult with law enforcement agencies from all over the world to help investigators and prosecutors understand the dynamics of these crimes and the personality makeup of the offenders responsible for them.

The FBI uses a unique two-part process to analyze violent crime scenes. This process, known as criminal investigative analysis, involves identifying every behavioral and forensic variable at a violent crime scene and then behaviorally interpreting these variables. Some of these variables include victimology; the victim selection process; offender risk level; offender–victim relationship; offender–victim verbal, physical, and sexual interaction; injury pattern to the victim and body disposal method and style of assault, including sexual assault; the degree of control exercised by the offender; the amount of planning involved in the crime; the degree of criminal sophistication; and forensic evidence recovered from the scene (Douglas et al., 1992; O'Toole, 1999; Ressler et al., 1988).

Singular crime scene behaviors are not isolated nor are they ascribed disproportionate significance over clusters of crime scene behaviors. Violent crime scene behaviors *must* be analyzed as an aggregate—the totality of the circumstances—to construct a behavioral blueprint of the crime and the personality of the offender (O'Toole, 1999; Ressler et al., 1988).

Once crime scene behaviors have been identified, their meaning must be interpreted. The ability to interpret crime scene behavior is the cumulative result of education, specialized training in a wide range of disciplines, and experience in reviewing and analyzing many cases. This cumulative experience, as well as knowledge of current empirical research in multiple disciplines, provides a strong foundation for a sound and reliable interpretation of a violent crime scene. However, the most important component for crime scene assessment, underpinning all the other qualifications, is the analyst's strong investigative background. This experience is absolutely essential to reliably interpret a crime scene. Without real experience, the analysis becomes primarily an academic effort.

CLASSIFYING CRIME SCENE BEHAVIOR

Classifying crime scene behavior is a cornerstone of criminal investigative analysis. Behavior classification systems are well documented in the literature on violent crime and crime scene analysis. Classification systems allow information about crime scenes, offender behavior, victims, forensics, etc., to be sorted and categorized for comparisons, analysis, and examination to develop a better understanding of theories of criminal behavior, violence, and violent offenders (Douglas et al., 1992; Ressler et al., 1988).

One of the earliest behavioral classification systems designed and used by the FBI for crime scene analysis is the organized–disorganized–mixed homicide scene paradigm. This system allows investigators to classify, along a continuum, the organizational structure of a homicide scene ("Crime Scene," 1985). Other behavioral classification paradigms have been developed to classify types of violence and violent offenders. For example, Salfati (2000) distinguished between instrumental and expressive aggression as seen in homicide scenes.

A well-known rape classification system designed by Groth, Burgess, and Holmstrom (1977) and modified by Hazelwood (1987) explains differences among rapists and their motivations based on offender behavior during the rape. Hazelwood and Warren (2000) developed a paradigm of serial sexual offenders. This paradigm distinguishes between two typologies of sexually violent offenders: the impulsive offender and the ritualistic offender. According to these authors, the distinctive nature of these offenders is evidenced in their victim selection process and crime scene behaviors. With the *Crime Classification Manual* (Douglas et al., 1992), violent crimes can be classified according to the primary intent of the offender. Classifying crimes this way allows investigators to better understand the components of the crime that can ultimately contribute to a quicker and more successful resolution. Investigators are able to classify crime scene behaviors in a way to better understand the personality of their suspect or suspects and their motivation (Douglas et al., 1992).

PSYCHOPATHY AND THE VIOLENT CRIME SCENE CLASSIFICATION SYSTEM

The empirical and clinical literature on psychopathy is extensive and extremely well documented, providing an excellent foundation upon which to base a violent crime scene classification system. Experts in the study and assessment of psychopaths have long agreed that psychopaths differ from other people in terms of how they present (Hare, 1998a, 1998b; Hervé, Ling, & Hare, 2000, Meloy, 1988). In many respects, psychopaths appear to be "qualitatively" different from other criminals, even from other violent criminals with long careers. Although the construct itself may be multidimensional, individuals high on the psychopathy dimensions (a strong dose of psychopathic features) may exhibit an "emergent" quality in which the quantitative differences in personality and behavior are so great as to give rise to an individual who is palpably different from those lower on the dimension (Guay, Ruscio, Knight, & Hare, 2005). (In much the same way, we view blood pressure as multidimensional. Someone at the extreme upper end of the continuum differs from others not only quantitatively but also qualitatively, at least in terms of the bodily processes and risk factors involved.) It is therefore reasonable to suggest that the distinctive nature of psychopathy will also be evident in unique behaviors at crime scenes. In fact, more and more empirical studies support the notion that psychopaths do behave differently at their crime scenes than do nonpsychopathic offenders.

Cornell et al. (1996) distinguished between psychopathic and nonpsychopathic offenders in their use of instrumental and reactive violence. A psychopath readily engages in both types of violence but is much more likely than others to use instrumental violence. Instrumental violence is unprovoked violence that is described as cold-blooded, purposeful, goal-directed, and in some instances predatory. In crimes involving instrumental violence, the victim does little or nothing to incite or threaten the offender. Instrumental violence does not require a preexisting relationship with the victim, and, in fact offenders who engage in instrumental violence are as likely to target strangers as victims. Woodworth & Porter (2002) suggested that even though nonpsychopaths are capable of engaging in instrumental violence, psychopaths demonstrate a preference for this type of violence.

Serial sexual killers can be considered the ultimate of violent offenders. Their crime scenes provide a rich environment in which to study the meshing of violence, sexuality, and psychopathy. For those psychopaths who become serial offenders, their lack of conscience, remorse, and empathy allows them to become human predators who engage in this unique type of unprovoked aggression and instrumental violence, without concern for the victims or others around them (Hare, 1993/1998; Woodworth & Porter, 2002). The comorbidity of psychopathy and sadism in sexual offending elevates the psychopath's threat to society and further distinguishes his crime scenes from those of other offenders. Serial murder is a dramatic and extreme example of instrumental, predatory violence (Dietz, Hazelwood, & Warren, 1990; Niehoff, 1999; Stone 2001).

Other research findings that support the notion that psychopaths manifest their personality traits and characteristics in a different way from that of other offenders at their crime scenes, include the following:

- A psychopath's violence is a more complex and distinctive form of violence than that of other violent offenders (Porter & Woodworth, 2005).
- A psychopath is more likely to commit an instrumental or cold-blooded, unprovoked homicide than is a nonpsychopath (Woodworth & Porter, 2002).
- Nonpsychopathic offenders are much more likely to engage in reactive violence, a type of violence in which the offender feels provoked by some real or imagined threat. Offenders engaging in reactive violence

are more likely to have some type of preexisting relationship with their victim (Cornell et al., 1996). Although a violent psychopath can also engage in reactive violence, his preference appears to be instrumental violence (Cornell et al., 1996; Woodworth & Porter, 2002).

- Clinical and empirical research and anecdotal evidence have indicated a connection between sadism, sexual sadism and psychopathy, particularly in serial killers (Dietz et al., 1990; Hare et al., 1999; Stone, 2001).
- A psychopathic offender is more likely to commit a sexually motivated homicide and to engage in significantly more gratuitous or excessive violence, including sadistic violence, than is a nonpsychopathic offender (Porter, Woodworth, Earle, Drugge, & Boer, 2003).
- Offenders whose victims includes *both* children and adults are more likely than not to be psychopaths, highly dangerous, and at great risk for reoffending (Porter et al., 2000; Rice & Harris, 1997).
- Male psychopaths are more geographically mobile than are nonpsychopaths (Hunter, Hemphill, Hare, & Anderson, 2003).

An FBI study by Dudek (2001) on single and serial prostitute murderers found that the serial offenders had significantly higher PCL–R Total scores than the single offenders. Factor 1 scores (interpersonal and affective) for the serial offenders were higher than scores for the single offenders. Dudek suggests that this difference could account for the serial offenders being "'sweet talkers' able to talk their victims beyond any forms of security screening they might employ" (p. 301). Dudek also found that serial killers had more jobs and more addresses than single offenders, suggesting a more transient lifestyle. The serial offenders in this study also evidenced significantly higher frequencies of prior adult and child sex offenses and higher numbers of deviant sexual interests.

In their study on psychopathy and unlawful confinement (kidnapping), Hervé, Mitchell, Cooper, Spidel, & Hare (2004) found that a high proportion of the offenders were psychopaths and that most of the cases involved instrumental violence.

Psychopathic offenders who act impulsively may not do so because of poor behavior controls but rather because they make a conscious decision to act out after only a very quick consideration of the consequences (Woodworth & Porter, 2002).

A psychopath's lack of empathy for his victims, compounded by his desire for thrill- and/or sensation-seeking, enable him to disregard the consequences of his actions and to engage in high-risk behaviors (Porter, Campbell, Woodworth, & Birt, 2001; Porter et al., 2000).

Motiveless Crimes?

An offender's motive is the purpose or intent for his committing the crime. The motive of a crime, including a violent crime or series of crimes, is more objective and may be inferred from a crime scene. For example, a sexual assault, a murder, a kidnapping, or a robbery is an objective, measurable event that can be observed at a crime scene. Offenders can have multiple motives for a single offense, and in serial offenses motive(s) can evolve over time (Myers, Husted, Safarik, & O'Toole, 2005; Safarik, Jarvis, & Nussbaum, 2000). Motive, however, is not synonymous with the offender's affective or emotional state. Affective state, what the offender is feeling at the time of the crime, is much more difficult to discern (Dietz, 1985). Despite this significant distinction, emotions are frequently identified as motives for crimes, particularly for violent crimes in which there is a great deal of violence and physical damage to the victim. In crimes involving extreme reactive violence, strong emotions, such as anger, rage, hatred, and hurt, are likely to underpin or fuel the offender's behavior. However, if the offender is a psychopath and the crime scene evidences gratuitous, excessive or sadistic violence, he may not have experienced strong, sustained emotions (Porter et al., 2003). In fact, ascribing an emotional state to a psychopath can be very problematic. Clinical and empirical research suggests that some psychopaths evidence a significant level of hypoemotionality, even when involved in excessively violent behavior (Herpertz et al., 2001). Niehoff (1999) indicates that psychopathic sex offenders are not necessarily angry with their victims; they just may not care about them. In fact, conflict may not be at all stressful for psychopaths (Niehoff, 1999). Conversely, for a particular type of psychopath, most notably the explosive psychopath, rage wounds on the victim may actually be the result of his greater impulsivity and more intense, primitive emotions which result in him overreacting to persons and events (see Hervé, chap. 17, this volume).

PSYCHOPATHY AND CRIME SCENE BEHAVIOR

Traits, characteristics, and behaviors that underpin the psychopathic construct seem to be fairly straightforward in terms of their definition. However, recognizing these same traits, characteristics, and behaviors in a violent crime scene can be much more difficult. For example, what does glib and superficially charming look like in a series of unsolved prostitute homicide scenes? Does the killer who targets prostitute victims manifest the same degree of glib and superficial charm as the killer who kidnaps middle-class women from their homes to sexually assault and murder them? If a serial murderer transports his murder victims to dump sites along remote, rural roads, is this behavior a manifestation of certain traits and characteristics within the psychopathic construct?

To better identify and interpret psychopathic behaviors manifested at a violent crime scene, four traits from the psychopathic construct are discussed: impulsivity, sensation-seeking, glib and superficial charm, and conning and manipulation.

Impulsivity and Sensation-Seeking

Impulsivity is an extremely important part of the psychopathic construct with respect to crime scene behavior. Impulsivity suggests that the offender only briefly considered the consequences of his actions before acting out (Woodworth & Porter, 2002). Impulsivity may be associated with sensation-seeking in which the offender uses circumstances, events, or situations to fulfill his need for excitement and/or thrill (Porter et al., 2003). Impulsivity and sensation-seeking can be manifested at a violent crime scene or a series of crime scenes in a number of ways.

Impulsivity can cause a crime to appear relatively spontaneous, unplanned, disorganized, and opportunistic. Acting impulsively results in behaviors that can put the offender at risk for being seen, identified, injured, or even apprehended. In a series of crimes, the offender's impulsivity can account for greater variation between crime scenes including: differences in victim age, race, and physical appearance; method of accessing victims; method of assault; injury pattern to the victims; choice of weapon; use of multiple weapons; and location and time of day during which the crime occurred.

A sensation-seeking offender needs particular situations, events, or circumstances to be present in his crimes to fulfill his need for high risk and thrill. This behavior, which is hyperexciting to the offender, usually involves risky behavior over and beyond what is necessary to complete the crime (Porter et al, 2003; Porter & Woodworth, 2005).

Impulsive, sensation-seeking behaviors may seem reckless, thoughtless, and even stupid or a result of the influence of drugs and/or alcohol. Some may describe high-risk or sensation-seeking offenders as just being lucky, even though they may successfully have committed a number of high-risk crimes. However, luck is not a variable in criminal investigative analysis. Luck is a nebulous concept that is neither measurable nor observable at a crime scene. High-risk crimes can generate significant public panic and fear in the community, and this response can fuel the sensation-seeking offender's behavior. For example, in a recent very high-profile sniper case, two offenders evaded identification and apprehension despite a tremendous unprecedented law enforcement response. The community's response was fear and panic. As the offenders continued their crime spree, some ascribed their success to luck. However, when viewed analytically, these crimes suggested offenders who were strongly driven, in part, by thrill- and sensation-seeking. They were able to make the most out of the law enforcement response, chaos, and public panic generated by their crimes. They were cool under the circumstances. If interviewed by police, they coolly offered a believable reason for being in the area and displayed no overt signs of stress or guilt. They found it thrilling and exciting to remain in the area after the shootings to watch the pandemonium they had created.

In another example, an offender entered an occupied middle-class home during the middle of the day to commit a sexual assault and murder. There was normal activity taking place in the neighborhood, and other residents were at home. The victim, who just recently had moved into that specific neighborhood, unexpectedly came home for lunch that day. Her roommate was away at the time.

This offender's decision to enter a residence under these circumstances was fraught with uncertainties; this crime was very high risk for him. Without prior knowledge of the dynamics of that residence and the neighborhood, the offender could have encountered a range of serious problems: nosey or watchful neighbors; service people; burglar alarms; a watchdog; a sleeping husband or boyfriend; and even an armed victim. However, the psychopathic offender may seek situations that allow him to satisfy his need for thrill and excitement. This offender would most likely not view his behavior as high risk. Rather, for him, these situations are exciting and challenging. The feelings of anxiety, worry, and stress that most of us would experience in the same situation were probably absent in this offender. Concerns about capture were only momentarily considered and then disregarded.

A psychopath's sensation-seeking and impulsivity will also be seen in other crimes he commits and in other noncriminal aspects of his life. In a linkage analysis of a series of similar crimes, the presence of impulsivity and high-risk behaviors are two variables, along with others, that can help to support an expert opinion for testimonial purposes that the crimes are behaviorally linked and the same offender is responsible.

Glib and Superficial Charm; Conning and Manipulative

Some psychopaths can seem charming, engaging, and even charismatic to others, including their victims. They are able to appear nonthreatening and incapable of violence. An example of how this particular psychopathic trait can be manifested at a crime scene is the manner in which an offender accesses his victim(s). Accessing a victim can be behaviorally described in terms of the interpersonal skills of the offender by their use of *any* one, or a combination, of the following approaches: (a) con; (b) ruse; (c) surprise; and (d) blitz (O'Toole & Safarik, personal communication, June 12, 2005).

In a *con* approach, the offender uses an interpersonal style, a certain persona, that is appealing and believable to the victim to obfuscate the threat he poses. The offender uses his verbal skills, his physical appearance, the promise of something, for example, a ride, dinner, money, sex, or drugs, as well as necessary props, to further his con. For example, in a serial murder case, a prolific serial killer convinced a number of prostitutes to get into his vehicle and drive away with him. To do this, he had children's toys visible on the floor of the vehicle. He also displayed a photograph of his son. The implication was he could not be a serial killer because he was a parent. The women who believed his con became his victims.

A *ruse* approach is a more specific and elaborate type of con. The offender fabricates a credible story in which there is some type of problem, and he needs help from the victim to solve the problem. In a ruse, the offender acts out a "role" in which he appears helpless, vulnerable, or in trouble. An example of a ruse was noted in another serial murder case that occurred in the Midwest. The offender dressed as a telephone repairman and approached victims in their middle-class homes. He told the women he needed access to their homes to fix the phone lines. Once inside the home, this offender initiated the attack.

A *surprise* approach can be described as an unexpected and sudden attack during which the offender attempts to gain immediate control of the victim. A surprise approach may or may not involve the use of injurious force. An example of a surprise approach involved a series of sexual assaults that occurred during early morning hours. The offender entered the victim's apartment through an open window. Once inside, the offender walked into the victim's bedroom and lay down next to her, stroking her arm until she woke.

A *blitz* assault is an immediate and overwhelming application of injurious physical force that incapacitates the victim. The offender attempts to gain immediate control of the victim and prevent resistance. An example in which a blitz assault was used involved a serial offender who walked up behind one of his victims and hit her over the head with a crow bar to incapacitate her and immediately control her. He then manually strangled her.

All four approaches can be used by psychopaths to access victims, and multiple approaches can be used on the same victim. The use of a particular approach can be a manifestation of the offender's particular psychopathy. For example, an offender can use a con or a ruse to manipulate the victim into lowering her guard and then use a blitz attack to ultimately incapacitate her. Successfully using a con or the more elaborate ruse requires a certain degree of verbal and manipulation skills for the offender to be convincing and believable to the victim. To lure a victim into a lethal situation requires convincing verbal skills (charm) and the ability to manipulate others. On the other hand, use of only the surprise attack or blitz assault suggests an offender who has no interest in or lacks the ability to talk with his victim. Porter and Woodworth (2005) suggested that "less intelligent psychopaths may resort to violence to compensate for their inferior abilities to manipulate others through language" (p. 21).

Identifying and accurately interpreting specific crime scene behaviors as indicative of psychopathy is a much-needed area of study. This type of research can provide critical insight into the offender's personality and will help law enforcement professionals focus their investigations by prioritizing investigative leads based on offender personality traits and characteristics. It would enable investigators to design and customize specific strategies, such as interview strategies, that work much more effectively with psychopaths. These include orchestrating the initial approach to the offender, preparing the right interview questions, setting up the interview room, choosing the right interviewer, and identifying effective interview themes. They can also assist investigators in linkage analysis—linking those crimes committed by the same offender—based on similar psychopathic traits and characteristics observed at crime scenes.

Empirical research involving violent crime scenes and the correlation of certain crime scene behaviors to the traits and characteristics in the psychopathic construct is necessary to be able to conclude, with any degree of certainty, that psychopathy is present. This research is currently being pursued at the FBI's BAU.

FOUR-FACET MODEL OF PSYCHOPATHY

Current empirical evidence suggests that psychopathy and its components, as measured by the PCL–R, are better described in dimensional than in categorical terms (Guay et al., 2005). As indicated in Table 11.1, psychopathy is underpinned by four clusters of items, or facets. Each item is scored 0, 1, or 2 and facet scores can range from 0 to 8 (four-item facets) or 0 to 10 (five-item facets). Detailed descriptions are provided by Hare (2003).

Facet 1: Interpersonal

The four items in this factor describe how an individual relates to and interacts with others. A high score on the factor reflects a manipulative, deceptive, conning, dominant, and controlling style of interaction.

Facet 2: Affective

The four items in this factor describe an individual's emotional landscape. A high score suggests that the individual's emotional life is shallow and relatively barren of normal deep-level feelings and that there is little or no concern for the feelings and welfare of others, except in an abstract, intellectual sense.

Facet 3: Lifestyle

The five items in this factor describe aspects of the individual's general lifestyle. A high score indicates that the individual leads an impulsive, nomadic lifestyle, with a tendency to live for the moment. He tends to become bored easily, is unlikely to remain in relationships or jobs for a long time, and is continually searching for new experiences and sensations.

Facet 4: Antisocial

The five items in this factor describe serious and generalized rule-breaking behaviors. A high score indicates that the individual engages in a varied and persistent antisocial lifestyle, with frequent and serious violations of social and legal expectations and standards from an early age. He may be easily offended, short-tempered, and aggressive and prone to engage in a wide variety of illegal activities.

SUBTYPES

The four-factor model has implications for the manner in which a psychopath presents. The affective features of psychopathy (Facet 2) are central to the construct (Bolt, Hare, Vitale, & Newman, 2004), but there is evidence that psychopaths can differ from one another in terms of the weighting of the traits, characteristics, and behaviors reflected in the other three factors (Hare & Neumann, 2005; Hervé, chap. 17, this volume). Experienced investigators understand this distinction because they have interviewed many violent, psychopathic offenders, including serial killers, all of whom are likely to be psychopathic but who differ from each other in terms of some aspects of their behavior and their crime scenes. For example, some serial killers are quite verbal, articulate, glib, and charming but others are less so. Some have extensive criminal histories and others have little, if any, formal criminal history. Some serial killers access their victims by relying on their verbal skills to convince their victims they are not dangerous and pose no threat. Other serial killers seem much more "Neanderthal" in how they access victims, using a surprise or blitz attack.

Hervé (chap. 17, this volume) identified four subtypes of offenders with high PCL–R scores: The *prototypical* psychopath, the *explosive* psychopath, the *manipulative* psychopath, and a fourth type referred to as the *sociopath* or *pseudo-psychopath*. The first three subtypes are underpinned by the affective traits of psychopathy, but they differ in the weighting of the other traits, characteristics, and behaviors. This variation in the psychopathic dimensions not only accounts for the differences in how these psychopaths present, but also in how they commit their crimes (Porter et al., 2003, Hervé, chap. 17, this volume). The fourth subtype lacks (relative to the other types) the Facet 2 (affective) features of psychopathy, all the while showing relatively high levels of the interpersonal, lifestyle, and antisocial features. These four types of psychopaths (i.e., offenders with high PCL–R scores) are described below.

Classic or Prototypical Psychopath

The classic or prototypical psychopath scores high in each of the four facets of psychopathy: affective, interpersonal, lifestyle, and antisocial (Bolt et al., 2004; Hare, 2003; Hervé, chap. 17, this volume). That is, he manifests all of the traits, characteristics and behaviors of psychopathy. He could be considered the "poster child" for psychopathy. A classic psychopathic sexual serial killer could be described as very manipulative, dominant, and controlling in his interactions with others. Although impulsive and sensation seeking, he would be criminally experienced, perhaps even to the point of being criminally sophisticated. Because of generalized rule breaking, including prior involvement in violent crime, he is likely to have spent time in jail and/or prison and, as a result, knows the importance of not leaving evidence at a scene. His criminal background is likely to show significant criminal versatility, including thefts, use of drugs, robberies, frauds, property crimes, assaults, and sex crimes. This criminal versatility is likely to include a degree of experimentation, which is underpinned by his tendency to become bored easily. Therefore, he imports change and variety into his crimes. For example, his methods of accessing victims and interacting with them will vary. He is likely to engage in excessive and gratuitous violence, which is not only indicative of absolute disregard for his victims but also is a reflection of hyperaggression.

The classic psychopath's crimes are likely to manifest evidence of careful planning within a domain of impulsivity and risk-taking, for example, occurring in the middle of the day in low-risk environments (middle-class homes in low-crime neighborhoods) and involving low-risk victims. Low-risk victims are victims whose lifestyle, habits and associates do not put them in jeopardy that could cause them to become the victim of a violent crime. When low-risk victims disappear, their disappearance tends to be noticed quickly and reported to law enforcement professionals. In contrast, high-risk victims are those whose lifestyle, habits, and/or associates (e.g., hitchhikers, prostitutes, or drug dealers) place them in jeopardy and, consequently, increase their vulnerability to becoming the victim of a violent crime. High-risk victims may lack regular accountability for their time and have periods of absences during which no one knows where they are, who they are with, or what they are doing. Therefore, the disappearance of a high-risk victim can go unnoticed and, therefore, unreported for a period of time.

The following case example is illustrative of two classic psychopaths who met while serving time together in prison. Both had extensive criminal histories reflecting significant criminal versatility.

Case Example 1

In a series of sadistic homicides that occurred a number of years ago in Southern California, five middle-class teenage girls were abducted and murdered over the course of 5 months. The bodies of four of the girls were discarded in remote areas and only partial remains of several of the victims were ultimately recovered. The nude body of the last victim was left on the front lawn of a home in an affluent neighborhood. Subsequent investigation identified two offenders who were arrested and ultimately convicted. During the investigation, an audiotape was recovered. On this audiotape, the last victim can be heard crying and screaming in almost an animal howl, as she is being physically tortured by one of the offenders. This particular offender, described as a sexual sadist,[2] maintained this torture tape for his continued personal sexual pleasure.

Some behaviors observed in this case manifest key traits of psychopathy: lack of remorse and guilt; callous lack of empathy for the victims; conning and manipulation; impulsivity; and criminal sophistication, a reflection of the

---

[2]Criminal sexual sadism, an extreme paraphilic behavior: The focus of sexual sadism involves an act in which the "individual derives sexual excitement from the psychological or physical suffering, including humiliation, of the victim" (APA, 1994).

offenders' criminal versatility. This series of murders occurred during a short period of time (weeks) and involved extreme criminal behavior: abduction, sexual sadism, and murder. These offenders continued their crimes until they were arrested. They did not stop themselves. In fact, they engaged in behaviors that enabled them to commit their crimes more successfully and without detection.

These offenders engaged in predatory behavior. They drove around specifically hunting for victims. They lured their victims into their van with promises of free rides and marijuana. These young girls were low-risk victims, although at the time of their abduction some of them were involved in activities, such as hitchhiking, that elevated their risk level. The offenders customized a van that enabled them to more efficiently abduct and restrain their victims while driving the freeways undetected. They preselected remote locations where they could ultimately take their victims to continue the attack. These offenders discarded the victims' bodies in separate locations that prevented and/or delayed their discovery and the retrieval of any forensic evidence that could connect them to the murders. There was no behavior manifested in these crimes to indicate that these offenders wanted to be caught or stopped.

These offenders lacked any empathy for their victims. Their victims were strangers, and the violence was instrumental, cold-blooded, sadistic, and unprovoked. In at least the last case, the violence was gratuitous. The victim was tortured, and her screams were memorialized on an audiotape. Despite her excruciating pain, these offenders did not stop. In fact, they specifically inflicted this degree of physical pain on this victim to elicit her response, as it was sexually gratifying.

Disposal of these victims' bodies also indicated that the offenders lacked empathy for their victims and felt no remorse or guilt for their crimes. Victims were left in remote areas where their remains were exposed to animal predation and a harsh environment, resulting in quick decomposition and body destruction. Some of the victims have never been found, and any forensic evidence that might have linked these offenders to the crimes has been lost forever. Based on the location of the body disposal sites, these offenders did not want the victims' bodies to be found, and there was no interest in giving their families closure.

Leaving the nude, tortured body of the last victim on the front lawn of someone's home was very arrogant. Although it guarantees the body will be found, it also shocks the community and demonstrates a strong disregard for the victim. This type of body disposal is intended to elicit a strong emotional response from the responding officers, the law enforcement community in general, and people in the community.

Explosive Psychopath

The explosive psychopath is less glib and superficially charming, conning, and manipulative than the classic psychopath. His psychopathy is manifested affectively, in his lifestyle, and in a background that includes antisocial behaviors and criminal versatility dating back to his adolescence, if not earlier. This psychopath is less likely to present as a talker or a con man. He takes action. As a serial killer, his approach to his victims would most likely be the surprise approach or blitz attack. Affectively, this offender experiences shallow emotions and will evidence a callous lack of empathy for others, as well as a lack of guilt and remorse for his actions. The explosive psychopath is less likely to blend in with a law-abiding community in which owning a home, being gainfully employed, and supporting a wife and family are a priority. The explosive psychopath is more reactive, and his emotions are more intense. He is more impulsive than other types, acting quickly without regard for consequences (Hervé, chap. 17, this volume). According to Hervé, what is particularly interesting about the explosive psychopath is that his motivation can be a result of "society's lack of attention" (p. 9) or his sense of persecution (also see Henderson, 1947). The explosive psychopath's motivation, in combination with his poor behavior controls, will cause him to react disproportionately to the triggering event. Nonetheless, he will fail to take responsibility for his destructive acts. This is an avid sensation or thrill seeker who, having no realistic future goals, often lives an overtly parasitic lifestyle (Hervé, chap. 17, this volume).

Manipulative Psychopath

The manipulative psychopath is interpersonally and affectively psychopathic, much like the classic psychopath, but his lifestyle and his background will evidence less criminal behavior and minimal criminal versatility. Because the manipulative psychopath exhibits fewer lifestyle and antisocial features of psychopathy, his life may appear normal. He may blend in better and *seem* more responsible and accomplished than other psychopaths. He is less likely to draw attention to himself, therefore enabling him to fly under law enforcement's radar screen. By acting more responsibly, he appears more socially acceptable. However, this appearance of living a responsible life is not due to his "sense of duty" and good citizenship but to his ability to con and manipulate people. Although he may come across as less overtly parasitic, this perception is probably due to his ability to use people in a more subtly deceptive way, thereby allowing his parasitic behavior to continue undetected for a longer period of time. Indeed, the manipulative psychopath uses his intellect to manipulate those around him to get what he wants. Some manipulative psychopaths may be more future oriented than others, and, therefore, are able to accomplish certain socially sanctioned long-term goals. For example, he may be married, employed full time, have attended school, graduated from college, own his own home, and/or be a church leader or a youth group leader (Hervé, chap. 17, this volume)

Because the manipulative psychopath is less antisocial, his *formal* criminal history (rap sheet) is likely to reflect few law enforcement contacts, if any, and his criminal behavior will evidence less versatility. If a manipulative psychopath is responsible for a series of unsolved homicides, identifying and interviewing all of the registered sex offenders in the area may very well be a waste of the investigator's time. Conversely, determining that a suspect from an objectively normal background has odd police contacts (e.g., a charge or conviction for something that would not be expected, such as drug trafficking, corporate crime, frauds and cons, or subcriminal activities–ethical violations), might make one start wondering if he or she is dealing with a manipulative psychopath (H. Hervé, electronic mail communication, July 7 and 12, 2005).

As a serial killer, the manipulative psychopath's crime scenes are likely to evidence less impulsiveness. They will seem less high risk and less spontaneous or spur of the moment. Their crimes will probably indicate more planning and control.

Fictional psychopathic serial killer Hannibal Lecter in the book and movie, *The Silence of the Lambs*, would be classified as a manipulative psychopath (Harris, 1988). Dr. Lecter had excellent interpersonal and manipulative skills. Affectively, he appeared to have no remorse for his murders and evidenced no empathy for his victims. However, he was a accomplished man. He graduated from college and medical school and had a psychiatric practice. Until his arrest, he seemed to live a normal life. He was not out robbing convenience stores, stealing cars, selling drugs, or otherwise engaging in criminal activity that would have brought him to the attention of law enforcement, but, instead, was living under a façade of normalcy.

In the real world, there are numerous cases of serial murders that drag on for years, and even decades, before the offender is identified and apprehended. This type of serial killer would most likely be a manipulative psychopath, a parasite able to go undetected for long periods.

The Pseudo-Psychopath (also known as the Sociopath)

Although this type of individual possesses many of the traits and characteristics of psychopathy, he lacks some of the crucial affective features of the disorder. The term *sociopath* seems appropriate here. The sociopath or pseudo-psychopath has a lifetime pattern of generalized and serious rule-breaking beginning at an early age. However, his development and criminal proclivities may be the result of early childhood exposure to an environment in which he was groomed into this type of behavior, for example, organized crime, drug trafficking, and so forth. According to H. Hervé (personal communication, July 7 and 12, 2005), "unlike idiopathic types who lack complex social emotions, these individuals are emotionally unstable and, therefore, more reactive and impulsive (in the true sense of the word); motivation likely reflects perceived wrongdoings of the past rather than current circumstances."

Clearly, understanding these subtypes will help explain subtle behavioral differences among psychopaths. Indeed, the experience at the National Center for the Analysis of Violent Crime suggests that the differences in how psychopaths manifest their particular blending of psychopathic features also distinguishes their crime scenes.

CHARACTERISTICS OF PSYCHOPATHY
AT A VIOLENT CRIME SCENE

In this section, descriptions of actual crime scene traits and characteristics indicative of psychopathy will be presented. There is no exhaustive list of crime scene behaviors that will irrefutably be indicative of psychopathy. Crime scene behaviors must be considered in their totality before any significance can be ascribed to them and interpretations made about the offender and his personality.

Case Example 2

A series of prostitute murders occurred in the Northwest over a 20-year period. An analysis of the crimes indicated the women initially went willingly with the killer. The women were strangled, and their bodies left in remote areas where they were never found or were so badly decomposed that there was little, if any, evidence that could be obtained.

These homicides evidenced thoughtful planning and control. The victims were considered high risk because of their lifestyle. The crimes occurred at night, and the victims were transported away from locations where they first encountered the offender. At that time, no usable forensic evidence was retrieved to connect the offender to the crimes. These homicides occurred over a period of years and then seemed to stop. Some in the law enforcement community believed this individual was remorseful for his behavior and, therefore, stopped killing. Behaviorally, however, the crime scenes were inconsistent with someone experiencing remorse or guilt for his actions. This person's behavior indicated that he did not want to be caught and, consequently, it was unlikely that he stopped killing; rather, he simply slowed down.

The following crime scene behaviors indicated that this offender was not impulsive but conning and manipulative in terms of the manner in which he accessed his victims and felt no remorse or guilt for his actions or empathy for his victims. First, the offender repeated his homicides over and over with the same degree of planning, control, and organization designed to prevent identification and capture. The deliberate continuation of this lethal predation, in such a methodical manner, strongly suggested that this individual's behavior was not affected by feelings of guilt or remorse.

Second, the victim selection process involved targeting prostitutes. Because of their lifestyle, prostitutes are considered at notoriously high risk for victimization. They can be victimized by a large number of people, thereby increasing the suspect pool exponentially. The greater the number of possible suspects, the lower is the risk that the offender will be singled out. Because of their high-risk lifestyles, prostitutes can be missing for long periods of time before their disappearance is even noted, let alone their bodies found and forensic evidence obtained. Putting time and distance between the offender and the victim minimizes the risk to the offender.

There was little variation in how this offender committed his crimes, and because of his consistency, lack of impulsivity, and lack of a need for sensation-seeking in his crimes, he was able to continue his lethal predation for years before he was apprehended. If psychopathic, this individual would fit the profile of a manipulative type.

Case Example 3

During a series of high-profile cases involving the murder of middle-class women, the offender approached his victims at their homes or, in at least one case, at her car. He made his approaches during hours when other people could have been in the home or seen or heard something. In several cases, the offender abducted the women out of their homes and transported them in his vehicle for a significant distance where he ultimately disposed of their nude bodies. There was variation in these crime scenes as a result of offender impulsivity. The victims were both White and Black females, ranging in age from early 20s to middle 40s. The injury pattern to the victims was varied. The time of day and the location of the assaults were not consistent. What was consistent in each crime scene was that the behavior was both very high risk and very impulsive, and the violence appeared to be instrumental—cold blooded, unprovoked, and predatory and, in some cases, excessive. While engaging in other high risk-impulsive crimes, the offender was subsequently identified by a surviving witness and convicted. If psychopathic, this individual would fit the classic profile.

Case Example 4

In a high-profile child abduction case in Northern California a number of years ago, the offender entered the home of a 12-year-old girl, who was hosting a slumber party for several of her friends. The victim's mother and younger sister were asleep in the next room. This was a middle-class neighborhood with a low incidence of crime. The time was approximately 10 p.m., and people were still awake in other homes in the neighborhood. The offender entered the home and went almost immediately to the victim's bedroom. He talked briefly to the girls before leaving the residence with the victim. He wore no mask or disguise, and the victim's friends were able to provide descriptions to law enforcement professionals. The two young witnesses initially thought the kidnapping was a joke, and once the offender left, they walked around the victim's home looking for her before notifying her mother. Approximately 45 days later, the victim was found nearly 1 hour away laying dead under a piece of plywood in a field along a well-traveled highway.

This crime was very high risk for the offender. The residence posed a significant number of potential problems for him. The victim and the girls could have screamed, waking the mother. A neighbor could have noticed something unusual and notified the police. There could have been an attack dog inside the home. The victim's mother could have awakened during the crime and had a gun or a knife.

Identification of the registered sex offenders in the area did not identify the offender. Following a 2-month investigation, the offender was identified. He was not a sex offender, and his criminal history did not reflect crimes involving children. Rather, his extensive criminal history reflected significant criminal versatility, and his crimes all manifested a high-risk/thrill component and gratuitous violence. If psychopathic, he would probably be explosive in nature.

SUMMARY

Violent crime scenes tell a story about the victim and the offender and their unique interaction. Psychopathy is an extremely well-researched personality disorder with specific traits, characteristics, and behaviors that are the hallmarks of this disorder. When a psychopath commits a violent crime, he leaves his signature at that scene—a signature we should be able to read if we understand psychopathy.

For many of us in law enforcement, psychopaths are an enigma. They walk and talk like us, and sometimes they cry during an interview or laugh with us as though they were our best friends. Their kids appear normal, and their wives seem to love them. If they are really good actors, they seem to be as offended by violent crime as we are. It is their appearance of normalcy that is so unsettling. At the end of a long, involved investigation when we finally meet that serial killer face-to-face, one of the first things we say is that he did not look like we expected. Psychopathy really is a frightening concept when you think about it: Psychopaths are people without a conscience, who are without guilt or remorse for the worst of crimes and feel nothing at all for their victims. They act with impunity when, how, and where they want.

Psychopaths are a tremendous challenge for law enforcement professionals, and those psychopaths who engage in serial violent crimes pose a particularly daunting challenge. A behavior classification system to analyze violent crime scenes that is based on the traits, characteristics, and behaviors of psychopathy would be a tremendous law enforcement tool. To enhance criminal investigative analysis, operationalizing the psychopathic construct based on crime scene evidence is a logical and much needed project. The FBI's BAU is pursuing this research through the study of serial killers and the specific psychopathy-related evidence they leave at their scenes. In addition to utilizing the traits, characteristics, and behaviors of psychopathy, crime scenes will also be sorted by key behaviors, such as paraphilic behaviors, selection of high- or low-risk victims, gender and age of the victim, offender race, victim access style, method of assault, sexual assault, presence or absence of gratuitous violence, body disposal, and so forth, to determine any correlation with the different facets of psychopathy.

The FBI's BAU continues to utilize the psychopathic construct and the four-factor model of psychopathy to study serial killers and their crime scenes to identify detailed behaviors that distinguish these offenders in terms of their specific type of psychopathy. Our goal and commitment to the law enforcement community by pursuing this research is to design a tool that will help law enforcement professionals identify and apprehend these offenders more quickly, prosecute them more successfully, and better educate the public about the phenomenon of serial killers within the psychopathic construct.

ACKNOWLEDGMENT

I acknowledge Dr. Robert Hare for his contributions, review, and editorial comments. I also thank Dr. Katherine Ramsland for her review and editorial comments and Kylie Neufeld for her editorial review and comments.

REFERENCES

American Psychiatric Association (1994). *Diagnostic and statistical manual of mental disorders* (4th ed.). Washington, DC: Author.

Bolt, D. M., Hare, R. D., Vitale, J. E., & Newman, J. P. (2004). A multigroup item response theory analysis of the Psychopathy Checklist–Revised. *Psychological Assessment, 16,* 155–168.

Cleckley H. (1976). *The mask of sanity* (5th ed.). St. Louis: Mosby.

Cooke, D. J. (1998). Psychopathy across cultures. In D. J. Cooke, A. E. Forth, & R. D. Hare (Eds.) *Psychopathy: Theory, research, and implications for society* (pp. 13–46). Dordrecht, The Netherlands: Kluwer.

Cornell, D. G., Warren, J., Hawk, G., Stafford, E., Oram, G., & Pine D. (1996). Psychopathy in instrumental and reactive violent offenders. *Journal of Consulting and Clinical Psychology, 64,* 783–790.

Crime scene and profile characteristics of organized and disorganized murderers. (1985, August). *FBI Law Enforcement Bulletin,* 18–25.

Dietz, P. E. (1985). Sex offender profiling by the FBI: A preliminary conceptual model. In M. H. Ben-Aron, S. J. Hucker, & C. D. Webster (Eds.), *Clinical criminology: The assessment and treatment of criminal behaviour* (pp. 207–219). Toronto, Ontario, Canada: M & M Graphics Ltd. in cooperation with the Clarke Institute of Psychiatry, University of Toronto.

Dietz, P. E., Hazelwood, R. R., & Warren, J. (1990). The sexually sadistic criminal and his offenses. *Bulletin of the American Academy of Psychiatry and the Law, 18,* 163–178.

Douglas, J., Burgess, A., Burgess, A., & Ressler, R. (1992). *Crime classification manual.* New York: Lexington Books.

Dudek, J. A. (2001). *When silenced voices speak: An exploratory study of prostitute homicide.* Unpublished doctoral dissertation, MCP Hahnemann University, Pennsylvania, PA.

Forth, A. E., Kosson, D., & Hare, R. D. (2003). *The Hare Psychopathy Checklist: Youth Version.* Toronto, Ontario, Canada: Multi-Health Systems.

Groth, A. N., Burgess, A. W., & Holmstrom, L. L. (1977). Rape: Power, anger and sexuality. *American Journal of Psychiatry, 134,* 1239–1243.

Guay, J., Ruscio, J., Knight, R. A., & Hare, R. D. (2005). *A taxometric analysis of the latent structure of psychopathy: Evidence for dimensionality.* Manuscript submitted for publication.

Hare, R. D. (1991). *The Hare Psychopathy Checklist–Revised.* Toronto, Ontario, Canada: Multi-Health Systems.

Hare, R. D. (1998). *Without conscience: The disturbing world of the psychopaths among us.* New York: Guilford Press. (Originally work published 1993)

Hare, R. D. (1998a). Psychopathy and its nature: Implications for the mental health and criminal justice systems. In T. Millon, E. Simonsen, M. Birket-Smith, & R. D. Davis (Eds.), *Psychopathy: Antisocial, criminal and violent behavior* (pp. 188–212). New York: Guilford Press.

Hare, R. D. (1998b). Psychopathy, affect and behavior. In D. J. Cooke, A. E. Forth, & R. D. Hare (Eds.), *Psychopathy: Theory, research, and implications for society* (pp. 105–138). Dordrecht, The Netherlands: Kluwer.

Hare, R. D. (1999). Psychopathy as a risk factor for violence. *Psychiatric Quarterly, 70,* 181–197.

Hare, R. D. (2003). *The Hare Psychopathy Checklist–Revised* (2nd ed.). Toronto, Ontario, Canada: Multi-Health Systems.

Hare, R. D., Cooke, D. J., & Hart, S. D. (1999). Psychopathy and sadistic personality disorder. In T. Millon, P. H. Blanney, & R. D. Davies (Eds.), *Oxford textbook of psychopathology* (pp. 555–584). New York: Oxford University.

Hare, R. D., & Neumann, C. S. (2005). Structural models of psychopathy. *Current Psychiatry Reports, 7,* 57–64.

Harris, G. T., Rice, M. E., & Cormier, C. A. (1991). Psychopathy and violent recidivism. *Law and Human Behavior, 15,* 625–637.

Harris, T. (1988). *The silence of the lambs.* New York: St. Martin's Press.

Hart, S. D., Cox, D. N., & Hare, R. D. (1995). *The Psychopathy Checklist: Screening Version.* Toronto, Ontario, Canada: Multi-Health Systems.

Hazelwood, R. (1987). Analyzing the rape and profiling the offender. In R. Hazelwood & A. Burgess (Eds.), *Practical aspects of rape investigation: A multidisciplinary approach* (pp. 169–199). New York: Elsevier.

Hazelwood, R., & Warren, J. (2000). The sexually violent offender: Impulsive or ritualistic? *Aggression and Violent Behavior, 5,* 267–279.

Henderson, D. K. (1947). *Psychopathic states* (2nd ed.). New York: W.W. Norton.

Herpertz, S. C., Werth, U., Lucas, G., Qunaibi, M., Schuerkens, A., Kunert, H., et al. (2001). Emotion in criminal offenders with psychopathy and borderline personality disorders. *Archives of General Psychiatry, 58,* 737–745.

Hervé, H. F., Ling, J. Y. H., & Hare, R. D. (2000, March). *Criminal psychopathy and its subtypes.* Paper presented at the American Psychology-Law Society, Division 41 of the American Psychological Association. New Orleans, Louisiana.

Hervé, H. F., Mitchell, D., Cooper, B. S., Spidel, A., & Hare, R. D. (2004). Psychopath and unlawful confinement: An examination of perpetrator and event characteristics. *Canadian Journal of Behavioural Science, 36,* 137–135.

Hunter, S. M., Hemphill, J. F., Hare, R. D., & Anderson, G. (2003, February). *Psychopathy and geographic mobility.* Paper presented at the 30th Annual Conference of the Western Society of Criminology, Vancouver, British Columbia, Canada.

Meloy, J. R. (1988). *The psychopathic mind: Origins, dynamics and treatment.* Northvale, NJ: Jason Aronson.

Myers, W. C., Husted, M. D., Safarik, M. S., & O'Toole, M. E. (2005). The motivation behind serial sexual homicide: Is it sex, power and control or anger? Manuscript in preparation.

Niehoff, D. (1999). *The biology of violence*. New York: The Free Press-Simon & Schuster.

O'Toole, M. E. (1999). Criminal profiling: The FBI uses criminal investigative analysis to solve crimes. *Corrections Magazine, 61*, 44–46.

O'Toole, M. E., & Safarik, M. (2005). *Serial murders: From victim access to body disposal— An overview of the terminology*. Personal communication, June 12, 2005.

Porter, S., Campbell, M. A., Woodworth, M., & Birt, A. R. (2001). A new psychological conceptualization of the sexual psychopath. In F. Columbus (Ed.), *Advances in psychology research* (Vol. VII, pp. 21–36). New York: Nova Science.

Porter, S., Fairweather, D., Drugge, J., Hervé, H., Birt, A., & Boer D. P. (2000). Profiles of psychopathy in incarcerated sexual offenders. *Criminal Justice and Behavior, 27*, 216–233.

Porter, S., & Woodworth, M. (2005). Patterns of violent behavior in the criminal psychopath. In C. Patrick (Ed.), *Handbook of Psychopathy*. New York: Guilford.

Porter, S., Woodworth, M., Earle, J., Drugge, J., & Boer, D. (2003). Characteristics of sexual homicides committed by psychopathic and nonpsychopathic offenders. *Law and Human Behavior, 27*, 459–470.

Ressler, R. K., Burgess, A., & Douglas, J. (1988). *Sexual homicide: Patterns and motives*. Lexington, MA: The Free Press.

Rice, M. E. & Harris, G. T. (1997). Cross-validation and extension of the Violence Risk Appraisal Guide for child molesters and rapists. *Law and Human Behavior, 21*, 231–241.

Safarik, M. E., Jarvis, J., & Nussbaum, K. (2000). Elderly female serial sexual homicide. *Homicide Studies, 4*, 294–307.

Salfati, G. C. (2000). The nature of expressiveness and instrumentality in homicide: Implications for offender profiling. *Homicide Studies, 4*, 265–291.

Stone, M. (2001). Serial sexual homicide; Biological, psychological, and sociological aspects. *Journal of Personality Disorders, 15*, 1–18.

Woodworth, M., & Porter, S. (2002). In cold blood: Characteristics of criminal homicides as a function of psychopathy. *Journal of Abnormal Psychology, 111*, 436–445.

12

The Psychopathic Batterer: Subtyping Perpetrators of Domestic Violence

Alicia Spidel, Gina Vincent, Matthew T. Huss, Jason Winters, Lindsey Thomas, and Don Dutton

As research regarding male perpetrators of domestic violence progresses, investigators have become increasingly aware of the extent and nature of the heterogeneity of this group (Dutton, 1995, 1998a; Holtzworth-Munroe & Stuart, 1994). Although scholars vary with respect to the labeling of male batterer subgroups, there is fair consistency in the personality traits, pathology, and battering patterns that define these subgroups (see Dutton 1998a; Huss & Langhinrichsen-Rohling, 2000; Tweed & Dutton, 1998, for reviews). One of these subgroups is known as the *generally violent/antisocial*. Despite striking similarities between the *generally violent/antisocial* batterers and men with psychopathic personality disorder, comprehensive assessments of psychopathy have yet to be integrated into the study or treatment of spousal batterers to any great extent. Instead, research has tended to rely on diagnostic criteria for antisocial personality disorder (APD) rather than on validated forensic assessments such as the Hare Psychopathy Checklist–Revised (PCL–R; Hare, 1991, 2003; Hart, Cox, & Hare, 1995).

Use of the appropriate Hare Psychopathy scales in domestic violence research could contribute significantly to our understanding of a specific type of male batterer. For example, psychopaths' repeated involvement in short-term marital relations might lead to distinct motives and patterns of intimate violence (Dutton & Kerry, 1999; Huss & Langhinrichsen-Rohling, 2000). If it can be established that a proportion of male batterers are psychopathic according to the PCL–R, the host of PCL–R research pertaining to the nature of the psychopath's violence could prove invaluable to understanding the causal mechanisms, assessing violence risk, and treating intimate violence within a subgroup of perpetrators. This chapter provides a foundation for the utility of the psychopathy construct in domestic violence research and clinical practice by hypothesizing about the nature of the psychopathic batterer, reviewing the evidence for psychopathy among batterers, and integrating knowledge about the etiology and treatment of psychopathy into the domestic violence literature.

THE ANTISOCIAL OR GENERALLY
VIOLENT BATTERER

Research has established that no single profile can be used to describe and understand male spousal assaulters. Several studies have defined subgroups of batterers based on psychological characteristics and the nature of violence (Gondolf, 1988; Hamberger & Hastings, 1985; Holtzworth-Munroe, Meehan, Herron, Rehman, & Stuart, 2000; Saunders, 1992) and suggested that consideration of these typologies is necessary when treating these individuals. A subtype of abusive males that could be classified as having antisocial features has emerged consistently across various batterer psychopathology studies and tested taxonomies (Dutton, 1998a; Gondolf, 1988, 1999; Gottman et al., 1995; Hamberger & Hastings, 1985; Hamberger, Lohr, Bonge, & Tolin, 1996; Hart, Dutton, & Newlove, 1993; Holtzworth-Munroe & Stuart, 1994; Langhinrichsen-Rohling, Huss, & Ramsey, 2000; Saunders, 1992; Tweed & Dutton, 1998). The features of males within this *generally violent/antisocial subgroup*, relative to other batterers, include a higher likelihood of engaging in violence outside of the home, having a criminal record, committing moderate to severe acts of spousal violence, and having antisocial personality disorder. In a study of men in treatment for spousal assault, Tweed and Dutton (1998) found generally violent batterers were more likely to exhibit dismissing attachment styles and less likely to express symptoms of trauma than borderline type batterers. On virtually all affective measures (e.g., depression and anxiety), the generally violent men scored below other groups, yet reported high violence scores.

Generally violent batterers appear to have unique motives for spousal violence. In his review, Dutton (1998b) noted that the generally violent (instrumental/undercontrolled) batterer's violence within an intimate relationship is often used for personal gain or control, in striking contrast to the explosive abuse characteristic of the avoidant or overcontrolled batterer subtype or the reactive, cyclical abuse stemming from the need to release tension characteristic of the borderline batterer. Finally, generally violent batterers seem to routinely lack empathy, have high acceptance of violence (Tweed & Dutton, 1998), and have high rates of drug dependency (Gottman et al., 1995).

RELEVANCE OF PSYCHOPATHY

Noting the striking similarities, Huss and colleagues (Huss, Covell, & Langhinrichsen-Rohling, in press; Huss & Langhinrichsen-Rohling, 2000) proposed that, within the antisocial and generally violent batterer type, there exists a subgroup of psychopaths who warrant different considerations in terms of treatment and risk. They persuasively argued for researchers to integrate forensic assessments of psychopathy into domestic violence research. It is important to clarify that although psychopathy and APD are synonymous on a conceptual level (indeed, the *Diagnostic and Statistical Man-*

ual of Mental Disorders, 4th ed., American Psychiatric Association, 1994, lists these constructs as one in the same) criteria sets for these disorders differ. The PCL–R identifies a smaller subgroup of offenders than any other nosological framework (Hare, Hart, & Harpur, 1991), who are more likely to commit future violence (e.g., Hemphill, Hare, & Wong, 1998; Salekin, Rogers, & Sewell, 1996), have biochemical and neuropsychological abnormalities (Raine, Lencz, & Taylor, 2003), and have low amenability to conventional forms of treatment (Ogloff, Wong, & Greenwood, 1990). This chapter refers to individuals with *psychopathy* as persons who would meet a diagnostic cutoff on a Hare Psychopathy Checklist (PCL) scale.

Psychopaths Versus Generally Violent Batterers

Huss and Langhinrichsen-Rohling (2000) highlighted several overlapping characteristics between psychopaths and generally violent batterers. First, they share a pattern of generalized violence that is not restricted to intimate relationships, a pattern that is more common among psychopathic than nonpsychopathic offenders (see Hare, 2003, for a review). Second, both generally violent batterers (Gottman et al., 1995) and psychopaths (Hemphill, Hart, & Hare, 1994; Mailloux, Forth, & Kroner, 1997) are likely to have heightened levels of alcohol use or drug dependency.

Another similarity regards physiological reactions to emotional stimuli. Psychopaths appear to have low skin conductance in the face of distressing stimuli, possibly indicative of slowed or more controlled physiological reactions (Blair, Jones, Clark, & Smith, 1997). In a study of domestic violence, Gottman et al. (1995) recorded psychophysiological responses of male batterers during heated debates with their partners, the expectation being that batterers would show heightened responses. To the contrary, one type of batterer (Type I) actually experienced a decrease in heart rate and skin conductance while watching a videotaped spousal conflict. Thus, the Type I batterers exhibited narrowed attentional foci on their partner but became internally calm in the face of an emotional argument.

Psychopaths and generally violent batterers are also similar with respect to some of their defining interpersonal and affective traits, such as manipulativeness, remorselessness, and callousness. Tweed and Dutton (1998) claimed that the generally violent men in their study tended "not to bond and treat relationships as though they were expendable" (p. 220). Given that generally violent batterers tend to commit frequent and moderate to severe acts of spousal violence, the ostensible lack of desire to desist the abuse may be evidence of not experiencing remorse. Despite the high frequency of abusive acts, Gottman et al. (1995) found that their antisocial or Type I batterers had lower separation or divorce rates than other batterers at the end of a 2-year follow-up period. Holtzworth-Munroe and Stuart (1994) proposed that skilled manipulation of their partners might enable these antisocial batterers to avoid or postpone separation for longer periods of time than other batterers.

Finally, psychopaths and generally violent spousal assaulters overlap in the use of *instrumental* violence, meaning violence that is planned and directed at personal gain, such as status, power, or money. This similarity is significant given that violence toward intimate partners and other loved ones is generally *reactive*, meaning that aggression is fueled by intense hostility in response to interpersonal conflict. Dutton and Kerry (1999) found that among uxoricides (wife killings) that could be classified for motive, 100% of men meeting the criteria for APD killed their wives for instrumental reasons (e.g., insurance benefits), whereas more reactive abandonment-related spousal killings were committed by men with avoidant/dependent personality types. The typical psychopathic offender is more likely to engage in instrumental violence than other offenders (Cornell et al., 1996). Although their proclivity for impulsive behavior frequently precludes extensive planning, psychopaths are capable of predatory violence that is both planned and opportunistic in nature (Hart & Dempster, 1997). In Hart and Dempster's words, psychopaths are "impulsively instrumental" (p. 226). These investigators found that psychopathic symptoms related to lifestyle impulsivity were associated with opportunistic predatory violence, whereas affective and interpersonal symptoms were related to planned violence.

Psychopaths' Motivations for Spousal Assault

Fair evidence exists for the presence of a psychopathic batterer subtype, but the pathway from psychopathy to spousal violence is still unclear. Psychopaths may be the most likely inmates to commit violence; however, they are the least likely to perpetrate violence on intimate partners, friends, or family (Williamson, Hare, & Wong, 1987). It is unlikely that the pattern of violence observed in psychopaths will be the same as that in men who offend primarily against intimate partners, who tend to be driven by emotions such as extreme jealousy (Dutton, van Ginkel, & Landolt, 1998), fear of abandonment, or general emotional volatility. Although jealousy in the psychopath may occur in the form of a narcissistic injury, the extent to which, for example, jealousy related to a fear of loss or abandonment, affects psychopaths, or is even experienced by psychopaths, is unknown. It has also been postulated that spousal assault is a consequence of intermittent explosive disorder, or explosive rage brought on by a neurological disorder (Elliot, 1977). However, as Dutton (1998a) noted, it is unlikely that this affective instability accounts for the behavior in psychopaths who appear to become calm when faced with heated arguments that may result in abuse. The lower incidence of intimate violence among psychopaths may be an artifact of the lack of emotional connections with others, making them less likely to engage in violence for emotional reasons.

Psychopaths probably enter marital relationships for reasons other than emotional connectedness. To understand the dynamic of violence between psychopaths and their spouses, one must first understand what would drive any emotionally uninvolved individual to enter into a marital or committed relationship of any type in the first place. As noted previously, generally violent batterers commonly commit acts of spousal violence for instrumental reasons. Hervé, Vincent, Kropp, and Hare (2001) suggested several instrumental reasons that psychopaths may be involved in a relationship that leads to spousal assault. One reason may stem from grandiosity and a need for status, which is satisfied by controlling or having power over another person. Another possibility is that spousal assault is motivated by purely sadistic needs, that is, a need to have someone on hand to torment. Hypothetically speaking, it is conceivable that psychopathic men may consider committed relationships as akin to a business union and, therefore, seek them out for financial advancement, other parasitic uses of a spouse's resources, or power. Power, control, sadism, and resources are, for the psychopath, also plausible motives for violence or coercion.

It is important to consider that, although violent psychopathic offenders have a tendency to engage in instrumental violence, reactive violence is still the most common for all offenders, including psychopaths (Hart & Dempster, 1997). Thus, the high occurrence of instrumental violence among psychopaths does not negate the possibility of reactive spousal violence brought on by sudden rage. Indeed, anecdotal evidence indicates that a psychopath who has incurred a narcissistic injury (e.g., public humiliation) at the hand of his spouse can easily react with violence (H. Hervé, personal communication, March 17, 2005).

Studies of Spousal Violence and the PCL

Although domestic violence researchers are beginning to consider the merits of including the PCL–R or PCL: Screening Version (PCL:SV; Hart, Cox, & Hare, 1995), few studies have attempted this. In a file-based study by Hervé et al. (2001), researchers scored the PCL–R (from files) and recorded the violence histories of 376 Canadian male prisoners. Inmates with histories of spousal violence (18% of the sample) were identified based on criminal records and unofficial documentation of assaults (including sexual) against intimate partners. Within the entire sample, spousal assault history was documented for 21% of high PCL–R scorers (cutoff = 30). Although only 13.8% of all low-scoring prisoners (PCL < 20) had a spousal assault history, 21.9% of all psychopaths had previously committed domestic violence, making them 1.6 times more likely to commit spousal violence. Thus, whereas high PCL–R scorers, relative to other inmates, were more likely to have at least one act of spousal violence documented, most batterers were not psychopathic.

The psychopathy construct may be more strongly associated with spousal violence when viewed as a dimensional trait. In a retrospective follow-up study, Grann and Wedin (2002) reported the predictive validity of file-based PCL–R scores for intimate violence in a sample of 88 violent offenders evaluated in a forensic psychiatric hospital in Sweden. PCL–R Total scores significantly detected reconvictions for spousal assault within 1 year after release (area under the curve = .71). Hilton, Harris, and Rice (2001) also examined the relationship of psychopathy and domestic violence in a sample of men who had been incarcerated in a maximum-security forensic facility. Using the PCL–R, they found a significant relationship between psychopathy and future spousal assault (r = .39). Although these studies are important, they are retrospective in nature and based on file reviews of adult offenders.

Data from samples of noninstitutionalized individuals paint a different picture. Huss and Langhinrichsen-Rohling (2005) assessed 131 self-referred and court-referred batterers in treatment using interview-based PCL:SV scores. The investigators found PCL:SV Factor 2 scores to be significantly higher among men classified as generally violent or as low-level antisocial than those classified as dysphoric/borderline or family-only batterers (PCL:SV total scores were significantly higher for generally violent than family-only batterers). The PCL:SV did not distinguish batterers with more versus less serious spousal violence histories or signs of maladjustment. However, PCL:SV scores were very low in this sample (M = 5.5). Similarly, Kropp and Hart (2000), in a prospective study of probationers receiving treatment for spousal assault, found that interview-based PCL:SV total scores did not discriminate between recidivists and nonrecidivists of spousal violence, but again, average scores were low.

To summarize, the relevance of psychopathic traits in the study of spousal assaulters may vary across settings. Among male offenders, psychopathic offenders are more likely than other male offenders to commit acts of spousal violence, and PCL–R scores may be significant predictors of spousal assault. However, most psychopathic offenders *do not* perpetrate violence against intimate partners, and most batterers *are not* psychopathic. On the surface, it seems that male psychopaths are highly likely to commit acts of violence in general and, on occasion, these acts may be perpetrated against an intimate partner. Unfortunately, the limited quantity and quality of research with offenders impede the interpretation and generalizability of findings. Results were dependent on criminal records and institutional documentation, meaning that findings could be an artifact of variability in reporting and the likelihood of getting caught. For example, the higher rates of spousal violence among psychopathic offenders in the Hervé et al. (2001) study may simply reflect more detailed file documentation for psychopaths as a consequence of more frequent incarcerations and extra attention from correctional staff to record even the most obscure incidents of violence.

The low prevalence of psychopathic traits among samples of noninstitutionalized individuals makes it difficult to recommend clinical use of the PCL in community treatment programs. The low prevalence of antisocial batterers in these studies may be indicative of a low prevalence in the community as a result of violent and antisocial behaviors leading to higher rates of incarceration. Alternatively, psychopaths may be unlikely to participate in community treatment programs even when court ordered because they are irresponsible and rarely accept responsibility for their actions.

ETIOLOGY OF THE PSYCHOPATHIC BATTERER

In weighing the evidence, it is conceivable that the psychopathic batterer is a distinct entity within the generally violent subtype. Integration of the etiological literature on psychopathy with that for perpetrators of spousal violence will increase our understanding of this group and guide treatment strategies. Popular etiological explanations for domestic violence are unlikely to explain the origins of such behavior within a psychopathic subgroup. Dutton (1998a) has persuasively argued that a triad of parental violence, shaming, and insecure attachment underlies the abusive personality with respect to borderline batterers. On the surface, these do not seem like plausible explanations for the generally violent batterer.

Numerous researchers have attempted to unearth an explanatory framework for understanding the development of the psychopathic personality. Compelling evidence for significant differences in the processing of information (particularly emotional information), affective/interpersonal characteristics, responses to various cognitive stimuli, and physiology between psychopaths and other offenders have focused attention toward genetic or psychoneurologic causes. These areas are covered in detail in other chapters and will not be detailed here. Instead, the focus of this section is on understanding the determinants of aggression in the psychopath as they relate to spousal assault.

Modeling of assaultive behavior against spouses may be a factor influencing spousal violence among psychopathic men. As Kropp and Hart (1997) discovered, the mere witnessing of family violence as a child or adolescent is the single most robust predictor of acts of spousal assault for the average batterer. There is some evidence for the impact of parental modeling on the expression of psychopathic traits. In their review, Forth and Burke (1998) noted that several family background variables might be linked to psychopathy to some extent. Specifically, research suggests that a generally negative home life or childhood abuse and neglect may exacerbate the behavioral expressions of psychopathy, namely by increasing the likelihood of violence, but does not increase the likelihood of having psychopathy. At the very least, it appears that childhood abuse may act to increase the likelihood of violence, including violence against intimate partners.

The occurrence of childhood abuse or neglect and witnessing of parental violence is a relevant developmental factor in the pathway to psychopathy and possibly later spousal violence for other reasons as well. Porter (1996) defined two phenotypically indistinguishable subtypes of psychopaths that differ with respect to causal pathways in his theory of secondary and primary psychopathy. The primary psychopath is the fundamental psychopath, born predisposed to an incapacity for forming affective bonds. The secondary psychopath develops by social forces that caused a "deactivation" of the affective system. These individuals reacted to traumatic childhood experiences such as abuse by shutting down their emotion or dissociating to cope. Neurobiological and developmental research results support the notion that an infant's affective interactions with the early human environment directly influence the maturation of brain structures that regulate future social and emotional functioning (Schore, 1994).

Subtyping psychopathy based on its causal mechanisms is potentially useful for the treatment and understanding of batterers. Hypothetically, secondary psychopaths should be more amenable to treatment than primary psychopaths because they may be capable of experiencing bonds and deep emotions. However, secondary psychopathy may make individuals prone to engage in intimate violence when presented with emotionally upsetting situations in interpersonal relationships, and they may react more intensely to emotionally arousing situations as a result of past trauma. Primary psychopathy may result in lower risk for spousal violence but is probably significantly more difficult to treat. Researchers have only just begun to study this theory empirically (e.g., Skeem, Andershed, & Johansson, 2004; Hervé, chap. 17, this volume).

Other determinants of aggression in the psychopath can involve a combination of the tendency to act on desires impulsively, an inability to delay gratification when seeking something they want, and the lack of interference of intense social emotions that for the rest of us act to inhibit violent responses (Newman, 1998; Newman & Wallace, 1993). Despite their seeming inability to experience deep emotions, psychopaths still undergo a high level of arousal in association with frustration or anger that can lead to reactive violence.

TREATMENT OF THE PSYCHOPATHIC BATTERER

When one is addressing the treatment needs of the psychopathic batterer, a crucial decision is to determine the primary focus of treatment—the psychopathy or the spousal violence. According to the treatment literature pertaining to psychopathy, regardless of the behaviors that they evince, the root of problematic behaviors and psychosocial maladjustment is the psychopathy. Therefore, this section focuses on treatment for psychopathy rather than treatment of spousal violence.

Conventional wisdom and empirical findings suggest that adult male psychopaths are generally untreatable. Ogloff et al. (1990), for example, examined treatment success for psychopaths in a therapeutic community treatment program. Relative to low PCL–R scorers, psychopaths were less likely to complete the program, performed more poorly while in treatment, and were significantly more likely to recidivate 1 year after release. Rice, Harris, and Cormier (1992) reported results from a quasi-experimental design comparing treated and untreated male forensic psychiatric patients for an average of 10.5 years after release. Among high PCL–R scorers, those who received treatment were significantly more likely to recidivate than the untreated group. A few studies demonstrated that treatment outcomes were differentially associated with facets of psychopathy. Treatment failure relates to interpersonal and affective traits rather than behavioral traits (Hare, Clark, Grann, & Thornton, 2000; Hobson, Shine, & Roberts, 2000; Hughes, Hogue, Hollin, & Champion, 1997).

A few studies were focused on treatment for spousal assault in PCL–R assessed batterers. Dunford (2000) evaluated 850 men who completed treatment for wife assault and found that psychopathic traits were associated with treatment failure. Dutton, Bodnarchuk, Kropp, Hart, and Ogloff (1997) found that APD *Millon Clinical Multiaxial Inventory–II* scores correlated significantly with partners' reports of post treatment group recidivism in men treated for wife assault.

Although the results appear dismal, significant methodological limitations in the extant psychopathy treatment studies preclude the conclusion that psychopaths are untreatable or likely to get worse after treatment (Hemphill & Hart, 2003; Salekin, 2002). None of these studies involved random assignment, and many did not include control groups. Several studies were retrospective, file-based, and used less than optimal outcome measures. Most importantly, none of these studies accounted for total time spent in treatment. Psychopathy is negatively correlated with attendance in treatment and strongly associated with dropout and disruptive behavior (see Hare, 2003). In the Rice et al. (1992) study, psychopaths received more punishments, which included lengthy confinements and other activities removing them from treatment. After accounting for length of time in treatment, Skeem and Mulvey (2001) recently reported that high PCL:SV scorers did drop out of treatment at a faster rate than low scorers, but their treatment outcomes did not differ from those of the low scorers who spent equivalent time in treatment. It should be noted, however, that the sample was civil psychiatric patients with low PCL:SV scores on average. Thus, it speaks more to the presence of psychopathic traits than to the presence of psychopathy per se.

There are several other considerations in the treatment of psychopathic offenders or spousal assaulters, besides the question as to whether they can be treated. Considerations in the development of treatment protocols for spousal violence that are tailored to the psychopathic batterer include what type of treatment modality (group vs. individual), the most effective type (i.e. cognitive behavioral), the high dropout rates found with psychopaths in treatment (Ogloff et al., 1990), and the high rates of dual diagnosis found in the psychopath (Hemphill et al., 1994; see Huss et al., in press; Huss & Langhinrichsen-Rohling, 2000, for reviews). Consideration for the psychopathic man's grandiosity and need for status is also essential. Treatment must be presented as a means for achieving his personal objectives (Hemphill & Hart, 2003; Losel, 1998), such as not being viewed as a batterer and confined in an institution. Based on the limited empirical and clinical evidence, Hemphill and Hart also advocated the use of motivational treatment programs geared toward the psychopaths' need for status and interpersonal contact, openness to novelty and proneness to boredom, and need for control. Cognitive–behavioral programs will be more effective than insight-oriented therapy or empathy training. Specifically, the information processing deficit found in psychopaths may suggest a behavioral approach, which teaches psychopaths to pause and rehearse before any goal-directed behavior while avoiding high-risk situations, may hold promise (Wallace, Schmitt, Vitale, & Newman, 2000). Clinicians should strive for what is likely to be the most effective approach, early prevention. The connection between exposure to violence in the home and/or abuse and neglect during childhood and adult general and spousal violence should direct attention to parent training programs and interventions.

RECOMMENDATIONS AND FUTURE DIRECTIONS

In summary, there are many similarities between psychopaths and generally violent batterers. Both are prone to acts of instrumental and severe spousal violence, generalized violence outside of the home, drug and alcohol dependence, recidivism and treatment resistance, and delayed or lacking psychophysiological responses to emotionally distressful situations compared with others. It may also be that these groups are perpetrators of the most severe and prevalent physical and emotional abuse within the batterer subtypes (Huss & Langhinrichsen-Rohling, 2000). It is important to establish the prevalence of psychopathy within the generally violent batterer subtype because the causal mechanisms and motivations underlying their acts of spousal violence are unlikely to be the same. In addition, the standard treatment that is recommended for batterers would not be likely to be effective with psychopathic batterers. Unfortunately, the connection between psychopathy and battering remains uncertain in light of significant disparities between incarcerated and community samples.

Clearly research is badly needed, particularly prospective studies of samples of institutionalized and community individuals that do not rely on archival data. Researchers of domestic violence and spousal batterers should direct attention to a number of factors. First, it is essential that domestic violence studies incorporate valid forensic assessments of psychopathy; namely, interview-based assessments with the Hare psychopathy scales. The lack of specificity in the diagnostic criteria for antisocial personality may cloud examination of the association between psychopathy and intimate violence. Further, the PCL–R permits investigations of psychopathy both categorically and dimensionally. Moreover, psychopathy recidivism and treatment researchers should routinely report analyses for separate classes of violence (e.g., spousal, sexual, and child abuse).

Second, as suggested by Cooke, Michie, Hart, and Clark (2004), researchers should examine the unique contribution of specific psychopathic symptom clusters (interpersonal style, affective deficits, and antisocial behavioral traits) to the nature of spousal violence to provide better clues as to batterers' motivations for committing these acts. As Huss and Langhinrichsen-Rohling (2000) noted, high loadings on particular PCL–R items or trait clusters might set men apart from other batterers in the domains of risk and treatment suitability irrespective of reaching the threshold for a psychopathy diagnosis. More specific personality profiles should lead to individualized treatment and, therefore, improvement in treatment effectiveness.

Finally, well-designed treatment outcome studies are desperately needed in the psychopathy field in general and with psychopathic batterers in specific. It is crucial that researchers incorporate multiple measures using multiple methods for treatment success and detailed documentation of time in treatment. Researchers in the field should strive to create designs with random assignment to traditional and nontraditional treatment conditions. Spousal assault treatment studies should incorporate the PCL–R routinely.

In the absence of empirical support, clinicians should consider the fact that psychopathic batterers will have unique responses to punishment and treatment for intimate violence. This recommendation is most applicable to clinicians treating spousal violence within incarcerated offender populations. The very low prevalence of psychopathic traits found in community treatment samples to date makes it difficult to justify the routine use of the PCL in the community at this time (Huss & Langhinrichsen-Rohling, 2005; Kropp & Hart, 2000). Instead, psychopathy, given its implications for management, treatment, and risk, could be assessed on a case-by-case basis. It is imperative that practitioners in the field determine whether a significant percentage of batterers are in fact psychopaths. As we have a solid basis of knowledge through the psychopathy literature, knowing that certain batterers are high in psychopathic traits can allow us to draw from this literature and make inferences about these individuals.

REFERENCES

American Psychiatric Association. (1994). *Diagnostic and statistical manual of mental disorders* (4th ed.). Washington, DC: The author.

Blair, R. J., Jones, L., Clark, F., & Smith, M. (1997). The psychopathic individual: A lack of responsiveness to distress cues. *Psychophysiology, 34*, 192–198.

Cooke, D. J., Michie, C., Hart, S. D., & Clark, D. A. (2004). Reconstructing psychopathy: Clarifying the significance of antisocial and socially deviant behavior in the diagnosis of psychopathic personality disorder. *Journal of Personality Disorders, 18*, 337–357.

Cornell, D. G., Warren, J., Hawk, G., Stafford, E., Oram, G., & Pine, D. (1996). Psychopathy in instrumental and reactive violent offenders. *Journal of Consulting and Clinical Psychology, 64*, 783–790.

Dunford, F. W. (2000). The San Diego Navy experiment: An assessment of interventions for men who assault their wives. *Journal of Consulting and Clinical Psychology, 68*, 468–476.

Dutton, D. G. (1995). *The domestic assault of women: Psychological and criminal justice perspectives* (2nd ed.). Vancouver, British Columbia, Canada: University of British Columbia Press.

Dutton, D. G. (1998a). *The abusive personality: Violence and control in intimate relationships*. New York: Guilford Press.

Dutton, D. G. (1998b). *Impulsivity in wife assault.* Unpublished manuscript, University of British Columbia, Vancouver, British Columbia, Canada.

Dutton, D. G., Bodnarchuk, M., Kropp, R., Hart, S. D., & Ogloff, J. (1997). Client personality disorders affecting wife assault post treatment recidivism. *Violence and Victims 12*, 37–50.

Dutton, D. G., & Kerry, G. (1999). Modus operandi and personality disorder in incarcerated spousal killers. *International Journal of Law and Psychiatry, 22*, 287–299.

Dutton, D. G., van Ginkel, C., & Landolt, M. A. (1996). Jealousy, intimate abusiveness, and intrusiveness. *Journal of Family Violence, 11*, 411–423.

Elliot, F. (1977). The neurology of explosive rage: The episodic dyscontrol syndrome. In M. Roy (Ed.), *Battered women: A psychosociological study of domestic violence.* New York: Van Nostrand.

Forth, A. E., & Burke, H. (1998). Psychopathy in adolescence: Assessment, violence, and developmental precursors. In D. J. Cooke, A. E. Forth, and R. D. Hare (Eds.), *Psychopathy: Theory, research and implications for society* (pp. 205–229), Dordrecht, The Netherlands: Kluwer Academic.

Gondolf, E. W. (1988). Who are these guys?: Towards a behavioral typology of batterers. *Violence and Victims, 3*, 187–203.

Gondolf, E. W. (1999). Characteristics of court-mandated batterers in four cities: Diversity and dichotomies. *Violence Against Women, 5*, 1277–1293.

Gottman, J. M., Jacobson, N.S., Rushe, R. H., Shortt, J. W., Babcock, J., La Tallade, J. J., et al. (1995). The relationship between heart rate reactivity, emotionally aggressive behavior, and general violence in batterers. *Journal of Family Psychology, 9*, 227–248.

Grann, M., & Wedin, I. (2002). Risk factors for recidivism among spousal assault and spousal homicide offenders. *Psychology, Crime, and Law, 8*, 5–23.

Hamberger, L. K., & Hastings, J. E. (1985). Personality correlates of men who abuse their partners: A cross-validation study. *Journal of Family Violence, 1*, 323–341.

Hamberger, L. K., Lohr, J. M., Bonge, D., & Tolin, D. F. (1996). A large sample empirical typology of male spouse abusers and its relationship to dimensions of abuse. *Violence and Victims, 6*, 151–158.

Hare, R. D. (1991). *The Hare Psychopathy Checklist–Revised.* Toronto, Ontario, Canada: Multi-Health Systems.

Hare, R. D. (2003). *Hare Psychopathy Checklist–Revised* (2nd ed.). Toronto, Ontario, Canada: Multi-Health Systems.

Hare, R. D., Clark, D., Grann, M., & Thornton, D. (2000). Psychopathy and the predictive validity of the PCL–R: An international perspective. *Behavioral Sciences and the Law, 18*, 623–645.

Hare, R. D., Hart, S. F., & Harpur, T. J. (1991). Psychopathy and the DSM-IV criteria for antisocial personality disorder. *Journal of Abnormal Psychology, 100*, 391–398.

Hart, S. D., Cox, D., & Hare, R. D. (1995). *Manual for the Psychopathy Checklist: Screening Version (PCL:SV).* Toronto, Ontario, Canada: Multi-Health Systems.

Hart, S. D., & Dempster, R. J. (1997). Impulsivity and psychopathy. In C. D. Webster and M. A. Jackson (Eds.), *Impulsivity: Theory, assessment, and treatment* (pp. 212–232). New York: Guilford Press.

Hart, S., Dutton, D. G., & Newlove, T. (1993). The prevalence of personality disorders among wife assaulters. *Journal of Personality Disorders, 7*, 329–341.

Hemphill, J., Hart, S. D., & Hare, R. D. (1994). Psychopathy and substance use. *Journal of Personality Disorders, 8*, 169–180.

Hemphill, J. F., Hare, R. D., & Wong, S. (1998). Psychopathy and recidivism: A review. *Legal & Criminological Psychology, 3*, 139–170.

Hemphill, J. F., & Hart, S. (2003). Forensic and clinical issues in the assessment of psychopathy. In A. M. Goldstein (Eds.), *Handbook of psychology: Forensic psychology* (Vol. 11, pp. 87–107). New York: Wiley.

Hervé, H., Vincent, G. M., Kropp, P. R., & Hare, R. D. (2001, April). *Psychopathy and Spousal Assault*. Presented at the 2001 founding conference of the International Association of Mental Health Services, Vancouver, British Columbia, Canada.

Hilton, N. Z., Harris, G. T., & Rice, M. E. (2001). Predicting violence by serious wife assaulters. *Journal of Interpersonal Violence, 16*, 408–423.

Hobson, J., Shine, J., & Roberts, R. (2000). How do psychopaths behave in a prison therapeutic community? *Psychology, Crime, and Law, 6*, 139–154.

Holtzworth-Munroe, A., Meehan, J. S., Herron, K., Rehman, U., & Stuart, G. L. (2000). Testing the Holtzworth–Munroe and Stuart (1994) batterer typology. *Journal of Consulting and Clinical Psychology, 68*, 1000–1019.

Holtzworth-Munroe, A., & Stuart, G. L. (1994). Typologies of male batterers: Three subtypes and the differences among them. *Psychological Bulletin, 116*, 476–497.

Hughes, G., Hogue, T., Hollin, C., & Champion, H. (1997). First-stage evaluation of a treatment programme for personality disordered offenders. *The Journal of Forensic Psychiatry, 8*, 515–527.

Huss, M. T., Covell, C. N., & Langhinrichsen–Rohling, J. (in press). Clinical implications for the assessment and treatment of antisocial and psychopathic domestic violence perpetrators. *Journal of Aggression, Maltreatment & Trauma.*

Huss, M. T., & Langhinrichsen–Rohling, J. (2000). Identification of the psychopathic batterer: The clinical, legal, and policy implications. *Aggression and Violent Behavior, 5*, 403–422.

Huss, M. T., & Langhinrichsen–Rohling, J. (2005, March). *Assessing the generalization of psychopathy to domestic violence perpetrators*. Paper presented at the 2005 conference of the American Psychology-Law Society, La Jolla, CA.

Kropp, P. R., & Hart, S. D. (1997). Assessing risk of violence in wife assaulters: The spousal assault risk assessment guide. In C. D. Webster and M. A. Jackson (Eds.), *Impulsivity: Theory, assessment, and treatment* (pp. 302–325). New York: Guilford Press.

Kropp, P. R., & Hart, S. D. (2000). The Spousal Assault Risk Assessment (SARA) Guide: Reliability and validity in adult male offenders. *Law and Human Behavior, 24*, 101–118.

Langhinrichsen–Rohling, J., Huss, M. T., & Ramsey, S. (2000). The clinical utility of batterer typologies. *Journal of Family Violence, 15*, 37–53.

Losel, F. (1998). Treatment and management of psychopaths. In D. C. Cooke, A. E. Forth, & R. D. Hare (Eds.), *Psychopathy: Theory, research and implications for society*. Dordrecht: The Netherlands: Kluwer Academic.

Mailloux, D. L., Forth, A. E., & Kroner, D. G. (1997). Psychopathy and substance use in adolescent male offenders. *Psychological Reports, 80*, 529–530.

Newman, J. P. (1998). Psychopathic behavior: An information processing perspective. In D. J. Cooke, A. E. Forth, and R. D. Hare (Eds.), *Psychopathy: Theory, research and implications for society* (pp. 81–104). Dordrecht, The Netherlands: Kluwer Academic.

Newman, J. P. & Wallace, J. F. (1993). Psychopathy and cognition. In K. S. Dobson, & P. C. Kendall (Eds.), *Psychopathology and cognition* (pp. 293–349). San Diego, CA: Academic Press.

Ogloff, J. R. P., Wong, S., & Greenwood, A. (1990). Treating criminal psychopaths in a therapeutic community program. *Behavioral Sciences and the Law, 8*, 181–190.

Porter, S. (1996). Without conscience or without active conscious? The etiology of psychopathy revisited. *Aggression and Violent Behavior, 1*, 179–189.

Raine, A., Lencz, T., & Taylor, K. (2003). Corpus callosum abnormalities in psychopathic antisocial individuals. *Archives of General Psychiatry, 60*, 1134–1142.

Rice, M. E., Harris, G. T., & Cormier, C. A. (1992). An evaluation of a maximum-security therapeutic community for psychopaths and other mentally disordered offenders. *Law and Human Behavior, 16*, 399–412.

Salekin, R. T. (2002). Psychopathy and therapeutic pessimism: Clinical lore or clinical reality? *Clinical Psychology Review, 22*, 79–112.

Salekin, R. T., Rogers, R., & Sewell, K. W. (1996). A review and meta-analysis of the Psychopathy Checklist and Psychopathy Checklist–Revised: Predictive validity of dangerousness. *Clinical Psychology: Science and Practice, 3*, 203–215.

Saunders, D. G. (1992). A typology of men who batter women: Three types derived from cluster analysis. *American Orthopsychiatry, 62*, 264–275.

Schore, A. N. (1994). *Affect regulation and the origin of the self: The neurobiology of emotional development.* Hillsdale, NJ: Lawrence Erlbaum Associates.

Skeem, J. L., Andershed H., & Johansson (2004, June). *Variants of psychopathy: An exploration.* Paper presented at the International Association of Forensic Mental Health Services conference, Stockholm, Sweden.

Skeem, J. L., & Mulvey, E. P. (2001). Psychopathy and community violence among civil psychiatric patients: Results from the MacArthur Risk Assessment Study. *Journal of Consulting and Clinical Psychology, 69*, 358–374.

Tweed, R. G. & Dutton, D. G. (1998). A comparison of impulsive and instrumental subgroups of batterers. *Violence and Victims, 13*, 3, 217–230.

Wallace, J. F., Schmitt, W. A., Vitale, J. E., & Newman, J. P. (2000). Experimental investigations of information-processing deficiencies in psychopaths: Implications for diagnosis and treatment. In C. B. Gacono (Ed.), *The clinical and forensic assessment of psychopathy: A practitioners guide* (pp. 87–110). Mahwah, NJ: Lawrence Erlbaum Associates.

Williamson, S., Hare, R. D., & Wong, S. (1987). Violence: Criminal psychopaths and their victims. *Canadian Journal of Behavioral Science, 19*, 454–462.

V

GENERALIZABILITY
OF THE CONSTRUCT

13

Using the Construct of Psychopathy to Understand Antisocial and Violent Youth

Paul J. Frick

Understanding the causes of aggressive and antisocial behavior has long been a priority of social science research. There are a number of reasons for the importance placed on such research. For example, antisocial youth often have numerous and severe psychosocial impairments including deficient educational achievement, poor social relationships, significant conflict with parents and teachers, involvement with the legal system, and high rates of emotional distress (Frick, 1998). As a result, chronic and severe antisocial behavior is one of the more debilitating forms of childhood psychopathology (Lambert, Wahler, Andrade, & Bickman, 2001). In addition, antisocial and delinquent behavior in youth is very costly to society, and these costs are both monetary and social (Zigler Taussig, & Black, 1992). The monetary costs include those associated with incarceration to prevent further offending for those youth who commit serious delinquent acts and the costs of repairing schools due to vandalism. The social costs include the inadequate and unsafe learning environments in schools created by the behaviors of antisocial youth and the reduced quality of life for the victims whose rights have been violated by the actions of these youth and for others living in high-crime neighborhoods.

As a result of the importance placed on this area of research, many studies of antisocial and aggressive youth have documented a number of correlates or *risk factors* that are associated with such behavior patterns. Table 13–1 provides a summary of some of the more commonly studied correlates. As evident from this list of risk factors, the correlates to antisocial behavior include factors that are intrinsic to the child, some that are present in the child's immediate psychosocial context, and others that reflect broader contextual factors that are present in the child's social ecology. The sheer number of factors that have been uncovered, the diverse processes underlying these factors, and the lack of independence among these processes have made it quite difficult to weave these findings into coherent, yet comprehensive, models for understanding the mechanisms involved in the etiology of serious antisocial and aggressive behavior in children and adolescents.

TABLE 13–1.
Summary of the Major Risk Factors Associated With Antisocial
and Delinquent Behavior in Youth

Risk Factors	Exemplar Studies
Dispositional	
Neurochemical abnormality	Kreusi et al., 1990
Autonomic irregularity	Raine, Venables, & Williams, 1990
Poor response inhibition/impulsivity	Moffitt, Lynam, & Silva, 1994
Reward dominant response style	O'Brien & Frick, 1996
Low verbal intelligence	Loney, Frick, Ellis, & McCoy, 1998
Academic underachievement	Frick et al., 1991
Deficits in social cognition	Dodge, Bates, & Petit, 1990
Contextual	
Parental psychopathology	Lahey et al., 1988
Family conflict	Amato & Keith, 1991
Inadequate socialization practices	Shelton, Frick, & Wootton, 1996
Peer rejection	Coie, Dodge, & Kupersmidt, 1990
Association with a deviant peer group	Keenan et al., 1995.
Impoverished living conditions	Peeples & Loeber, 1994
Exposure to violence	Richters & Martinez, 1993

Note: The organization into dispositional and contextual factors is not meant to imply a nature–nurture distinction but is used solely as an organizational heuristic. Data from Frick (1998).

It is clear from this research, however, that a focus on any single risk factor or process will be inadequate to account for even a minimal amount of variance in any measure of antisocial behavior. Similarly, any single factor or process will be inadequate to account for the development of antisocial and violent behavior in any individual child or adolescent. As a result, there is a growing number of multivariate models being developed to explain the etiology of antisocial and aggressive behavior in which the operation of multiple causal processes are considered. One common type of multivariate model is the "cumulative risk model," which proposes that it is the accumulation of multiple handicapping conditions and vulnerabilities that best explains the development of severe antisocial behavior in children and adolescents (e.g., Loeber, 1990). For example, any one of the vulnerabilities from Table 13–1 (e.g., poor response inhibition) may convey only moderate risk for a child developing antisocial behavior. However, in combination with other risk factors (e.g., inadequate socializing experiences or impoverished living conditions), the risk for antisocial outcomes can be quite high (see Colder, Lochman, & Wells, 1997; Lynam et al., 2000, for examples).

The recognition that multiple influences operate in the development of antisocial behavior is quite important. However, there is yet another level of complexity that is important to integrate into these causal models. That is, different groups of children and adolescents who show severe antisocial and aggressive behavior may do so as a result of very different causal processes. This is one hallmark of a developmental psychopathology approach to understanding any developmental outcome, including antisocial behavior. This approach recognizes that children can develop the same type of behavioral disturbance through very different developmental pathways (Frick, Cornell, Barry, Bodin, & Dane, 2003). This conceptualization has important implications for how research should be conducted to advance our understanding of the causal processes related to antisocial behavior (Richters, 1997). It also has important implications for intervention by suggesting that the same type of intervention will most likely not be appropriate for all antisocial youth (Frick, 1998, 2001). Given both the theoretical and applied importance of understanding the different developmental pathways to antisocial and aggressive behavior, an important focus of research has been to uncover subgroups of antisocial or delinquent youth whose behavior problems seem to have developed through distinct causal trajectories.

THE CHILDHOOD AND ADOLESCENT-ONSET DISTINCTION

There have been numerous attempts to define meaningful subtypes of aggressive and antisocial children or delinquent youth (see Frick & Ellis, 1999, for a review). One approach that has achieved widespread acceptance is the distinction between children who begin showing severe conduct problems in childhood and those whose onset of severe antisocial behavior coincides with the onset of puberty. This approach has been incorporated into the diagnostic nomenclature for conduct disorder in the most recent versions of the *Diagnostic and Statistical Manual of Mental Disorders* (American Psychiatric Association, 1994, 2000). Children in the childhood-onset group often begin to show mild conduct problems as early as preschool or early elementary school, and their behavioral problems tend to increase in rate and severity throughout childhood and into adolescence (Lahey & Loeber, 1994). In contrast, the adolescent-onset group do not show significant behavioral problems in childhood, but they begin exhibiting significant antisocial and delinquent behavior coinciding with the onset of adolescence (Hinshaw, Lahey, & Hart, 1993; Moffitt, 1993). In addition to the different patterns of onset, there are important differences in the outcome of these two groups of antisocial youth. Specifically, the childhood-onset group is much more likely to continue to show antisocial and criminal behavior through adolescence and into adulthood compared with the adolescent-onset group, whose antisocial and delinquent behavior is often confined to the adolescent period (Frick & Loney, 1999).

More relevant to causal theory, however, is the fact that research has found that the two groups of antisocial youth show important differences in their association with many of the risk factors to antisocial behavior. These differences are summarized in Table 13–2 (see also Moffitt & Caspi, 2001). Many

TABLE 13–2.
Differential Correlates to Childhood-Onset and Adolescent-Onset Conduct Disorder

Childhood-Onset	Adolescent-Onset
High rates of aggression/violence	Nonviolent antisocial behavior
Family dysfunction	Endorsement of unconventional values
Neuropsychological/intellectual deficits	Rejection of traditional status hierarchies
Autonomic irregularities	Deviant peer group
Impulsivity/ADHD	
Deficits in social cognition	
Deviant peer group	
Cold and callous interpersonal style	

Note. Data from Frick (1998), Moffitt (1993), and Moffitt & Caspi (2001).

of the dispositional (e.g., cognitive and neuropsychological dysfunction) and contextual (e.g., family dysfunction) correlates that have been associated with severe antisocial behavior seem primarily associated with the childhood-onset subtype, whereas the adolescent-onset subtype has characteristics that seem to be exaggerations of normal developmental processes common in adolescence (e.g., rejecting traditional status hierarchies). The differences between children in the two trajectories suggest that there may be different mechanisms leading to the antisocial behavior across these groups. For example, Moffitt (1993) proposed that children in the childhood-onset group develop their problem behavior through a transactional process of a difficult and vulnerable child who often also experiences an inadequate rearing environment (see also Hinshaw et al., 1993). This dysfunctional transactional process leads to enduring vulnerabilities in these children that negatively influence their psychosocial adjustment throughout their lives. In contrast, children in the adolescent-onset pathway are not viewed as having enduring vulnerabilities. Their antisocial behavior is seen as an exaggeration of the normative developmental process of identity formation that takes place in adolescence. Their engagement in antisocial and delinquent behaviors is conceptualized as a misguided attempt to obtain a subjective sense of maturity and adult status in a way that is encouraged by an antisocial peer group.

THE CONSTRUCT OF PSYCHOPATHY

The childhood-onset and adolescent-onset distinction illustrates one method for designating distinct pathways to explain the development of antisocial and aggressive behavior in youth. Similar issues in developing and testing causal models have been faced in research on violent and antisocial adults. Specifically, it is clear that antisocial and criminal adults are not a homogeneous group, and there have been numerous methods used to designate subtypes of criminal offenders. The construct of psychopathy, which focuses on a particular affective (e.g., lacking guilt and empathy, poverty of emotions), self-referential (e.g., grandiose sense of importance), interpersonal (e.g., callous use of others), and behavioral (e.g., impulsive and irresponsible) style, has proven to be useful for designating one important subgroup of antisocial adults (see Hare, Hart, & Harpur, 1991; Hart & Hare, 1997, for reviews). In short, research suggests that antisocial individuals who show these psychopathic traits exhibit a particularly high rate of violence, both inside and outside of forensic institutions. Further, their violence is more likely to include (but not be limited to) premeditated and instrumental violent acts (e.g., to obtain goods or services or for social dominance; see also Cornell et al., 1996; Woodworth & Porter, 2002). Possibly one of the most important findings for the construct in terms of its applied importance is the finding that psychopathic traits predict recidivism, especially violent recidivism, when an individual is released from an institution (Hart, Kropp, & Hare, 1998; Serin, 1993; Serin, Peters, & Barbaree, 1990). However, in addition to the predictive utility of the construct, psychopathy also appears to be important for causal theories of antisocial and criminal behavior. Specifically, antisocial individuals who show psychopathic traits are more likely to show deficits in the way they experience emotion compared with incarcerated individuals without these traits (Hare et al., 1991). However, they are less likely to show deficits in intelligence and are less likely to have adverse family backgrounds (Hare et al., 1991). These results suggest that the causal factors that may underlie the antisocial behavior of persons with and without psychopathic traits may be different (Hare, 1998).

The importance of the construct of psychopathy for understanding antisocial adults, combined with the finding that most psychopathic individuals have antisocial and criminal histories that begin before adulthood (Hart & Hare, 1997), raises the important questions as to (a) whether or not developmental precursors to psychopathic traits can be identified in samples of antisocial youth and (b) how these precursors would fit in existing models for explaining antisocial behavior in youth.

There have been several attempts to extend the construct of psychopathy to youth. For example, Lynam (1996) suggested that many of the behavioral (e.g., severe aggression and poorer prognosis) and neuropsychological (e.g., executive functioning deficits) characteristics of children with a combined diagnosis of conduct disorder and attention deficit hyperactivity disorder (ADHD) are similar to those found in adults with psychopathic traits. In addition, Moffitt, Caspi, Dickson, Silva, and Stanton (1996) reported that many children in the childhood-onset group show a personality profile characterized by impulsive and impetuous behavior and a cold, callous, alienated, and suspicious interpersonal style. They explicitly note that these traits are quite consistent with descriptions of adults with psychopathy.

Based on these findings, it is likely that the developmental precursors to psychopathy are to be found within children who show a childhood onset of their antisocial behavior and within those who may show high rates of impulsivity associated with the diagnosis of ADHD. However, it also possible that a more specific focus on the affective, self-referential, and interpersonal traits that have been hallmarks of adult conceptualizations of psychopathy will lead to a more refined designation of a developmental precursor to this construct. This possibility is most directly supported by the findings of Barry et al. (1999) in which preadolescent children referred to a mental health clinic were divided into those without ADHD or conduct problems, those with ADHD alone, those with ADHD and conduct problems, and those with ADHD, conduct problems, and traits associated with psychopathy. It was only the last group, the group that showed high rates of the callous and unemotional traits associated with the construct of psychopathy, who showed features that are characteristic of adults designated as psychopathic.

Before describing in more detail a line of research that has focused specifically on the interpersonal and affective characteristics of psychopathy in children, it is important to highlight both the promise and dangers of this type of research. The promise is that it has the potential to designate another important developmental pathway to antisocial behavior in youth, one that involves a particularly severe pattern of aggression and violence, and one that may involve distinct causal processes, as suggested by the research conducted with adults. Also, studying the processes related to psychopathy early in development may provide an important method for disentangling the causal processes related specifically to this constellation of personality traits compared with those processes related to antisocial behavior more generally. That is, it is difficult to determine in incarcerated adult samples what might be causally related to psychopathic traits and what might be a cause or a consequence of a lifelong pattern of antisocial behavior and the concomitant problems in adjustment (e.g., low educational achievement, extended periods of incarceration, or substance abuse) that often accompany such behavior. Furthermore, by understanding the early processes involved in the development of psychopathic traits, interventions may be implemented at a period in development when the traits or their resulting behavioral manifestations are more amenable to treatment (Frick, 1998, 2001).

Despite this promise, there are legitimate concerns about applying the construct of psychopathy to children (see Quay, 1987; Steinberg, 2002). The first concern is the negative connotations that the label of *psychopathy* has for many professionals and the lay public. For many, this label designates by definition a person who will not respond to treatment and who is likely to show a lifelong pattern of antisocial and criminal behavior (Quay, 1987). Although such predictive validity has been fairly well established for antisocial adults with psychopathy (Hemphill, Hare, & Wong, 1998), the validity of these assumptions for childhood manifestations of the construct has not been established (Edens, Skeem, Cruise, & Cauffman, 2001). In fact, there is good reason to believe that the same level of stability will not be found in children, given that personality traits in general are often less stable in children than they are in adults (Buss, 1995). The second concern is that psychopathy implies an intrinsic and biological basis to the dysfunction and one that is not highly modifiable by environmental circumstances (Steinberg, 2002). This assumption is somewhat questionable even in adults (Weiler & Widom, 1997; Widom, 1989). However, it is even more questionable in children, whereby there is strong evidence for the important role of a child's psychosocial environment in shaping personality traits, even if the basic temperamental underpinnings have a neurobiological basis (Buss, 1995).

Given that the stability and amenability to contextual influences of psychopathic traits have been inadequately tested in children and are likely to be different than is often assumed from research with adults, the logical question is why explicitly tie research on youth to a label that has such connotations. Unfortunately, the common alternative to *explicitly* applying the concept of psychopathy to children is to *implicitly* consider all or a large percentage of antisocial children as showing a "childhood manifestation of psychopathy" (e.g., Richters & Cicchetti, 1993). This alternative is even more problematic because many of the malignant, impairing, and unique dispositional features associated with adult psychopathy may apply to only a small subset of such children. Furthermore, there have been attempts in the past to apply the construct of psychopathy to youth using an alternative label in an effort to avoid the negative connotations associated with the term psychopathy, such as using the term *undersocialized aggressive* to label a subgroup of children with conduct disorder or to designate a subgroup of juvenile delinquents (Quay, 1987). However, the failure to explicitly tie the construct to research on psychopathy led to great confusion over the core features of undersocialized aggression, and this resulted in many very different operational definitions of the construct (Frick & Ellis, 1999; Hinshaw et al., 1993). As a result, research findings were inconsistent and hard to integrate because of the widely varying definitions, eventually leading to the term being dropped from many standard methods of subtyping antisocial children and adolescents.

In summary, concerns about the negative connotations associated with the term psychopathy are quite important and their inappropriateness to the construct as it may be expressed earlier in development needs to be recognized. However, by being more precise in defining early signs of psychopathy, we can begin to accumulate a research base from which to address the critical questions concerning the stability of these traits at various stages of development and concerning the complex interaction between various types of causal factors that may be involved in the development of these traits. By avoiding explicit and clearly defined links to the construct of psychopathy, one is left with implicit and idiosyncratic applications of the construct to youth. Such imprecision hampers the accumulation of a body of research from which to understand the developmental processes involved in the etiology of these traits.

THE STRUCTURE OF PSYCHOPATHIC TRAITS IN CHILDREN

A basic issue in extending the construct of psychopathy to children is determining the structure or "dimensionality" of the construct in samples of youth. One difficulty in addressing this issue is that there is no consensus as to the structure of psychopathy in adults. Research suggests that psychopathic traits in adults form multiple dimensions, but the exact number and content of these dimensions is unclear (e.g., Cooke & Michie, 2001; Harpur, Hare, & Hakstian, 1989; Lilienfeld & Andrews, 1996). There is evidence for the multidimensionality of psychopathic traits in children as well. Parent and teacher ratings of traits associated with psychopathy, but modified to be developmentally appropriate (Frick & Hare, 2001) were factor analyzed in a sample of 1,136 elementary school-aged children (Frick, Bodin, & Barry, 2000). These ratings could be divided into three dimensions: a Callous–Unemotional dimension, a Narcissism dimension, and an Impulsivity dimension. Behaviors defining these factors are provided in Table 13–3. These dimensions are somewhat different from the two-dimensional structure found in an earlier factor analysis of the same behaviors by Frick, O'Brien, Wootton, and McBurnett (1994) using 92 clinic-referred children between the ages of 6 and 13. In this sample, behaviors indicative of Narcissism and Impulsivity were highly intercorrelated and did not form separate factors.

These somewhat inconsistent findings suggest that the dimensionality of psychopathy in children and adolescents requires further testing in different samples (e.g., Vitacco, Rogers, & Neumann, 2003). However, there are several reasons for considering the three-factor solution as the primary method for viewing the dimensionality of psychopathy in children until more data are accumulated. First, the community sample in which this factor structure emerged was much larger than the clinic sample and, therefore, it is likely to

TABLE 13–3.
A Summary of the Three Dimensions Emerging from Factor Analyses
of Psychopathic Traits in Children

Narcissism	Impulsivity	Callous–Unemotional
Thinks more important than others	Acts without thinking; does not plan ahead	Is unconcerned about feelings of others
Brags excessively	Engages in risky activities	Does not feel bad or guilty over misdeeds
Uses or "cons" others	Blames others for mistakes	Is unconcerned about schoolwork
Teases others	Gets bored easily	Does not keep promises
Becomes angry when corrected		Does not show emotions
Emotions seem shallow		Does not keep the same friends

Note. Dimensions are based on the factor analyses of the APSD (Frick & Hare, 2001) reported in Frick et al. (2000). Items are placed in order of their factor loadings on the individual dimensions. The item, "Lies easily and skillfully" from the APSD did not load consistently on any of the three dimensions and is not included in the table.

provide a more stable factor structure. Second, when the three-factor structure was "forced" in an expanded clinic sample from the one reported by Frick et al. (1994) using confirmatory factor analyses, it showed an adequate fit in this sample, albeit not being incrementally better than the two-factor solution (Frick et al., 2000). Third, this three-factor structure corresponds closely with the three (Cooke & Michie, 2001) and four (Hare, 2003) factor structures that are emerging in many adult samples using the Psychopathy Checklist–Revised (PCL–R; Hare, 1991). The additional fourth factor emerging in some samples includes an antisocial and criminal behavior dimension and items assessing this dimension were not included in the assessment of children. Fourth, the Narcissism and Impulsivity dimensions appear to have some important differences in their correlations with other variables. For example, the Narcissism dimension appears to be somewhat more highly correlated with diagnostic criteria for oppositional defiant disorder, whereas the Impulsivity dimension appears somewhat more strongly associated with criteria for ADHD (Frick et al., 2000). Similarly, these dimensions have very different correlates when they are studied separately in adults (Lilienfeld & Andrews, 1996). By separating these dimensions, one can study the differential correlates of these dimensions in children to better evaluate their divergent validity in children and adolescents.

PSYCHOPATHIC TRAITS AND THE SEVERITY OF ANTISOCIAL BEHAVIOR

As mentioned previously, one important use of measures of psychopathy in adults has been to designate incarcerated individuals who show an especially severe and violent pattern of behavior and who show a poor response to treatment (see Hare et al., 1991; Hemphill et al., 1998). Therefore, a key question in extending the construct to youth is whether it also may be useful for designating a subgroup of children with particularly severe conduct problems. However, to interpret this literature, an important conceptual issue is whether one should use high scores on all three dimensions as the index of psychopathy or whether scores on one of the three dimensions is most important. How to conceptualize the core dimension or dimensions of psychopathy is still open to debate (see Hart & Hare, 1997; Lilienfeld & Andrews, 1996). However, in both clinic-referred and community samples of preadolescent children, most children with severe conduct problems tend to score high on both the Impulsive and Narcissistic dimensions (Christian, Frick, Hill, Tyler, & Frazer, 1998; Frick et al., 2000). As a result, these two dimensions are not useful for distinguishing between subtypes of children with conduct problems, at least before adolescence. In contrast, only a minority of children with severe conduct problems show high rates of callous and unemotional (CU) traits. Therefore, these traits do appear to be the most useful for designating subgroups within antisocial youth, consistent with some evidence from adult samples (Hare, 1998; Patrick, 2001).

To illustrate this, Christian et al. (1997) conducted a cluster analysis of psychopathic traits and conduct problems in a sample of clinic-referred children ages 6–13. Children with severe conduct problems, most of whom met the criteria for a conduct problem diagnosis, clustered into two groups. One group was high on conduct problems and had high scores on the Impulsivity and Narcissism dimensions, whereas the other conduct problem group showed high scores on the Impulsivity and Narcissism dimensions but also exhibited significantly more CU traits. Importantly, despite both groups showing high rates of conduct problem diagnoses, the group that was high on CU traits (a) showed a more severe and varied pattern of conduct problems, (b) had stronger family histories of antisocial personality disorder, and (c) had higher rates of police contacts, all of which have proven to predict severity and stability of conduct problems in preadolescent children (Frick & Loney, 1999).

There is also evidence that psychopathic traits designate a particularly severe and violent type of adolescent juvenile offender. For example, several studies have found that psychopathy measures predict reoffending, especially violent reoffending, in incarcerated adolescents (Brandt, Kennedy, Patrick, & Curtin, 1997; Forth, Hart, & Hare, 1990; Toupin, Mercier, Dery, Cote, & Hodgins, 1995). Importantly, in many of the studies, psychopathic traits were more strongly related to violent reoffending than to reoffending in general (Brandt et al., 1997; Forth et al., 1990). There is also evidence that the relation between psychopathy and violence may be specific to a certain type of violent offending. For example, Caputo, Frick, and Brodsky (1999) reported that CU traits (but not other dimensions of psychopathy) differentiated violent sex offenders from other violent offenders and non-violent offenders. Violent sex offenders tend to be the most violent juvenile offenders overall and they tend to show a very predatory and instrumental pattern of violence compared to other juvenile offenders. Kruh, Frick, and Clements (2005) reported on a group of incarcerated adolescents and young adults who had all committed offenses as juveniles that were judged serious enough to lead them to be referred for trial and sentencing as adults. As a result, the sample was a serious offender group with a very high rate of violent offending. In this sample, a measure of psychopathy predicted a pattern of violence that included more premeditated and instrumental violence, more sadistic violence, repeated violence against the same victim, and violence that resulted in more serious injuries to the victims. In contrast, the violent offending of those low on psychopathic traits tended to be confined to reactive types of violence involving instances of perceived provocation and involving only single acts of violence against a victim.

In general, these studies suggest that in clinic-referred and forensic samples, the traits associated with psychopathy tend to designate a group of antisocial youth who show a more severe pattern of antisocial behavior and one that is associated with more violence and aggression, especially violence of an instrumental and predatory nature. In one of the few studies to test the association between psychopathic traits and severity of antisocial behavior in a nonreferred sample, Frick, Cornell, Barry, et al. (2003) reported on a sample of 98 children recruited from elementary schools in two school districts in the southeastern United States. These children were identified in a screening of 1,136 children in grades 3, 4, 5, and 6. The sample of 98 children were selected to fill a 2×2 design based on whether they were rated by parents and teachers as showing high or low rates of conduct problem and high or low rates of CU traits. Level of conduct problems, level of aggression, and self-reported delinquency were assessed approximately 1 year after the initial screening. Both CU traits and conduct problems predicted conduct problem severity 1 year later, although the initial level of conduct problems seemed to be the more important predictor. However, there was an interaction between CU traits and conduct problems in the prediction of aggression, with the group high on both CU traits and conduct problems showing very high levels of aggression. Furthermore, the association with aggression was different depending on whether or not reactive or instrumental aggression was studied. This difference is illustrated in Fig. 13–1. Specifically, children with both CU traits and conduct problems showed high levels of both reactive and instrumental aggression. However, children with conduct problems without CU traits showed overall lower levels of aggression compared with the combined group and were only different from non-conduct problem control children on reactive forms of aggression. In terms of self-reported delinquency, CU traits but not conduct problems were a significant predictor of self-reported delinquency 1 year later. This effect is illustrated in Fig. 13–2. Children with conduct problems and CU traits had very high rates of self-reported delinquency, as did children with CU traits without conduct problems. Follow-up analyses revealed that this

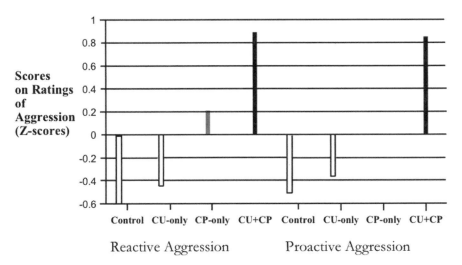

FIGURE 13–1.   Different levels and type of aggression in children with conduct problems (CP) with and without callous-unemotional (CU) traits in a nonreferred sample ($n = 98$) (Frick, Cornell, Barry, et al., 2003).

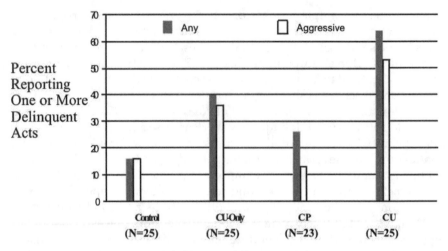

FIGURE 13–2.   Percentage of children reporting any delinquent acts and any violent delinquent acts in a sample of nonreferred children ($n = 98$) selected from large community-wide screening (Frick, Cornell, Barry, et al., 2003).

result was largely due to the older girls in this group. The girls with CU traits reported a high rate of delinquent behavior, despite not being rated as showing conduct problems by parents or teachers 1 year earlier. In contrast, children with conduct problems without CU traits did not self-report a high rate of delinquency. In summary, the results of this study in a nonreferred sample suggest that CU traits are important for predicting more aggression, particularly more instrumental aggression, in children with conduct problems and for predicting self-report of delinquency, even in the absence of conduct problems.

PSYCHOPATHY AND DEVELOPMENTAL PATHWAYS TO ANTISOCIAL BEHAVIOR

As mentioned previously, the construct of psychopathy has been useful in adult forensic samples for designating a group of antisocial individuals who seem to have different causal mechanisms underlying their criminal behavior. As a result, an important issue in extending the construct to youth is whether psychopathic traits designate children and adolescents with conduct problems who (a) show characteristics that are similar to those of adults with psychopathy and (b) show characteristics that are different from those of other antisocial youth. The available research related to both of these issues is quite promising.

To summarize this research, it appears that high levels of CU traits are more likely to be characteristic of children who show a childhood-onset type of conduct disorder (Moffitt et al., 1996; Silverthorn, Frick, & Reynolds, 2001).

However, these traits appear to designate a group of children *within* the childhood-onset category that have several unique characteristics. Specifically, antisocial children and adolescents with high levels of CU traits show more thrill- and adventure-seeking tendencies (Frick, Lilienfeld, Ellis, Loney, & Silverthorn, 1999; Frick, Cornell, Bodin, et al., 2003), show less sensitivity to cues to punishments when a reward-oriented response set is primed (Fisher & Blair, 1998; Frick, Cornell, Bodin, et al., 2003; O'Brien & Frick, 1996), and are less reactive to emotional words (Frick, Cornell, Bodin, et al., 2003; Loney, Frick, Clements, Ellis, & Kerlin, 2003) and threatening stimuli (Blair, 1999) than other youth with conduct problems. Furthermore, antisocial children and adolescents high on CU traits are less distressed by the negative effects of their behavior on others (Frick et al., 1999; Pardini, Lochman, & Frick, 2003), are more impaired in their moral reasoning and empathic concern toward others (Fisher & Blair, 1998; Pardini et al., 2003), and expect more instrumental gain (e.g., obtaining goods or social goals) from their aggressive actions than antisocial youth without these traits (Pardini et al., 2003).

Given that much of this research has focused on dividing children with childhood-onset conduct problems into those high and low on CU traits, it is not clear whether or not these characteristics are associated with CU traits or whether they are uniquely associated with a combination of antisocial behavior and CU traits. Most researchers have used clinic-referred or forensic samples in which children who may show CU traits but without conduct problems are not likely to be represented. The one exception is the study by Frick, Cornell, Bodin, et al., (2003) described previously in which a group of children who were high on CU traits but low on conduct problems were identified in a community-wide screening. These authors reported that thrill- and adventure-seeking tendencies and a reward dominant response style were associated with CU traits, irrespective of the presence of conduct problems. This finding is illustrated in Fig. 13–3, which shows the results of a computer task in which there is an increasing ratio of punished to rewarded responses and children must learn to quit playing as the rates of punished responses (i.e., loss of points) increase to earn prizes (see O'Brien & Frick, 1996, for a description of this task). As illustrated in Fig. 13–3, children with CU traits played significantly more trials despite the increasing rates of punished responses, thus supporting the contention that they show a more reward oriented response style. Of importance, this association between CU traits and number of trials played on the task was present irrespective of the level of conduct problems.

These findings suggest that children with conduct problems who also have CU traits show many of the characteristics that have been associated with psychopathy in adult samples. Furthermore, these characteristics differentiate them from other children and adolescents with severe conduct problems and can be integrated into a model to explain the development of CU traits, as illustrated graphically in Fig. 13–4. The first part of the model specifies that CU traits designate one subgroup of children *within* the childhood-onset trajectory of conduct disorder who are more likely to have a temperamental style that

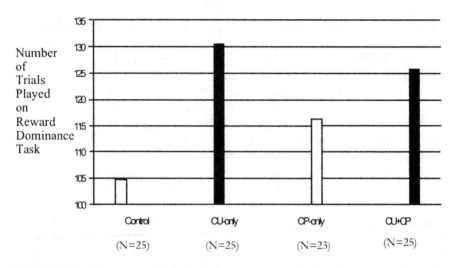

FIGURE 13–3. Number of trials played on a computer task with an increasing ratio of punished (loss of points) to rewarded (gain of points) trials in a sample of non-referred children (*n* = 98) (Frick, Cornell, Bodin, et al., 2003).

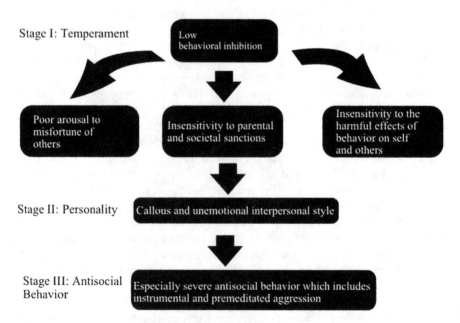

FIGURE 13–4. A proposed theoretical model to explain the developmental pathway to childhood-onset conduct problems involving CUtraits.

has been labeled as *low behavioral inhibition* or *behaviorally uninhibited*. Low behavioral inhibition is characterized physiologically by underreactivity in the autonomic nervous system, and behaviorally by low fearfulness to novel or threatening situations and poor responsiveness to cues to punishment (Kagan & Snidman, 1991; Rothbart, 1989). The characteristics of a behaviorally uninhibited temperament are consistent with the characteristics of antisocial youth who are high on CU traits, such as showing a preference for thrill- and adventure-seeking activities (i.e., low fearfulness), being insensitive to punishment cues, and being generally less reactive to negative emotional stimuli (see Hare, 1998; Lykken, 1995, for similar theories in adults).

The second part of the model specifies that this temperament can be related to the development of a callous and unemotional interpersonal style in several ways (see Kochanska, 1993, for seven different theories to account for this link). For example, this temperament could place a child at risk for missing some of the early precursors to empathetic concern that involve emotional arousal evoked by the misfortune and distress of others (see also Blair, 1999). Also, it could lead a child to be relatively insensitive to the prohibitions and sanctions of parents and other socializing agents. Finally, this temperament could place a child at risk for developing an interpersonal style in which the child becomes so focused on the potential rewards and gains involved in using aggression to solve conflictual encounters that he or she ignores potentially harmful effects of this behavior on others (see Kochanska, 1991, 1995, for tests of these proposed mechanisms). Again, each of these potential mechanisms is consistent with the characteristics of antisocial youth high on CU traits uncovered in research.

The third part to the developmental model illustrated in Fig. 13–4 specifies that this personality pattern can place a child at high risk for showing a particularly severe and violent pattern of behavior. Even more specifically, such an affective and interpersonal style can make a child or adolescent more likely to act in a premeditated and instrumental manner in which the rights of others are disregarded without concern for their feelings.

In addition to these three explicit parts to the developmental model outlined in Fig. 13–4, there are several implicit aspects to the model. First, by conceptualizing the components in three stages, it acknowledges that not all children will progress through all stages. That is, not all children with a behaviorally uninhibited temperament will develop a personality characterized by CU traits. Further, not all children with CU traits will necessarily display severe antisocial and aggressive behavior. Second, the model does not specify for whom the term psychopathy should be applied. That is, it clearly suggests that the CU traits are what differentiate children in this pathway from other children who show severe antisocial and aggressive behavior, as suggested by the data presented previously. However, it does not specify whether or not children who show CU traits should be considered as showing developmental precursors to psychopathy or whether the construct should be reserved for those who have progressed through all three stages and show both CU traits and severe antisocial behavior. This purposeful omission is based, in part, on the fact that this is an unresolved issue in the adult research as well (see Hart & Hare, 1997) and, in part, in recognition of the need for much more data on the validity of either conceptualization for predicting adult adjustment. Third, the model does not specify the causes of the behaviorally uninhibited temperament. Although this temperament has been tied to the functioning of specific biological systems (see Blair & Frith, 2000; Kagan & Snidman, 1991), it is not clear whether this pattern of biological functioning is inherited, acquired, or both.

Another important implication of this model is that only a small percentage of children with severe conduct problems show characteristics that have been associated with psychopathy. Even more specifically, this small percentage appear to be children within the most severe trajectory of conduct disorder (i.e., the childhood-onset group). This finding suggests that there is a large group of youth with severe conduct problems for whom the causal processes leading to their problem behavior are not explained well by this model. However, the studies that have distinguished between children with and without CU traits within the childhood-onset group provide some clues as to the mechanisms involved in the development of conduct problems in children without these traits (Frick & Morris, 2004). For example, antisocial children who do not show CU traits have conduct problems that are more strongly associated with dysfunctional parenting practices (Wootton, Frick, Shelton, & Silverthorn, 1997) and with deficits in verbal intelligence (Loney, Frick, Ellis, & McCoy, 1998). Also, the antisocial youth who do not show CU traits exhibit high levels of emotional distress (Frick et al., 1999), are more reactive to the distress of others in social situations (Pardini et al., 2003), and are highly reactive to negative emotional stimuli (Loney et al., 2003). In addition, as illustrated by the findings in Fig. 13–1, children with conduct problems who are not elevated on CU traits are less likely to be aggressive than those who are high on CU traits. When they do act aggressively, however, their aggression is more likely to be reactive in nature and in response to real or perceived provocation by others.

These findings suggest that very different mechanisms are operating in the development of conduct problems for children who do not show high rates of CU traits. One potential model to account for these different mechanisms is illustrated in Fig. 13–5. That is, children with conduct problems without CU traits seem to have problems more specifically associated with poor behavioral and emotional regulation characterized by very impulsive behavior and high levels of emotional reactivity. Such poor emotional regulation can result from a number of interacting causal factors, such as inadequate socialization experiences, deficits in verbal intelligence, or temperamental problems in response inhibition and high emotional reactivity (see Frick & Morris, 2004, for a more extended discussion of this pathway). The problems in emotional regulation can lead to very impulsive and unplanned aggressive and antisocial acts for which the child may be remorseful afterwards but still have difficulty controlling in the future. The problems in emotional regula-

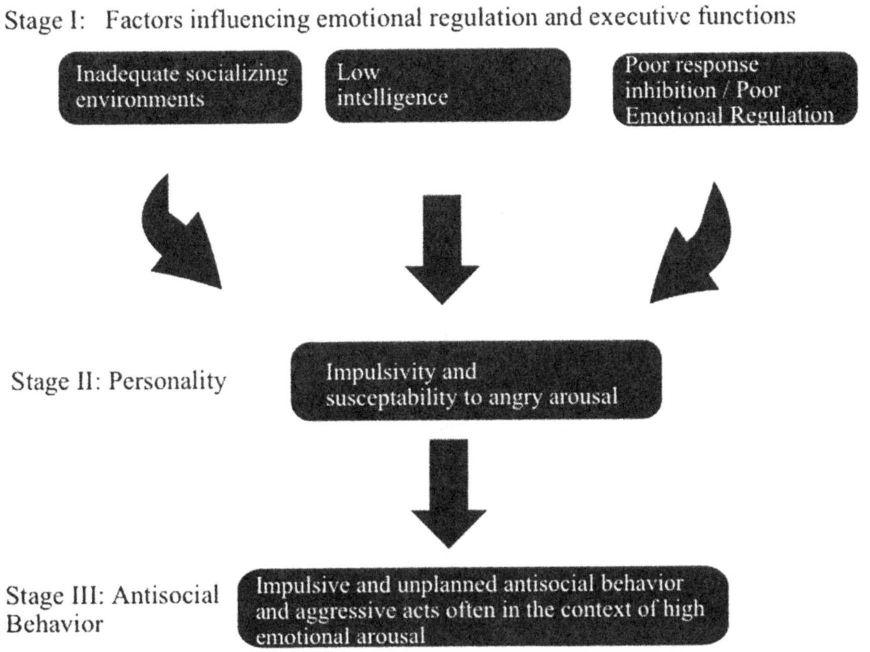

Stage I: Factors influencing emotional regulation and executive functions

FIGURE 13–5. A proposed theoretical model to explain the developmental pathway to childhood-onset conduct problems involving primarily impulsive aggressive and antisocial acts.

tion can also make a child particularly susceptible to becoming angry due to perceived provocations from peers leading to violent and aggressive acts within the context of high emotional arousal.

There are a few important points to be made about the developmental mechanisms proposed for this pathway to childhood-onset conduct problems. First, like the model outlined for children with CU traits in Fig. 13–4, not all children will progress through all stages of this model. For example, not all children with low verbal intelligence will develop an impulsive personality style and not all impulsive individuals will develop conduct problems and reactive aggression. Second, and also like the model outlined for children with CU traits, this model includes multiple mechanisms and allows for the interaction and transaction of biological and contextual influences in shaping a child's personality and behavior. Third, a noticeable difference from the model outlined for children with CU is that temperamental differences in response inhibition or emotional reactivity are included as only one of many different mechanisms that can contribute to the development of the impulsive personality style. This reflects a belief that the causal mechanisms involved in this pathway are likely to be much more heterogeneous than those that are operating in the pathway for children with CU traits.

SUMMARY AND CLINICAL IMPLICATIONS

The research reviewed in this chapter suggests that extending the construct of psychopathy earlier in development could have potentially important implications for our understanding of antisocial and aggressive youth. Before highlighting this great potential, it is also important to note that this research is in a very early stage, especially when compared with the many decades of research conducted on the construct of psychopathy in adults. Much of the research has been conducted by only a few research groups using overlapping and often limited samples. This limited research base, combined with the aforementioned dangers in applying the label of psychopath to youth, make it important that any summary of this research and its implications be made within the context of a clear delineation of its limitations.

Some of these limitations have been noted at various places in the chapter. For example, the factor structure of psychopathic traits in children still requires further study to determine the most useful method of conceptualizing the psychological dimensions that constitute this construct. Also, the optimal method of assessing these traits still needs to be tested in terms of the most appropriate content, method (e.g., ratings scales, and interviews), and sources (e.g., report of others, self-report, and interview impressions). A determination of the best method of assessment is likely to be complicated greatly by the fact that the optimal content, method, and source may depend on the age of the child being assessed, as is the case for the assessment of many psychosocial constructs in youth (Kamphaus & Frick, 2002).

In addition to these basic measurement issues, there are a number of additional limitations in the validation of the construct of psychopathy in children and adolescents at present. For example, there is very limited normative data available to show the natural variation of the traits associated with psychopathy across development. Also, the available research suggests that children with conduct problems and adolescents adjudicated as delinquent who show CU traits seem to show a more severe and violent pattern of behavior. However, this research has been largely correlational, and much more work is needed to determine the predictive validity of these traits. It is also important to note that the theoretical models outlined in Figs. 13–4 and 13–5, which use the presence or absence of CU traits to designate unique pathways to severe antisocial behavior, involve testable predictions to guide future research. However, as such research is conducted, modification of these models is likely to be needed to reflect these findings. Finally, one of the greatest sources of promise in extending the construct of psychopathy to children, but is to date an area that remains untested, is whether the construct and the use of it to designate distinct pathways to antisocial behavior aids in the prevention and treatment of antisocial and violent youth (Frick, 1998, 2001).

Clearly, there is a significant amount of research that remains to be conducted before the usefulness of extending the construct of psychopathy can be fully evaluated. Equally clear, however, is the fact that the findings to date are quite encouraging and make continued research in this area an important endeavor. Consistent with the findings in adults (Hare et al., 1991; Hart & Hare, 1997), the characteristics associated with psychopathy seem to designate a unique subgroup of antisocial and delinquent youth who show a more severe pattern of behavior, one that is characterized by high rates of aggression and violence. This finding in and of itself suggests that attempts to understand and reduce the incidence of youth violence are likely to be advanced by gaining a better understanding of children and adolescents with these traits. Furthermore, and also consistent with the adult literature, CU traits seem to designate a group of antisocial youth who show some unique characteristics implying (but not proving) that different mechanisms underlie their antisocial behavior in comparison with other children with conduct problems.

In this chapter, theoretical models specifying these different mechanisms were presented. As mentioned previously, the predictions based on these models require much more testing. However, these models, which use CU traits to delineate one distinct pathway, have the potential for advancing and integrating several past methods of subtyping children with severe conduct problems and adolescents adjudicated as delinquent (Frick & Ellis, 1999). For example, they suggest that the children with the childhood-onset subtype of conduct disorder may be divided even further into subgroups that differ on both temperamental and contextual processes, and this division may explain some of the differences found among children who show different forms of aggression (Crick & Dodge, 1996; Pardini et al., 2003). Furthermore, these models reinforce the more general issue of the need to conceptualize severe conduct problems, not as a unitary developmental outcome for which a single general causal model can be developed, but as a heterogeneous group of problems, in which there can be widely varying mechanisms operating across children. This conceptualization has important implications for how research is designed and data are analyzed (Richters, 1997).

This method for conceptualizing developmental pathways and the potential usefulness of CU traits for designating one distinct pathway also has some important implications for prevention and treatment. That is, this conceptualization supports the need for interventions that are more individualized to the specific needs of individual children and adolescents with severe conduct problems rather than an attempt to find the single best intervention approach (see Frick, 1998; 2001, for a further discussion of this issue). In addition, most interventions that have been systematically developed and tested for the treatment of severe antisocial behavior in youth have largely focused on the processes that are most important for children who do not show CU traits. For example, helping parents to use more effective behavior management strategies, helping children to control their anger and impulsivity, and helping children to use better social problem-solving skills have all been key components to most treatment packages for children and adolescents with severe conduct problems (Frick, 1998; 2001). As we learn more about antisocial youth with CU traits, it is hoped that additional interventions can be developed and tested to more specifically address the processes underlying the antisocial behavior in these children. For example, interventions that are implemented early in development to promote empathy development and internalization of values or that use motivational strategies capitalizing on the reward-oriented response style and appeal to a child's self-interest may be more effective for youth who show CU traits. This contention is only speculative at this point, because controlled studies of these types of interventions with children who show CU traits have not been conducted. However, it does illustrate how an increased understanding of the processes specifically related to these traits can eventually lead to more effective intervention approaches for this particular group of antisocial youth.

Finally, our developmental model of psychopathy could provide a more explicit link to the literature on adult psychopathy and some of the rich theoretical discussions of the basic processes underlying psychopathic behavior (e.g., Hare, 1998; Lykken, 1995; Newman, 1998). As previously mentioned, this link to the adult literature can also have harmful effects if potential developmental considerations concerning the stability and influence of the child's psychosocial context are ignored. However, the link provides researchers and clinicians alike with a more precise conceptualization of what may be childhood manifestations of psychopathy. This conceptualization can have a very immediate clinical application by alerting professionals to the fact that not all children who exhibit severe antisocial behavior, even those who can be diagnosed with a conduct disorder, should be considered as "budding psychopaths." Instead, it suggests that this label may be best reserved for a very distinct and relatively small subgroup of antisocial children and adolescents. This chapter provides a glimpse of the emerging picture that is being formed of this group of children. As this picture develops further, it may provide us with our best chance of reducing the impact of psychopathic behaviors on our society by allowing us to alter the development of these traits early in life, when they may be more malleable.

ACKNOWLEDGMENT

Work on this chapter was supported by Grant MH55654 from the National Institute of Mental Health.

REFERENCES

Amato, P. R., & Keith, B. (1991). Parental divorce and the well-being of children: A meta-analysis. *Psychological Bulletin, 110*, 26–46.

American Psychiatric Association (1994). *The diagnostic and statistical manual of mental disorders* (4th ed.). Washington, DC: Author.

American Psychiatric Association (2000). *The diagnostic and statistical manual of mental disorders* (4th ed., text revision). Washington, DC: Author.

Barry, C. T., Frick, P. J., Grooms, T., McCoy, M. G., Ellis, M. L., & Loney, B. R. (2000). The importance of callous-unemotional traits for extending the concept of psychopathy to children. *Journal of Abnormal Psychology, 109*, 335–340.

Blair, R. J. R. (1999). Responsiveness to distress cues in the child with psychopathic tendencies. *Personality and Individual Differences, 27*, 135–145.

Blair, R. J. R., & Frith, U. (2000). Neurocognitive explanations of the antisocial personality disorders. *Criminal Behavior and Mental Health, 10*, 66–81.

Brandt, J. R., Kennedy, W. A., Patrick, C. J., & Curtin, J. J. (1997). Assessment of psychopathy in a population of incarcerated adolescent offenders. *Psychological Assessment, 9*, 429–435.

Buss, A. H. (1995). *Personality: Temperament, social behavior, and the self.* Boston: Allyn & Bacon.

Caputo, A. A., Frick, P. J., & Brodsky, S. L. (1999). Family violence and juvenile sex offending: Potential mediating roles of psychopathic traits and negative attitudes toward women. *Criminal Justice and Behavior, 26*, 338–356.

Christian, R., Frick, P. J., Hill, N., Tyler, L. A., & Frazer, D. (1997). Psychopathy and conduct problems in children: II. Subtyping children with conduct problems based on their interpersonal and affective style. *Journal of the American Academy of Child and Adolescent Psychiatry, 36*, 233–241.

Coie, J. D., Dodge, K. A., & Kupersmidt, J. B. (1990). Peer group behavior and social status. In S. R. Asher & J. D. Coie (Eds.), *Peer rejection in childhood* (pp. 17–59). New York: Cambridge University Press.

Colder, C. R., Lochman, J. E., & Wells, K. C. (1997). The moderating effects of children's fear and activity level on relations between parenting practices and childhood symptomology. *Journal of Abnormal Child Psychology, 25*, 251–263.

Cooke, D. J., & Michie, C. (2001). Refining the construct of psychopathy: Towards a hierarchical model. *Psychological Assessment, 13*, 171–188.

Cornell, D. G., Warren, J., Hawk, G., Stafford, E., Oram, G., & Pine, D. (1996). Psychopathy in instrumental and reactive violent offenders. *Journal of Consulting and Clinical Psychology, 64*, 783–790.

Crick, N. R., & Dodge, K. A. (1996). Social information-processing mechanisms in reactive and proactive aggression. *Child Development, 67*, 993–1002.

Dodge, K. A., Bates, J. E., & Pettit, G. S. (1990). Mechanisms in the cycle of violence. *Science, 250*, 1678–1683.

Edens, J., Skeem, J., Cruise, K., & Cauffman, E. (2001). The assessment of juvenile psychopathy and its association with violence: A critical review. *Behavioral Sciences & the Law, 19*, 53–80.

Fisher, L., & Blair, R. J. R. (1998). Cognitive impairment and its relationship to psychopathic tendencies in children with emotional and behavioral difficulties. *Journal of Abnormal Child Psychology, 26*, 511–519.

Forth, A. E., Hart, S. D., & Hare, R. D. (1990). Assessment of psychopathy in male young offenders. *Psychological Assessment, 2*, 342–344.

Frick, P. J. (1998). *Conduct disorders and severe antisocial behavior.* New York: Plenum.

Frick, P. J. (2001). Effective interventions for children and adolescents with conduct disorder. *The Canadian Journal of Psychiatry, 46*, 26–37.

Frick, P. J., Bodin, S. D., & Barry, C. T. (2000). Psychopathic traits and conduct problems in community and clinic-referred samples of children: Further development of the Psychopathy Screening Device. *Psychological Assessment, 12*, 382–393.

Frick, P. J., Cornell, A. H., Barry, C. T., Bodin, S. D., & Dane, H. A. (2003). Callous-unemotional traits and conduct problems in the prediction of conduct problem severity, aggression, and self-report of delinquency. *Journal of Abnormal Child Psychology, 31*, 457–470.

Frick, P. J., Cornell, A. H., Bodin, S. D., Dane, H. A., Barry, C. T., & Loney, B. R. (2003). Callous-unemotional traits and developmental pathways to severe conduct problems. *Developmental Psychology, 39,* 246–260.

Frick, P. J., & Ellis, M. L. (1999). Callous-unemotional traits and subtypes of conduct disorder. *Clinical Child and Family Psychology Review, 2,* 149–168.

Frick, P. J., & Hare, R. D. (2001). *The Antisocial Process Screening Device.* Toronto, Ontario, Canada: Multi-Health.

Frick, P. J., Kamphaus, R. W., Lahey, B. B., Loeber, R. Christ, M. A. G., Hart, E. L., et al. (1991). Academic underachievement and the disruptive behavior disorders. *Journal of Consulting and Clinical Psychology, 59,* 289–294.

Frick, P. J., Lilienfeld, S. O., Ellis, M. L., Loney, B. R., & Silverthorn, P. (1999). The association between anxiety and psychopathy dimensions in children. *Journal of Abnormal Child Psychology, 27,* 381–390.

Frick, P. J., & Loney, B. R. (1999). Outcomes of children and adolescents with conduct disorder and oppositional defiant disorder. In H. C. Quay & A. Hogan (Eds.), *Handbook of disruptive behavior disorders* (pp. 507–524). New York: Plenum.

Frick, P. J., & Morris, A. S. (2004). Temperament and developmental pathways to conduct problems. *Journal of Clinical Child and Adolescent Psychology, 33,* 54–68.

Frick, P. J., O'Brien, B. S., Wootton, J. M., & McBurnett, K. (1994). Psychopathy and conduct problems in children. *Journal of Abnormal Psychology, 103,* 700–707.

Hare, R. D. (1991). *The Hare Psychopathy Checklist-Revised.* Toronto, Ontario, Canada: Multi-Health Systems.

Hare, R. D. (1998). Psychopathy, affect, and behavior. In D. J. Cooke, A. E. Forth, & R. D. Hare (Eds.), *Psychopathy: Theory, research, and implications for society* (pp. 105–138). Dordrecht, The Netherlands: Kluwer Academic.

Hare, R. D. (2003). *Hare Psychopathy Checklist–Revised (PCL-R): Technical Manual* (2nd ed.). Toronto, Ontario, Canada: Multi-Health Systems.

Hare, R. D., Hart, S. D., & Harpur, T. J. (1991). Psychopathy and the DSM-IV criteria for antisocial personality disorder. *Journal of Abnormal Psychology, 100,* 391–398.

Harpur, T. J., Hare, R. D., & Hakstian, A. R. (1989). Two-factor conceptualization of psychopathy: Construct validity and assessment implications. *Psychological Assessment, 1,* 6–17.

Hart, S. D., & Hare, R. D. (1997). Psychopathy: Assessment and association with criminal conduct. In D. M. Stoff, J. Brieling, & J. Maser (Eds.), *Handbook of antisocial behavior* (pp. 22–35). New York: Wiley.

Hart, S. D., Kropp, P. R., & Hare, R. D. (1988). Performance of male psychopaths following conditional release from prison. *Journal of Consulting and Clinical Psychology, 56,* 227–232.

Hemphill, J. F., Hare, R. D., & Wong, S. (1998). Psychopathy and recidivism: A review. *Legal and Criminological Psychology, 3,* 139–170.

Hinshaw, S. P., Lahey, B. B., & Hart, E. L. (1993). Issues of taxonomy and co-morbidity in the development of conduct disorder. *Development and Psychopathology, 5,* 31–50.

Kagan, J., & Snidman, N. (1991). Temperamental factors in human development. *American Psychologist, 46,* 856–862.

Kamphaus, R. W., & Frick, P. J. (2002). *Clinical assessment of child and adolescent personality and behavior* (2nd ed.). Boston: Allyn & Bacon.

Keenan, K., Loeber, R., Zhang, Q., Stouthamer-Loeber, M., & Van Kammen, W. B. (1995). The influence of deviant peers on the development of boys' disruptive and delinquent behavior: A temporal analysis. *Development and Psychopathology, 7,* 715–726.

Kochanska, G. (1991). Socialization and temperament in the development of guilt and conscience. *Child Development, 62*, 1379–1392.

Kochanska, G. (1993). Toward a synthesis of parental socialization and child temperament in early development of conscience. *Child Development, 64*, 325–347.

Kochanska, G. (1995). Children's temperament, mothers' discipline, and security of attachment: Multiple pathways to emerging internalization. *Child Development, 66*, 597–615.

Kreusi, M. J. P., Rapoport, J. L., Hamburger, S., Hibbs, E., Potter, W. Z., Lenane, M., et al. (1990). Cerebrospinal fluid monamine metabolites, aggression, and impulsivity in disruptive behavior disorders of children and adolescents. *Archives of General Psychiatry, 47*, 419–426.

Kruh, I. P., Frick, P. J., & Clements, C. B. (2005). Historical and personality correlates to the violence patterns of juveniles tried as adults. *Criminal Justice and Behavior, 32*, 69–96.

Lahey, B. B., & Loeber, R. (1994). Framework for a developmental model of oppositional defiant disorder and conduct disorder. In D. K. Routh (Ed.). *Disruptive behavior disorders in childhood* (pp. 139–180). New York: Plenum.

Lahey, B. B., Piacentini, J. D., McBurnett, K., Stone, P., Hartdagen, S. E., & Hynd, G. W. (1988). Psychopathology and antisocial behavior in the parents of children with conduct disorder and hyperactivity. *Journal of the American Academy of Child and Adolescent Psychiatry, 27*, 163–170.

Lambert, E. W., Wahler, R. G., Andrade, A. R., & Bickman, L. (2001). Looking for the disorder in conduct disorder. *Journal of Abnormal Psychology, 110*, 110–123.

Lilienfeld, S. O., & Andrews, B. P. (1996). Development and preliminary validation of a self-report measure of psychopathic personality. *Journal of Personality Assessment, 66*, 488–524.

Loeber, R. (1990). Development and risk factors of juvenile antisocial behavior and delinquency. *Clinical Psychology Review, 10*, 1–41.

Loney, B. R., Frick, P. J., Clements, C. B., Ellis, M. L., & Kerlin, K. (2003). Callous-unemotional traits, impulsivity, and emotional processing in antisocial adolescents. *Journal of Clinical Child and Adolescent Psychology, 32*, 66–80.

Loney, B. R., Frick, P. J., Ellis, M., & McCoy, M. G. (1998). Intelligence, psychopathy, and antisocial behavior. *Journal of Psychopathology and Behavioral Assessment, 20*, 231–247.

Lykken, D. T. (1995). *The antisocial personalities*. Hillsdale, NJ: Lawrence Erlbaum Associates.

Lynam, D. R. (1996). Early identification of chronic offenders: Who is the fledgling psychopath? *Psychological Bulletin, 120*, 209–234.

Lynam, D. R., Caspi, A., Moffitt, T. E., Wikstrom, P. H., Loeber, R., & Novak, S. (2000). The interaction between impulsivity and neighborhood context on offending: The effects of impulsivity are stronger in poorer neighborhoods. *Journal of Abnormal Psychology, 109*, 563–574.

Moffitt, T. E. (1993). Adolescence-limited and life-course persistent antisocial behavior: A developmental taxonomy. *Psychological Review, 100*, 674–701.

Moffitt, T. E., & Caspi, A. (2001). Childhood predictors differentiate life-course persistent and adolescence-limited antisocial pathways in males and females. *Development and Psychopathology, 13*, 355–376

Moffitt, T. E., Caspi, A., Dickson, N., Silva, P., & Stanton, W. (1996). Childhood-onset versus adolescent-onset antisocial conduct problems in males: Natural history from ages 3 to 18 years. *Development and Psychopathology, 8*, 399–424.

Moffitt, T. E., Lynam, D., & Silva, P. A. (1994). Neuropsychological tests predict persistent male delinquency. *Criminology, 32,* 101–124.

Newman, J. P. (1998). Psychopathic behavior: An information processing perspective. In D. J. Cooke, A. E. Forth, & R. D. Hare (Eds.), *Psychopathy: Theory, research, and implications for society* (pp. 81–104). Dordrecht, The Netherlands: Kluwer Academic.

O'Brien, B. S., & Frick, P. J. (1996). Reward dominance: Associations with anxiety, conduct problems, and psychopathy in children. *Journal of Abnormal Child Psychology, 24,* 223–240.

Pardini, D. A., Lochman, J. E., & Frick, P. J. (2003). Callous/unemotional traits and social cognitive processes in adjudicated youth. *Journal of the American Academic of Child and Adolescent Psychiatry, 42,* 364–371.

Patrick, C. J. (2001). Emotional processes in psychopathy. In A. Raine & J. Sanmartin (Eds.), *Violence and psychopathy* (pp. 57–77). New York: Kluwer Academic.

Peeples, F., & Loeber, R. (1994). Do individual factors and neighborhood context explain ethnic differences in juvenile delinquency? *Journal of Quantitative Criminology, 10,* 141–157.

Quay, H. C. (1987). Patterns of delinquent behavior. In H. C. Quay (Ed.), *Handbook of juvenile delinquency* (pp. 118–138). New York: Wiley.

Raine, A., Venables, P. H., & Williams, M. (1990). Relationships between central and autonomic measures of arousal at age 15 and criminality at age 24 years. *Archives of General Psychiatry, 47,* 1003–1007.

Richters, J. E. (1997). The Hubble hypothesis and the developmentalist's dilemma. *Development and Psychopathology, 9,* 193–230.

Richters, J. E., & Cicchetti, D. (1993). Toward a developmental perspective on conduct disorder. *Development and Psychopathology, 5,* 1–4.

Richters, J. E., & Martinez, P. (1993). The NIMH community violence project: Vol. 1: Children as victims of and witnesses to violence. *Psychiatry, 56,* 7–21.

Rothbart, M. K. (1989). Temperament in childhood: A framework. In G. A. Kohnstamm, J. A. Bates, & M. K. Rothbart (Eds.), *Temperament in childhood* (pp. 59–73). New York: Wiley.

Serin, R. C. (1993). Diagnosis of psychopathology with and without an interview. *Journal of Clinical Psychology, 49,* 367–372.

Serin, R. C., Peters, D. V., & Barbaree, H. V. (1990). Predictors of psychopathy and release outcome in a criminal population. *Psychological Assessment: A Journal of Consulting and Clinical Psychology, 2,* 419–422.

Shelton, K. K., Frick, P. J., & Wootton, J. (1996). The assessment of parenting practices in families of elementary school-aged children. *Journal of Clinical Child Psychology, 25,* 317–327.

Silverthorn, P., Frick, P. J., & Reynolds, R. (2001). Timing of onset and correlates of severe conduct problems in adjudicated girls and boys. *Journal of Psychopathology and Behavioral Assessment, 23,* 171–181.

Steinberg, L. (2002). The juvenile psychopath: Fads, fictions, and facts. *National Institute of Justice Perspectives on Crime and Justice,* (Vol. V). Washington, DC: National Institute of Justice.

Toupin, J., Mercier, H., Dery, M., Cote, G., & Hodgins, S. (1995). Validity of the PCL–R for adolescents. *Issues in Criminological and Legal Psychology, 24,* 143–145.

Vitacco, M. J., Rogers, R., & Neumann, C. S. (2003). The Antisocial Process Screening Device: An examination of its construct and criterion validity. *Assessment, 10,* 143–150.

Weiler, B. L., & Widom, C. S. (1996). Psychopathy and violent behavior in abused in neglected young adults. *Criminal Behaviour and Mental Health, 6*, 253–271.

Widom, C. S. (1989). Does violence beget violence? A critical examination of the literature. *Psychological Bulletin, 106*, 3–28.

Woodworth, M., & Porter, S. (2002). In cold blood: Characteristics of criminal homicides as a function of psychopathy. *Journal of Abnormal Psychology, 111*, 436–445.

Wootton, J. M., Frick, P. J., Shelton, K. K., & Silverthorn, P. (1997). Ineffective parenting and childhood conduct problems: The moderating role of callous-unemotional traits. *Journal of Consulting and Clinical Psychology, 65*, 301–308.

Zigler, E., Taussig, C., & Black, K. (1992). Early childhood intervention: A promising preventive or juvenile delinquency. *American. Psychologist, 47*, 997–1006.

14

Psychopathy in Youth: A Valid Construct?

Adelle E. Forth and Angela S. Book

The Hare Psychopathy Checklist (PCL; Hare, 1980) and its Revision (PCL–R; Hare, 1991, 2003) have been instrumental in creating a scientific basis for investigating the construct of psychopathy in adults. In developing the PCL, Robert Hare provided a psychometrically sound assessment instrument to identify psychopaths as adults that has led to enormous strides in our understanding of this complex disorder. In the two decades since the PCL was first published a significant amount of research on psychopathy has been done. Consider the number of dissertations related to psychopathy since 1960: Between 1961 and 1970 there were eight, between 1971 and 1980 there were 13, between 1981 and 1990 there were 17, between 1991 and 2000 there were 107, and between 2001 and 2004 there were 69.

Although most research on psychopathy has explored its characteristics in adults, a growing number of studies are now being focused on the developmental antecedents of psychopathy. Many researchers and clinicians believe that psychopathic traits and behaviors are manifested early in life (Forth & Mailloux, 2000; Frick, 1998; Johnson & Cooke, 2004; Lynam, 2002; Saltaris, 2002). Consequently, researchers have proposed various instruments designed to identify psychopathic traits early in development. Some of these measures use youth (e.g., the Youth Psychopathic Traits Inventory, Andershed, Gustafson, Kerr, & Stattin, 2002; the Psychopathy Content Scale, Murrie & Cornell, 2000; and the Millon Adolescent Clinical Inventory Scales, Salekin, Ziegler, Larrea, Anthony, & Bennett, 2003) or parent and teacher self-reports (the Child Psychopathy Scale [CPS], Lynam, 1997; and the Antisocial Process Screening Device [APSD]; Frick & Hare, 2001), whereas others utilize a combination of a structured interview and file information (Psychopathy Checklist: Youth Version [PCL:YV]; Forth, Kosson, & Hare, 2003).

The goal of this chapter is to summarize work exploring the antecedents of psychopathy in adolescents and to consider some of the issues raised by such work. The chapter begins with a rationale for doing research on the etiology of psychopathy from both theoretical and pragmatic perspectives. The next section describes what to look for in a measure of psychopathic traits in youth, based, in part, on Cleckley's (1941, 1982) observations about youth with psychopathic characteristics. Next, the PCL:YV is described. The PCL:YV is an instrument derived from the PCL–R designed to measure psychopathy in adolescents aged 12–18 years. It has been used extensively in much of the research investigating psychopathy in youth. Following the description of the PCL:YV is a section in which we review several issues surrounding the existence of psychopathy in youth, including its stability during adolescence, the possibility of mistakenly characterizing the range of adolescent behaviors as markers for psychopathy, and the potential consequences of labeling youth as psychopaths. Next, the predictive utility of the PCL:YV is presented. In this section we describe studies that assess how well youth psychopathy measures predict antisocial and criminal behaviors.

PROVIDING A RATIONALE FOR INVESTIGATING PSYCHOPATHY IN YOUTH

Converging evidence exists for a strong association between psychopathy and serious repetitive crime, violent behavior, and a poor treatment prognosis (Hare 1998; Hare, Clark, Grann, & Thornton, 2000; Hemphill, Hare, & Wong, 1998; Ogloff, Wong, & Greenwood, 1990; Rice, Harris, & Cormier, 1992; Seto & Barbaree, 1999). The nature of psychopathic offenders' violence differs from that of other offenders. Psychopathic offenders are more likely than other offenders to commit instrumental violent offenses, including homicide (Cornell, Warren, Hawk, Stafford, Oran, & Pine, 1996; Williamson, Hare, & Wong, 1987; Woodworth & Porter, 2002). Clearly, adults with psychopathic characteristics constitute a group that requires a disproportionate amount of resources from the criminal justice system. Identifying youth with similar characteristics is important because they may be more likely than other youth to become persistent high-rate serious offenders as adults. Of equal interest are those youth who manifest psychopathic features, but who do not go on to exhibit negative outcomes. Knowledge of protective processes may have the potential to alter the direction of trajectories. Although evidence for the successful treatment of adult psychopaths is limited (D'Silva, Duggan, & McCarthy, 2004), it is possible that psychopathic traits in youth are more malleable with appropriate intervention. Finally, investigations of the construct of psychopathy in youth will hopefully lead to a better understanding of the causal mechanisms and help to delineate the psychological, social, and biological correlates underlying psychopathy. Taken together these reasons justify the importance of studying the construct of psychopathy in youth.

WHAT TO LOOK FOR IN A MEASURE OF PSYCHOPATHIC TRAITS IN YOUTH

Most contemporary descriptions of psychopathy are linked to the work of Cleckley (1941) who provided rich clinical descriptions of psychopaths. Cleckley described the emergence of psychopathic features during adolescence and highlighted the range of traits and behaviors he thought distinguished psychopathy in adolescents and adults. He described interpersonal features, such as egocentricity and manipulativeness, affective features, such as shallow and short-lived emotions and lack of remorse, and behavioral features, such as impulsivity, irresponsibility, and the likelihood of engaging in antisocial acts.

In one case study, Cleckley (1982) described the case of Gregory. Cleckley first assessed and treated Gregory when he was 13 years old and then again when he was 25 years old. Descriptions of Gregory as a child and adolescent indicate that he ". . . At times gave a remarkably convincing impression of having changed profoundly and of having gained crucial insight. . . . Any remorse shown by this boy is staged. . . . Tells lies freely and convincingly. . . . Superficial expressions of affection to mother but these apparently have little reality. . . . Mother says patient was a problem since he began to walk. . . ." (p. 84). Cleckley describes how prolonged and repeated attempts to treat Gregory were unsuccessful. He describes Gregory's psychiatrist as having ". . . gone beyond the ordinary call of medical duty in his almost heroic efforts to rehabilitate Gregory. Despite these efforts and those of other psychiatrists, psychologists, social workers, teachers, clergymen, and others, Gregory continued in his destructive, irresponsible, and antisocial patterns of behavior" (p. 85).

Recently, two groups have attempted to identify the core features of psychopathy in youth using prototypicality analyses. Salekin, Rogers, and Machin (2001) asked 511 child psychologists and Cruise, Colwell, Lyons, and Baker (2003) asked 424 juvenile detention and probation officers to identify the core features of psychopathy in male and female adolescents. Highly prototypical features included a wide range of interpersonal (e.g., lies easily and skillfully and acts charming in ways that seem insincere), affective (e.g., does not feel bad or guilty and emotions seem shallow), behavioral (e.g., impulsivity and often loses temper), and antisocial (e.g., used a weapon causing serious harm and had a previous juvenile court case) traits. Similar features of psychopathy were rated as prototypical in both male and female youth.

A range of methodologies (self-report, informant rating, and expert rating) have been used to assess psychopathic traits in youth. We suggest that measures of psychopathic traits in youth should include the following:

1. Scores reflect levels of the traits and behaviors that are non-normative.
2. Items should be sensitive to age-appropriate manifestations.
3. A range of interpersonal, affective, lifestyle, and antisocial characteristics should be covered.
4. Scores reflect stable dispositions and not transitory problems.
5. Scores should be based on multiple sources of information.

An assessment instrument that does meet the above criteria is the PCL:YV. It is a rating scale designed to measure psychopathic traits and behaviors in male and female adolescents aged 12 to 18 years. The PCL:YV emphasizes the need for multidomain and multisource information to adequately assess psychopathic traits. It consists of 20 items that measure the interpersonal, affective, and behavioral dimensions considered to be fundamental to the construct of psychopathy. The PCL:YV manual provides detailed item descriptions and examples of sources of information to use when rating items. Each item is scored a 2 (*definitely applies*), 1 (*applies to some extent*), or 0 (*definitely does not apply*). The item scores are summed to obtain a total score ranging from 0 to 40. Several sources of information are needed to score the PCL:YV, namely, a semistructured interview with the youth and a review of available file and collateral information. The interview covers information about past history and current functioning; including school history and adjustment, work history and goals, family background and current functioning, interpersonal relationships, substance use, attitudes and emotions, and childhood and adolescent antisocial behaviors. The type and amount of file information will vary across settings; however, adequate file information from a variety of social contexts, such as home, community, and school, is required. Some researchers (Campbell, Porter, & Santor, 2004; Gretton, Hare, & Catchpole, 2004; Gretton, McBride, Hare, O'Shaughnessy, & Kumka, 2001; Marczyk, Heilbrun, Lander, & DeMatteo, 2003; O'Neill, Lidz, & Heilbrun, 2003a, 2003b) have used extensive file information, exclusively, to generate PCL:YV scores. Although not optimal, file-only PCL:YV scores are acceptable when one is conducting an archival study and/or when it is impossible to conduct an interview. File-only assessments limit the information necessary for scoring items dealing with affective and interpersonal styles.

Measuring Psychopathic Traits in Youth: What Are the Challenges?

A number of concerns and issues have been raised about the attempt to measure psychopathic features in youth. These concerns relate to both to the challenges of assessing traits in samples of children and adolescents and the possible consequences of providing a measure of psychopathy for clinical forensic practice in this group (Edens, Skeem, Cruise, & Cauffman, 2001; Hart, Watt, & Vincent, 2002; Lyon & Ogloff, 2000; Seagrave & Grisso, 2002; Zinger & Forth, 1998).

Edens et al. (2001) and Seagrave and Grisso (2002) have argued that some psychopathic traits and behaviors that are incorporated in measures of psychopathy are transient normal developmental characteristics of youth. These authors contended that developmental issues may influence the measurement of interpersonal, affective, and social deviance features of psychopathy. Because of changes in perspective-taking ability and cognitive functions, developing an autonomous identity, and susceptibility to peer influences, youth may appear to be grandiose, lacking remorse or empathy, manipulative, sensation-seeking, impulsive, and lacking goals. Measures of youth psychopathy that fail to take into account normative adolescent patterns of behavior may produce scores that are spuriously high, and overestimate the level of psychopathic traits in adolescent samples.

If psychopathic traits are features of normative adolescent development one might expect there to be a negative correlation between age at the time of assessment and psychopathic features. That is, younger adolescents would appear to be more psychopathic than their older adolescent counterparts. Most studies using the PCL:YV have not found an association between age at time of assessment and PCL:YV Total scores (Corrado, Vincent, Hart, & Cohen, 2004; Forth et al., 2003; Murrie, Cornell, Kaplan, McConville, & Levy-Elkon, 2004; O'Neill et al., 2003a). However, it is possible that certain clusters of psychopathic features may be more strongly associated with age. For example, Brandt, Kennedy, Patrick, and Curtin (1997) reported a negative association between items measuring lifestyle and antisocial features and age at time of assessment ($r = -.21$).

The prevalence of psychopathic traits in nonoffender community samples of adolescents remains largely untested. Community samples of older adolescents score very low on psychopathic traits measured by the PCL:YV (Forth et al., 2003). Future studies are needed on the prevalence of psychopathic traits in community samples of younger adolescents.

Adolescence is a period of substantial change in biological, psychological, and social systems (Spear, 2000). Arnett (1999) revisits the view put forth by Hall in 1904 that adolescence is a period of "storm and stress." Given the problems characteristic of adolescence, the question is, How much change occurs in personality traits during adolescence? There is an ongoing debate on the stability of personality traits across the age span. Roberts and DelVecchio (2000), in a meta-analysis of the rank order consistency of personality traits (do people retain the same rank ordering on trait dimensions over time), reported that trait consistency increased from .31 in childhood, to .47 in adolescence, to .54 in young adults, to .64 at age 30 and reached a plateau between ages 50 and 70 at .74. McCrae et al. (2002) used longitudinal, cross-sectional, and cross-cultural studies to assess the mean level of consistency (do people increase or decrease in trait dimensions over time) in the Big five factors of personality in adolescence. Between age 12 and age 18 there were no consistent changes in mean levels of Extraversion, Agreeableness, or Conscientiousness for boys or girls, there were modest increases for boys and girls in Openness to Experience, and girls increased in Neuroticism. These results suggested that adolescents show less fluidity in personality traits than what might be anticipated.

In many of the existing longitudinal studies of personality traits samples have been drawn from educated populations (adolescents in schools or young adults in university). In these samples, there may be higher levels of consistency in personality traits than in other samples (e.g., adolescent offenders). For example, Lahey, Loeber, Burke, Rathouz, and McBurnett (2002) found in a sample of male clinic-referred boys that, although there was no significant mean change in conduct disorder symptoms across a 7-year longitudinal study, there were marked individual differences in conduct disorder symptoms over time.

What is needed most is longitudinal research to tracks the stability of psychopathic traits from early adolescence through adulthood in different samples of youth. This critical research has yet to be conducted. It is not known what proportion of adolescents with few, some, or many psychopathic traits will manifest a similar number of traits when reassessed as adults.

There has been only one published study in which the test–retest reliability of the PCL:YV was assessed in a sample of incarcerated youth. Skeem and Cauffman (2003) reported intraclass correlation coefficients of .66 for the PCL:YV total score over a 1-month follow-up. Given the short follow-up period, this stability estimate is much lower than that from research measuring the stability of psychopathic traits in adult offenders (Schroeder, Schroeder, & Hare, 1983: stability of .89 over a 10-month period; Rutherford, Cacciola, Alterman, McKay, & Cook, 1999: stability of .60 for men and .65 for women over 2 years).

Much higher rates of stability have recently been reported in community youth using the APSD from late childhood to early adolescence (Frick, Kimonis, Dandreaus, & Farell, 2003). Using parent ratings, the intraclass correlation coefficients for 2 to 4 years ranged from .88 to .80. Much lower intraclass correlation coefficients were obtained in comparing parental ratings at Time 1 with youth self-report at later time periods (.46 to .51). It is not surprising that lower estimates are found when parental ratings are compared with youth ratings because these estimates include not only temporal changes but also variance associated with different raters. Although relatively high levels of stability were found, the pattern of change indicated that children rated high on psychopathic traits tended to show less severe levels of these traits across time. Very few children who were rated low on psychopathic traits in late childhood developed significant levels of these traits in early adolescence.

What accounts for the stability of personality traits? Roberts and DelVecchio (2000) described five mechanisms that are postulated to enhance personality trait consistency: the environment, genes, psychological factors, person–environment transactions, and identity structure. One factor that could account for personality trait consistency in psychopathy is genetics. Recently, researchers have begun to examine the etiology of psychopathic traits in large-scale twin studies. With use of community samples of monozygotic and dizygotic twin pairs, the genetic and environmental influences on psychopathic traits have been studied in adults (Blonigen, Carlson, Krueger, & Patrick, 2003), adolescents (Larsson, Andershed, & Lichtenstein, in press; Taylor, Loney, Bobadilla, Iacono, & McGue, 2003), and children (Viding, Blair, Moffit, & Plomin, in press). Taken together, these studies indicate that genetic and nonshared environmental factors play salient roles in the development of psychopathic traits from childhood through adulthood in community samples.

Cicchetti and Rogosch (1996) described two concepts they consider to be important when one is studying developmental psychopathology: multifinality and equifinality. Both of these concepts are central to attempts to measure psychopathic traits in youth. The concept of multifinality proposes that individuals may share similar traits at one point in development but that diverse outcomes may evolve. Individuals will vary in the other risk factors and protective factors that eventually interact to lead to different disorders or even adaptive functioning. For example, not all youth with conduct disorder manifest antisocial personality disorder as adults (Robins, 1966): some developed substance use disorders, others developed schizophrenia, and some exhibited normal adaptation. An important goal for researchers studying psychopathy in youth is to identify these risk and protective factors that lead to diverse outcomes.

The concept of equifinality proposes that a common outcome or psychopathology probably results from diverse processes across different individuals. Thus, there might be different developmental pathways to psychopathy. For example, some adolescents who manifest psychopathic traits in childhood or adolescence may have a genetic predisposition for the development of these traits. Other adolescents may have grown up in a home where they witnessed or experienced violence and where they were provided with little warmth, structure, or discipline. Forth and Burke (1998) speculated that ". . . there might be different etiological pathways for the development of the distinct facets of psychopathy" (p. 224). If multiple pathways are discovered for the development of psychopathy, this knowledge would provide essential information for the development of prevention, treatment, and management strategies (see Brinkley, Newman, Widiger, & Lynam, 2004, for a review).

Hart, Watt, and Vincent (2002) raised the question whether psychopathy might manifest differently in youth than in adults. The distinction between homotypic and heterotypic continuity has implications for the measurement of psychopathic features across the life span. Homotypic continuity is the "identical behavioral expression of an underlying process across different developmental periods" (Cicchetti & Rogosch, 2002, p. 13). Heterotypic continuity represents "the manifestation of the same underlying process through different behavioral presentations at different developmental periods" (Cicchetti & Rogosch, 2002, p. 13). For example, how a 6-, 16-, or 36-year-old manifests poor frustration tolerance is likely to be different. Consideration of age-appropriate manifestations of psychopathic traits is essential both in adolescence but also across the age span—children, adults, and elderly.

Measuring Psychopathy in Youth: What Are the Potential Consequences?

Assuming that psychopathic traits can be identified in youth, there are legitimate concerns about how that information might be used in clinical or forensic decision-making. One critical concern that is often raised is the potentially grave consequences of labeling a youth as a psychopath. As described by Lyon and Ogloff (2000) "psychopathy is a powerful pejorative diagnostic label that can exert a profound influence over the legal decisions rendered in courts" (p. 139). The construct of psychopathy has been applied to adolescents in court proceedings before the publication of youth psychopathy measures. In some cases, mental health professionals appeared to have used unstructured clinical judgments to label a youth a psychopath, used the adult version of the PCL–R to assess psychopathy, or equated the diagnosis of conduct disorder with psychopathy.

The reliability and validity of these unstructured clinical judgments are unknown. Using an assessment instrument validated for use in adults with adolescents prior to research results support its validity is unethical. Finally, although psychopathic traits and CD symptoms are moderately and positively associated (Kosson, Cyterski, Steuerwald, Neumann, & Walker-Matthews, 2002; Salekin, Neumann, Leistico, DiCicco, & Duros, 2004), they do not correspond to identical constructs.

There are two published measures of psychopathy available to be used for clinical or forensic purposes. The authors of both these measures warn explicitly against using a categorical label. The authors of the PCL:YV manual address the issue of labeling, stating that "users not use the PCL:YV to diagnose adolescents as psychopaths for clinical or forensic purposes" (Forth et al., 2003, p. 16). The authors of the APSD caution that there is a ". . . strong rationale for never using the APSD to assign a child the label of psychopath" (Frick & Hare, 2001, p. 9).

In adult samples, the issue has been raised that the PCL–R may be used to divert offenders from treatment programs (Hare et al., 2000). In their study, Richards et al. (2003) removed inmates from the treatment program with PCL–R scores at or above 30. Seagrave and Grisso (2002) are concerned that the "assumption of untreatability" associated with adult psychopathy might be extended to youth. In jurisdictions where limited resources are being provided for rehabilitation, this is certainly a potential risk. It is crucial that measures of psychopathy not be used to exclude adolescents with psychopathic traits from intervention. We still do not know enough about the malleability of psychopathic traits in adolescents and their responsivity to treatment.

PREDICTIVE UTILITY OF THE PSYCHOPATHY CONSTRUCT IN YOUTH

If psychopathy is to be a useful construct in adolescence, it must have demonstrated predictive validity. More specifically, the types of behavior predicted by psychopathy scores in adolescence should mirror the behaviors predicted by PCL–R scores in adulthood. Studies conducted with youth have shown that youth psychopathy measures are predictive of the same types of antisocial and criminal behaviors found in adult psychopaths.

Before the predictive validity of psychopathy is demonstrated, however, it is important to note a few related to measuring this trait in adolescents. First, the validity of such measurements appears to be contingent on using the affective and interpersonal traits associated with psychopathy in combination with antisocial behavior. For example, in a study on 259 adolescent male young offenders, Vincent, Vitacco, Grisso, and Corrado (2003) found that using disruptive behavioral and impulsive symptoms alone did not identify "fledgling psychopaths." They stated that assessments disregarding callous–unemotional traits might result in high false-positive rates among adolescent offenders. Similarly, Salekin et al. (2004) found that the PCL:YV, which includes affective and interpersonal symptoms of psychopathy, was able to predict future antisocial behavior beyond simply looking at disruptive behavior disorders. Such findings suggest that it is not only important but also essential that researchers and clinicians use the affective and interpersonal traits associated with psychopathy as they add to the predictive validity of the construct. The use of these traits may help to identify a subset of adolescent serious offenders who are likely to be psychopathic later in life. The studies that are the focus of the remainder of this chapter will be those in which these traits were incorporated into the assessment of psychopathy.

A second issue in the assessment of the construct of psychopathy in youth is the comparison of self-report and ratings versus clinical interview combined with file review. Murrie and Cornell (2002) found that briefer measures relying on self-report and/or staff ratings (the APSD Self-Report and APSD Staff Rating) were not successful as screening measures to identify youths who score high on the PCL:YV and that correlations between these instruments and the PCL:YV are lower than would be expected ($r = .30$ for self report and $r = .35$ for staff ratings). In this chapter, therefore, we will focus on studies that used the PCL:YV, although relationships with other scales, such as the APSD and the modified CPS, will be addressed. Unless otherwise noted, psychopathy scores will refer to modified PCL–R or PCL:YV scores.

General Antisocial Behavior

In adulthood, psychopathy has been associated with indicators of antisocial behavior that spans many contexts (Hare, 2003), such as aggression (Book & Quinsey, 2004), self-directed aggression (Verona, Patrick, & Joiner, 2001), behavioral problems within institutions (Buffinton-Vollum, Edens, Johnson, & Johnson, 2002; Hare et al., 2000; Heilbrun et al., 1998; Shine & Hobson, 2000), and poor treatment process and outcomes (Hare et al., 2000; Rice et al., 1992; Seto & Barbaree, 1999).

Much of the literature regarding the relationship between psychopathy and indicators of antisocial behavior in youth mirrors the literature on adult psychopaths, and like their adult counterparts, psychopathic youth tend to exhibit problems in many areas, including the academic and social spheres. For example, researchers have found that psychopathic youth were more likely to have academic problems (Ridenour, Marchant, & Dean, 2001). Further, psychopathy in youth is correlated with a history of behavior problems at school, and, not surprisingly, with expulsion from school (Campbell et al., 2004), and youth scoring high on the PCL:YV also tend to get into significantly more physical fights per year than lower-scoring adolescents (Salekin et al., 2004). However, psychopathic youth do not appear to have excessive problems at home (antisocial influence, number of disruptions in living situation, or single parent; Campbell et al., 2004).

There is also a clear link between psychopathy and overall aggression in adolescents. Stafford and Cornell (2003) found that modified PCL–R scores were positively correlated with self-reported overall aggression, verbal aggression, aggression toward peers, and covert aggression. Interestingly, youths scoring high on psychopathic traits reported using both instrumental and reactive aggression, whereas youth with fewer psychopathic traits reported only engaging in reactive aggression. Psychopathic youth appear to be more likely to be aggressive toward themselves, consistent with the adult literature (Verona et al., 2001). Gretton (1998) found that adolescents scoring higher on psychopathy were more likely to have a history of self-injury, and Stafford and Cornell (2003) reported a correlation of .16 between psychopathy and self-directed aggression.

According to the manual for the PCL:YV (Forth et al., 2003), there is a "tendency of those with many psychopathic features to take risks, defy authority, and act impulsively" (p. 78). This is evidenced by the problematic behaviors observed within institutions. Several researchers have found a link between psychopathy in youth, as measured by the PCL:YV, and the number of infractions or conduct reports. For example, Campbell et al. (2004) found that PCL-YV scores were positively associated with self-reported delinquency and aggressive behavior. Further, psychopathic traits were related to a violent and versatile criminal history, although PCL:YV scores were not related to official criminal records for total violent, nonviolent, and technical violation convictions. Spain, Douglas, Poythress, and Epstein (2004) also found a significant correlation between PCL:YV scores and the rate of infractions, although correlations were stronger for other measures of psychopathy (APSD and modified CPS). Psychopathy is also positively correlated with escape or attempted escape from the institution (Gretton et al., 2001) and the number of violent or aggressive infractions (Brandt et al., 1997; Forth, Hart, & Hare, 1990; Murrie et al., 2004). Although most of the literature has pointed to moderate relations between psychopathy and number of problems within institutions, Edens, Poythress, and Lilienfeld (1999) found that modified PCL–R scores were NOT associated with nonaggressive or aggressive infractions, unless all types of infractions were combined ($r = .28$).

There have been few studies measuring the association between treatment outcome and psychopathic traits in youth. As with adult psychopaths, the literature on treatment process and outcomes is not very promising, regardless of which measure of psychopathy was used in a given study. For example, Falkenbach, Poythress, and Heide (2003) found that two self-report psychopathy scales (APSD and modified CPS) were predictive of program noncompliance in a juvenile diversion program. In another study, Spain et al.

(2003) reported a positive association between the APSD and modified CPS and the number of days participants took to reach the second level of a treatment program. However, no relationship was found between PCL:YV scores and the number of days needed to reach the next level of the treatment program. Finally, O'Neill et al. (2003b) reported that psychopathic characteristics were related to treatment process and outcome variables, including attrition, lack of participation, substance use, and lack of clinical improvement.

Overall, the findings in the youth literature are similar to what has been observed in adult psychopaths. Psychopathic youth tend to be more aggressive, have problems in multiple contexts, and have more institutional infractions (especially of a violent nature). Psychopathy in youth, then, can be said to be predictive of general antisocial behaviors, as it is in adults.

Criminal Activity

In adults, psychopathy is associated with earlier onset of criminal activity (Hemphill, Templeman, Wong, & Hare, 1998; Moltó, Poy, & Torrubia, 2000), frequency and versatility of crime (Hare & McPherson, 1984; Kosson, Smith, & Newman, 1990; Porter, Birt, & Boer, 2001; Tengström, A., Hodgins, S., Grann, M., Långström, N., & Kullgren, 2004; Wong, 1984), instrumental motives for violence (Cornell et al., 1996; Woodworth & Porter, 2002; Serin, 1991), stability of antisocial behavior (Hare, 2003), and general and violent recidivism (Hemphill & Hare, 2004; Hemphill et al., 1998; Rice & Harris, 1997; Salekin, Rogers, & Sewell, 1996). Psychopathy in youth, then, should correlate with these variables if measures such as the PCL:YV have predictive utility.

In adults, psychopathy is negatively associated with age of onset for criminal activity. This finding appears to generalize to the adolescent population, as well. Vincent et al. (2003), for instance, found that male young offenders scoring high on psychopathy received their first convictions at significantly younger ages than those scoring lower. Further, Salekin et al. (2004) found a negative relationship between the age of onset of antisocial behavior and PCL:YV scores, although the relationship was not significant. Many other researchers have reported the same relationship between PCL:YV scores and age of onset for nonviolent and violent offenses (Brandt et al., 1997: age at first arrest only; Forth, 1995; Forth et al., 1990). However, Kosson et al. (2002) reported finding no correlation between the PCL:YV and age at first trouble with the law, and O'Neill et al. (2003a) reported that the PCL:YV was not significantly correlated with age of onset for drug use.

Adolescents with psychopathic traits are similar to adult psychopaths in both frequency and versatility of criminal behaviors. Campbell et al. (2004) found that PCL:YV scores were correlated with self-report measures of delinquency and aggression, and Vincent et al. (2003) reported that adolescents scoring higher on psychopathy have significantly more prior convictions and more violent convictions than adolescents scoring lower on the PCL:YV. Further, Kosson et al. (2002) found medium to large correlations between psychopathy and the number of nonviolent charges, the number of violent charges, the total number of charges, and the number of different offense types.

Psychopathy in adults is also correlated with instrumental motives for violence and severity of crime; this relation appears to hold true across adolescence. Brandt et al. (1997) found that the core personality component of the PCL–R (Factor 1) was related to offense severity, and Murrie et al. (2004) reported a significant positive correlations between PCL:YV scores and measures of offense severity, including "victim required medical attention" ($r = .30$) and "use of weapons in violent offense" ($r = .32$). Further, Murrie et al. reported a moderate correlation between PCL–R scores and instrumental motives of prior violence ($r = .36$).

At this point, it is not clear whether the criminal behavior of adolescents who score high on psychopathy is stable across adolescence, a stability that is characteristic of adult psychopaths. Forth and Burke (1998), for example, found no significant differences for nonviolent offending across age periods (13 to 20.5). Interestingly, though, the high psychopathy group showed more violence in first and last time periods. Gretton (1998), however, found that there was some stability in criminal behavior in individuals scoring high on the PCL:YV. Participants in the high psychopathy group (compared with those scoring lower) committed more nonviolent offenses in late adolescence, committed more violent offenses in early and late adolescence, and continued to be more violent in early adulthood.

When one is evaluating predictive validity, it is obviously essential to examine the relationships between instruments assessing psychopathy and risk assessment. In adults, psychopathy is incorporated in risk assessment measures, such as the Violence Risk Appraisal Guide (Quinsey, Harris, Rice, & Cormier, 1998) and the HCR-20 (Webster, Douglas, Eaves, & Hart, 1997). Of importance, PCL:YV scores are correlated with youth risk assessment measures, such as the Youth Level of Service/Case Management Inventory (Hoge & Andrews, 2002) and the Structured Assessment of Risk for Violence in Youth (Borum, Bartel, & Forth, 2002) total risk score (Forth et al., 2003).

Because psychopathy in adult offenders is positively correlated with recidivism (or negatively correlated with time to reoffend), the evaluation of the predictive utility of a youth measure of psychopathy, such as the PCL:YV, must incorporate relationships with recidivism. A number of studies have linked psychopathy in adolescence to recidivism. Several studies have shown that psychopathy in adolescents is positively correlated with juvenile recidivism (Corrado et al., 2004; Toupin, Mercier, Dery, Côté, & Hodgins, 1995). Furthermore, adolescent offenders who score higher on psychopathy have higher base rates for both nonviolent and violent offenses (Vincent et al., 2003). Survival analyses of the same data set showed that psychopathic offenders were charged with any offense and nonviolent offenses approximately four times as quickly as low scorers. For violent reoffense, the high psychopathy group had a significantly shorter survival time than the other groups. Similarly, Catchpole and Gretton (2003) found that adolescents who recidivated within 1 year had a 78% chance of scoring higher on the PCL:YV than nonrecidivists. Survival analyses confirmed that PCL:YV scores were able to differentiate those who were more likely to reoffend. These results were similar for adolescents who violently reoffended (74% chance of scoring higher on PCL-YV). Other measures of juvenile psychopathy (APSD and modified CPS) have also exhibited positive correlations with self- and parent-reported recidivism (Falkenbach et al., 2003).

Whereas most youth studies have shown links between psychopathy and both violent and nonviolent recidivism, Forth et al. (1990) found that the relationship was specific to violent reoffense. They reported a modest correlation between modified PCL–R scores in mid-adolescence and the number of charges or convictions for violent offense late in adolescence (27-month follow-up) but found no evidence for a relationship with general recidivism. Similarly, Brandt et al. (1997) found that low scorers on PCL–R took the longest time to reoffend violently, whereas high scorers had the shortest time to violent reoffense. Although the groups did differ on both violent and any recidivism, there were no differences between the groups in nonviolent recidivism alone. Even with a 10-year follow-up, the pattern appears to hold. High PCL:YV scores predicted risk for violent reoffense, even after controlling for CD symptoms (Gretton et al., 2004), but this relationship was nonexistent for nonviolent and sexual recidivism.

The overall pattern of associations between psychopathy measures in youth and a variety of antisocial and criminal behaviors is consistent with what has been found in research with adults. Psychopathy scores in youth appear to be predictive of type, amount, and severity of criminal behavior and the age of onset for criminal behavior. Further, there is a clear link between psychopathy and violent recidivism, with mixed results for nonviolent/general recidivism. These findings suggest that adolescent psychopathy measures, such as the PCL:YV, have predictive utility.

SUMMARY AND CONCLUSIONS

Psychopathy in adulthood has its roots in behaviors and traits that are measurable during adolescence. In this chapter we have argued that the precursors of adult psychopathy can be observed and measured reliably in youth. Measurement of psychopathy in youth requires a measurement instrument. Instruments designed to measure psychopathy in youth must meet five basic criteria: First, youth who are deemed psychopathic should have scores that reflect non-normative levels of the traits and behaviors associated with psychopathy. Second, measurement instruments must have items that are consistent with age-appropriate manifestations. Third, the instrument must provide coverage of a range of interpersonal, affective, lifestyle, and antisocial characteristics associated with psychopathy. Fourth, scores should reflect stable dispositions and not transitory problems. Fifth, scores derived from the instrument should be based on multiple sources of information. The PCL:YV is a test instrument that meets these criteria.

Various concerns surround the claim that psychopathy is manifested in youth. The first concern is that psychopathy is an unstable trait in adolescents. Results from a number of studies suggest that personality traits and behaviors are stable during adolescence. Many of these traits and behaviors overlap psychopathic traits and behaviors. The second concern is the possibility that transitory normative adolescent traits could be mistaken for more stable psychopathic traits. Research indicates that normal adolescents typically do not engage in the same number and extent of extreme behaviors that are characteristic of psychopathic adolescents. The third concern is the potential consequence of labeling youth as psychopaths. Authors of instruments designed to measure psychopathy, such as the PCL:YV, address this issue directly by warning against using the label *psychopath* because of its pejorative connotations, particularly with respect to labeling and access to intervention. It is incumbent upon clinicians who use youth psychopathy measures to ensure that they do not go beyond the current empirical literature and to acknowledge the limitations of the research. Moreover, until longitudinal studies are completed, assuming a high degree of stability of psychopathic traits from adolescence to adulthood is unwarranted.

ACKNOWLEDGMENT

The authors are grateful to Heather Gretton for her helpful comments and suggestions during the preparation of this chapter.

REFERENCES

Andershed, H., Gustafson, S. B., Kerr, M., & Stattin, H. (2002). The usefulness of self-reported psychopathy-like traits in the study of antisocial behaviour among non-referred adolescents. *European Journal of Personality, 16*, 383–402.

Arnett, J. J. (1999). Adolescent storm and stress, reconsidered. *American Psychologist, 54*, 317–326.

Blonigen, D. M., Carlson, S. R., Krueger, R. F., & Patrick, C. J. (2003). A twin study of self-reported psychopathic personality traits. *Personality and Individual Differences, 35*, 179–197.

Book, A. S., & Quinsey, V. L. (2004). Psychopaths: Cheaters or warrior-hawks? *Personality and Individual Differences, 36*, 33–45.

Borum, R., Bartel, P., & Forth, A. (2002). *Manual for the Structured Assessment for Violence Risk in Youth (SAVRY). Consultation version.* Tampa, FL: Florida Mental Health Institute at University of South Florida.

Brandt, J. R., Kennedy, W. A., Patrick, C. J., & Curtin, J. J. (1997). Assessment of psychopathy in a population of incarcerated adolescent offenders. *Psychological Assessment, 9*, 429–435.

Brinkley, C. A., Newman, J. P., Widiger, T., & Lynam, D. (2004). Two approaches to parsing the heterogeneity of psychopathy. *Clinical Psychology: Science and Practice, 11*, 69–94.

Buffington-Vollum, J. K., Edens, J. F., Johnson, D. W., & Johnson, J. K. (2002). Psychopathy as a predictor of institutional misbehavior among sex offenders: A prospective replication. *Criminal Justice and Behavior, 29*, 497–511.

Campbell, M. A., Porter, S., & Santor, D. (2004). Psychopathic traits in adolescent offenders: An evaluation of criminal history, clinical, and psychosocial correlates. *Behavioral Sciences and the Law, 22*, 23–47.

Catchpole, R. E. H., & Gretton, H. M. (2003). The predictive validity of risk assessment with violent young offenders: A 1-year examination of criminal outcome. *Criminal Justice and Behavior, 30*, 688–708.

Cicchetti, D., & Rogosh, F. A. (1996). Equifinity and multifinity in developmental psychopathology. *Development and Psychopathology, 8*, 597–600.

Cicchetti, D., & Rogosch, F. A. (2002). A developmental psychopathology perspective on adolescence. *Journal of Consulting and Clinical Psychology, 70*, 6–20.

Cleckley, H. (1941). *The mask of sanity: An attempt to clarify some issues about the so called psychopathic personality.* St. Louis: Mosby.

Cleckley, H. (1982). *The mask of sanity* (4th ed). New York: Mosby.

Cornell, D. G., Warren, J., Hawk, G., Stafford, E., Oram, G., & Pine, D. (1996). Psychopathy in instrumental and reactive violent offenders. *Journal of Consulting and Clinical Psychology, 64*, 783–790.

Corrado, R. R., Vincent, G. M., Hart, S. D., & Cohen, I. M. (2004). Predictive validity of the Psychopathy Checklist: Youth Version for general and violent recidivism. *Behavioral Sciences and the Law, 22*, 5–22.

Cruise, K. R., Colwell, L. H., Lyons, P. M., & Baker, M. D. (2003). Prototypical analysis of adolescent psychopathy: Investigating the juvenile justice perspective. *Behavioral Sciences and the Law, 21*, 829–846.

D'Silva, K., Duggan, C., & McCarthy, L. (2004). Does treatment really make psychopaths worse? A review of the evidence. *Journal of Personality Disorders, 18*, 163–177.

Edens, J. F., Poythress, N. G., & Lilienfeld, S. O. (1999). Identifying inmates at risk for disciplinary infractions: A comparison of two measures of psychopathy. *Behavioral Sciences and the Law, 17*, 435–443.

Edens, J. F., Skeem, J. L., Cruise, K. R., & Cauffman, E. (2001). Assessment of "juvenile psychopathy" and it's association with violence: A critical review. *Behavioral Sciences and the Law, 19*, 53–80.

Falkenbach, D. M., Poythress, N. G., & Heide, K. M. (2003). Psychopathic features in a juvenile diversion population: Reliability and predictive validity of two self-report measures. *Behavioral Sciences and the Law, 21*, 787–805.

Forth, A. E. (1995). *Psychopathy and young offenders: Prevalence, family background, and violence. Program Branch Users Report.* Ottawa, Ontario, Canada: Ministry of the Solicitor General of Canada.

Forth, A. E., & Burke, H. (1998). Psychopathy in adolescence: Assessment, violence, and developmental precursors. In D. J. Cooke, A. E. Forth, & R. D. Hare (Eds.), *Psychopathy: Theory, research, and implications for society* (pp. 205–229). Dordrecht, The Netherlands: Kluwer Academic Publishers.

Forth, A. E., Hart, S. D., & Hare, R. D. (1990). Assessment of psychopathy in male young offenders. *Psychological Assessment, 2*, 342–344.

Forth, A. E., Kosson, D. S., & Hare, R. D. (2003). *Hare Psychopathy Checklist: Youth Version. Technical manual.* Toronto, Ontario, Canada: Multi-Health Systems.

Forth, A. E., & Mailloux, D. L. (2000). Psychopathy in youth: What do we know? In C. B. Gacono (Ed.), *The clinical and forensic assessment of psychopathy: A practitioner's guide* (pp. 25–54). Mahwah, NJ: Lawrence Erlbaum Associates.

Frick, P. J. (1998). Callous-unemotional traits and conduct problems: Applying the two-factor model of psychopathy to children. In D. J. Cooke, A. E. Forth, & R. D. Hare (Eds.), *Psychopathy: Theory, research, and implications for society* (pp. 161–187). Dordrecht, The Netherlands: Kluwer Academic.

Frick, P. J., & Hare, R. D. (2001). *The Antisocial Process Screening Device.* Toronto, Ontario, Canada: Multi-Health Systems.

Frick, P. J., Kimonis, E. R., Dandreaux, D. M., & Farell, J. M. (2003). The 4 year stability of psychopathic traits in non-referred youth. *Behavioral Sciences and the Law, 21,* 713–736.

Gretton, M. H. (1998). Psychopathy and recidivism in adolescence: A ten-year retrospective follow-up [Abstract]. *Dissertation Abstracts International, 59,* 6488.

Gretton, H. M., Hare, R. D., & Catchpole, R. E. H. (2004). Psychopathy and offending from adolescence to adulthood: A 10-year follow-up. *Journal of Consulting and Clinical Psychology, 72,* 636–645.

Gretton, H. M., McBride, M., Hare, R. D., O'Shaughnessy, R., & Kumka, G. (2001). Psychopathy and recidivism in adolescent sex offenders. *Criminal Justice and Behavior, 28,* 427–449.

Hare, R. D. (1980). A research scale for the assessment of psychopathy in criminal populations. *Personality and Individual Differences, 1,* 111–119.

Hare, R. D. (1991). *The Hare Psychopathy Checklist–Revised.* Toronto, Ontario, Canada: Multi-Health Systems.

Hare, R. D. (1998). Psychopaths and their nature: Implications for the mental health and criminal justice systems. In T. Millon, E. Simonson, M. Burket-Smith, & R. Davis (Eds.), *Psychopathy: Antisocial, criminal, & violent behavior* (pp. 188–212). New York: Guilford Press.

Hare, R. D. (2003). *Manual for the Revised Psychopathy Checklist* (2nd ed.). Toronto, Ontario, Canada: Multi-Health Systems.

Hare, R. D., Clark, D., Grann, M., & Thornton, D. (2000). Psychopathy and the predictive validity of the PCL–R: An international perspective. *Behavioral Sciences and the Law, 18,* 623–645.

Hare, R. D., & McPherson, L. M. (1984). Violent and aggressive behavior by criminal psychopaths. *International Journal of Law and Psychiatry, 7,* 35–50.

Hart, S. D., Watt, K. A., & Vincent, G. M. (2002). Commentary on Seagrave and Grisso: Impressions of the state of the art. *Law and Human Behavior, 26,* 241–245.

Heilbrun, K., Hart, S. D., Hare, R. D., Gustafson, D., Nunez, C., & White, A. (1998). Inpatient and post-discharge aggression in mentally disordered offenders: The role of psychopathy. *Journal of Interpersonal Violence, 13,* 514–527.

Hemphill, J. F., & Hare, R. D. (2004). Some misconceptions about the Hare PCL–R and risk assessment: A reply to Gendreau, Goggin, and Smith. *Criminal Justice and Behavior, 31,* 203–243.

Hemphill, J. F., Hare, R. D., & Wong, S. (1998). Psychopathy and recidivism: A review. *Legal and Criminological Psychology, 3,* 141–172.

Hemphill, J. F., Templeman, R., Wong, S., & Hare, R. D. (1998). Psychopathy and crime: Recidivism and criminal careers. In D. J. Cooke, A. E. Forth, & R. D. Hare (Eds.), *Psychopathy: Theory, research, and implications for society* (pp. 375–399). Dordrecht, The Netherlands: Kluwer Academic.

Hoge, R., & Andrews, D. (2002). *The Youth Level of Service/Case Management Inventory.* Toronto, Ontario, Canada: Multi-Heath Systems.

Johnson, L., & Cooke, D. J. (2004). Psychopathic-like traits in childhood: Conceptual and measurement concerns. *Behavioral Sciences and the Law, 22,* 103–125.

Kosson, D. S., Cyterski, T. D., Steuerwald, B. L., Neumann, C. S., & Walker-Matthews, S. (2002). The reliability and validity of the Psychopathy Checklist: Youth Version in nonincarcerated adolescent males. *Psychological Assessment, 14*, 97–109.

Kosson, D. S., Smith, S. S., & Newman, J. P. (1990). Evaluating the construct validity of psychopathy in Black and White male inmates: Three preliminary studies. *Journal of Abnormal Psychology, 99*, 250–259.

Lahey, B. B., Loeber, R., Burke, J., Rathouz, P. J., & McBurnett, K. (2002). Waxing and waning in concert: Dynamic comorbidity of conduct disorder with other disruptive and emotional problems over 17 years among clinic-referred boys. *Journal of Abnormal Psychology, 111*, 556–567.

Larsson, H., Andershed, H., & Lichtenstein, P. (in press). A genetic factor explains most of the variation in the psychopathic personality. *Journal of Abnormal Psychology*.

Lynam, D. R. (1997). Pursuing the psychopath: Capturing the fledgling psychopath in a nomological net. *Journal of Abnormal Psychology, 106*, 425–438.

Lynam, D. R. (2002). Fledgling psychopathy: A view from personality theory. *Law and Human Behavior, 26*, 255–259.

Lyon, D. R., & Ogloff, J. R. P. (2000). Legal and ethical issues in psychopathy assessment. In C.B. Gacono (Ed.), *The clinical and forensic assessment of psychopathy: A practitioner's guide* (pp. 139–173). Mahwah, NJ: Lawrence Erlbaum Associates.

Marczyk, G. R., Heilbrun, K., Lander, T., & DeMatteo, D. (2003). Predicting juvenile recidivism with the PCL:YV, MAYSI, and YLS/CMI. *International Journal of Forensic Mental Health, 2*, 7–18.

McCrae, R. R., Costa, P. T., Terracciano, A., Parker, W. D., Mills, C. J., De Fruyt, F., & Mervielde, I. (2002). Personality trait development from age 12 to age 18: Longitudinal, cross-sectional and cross-cultural analyses. *Journal of Personality and Social Psychology, 83*, 1456–1468.

Moltó, J., Poy, R., & Torrubia, R. (2000). Standardization of the Hare Psychopathy Checklist–Revised in a Spanish prison sample. *Journal of Personality Disorders, 14*, 84–96.

Murrie, D. C., & Cornell, D. G. (2000). The Millon adolescent clinical inventory and psychopathy. *Journal of Personality Assessment, 75*, 110–125.

Murrie, D. C., & Cornell, D. G. (2002). Psychopathy screening of incarcerated juveniles: A comparison of measures. *Psychological Assessment, 14*, 390–396.

Murrie, D. C., Cornell, D. G., Kaplan, S., McConville, D., & Levy-Elkon, A. (2004). Psychopathy scores and violence among juvenile offenders: A multi-measure study. *Behavioral Sciences and the Law, 22*, 49–67.

O'Neill, M. L., Heilbrun, K., & Lidz, V. (2003a). Adolescents with psychopathic characteristics in a substance abusing cohort: Treatment process and outcomes. *Law and Human Behavior, 27*, 299–314.

O'Neill, M. L., Lidz, V., & Heilbrun, K. (2003b). Predictors and correlates of psychopathic characteristics in substance abusing adolescents. *International Journal of Forensic Mental Health, 2*, 35–45.

Ogloff, J., Wong, S., & Greenwood, A. (1990). Treating criminal psychopaths in a therapeutic community program. *Behavioral Sciences and the Law, 8*, 181–190.

Porter, S., Birt, A. R., & Boer, D. P. (2001). Investigation of the criminal and conditional release profiles of Canadian Federal offenders as a function of psychopathy and age. *Law and Human Behavior, 25*, 647–661.

Quinsey, V. L., Harris, G. T., Rice, M. E., & Cormier, C. A. (1998). *Violent offenders: Appraising and managing risk.* Washington, DC: American Psychological Association.

Rice, M. E., & Harris, G. T. (1997). Cross-validation and extension of the Violence Risk Appraisal Guide for child molesters and rapists. *Law and Human Behavior, 21,* 231–241.

Rice, M. E., Harris, G. T., & Cormier, C. A. (1992). An evaluation of a maximum security therapeutic community for psychopaths and other mentally disordered offenders. *Law and Human Behavior, 16,* 399–412.

Richards, H. J., Casey, J. O., & Lucente, S. W. (2003). Psychopathy and treatment response in incarcerated female substance abusers. *Criminal Justice & Behavior, 30,* 251–276.

Ridenour, T. A., Marchant, G. J., & Dean, R. S. (2001). Is the psychopathy checklist revised clinically useful for adolescents? *Journal of Psychoeducational Assessment, 19,* 227–238.

Roberts, B. W., & DelVecchio, W. F. (2000). The rank-order consistency of personality from childhood to old age: A quantitative review of longitudinal studies. *Psychological Bulletin, 126,* 3–25.

Robins, L. M. (1966). *Deviant children grown up.* Baltimore: Williams & Wilkins.

Rutherford, M. J., Cacciola, J. S., Alterman, A. I., McKay, J. R., & Cook, T. G. (1999). Two-year test-retest reliability of the Psychopathy Checklist–Revised in methadone patients. *Assessment, 6,* 285–291.

Salekin, R. T., Neumann, C. S., Leistico, A. R., DiCicco, T. M., & Duros, R. L. (2004). Construct validity of psychopathy in a young offender sample: Taking a closer look at psychopathy's potential importance over disruptive behavior disorders. *Journal of Abnormal Psychology, 113,* 416–427.

Salekin, R. T., Rogers, R., & Machin, D. (2001). Psychopathy in youth: Pursuing diagnostic clarity. *Journal of Youth and Adolescence, 30,* 173–194.

Salekin, R. T., Rogers, R., & Sewell, K. (1996). A review and meta-analysis of the Psychopathy Checklist and Psychopathy Checklist–Revised: Predictive validity of dangerousness. *Clinical Psychology: Science and Practice, 3,* 203–215.

Salekin, R. T., Ziegler, T. A., Larrea, M. A., Anthony, V. L., & Bennett, A. D. (2003). Predicting dangerousness with two Millon Adolescent Clinical Inventory Psychopathy Scales: The importance of egocentric and callous traits. *Journal of Personality Assessment, 80,* 154–163.

Saltaris, C. (2002). Psychopathy in juvenile offenders: Can temperament and attachment be considered as robust developmental precursors? *Clinical Psychology Review, 22,* 729–752.

Schroeder, M., Schroeder, K., & Hare, R. D. (1983). Generalizability of a checklist for assessment of psychopathy. *Journal of Consulting and Clinical Psychology, 51,* 511–516.

Seagrave, D., & Grisso, T. (2002). Adolescent development and the measurement of juvenile psychopathy. *Law and Human Behavior, 26,* 219–239.

Serin, R. C. (1991). Psychopathy and violence in criminals. *Journal of Interpersonal Violence, 6,* 423–431.

Seto, M. C., & Barbaree, H. E. (1999). Psychopathy, treatment behavior, and sex offenders recidivism. *Journal of Interpersonal Violence, 14,* 1235–1248.

Shine, J. H., & Hobson, J. A. (2000). Institutional behaviour and time in treatment among psychopaths admitted to a prison-based therapeutic community. *Medicine, Science, and the Law, 40,* 327–335.

Skeem, J. L., & Cauffman, E. (2003). Views of the downward extension: Comparing the Youth Version of the Psychopathy Checklist with the Youth Psychopathic Traits Inventory. *Behavioral Sciences and the Law, 21,* 737–770.

Spain, S. E., Douglas, K. S., Poythress, N. G., & Epstein, M. (2004). The relationship between psychopathic features, violence, and treatment outcome: The comparison of three youth measures of psychopathic features. *Behavioral Sciences and the Law, 22*, 85–102.

Spear, L. P. (2000). The adolescent brain and age-related behavioral manifestations. *Neuroscience and Behavioral Reviews, 24*, 417–463.

Stafford, J. E., & Cornell, D. (2003). Psychopathy scores predict adolescent inpatient aggression. *Assessment, 10*, 102–112.

Taylor, J., Loney, B. R., Bobadilla, L., Iacono, W. G., & McGue, M. (2003). Genetic and environmental influences on psychopathy trait dimensions in a community sample of male twins. *Journal of Abnormal Child Psychology, 31*, 633–645.

Tengström, A., Hodgins, S., Grann, M., Långström, N., & Kullgren, G. (2004). Schizophrenia and criminal offending: The role of psychopathy and substance use disorders. *Criminal Justice and Behavior, 31*, 367–391.

Toupin, J., Mercier, H., Dery, M., Côté, G., & Hodgins, S. (1995). Validity of the PCL–R for adolescents. *Issues in Criminological and Legal Psychology, 24*, 143–145.

Verona, E., Patrick, C. J., & Joiner, T. A. (2001). Psychopathy, antisocial personality, and suicide risk. *Journal of Abnormal Psychology, 110*, 462–470.

Viding, E., Blair, R. J. R., Moffitt, T. E., & Plomin, R. (2005). Evidence for substantial genetic risk for psychopathy in 7-year-olds. *Journal of Child Psychology and Psychiatry, 46*, 592–597.

Vincent, G. M., Vitacco, M. J., Grisso, T., & Corrado, R. R. (2003). Subtypes of adolescent offenders: Affective traits and antisocial behavior patterns. *Behavioral Sciences and the Law, 21*, 695–712.

Webster, C. D., Douglas, K. S., Eaves, D., & Hart, S. D. (1997). *HCR-20: Assessing risk for violence (Version 2)*. Burnaby, BC: Mental Health, Law, and Policy Institute. Simon Fraser University.

Webster, C. D., & Jackson, M. A. (1997). *Impulsivity: Theory, assessment, and treatment*. New York: Guilford Press.

Williamson, S. E., Hare, R. D., & Wong, S. (1987). Violence: Criminal psychopaths and their victims. *Canadian Journal of Behavioral Science, 19*, 454–462.

Wong, S. (1984). *Criminal and institutional behavior of psychopaths* (Programs Branch Users Report). Ottawa, Ontario, Canada: Ministry of the Solicitor-General of Canada.

Woodworth, M., & Porter, S. (2002). In cold blood: Characteristics of criminal homicides as a function of psychopathy. *Journal of Abnormal Psychology, 111*, 436–445.

Zinger, I., & Forth, A. (1998). Psychopathy and Canadian criminal proceedings: The potential for human rights abuses. *Canadian Journal of Criminology, 40*, 237–276.

15

Psychopathy in Women: A Valid Construct With Clear Implications

Rebecca Jackson and Henry Richards

As early as Cleckley's (1941/1976) original formulation of the modern understanding of psychopathy, women were included among those manifesting the disorder. Indeed, Cleckley provided clinical descriptions of two such women, emphasizing the maladaptive personality traits, such as callousness and remorselessness, that have come to be accepted as the defining features of psychopathy. Despite their prominence in early conceptualizations of the disorder, women have only been studied in the psychopathy research literature for a short time.

Although psychopathy is the primary focus of this chapter, the related concepts of antisocial personality disorder (ASPD) and conduct disorder (CD) are also briefly used in providing a richer discussion of the expression of the disorder across gender. The trend toward investigating differential expression of externalizing disorders, such as ASPD and CD, is directly relevant to this discussion of psychopathy. The chapter then focuses on psychopathy, primarily as it is assessed by the Psychopathy Checklist–Revised (PCL–R).

A consistent finding across the literature is that, compared with males, females evidence lower rates of ASPD, CD, and psychopathy. Among the possible explanations for this are (a) gender bias in the diagnostic criteria and/or (b) true gender differences in the core features of the disorders. In terms of conduct disorder, the diagnostic criteria are heavily weighted in favor of antisocial behaviors more often exhibited by boys than by girls. For example, boys more often engage in physical fighting, cruelty to animals, and fire-setting (Goldstein, Poers, McCusker, & Mundt, 1996). Because boys more often engage in these behaviors, and these behaviors make up the diagnostic criteria, boys are more likely to be diagnosed with the disorder. For instance, Zoccolillo and colleagues (Zoccolillo, 1993; Zoccolillo, Tremblay, & Vitaro, 1996) demonstrated that slightly changing the diagnostic criteria for CD resulted in an increase in the percentage of girls meeting diagnostic criteria from 6% to 35%, with a false positive rate of only 1%. Similarly, the diagnostic criteria for ASPD may be weighted more heavily with antisocial behaviors more likely to be expressed by males (Goldstein et al., 1996). Alternatively, true differences may exist in the disorder. For example, Silverthorn and Frick (1999; see also Silverthorn, Frick, & Reynolds, 2001) argue that the childhood-onset type of CD is not applicable to girls, as they most often begin antisocial behavior later in adolescence. Instead, a delayed-onset type has been advanced for girls that is behaviorally similar to the childhood onset of CD displayed in boys (Silverthorn et al., 2001).

Sampling bias is an additional source of gender differences in regard to these disorders (Hartung & Widiger, 1998). For example, Hartung and Widiger suggested that the conclusion that a particular personality disorder is more prevalent in men, based on research conducted at a Veteran's Administration hospital, is likely to be misleading. Because more men than women will typically present to a veteran's hospital, the sample is likely to be biased. A natural parallel exists with ASPD research in that most research on ASPD is conducted in jails and prison, where the majority of inmates are male.

However, studies conducted with nonincarcerated samples suggested that sampling bias is not responsible for observed gender differences in prevalence. In a large-scale epidemiological study of community adults, Mulder, Wells, and Bushnell (1994) compared men and women meeting the criteria for ASPD. The results suggest that, diagnostic criteria aside, important gender differences exist in the expression of the disorder. For example, men engaged in more criminal behavior, whereas women had more difficulties in interpersonal relationships and with lying. In addition, women with ASPD experienced greater diagnostic comorbidity of depressive and anxiety disorders. Women also reported more troubled personal lives, with higher rates of marriage dissolution and more dysfunctional childhoods.

The diagnostic criteria for both CD and ASPD are also heavily weighted in favor of dysfunctional or unlawful behavior and, therefore, may be more biased towards males. The introduction of the PCL and PCL–R has allowed for the systematic study of this disorder that extends beyond behavioral manifestations. Of particular interest is the fact that the PCL–R assesses the personality and relationship features of the disorder that previous researchers have found to be more central in women than in men with ASPD. In this chapter we review the available literature regarding psychopathy in females, primarily as it is assessed by the PCL or PCL–R.

An earlier review by Vitale and Newman (2001a) provided an excellent summary of the use of the PCL–R with women. Much of the research reviewed by those authors suggested that the PCL–R is a reliable and valid measure when used with females. The research conducted up to that point was largely descriptive in nature; only a few studies had investigated the PCL–R's predictive validity, factor structure, and laboratory correlates. In this chapter we will provide a brief overview of earlier studies. For a more comprehensive review of these studies, interested readers should refer to Vitale and Newman (2001a). For the reader's convenience, an annotated summary of female-specific research reviewed in the current chapter is provided in Table 15–1.

TABLE 15–1.
Summary of Research Finding of Psychopathy in Females

Variable	Findings
Severity	Women obtain lower PCL–R and PCL:SV scores than do men in incarcerated, forensic, treatment/clinical, and non-criminal populations (Darke et al., 1998; Forth et al., 1996; Grann, 2000; Jackson et al., 2002; Richards et al., 2003; Rutherford et al., 1996; Salekin et al., 1997).
Base Rates	Base rates of female psychopathy are typically lower than in comparable male samples (Grann, 2000; Jackson et al., 2002; Rutherford et al., 1996; Salekin et al., 1997; Vitale & Newman, 2001).
Criminal History Density	A moderate relationship exists between density of criminal and violent offending with psychopathy scores (Cooke, 1995; Rutherford et al., 1996).
Institutional Maladjustment	Institutional and program related behavior are significantly related to psychopathy (Richards et al., 2003) and antisocial personality disorder (Salekin et al., 1997).
Recidivism	Although female psychopaths recidivate at lower levels (Salekin et al., 1998), the PCL–R, particularly Factor 1, is a valid predictor (Salekin et al., 1998; Richards et al., 2003).
Two-Factor Model	Little support for the traditional two-factor model with female samples (Darke et al., 1998; Jackson et al., 2002; Salekin et al., 1997; Warren et al., 2003).
Three- and Four-Factor Models	Some support for the three factor model in female samples (Jackson et al., 2002), with mixed results reported for the four-factor model (Hare, 2003; Warren et al., 2003).
Laboratory Correlates	Psychopathic females appear to suffer from similar emotion regulation deficits as males (Sutton et al., 2002), but response modulation deficits have not been replicated (Vitale & Newman, 2001b).

THE NATURE OF PSYCHOPATHY

Because other chapters in this volume include a description of the nature of the psychopathy construct in detail, only a brief description is provided here. As noted at the outset, modern conceptualizations of psychopathy have their roots with Cleckley's influential, *The Mask of Sanity*, in which he outlines a disorder in which certain individuals suffer from a constellation of personality and behavioral traits that make them qualitatively different from other psychiatric patients. These patients were grandiose, impulsive, and cold-hearted while at the same time being charming and engaging. Women as well as men were included in these descriptions, although male psychopaths have been the focus of the majority of clinical and research attention until recently.

Psychopaths can be thought of as suffering from certain affective and behavioral deficits and excesses—excesses in terms of grandiosity, promiscuity, and manipulation, and deficits in terms of remorse, behavioral controls, and genuine emotional experience. More traditionally, psychopathy has been understood as consisting of two related underlying dimensions or factors. Factor 1 consists of the emotional–affective traits associated with the disorder such as callousness, remorseless, and grandiosity. Factor 2 describes a chronically antisocial lifestyle (Hare et al., 1990; Harpur, Hakstian, & Hare, 1988; Harpur, Hare, & Hakstian, 1989).

Until recently, this two-factor structure has been accepted as the most useful conceptualization. As a result, in much of the research to date on psychopathy and its dimensions this conceptualization has been used. Although recent researchers have questioned the adequacy of this model (see the section on factor analytic studies later in the chapter), the two-factor model is useful in understanding the broad dimensions of the disorder. Many of the findings reviewed here discussed psychopathy in these broad terms and have led to a finer understanding of its expression.

Research over two decades has demonstrated that psychopathy is a reliable and valid construct with clear implications for violence prediction, treatment response, recidivism, and institutional adjustment. As the premier assessment measure of psychopathy, PCL–R studies are undeniably important in understanding the construct. Many similarities across gender have been established in existing research, which has also highlighted the differences. As will be discussed here, some of the research suggests that the PCL–R does not sufficiently capture the psychopathy construct as it manifests in women or perhaps that psychopathy at its core differs across gender. Although this is one important aspect of psychopathy, it is not likely to be the whole picture. Thus, in this chapter we review the extant literature on psychopathy in females, but also strive to extend the thinking about this construct beyond that obtained by its assessment with the PCL–R.

SEVERITY AND PREVALENCE OF PCL–R PSYCHOPATHY IN WOMEN

One consistent finding is that females have lower PCL–R scores than their male counterparts. With one notable exception (Louth, Hare, & Linden, 1998), this finding holds across incarcerated (Jackson, Rogers, Neumann, & Lambert, 2002; Richards, Casey, & Lucente, 2003; Salekin, Rogers, & Sewell 1997), forensic psychiatric (Grann, 2000), and treatment samples (Rutherford, Cacciola, Alterman, & McKay, 1996). Indeed, Hare (2003) reported total scores in his normative samples that were ~3 points lower than those in males ($M_{males} = 22.1$ vs. $M_{females} = 19.0$). As with males, lower scores are typically found in treatment and clinical samples (Darke et al., 1998; Rutherford, Alterman, Cacciola, & McKay, 1998; Rutherford, Cacciola, Alterman, & McKay, 1996), with slightly higher scores in incarcerated samples ($M = 20.04$;

Jackson et al., 2002; Salekin, Rogers, Ustad, & Sewell, 1998). The trend extends also to noncriminal samples in which males scored significantly higher than females on nearly all the items (Forth, Brown, Hart, & Hare, 1996).

In addition to lower dimensional ratings of psychopathy, lower base rates of PCL–R measured psychopathy are found in female samples, although the overlap is considerable. Hare (2003) reported the base rate in correctional and forensic populations to be approximately 15%–25%. With females, published reports indicate a typical range of 11%–16%, although some Canadian studies have reported base rates as high as 30% (Louth et al., 1998). Base rates tend to be lower in U.S. correctional settings and lowest in treatment settings (Rutherford et al., 1996). In fact, in Rutherford et al.'s study of females in a methadone treatment program, none exceeded the PCL–R recommended cut score of 30. The base rate depends not only on the type of sample (e.g., treatment vs. offender), but perhaps also on geography. The highest base rates were found in Canadian correctional institutions (Louth et al., 1998; Strachan, 1993). Differences in sentencing practices between the U.S. and Canada may contribute to the differences in base rates.

Despite the differences in descriptive scores across gender, the PCL–R is considered to be a reliable measure of the psychopathy construct in women (Vitale & Newman, 2001a). As Vitale and Newman argue, the psychopathy construct and the PCL–R must also predict certain important behaviors that are theoretically related to psychopathy to be maximally useful. Important external correlates related to psychopathy include institutional maladjustment and treatment compliance, recidivism, and criminal behavior density and versatility. Although the PCL–R is used in the majority of research concerning psychopathy, alternate measures of the construct or related constructs are also used (e.g., ASPD). The discussion now turns to those important external correlates.

OFFENSE HISTORY AND CRIMINAL VERSATILITY

Male psychopaths are significantly more likely than nonpsychopaths to commit physical violence and otherwise aggressive behavior. The relationship between crime, particularly violent crime, and psychopathy has been well established in male offenders (e.g., Brinkley, Schmitt, Smith, & Newman, 2001; Porter, Birt, & Boer, 2001). For example, Porter et al. reported that offenders who scored high on the PCL–R committed significantly more violent and nonviolent crimes than low scorers. Factor 1 was significantly, although modestly, related to violent and nonviolent crimes ($r = .11$), whereas Factor 2 was more strongly related to both nonviolent ($r = .33$) and violent ($r = .26$) offenses.

The relationship between criminal offenses, including violent offenses, and psychopathy may be even stronger for women. Loucks and Zamble (2000; as cited by Hare, 2003) reported that the relationships between PCL–R Total, Factor 1, and Factor 2 and total convictions were .49, .43, and .42

respectively, and .46, .29, and .36 with total violent convictions. In related studies, Cooke (1995) also found a gender difference in the relationship between a diagnosis of psychopathy and general offending ($r = .35$ for females vs. .20 for males). Among methadone patients, the number of arrests among females was significantly correlated with total PCL–R scores (Rutherford et al., 1996). Among males, this relationship was nonsignificant (Rutherford, Alterman, Cacciola, & McKay, 1997). The bulk of evidence appears to suggest that psychopathy accounts for more variance in the expression of violent and criminal acts in female offenders and substance abusers than it perhaps does for males. It is not known whether this relationship would also hold true for other populations, such as female forensic psychiatric patients.

Kosson, Smith, and Newman (1990) reported that among male offenders, psychopaths had significantly more types of convictions than the nonpsychopaths. Simourd and Hoge (2000) replicated this result, finding greater criminal versatility among male psychopaths. Although factor analytic evidence suggests that criminal versatility is an important component in explaining psychopathy among females (Jackson, 2001; Salekin et al, 1997), there are no published reports of a systematic investigation of this variable.

INSTITUTIONAL MALADJUSTMENT

Psychopaths in general commit more institutional infractions than do nonpsychopaths, particularly infractions of the more serious variety (Edens et al., 2002; Hare, Clark, Grann, & Thornton, 2000; Kroner & Mills, 2001). Psychopathy is significantly related to verbal and physical acting out (Edens et al., 2002), assaults on staff (Hare et al., 2000), and general prison misconduct (Hare et al., 2000). Only three groups to date have investigated the relationship between psychopathy and institutional infractions among female inmates, with results generally confirming those found among males (Loucks & Zamble, 2000; Richards et al., 2003; Salekin et al., 1998).

In a large substance abuse treatment study of incarcerated females, Richards, Casey, and Lucente (2003) provided a detailed analysis of institutional and treatment program infractions during three time periods: Pre-program infractions, In-program infractions, and Post-program infractions. Using partial correlations, the authors correlated the number of infractions in each observation period while controlling for the number of days at risk for infractions. Institutional infractions included violent, disruptive, other serious, lesser, and total infractions. In addition, program-related infractions, including drug-related infractions and noncompliance with urinalysis, were analyzed by PCL–R score. Overall, women higher in psychopathy were more problematic and incurred more institutional and program-related infractions.

During the Pre-program period, Factor 1, Factor 2, and PCL–R total scores were significantly related to violent, disruptive, lesser, and total infractions. Other serious infractions were uniquely related to Factor 2 scores. During the In-program period, the pattern of results was essentially the same, except that

Factor 1 was no longer significantly related to violent infractions. This finding raises interesting hypotheses regarding whether higher rates of the personality and emotional traits associated with Factor 1 allow women to modify their behavior to be more conducive to treatment progress.

Although the relationship between drug-related infractions and psychopathy was not significant either Pre-program or In-program, this may be partly explained by the significant association between psychopathy and urinalysis avoidance. Women highest in psychopathy were most likely to avoid providing a urine sample by not appearing for appointments or providing non-valid excuses to staff.

In an interesting methodological approach to measuring institutional adjustment, Salekin et al. (1997) administered the Personality Disorder Examination (PDE), the Personality Assessment Inventory (PAI), and the PCL–R to a sample of female inmates. In addition, they asked correctional officers to provide ratings on each inmate on the following dimensions: violence, verbal aggression, noncompliance, manipulation, remorse, and danger. Surprisingly, neither Factor 1, Factor 2, nor the PCL–R Total score was significantly related to any of these dimensions as rated by the correctional officers. However, each was significantly related to ASPD as measured by the PDE. In addition, inmates' self-reported antisocial behaviors, as measured by the PAI, were significantly correlated with correctional officers' ratings of violence, verbal aggression, manipulation, and danger.

RECIDIVISM

Despite its development as strictly a measure of a psychological construct (Hare, 2003), the PCL–R has been shown to be a robust predictor of general and violent recidivism. Psychopaths are more likely to recidivate than non-psychopaths and commit new crimes faster than nonpsychopaths (Hart, Kropp, & Hare, 1988; Serin, Peters, & Barbaree, 1990). For example, Serin (1996) administered the PCL–R to 81 male prison inmates before their conditional release from prison. The average follow-up time was 30 months. The failure rate was 57% for the entire sample, 38% for nonpsychopaths (PCL–R score <18), 54% for inmates with scores in the middle range, and 85% for the psychopaths (PCL–R score >28). Dichotomous outcome, that is, success or failure, was most highly correlated with PCL–R Factor 2 ($r = .36$) and Total scores ($r = .31$) and to a much lesser extent with Factor 1 scores ($r = .14$). Similarly, in a meta-analysis conducted by Hemphill, Hare, and Wong (1998), general recidivism was more strongly correlated with Factor 2 than with Factor 1 psychopathy scores.

Male psychopaths have also been shown to recidivate more rapidly, spending fewer offense-free days in the community than their nonpsychopathic counterparts. Porter et al. (2001) demonstrated that psychopaths (PCL–R score ≥30) recidivated significantly faster than did the nonpsychopaths. Of particular interest, these authors also found a strong interaction between psychopathy score, age, and survival rate. Among nonpsychopaths, the number of successful days increased dramatically over 40, consistent with the clinical notion that those with antisocial personality "burn-out" after age 40. Among psychopaths, successful days after release remained steady and even decreased after age 40.

Similar trends are seen for violent recidivism. For example, Serin and Amos (1995) found that the violent failure rate for psychopathic offenders was 35% compared with 23% for nonpsychopathic offenders. In a meta-analysis consisting of 18 PCL or PCL–R prediction studies (Salekin, Rogers, & Sewell, 1996), the mean effect size for violent outcome was .79, a large effect. The mean effect size for general recidivism was lower but was still moderate ($d = .55$). Salekin et al. concluded that the PCL–R was "unparalleled" as a risk assessment instrument (but see Gendreau, Goggin, & Smith, 2002, for an alternative view). Further, the authors reported that Factor 2 was a stronger predictor of both violent and general recidivism than Factor 1 and offered the opinion that individuals with psychopathy based primarily on Factor 1 items may pose less of a risk than individuals whose scores are weighed heavily with Factor 2 items.

Psychopathy, as measured by the PCL–R, has received so much support as a violence risk assessment measure; it is by far the most heavily weighted risk factor on the Violence Risk Appraisal Guide (Harris, Rice, & Quinsey, 1993), perhaps the most well-validated violence risk assessment instrument. It also figures prominently on other violence risk assessment instruments, including the HCR-20 (Webster, Douglas, Eaves, & Hart, 1997).

Despite the dozens of articles and chapters devoted to psychopathy's ability to predict violence and recidivism, little is known regarding the relationship between psychopathy and recidivism, particularly violent recidivism, among females. The first published report appeared in 1998 (Salekin, Rogers, Ustad, & Sewell, 1998), with only a few being published since then. Preliminary evidence suggests that significant gender differences exist in females' rates of recidivism, as well as their psychopathy-related risk factors. These studies demonstrate the need for gender-specific research in the area of psychopathy and highlight the degree of caution needed in trying to extend research findings to new populations.

Salekin et al. (1998) followed up on 78 female offenders (primarily Caucasian) 1 year after their release from a large urban jail. In addition to the PCL–R and its factors, the authors included related constructs of ASPD and aggressiveness, as measured by the PDE and the PAI. The overall recidivism rate for the sample was 41%, considerably lower than the recidivism rate found in male samples (approximately 60%; Serin, 1996).

Categorically, 12.9% of the sample was classified as PCL–R psychopaths ($\geq$30). Only 50% of these psychopathic offenders recidivated during the follow-up period. Reports with male offenders indicate that up to 85% of psychopaths reoffend (Hare et al., 2000; Serin, 1996). In contrast to findings with male offenders, only Factor 1 of the PCL–R was significantly related to recidivism in this female sample ($r = .26$). The Antisocial (ANT) scale of the PAI

(r =.26) and the Antisocial egocentricity (ANT–E) subscale (r = .27) were also significantly related to future recidivism. Self-reported aggression (r = .29), specifically verbal aggression and aggressive attitude, were most highly related (r = .29 and .25, respectively). Interestingly, self-ratings of physical aggression were not related to future criminality. Overall, personality and interpersonal factors contributed more to females' recidivism than did various behavioral indicators. Clearly, this finding has important implications for the risk assessment and management of female offenders.

Because of the small number of psychopaths (n = 10) in the sample, the point–biserial correlations reported earlier may have been attenuated. Utilizing the PCL–R, the PDE, and PAI dimensionally, Salekin et al. (1998) also conducted receiver operator characteristic analysis. Each of the psychopathy and ASPD measures predicted recidivism in this sample moderately at best (.64, .64, and .59 for ANT, PCL–R, and PDE, respectively). Finally, the authors entered the relevant scales and subscales into a discriminant function analysis. Again, Factor 1 of the PCL–R, ANT–E, and Aggression–Verbal (AGG-V) scales emerged as the strongest predictors of recidivism.

In a much larger study of incarcerated women (n = 404; primarily African American) Richards et al. (2003) collected re-arrest and reincarceration data for a subset of 239 participants who had at least 90 days of treatment. The average follow-up time was a little more than a year (13.93 months), during which time 29.7% were charged with a new offense. Of note, there were no psychopaths classified by a PCL–R score ≥30 in this study owing to their exclusion from the larger drug treatment study. Despite their removal, the overall mean PCL–R Total score was 15.00 (SD = 7.07), similar to the mean for females in other treatment samples.

Surprisingly, psychopathy scores were not related to re-arrest. However, consistent with findings with male offenders, a significant relationship existed between number of days in the community and psychopathy scores (r = −.24, p < .01). Women in the low psychopathy group spent significantly more offense-free days in the community (525 days, SD = 325) than did women in the high psychopathy group (321 days, SD = 252).

To control for time at risk, Cox regression analysis was performed. Only Factor 1 of the PCL–R contributed to the prediction of recidivism. A 1-point increase above the group mean Factor 1 score was associated with an ~11% increase in hazard for arrest. Treatment condition, days in treatment, and PCL–R Total and Factor 2 scores all failed to predict time to arrest.

Neither Salekin et al. (1998) nor Richards et al. (2003) investigated violent recidivism as separate from general recidivism. However, in terms of general recidivism, females high in Factor 1 appear to be at greater risk of community failure, directly in contrast to the evidence regarding male offenders (see, e.g., Salekin et al., 1996). Very little is known about patterns of female violence, particularly as it relates to psychopathy and its components. Patterns of violence among male psychopaths suggest that males higher in Factor 1 may be at greater risk of committing violence characterized as instrumental or predatory, whereas primarily Factor 2 dominant psychopaths may be more reactive in their violence. Whether this pattern is similar for female offenders remains uninvestigated, although gender differences in violence base rates suggested that this pattern may not generalize. Women have lower rates of violent behavior and, when committed, violence is more often toward a partner or family member in the midst of an argument. Given these gender differences, would Factor 1 be as important a predictor of violence in women as it is for general offending? Or would the lack of behavioral controls and general impulsivity associated with Factor 2 be more likely to predict the type of violence typically perpetrated by women? Naturally, more research is necessary before any conclusions can be drawn regarding the pattern of violence in women and the potential for differential relationships to the PCL–R factors.

THE LATENT STRUCTURE OF FEMALE PSYCHOPATHY

Psychopathy can be understood as consisting of a "constellation of affective, interpersonal, and behavioral characteristics" (Hare, 1996). Exploratory factor analytic and confirmatory factor analytic studies are used to investigate the number and nature of these underlying constructs, in addition to how well particular items measure the theoretical constructs in question. Recent research on the exact nature of these underlying dimensions, as well as gender differences, or lack thereof, in factor structure has generated a great deal of renewed interest regarding the "proper" factor structure of psychopathy. More information about the nature of these studies can be found in other chapters of this volume (see, e.g., Bolt, chap. 5, this volume; Neumann, Kosson, & Salekin, chap. 4, this volume). Instead, in this section we will discuss current research in terms of its implications for understanding and describing psychopathy as it manifests in females.

The two-factor conceptualization of psychopathy (Hare et al., 1990; Harpur et al., 1988, 1989) has dominated the majority of research efforts and clinical understanding of this disorder. Because the PCL and PCL–R were validated on Caucasian males, little was known regarding the underlying dimensions among females. Salekin, Rogers, and Sewell (1997) provided the first published factor analytic study with female offenders. Using exploratory techniques, Salekin et al. (1997) demonstrated that an alternative two-factor structure most appropriately represented the underlying construct of psychopathy in females. Although the dimensions were essentially consistent with that found in males (i.e., a personality related dimension and a behaviorally related dimension), important differences were also found. First, many items cross-loaded with the female sample, suggesting that some items were equally characteristic of each dimension. Second, two items loaded significantly in the female sample that had not previously been included in the two-factor conceptualization of psychopathy in males. These items, promiscuity and criminal versatility, loaded substantially onto the behavioral factor. With confirmatory factor analytic approaches, the traditional two-factor model has also been rejected with female patients receiving methadone (Darke et al., 1998), as well as jail and prison inmates (Jackson et al., 2002; Warren et al., 2003).

The paradigm shift that occurred with the publication of Cooke and Michie's (2001) three-factor model of psychopathy proved important for the conceptualization of female psychopathy as well. The three-factor model deconstructs the traditional Factor 1 into two related dimensions of Arrogant and Deceitful Interpersonal style and Deficient Affective Experiences. Notably, it also truncates the traditional Factor 2 by eliminating the items directly related to criminal and otherwise antisocial activity, resulting in a Lifestyle factor. Utilizing confirmatory factor analytic techniques, Jackson et al. (2002) demonstrated an adequate fit for the three-factor model with female offenders. Unfortunately, the three-factor model also excludes promiscuity and criminal versatility, suggested by Salekin et al. (1997; see also Jackson, 2001) as being important to the underlying disorder in females. The likely conclusion is that psychopathy in females can be partially understood in terms of Cooke and Michie's three-factors, yet important information regarding the expression of psychopathy is not captured by existing models.

Most recently, Hare (2003) introduced an alternative conceptualization of psychopathy. This four-factor (or facet) model retains the broad dimensions of personality and behavior, but deconstructs each of these broad dimensions into facets. Cooke and Michie's (2001) Interpersonal, Affective, and Lifestyle factors were retained, and an Antisocial facet, consisting of the criminal or antisocial items (including criminal versatility), was added. Using a sample of female prison inmates, Warren et al. (2003) found only a moderate fit for this four-factor model.

Utilizing item response theory, Bolt, Hare, Vitale, and Newman (2004) conducted differential item functioning (DIF) analyses of the PCL–R with several groups, including female offenders. Compared with results in the reference group of male offenders, items measuring antisocial behavior (i.e., items on Facets 3 and 4) evidenced more DIF than the more personality based items on Facets 1 and 2. Specifically, large differences were seen in the items measuring early behavior problems, juvenile delinquency, and criminal versatility, with females obtaining lower scores on these behaviorally based items. The lack of DIF for the majority of the personality based items seems to support the notion of core personality traits associated with psychopathy that can be reliably measured and used to distinguish psychopathic from nonpsychopathic individuals, regardless of gender.

Without exception, the research to date regarding the factor structure of psychopathy in females has been a reaction to findings with males. Exploratory factor analytic studies (e.g., Salekin et al., 1997) suggested that a model of psychopathy built exclusively for females may differ in important ways. For example, promiscuity would be likely to emerge as a significant component of a behavioral or lifestyle factor (Grann, 2000; Salekin et al., 1997). Existing models, although providing an adequate fit to female samples, probably describe only a small portion of psychopathic behavior in women.

LABORATORY STUDIES

The hypothesis that gender differences exist in the core features of psychopathy begs the question, What are the core deficits? Cleckley (1941/1976) hypothesized that psychopaths suffer from an affective or information processing deficit that predisposes them to commit acts that are harmful to themselves as well as society. Information processing deficits, of both the cognitive and emotional variety, have been researched primarily through the use of laboratory experimental paradigms. Among males, the information processing deficit hypothesis has generated a great deal of support. Only recently have researchers tested this hypothesis with females. Tentative conclusions suggest that information processing deficits exist but may be more linked to the processing of emotional, rather than cognitive, information. The studies reviewed here begin to shape the laboratory exploration of psychopathy in females and serve to generate important hypotheses for future investigations.

Cognitive/Behavioral Deficits

Newman (1998) advanced the response modulation hypothesis to help explain why psychopaths continue in a dominant response set (response perseveration), even when it is detrimental to them. Response modulation refers to brief, relatively automatic shifts of attention from the implementation of goal-directed behavior to the evaluation of the behavior (a shift from content to process). Most individuals will attend to peripheral cues and use that information to alter their behavior accordingly.

A computerized card task has become a popular paradigm with which to test response perseveration among psychopaths. In essence, the card task sets up a dominant response to continue playing the game by setting the initial odds of winning quite high. Over the course of the game, the odds of winning decrease. Psychopathic males end up losing more money than nonpsychopathic males, presumably because they are less aware of the changing odds or less likely to change their behavior based on the changing odds. This behavior is an experimental analog to the observations that psychopathic offenders appear to ignore the punishing consequences of their behavior, such as loss of freedom during incarceration, while concentrating on rewarding consequences, such as the opportunity for status within prison inmate hierarchies. These experimental results have been replicated extensively with psychopathic males to the extent that response modulation is considered a core deficit in psychopathy (Newman, 1998).

In the only published attempt to replicate these results with female psychopaths, Vitale and Newman (2001b) used the card task with a sample of 112 female offenders. In this study, they did not find support for the response modulation hypothesis with females. Specifically, women classified as psychopaths did not play significantly more cards than their nonpsychopathic counterparts. When used dimensionally, no relationship existed between PCL–R score and number of cards played. Likewise, psychopathic women did not lose more money during the game than the nonpsychopathic women.

As the first study of its kind, no firm conclusions may be drawn from Vitale and Newman's (2001) results. Important limitations in this study exist, most notably the small number of women meeting the cutoff for psychopathy classification ($n = 11$). The authors also suggested that the PCL–R may not adequately assess psychopathy in women, and therefore failed to classify the participants properly. Other possible hypotheses for the observed difference are perhaps more closely related to the current discussion of gender differences. For the sake of argument, let us suppose that the current results (no behavioral inhibition deficits in psychopathic females) are replicated in a dozen studies using the card-playing task. The hypothesis of behavioral disinhibition or response modulation deficits still would not be disconfirmed. The hypothesis suggests that once a goal is set and motivation to meet that goal is present, the behavior becomes "locked in." Quite possibly, winning money is not a sufficiently motivating goal for females. In other words, the response modulation deficit may still exist, but it has not been activated by the current paradigm. The underlying gender difference may be not in the deficit but in the value or desirability of the given goal.

Newman and Wallace (1993) advanced two other personality traits, in addition to psychopathy, that may account for response modulation deficits in offenders: anxiety and impulsivity. Although impulsivity has not been investigated as a potential source of response modulation deficits in women, an investigation of response modulation and trait anxiety has been recently conducted with this population (MacCoon & Newman, 2003). In a computerized picture–word task involving threatening and nonthreatening cues, high-anxious female offenders (neurotic introverts), contrasted with control participants, were more vigilant to peripheral cues and made more task errors. In effect, they found peripheral cues more relevant than primary cues. This type of dysregulation in the presence of punishment is the opposite of the response modulation deficit demonstrated in male psychopaths, in which punishment is discounted within a reward-dominant context. Unfortunately, although PCL–R data were collected, the currently published report does not contain data relating psychopathy to the observed response modulation failure in the high-anxious group. Also, no parallel study has been performed using male offenders as participants.

Emotional Deficits

Patrick and colleagues (see, e.g., Patrick, 1994; Patrick, Bradley, & Lang, 1993) designed a series of experiments with which they found that male psychopaths did not show the expected blink–startle response when exposed to emotionally arousing stimuli. Specifically, these experiments have individuals view pictures with various emotional valence: positive, neutral, and unpleasant.

During viewing, sudden auditory stimuli are presented. Nonpsychopaths exhibit a larger blink response while viewing unpleasant stimuli than pleasant stimuli (relative to neutral stimuli). In contrast, psychopaths' blink response was smaller to both pleasant and unpleasant stimuli than to neutral stimuli. This deficit was most related to the traditional Factor 1 of psychopathy, the emotional–affective domain.

In an effort to replicate this emotion processing deficit with female offenders, Sutton, Vitale, and Newman (2002) tested 172 offenders (24 psychopaths or 13.9%) with the picture perception paradigm. In addition, they examined the role of trait anxiety in modulating startle response, an investigation that has not been performed using male psychopaths. They found that female psychopaths exhibited a blink–startle response similar to that of their male counterparts. Differences in the blink–startle response were most pronounced for low-anxiety psychopaths with both high Factor 1 and Factor 2 scores. As with male samples, female subjects responded more normally when probes were presented later during the presentation of pictures. In sum, it appears that psychopaths of both genders have a delayed, rather than absent, emotional response (Levenston, Patrick, Bradley & Lang, 2000). It is unclear from current studies, however, whether emotional responding is modulated by trait anxiety in male psychopaths, as is the case for females. Testing whether this pattern will generalize across genders is important because the relationship between anxiety and the phenotypic expression of psychopathy may be different for males and females. For example, as previously mentioned, females with ASPD generally report higher levels of anxiety than do males with this disorder. Also, in a large sample study of personality correlates of psychopathy using a NEO-Personality Inventory–Revised-based Psychopathy Resemblance Index, Miller, Lynam, Widiger, and Leukenfeld (2001) found significant negative relationships between psychopathy resemblance and generalized anxiety symptoms of worries ($-.17, p < .01$) and social phobia ($-.22, p < .001$) for women, whereas for males the corresponding correlations were nonsignificant ($-.06$ and $-.16$, respectively).

HYPOTHESES REGARDING THE CAUSES
OF DIFFERENTIAL PHENOTYPIC EXPRESSION
OF PSYCHOPATHY BY GENDER

Because considerable controversy and lack of certainty regarding the central deficits and defects underlying psychopathy still remain, it is not surprising that the explanation of observed gender differences is similarly controversial and uncertain. A range of psychosocial and biological factors and their interaction remain viable candidates. Because exploring these differences may ultimately inform the entire endeavor of understanding psychopathy, several lines of thinking which implicate factors that may in the future result in fruitful empirical investigations are discussed.

Psychosocial Hypotheses Regarding Differential
Phenotypic Expression of Psychopathy

Because the socialization and social role expectations for males and females differ markedly in most societies, psychosocial explanations of the origin of differences in psychopathy have an obvious appeal. Girls are taught and encouraged to practice interpersonal and emotional skills such as sharing, negotiation, and empathy. Throughout the lifespan, females are more frequently called upon to act as caregivers and to provide emotional support to others. Aggression, tough-minded, self-centered behavior and open self-assertion in girls may be met with relatively frequent and consistent disapproval and punishment, whereas corresponding behaviors in boys may be met with a wider range of responses, including frank approval and reward, emotional and behavioral ambivalence, and ignoring of the behavior as being gender consistent, as in the idiom "boys will be boys." Cultural values of the traditional family in most societies prepare girls to become primary care providers for children and elderly and sick persons and to submit to male direction and control. Stronger prohibitions against females than males engaging in sexual activity outside of marriage exist in most societies, and such mores may even condemn sexual interest on the part of women in any context. Girls and women may be cautioned more frequently about the harmful features of environments and activities, and others may draw attention to the inadequacies of females rather than to their capabilities in dealing with challenges. This complex system of gender-related social roles, expectations, and reinforcements may attenuate aggressive and hedonistic motivations while accentuating harm avoidance, social anxiety, and the acquisition of social and emotional skills in girls, resulting in a pattern of influences on development that run counter to the aggression, hedonism, and emotional–interpersonal retardation of psychopathy.

Biological Hypotheses Regarding Differential
Phenotypic Expression of Psychopathy

Differential phenotypic expression of personality can be based in genetically heritable characteristics, acquired physical deficits, environmental or experiential factors, or the interaction of these causes. Twin studies suggest that the heritability of normal personality traits is within the range of 40% to 60%, similar to the heritability of antisocial behaviors and psychopathy. In the case of psychopathy, it is likely the genetic component displays incomplete penetrance; that is, there are several phenotypes, showing degrees of expression and responsivity of expression to environmental conditions. Unlike speculations regarding differential expression in psychopathy in regard to race, in which a clear genetic basis separate from social construction of the race concept is absent, in regard to gender a clear genetic difference does exist in the sex chromosomes that determine primary and secondary sexual characteristics which, in turn, govern the types and typical serum levels of hormones.

Reports of gender-based differences in the expression of heritable characteristics having an impact on complex behaviors are increasingly being seen in the scientific literature. For example, a gender-specific association between the frequency of suicide attempts and their lethality with bimorphism in a serotonin transporter cell has been reported, such that one form of the transporter, but not the other, was associated with increased suicidality and lethality, in women, but not in men (Baca-Garcia et al., 2002). For anxiety, a trait found to be a moderator in regard to psychopathy correlates, studies in two independent samples revealed that the 5-HTT polymorphism (involved in modulation of serotonin uptake) accounts for 3%–4% of the total variation and 7%–9% of the inherited variance in neuroticism in individuals as well as siblings (Lesch et al., 1996); however, this finding was not replicable for a female sample (Du, Bakish, & Hrdina, 2000), suggesting to the investigators that gender differences exist in the contribution of genetic factors to the behavioral phenotypes defined primarily by neuroticism.

Not surprisingly, notions concerning differential expression of psychopathic core traits by gender have appeared recurrently in the theoretical literature and have been the subject of some empirical investigations. The majority of these efforts have focused on the rates of and comorbidity among four disorders: ASPD, borderline personality disorder, histrionic personality disorder, and somatization disorder (Cale & Lilienfeld, 2002). Two of these disorders, somatization disorder and histrionic personality disorder, were previously conceptualized in classical psychiatry under the rubric of hysteria. The symptoms of hysteria included conversion disorders, somatization of feeling states, a tendency to dissociate in conflict situations, and an overly dramatic, attention-getting style. These symptoms relate to hyperemotionality and were classically interpreted as forms of nonverbal communication of unconscious, often unacceptable, relationship concerns, symptomatic themes that are on the surface far removed from, if not the inverse of, the psychopathic lack of interpersonal bonding, and relative indifference to affective aspects of experience. Males have a higher frequency of ASPD and lower rate of occurrence and comorbidity of the remaining disorders when contrasted with females. Some theorists have viewed these different rates of diagnosis as a matter of differential thresholds between males and females for the level of severity required for the overt expression of psychopathology of a given type. Others have viewed these differences from the perspective of social construction of behavior, i.e., as the result of the influence of gender roles or from diagnostic bias due to gender stereotyping of female behavior. Most empirical studies of these issues have suffered from the use of low-validity measures of psychopathy (i.e., measures other than the Hare PCL and PCL–R), the use of small sample sizes, or the failure to directly test the hypothesis of gender differences with appropriate statistical techniques. For example, as early as the 1970s, Cloninger, Christiansen, Reich, and Gottesman (1978) had explored gender differences in the familial transmission of *sociopathy* and the role of sociopathy and hysteria (the partial proto-type of current formulations of somatization disorder and histrionic person-ality disorder) in antisocial behavior in females, concluding that differences between males and females in regard to criminality were due to familial influences.

Deficient psychophysiological arousal/arousability was recently identi-fied by Eysenck (1996) as a candidate for understanding the central deficit in psychopathy. Eysenck viewed arousal/arousability as an underlying general psychobiological trait with a high genetic load that is associated with high extroversion and high psychoticism in his three-factor model of personality. Relevant to the issue of possible gender differences in psychopaths, he pro-posed that testosterone and monoamine oxidase exacerbate the effects of poor arousability on criminal behavior. As a consequence of the typically lower titrates of these biochemicals in females, they provide a similar mod-erating effect for female behavior. Monoamine oxidase has been shown to be negatively correlated with criminal activity and PCL–R scores (Lidberg et al., 1985; Stalenheim, 2001). This relationship was shown to be highly sta-ble over time and predictive of criminal recidivism and correlated with per-sonality measures (Karolinska Scale of Personality). In violent recidivists, there was a remarkably high correlation between triiodothyronine levels and Karolinska Scale of Personality Irritability and Detachment. Thyroid hor-mones such as triiodothyronine and thyroxine have been suggested as mark-ers for psychopathy, based on their significant correlations with both psy-chopathy (PCL–R Total score and Factor 2 scores) and repeated violent criminality (Stålenheim, Knorring, & Wide, 1998).

Overall, low monoamine oxidase activity, which is more characteristic of males than females, is associated with agitated behavior and disinhibition and may reflect some of the mediating effects of serotonin and sex hormones (especially androgens) on criminal behavior (Ellis, 1991). Although these hor-mones are responsive to ongoing stress and to previous life experience, pre-senting viable environmental and experiential hypotheses, on average it is reasonable to assume that they may contribute to some extent to observed differences between males and females in regard to frequency, severity, and expression of psychopathy.

SUMMARY AND CONCLUSIONS

Studies of psychopathy in women have advanced considerably beyond the early case anecdotes of Cleckley and others. Although interest continues in related and analogous disorders (antisocial personality disorder) and in gen-der differentiated comorbidity (for example with histrionic personality dis-order and somatization disorder), the PCL–R operationalization of psy-chopathy in women offenders, as with their male counterparts, has resulted in the most productive lines of investigation. These studies have demon-strated that women offenders can be reliably assessed using the PCL–R. Most

PCL–R items function similarly in male and females, although with a few nuances, such as sexual promiscuity and criminal versatility relating differently by gender to the underlying disorder. The factor structure of the PCL–R in women appears to be better represented by three- or four-factor solutions than by the original two-factor solution.

In regard to validity, the lower rates of recidivism in women may account for the somewhat lower correlations of recidivism to the PCL–R in women compared with men. In contrast to general recidivism, several studies have shown that psychopathy accounts for more variance in violent crimes and criminal versatility in women than in men and that the affective interpersonal items of the traditional Factor 1 are more predictive than the lifestyle and antisocial items of Factor 2.

The study of laboratory correlates of psychopathy in women remains at a preliminary stage. On the one hand, it has not been demonstrated that female psychopaths have the same passive avoidance learning response modulation deficit that has been replicated in males. Differences in trait anxiety and differential valuing of motivating characteristics of the laboratory tasks may account for the absence of this deficit in women. On the other hand, women psychopaths have the same pattern of startle paradigm affective deficit as their male counterparts, suggesting that the core emotional deficit may generalize across gender, even if a core attentional deficit may be moderated by gender-related variables.

Future research in the area of psychopathy would be greatly benefited by further replication of previous studies performed on male offenders and generation of new models with the female psychopaths specifically in mind. Researchers examining the downward extensions of psychopathy into childhood and adolescence should posit and explore differential pathways for males and females, and a few key biological markers, related to but not identical with gender, should be included in such a research agenda. Similarly, the role of childhood sexual and physical abuse in promoting the development of psychopathy may differ by gender, due to both differences in the likelihood of victimization and also differences in the range of responses available to the child and to the social meaning of externalizing versus internalizing responses to abuse. Replications of laboratory cognitive affective correlates may require significant modification of techniques for female offenders. For example, the type of reward, such as visitation time or telephone tokens for money might provide greater motivation for females, and may better differentiate between types of psychopaths than do small monetary rewards. Because women often are more relationally oriented versus task oriented than men, studies examining the importance of a clinical interview in the assessment of psychopathy, the role of gender of the interviewer, and the value of relating to the experimenter in laboratory studies might yield patterns that are of little significance in men. Finally, although the behavior and social impact of male noncriminal psychopaths, such as those seen in the corporate world, has only recently been initiated, a parallel investigation of female psychopaths is also possible. Settings and careers that are primarily populated by women and activities such as childrearing, especially when legal disputes arise, might be particularly promising arenas in this regard.

REFERENCES

Baca-Garcia, E., Vaquero, C., Diaz-Sastre, C., Saiz-Ruiz, J., Fernandez-Piqueras, J., & de Leon, J. (2002). A gender-specific association between the serotonin transporter gene and suicide attempts. *Neuropsychopharmacology, 26*, 692–695.

Bolt, D. M., Hare, R. D., Vitale, J. E., & Newman, J. P. (2004). A multigroup item response theory analysis of the Psychopathy Checklist–Revised. *Psychological Assessment, 16*, 155–168.

Brinkley, C. A., Schmitt, W. A., Smith, S. S., & Newman, J. P. (2001). Construct validation of a self-report psychopathy scale: Does Levenson's self-report scale measure the same construct as Hare's Psychopathy Checklist–Revised? *Personality and Individual Differences, 31*, 1021–1038.

Cale, E. M., & Lilienfeld, S. O. (2002). Sex differences in psychopathy and antisocial personality disorder. A review and integration. *Clinical Psychology Review, 22*, 1179–1207.

Cleckley, H. (1976). *The mask of sanity*. St. Louis: Mosby. (Original work published 1941)

Cloninger, C. R., Christiansen, K. O., Reich, T., & Gottesman, I. I. (1978). Implications of sex differences in the prevalences of antisocial personality, alcoholism, and criminality for familial transmission. *Archives of General Psychiatry, 35*, 941–951.

Cooke, D. J. (1995). Psychopathic disturbance in the Scottish prison populations: Cross-cultural generalizability of the Hare Psychopathy Checklist. *Psychology, Crime, and Law, 2*, 101–118.

Cooke, D. J., & Michie, C. (2001). Refining the construct of psychopathy: Towards a hierarchical model. *Psychological Assessment, 13*, 171–188.

Darke, S., Kaye, S., & Finlay-Jones, R. (1998). Antisocial personality disorder, psychopathy, and injecting heroin use. *Drug and Alcohol Dependence, 52*, 63–69.

Du, L., Bakish, D., & Hrdina, P. D. (2000). Gender differences in association between serotonin transporter gene polymorphism and personality traits. *Psychiatric Genetics, 10*, 159–164.

Edens, J. F., Buffington-Vollum, J. K., Colwell, K. W., Johnson, D. W., & Johnson, J. K. (2002). Psychopathy and institutional misbehavior among incarcerated sex offenders: A comparison of the Psychopathy Checklist–Revised and the Personality Assessment Inventory. *International Journal of Forensic Mental Health, 1*, 49–58.

Ellis, L. (1991). Monoamine oxidase and criminality: Identifying an apparent biological marker for antisocial behavior. *Journal of Research in Crime & Delinquency, 28*, 227–251.

Eysenck, H. J. (1996). Personality theory and the problem of criminality. In *Criminological perspectives: A reader* (pp. 81–98). Thousand Oaks, CA: Sage.

Forth, A. E., Brown, S. L., Hart, S. D., & Hare, R. D. (1996). The assessment of psychopathy in male and female noncriminals: Reliability and validity. *Personality and Individual Differences, 20*, 531–543.

Gendreau, P., Goggin, C., & Smith, P. (2002). Is the PCL–R really the "unparalleled" measure of offender risk? A lesson in knowledge cumulation. *Criminal Justice and Behavior, 29*, 397–426.

Goldstein, R. B., Powers, S. I., McCusker, J., & Mundt, K. A. (1996). Gender differences in the manifestations of antisocial personality disorder among residential drug abuse treatment clients. *Drug and Alcohol Dependence, 41*, 35–45.

Grann, M. (2000). The PCL–R and gender. *European Journal of Psychological Assessment, 16*, 147–149.

Hare, R. D. (1996). Psychopathy: A clinical construct whose time has come. *Criminal Justice and Behavior, 23*, 25–54.

Hare, R. D. (2003). *Hare PCL–R Technical Manual* (2nd ed.). Toronto, Ontario, Canada: Multi-Health Systems.

Hare, R. D., Clark, D., Grann, M., & Thornton, D. (2000). Psychopathy and the predictive validity of the PCL–R: An international perspective. *Behavioral Sciences and the Law, 18*, 623–645.

Hare, R. D., Harpur, T. J., Hakstian, A. R., Forth, A. E., Hart, S. D., & Newman, J. P. (1990). The revised Psychopathy Checklist: Reliability and factor structure. *Psychological Assessment, 2*, 338–341.

Harpur, T. J., Hakstian, A. R., & Hare, R. D. (1988). Factor structure of the Psychopathy Checklist. *Journal of Consulting and Clinical Psychology, 56*, 741–747.

Harpur, T. J., Hare, R. D., & Hakstian, A. R., (1989). Two-factor conceptualization of psychopathy: Construct validity and assessment implications. *Psychological Assessment, 1*, 6–17.

Harris, G. T., Rice, M. E., & Quinsey, V. L. (1993). Violent recidivism of mentally disordered offenders: The development of a statistical prediction instrument. *Criminal Justice and Behavior, 20*, 315–335.

Hart, S. D., Kropp, P. R., & Hare, R. D. (1988). Performance of psychopaths following conditional release from prison. *Journal of Consulting and Clinical Psychology, 56*, 227–232.

Hartung, C. M., & Widiger, T. A. (1998). Gender differences in the diagnosis of mental disorders: Conclusions and controversies of the DSM-IV. *Psychological Bulletin, 123*, 260–278.

Hemphill, J. F., Hare, R. D., & Wong, S. (1998). Psychopathy and recidivism: A review. *Legal and Criminological Psychology, 3*, 139–170.

Jackson, R. L. (2001). *Assessment of psychopathy in incarcerated females.* Unpublished master's thesis. University of North Texas.

Jackson, R. L., Rogers, R., Neumann, C. S., & Lambert, P. L. (2002). Psychopathy in female offenders: An investigation of its underlying dimensions. *Criminal Justice and Behavior, 29*, 692–704.

Kosson, D. S., Smith, S. S., & Newman, J. P. (1990). Evaluating the construct validity of psychopathy in Black and White male inmates: Three preliminary studies. *Journal of Abnormal Psychology, 99*, 250–259.

Kroner, D. G., & Mills, J. F. (2001). The accuracy of five risk appraisal instruments in predicting institutional misconduct and new convictions. *Criminal Justice and Behavior, 28*, 471–489.

Lesch, K.-P., Bengel, D., Heils, A., Sabol, S. Z., Greenberg, B. D., Petri, S., et al. (1996). Association of anxiety-related traits with a polymorphism in the serotonin transporter gene regulatory region. *Science, 274*, 1527–1531.

Levenston, G. K., Patrick, C. J., Bradley, M. M., & Lang, P. J. (2000). The psychopath as observer: Emotion and attention in picture processing. *Journal of Abnormal Psychology, 109*, 373–385.

Lidberg, L., Modin, I., Oreland, L., Tuck, J. R., & Gillner, A. (1985). Platelet monoamine oxidase activity and psychopathy. *Psychiatry Research, 16*, 339–343.

Louth, S. M., Hare, R. D., & Linden, W. (1998). Psychopathy and alexithymia in female offenders. *Canadian Journal of Behavioural Science, 30*, 91–98.

MacCoon, D. G., & Newman, J. P. (2003). Dysregulation in high-anxious female prisoners: Attentionally mediated? *Cognitive Therapy and Research, 27*, 681–696.

Miller, J. D., Lynam, D. R., Widiger, T. A., & Leukefeld, C. (2001). Personality disorders as extreme variants of common personality dimensions: Can the Five-Factor Model adequately represent psychopathy? *Journal of Personality, 69*, 253–276.

Mulder, R. T., Wells, J. E., & Bushnell, J. A. (1994). Antisocial Women. *Journal of Personality Disorders, 8*, 279–287.

Newman, J. P. (1998). Psychopathic behavior: An information processing perspective. In D. J. Cooke, A. E. Forth, & R. D. Hare (Eds.), *Psychopathy: Theory, research and implications for society* (pp. 81–104). Dordrecht, The Netherlands: Kluwer Academic.

Newman, J. P., & Wallace, J. F. (1993). Diverse pathways to deficient self-regulation: Implications for disinhibitory psychopathology in children. *Clinical Psychology Review, 13*, 699–720

Patrick, C. J. (1994). Emotion and psychopathy: Startling new insights. *Psychophysiology, 31*, 319–330.

Patrick, C. J. Bradley, M. M., & Lang, P. J. (1993). Emotion in the criminal psychopath. Startle reflex modulation. *Journal of Abnormal Psychology, 103*, 82–92.

Porter, S., Birt, A. R., & Boer, D. P. (2001). Investigation of the criminal and conditional release profiles of Canadian federal offenders as function of psychopathy and age. *Law and Human Behavior, 25*, 647–661.

Richards, H. J., Casey, J. O., & Lucente, S. W. (2003). Psychopathy and treatment response in incarcerated female substance abusers. *Criminal Justice and Behavior, 30*, 251–276.

Rutherford, M. J., Alterman, A. I., Cacciola, J. S., & McKay, J. R. (1997). Validity of the Psychopathy Checklist–Revised in male methadone patients. *Drug and Alcohol Dependence, 44*, 143–149.

Rutherford, M. J., Alterman, A. I., Cacciola, J. S., & McKay, J. R. (1998). Gender differences in the relationship of antisocial personality disorder criteria to Psychopathy Checklist–Revised scores. *Journal of Personality Disorders, 12*, 69–76.

Rutherford, M. J., Cacciola, J. S., Alterman, A. I., & McKay, J. R. (1996). Reliability and validity of the Revised Psychopathy Checklist in women methadone patients. *Assessment, 3*, 43–54.

Salekin, R. T., Rogers, R., & Sewell, K. W. (1996). A review and meta-analysis of the Psychopathy Checklist and Psychopathy Checklist–Revised: Predictive validity of dangerousness. *Clinical Psychology: Science and Practice, 3*, 203–215.

Salekin, R. T., Rogers, R., & Sewell, K. W. (1997). Construct validity of psychopathy in a female offender sample: A multitrait–multimethod evaluation. *Journal of Abnormal Psychology, 106*, 576–585.

Salekin, R. T., Rogers, R., Ustad, K. L., & Sewell, K. W. (1998). Psychopathy and recidivism among female inmates. *Law and Human Behavior, 22*, 109–128.

Serin, R. C. (1996). Violent recidivism in criminal psychopaths. *Law and Human Behavior, 20*, 207–217.

Serin, R. C., & Amos, N. L. (1995). The role of psychopathy in the assessment of dangerousness. *International Journal of Law and Psychiatry, 18*, 231–238.

Serin, R. C., Peters, R. D., & Barbaree, H. E. (1990). Predictors of psychopathy and release outcome in a criminal population. *Psychological Assessment: A Journal of Consulting and Clinical Psychology, 2*, 419–422.

Silverthorn, P., & Frick, P. J. (1999). Developmental pathways to antisocial behavior: The delayed-onset pathway in girls. *Development and Psychopathology, 11*, 101–126.

Silverthorn, P., Frick, P. J., & Reynolds, R. (2001). Timing of onset and correlates of severe conduct problems in adjudicated girls and boys. *Journal of Psychopathology and Behavioral Assessment, 23*, 171–181.

Simourd, D. J., & Hoge, R. D. (2000). Criminal psychopathy: A risk-and-need perspective. *Criminal Justice and Behavior, 27*, 256–272.

Stålenheim, E. G. (2001). Relationships between attempted suicide, temperamental vulnerability, and violent criminality in a Swedish forensic psychiatric population. *European Psychiatry, 16*, 386–394.

Stålenheim, E. G., von Knorring, L., & Wide, L. (1998). Serum levels of thyroid hormones as biological markers in a Swedish forensic psychiatric population. *Biological Psychiatry, 43*, 755–761.

Strachan, C. E. (1993). *The assessment of psychopathy in female offenders*. Unpublished doctoral dissertation. University of British Columbia, Vancouver, Canada.

Sutton, S. K., Vitale, J. E., & Newman, J. P. (2002). Emotion among women with psychopathy during picture perception. *Journal of Abnormal Psychology, 111*, 610–619.

Vitale, J. E., & Newman, J. P. (2001a). Using the Psychopathy Checklist–Revised with female samples: Reliability, validity, and implications for clinical utility. *Clinical Psychology: Science and Practice, 8*, 117–132.

Vitale, J. E., & Newman, J. P. (2001b). Response perseveration in psychopathic women. *Journal of Abnormal Psychology, 110*, 644–647.

Warren, J. I., Burnette, M. L., South, S. C., Chauhan, P., Bale, R., Friend, R., & VanPatten, I. (2003). Psychopathy in women: Structural modeling and comorbidity. *International Journal of Law and Psychiatry, 26*, 223–242.

Webster, C. D., Douglas, K. S., Eaves, D., & Hart, S. D. (1997). *HCR-20: Assessing risk for violence*. Lutz, FL: Psychological Assessment Resources.

Zoccolillo, M. (1993). Gender and the development of conduct disorder. *Development and Psychopathology, 5*, 65–78.

Zoccolillo, M., Tremblay, R., & Vitaro, F. (1996). DSM-III–R and DSM-III criteria for conduct disorder in preadolescent girls: Specific but insensitive. *Journal of the American Academy of Child and Adolescent Psychiatry, 35*, 461–470.

16

From Darkness Into the Light: Psychopathy in Industrial and Organizational Psychology

Paul Babiak

In this chapter I provide a brief review of the research to date on psychopaths working in business settings. I begin by tracking the evolution of psychopathy research in industrial–organizational (I–O) psychology and providing evidence that psychopaths do appear able to infiltrate the corporate world. A model explaining the psychopath's ability to prosper within the business world through manipulation and conning is then presented. Issues pertaining to the assessment of psychopathy in I–O settings are then discussed, following which a new instrument—the B-Scan 360—is introduced. I conclude with future directions and implications for society.

PSYCHOPATHS AT WORK

As an industrial-organizational (I–O) psychologist, I get the chance to study people doing what most of us spend much of our lives doing—working. Whether we love our work or hate our work, we tend to do a lot of it, and this offers the I–O psychologist plenty of opportunity for study. The field itself has evolved from its "industrial" psychology roots, which focused on employee selection, performance improvement, and understanding job satisfaction and the characteristics that define the ideal employee to now include more "organizational" variables, such as group dynamics, leadership research, and overall organizational effectiveness and development. As an applied field of study, the research is very often conducted in real time, with real people doing real work. Laboratory experiments are also conducted and a rich empirical base has evolved from both of these approaches. In true scientist–practitioner fashion, it is common for a researcher to take his or her observations, develop a model and then test it both in the laboratory and organizational settings. Much of the research results are then used to solve real-life problems, as the ultimate goal of our research is to improve organizational and personal effectiveness.

The study of personality as an important individual difference variable by I–O psychologists has grown in popularity during the past 15 years. Until recently, much of this research has focused on normal or *bright side* traits—those personality characteristics thought to be associated with good leadership, effective teamwork, and productive work performance (see Hogan, 1991, for an excellent review). The negative aspects of personality—referred to as the *dark side*—and the impact they have on coworkers and performance have received far less attention, except from a few researchers. The study of the dysfunctional aspects of personality has taken somewhat longer to gain acceptance, except in professions in which the potential impact of dark side traits is of great importance, such as in selection of police, firefighters, and other public safety staff. The primary outcome variables studied include supervisory ratings of performance on the positive side and counterproductive work behavior on the negative side.

Psychopathy, as defined by the Hare Psychopathy Checklist–Revised (PCL–R; Hare, 1991), is one personality construct that has received little attention by I–O investigators. Moreover, arguments *against* investigating psychopathy in business settings have included its low base rate, the fact that other variables already included in I–O research "look" like psychopathy, its clinical nature, and the sensationalist connotations of the term *psychopath*. The low base rate problem, which in an applied field means that there is *no* real problem to solve, has been especially difficult to counteract, because case studies are rarely reported in the I–O literature except to illustrate major empirical findings. Both narcissism and Machiavellianism have been studied in organizations, and these studies offer convincing, acceptable explanations for some psychopathic-like behaviors commonly observed without the need to enter clinical or forensic arenas.

Certainly, if headlines of major newspapers are to be believed, psychopaths, or at least people acting like them, abound in business, in academia, in medicine, on the Internet, and in some governments. Although this publicity may help forensic psychologists, psychiatrists, and profilers to gain research support, the association of psychopathy with serial killers and other high-profile (or highly violent or prolific) criminals tends to dampen the interest of business folks from participating in research. Many people, of course, feel that their boss *is* a psychopath; some feel they may be married to one, and almost everyone is curious to know how to spot them. Until several years ago, few corporations were willing to investigate even the most benign dark side traits among their employees, let alone psychopathy. However, in this post-9/11 world, the realization that freedom requires vigilance has opened the door to understanding the role psychopathy may play in workplace violence, white-collar crime, bullying on the job, and Internet crime and terrorism, all real problems behind the sensationalist headlines. In addition, the persistence of I–O researchers over the years in pursuing their agendas has helped.

INTRODUCTION AT THE NATO ADVANCED
STUDY INSTITUTE ON PSYCHOPATHY

Two I–O psychologists, Sigrid Gustafson, then at Virginia Polytechnic Institute, and Paul Babiak, the author of this chapter, and an organization development consultant, were, perhaps, the only I–O psychologists interested in the topic during the mid-1990s and were therefore invited to participate in the NATO Advanced Study Institute on Psychopathy in Alvor, Portugal in 1995 (organized by Robert D. Hare). This conference opened the door for legitimizing industrial research efforts by allowing these researchers to share their findings with the forensic and clinical psychologists and psychiatrists who attended this meeting and get the perspective of those who work routinely with criminal psychopaths.

Several questions were raised during the discussions as other researchers considered the possibility that individuals with psychopathic personalities could be working in corporations. The first question was, How could a psychopathic individual pass through the rigors of the typical corporate screening process, outshine other candidates with good credentials, and ultimately land a job? The second, and perhaps more interesting question to those who work with criminal psychopaths, was, Why would a psychopath want to work in industry anyway? Going to work is typically seen as drudgery and the business world as too confining to foster personal freedom. A third question, following quite naturally from the others, was, How long can a psychopath, once hired, survive in a company before his or her manipulative and deceitful behaviors reach the notice of management, and the person is terminated.

At the NATO Advanced Study Institute, in an attempt to address the question, I presented six case studies of individuals with psychopathic personalities who were working in industry (Babiak, 1995a; 1995b). These individuals were successfully manipulating their coworkers and bosses, as well as circumventing much of their organizations' human resource and financial systems. Contrary to expectations that their antisocial and deceitful manipulative behaviors would lead them to failure, they were readily accepted into the management ranks and were experiencing career success. These individuals, with PCL–R scores ranging from 25.6 to 31.3 and PCL: Screening Version (PCL:SV; Hart, Cox, & Hare, 1995) scores ranging from 17 to 19 (see later for methods used to score PCLs in industrial settings), were psychopaths who had successfully been hired and were systematically manipulating other employees to set up scams whereby they could draw large salaries for limited work, prey on coworkers, and move into higher levels of power.

One question raised by this finding was whether these individuals were actually "ideal employees." In fact, 5 of the 6 were identified as future management candidates, and two of these were rated on their corporate succession plan as "high potential" employees. All were deemed charming and likeable, conscientious, intelligent or bright, effective at what they did, and high performers. However, only a small group in the organization (albeit those in power) maintained this view, whereas many others reported observing negative behaviors. According to these detractors, the subjects manipulated their bosses and coworkers, they were deceitful, lied, actually did minimal work (relying on those they controlled to do their job), created interpersonal conflict among their coworkers, abused some fellow employees (even to the point of bullying), and lied about their experience and education on their résumés. Many were padding their expense accounts and at least two were taking company property to sell on the side. When questioned about overspending his expense budget, one subject said to his boss, "I feel like a kid in a candy store!" Despite all of this, the perception of upper management did not change, and the subjects continued to experience career success.

I believe that these individuals were able to manipulate coworkers more easily because of the organizational chaos their respective companies were experiencing. In each of these cases, their corporations were undergoing major changes such as downsizing, mergers, or acquisitions. I believe that the organizational chaos of these transitions was acting as an attractant for them, as well as a cover for their psychopathic behaviors.

Sigrid Gustafson, now at the American Institutes for Research, in Washington, D. C., reported on her groundbreaking work on subclinical psychopaths in a college student population. Gustafson & Ritzer (1995) used several pattern-oriented methodologies to analyze responses to items from the Narcissistic Personality Inventory, the California Psychological Inventory, the Crowne and Marlowe Social Desirability Scale, and the Self-Report Psychopathy Scale (Hare, Hemphill, & Paulhus, 2002). Her results across two samples confirmed the robustness and the stable prevalence of a pattern of narcissism and antisocial behavior that she called *aberrant self-promotion* (ASP). The meaningfulness of the ASP pattern was validated against PCL–R scores. PCL–R scores were significantly higher for the ASP group than for the non-ASP group. The average PCL–R scores differed by 9 points, with virtually no overlap of scores between the two groups. In addition, aberrant self-promoters, compared with their non-ASP counterparts, exhibited more antisocial behavior, in the form of committing parking violations, committing rule violations for which they received sanctions from the university, engaging in public drunkenness, university arrests, and self-report of criminality, etc. Thus, Gustafson was able to show that ASPs were a subclinical form of psychopathy, differing from their criminal counterparts in degree but not in kind.

FIRST SOCIETY FOR INDUSTRIAL
AND ORGANIZATIONAL PSYCHOLOGY
SYMPOSIUM ON PSYCHOPATHY

Research on the relationship between counterproductive work behavior and some personality variables (i.e., The Big Five, Conscientiousness, and

Narcissism) had increased over recent years, but psychopathy had yet to stimulate any serious attention from I–O psychologists. The first I–O symposium dedicated to psychopathy was conducted at the annual conference of the Society for Industrial and Organizational Psychology in 1996. This symposium was designed to introduce psychopathy as a viable variable for organizational study to the I–O community and to familiarize those new to the rich field of existing research. Because psychopathy was such a new concept to I–O, it was critical to start the symposium by addressing this knowledge gap of the attendees. Robert D. Hare traced the evolution of the current understanding of psychopathy from the "murky past" of clinical evaluation, through the development of the PCL–R, up to his latest observations of the brains of psychopaths using functional magnetic resonance imaging technology. Hare impressed upon the large audience of distinguished I–O researchers, as well as graduate students, that psychopaths do, in fact, exist in business and that further research by I–O psychologists is desperately needed.

Subsequently, I reviewed the results of eight industrial case studies assessed using the PCL–R and PCL:SV (Babiak, 1996). Seven of the 8 individuals scored at or above the cutoff for psychopathy. The other individual approached the cutoff for psychopathy but did not quite reach it. The PCL–R and PCL:SV Total and Factor 1 and 2 scores for this sample are shown in Table 16–1.

The Total PCL–R scores ranged from 24.7 to 32.9, Factor 1 scores ranged from 14 to 16, and Factor 2 scores ranged from 7.7 to 12.9. Unlike criminal psychopaths that score high on both factors and nonpsychopathic criminals that tend to have low/moderate Factor 1 scores and high Factor 2 scores, the individuals from corporate settings had high Factor 1 scores and low/moderate Factor 2 scores, exhibiting a profile that I hypothesized characterizes the noninstitutionalized industrial or corporate psychopath.

TABLE 16–1.
PCL–R and PCL:SV Scores of Corporate Psychopaths

Case	PCL–R			PCL:SV		
	Factor 1	Factor 2	Total	Factor 1	Factor 2	Total
Dave	15	11.6	29.4	11	8	19
Bob	16	11.6	31.3	12	7	19
Ron	15	11.6	30.6	11	8	19
Jim	15	11.6	29.4	11	8	19
Ev	15	10.1	27.8	11	6	17
Carol	14	10.3	25.6	12	7	19
Harry	16	12.9	32.9	12	9	22
Gus	15	7.7	24.7	11	5	16

HOW PSYCHOPATHS MANIPULATE
ORGANIZATIONS—A MODEL

In open society, the psychopathic process involves identifying a victim
(a *mark*), setting up and running the scam (using and abusing the victim), and
then moving on to another mark, usually in a different venue (e.g., different
city or state). Potential discovery is circumvented through clever lying, deceit,
sometimes violence, and ultimately moving on to another target. From the
group dynamics perspective, corporate settings, being closed social systems,
differ in important ways from open society within which psychopaths normally operate, which, in theory, should make it difficult for the psychopath
to operate. In work organizations, the psychopathic employee's attempts at
swindling would meet with limited success because his or her abusive behavior would be obvious to fellow employees worked with on a daily basis.
Having to report to a steady job everyday would make moving on to different
targets difficult in the confines of an organization. In addition, business
processes such as performance management (including annual appraisals and
written goals and measures), would, if properly administered, make hiding
poor performance rather difficult. However, this is not at all what I found.

In the cases studied, I discovered that these *successful* psychopaths had
covered their tracks by creating and then effectively managing *discrepant
perceptions* among coworkers. In fact, some coworkers were completely taken
in by the scam, becoming avid supporters and protectors, whereas others
became detractors and tried to unseat the psychopath. Interestingly, the few
detractors, regardless of their rank, were unable to convince the supporters to
change their views.

Confidential interviews with coworkers suggested that there might be two
factors that facilitated the creation of this split among the observers: the
amount of *time* the individual actually spent in the presence of the psychopath (that is, interacting with him or her frequently versus infrequently),
and the *utility* of an individual to satisfying the psychopath's needs. In all
samples, four roles emerged, as outlined in Table 16–2.

Supporters were of two types, differing mainly in their level of interaction with the psychopath at hand. One subgroup of supporters consisted
primarily of high-level individuals—those with formal organizational
power—who interacted with the psychopathic subject infrequently (most
executives in these organizations had very busy travel schedules), but who
were nonetheless impressed by what they saw and reported that they liked
him or her very much. In fact, several acted like the psychopaths' *patrons*,
protecting and defending them from the criticisms of other organization
members when needed. I hypothesized that their organizational power and
influence made these executives attractive targets, and the limitation of brief
intermittent meetings actually allowed for controlled presentations (i.e.,
manipulation) by the psychopath.

A second subgroup of supporters was made up of peers and lower level
employees who had informal influence over various organizational resources

TABLE 16–2.
Psychopathic Manipulation Leads to the Formation of Discrepant
Views Among Coworkers

	Low Utility	*High Utility*
	PATSIES	PAWNS
Frequent interaction	Have lost power and are no longer useful to the psychopath	Have "informal power" and influence over resources the psychopath wants
	ORGANIZATION POLICE	*PATRONS*
Infrequent interaction	Can thwart or frustrate the psychopath	Have "formal power" and can protect and defend the psychopath

Copyright 1995 by Paul Babiak, PhD.

(e.g., access to executives, accounting functions, funding, the "grapevine," and so forth). Some of these individuals described themselves as close friends of the subjects, and a few even did the psychopaths' work. Those fulfilling this latter role, that is, covering for inadequate work performance, were labeled *soul mates*, to capture the reports of some observers that these individuals seemed to be fixated on pleasing the psychopath. Individuals who were doing the psychopath's job for him or her were found in more than half the samples. Because most of these individuals were seen (by coworkers, as well as first-hand observation of this author) as being manipulated by the psychopath, they were labeled *pawns*.

The detractor group was also composed of two subgroups, differing in terms of their frequency of interaction with the psychopathic subjects. One subgroup was labeled the *organizational police* because they tended to be in traditional business control functions such as auditing, corporate security, and human resources. They dealt with the psychopathic subjects only on rare occasions, yet they reported neither liking nor trusting them. I believe that professional training or experience made them especially sensitive to the psychopath's manipulation attempts.

The other subgroup, labeled *patsies*, was composed of individuals who had formerly been supporters, that is, *pawns*, but who had realized either that they had been manipulated or had been "discarded" by the psychopath because they were no longer useful. Despite extremely negative things to report about the psychopathic subjects, a few of these coworkers reported regretting that the "special relationship" that they had had with the psychopaths had ended, even to the point of blaming themselves for the falling out!

The question of how these groups were formed or, in group dynamics terms, how the psychopaths were able to manipulate coworkers into playing these roles is addressed by a model of psychopathic manipulation summarized in Fig. 16–1.

This model is an attempt to answer the question of how the psychopathic employee could influence the organization and its members. The first phase of the process involves the psychopath gaining entry into the organization. This is far easier than expected because of his or her ability to charm hiring managers and other decision makers, who are often not trained in effective interviewing techniques. Also, and more importantly, some of the overt behaviors exhibited by psychopaths are misinterpreted as leadership traits. Many companies faced with fast-paced change seek those with raw leadership talent whom they can groom and promote quickly; it is very possible that a clever psychopath can create a façade of the ideal candidate. Table 16–3 suggests some of the common psychopathic personality traits that can be misinterpreted as leadership traits by unsuspecting executives and corporations.

Referring to Fig. 16–1, Phase 2, having successfully passed through the selection process, the psychopathic new employee begins assessing the utility of other employees by meeting and greeting as many people as possible. During this phase, potential targets—*pawns* and *patrons*—are identified for further manipulation, as are potential rivals. An outgrowth of this process is an *influence network* comprising a series of one-on-one relationships, many of which develop into "psychopathic bonds" that capitalize on the socio-emotional needs (and often, weaknesses) of the coworkers.

During the manipulation phase (Fig. 16–1, Phase 3), the psychopath sets about to create a façade or, on a grander scale, a "psychopathic fiction" about

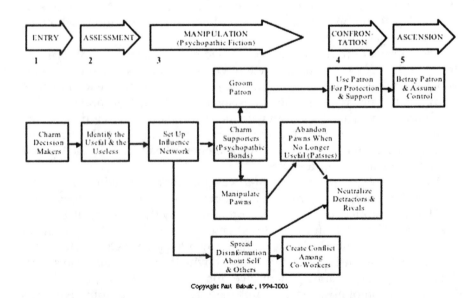

FIGURE 16–1.   The five-phase psychopathic manipulation process.

TABLE 16–3.
Psychopathic Features and the Leadership Labels We Give Them

Psychopathic Features	Corporate Labels
Charm and charisma	"Leadership"
Taking about lofty ideas/goals	"Visioning"
Conning and manipulation	"Motivating"; "Influential"; "Persuasive"
Lack of remorse or guilt for hurtful behavior	"Can make hard decisions"; "Action oriented"
Impulsivity; No fear	"High Energy"; "Courage"
Has no emotions (affect)	"Controls emotions"; "Strong"
Grandiose self-appraisal	"Self-confidence"
Thrill-seeking and need for stimulation	"Ability to multi-task"

him- or herself to better influence coworkers and management. In society, this might involve creating an image of trustworthiness and sincerity (e.g., convincing the target that one is the perfect life partner is the basis for many "sweetheart" and "Romeo" scams) and then moving in for the con. In an organization, the psychopathic fiction is *to create an impression of one as an ideal leader, someone worthy of increased trust from higher-ups, who belongs on the corporate succession plan, and who has executive leadership qualities.* Career success for these individuals is dependent on the skill of the psychopath in maintaining the credibility of the psychopathic fiction. To effectively establish credibility requires the psychopath to spread positive disinformation about him or herself (that he or she is an ideal leader), and negative disinformation about potential rivals and detractors (e.g., that they are jealous, incompetent, or dishonest). Because the source of the information is rarely traceable within the complex influence network, the psychopath is able to control perceptions about himself or herself and others.

Over time, of course, there is the risk of coworkers' sharing information about the psychopath's antisocial (dark side) traits and behaviors with each other and thereby validating their growing suspicions. As part of his or her cover, the psychopath instigates conflicts among coworkers so that they minimize their communications and divert their attention. A clever psychopath can come across as supportive and understanding while making one's close friend and colleague seem like a traitor.

Inevitably, some *pawns* lose their utility to the psychopath and are no longer needed for the scam, so they are abandoned. This drastic and abrupt change in relationship from seemingly close (in some cases, even intimate) to cold and distant creates dissonance in some victims as they realize that they have been used. This characterizes Phase 4 (see Fig. 16–1) of the process where confrontation between *pawns* (now feeling like *patsies*) and the psychopath can occur. Again, through the influence network, the psychopath is able to effectively disparage the reputations of detractors if they attempt to make trouble with management authorities, relying, if necessary, on the *patron* for protection and support.

Phase 5 is the culmination of the process and occurs when the psychopath successfully unseats his or her *patron* and assumes the position and control the *patron* once had. Now, having successfully moved into a new situation (e.g., in the cases I studied this was primarily a promotion to a higher position within the company—often the boss's), the psychopathic drama continues as new and different players enter. With a major political coup under his or her belt, the psychopath moves on to a new (and often bigger) game, reassessing the utility of coworkers and extending his or her influence deeper into the organization.

PSYCHOPATHIC NESTING GROUNDS

Organizations in transition are more prone to psychopathic manipulation of this sort than those that are stable (Babiak, 1995, 2000a, 2000b, 2000c). "Transitioning" organizations, which have included many major corporations since the 1980s, are those forced by marketplace demands to undergo dramatic change to survive. Traditional hierarchical organizations with strong centralized policies and procedures have moved toward flatter, more free-form structures, eliminating many middle-management positions and decentralizing decision making. These changes have necessarily led to changing roles for employees and increasing focus on leadership. This focus requires that older human resource systems such as performance management (which traditionally focused on solidifying goals and objectives) and reward systems (previously rewarding conformity, status quo, and compliance) be updated and made more flexible as well.

Herein lies the problem. During times of chaos, an organization is at its weakest point and prone to manipulation. First, it takes time to create flexible yet effective new systems. The development of more appropriate measures can lag business growth itself. The psychopath has a great advantage in this environment. With the organization in flux around him or her, inadequate controls and measures make it easier to hide antisocial behavior, while his or her disdain for rules and regulations is accommodated. Increased corporate rewards for risk-taking and nonconformity can offer the psychopath faster career movement than before. Second, whereas employees and managers are typically distressed by dramatic change, psychopaths thrive on the freedom they experience in situations that lack structure and stability. Psychopaths are attracted to transitioning organizations because of the stimulation they afford, which satisfies their thrill-seeking needs.

The implication for future organizations is to recruit candidates who are comfortable with a fast-paced environment and who are bright, have social skills, and demonstrate leadership traits. As noted before, the psychopathic candidate can easily demonstrate these traits, thus putting a hiring manager at a distinct disadvantage. The ability to differentiate between psychopaths and nonpsychopaths in this regard is difficult, even for those who make a career of studying them, as many researchers reading this book know all too well. All of the characteristics of the transitioning organization are good and necessary in today's business environment, but their success relies on the belief that one hires only good, honest, sincere, compassionate, and straightforward people. Without adequate control mechanisms (e.g., recruitment, performance management, and succession planning), this may not always be the case.

SELF-REPORT ASSESSMENTS OF PSYCHOPATHY FOR BUSINESS APPLICATION

Much of the assessment work that is done in organizations relies on self-report measures of personality, most often Machiavellianism and narcissism. An important question is whether corporate psychopaths are any different from Machiavellians. Both seem to be cold and calculating, devoid of emotion, self-motivated, and lacking in empathy for those they hurt. Russell (1996), addressing this question, reported on a laboratory game simulation comparing the performance of Machiavellians (Machs) and Gustafson's Aberrant Self-Promoters (ASPs). This simulation required participants to compete as well as to cooperate with others to win. Russell found that Machs kept their word, were liked by others on the teams, and forged successful alliances with representatives of other constituencies. In contrast, ASPs reneged on their bargains and were disliked by their teammates. Moreover, when the proposed legislation issues were emotionally charged (i.e., a proposal to raise the drinking age or a proposal to abolish abortion rights), Machs also garnered more points, by winning votes from others for the positions they espoused, than did the ASPs, who tended to sacrifice their constituencies in favor of representing their own personal opinions on these emotion-laden topics. Russell concluded that Machiavellians were different from psychopaths.

Before the introduction of psychopathy to the applied psychology literature, narcissism had been the critical variable in the study of leadership. Most researchers used the Narcissistic Personality Inventory (Raskin & Terry, 1988). O'Shea and Gustafson (2000) conducted an item response theory analysis of the Narcissistic Personality Inventory in an attempt to assess how robust the items were, given some criticism that the instrument was out of date. Analyzing their results, they were able to clarify the theoretical underpinnings of the dimension and, with subsequent modifications, created new items that discriminate more sharply and at a higher level of the trait. With this revised instrument, they are beginning to explore the relationship between psychopathy and narcissism.

The validity of any selection instrument depends on the willingness of the test taker to respond to the items honestly. Because important life decisions are often made, in part, based on test results, it is natural for job candidates to attempt to make the best impression they can when responding. A major area of study in I–O psychology revolves around solving the problem of job applicants "faking good" or "faking bad," including the motivations, ability, and impact on the outcome (Sackett & Harris, 1984). Previous criticism of fake-good and fake-bad research using student samples suggested that the unreal nature of applying for a job in a laboratory setting adversely influences the results obtained. This adverse influence would be even more so in the case of psychopaths because of their proclivity for lying, thereby raising questions about the transferability of the results.

Offering the alternative point of view—that self-report indicators are useful to assess psychopathy—Hare, in the 1996 symposium discussed earlier, dramatically illustrated the power of the psychopath to manipulate paper and pencil instruments, as well as the criminal justice system. A large number of psychologists attending the symposium were shown a video case study of a criminal subject and subsequently presented with three valid Minnesota Multiphasic Personality Inventory (MMPI) profiles: a schizophrenic, a traditional MMPI 4–9 psychopath (or, more accurately, antisocial), and an individual with mixed anxiety/antisocial behavior. The group was asked to identify the profile of the subject they had just observed on the video. After some debate, consensus was reached on the MMPI Psychopathic Deviate (Pd)–Hypomania (Ma) (4–9) profile, which was once used to assess psychopathy in psychiatric settings. In fact, the subject had actually produced *all* of the profiles at different times in his incarceration, depending on the outcome he desired at the time. Not only did this demonstrate that the MMPI (a reputable instrument) is prone to faking, but a known psychopath (PCL–R Total = 40), motivated by a desired outcome accomplished the faking without detection and got the outcomes he wanted (transfers between prison and forensic hospital setting). This underscored Hare's arguments that it would be extremely difficult, and perhaps impossible, to accurately identify a psychopath using self-report measures.

Gustafson (1999) has since offered a new and very different approach to the measurement of aberrant self-promotion (subclinical psychopathy), using the conditional reasoning technique developed originally by James (1988, 1998). Although this paper and pencil instrument is made up of items that tap the underlying motivation, biases, and assumptions of respondents, the items, however, appear to test-takers to be part of a logical reasoning test. The answers chosen, according to the conditional reasoning model, reflect the subjects' implicit views of themselves and the world. Gustafson concluded that conditional reasoning items were successful in identifying the underlying assumptions of the ASPs in her samples, including their narcissism (grandiosity, lack of empathy, callousness, superiority, and dominance) and antisocial behavior (impulsiveness, irresponsibility, poor behavioral controls and sensation-seeking), as validated against scores on the measurement instrument used in her previous research. In follow up studies, using revised items for the ASP conditional reasoning instrument, Gustafson (2000) was able to demonstrate sharper discrimination between ASPs and non-ASPS among two U. S. samples and one Swedish sample.

B-SCAN 360

There are certainly individuals in organization who exhibit some psycho-pathic-like features, but who are otherwise honest, productive, and success-ful. Many high-potential employees are considered "diamonds in the rough" by their organizations: individuals with some behavioral flaws, but who are on accelerated career paths because decision makers in the organization see management and leadership talent and are willing to invest in the develop-ment of this potential. Although the PCL–R, PCL:SV, and the P-Scan (Hare & Hervé, 2003) have been invaluable tools for assessing psychopathic-like behavior in organizations for the purpose of research, the identification of these behaviors using clinical tools developed for use in forensic settings for business decision making is not justified. Robert Hare and I have begun the development of an instrument for use in business settings. This instrument is based upon Hare's four-factor model of psychopathy, and my work defin-ing the features of the corporate psychopath (Babiak & Hare, in press).

In an attempt to identify those features of psychopathic thoughts and behaviors that are applicable to business environments, Babiak, Hare, and Hemphill (1999) experimented with a 12-item self-report instrument. Items for the Psychopathic Thought Questionnaire were modeled after business behaviors described in biographies of famous (and infamous) business peo-ple showcased in the *Wall Street Journal* (p. 1 lead articles). During a pilot test, more than 30,000 individuals responded to the web-enabled survey. A sample of 4,000 individuals with sufficiently complete data were identified for further analysis. Hemphill conducted a factor analysis yielding two factors, as noted in Table 16–4. Factor 1 seemed to include leadership-like thought, whereas Factor 2 reflected a caustic attitude toward others. The results of this study formed part of the basis for the development of the B-Scan to be dis-cussed later.

Initially, management development and succession planning ratings of more than 300 managers from several organizations were reviewed for con-tent. Development plans included descriptions of counterproductive atti-tudes, behaviors, and judgments that were in need of improvement for the candidate to be promoted into higher levels of management and leadership positions. To varying degrees, all of these items were believed to be impor-tant determinants of continued career movement in the company.

The behavioral descriptions were reviewed for possible examples of psy-chopathic behaviors and characteristics as described by Hare, Babiak, and

TABLE 16–4.
Two Factors From the Psychopathic Thought Questionnaire

Item	Factor 1	Factor 2
Charms others	.67*	−.07
Uses people	.64*	.10
A risk taker	.62*	.06
Believes in winners and losers	.60*	−.02
Does "what it takes"	.51*	.37
Makes impulsive decisions	.45*	.22
Believes lying is necessary	.15	.61*
Is an unrecognized talent	−.10	.54*
It's a waste to worry	.23	.53*
Does not admit mistakes	−.01	.49*
It's a waste to plan	.01	.35
Prefers vague rules	.19	.34

*$p < .05$.

others. Although some had more obvious potential than others (e.g., stealing vs. using jargon to impress others), a collection of about 200 items was selected for further investigation. These items were pilot-tested with two groups. One group comprised business executives, primarily vice presidents and directors. They were asked to rate the degree of appropriateness of each behavior for a prototypical manager or leader in a large organization. The ratings varied from those thought not to be issues to those that would raise serious concern.

The second group comprised I–O and forensic psychologists who are experts in the assessment of psychopathy using the PCL–R (most had been trained by Robert Hare and Adelle Forth). These individuals were asked to evaluate the potential relationship of these behaviors to psychopathy or one of its characteristics.

Items that were deemed significant by both groups were retained. These items were viewed by the executives to be behavioral or performance issues requiring attention and as possible indicators of psychopathic tendencies by the psychopathy experts. One hundred and seven items were included in the research version of the B-Scan 360. They were grouped by the authors into 16 scales and ultimately fit into the four-factor Hare model of psychopathy. In its current research version form, the B-Scan 360 yields 16 scale scores (from 0 to 12 each), 4 facets (from 0 to 48 each), and a total score. The instrument is completed by those familiar with the work performance or the on-the-job behavior of the subject, typically the boss, peers, and subordinates. Respondents are asked to indicate how descriptive each item is of the person in question (*descriptive* = 2; *somewhat descriptive* = 1; *not descriptive* = 0).

In a preliminary study, nonpsychologist business associates of the writer (8 of whom are/were members of the organizations from which the subjects previously reported worked) were asked to field-test the B-Scan items. All who agreed to participate were asked to "evaluate a hypothetical manage-ment development candidate who might benefit from behavioral feedback" using the B-Scan. They understood that they would not receive the results of their participation, but that their data as well as their personal feedback would be useful to the authors in further development of the B-Scan. Seven of the assessors used the B-Scan 360 to rate individuals who had previously been evaluated (by this writer) using the PCL–R and PCL:SV. The business associates were not aware of this previous research (the identities of these subjects have never been revealed). Their assessments are shown in graphical form in Fig. 16–2.

Although this is not a rigorous study and the sample size is small, the results are interesting. It is interesting to note that "Gus," the individual who just missed the cutoff of 25 on the PCL–R (at 24.7 prorated) had a profile con-siderably *lower* than that of the others. Upon re-review of my notes, I recalled that he appeared to be more honest than the others in the sample, but the proximity of his score to the cutoff led to his inclusion in the data set.

Current validation research with the B-Scan looks promising. The results of two samples, one a group of high performing directors and executives at a major U. S. company and the other a group of persons convicted of economic crimes, are beginning to show some differentiation. Preliminary alphas are

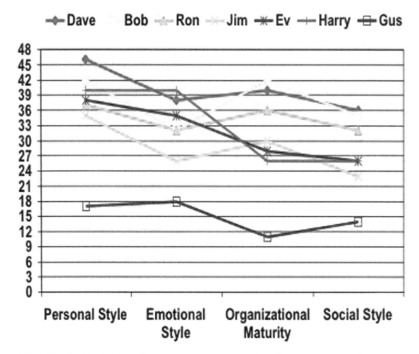

FIGURE 16–2.   B-Scan facet scores for a sample of corporate psychopaths.

quite good and studies with new groups are moving forward with no change to the items yet.

CONCLUSION

In conclusion, and perhaps to underscore the importance of studying psychopaths in organizations, I want to update the reader on the whereabouts of my original sample of eight. As of this writing, only one lost his job, but left the organization with a healthy financial package, and moved into a higher-level job at a competitor. Two were promoted into a higher-level position with the acquiring company following mergers, whereas another survived a merger by being selected for the transitional team and then was in a position to determine who would stay in (i.e., his supporters) and who would leave (i.e., his detractors) the new organization. Two from this sample have been promoted at least once and are still with their original companies, and one whose employer had gone out of business has "disappeared." Gus, whose psychopathy is now in question, has had a good career, ultimately rising to the position of vice president and recently retiring with his wife.

Research on psychopathy in organizations is moving forward; business managers are now asking how they might participate in studies, and graduate students are exploring field research that in recent memory would have been unthinkable. There are still concerns and issues to be addressed, of course, and issues of confidentiality, anonymity, and ethics are important considerations, not the least of which is the suggestion (by many in business) that some aspects of psychopathy may be a good thing for companies to look for in their new hires. Clearly, the expansion of research that is focused on business-critical variables and ultimately leads to positive behavior change and performance improvement, will also contribute to our theoretical understanding of psychopathy as manifested in organizational settings.

REFERENCES

Babiak, P. (1995a). When psychopaths go to work: A case study of an industrial psychopath. *Applied Psychology: An International Review, 44,* 171–188.

Babiak, P. (1995b). *Psychopathic manipulation in organizations: Pawns, patrons, and patsies.* Paper presented at the NATO Advanced Study Institute, Psychopathy: Theory, Research, and Implications for Society, Alvor, Portugal.

Babiak, P. (1996). Industrial psychopaths: Organizational manipulation and career success. In P. Babiak (Chair), *Shining light on the dark side: Psychopaths in organizations.* Symposium conducted at the 11th Annual Conference of the Society for Industrial and Organizational Psychology, San Diego, CA.

Babiak, P. (2000a). Psychopathic manipulation at work. In C. B. Gacono (Ed.), *The clinical and forensic assessment of psychopathy: A practitioner's guide.* Mahwah, NJ: Lawrence Erlbaum Associates.

Babiak, P. (2000b). Psychopaths in the organization. In R. Restak (Chair), *Controversies in neuropsychiatry—psychopathy.* Symposium conducted at the 11th Annual Meeting of the American Neuropsychiatric Association, Fort Myers, FL.

Babiak, P. (2000c). Scanning for psychopathy. In S. Gustafson (Chair), *Personality in the shadows: A continuum of destructiveness.* Symposium conducted at the 15th Annual Conference of the Society for Industrial and Organizational Psychology, New Orleans, LA.

Babiak, P. & Hare, R. D. (in press). *The B-Scan 360–Manual.* Toronto, Ontario, Canada: Multi-Health Systems.

Babiak, P., Hare, R. D., & Hemphill, J. (1999). Help wanted: Psychopaths please apply. In P. Babiak (Chair), *Liars of the dark side: Can personality interfere with personality measurement?* Symposium conducted at the 14th Annual Conference of the Society for Industrial and Organizational Psychology, Atlanta, GA.

Gustafson, S. B. (1995). *The psychopath as aberrant self-promoter.* Paper presented at the NATO Advanced Study Institute, Psychopathy: Theory, Research, and Implications for Society, Alvor, Portugal.

Gustafson, S. B. (1999). Out of their own mouths: A conditional reasoning instrument for identifying aberrant self-promoters. In P. Babiak (Chair), *Liars of the dark side: Can personality interfere with personality measurement?* Symposium conducted at the 13th Annual Conference of the Society for Industrial and Organizational Psychology, Atlanta, GA.

Gustafson, S. B. (2000). Personality and organizational destructiveness: Fact, fiction, and fable. In L. R. Bergman, R. B. Cairns, L. Nilsson, & L. Nystedt (Eds.), *Developmental science and the holistic approach.* Mahwah, NJ: Lawrence Erlbaum Associates.

Gustafson, S. B., & Ritzer, D. R. (1995). The dark side of normal: A psychopathy-linked pattern called aberrant self-promotion. *European Journal of Personality, 9,* 147–183.

Hare, R. D. (1991). *The Hare Psychopathy Checklist–Revised.* Toronto, Ontario, Canada: Multi-Health Systems.

Hare, R. D., Hemphill, J. F., & Paulhus, D. (2002). *The Self-Report Psychopathy Scale–II (SRP–II).* Manual in preparation.

Hare, R. D., & Hervé, H. (2003). *The Hare P-Scan: Research version 2.* Toronto, Ontario, Canada: Multi-Health Systems.

Hart, S. D., Cox, D. N., & Hare, R. D. (1995). *The Psychopathy Checklist: Screening Version.* Toronto, Ontario, Canada: Multi-Health Systems.

Hogan, R. T. (1991). Personality and personality measurement. In M. D. Dunnette & L. M. Hough (Eds.), *Handbook of industrial and organizational psychology* (pp. 873–919). Palo Alto, CA: Consulting Psychologists Press.

Hogan, R., Raskin, R., & Fazzini, D. (1990). The dark side of charisma. In K. E. Clark & M. B. Clark (Eds.), *Measures of leadership* (pp. 343–354). West Orange, NJ: Leadership Library of America.

James, L. R. (1988). Measurement of personality via conditional reasoning. *Organizational Research Methods, 1,* 131–163.

James, L. R. (1998). Measurement of relative motive strength via conditional reasoning. *Organizational Research Methods Journal, 1,* 131–163.

O'Shea, G., & Gustafson, S. B. (2000). Improving the measurement of narcissism: A revised instrument. In S. Gustafson (Chair), *Personality in the shadows: A continuum of destructiveness.* Symposium conducted at the 15th Annual Conference of the Society for Industrial and Organizational Psychology, New Orleans, La.

Raskin, R., & Terry, R. (1988). A principal-components analysis of the Narcissistic Personality Inventory and further evidence of its construct validity. *Journal of Personality and Social Psychology, 54*, 890–900.

Russell, D. (1996). *Aberrant self-promotion versus Machiavellianism: A differentiation of constructs.* Unpublished master's thesis, Virginia Polytechnic Institute and State University, Blacksburg.

Sackett, P. R., & Harris, M. M. (1984). Honesty testing for personnel selection: A review and critique. *Personnel Psychology, 37*, 221–245.

VI

PSYCHOPATHIC SUBTYPES:
MEASUREMENT AND
IMPLICATIONS

17

Psychopathic Subtypes: Historical and Contemporary Perspectives

Hugues Hervé

> Classifications owe their existence to an economizing principle of the human intellect. Indeed, if we're to renounce classifications—we also condemn ourselves to treat every new experience as the first one. (Riese, 1945, as cited in Werlinder, 1978, p. 186)

By definition, those individuals who meet the Hare Psychopathy Checklist–Revised (PCL–R: Hare, 1991) criteria for psychopathy share many common features; that is, they possess high levels of the interpersonal, affective, life-style, and behavioral facets of the disorder (for an explanation of the facets of psychopathy, see Hare, 2003). Nonetheless, although similar to one another in many respects, especially relative to nonpsychopaths, theory and clinical experience indicate that psychopaths differ from one another in several ways, particularly with respect to the interpersonal, lifestyle, and behavioral manifestations of the disorder. In early conceptions of psychopathy reflecting in-depth clinical observations, in fact, the construct was described in terms of subtypes (e.g., Arieti, 1967; Henderson, 1947; Karpman, 1955). Indeed, as I hope to demonstrate, the investigation of psychopathic subtypes has a very rich clinical history. Unfortunately, this topic lost momentum in the mid-to-late 20th century, a time when the need for a common nomenclature understandably took precedence over the clinical refinement of the construct (for further details, see Hervé, chap. 2, this volume). As Cleckley noted, "before these fine distinctions can be made to any good purpose, there must first appear some recognition of the basic group that is to be further differentiated" (1941/1988, p. 229).

With the advent of the Hare PCL–R, this issue was addressed. The field finally had a reliable and valid assessment tool, one that stayed true to its clinical foundation (see Hervé, chap. 2, this volume). Consequently, theorists, clinicians, and researchers were once again able to turn their attention to the study of psychopathic subtypes. Yet, this area remains largely ignored. The limited research that has been conducted has not only supported theories of old but also led to further insights into the various masks of psychopathy. After reviewing the clinical foundation on which current research lies, I will present recent empirically derived typologies, as well as related research and theories highlighting differences among psychopaths. I hope that this chapter will stress the need for a greater focus upon individual differences, which I believe is imperative if the field is to advance in any significant manner.

INSIGHTS FROM THE CLINICAL TRADITION

The notion that psychopaths differ in presentation and behavior has long been noted in the clinical literature (Arieti, 1963; Cleckley, 1941/1988; Hare, 1970, 1998c; Henderson, 1947; Karpman, 1941; Partridge, 1928). However, the diagnostic confusion surrounding psychopathy from the 18th to mid-to-late 20th century was, in part, the reason that subtypes were clinically apparent (see Hervé, chap. 2, this volume). Obviously, if one throws a bunch of apples, oranges, and pears into a basket one will later see that it contains different types of fruits. Nonetheless, a review of this literature with the Hare (1991) psychopath in mind reveals that many of these early investigators were on the right track.[1]

Idiopathic Psychopaths versus Pseudopsychopaths[2]

Clearly, when one is investigating variants within a construct, the easiest and most obvious distinction to be made is to separate exemplars from impersonators: Distinct disorders are presumably easier to distinguish, both clinically and empirically, than variants of the same condition. Although Karpman (1941) has been credited for first promoting this distinction (see Poythress & Skeem, 2005; Skeem, Poythress, Edens, Lilienfeld, & Cale, 2003), he was in fact not the first nor the only one in his cohort to do so. Indeed, Partridge (1928), via a qualitative analysis of 50 male and female psychopaths (i.e., individuals diagnosed as such by hospital staff[3]), was the first to suggest that the overt manifestation of psychopathy may evolve from various (in this case two) unique developmental pathways: one with a family history of psychopathy (*delinquent* and *inadequate*) and, therefore, a biologically predetermined (genotype) and one with no such family history but raised in chaotic families (*general incompatible* or *emotionally unstable*) and, therefore, the product of environment (phenotype; also see McCord & McCord, 1964). Nevertheless, Karpman was a visible advocate for the clinical importance of

---

[1]*Psychopathy* refers to the Hare PCL–R (Hare, 1991) conceptualization unless otherwise specified.

[2]The terms *idiopathic* and *pseudo* were used as they do not imply gradation, as does the primary–secondary distinction, which I believe is misleading. Furthermore, the term *pseudopsychopathy* was deemed more appropriate than *secondary* or *symptomatic* as it highlights the fact that this type of individual does not suffer from psychopathy but from a yet unspecified condition.

[3]It should be noted that Partridge (1928) rooted his work in a clear and relatively accurate conceptualization of psychopathy (see Hervé, chap. 2, this volume).

such a distinction (*primary* or *idiopathic* and *secondary* or *symptomatic*; 1941, 1946, 1948a, 1948b, 1950, 1955, 1961), as was Arieti (*idiopathic psychopaths* and *pseudopsychopaths*; 1963, 1967). Indeed, both felt it crucial to separate personality deviations that "appear as secondary manifestations in practically all psychiatric conditions from the syndromes in which they constitute the basic pathology" (Arieti, 1963, p. 301).

By definitions, idiopathic psychopaths and pseudopsychopaths share many common features. Both show a chronic pattern of affective dullness toward others, as well as grandiosity, deception, manipulation, and social maladjustment, including varied antisocial behaviors. They are entitled, egocentric, callous, remorseless, irresponsible, and impulsive individuals who live life according to personal rather than social rules or norms. Indeed, their differences lie less in the manner in which they present to the world than in their underlying pathology.

According to Arieti (1967) and, to a lesser extent, Karpman (1941, 1948a), idiopathic psychopathy is the result of an underlying pathology in which individuals, to use Arieti's terms, are without long-circuited (lasting, complex) emotions (LCEs), emotions that to the rest of us are central in moderating (motivating-inhibiting) behavior (be it antisocial or not). Consequently, they are free to act upon their short-circuited (fleeting) emotions, impulses, or urges (SCEs). To these authors, their pathology (LCE deficit) reflects a lack of development in this sphere rather than some kind of developmental arrest. No matter how hard and long one searches, no other cause to their disorder can be found. Early and adult socializing effects, irrespective if positive or negative, have little effect on the course of the disorder other than influencing its manifestation (i.e., environment affects their behaviors not their personality; Arieti, 1963; Karpman, 1950; Partridge, 1928; for a more contemporary view, see Hare, 1998b, 1998c). Comorbidity (e.g., paranoia, paraphilia, etc,), when present, is only of secondary importance and typically manifests in a manner consistent with their underlying pathology, that is, in an egocentric, callous, and remorseless fashion. It is this biologically predetermined LCE deficit that is instrumental in distinguishing idiopathic psychopathy from other disorders (Arieti, 1967; for a more contemporary view, see Patrick, chap. 8, this volume). Indeed, pseudopsychopaths are viewed as having the capacity to experience LCEs. However, in light of their main nonpsychopathic pathology (see later), their LCEs are essentially fleeting, unstable, overridden, dormant or dismissed, thereby rendering them functionally ineffective in controlling behavior. That is, their pathology is characterized by a disruption of LCEs, rather than a LCE deficit. This disruption is believed to occur due to an arrest in (rather than lack of) development, leaving them filled with *intra-psychic* or internal conflicts (i.e., anxiety, urges, and the like; Arieti, 1963; Karpman, 1946, 1961; Partridge, 1928). In other words, while the idiopathic psychopath is hard to the core, the symptomatic psychopath is "tough on the outside and soft on the inside" (Alexander & Healey, as cited in Karpman, 1948b, p. 487).

By extension, idiopathic and pseudo-psychopaths are also believed to experience SCEs for different reasons and in a manner consistent with their unique developmental pathways. Having a congenital LCE deficit, the SCEs of idiopathic types are never regulated and, therefore, largely reflect their current wishes or conditions (i.e., external triggers). In contrast, having developmentally disrupted LCEs, the SCEs of pseudopsychopaths largely reflect past grudges or frustrations (i.e., internal triggers). Although both, for example, are prone to engage in aggressive behavior of a callous nature, the idiopathic psychopath does so as an opportunity surfaces, whereas the pseudopsychopath does so for retribution for some past wrongdoing, be it real or imagined (Partridge, 1928). The end result is that both types primarily interact with the world on the basis of their immature impulses or urges (SCEs), which is why pseudopsychopaths present such a convincing psychopathic façade.

Subtle yet clinically significant differences are nevertheless apparent. On the one hand, idiopathic psychopaths, being free from internal conflicts and from the moderating influence of LCEs, consciously (i.e., instrumentally, objectively, and uninhibitedly) seek to gratify their primitive needs as quickly and easily as possible and no matter the consequences for those around them: "We are dealing here with something beyond a fight against ethical principles or against the superego, and something beyond an acting out in accordance with the unconscious sanction of the parents" (Arieti, 1967, p. 246). As a result, they display, from an early age, a grandiose and entitled attitude that leads them to guiltlessly and remorselessly seek immediate gratification through callous, parasitic, manipulative, impulsive, aggressive, and other antisocial (or unethical) behaviors. Yet, although their actions may appear impulsive to an observer, this is not always the case (Arieti, 1967; Karpman, 1948b, 1961). Their lack of social emotions gives them access to a wider range of alternatives to choose from, from the relatively prosocial to the downright sadistic, in their quest to satisfy their psychopathic needs. Caring only for themselves and having little concern for the future, they often choose the path of least resistance, which, to a future-oriented observer, may seem rash or irrational. Once a path is chosen, their affective and social blindness enables them to quickly put their plan into action without any concerns for injuries to others. The result is that the individual appears impulsive, rash, irrational, and/or reactive to an observer although, in reality, his or her plan came about in a calm, methodical, and instrumental fashion.

On the other hand, the pseudopsychopath, unlike the idiopathic type, has a conscience, albeit a very disturbed, conflicted, or uneven one (Arieti, 1967; Karpman, 1948b). Lacking LCE stability and filled with internal conflict, pseudopsychopaths are chronically sensitive to criticism and characteristically worry about their current misfortunes (Arieti, 1963; Karpman, 1946, 1955, 1961; Partridge, 1928). Rather than taking responsibility for their problems, they believe circumstances or other people are at fault (i.e., take on a victim role or suspect others of contriving against them), which typically leads to suspiciousness, feelings of hostility, and/or signs of dissatisfaction or unhappiness (i.e., anxiety in the form of frustration). In light of early socializing effects (i.e., overindulging or traumatic, neglectful, or invalidating upbringings; Karpman, 1950, 1955; Levy, 1950; McCord & McCord, 1964; Partridge, 1929, 1930), these individuals learned to express their underlying pathology and hostile feelings in callous, guiltless, irresponsible, impulsive, and aggressive ways. Consequently, they are unconsciously (i.e., reactively or subjectively) motivated to meet their needs in a quick, sometimes compulsive, fashion: "Although the actions of these patients seem consciously motivated, it is the unconscious motivation (generally defiance of parents [and later society]) which [generally] directs their behavior" (Arieti, 1967, p. 244). The greater the intensity of their underlying pathology, the more impulsively (i.e., reactively, without much forethought) they act out against society and, consequently, the more psychopathic they appear to be. Therefore, to the pseudopsychopath, psychopathy itself is only of secondary or superficial importance, with the underlying pathology being of primary psychiatric significance.

According to Karpman (1941, 1946, 1948a, 1955) and Arieti (1963, 1967), various conditions could manifest as pseudopsychopathy, including psychoneuroses and character neuroses (e.g., mania and histrionic; also see Henderson, 1947; Millon & Davis, 1998; Murphy & Vess, 2003; Partridge, 1929, 1930), pre- or postpsychotic syndromes (e.g., preactive phases of schizophrenia or schizophrenia in remission; also see Blackburn & Coid, 1999; Henderson, 1947), and organic conditions (e.g., postencephalitic patients and those with lesions to the prefrontal lobes; also see Damasio, Tranel, & Damasio, 1990), all of which share in common a propensity for irresponsible, impulsive, and callous antisocial behavior with little regard for the consequence of their actions. Unfortunately, aside from these clinically based speculations, the refinement of the classification of pseudopsychopathy has received no focused attention.[4] In contrast, the identification of idiopathic subtypes has a long history, rooted in rich clinical descriptions.

Idiopathic Subtypes

The notion that idiopathic psychopathy may in fact come in various forms can be traced back to Germany in the work of Kraepelin (1907/1981, 1913, 1915, as cited in Werlinder, 1978; also see Partridge, 1930) and his successor, Schneider (1950/1958). Although living in a time when diagnostic confusion over the concept of psychopathy prevailed,[5] these influential clinicians proposed several different types of *psychopathies* (i.e., personality disorders), three of which appear to reflect (to one degree or another) psychopathy as it is defined today (see Hervé, chap. 2, this volume). Although intellectually intact and aware of social norms, individuals manifesting each type fail to

---

[4]Although Lykken (1995) broached this topic, his work was not specific to PCL–R psychopaths and, therefore, his sociopathic subtypes will not be reviewed here.

[5]Although Prichard (1835, as cited in Werlinder, 1978) proposed variants of psychopathy much earlier, his work reflected the heterogeneity of his classification rather than psychopathy per se (see Hervé, chap. 2 this volume).

experience these norms emotionally and, therefore, feel justified in acting in whatever way they choose. Their differences lie in the extent to which they display the various facets of the disorder.

The Classic Psychopath

The first idiopathic type noted in the literature depicts a classic (and often sensational) case of psychopathy and, therefore, can be referred to as the *classic psychopath*. Based on Lombroso's theories (1887, as cited in Werlinder, 1978), Kraepelin (1907/1981, 1913) was the first to describe this subtype, that is, the *born criminal*. Since then, this type has been depicted in the typologies of Schneider (*affectionless*; 1950/1958), Partridge (*delinquent*; 1928), Henderson (*aggressive–murderer*; 1947), and, most recently, Millon and Davis (*malevolent*; 1998) and Murphy and Vess (*sadistic*; 2003). According to these authors, the classic psychopath is an individual who, from an early age, shows a chronic pattern of affective dullness toward others (i.e., devoid of social, complex, or LCEs) and, therefore, characteristically acts upon his or her primitive instincts and urges without restraint. Classic psychopaths are morally blind, callous, hostile, vindictive, remorseless, boastful, egocentric, entitled, and irresponsible and are prone to deceit, manipulation, violence, and varied antisocial activities. Being immune to any attempt at rehabilitation, refusing to plan for the future, and caring little for the consequences of their actions, they show a pattern of social maladjustment that is chronic and unrelenting (Henderson, 1947; Kraepelin, 1907/1981, 1913; Partridge, 1928; Schneider, 1950/1958). Given their nature, they present as reactive, opportunistic, and egotistical sensation seekers whose aggression is characteristically impulsively goal-driven, ruthless, and callous and conducted with an insensitivity for others which is almost "inhuman" (Henderson, 1947). These are the most instrumental and sadistic of psychopaths: Individuals who relish in the pain, both physical and emotional, they cause others (Henderson, 1947; Millon & Davis, 1998; Murphy & Vess, 2003).

The Explosive Psychopath

The second type depicted refers to an individual who displays his or her psychopathy in very antisocial, impulsive and aggressive ways and, therefore, is referred to as the *explosive psychopath*. Again, this type of psychopath can be traced back to Kraepelin's (1907/1981, 1913) and Schneider's (1950/1958) typologies (*impulsive* and *explosive*, respectively), as well as to the work of Henderson (*aggressive–epileptoid*; 1947), Karpman (*aggressive–predatory*; 1946, 1948b, 1955), Arieti (*simple*; 1967), Millon and Davis (*abrasive*; 1998), and Murphy and Vess (*antisocial*; 2003). Across these various accounts, explosive psychopaths, like other idiopathic types, are viewed as grandiose, egotistical, entitled individuals who are impervious to change and have a complete lack of social emotions, such as empathy, love, guilt, and remorse and, consequently, are uninhibited in their selfish pursuits. Living entirely in the present and spending little or no time worrying about the future, they chronically disregard the rights and feelings of others, as well as accepted social norms. Although similar to the other types in many important ways, their psychopathy is nevertheless unique. Their instincts and urges are more primitive (e.g., sex, food, and fun; Arieti, 1963), and their emotions are more shallow and reactive (e.g., tension, worry, frustration, and especially hate; Karpman, 1946, 1948b, 1955). As a result, they present as highly emotional and interpersonally reactive individuals, with very poor behavioral controls and a proneness to overreact to insignificant events. They are more suspicious than other types, not due to some paranoid process but out of projection of their own predatory, instrumental outlook onto others. Indeed, their acts appear motivated by society's lack of attention, or conversely, to its persecution (Henderson, 1947). As a result, they are characterized by intentional and overt antagonistic, vindictive, and antisocial attitudes and behaviors, and seek conflict no matter the circumstance, yet blame others for its occurrence. Their drives are so intensely experienced that they require immediate gratification, resulting in the use of short-term, impulsive-like strategies. Accordingly, while idiopathic in pathology, they may appear similar to (and even be mistaken for) pseudopsychopaths. To the explosive psychopath, insight is limited to finding ways to satisfy needs (i.e., actively take what they want and live by their own rules), which are characteristically aggressive, callous, and predatory (Arieti, 1963; Henderson, 1947; Karpman, 1946, 1948b, 1955). According to Arieti (1963, 1967), many are endowed with "inadequate" personalities and, consequently, lack the intellect to achieve their pretentious goals. However, they will nevertheless pursue their goals, resulting in a lifestyle characterized by emotional reactivity and active aggressive predation.

The Manipulative Psychopath

Finally, the third type consistently depicted is one in which deceptive features are paramount to psychopathy. These individuals, who I refer to as *manipulative psychopaths,* can be seen in the classifications of Kraepelin (*liars and swindlers;* 1907/1981, 1913), Schneider (*attention seekers;* 1950/1958), Partridge (*inadequate;* 1928), Henderson (*passive* or *inadequate;* 1947), Karpman (*passive–parasitic;* 1946, 1948b, 1955), Arieti (*complex;* 1963, 1967), Millon and Davis (*unprincipled* or *covetous;* 1998), and Murphy and Vess (*narcissistic;* 2003). Like the other idiopathic types, these are demanding and egotistical individuals who, devoid of complex, social emotions and prone to boredom, act in a selfish, irresponsible, remorseless, and immature manner with little care for consequences, responsibilities, and/or the future. However, their needs are less primitive (i.e., power, control, and fame), their emotions (i.e., SCEs) less intense, and their insights more complex (Arieti, 1963). They rely on their greater intellect to achieve longer ranging goals (i.e., get what they want *and* get away with it) and, as such, their seemingly "long-circuited [intellectual] mechanisms are in the service of short-circuited [emotional] ones" (Arieti, 1967, p. 257), thereby enabling them to exert some control over their psychopathy. They are characteristically grandiose, entitled, glib, and superficially charming (i.e., "flowers without perfume"; Henderson, 1947, p. 68), linguistically talented (i.e., can tell convincing stories), interpersonally skilled (i.e., can easily read others and situations), and indifferent to the evaluations and complaints of others and gain intrinsic joy from their deceptive actions (Henderson, 1947; Karpman, 1955; Kraepelin, 1907/1981, 1913; Millon & Davis, 1998; Partridge, 1930). Overall, they are less aggressive and impulsive than the other types and prefer passive parasitic pursuits to active predation, making them especially well suited to pursue subcriminal or white-collar criminal activities, which take longer to come to fruition. Like parasites, they attach themselves to others, on whom they depend to satisfy their selfish needs. Unlike most parasites, they may destroy their hosts, at which point they guiltlessly move on to another. If hosts are unavailable, they may resort to aggression but only as required by the situation and generally in a manipulative manner (i.e., use threats rather than violence). Indeed, as long as they get what they want, they are superficially docile and obedient. Their true nature, although initially masked, eventually surfaces as they repeatedly fail to show any warmth toward others, honor contracts, or return favors (Henderson, 1947; Karpman, 1955). Indeed, they prefer to revel in the pain of others rather than act in any altruistic manner.

Cleckley's Position

Clearly, the distinctions between classic, explosive, manipulative, and pseudopsychopaths, if in fact valid, have important clinical implications. Indeed, even Cleckley (1941/1988), who explicitly objected to typological efforts before a common nomenclature was adopted, implicitly supported the notion that idiopathic psychopathy might come in various shapes and sizes. In his influential book, *The Mask of Sanity*, he alluded to two variants of psychopathy by devoting separate chapters for "the disorder in full clinical manifestation" (p. 29) and for "incomplete manifestations or suggestions of the disorder" (p. 188). Although Cleckley (1941/1988) did not suggest these types to be separate entities per se but, instead, different gradations of the disorder, it could be argued that notable differences in one's level of psychopathy could just as well be indicative of categorical differences (e.g., Harris, Rice, & Quinsey, 1994; Skilling, Quinsey, & Craig, 2001). Furthermore, Cleckley's own renditions paralleled the classifications of others, therefore suggesting that his two groups are more than a reflection of gradation.

According to Cleckley, some psychopaths (i.e., full manifestation) are entirely at the mercy of their immature emotional reactions. As a result, they focus solely on immediate gratification without forethought on how to avoid detection and, therefore, are unable to mask their psychopathy for any considerable amount of time. They demonstrate, from an early age, a chronic and unbending propensity toward an antisocial lifestyle that is characterized by irresponsibility, impulsivity, aggression, and an inability to learn from experience. They are unable to use their psychopathy to their advantage, as if their disorder is completely out of their control. This description, as well as the case examples he provided, appears to characterize both classic and explosive psychopaths. Arguably, his failure to differentiate these two types reflected his focus on differentiating psychopaths based solely on their antisocial propensities. As a result, Cleckley was unable to see the trees through the forest: Both classic and explosive types are, by definition, highly antisocial. Presumably, classic psychopaths' antisociality is motivated more by their beliefs that they have the right to bleed society, whereas explosive types are motivated by their need to get back at society for its perceived persecution.

In contrast, Cleckley found other psychopaths (i.e., incomplete manifestation) to be no less psychopathic in terms of underlying pathology but nevertheless able to exert some control over (and, therefore, mask) their disorder. Like all psychopaths, they are focused on self-gratification but, unlike others, they place a considerable amount of forethought into avoiding detection. In addition, they are less overtly aggressive, relying instead on manipulation and intimidation for goal achievement. Consequently, they appear to be able to adjust to life's demands and live as part of society as, for example, businessmen, lawyers, and politicians (for recent work on the subject, see Babiak, chap. 16, this volume). However, the manner in which they function within society is wholly psychopathic, in that they use their grandiose, entitled, callous, manipulative, and parasitic ways to satisfy their selfish needs for power, fame, and fortune within the niches they have carved out for themselves (also see Hare, 1998b, 1998c). In other words, these psychopaths are overtly responsible in life but psychopathic in its pursuit (Cleckley, 1941/1988). Clearly, these features depict manipulative psychopaths in that these individuals are able to utilize compensatory intellectual mechanisms while chasing their immature emotional needs.

In regards to pseudopsychopaths, Cleckley arguably avoided the topic altogether given the fact that his focus was clearly on delineating idiopathic psychopaths, as exemplified by the title of his work: *"The Mask of Sanity."*

Limitations of Clinically Defined Subtypes

It is important to highlight the fact that the typologies reviewed in the preceding section, although clinically and theoretically significant, were not empirically derived but were based on clinical intuition and observations. As a result, very little is known to this date regarding the reliability, validity, and/or generalizability of these subtypes. Moreover, there is reason to believe that the aforementioned classifications reflected, at least in part, clinical confounds. First, the lack of a clear definition guiding clinicians in their work probably resulted in many false-positives, reflecting not pseudopsychopaths but different conditions altogether, that is, individuals who were nonpsychopathic in both pathology and behavior (Hervé, chap. 2, this volume). A recent example of this type of error can be seen in the typology of Millon and Davis (1998): Their *disingenuous, spineless,* and *malignant* types appear more conceptually related to DSM notions of histrionic, obsessive-compulsive, and paranoid personality disorders, respectively, than to psychopathy. That Millon and Davis (1998) mislabeled these individuals as psychopathic is probably due to the fact that they admittedly did not base their typology solely on the PCL–R psychopath but more generally on behaviorally related disorders depicted in various diagnostic systems, such as the *DSM–III* and International Classification of Diseases. In other words, their focus was on antisocial variants rather than on psychopathic ones. Interestingly, in the one clinical typology that was focused solely on the PCL–R, four types of psychopaths were identified (Murphy & Vess, 2003): the sadistic (classic), antisocial (explosive), narcissistic (manipulative), and borderline (pseudo).

Second, because research has demonstrated that clinical impressions often lack reliability and/or validity (Melton, Petrila, Poythress, & Slobogin, 1997; Monahan, 1995), clinical typologies may have been tainted by clinical contaminants, such as impression management and diagnostic comorbidity. Impression management is a fundamental feature of psychopathy (Hare, Forth, & Hart, 1989). Because clinical impressions of psychopaths can be biased in an impression management congruent manner (see Porter & Woodworth, 2006; Rogers et al., 2002), typologies of old may reflect both intraindividual (i.e., within subject) and interindividual (i.e., between subject) heterogeneity (variability). For example, Arieti's dyssocials (1967) basically are manipulative psychopaths who found a niche (i.e., antisocial group/gang). Like the manipulative types, they use long-circuited mechanisms (i.e., loyalty) for short-circuited purposes (e.g., sanctioned antisocial actions). Presumably, their reported loyalty may help them deflect responsibility in certain situations. Similarly, the malevolent and tyrannical subtypes proposed by Millon and Davis (1998), each of which are predisposed toward aggressive and callous acts, may be the same subtype (classic), reporting their violent tendencies differently.

Definitions of subtypes based on the presence of comorbid clinical disorders need to be avoided in typologies, as such disorders probably reflect dual diagnosis issues rather than subtyping (Blashfield & Livesley, 1999). If this is not done, the typology may become invalid solely based on the successful treatment of the secondary condition. This issue is especially important within this context, as psychopathy is known to coexist with other disorders (e.g., Hart & Hare, 1989; Stålenheim & von Knorring, 1996). The link between psychopathy and schizophrenia, for example, brings into question the paranoid-like subtype referred to by Henderson (*passive–schizoid;* 1947), Arieti (*paranoiac;* 1967), and Millon and Davis (*malignant,* 1998). These individuals may have psychopathy and a subclinical form of schizophrenia. Similarly, the link between psychopathy and deviancy (Rice & Harris, 1997) makes Henderson's *aggressive sex-variant* type and Millon and Davis' (1998) *tyrannical* type suspect. These individuals may simply be both psychopathic and deviant (be it sexual or not).

To avoid such confounds, those determining typologies need to ensure that the concept under investigation is operationally defined in a valid and reliable manner and use classification variables that reflect stable (i.e., trait not state) intersubject variability (for a review of classification, see Blashfield & Livesley, 1999).[6] A possible solution is to investigate PCL–R identified psychopaths using reliable and valid personality traits as classification variables and replicate the identified classification system across various samples, each with unique characteristics (e.g., differ in age, race, gender, comorbidity, and so forth), as any variation in findings would bring the typology into doubt (Everitt, Landau, & Leese, 2001; Hair, Anderson, Tatham, & Black, 1998).

EMPIRICALLY GROUNDED TYPOLOGIES

Irrespective of the limitations associated with previous typologies, the idea that clinically meaningful subtypes of psychopathy can be identified is worth investigating. Not only would such research increase the diagnostic sensitivity and specificity of psychopathy, but it may also highlight important risk and protective factors specifically associated with this socially devastating disorder, factors that have yet to receive proper empirical attention. Since its introduction, the PCL–R has enabled the investigation of psychopathy and its subtypes to proceed in a much more specific and sensitive manner.[7]

Empirical Differences Among Psychopaths

Indeed, there is mounting evidence to support the view that psychopaths, although unquestionably different as a group from nonpsychopaths, may vary from one another in certain important respects.

Low- and High-Anxious Psychopaths

The notion that some types may differ in terms of their ability to experience anxiety has received the most empirical attention. This area of inquiry stems from various clinical accounts depicting idiopathic psychopaths as incapable of experiencing pathological anxiety, that is, long-circuited or future-oriented anxiety as seen, for example, in the spectrum of anxiety disorders (e.g., Arieti, 1963; Cleckley, 1941/1988; Karpman, 1955; McCord & McCord, 1964). In contrast, pseudopsychopaths, given their unique pathology, are presumably susceptible to both anxiety disorders and, given internal conflicts, anxiety in the form of chronic tension or worry (Arieti, 1963; Karpman, 1961; Porter, 1996). In partial support of this theory, Kosson, Smith,

---

[6]State variables can be useful in establishing concurrent or divergent validity (see Skeem et al., 2003).

[7]Only research in which the Hare PCL scales were used will be reviewed as these are the only tools validated for the assessment of psychopathy.

and Newman (1990) found some psychopaths to score highly on self-report measures of anxiety (also see Schmitt & Newman, 1999). Intrigued by this finding, Newman and his colleagues began separating high- and low-anxious psychopaths in their research and, as a result, found them to differ on various experimental tasks (e.g., Arnett, Smith, & Newman, 1997; Kosson & Newman, 1995; Newman & Schmitt, 1998; Newman, Wallace, Schmitt, & Arnett, 1997). For example, whereas low-anxious psychopaths show deficits in passive avoidance (i.e., inhibition of response), high-anxious psychopaths show no such deficit, performing as if nonpsychopathic. Further research showed low anxious psychopaths to have specific difficulty integrating peripheral information once engaged in reward-seeking behavior, an attentional rigidity not seen in high anxious psychopaths (Newman, 1998). According to Newman (also see Lykken, 1995), these findings indicate that low-anxious psychopaths, as theory would predict (Fowles, 1980), either have an overly active behavioral activation system (are very sensitive to reward; Gorenstein & Newman, 1980) or a malfunction in communication between the behavioral inhibition system and the behavioral activation system (i.e., response modulation deficit; Patterson, Kosson, & Newman, 1987). Because high-anxious psychopaths show no such deficit, these findings could be interpreted as supporting the idiopathic–pseudo distinction (Skeem et al., 2003).

However, in light of other contradictory findings and methodological concerns regarding this line of research, this conclusion is premature. Several groups, for example, have failed to find differences between low- and high-anxious psychopaths on similar, as well as other, experimental tasks (e.g., Arnett, Smith, & Newman, 1997 [Experiment 2]; Brinkley, Newman, Harpur, & Johnson, 1999; Doninger & Kosson, 2001; Howard, Payamal, & Neo, 1997). More importantly, their measure of anxiety, which typically relies on the Minnesota Multiphasic Personality Inventory (MMPI)/MMPI-II Welsh Anxiety Scale (WAS; Welsh, 1956), is of questionable validity for measuring anxiety (Butcher et al., 2001; Greene, 2000). Although some studies suggest that higher scorers are likely to report more symptoms of anxiety, other research suggests that this scale simply measures general maladjustment, with higher scorers being less well adjusted (Butcher et al., 2001; Greene, 2000). Paradoxically, Newman himself (Schmitt & Newman, 1999) found that the WAS only correlated mildly with other anxiety measures ($r = 0.40$–0.63). In addition, although norms exist for the WAS, these researchers typically separated participants based on the sample median, the logic of which is unclear. Finally, self-report measures (especially the WAS) may not be adequate to assess the anxiety differences between idiopathic psychopaths and pseudopsychopaths. Specifically, although pseudopsychopaths, given their internal conflicts, are more likely to report a chronic type of anxiety (i.e., worry and tension) at any given time, the idiopathic psychopath (especially the explosive type), whose incarceration blocks his ability to satisfy his or her SCEs, may report experiencing frustration, tension, and worry in light of his or her current situation. The result is that each type would be undifferentiated on global measures of anxiety. Moreover, the possibility remains that Newman et al.'s low- and high-anxious psychopaths, rather than reflecting an idiopathic–pseudo division, could simply be two idiopathic types, with the former being classic and the latter explosive, as suggested by recent research (see Hicks, Markon, Patrick, Krueger, & Newman, 2004). Whereas two groups of PCL–R-identified psychopaths were differentiated via cluster analysis, group differences suggested a classic–explosive distinction rather than the primary–secondary division advocated (see Hicks et al., 2004). Not only did their two groups not differ on Factor 1 of the PCL–R, but their account of their emotionally stable (high-anxious or primary) psychopath admittedly depicted a "classic" type (p. 283), whereas their findings pertaining to their aggressive (low-anxious or secondary) type arguably reflected explosive psychopathy rather pseudopsychopathy (e.g., lower IQ, a tendency to be easily upset, disinhibited, undercontrolled, aggressive, and a view of the world as threatening).

The concerns raised in regards to this line of research also calls into question Schmitt and Newman's (1999) critique of the PCL–R. These authors suggested that the PCL–R's inability to explicitly account for anxiety, or the lack thereof, weakens its construct validity in that it cannot differentiate primary (idiopathic) from secondary (pseudo-) psychopathy.[8] However, anxiety (at least as measured by these authors) may not be key to differentiating idiopathic from pseudo types, especially because we do not yet know whether the pseudo category contains subtypes of its own. Moreover, my own line of research suggests that the PCL–R, given its facet structure, might in fact be well suited to identify subtypes of psychopaths (see later). Finally, it is important to note that matters of differential diagnosis, in the real world, are the duty of clinicians, not instruments. Indeed, in my own practice, I have had to clinically override PCL–R findings (e.g., diagnosing an individual with a total score of 34 as borderline rather than psychopathic). It should be noted, however, that diagnostic overrides, while appropriate, should not generalize to risk prediction. The research is clear: the higher the score the higher the risk!

Linguistic Differences Among Psychopaths

Recent findings also support the notion that PCL–R psychopaths may differ from one another in terms of their interpersonal skills. For example, Gretton (1998), as part of a larger study, found that some adolescent offenders with high scores on the Psychopathy Checklist: Youth Version (Forth, Kosson, & Hare, 2004) tended to be more aggressive in their crimes whereas others tended to be more manipulative. Further analyses revealed that the aggressive psychopaths had lower verbal intelligence quotients than performance intelligence quotients (i.e., VIQ < PIQ) on the Wechsler Intelligence Scale for Children (WISC-III) and that the manipulative group showed the opposite pattern (i.e., VIQ > PIQ). Similar linguistic differences were also observed by Roussy (1999): Psychopaths demonstrating behavioral problems

---

[8]Note, however, that the PCL–R's interpersonal and affective items implicitly take into account the psychopath's lack of anxiety, as well as other emotions (Hare, 1991).

as children achieved lower VIQ scores and educational performances in adulthood than those psychopaths with unremarkable backgrounds. Given evidence suggesting that delayed language development appears to be a contributing factor to antisociality at later ages (Stattin & Klackenberg-Larsson, 1993), these findings not only lend support to the distinction between manipulative and explosive psychopaths but also point to developmental precursors of each subtype, with the latter possibly being developmentally delayed in their language acquisition compared with the former. In addition, given that many interpersonal skills (e.g., manipulation, superficial charm, and so forth) rely heavily on language, the findings support the clinical speculations regarding psychopathic variability in interpersonal presentation.

Successful Versus Unsuccessful Psychopaths

Research is also starting to show support for the idea that PCL–R psychopaths differ from one another with respect to the lifestyle manifestations of the disorder (see Hare, 1998c). For example, although in research psychopaths have been identified as having a high risk to recidivate, the fact remains that not all psychopaths reoffend (for a review, see Hemphill, Hare, & Wong, 1998). Although some of these apparently successful psychopaths may have simply moved to avoid detection, have gotten "better" at committing crimes, or died, the fact that not all psychopaths recidivate indicates behavioral variability (Skeem et al., 2003). That successful psychopaths may differ in significant ways from unsuccessful psychopaths is further supported by a recent study conducted by Ishakawa, Raine, Lencz, Bihrle, and Lacasse (2001). These investigators compared the autonomic reactivity, executive functioning, and psychosocial and criminal histories of successful and unsuccessful PCL–R psychopaths recruited from the community, with success defined as not ever having been convicted of an offense. Results indicated that although unsuccessful psychopaths showed the predicted decreased autonomic reactivity (Hare, 1970, 1978; Raine, 2002), successful psychopaths actually showed heightened autonomic reactivity, stronger executive functioning, and greater childhood parental absence. This finding suggests that successful and unsuccessful psychopaths, although identical in respects to the core features of psychopathy (i.e., successful and unsuccessful psychopaths did not differ on Factor 1), may have different underlying pathologies (Ishakawa et al., 2001). Although these finding are limited in light of the psychopathy assessments used (i.e., lower psychopathy thresholds and limited collateral information), they are nevertheless theoretically appealing in that they lend further support to the notion that there may be different pathways to psychopathy.

Theoretically Derived Subtypes

Based on such findings, the post-Psychopathy Checklist (PCL) era has also seen a resurgence of theories on the topic. Although little attention has been paid to idiopathic variations (other than noting how environment influences the course of the disorder; Hare, 1998b, 1998c), important insights along the idiopathic–pseudo dimension are emerging.

Mealey's Theory

Mealey (1995a, 1995b) proposed a sociobiological evolutionary theory of *primary* (idiopathic) and *secondary* (pseudo-) sociopathy (i.e., psychopathy). Based on a review of the empirical and theoretical literature on the developmental pathways to sociopathy and antisocial personality disorder and on evolutionary models of emotions and game theories (i.e., theories explaining evolution in terms of adaptations stemming from competitive strategies for successful genetic reproduction), Mealey (1995a) proposed two etiological pathways to psychopathy, much like those proposed by Partridge (1928, 1930) and McCord and McCord (1964).

On the one hand, primary psychopathy reflects a genotype characterized by an autonomic hyposensitivity to arousal and a certain biologically predetermined temperament or personality that, in combination, make individuals particularly nonresponsive to cues required for the normal development of social emotions and morality. Because intellect is unaffected, primary psychopaths' cognitive development occurs normally except for the fact that it is devoid of emotional depth. As a consequence, their cognitions are purely instrumental, serving only themselves and their needs, which is consistent with their offense pattern (Cornell et al., 1996; Woodworth & Porter, 2002). In other words, Mealey (1995a) proposed that primary psychopaths are biologically predisposed against the development of LCEs but development of their SCEs is relatively intact. Having no inhibitory emotions, they play the game of life purely on a cost-benefit approach, which is based on immediate gratification with no care for cooperation or for the consequences of their actions. On the other hand, secondary psychopaths reflect a phenotype that developed through exposure to environmental risk factors (e.g., disadvantaged social milieu or childhood abuse or neglect) in individuals who are only mildly genetically predisposed to psychopathy (also see Blackburn, 1979; Porter, 1996). Unlike the primary psychopath, the secondary psychopath is hypothesized to have developed relatively normally both emotionally and cognitively. However, because of a chaotic childhood that leaves them socially, academically, and reproductively disadvantaged in respect to their peers, they seek out alternate and typically antisocial peer groups in which they can prosper. Through involvement in, and competition within such groups, the secondary psychopath develops an instrumental attitude toward life that, although mimicking psychopathy, is nevertheless not devoid of affect. On the PCL–R, Mealey (1995b) speculated that whereas her primary psychopaths would score high on Factor 1 (i.e., the interpersonal/affective factor) of the PCL–R and variably on Factor 2 (i.e., the lifestyle/behavioral factor), her secondary psychopaths would only score high on Factor 2, suggesting that this latter type in fact reflects an antisocial rather than a psychopathic personality.

Lykken's Theory

Like Mealey, Lykken (1995) proposed two types of severe antisocial conditions: psychopathy and sociopathy. On the one hand, he suggested that psychopathy is a biologically predisposed disorder rooted in a deficient fear response. Throughout development, psychopaths, being relatively insensitive to fear conditioning, fail to learn from punishment and, consequently, mature into self-gratifying adults with little care for the consequences of their actions. On the other hand, he described sociopathy as an environmental adaptation in which antisocial lifestyles and attitudes are required for survival. From an early age, sociopaths, who grow up within disadvantaged milieus, feel rejected by mainstream society and, therefore, gravitate toward antisocial groups. Within such groups, sociopaths develop their antiauthoritarian views and antisocial ways. As a result, they present much like psychopaths. However, their need for self-gratification is born out of retribution rather than some deficient biological system. Consequently, although they may care little for the consequences of their actions upon their victims, one would expect that they are very much concerned with how their actions affect themselves and their associates.

Lykken's (1995) theory therefore includes a genotype and phenotype for personality conditions typified by severe antisociality and, as such, is quite similar to the model proposed by Mealey (1995a) and to the developmental views of psychopathic subtypes put forward by both Partridge (1930) and McCord and McCord (1964). However, his theory fails to account for the specific psychological mechanism(s) that lead to sociopathy and, furthermore, the evidence for his distinction has been mixed, especially in regards to the fear-conditioning hypothesis of psychopathy (Hare, 1978; Raine, 2002). One possible explanation for such inconsistent findings is that poor fear conditioning, which is thought to stem from low autonomic activity, may not be unique to psychopathy but simply characteristic of antisociality (Patrick, chap. 8, this volume; Raine, 1997; 2002; Raine, Lencz, Bihrle, LaCasse, & Colletti, 2000).

Raine's Theory

Based on literature reviews, Raine (1997, 2002) speculated that many of the features of antisociality, including low autonomic arousal, fearlessness, emotional bluntness, attentional and other cognitive deficits, social processes, and antisocial behaviors, are either closely or more distally related to neurocognitive executive functions, which are themselves rooted within the prefrontal cortex. He proposed that prefrontal deficits are central to the development of antisociality. More germane to the present topic, he noted that the nature of the deficit and the psychosocial context in which it develops might help explain the various pathways to antisociality reported in the literature. For example, he proposed that early, lifelong, and severe patterns of antisociality might result from early damage to or dysfunctions of the prefrontal cortex in individuals from disadvantaged environments. However, a similarly disordered individual from a relatively unremarkable environment may develop into a prosocial member of society or, at the very least, may be much less anti-social than his disadvantaged counterpart. In contrast, individuals with no prefrontal damage are much less likely to become antisocial, unless environ-mentally induced to do so (i.e., come from disadvantaged backgrounds). Indeed, environmental demands might act to overload intact prefrontal resources and, therefore, lead to antisocial acts. This overloading hypothesis is thought to occur in individuals whose prefrontal cortex is structurally nor-mal but functionally limited in some way. For example, one's prefrontal cortex might be late to mature (i.e., the prefrontal cortex maturation process continues into the 20s and beyond; Raine, 2002), and/or the demands of a sit-uation may simply be too overwhelming for one's executive functioning capacities. If such demands occur early enough in one's development and are chronic in nature, they may result in permanent functional prefrontal dys-functions that result in chronic rather than situational antisociality (Raine, 1997). Thus, Raine's theory appears to provide the etiological background missing in Lykken's work. Although all forms of psychopathy/sociopathy are likely to be characterized by fearlessness, the fearlessness found in geno-typic and phenotypic versions probably results from biological and environ-mental mechanisms, respectively. Unfortunately, neither Raine's nor Lykken's theory has been empirically validated.

Porter's Theory

Porter (1996) also proposed two pathways to psychopathy, one resulting in what he termed the *fundamental* (i.e., idiopathic) psychopath and the other in the *secondary* (i.e., pseudo-) psychopath. Influenced by Hare's work, Porter (1996) believed psychopathy to be a disorder of affect (i.e., emotional blind-ness) that results in an individual whose mental or cognitive life is devoid of emotional meaning. Like others, he speculated that such a clinical presen-tation could result from both biological and environmental events. On the one hand, fundamental psychopathy was believed to be a genotype in which deep-rooted deviant biological processes, probably within the limbic sys-tem, precluded any emotional development. That is, Porter viewed funda-mental psychopathy as a biologically predisposed disorder. On the other hand, secondary psychopathy was believed to be a phenotype in which there is a predisposition not to psychopathy proper but to some posttraumatic stress response (i.e., perhaps via dissociative processes in which emotions are separated from cognitions) that, if activated within childhood by some trau-matic event (e.g., abuse), interrupts or postpones emotional development. Interestingly, recent research suggests childhood traumas to be important to the manifestation of adult psychopathy (Forth & Burke, 1998). For example, Harris, Rice, and Lalumiere (2001) found inadequate, antisocial parenting to be related to adult psychopathy, and Steadman et al. (2000) found adult psychopaths with a history of childhood sexual abuse to be at greater risk for future violence than those with no such history. Unfortunately, although distally supporting Porter's model as well, information regarding preabuse functioning was not available and, therefore, it is unknown whether or not the abuse caused (pseudo-) psychopathy or simply affected its (idiopathic) trajectory.

Empirically Derived Typologies

The clearest evidence supporting the notion that clinically relevant subtypes of psychopaths do in fact exist comes from an emerging body of research relying specifically on classification methodologies.

Blackburn and Coid's Subtypes

Based on cluster analyses of the *DSM-III* personality disorder criteria, Blackburn and Coid (1999), for example, found six subtypes of violent offenders: antisocial–narcissistic, paranoid–antisocial, borderline–antisocial–passive–aggressive, borderline, compulsive–borderline, and schizoid. On the PCL–R the first three groups were no different from one another but scored significantly higher than all of the other groups (PCL–R = 32.08, 32.60, 31.62, 20.80, 17.62, and 17.85, respectively) and more than three quarters met the criteria for psychopathy (76%, 80%, and 77%, respectively). Consistent with the literature on psychopathy (Hare, 1996; 1998a), further analyses revealed these psychopathic groups to be more antisocial than their nonpsychopathic counterparts. Head-to-head comparisons revealed the paranoid–schizoid type to have the highest lifetime history of psychotic disorders and the borderline–antisocial–passive–aggressive type to have the highest lifetime history of affective and anxiety disorders. In addition, the paranoid–schizoid type had more convictions for fraud and fewer for robbery and firearm offenses than the antisocial–narcissistic subtype. When compared with nonpsychopaths, the antisocial–narcissistic and paranoid–antisocial subtypes scored significantly higher on Factor 1 of the PCL–R (i.e., interpersonal and affective traits) and the borderline–antisocial–passive–aggressive subtypes on Factor 2 (i.e., lifestyle traits). According to Blackburn and Coid (1999), their findings supported their earlier work on primary (or idiopathic) and secondary (or pseudo-) psychopaths, with the narcissistic–antisocial subtype described as primary psychopaths and the borderline–antisocial–passive–aggressive and paranoid–antisocial subtypes as secondary psychopaths. However, it could be argued that their antisocial–narcissistic type depicted classic (or possibly explosive) psychopaths, and their paranoid-antisocial type idiopathic manipulative psychopaths (e.g., they engage in more fraud-type crimes and have high Factor 1 scores) with comorbid mental health problems. Unfortunately, as this research was conducted before the development of the PCL–R facet structure, each group's predominant psychopathic features remains unknown. Nonetheless, the theory that one or more types of psychopaths may present with features of other personality disorders has received some empirical support (Alterman et al., 1998; Meloy, & Gacono, 1993; Raine, 1992).

Alterman et al.'s Subtypes

Using a similar methodology (i.e., cluster analyses of measures indexing antisocial attitudes and personality traits, including a shortened version of the PCL–R), Alterman et al. (1998) found six replicable and temporally stable clusters, each of which had unique criminal and psychiatric (Axis I or II) histories. Of special interest to the present discussion were their early-onset, high antisociality (Type 1), late-onset, high antisociality (Type 2), and psychopathic, moderate antisociality (Type 5) subtypes. Type 1 individuals were characterized by a significant and long history of criminal involvement, drug and alcohol problems, and social maladjustment, as well as by high levels of anxiety and depression, hostility, and paranoid, borderline, and sadistic personality features. Type 2 individuals were similar to Type 1 individuals except that they reflected relatively less antisociality in youth and more features of histrionic and narcissistic personalities. Compared with Types 1 and 2, Type 5 individuals showed a similar adult criminal pattern but less youth antisociality, less problems in social spheres, and markedly less anxiety, guilt, and depression than individuals of any other type. At a superficial level, Types 1, 2, and 5 appear in many respects similar to the descriptions of pseudo-, explosive (or possibly classic), and manipulative psychopaths, respectively. However, none of these individuals actually met the diagnostic criteria for psychopathy (mean PCL–Rs for Types 1, 2, and 5 were 21, 23, and 20, respectively; the diagnostic cutoff on 17 items = 25.5). Although lower PCL–R scores could simply reflect lower Factor 2 elevations, as would be expected in a nonforensic sample (participants were male patients receiving methadone), PCL–R factor comparisons were not conducted because of a relatively high interfactor correlation ($r = 0.65$). Like the Blackburn and Coid (1999) study, this investigation, although suggestive of subtypes, tells us little about how individuals diagnosed with psychopathy may differ from one another with respect to the degree to which they display the core features of the disorder.

Frick's Subtypes

The emerging research by Frick and his colleagues on psychopathic children has started to shed some light on this issue (e.g., Christian, Frick, Hill, Tyler, & Fraser, 1997; Frick, Bodin, & Barry, 2001; also see Skeem et al., 2003). Based on a child-appropriate version of the PCL–R (i.e., a parent-teacher rating scale; the Antisocial Process Screening Device [APSD]: Frick & Hare, 2001), Frick and colleagues investigated whether the APSD factor structure could identify different personality types in clinic-referred (mean age = 9 [*SD* = 2.0]; Christian et al., 1997) and community samples of children (mean age =

11 [SD = 1.6]; Frick et al., 2001).[9,10] Together, these studies suggest that children with behavioral problems can be differentiated in a manner similar to that seen in adult populations. The psychopathic conduct/high psychopathy groups, possessing high levels of the interpersonal (ASPD Narcissistic facet), affective (Callous–Unemotional facet), and behavioral (Impulsive facet and symptoms of oppositional defiant and conduct disorders) traits of psychopathy, appear similar in description to classic psychopaths. These youths displayed the greatest amount of youth antisociality. The characteristics of the callous–unemotional group and, to a lesser degree, the mild callousness group, each displaying significant levels of the affective traits of psychopathy but having relatively few behavioral problems, may be precursors to adult manipulative psychopathy. The pure narcissistic type, showing a general self-centeredness and significant behavioral problems, evokes pictures of the adult explosive psychopath. Finally, the impulsive conduct–pure impulsive group, showing significant behavioral problems in the absence of affective and interpersonal psychopathic traits, may, depending on further socialization factors, develop into a type of pseudopsychopath. However, all of this remains speculative as the long-term course of these subtypes has yet to be investigated (Edens, Skeem, Cruise, & Cauffman, 2001; Skeem et al., 2003). Nonetheless, Frick's work has theoretical appeal and, more importantly, his methodology, using psychopathy facets to identify subtypes, is a significant step forward in this area.

Hervé's Subtypes

My own work on the subject, albeit in its infancy, is thus far the only research to focus both on PCL–R-identified psychopaths (PCL–R ≥ 27[11]) and on identifying (or classifying) subtypes based on the predominance of psychopathic features, as indexed by the three- and four-facet structure of the PCL–R. Using exploratory (hierarchical) and confirmatory (nonhierarchical) cluster analytical procedures in a sample of 202 adult North American male correctional inmates (Hervé, Ling, & Hare, 2000), four groups emerged in a consistent (i.e., a four-cluster solution was the most consistent across algorithms) and stable (i.e., group assignment [kappa] across algorithms ranged

---

[9]Given the age group considered, personality, in this respect, is loosely defined to refer to relatively stable interpersonal, emotional, and behavioral traits (see Edens et al., 2001; Frick, 2000, for reviews of ethical and methodological issues in the assessment of psychopathy in youth).

[10]Like the PCL–R factor structure, the APSD factor structure has evolved, changing from a two factor (i.e., callous–unemotional and impulsive–conduct problem) to a three-factor (i.e., callous–unemotional, narcissistic, and impulsive) structure (Christian et al., 1997; Frick et al., 2001, respectively).

[11]Although a cutoff of 30 is typically recommended, a cutoff of 27 was used as it is approximately 1 standard error of measurement below the recommended cutoff and, therefore, takes into account the measurement error associated with a cutoff score of 30. Consequently, it should either correct for false-negatives (i.e., by including participants in emerging clusters) or result in false-positives (i.e., by creating an independent cluster).

from 0.67 to 0.96, $p < .001$) fashion, each differing in the extent to which they displayed the interpersonal, affective, and lifestyle features of psychopathy (Cooke & Michie, 2001). The first group appeared conceptually similar to the descriptions of classic psychopaths. They had the highest overall PCL–R scores and scored highly on all three facets (i.e., showed all the characteristics of the disorder to high levels). The second group was interpreted as representing explosive psychopaths as they had the second highest PCL–R elevations and scored relatively low (for psychopaths, that is) on the interpersonal facet but high on the affective and lifestyle facets.[12] The third group appeared to depict manipulative psychopaths; that is, individuals who scored highly on the interpersonal and affective facets but relatively low on the lifestyle facet. Finally, the fourth group seemed to subsume pseudopsychopaths. These individuals, who had the lowest PCL–R scores, showed the interpersonal and behavioral characteristics of the disorder but not the affective ones, at least not to the same degree as the other groups. When similar procedures were employed using the newly developed four-facet PCL–R structure (see Hare, 2003), a four-cluster solution was again the one that proved to be the most statistically rigorous and representative of the sample (Hervé, 2004). Not only was the resulting pattern virtually identical to the one found with the three-facet model (i.e., in regards to the domains that these models share in common), but also the additional facet further differentiated the subtypes in a clinically and theoretically predictable manner, both from one another and relative to inmates who score low and moderate on the PCL–R (see Fig. 17–1). That is, manipulative psychopaths scored relatively lower than all other subtypes on the domain of early and persistent antisocial behavior. These results support the long-held belief that highly psychopathic individuals differ from one another with respect to the degree to which they embody the core interpersonal, affective, lifestyle, and behavioral characteristics of the disorder.

Nonetheless, the possibility that the identified typology was unique to the sample studied remained a viable possibility. If the subtypes reflect some *natural* psychopathic phenomenon, then one would expect them to emerge in various samples, irrespective of age, race, culture, gender, and/or psychiatric comorbidity (Blashfield & Livesley, 1999; Everitt et al., 2001). In line with this notion, the same four subtypes (classic, explosive, manipulative, and pseudo) were found in six other forensic samples of psychopaths via confirmatory (i.e., nonhierarchical) cluster analyses (Hervé, 2002[13]): 443 adult male correctional inmates from the United States, 167 adult male correctional inmates from England, 238 African American male correctional inmates, 292 North American female correctional inmates, 142 Swedish forensic

---

[12]Initially, I referred to this type as "macho" psychopaths but, based on my reading of the literature and clinical experience, I now find "explosive" to be a more accurate description.

[13]This research was based on the three-facet PCL–R structure as it was conducted before the development of the four-facet structure. However, four-facet analyses will be conducted in the near future.

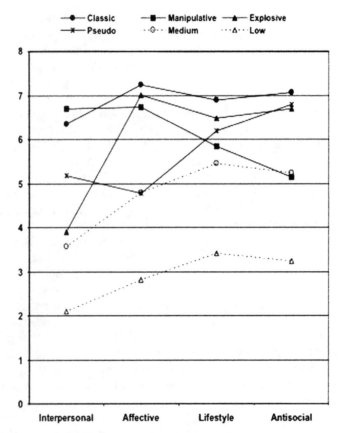

FIGURE 17–1.   Mean PCL–R (2nd ed.) facet scores for psychopathic subtypes (classic, manipulative, explosive, and pseudo) and medium and low psychopathy groups for a sample of adult Canadian male federal inmates.

psychiatric male patients, and, most recently, 105 adolescent male and female correctional inmates (Spidel, Hervé, Hemphill, & Bartel, 2005). At the very least, these findings support the notion that psychopaths can be reliably classified into four clinically and theoretically meaningful types. Because the classification generalized across diverse populations, it also appears that these types do not reflect unique sample characteristics but instead true differences among psychopaths, differences that are unaffected by age, gender, psychiatric comorbidity, race, or culture.

While reliable, little is yet known about the validity of this classification. The one study conducted (Hervé, 2002), however, suggests that this line of research is worth pursuing. Based on the three-facet classification (and therefore avoiding criterion contamination), I found the four subtypes to differ from one another and from nonpsychopathic offenders with respect to their criminal histories (i.e., convictions). Specifically, prototypical psychopaths and pseudopsychopaths engaged in a greater number of crimes across their criminal careers and were more likely to have defied authority (i.e., escape, obstruction, and court violations) than were the explosive and manipulative psychopaths, with the latter being the least criminally problematic, especially in regard to severe interpersonal violence (i.e., murder, sexual and simple assault, and kidnapping). Pseudo- and macho psychopaths also engaged in more destructive (e.g., arson, vandalism, and threat) and less fraudulent crimes than did other psychopaths, especially manipulative ones. Although the design was unbalanced (i.e., 65 classic, 11 manipulative, 29 macho, 27 pseudo, 89 medium, and 62 low), admittedly, as this was a sample of convenience, and there were low base rates for various crime categories (e.g., violent crimes, anger-related crimes [vandalism, arson, and threat], and some types of frauds), these findings support the validity of the current typology in a theoretically meaningful manner. Nonetheless, not all predictions held. For example, whereas manipulative psychopaths were found to engage in more fraud for needs (food and shelter) than other types, they were not found to be more likely to con others out of money. Accordingly, additional validity studies are required before these findings are applied to practice. Overall, my research thus far has, at the very least, set the foundation for further research into this topic, in that reliability sets the parameters of validity (Glass & Hopkins, 1996).

CONCLUSION

Clinical experience suggests that psychopaths differ from one another in several ways, particularly with respect to the core interpersonal, affective, lifestyle, and behavioral features of the disorder. Indeed, historical and theoretical renditions consistently depict psychopathy as a higher order construct that manifests itself in several unique ways. This observed variability has led to the notion that psychopathy may in fact subsume subtypes. Clinical and theoretical accounts, for example, have highlighted the possibility of both genotype (i.e., idiopathic, primary, and fundamental) and phenotype (i.e., pseudo, symptomatic, and secondary) versions of psychopathy, with the former being the product of nature and the latter of nurture. In addition, several different sightings of the genotype have been reported, including one that embodies all aspects of the disorder (i.e., classic), one that manifests itself in parasitic ways (i.e., manipulative), and one in which aggressive and antisocial impulses predominate (i.e., the explosive). In these cases, environmental factors are thought to account for the differences. However, comorbid biological deficits in autonomic functioning and in various neurocognitive domains (e.g., in the prefrontal and temporal areas) cannot be ruled out (Raine, 2002; Patrick, chap. 8, this volume).

Clearly, the implications of this line of inquiry are many (see Murphy & Vess, 2003; Poythress & Skeem, 2005; Skeem et al., 2003). Indeed, understanding individual differences within the construct of psychopathy (as well as more generally) will likely lead to advancements in theory (e.g., etiology of psychopathy and its subtypes), investigative psychology (e.g., criminal profiling, credibility assessment), offender management (e.g., internal security; risk prediction), and treatment (e.g., idiopathic vs. pseudo). This line of research also has implications for the debate on whether psychopathy, as assessed by the PCL–R, is a categorical or a continuous trait (Hare, 1996, 1998a; Harris et al., 1994). This debate has typically been viewed as having only one outcome, that is, psychopathy is either categorical (i.e., different in kind) or dimensional (i.e., different in degree). However, perhaps the PCL–R assesses both a categorical and a dimensional entity (Mealey, 1995b). The categorical concept may apply only to idiopathic psychopaths, whose biologically rooted emotional deficit sets them apart from other individuals. Pseudopsychopathy may be a dimensional concept reflecting different life trajectories. As such, the intensity of the environmental agent (e.g., acute vs. chronic childhood traumas) leading to pseudopsychopathy, in combination with other developmental events (e.g., poor parenting, delinquent subculture, etc.), would set the level at which an affected individual displays his or her psychopathy.

Unfortunately, although the topic has received some empirical attention in recent years, studies in this area have either not been specific to psychopathy (e.g., Alterman et al., 1998; Blackburn, 1975), have utilized limited methodologies (Blackburn & Coid, 1999; Hicks et al., 2004), or remain largely invalidated (Frick et al., 2001; Hervé, 2002). For this line of research to efficiently prosper, researchers need to limit their investigations to psychopaths as defined by the Hare PCL. Self-report measures of psychopathy, although useful for screening purposes, are not diagnostic tools and, moreover, are arguably of limited validity (i.e., biased toward the behavioral features of the disorder; see Hare, 1985). As noted by Cleckley (1941/1988) and consistent with rules of classification (Blashfield & Livesley, 1999), the entity under investigation needs to be reliably and validly defined; only then can refinements to methodology be made. In addition, classification variables need to reflect stable traits that are measured in a reliable and valid manner; again, self-reports are of limited use. That psychopathy can co-occur with other disorders is not debatable, nor is the likelihood that subtypes will be found to be prone to different comorbid psychiatric conditions. The concern with this approach to classification is that it fails to inform how individuals with a specific diagnosis differ in respect to the disorder itself. As a result, when the comorbid condition is not present (i.e., premorbid states or states in remission), the identified subtypes essentially disappear, resulting in a typology that lacks temporal stability. Given the infancy of this line of research, we also need to be open to the possibility that yet unidentified variants exist (Poythress & Skeem, 2005). Indeed, there are likely to be, for example, various types of pseudopsychopaths; early and chronic disruptions in complex, social emotions may result from childhood psychosocial stressors, disease, and/or acquired brain trauma. Similarly, the use of exploratory (rather than confirmatory) methodologies will be essential when researchers attempt to generalize findings (e.g., to nonincarcerated samples). Failing to pursue a more refined typology will only serve to limit the sensitivity and specificity of our work, resulting—given the nature of the beast—in undo harm for society in general and victims in particular. Finally, greater emphasis should be placed on integrating rather than debating findings, the former arguably being the most challenging. I suspect that the various typological approaches taken, such as those founded on etiology, autonomic reactivity, psychiatric comorbidity, fear conditioning, and/or perceived anxiety, are not mutually exclusive but simply different parts of the puzzle.

ACKNOWLEDGMENT

The views expressed are those of the authors, and do not necessarily reflect the position of the Forensic Psychiatric Hospital.

I acknowledge Kristin Kendrick, BA, and John Yuille, PhD, for their helpful comments.

REFERENCES

Alterman, A. I., McDermott, P. A., Cacciola, J. S., Rutherford, M. J., Boardman, C. R., McKay, J. R., & Cook, T. G. (1998). A typology of antisociality in methadone patients. *Journal of Abnormal Psychology, 107*, 412–422.

Arieti, S. (1963). Psychopathic personality: Some views on its psychopathology and psychodynamics. *Comprehensive Psychiatry, 4*, 301–312.

Arieti, S. (1967). *The intrapsychic self: Feeling, cognition, and creativity in the health and mental illness.* New York: Basic Books.

Arnett, P. A., Smith, S. S., & Newman, J. P. (1997). Approach and avoidance motivation in psychopathic criminal offenders during passive avoidance. *Journal of Personality and Social Psychology, 72*, 1413–1428.

Blackburn, R. (1975). An empirical classification of psychopathic personality. *British Forensic Psychiatry, 127*, 456–460.

Blackburn, R. (1979). Cortical and autonomic arousal in primary and secondary psychopaths. *Psychophysiology, 16*, 143–150.

Blackburn, R., & Coid, J. (1999). Empirical clusters of DSM-III personality disorders in violent offenders. *Journal of Personality Disorders, 13*, 18–34.

Blashfield, R. K., & Livesley, W. J. (1999). Classification. In T. Millon, P. H. Blaney, & R. D. Davis (Eds.), *Oxford textbook of psychopathology* (pp. 3–28). New York: Oxford University Press.

Brinkley, C. A., Newman, J. P., Harpur, T. J., & Johnson, M. M. (1999). Cohesion in texts produced by psychopathic and nonpsychopathic criminal inmates. *Personality and Individual Differences, 26*, 873–885.

Butcher, J. N, Graham, J. R., Ben-Porath, Y. S., Tellegen, A., Dahlstrom, W. G., & Kaemmer, B. (2001). *Minnesota Multiphasic Personality Inventory–2: Manual for administering, scoring, and interpretation* (2nd ed.). Minneapolis, MN: University of Minnesota Press.

Christian, R. E., Frick, P. J., Hill, N. L., Tyler, L., & Fraser, D. R. (1997). Psychopathy and conduct problems in children: II. Implications for subtyping children with conduct problems. *Journal of the American Academy of Child and Adolescent Psychiatry, 36*, 233–241.

Cleckley, H. (1988). *The mask of sanity* (5th ed.). St. Louis, MO: Mosby. (Original work published in 1941)

Cooke, D. J., & Michie, C. (2001). Refining the construct of psychopathy: Towards a hierarchical model. *Psychological Assessment, 13*, 171–188.

Cornell, D., Warren, J., Hawk, G., Stafford, E., Oram, G., & Pine, D. (1996). Psychopathy in instrumental and reactive violent offenders. *Journal of Consulting and Clinical Psychology, 64*, 783–790.

Damasio, A., Tranel, D., & Damasio (1990). Individuals with sociopathic behavior caused by frontal damage fail to respond to social stimuli. *Behavioral Brain Research, 41*, 81–94.

Doninger, N. A., & Kosson, D. S. (2001). Interpersonal construct systems among psychopaths. *Personality and Individual Differences, 30*, 1263–1281.

Edens, J. F., Skeem, J. L., Cruise, K. R., & Cauffman, E. (2001). Assessment of "juvenile psychopathy" and its association with violence: A critical review. *Behavioral Sciences and the Law, 19*, 53–80.

Everitt, B. S., Landau, S., & Leese, M. (2001). *Cluster analysis* (4th ed.). New York: Oxford University Press.

Forth, A. E., & Burke, H. C. (1998). Psychopathy in adolescence: Assessment, violence, and developmental precursors. In D. J. Cooke, A. E. Forth, & R. D. Hare (Eds.), *Psychopathy: Theory, research, and implications for society* (pp. 205–229). Dordrecht, The Netherlands: Kluwer Academic.

Forth, A. E., Kosson, D. S., & Hare, R. D. (2004). *The Psychopathy Checklist: Youth Version (PCL:YV)*. Toronto, Ontario, Canada: Multi-Health Systems.

Fowles, D. C. (1980). The three arousal model: Implications of Gray's two-factor learning theory for heart rate, electrodermal activity, and psychopathy. *Psychophysiology, 17*, 87–104.

Frick, P. J. (2000). The problems of internal validation without a theoretical context: The different conceptual underpinnings of psychopathy and the disruptive behavior disorder criteria. *Psychological Assessment, 12*, 451–456.

Frick, P. J., Bodin, S. D., & Barry, C. T. (2001). Psychopathic traits and conduct problems in community and clinic-referred samples of children: Further development of the Psychopathy Screening Device. *Psychological Assessment, 12*, 382–393.

Frick, P., & Hare, R. D. (2001). *The Antisocial Processes Screening Device: Technical manual*. Toronto, Ontario, Canada: Multi-Health Systems.

Glass, G. V., & Hopkins, K. D. (1996). *Statistical methods in education and psychology* (3rd ed.). Boston, MA: Allyn & Bacon.

Gorenstein, E. E., & Newman, J. P. (1980). Disinhibitory psychopathology: A new perspective and a model for research. *Psychological Review, 87*, 301–315.

Greene, R. L. (2000). *The MMPI-2: An interpretive manual* (2nd ed.). Boston: Allyn & Bacon.

Gretton, H. M. (1998). *Psychopathy and recidivism in adolescence: A ten-year retrospective follow-up*. Unpublished doctoral dissertation, University of British Columbia, Vancouver, British Columbia, Canada.

Hair, J. F., Anderson, R. E., Tatham, R. L., & Black, W. C. (1998). *Multivariate data analysis* (5th ed.). Upper Saddle River, NJ: Prentice Hall.

Hare, R. D. (1970). *Psychopathy: Theory and research*. New York: Wiley.

Hare. R. D. (1978). Electrodermal and cardiovascular correlates of psychopathy. In R. D. Hare & D. Schalling (Eds.), *Psychopathic behavior: Approach to research* (pp. 107–144). New York: Wiley.

Hare, R. D. (1985). A comparison of procedures for the assessment of psychopathy. *Journal of Consulting and Clinical Psychology, 53*, 7–16.

Hare, R. D. (1991). *The Hare Psychopathy Checklist–Revised*. Toronto, Ontario, Canada: Multi-Health Systems.

Hare, R. D. (1996). Psychopathy: A clinical construct whose time has come. *Criminal Justice and Behavior, 23*, 25–54.

Hare, R. D. (1998a). Psychopathy, affect, and behavior. In D. Cooke, A. Forth, & R. Hare (Eds.). *Psychopathy: Theory, research, and implications for society* (pp. 105–137). Dordrecht, The Netherlands: Kluwer Academic.

Hare, R. D. (1998b). The Hare PCL–R: Some issues concerning its use and misuse. *Legal and Criminological Psychology, 3*, 99–119.

Hare, R. D. (1998c). *Without conscience: The disturbing world of the psychopaths among us*. New York: Guilford Press.

Hare, R. D. (2003). *The Hare Psychopathy Checklist–Revised* (2nd ed.). Toronto, Ontario, Canada: Multi-Health Systems.

Hare, R. D., Forth, A. E., & Hart, S. D. (1989). The psychopath as prototype for pathological lying and deception. In J. C. Yuille (Ed.), *Credibility assessment* (pp. 24–49). Dordrecht, The Netherlands: Kluwer Academic.

Harris, G. T., Rice, M. E., & Lalumière, M. (2001). Criminal violence: The role of psychopathy, neurodevelopmental insults, and antisocial parenting. *Criminal Justice and Behavior, 28*, 402–426.

Harris, G. T., Rice, M. E., & Quinsey, V. L. (1994). Psychopathy as a taxon: Evidence that psychopaths are a discrete class. *Journal of Consulting and Clinical Psychology, 62*, 387–397.

Hart, S. D., & Hare, R. D. (1989). Discriminant validity of the Psychopathy Checklist in a forensic psychiatric population. *Psychological Assessment, 1*, 211–218.

Hemphill, J. F., Hare, R. D., & Wong, S. (1998). Psychopathy and recidivism: A review. *Legal and Criminological Psychology, 3*, 141–172.

Henderson, D. K. (1947). *Psychopathic states* (2nd ed.). New York: W. W. Norton.

Hervé, H. F. (2002, June). Criminal psychopathy and its subtypes: Implications for the assessment of risk as a function of psychopathy. In S. Porter (Chair), *Investigations of aggression and violence as a function of psychopathy in both children and adults*. Symposium conducted at the 62nd Annual Convention of the Canadian Psychology Association, Vancouver, British Columbia, Canada.

Hervé, H. F. (2004, March). Psychopathic subtypes and their crimes: A validation study. In H. Hervé (Chair), *Psychopaths and their crimes: Towards a more refined understanding*. Symposium conducted at the American Psychology-Law Society, Division 41 of the American Psychological Association, Scottsdale, AZ.

Hervé, H. F., Ling, J. Y. H., & Hare, R. D. (2000, March). *Criminal psychopathy and its subtypes*. Paper presented at the American Psychology-Law Society, Division 41 of the American Psychological Association, New Orleans, LA.

Hicks, B. M., Markon, K. E., Patrick, C. J., Krueger, R. F., & Newman, J. P. (2004). Identifying psychopathy subtypes on the basis of personality structure. *Psychological Assessment, 16*, 276–288.

Howard, R. C., Payamal, L. T., & Neo, L. H. (1997). Response modulation deficits in psychopaths: A failure to confirm and a reconsideration of the Patterson–Newman model. *Personality and Individual Differences, 22*, 707–717.

Ishakawa, S. S., Raine, A., Lencz, T., Bihrle, S., & Lacasse, L. (2001). Autonomic reactivity and executive functions in successful and unsuccessful criminal psychopaths from the community. *Journal of Abnormal Psychology, 110*, 423–432.

Karpman, B. (1941). On the need of separating psychopathy into distinct clinical types: The symptomatic and the idiopathic. *Journal of Criminal Psychopathology, 3*, 112–137.

Karpman, B. (1946). Psychopathy in the scheme of human typology. *Journal of Nervous and Mental Disease, 103*, 276–288.

Karpman, B. (1948a). The myth of the psychopathic personality. *American Journal of Psychiatry, 104*, 523–234.

Karpman, B. (1948b). Conscience in the psychopath: Another version. *American Journal of Orthopsychiatry, 18*, 455–491.

Karpman, B. (1950). Psychopathic behavior in infants and children: A critical survey of the existing concepts. *American Journal of Orthopsychiatry, 21*, 223–272.

Karpman, B. (1955). Criminal psychodynamics: A platform. *Archives of Criminal Psychodynamics, 1*, 3–100.

Karpman, B. (1961). The structure of neuroses: With special differentials between neurosis, psychosis, homosexuality, alcoholism, psychopathy and criminality. *Archives of Criminal Psychodynamics, 4*, 599–646.

Kosson, D. S., & Newman, J. P. (1995). An evaluation of Mealey's hypotheses based on Psychopathy Checklist-identified groups. *Behavioural and Brain Sciences, 18*, 562–563.

Kosson, D. S., Smith, S. S., & Newman, J. P. (1990). Evaluation of the construct validity of psychopathy in Black and White male inmates: Three preliminary studies. *Journal of Abnormal Psychology, 99*, 250–259.

Kraepelin, E. (1981). *Clinical psychiatry* (2nd English ed., A. R. Diefendorf, Trans.). New York: Scholars' Facsimiles & Reprints. (Original work published in 1907)

Kraepelin E. (1913). *Lectures on clinical psychiatry* (3rd English ed., T. Johnstone, Trans.). New York: William Wood.

Levy, D. M. (1950). The deprived and indulged forms of psychopathic personality. *American Journal of Orthopsychiatry, 21*, 250–254.

Lykken, D. T. (1995). *The antisocial personalities*. Hillsdale, NJ: Lawrence Erlbaum Associates.

McCord, W., & McCord J. (1964). *The psychopath: An essay on the criminal mind*. Princeton, NJ: D. Van Nostrand.

Mealey, L. (1995a). The sociobiology of sociopathy: An integrated evolutionary model. *Behavioral and Brain Sciences, 19*, 523–540.

Mealey, L. (1995b). Primary sociopathy (psychopathy) is a type, secondary is not. *Behavioral and Brain Sciences, 19*, 579–599.

Melton, G. B., Petrila, J., Poythress, N. G., & Slobogin, C. (1997). *Psychological evaluations for the courts: A handbook for mental health professionals and lawyers* (2nd ed.). New York: Guilford Press.

Meloy, J. R., & Gacono, C. B. (1993). A borderline psychopath: "I was basically maladjusted. . . ." *Journal of Personality Assessment, 61*, 358–373.

Millon, T., & Davis, R. D. (1998). Ten subtypes of psychopathy. In T. Millon, E. Simonson, M. Burket-Smith, & R. Davis (Eds.), *Psychopathy: Antisocial, criminal, and violent behavior* (pp. 161–170). New York: Guilford Press.

Monahan, J. (1995). *The clinical prediction of violent behavior*. Northvale, NJ: Jason Aronson.

Murphy, C., & Vess, J. (2003). Subtypes of psychopathy: Proposed differences between narcissistic, borderline, sadistic, and antisocial psychopaths. *Psychiatric Quarterly, 74,* 11–29.

Newman, J. P. (1998). Psychopathic behavior: An information processing perspective. In D. Cooke, A. Forth, & R. Hare (Eds.), *Psychopathy: theory, research, and implications for society* (pp. 81–105). Dordrecht, The Netherlands: Kluwer Academic.

Newman, J. P., & Schmitt, W. A. (1998). Passive avoidance in psychopathic offenders: A replication and extension. *Journal of Abnormal Psychology, 107,* 527–532.

Newman, J. P., Wallace, J. F., Schmitt, W. A., & Arnett, P. A. (1997). Behavioral inhibition system functioning in anxious, impulsive and psychopathic individuals. *Personality and Individual Differences, 23,* 583–592.

Partridge, G. E. (1928). A study of 50 case of psychopathic personalities. *American Journal of Psychiatry, 7,* 953–974.

Partridge, G. E. (1929). Psychopathic personality and personality investigation. *American Journal of Psychiatry, 8,* 1053–1055.

Partridge, G. E. (1930). Current conceptions of psychopathic personality. *American Journal of Psychiatry, 10,* 53–99.

Patterson, C. M., Kosson, D. S., & Newman, J. P. (1987). Reaction to punishment, reflectivity, and passive avoidance learning in extraverts. *Journal of Personality and Social Psychology, 52,* 565–575.

Porter, S. (1996). Without conscience or without active conscience? The etiology of psychopathy revisited. *Aggression and Violent Behavior 1,* 1–11.

Porter, S., & Woodworth, M. (2006). "I'm sorry I did it . . . but he started it:" A comparison of the official and self-reported homicide descriptions of psychopaths and non-psychopaths. *Law & Human Behavior.*

Poythress, N. G., & Skeem, J. L. (2005). Disaggregating psychopathy: Where and how to look for subtypes. In C. Patrick (Ed.), *Handbook of psychopathy.* New York: Guilford Press.

Raine, A. (1992). Schizotypal and borderline features in psychopathic criminals. *Personality and Individual Differences, 13,* 717–721.

Raine, A. (1997). Antisocial behavior and psychophysiology: A biosocial perspective and a prefrontal dysfunction hypothesis. In D. Stoff, J. Breiling, & J. D. Maser (Eds.), *Handbook of Antisocial Behavior* (pp. 289–304). New York: Wiley.

Raine, A. (2002). Biosocial studies of antisocial and violent behavior in children and adults: A review. *Journal of Abnormal Child Psychology, 30,* 311–316.

Raine, A., Lencz, T., Bihrle, S., LaCasse, L., & Colletti, P. (2000). Reduced prefrontal gray matter volume and reduced autonomic activity in antisocial personality disorder. *Archives of General Psychiatry, 57,* 119–127.

Rice, M. E., & Harris, G. T. (1997). Cross-validation and extension of the Violence Risk Appraisal Guide for child molesters and rapists. *Law and Human Behavior, 21,* 231–241.

Rogers, R. Vitacco, M. J., Jackson, R. L., Martin, M., Collins, M., & Sewell, K. W. (2002). Faking psychopathy? An examination of response styles with antisocial youth. *Journal of Personality Assessment, 78*(1), 31–47.

Roussy, S. (1999). *Psychopathi et lateralisation du traitment des stimuli emotionnels inaccessibles a la cognition linguistic (Psychopathy and lateralization during the processing of emotional stimuli that are inaccessible to linguistic cognitions).* Unpublished doctoral dissertation, University of Montreal, Montreal. Quebec, Canada.

Schmitt, W. A., & Newman, J. P. (1999). Are all psychopathic individuals low-anxious? *Journal of Abnormal Psychology, 108,* 353–358.

Schneider, K. (1958). *Psychopathic personalities* (9th ed., M. Hamilton, Trans.). London: Cassell. (Original work published in 1950)

Skeem, J. L., Poythress, N., Edens, J. F., Lilienfeld, S. O., & Cale, E. M. (2003). Psychopathic personality or personalities? Exploring potential variants of psychopathy and their implications for risk assessment. *Aggression and Violent Behaviour, 8,* 513–546.

Skilling, T. A., Quinsey, V. L., & Craig, W. M. (2001). Evidence of a taxon underlying serious antisocial behavior in boys. *Criminal Justice and Behavior, 28,* 450–470.

Spidel, A., Hervé, H., Hemphill, J., & Bartel, P. (2005, July). *An exploratory study of subtypes of psychopathy in adolescent offenders.* Poster presented at the 1st conference for the Society for the Scientific Study of Psychopathy in Vancouver, British Columbia, Canada.

Stålenheim, E. G., & von Knorring, L. (1996). Psychopathy and Axis I and Axis II psychiatric disorders in a forensic psychiatric population in Sweden. *Acta Psychiatrica Scandinavica, 94,* 217–223.

Stattin, H., & Klackenberg-Larsson, I. (1993). Early language and intelligence development and their relationship to future criminal behavior. *Journal of Abnormal Psychology, 102,* 369–378.

Steadman, H. J., Silver, E., Monahan, J., Appelbaum, P. S., Robbins, P. C., Mulvey, E. P., et al. (2000). A classification tree approach to the development of actuarial violence risk assessment tools. *Law and Human Behavior, 24,* 83–100.

Welsh, G. (1956). Factor dimensions A and R. In G. S. S. Welsh & W. G. Dahlstrom (Eds.), *Basic readings on the MMPI in psychology and medicine* (pp. 264–281). Minneapolis: University of Minnesota Press.

Werlinder, H. (1978). *Psychopathy: A history of the concepts. Analysis of the origin and development of a family of concepts in psychopatho*logy. Stockholm, Sweden: Almqvist & Wiksell International.

Woodworth, M., & Porter, S. (2002). In cold blood: Characteristics of criminal homicides as a function of psychopathy. *Journal of Abnormal Psychology, 111,* 436–445.

18

The Heterogeneity of Incarcerated Psychopaths: Differences in Risk, Need, Recidivism, and Management Approaches

Stephen C. P. Wong and Grant Burt

Psychopathy is a serious personality disorder marked by a constellation of affective, interpersonal, and behavioral characteristics (Hare, 1993/1998, 1996). Affectively, psychopaths are emotionally shallow, selfish, callous, and lack any remorse. Interpersonally, psychopaths are cunning, deceitful, and manipulative. Behaviorally, psychopaths are irresponsible and impulsive and lack realistic long-term goals. The Psychopathy Checklist–Revised (PCL–R; Hare, 1991, 2003) is the most widely used instrument to assess this personality disorder.

Most studies investigating the psychopath's risk to recidivate, to violate conditional release, and so forth compared psychopaths with nonpsychopaths. Consistently, psychopaths are at a higher risk to engage in antisocial behaviors and are also more difficult to manage and treat than nonpsychopaths (for review see Hemphill, Hare, & Wong, 1998; Salekin, 2002; Wong, 2000; Wong & Hare, 2005). Understandably, correctional managers, mental health professionals, decision makers (e.g., parole board members), supervisors, and line staff will give this group of high-risk offenders with personality disorders very close scrutiny. To do their jobs properly, the staff require reliable and valid information about the psychopathic personality, as well as the similarities and differences among them, so that their interventions and management approaches could be more prescriptive and less indiscriminate.

However, an observation that has not received much attention is the fact that psychopaths are not homogenous with respect to their likelihood to violate societal rules. For example, a significant proportion of psychopaths do not commit serious or violent offenses even after long follow-up periods. Serin and Amos (1995) found that no less than 20% to 30% of psychopaths did not receive a conviction after as long as 8 years of freedom in the community. In a sample of Swedish offenders released from correctional and psychiatric facilities, 35% with PCL–R ratings >32 did not have a violent re-conviction after 8 years of follow-up (Grann, Långström, Tengström, & Kullgren, 1999). In a sample of 278 male prisoners from the English Prison Service, 61.8% with a PCL–R of score of ≥25 did not have a violent re-conviction within 2 years following release (Hare, Clark, Grann, & Thornton, 2000). Similarly, Hemphill, Newman, and Hare (2003; as cited in Hare, 2003) found that about 67% of a group of White and African Americans male offenders in Wisconsin rated ≥30 on the PCL–R did not reoffend violently after an average of 7 years of follow-up. Many of the psychopaths who did not commit a serious offense, nonetheless, might have committed a less seri-ous nonviolent or some undetected antisocial act (see Wilson, 2001). One of the first studies to examine the outcome of conditional release also indicated that 34.8% of those rated ≥34 on the Psychopathy Checklist (PCL) had not violated conditional release (Hart, Kropp & Hare, 1988). In another study of parole release outcome, 67% of offenders rated >31 on the PCL did not fail on parole (Serin, Peters, & Barbaree, 1990). The vast majority of psychopaths who recidivated did so within 2–3 years of their release (Hemphill et al., 1998). Those who survived beyond this window without recidivating were not likely to recidivate thereafter (e.g., Serin & Amos, 1995; Wintrup, Coles, Hart, & Webster, 1994). The available evidence indicates that differences in the risk to recidivate, including parole violation, among psychopaths are not trivial.

We should not assume that incarcerated psychopaths are homogenous in their risk, need, institutional behaviors, or their response to treatment. Knowing more about the differences among psychopaths should lead to bet-ter management, treatment, and supervision of these offenders. As mental health professionals we are also duty bound to respect individual differences in our clients when we provide services to them (Canadian Psychological Association, 2000). Individuals deemed to be psychopathic are no excep-tion. Of particular interest are the differences between released psychopaths who recidivated and those who did not because the safe release of all offend-ers, in particular high-risk psychopathic offenders, are of major concern to prison and mental health authorities. Although there have been some attempts to identify subtypes of psychopaths (Blackburn, 1975; Hervé & Hare, 2002; also see Hervé, chap. 17, this volume), there is no research com-paring psychopaths who reoffend after release with psychopaths who do not. We will report research results of such a comparison focusing on the fol-lowing area of investigation: differences in risk, criminogenic need linked to violence, and recidivism. A discussion of the implications of the observed differences for the treatment and management for psychopathic offenders is also provided.

RISK

Risk refers to the offender's overall likelihood to recidivate. Differences in risk between psychopaths and nonpsychopaths are well established. However, differences in risk for violent recidivism among psychopaths have not been investigated.

CRIMINOGENIC NEED

Criminogenic need refers to the offender's dynamic or changeable factors that, directly or indirectly, cause the offender to commit crimes (Andrews & Bonta, 2003; Wong & Hare, 2005). The Need Principle (Andrews & Bonta, 2003) posits that treatment to reduce the risk of recidivism should target the individual's criminogenic needs. Similarly, treatment to reduce violence should target criminogenic needs linked to violence. The criminogenic need profile of a psychopath would help to identify the type of treatment that psychopaths would require to reduce their risk of violence. During treatment, psychopaths can easily sidetrack inexperienced staff into working with them on vague and nonspecific treatment goals unrelated to their violence and criminality. An assessment that clearly identifies a psychopath's criminogenic needs would provide much needed structure to the treatment plan, thus alleviating the problems of the psychopath trying to usurp the treatment agenda.

RISK, CRIMINOGENIC NEED, AND RECIDIVISM

It is important is understand, among psychopaths, the link between their risk, need, and violent recidivism to ensure that we do the right things to help them manage their risk when they are released back to the community.

To address these issues, we, in Part 1 of this chapter, compare the risk and need characteristics of two groups of treated psychopathic offenders: one group recidivated violently within 5 years after release into the community, the other group did not. Parole decisions and outcomes were also compared. In Part 2, we provide a set of guidelines for the management of incarcerated psychopathic offenders.

PART 1: THE RECIDIVATED AND NON-RECIDIVATED PSYCHOPATHS

The following summarizes an investigation in which we compared a group of psychopaths who had recidivated with one or more violent conviction(s) (recidivated psychopaths [RPs]) with another group of psychopaths who had not recidivated violently (nonrecidivated psychopaths [NRPs]) after release to the community for 5 years. Both groups had virtually identical mean PCL–R ratings and received treatment in a forensic mental health facility. We investigated the differences between the RPs and the NRPs in terms of risk, need, and other correctional management outcomes such as the granting and successful completion of parole.

Method

Sample

The sample comprised male federal offenders serving sentences of 2 years or more, who were admitted to the Regional Psychiatric Centre (RPC), Saskatoon, Saskatchewan, between 1981 and 1998 for treatment. All of them had completed at least 4 months of treatment in the violent offender treatment program. The RPC, a multilevel security institution within the Correctional Service of Canada, is an accredited inpatient mental health facility. It provides assessment and specialized high-intensity treatment programs for sexual offenders, violent offenders, and male and female offenders with major mental illnesses.

A sample of offenders who were treated in the violent offender program and received a PCL/PCL–R score of ≥25 were identified. Their pretreatment and postrelease criminal records were obtained using the Canadian Police Information Centre (CPIC) database[1] and through Interpol. Offenders in our sample who were reconvicted of a violent offense within 5 years of release to the community after treatment at RPC were deemed the RPs; those who were not reconvicted of a violent offense within the same period of time were the NRPs. The 5-year follow-up window was based, in part, on the observation that the mean number of violent convictions per year for the sample was .33 ($SD = .22$). It follows that more than 1.6 violent convictions would be expected to have occurred within the 5-year follow-up window which was deemed to be of adequate length to reasonably detect the presence of new convictions. It is entirely possible that individuals may recidivate outside the 5-year window and would be false-negatives according to our criteria for NRPs. The final sample included 123 offenders[2]: 58 NRPs (47.2%) and 65 RPs (52.8%).

The mean age (standard deviation in parentheses) of the sample on release to the community was 31.31 (6.84) years. Sixty-six offenders were Caucasian and 55 were of First Nations background. There was a slightly larger proportion of Caucasian offenders in the NRP group (63.8%) than in the RP group (44.6%), but the difference was not significant. At the time of incarceration, all offenders were serving federal sentences of 2 years of more in Alberta, Saskatchewan, or Manitoba in Canada.

All offenders in our sample had very significant criminal histories. Before RPC admission, they had a mean of 4.34 (2.69) violent convictions and 15.68

---

[1]A computerized information system operated by the Royal Canadian Mounted Police that captures all Canadian Criminal Code violations. The identities of criminal record entries in CPIC are verified by fingerprinting.

[2]Of the original identified sample ($n = 144$), 21 offenders were lost to follow-up for the following reasons: 13 were never released into the community after their stay at RPC up to the time of data collection, the criminal records of 6 offenders could not be accessed, 1 offender died within the first 5 years of his community release, and 1 offender was deported immediately upon release.

(12.41) nonviolent convictions. They started offending in their mid-teens ($M = 16.99$, $SD = 1.86$) and had their first adult violent conviction by their early 20s ($M = 20.37$, $SD = 4.21$).

The PCL/PCL–R ratings were completed by psychologists or research assistants who were trained to use the instrument. Scores on the PCL when they were administered were converted to PCL–R scores as described by Hare (1991).

Measurement of Risk and Need

The risk of violent recidivism and the criminogenic needs linked to violence were measured by the Violence Risk Scale (VRS; Wong & Gordon, 2001–4). The VRS was developed to assess quantitatively the level of risk of violence and treatment readiness, to identify treatment targets and areas of strength, and to quantitatively measure changes in risk after treatment. The VRS measures the level of pretreatment risk using 6 static and 20 dynamic risk items (see Fig. 18–1 for a list of the dynamic items). Each VRS static and dynamic risk item is rated on a 4-point scale (0, 1, 2, and 3). The static items are designed to measure the individual's track record of violence based on past incidences and convictions of violence. Most of the dynamic items are rated based on how closely each item relates to the offender's use of violence; the higher the rating, the more the item (e.g., Criminal Attitude) is the direct or indirect cause

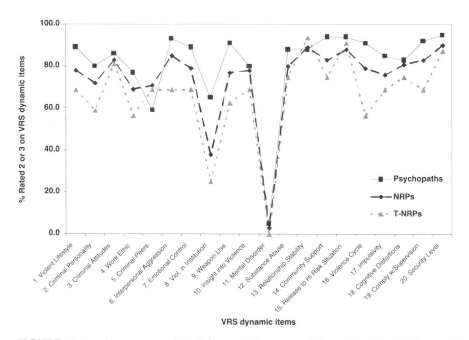

FIGURE 18–1.   Percentage of VRS dynamic items rated 2 or 3 for RPs, NRPs, and t-NRPs.

of violence in the offender's lifetime functioning. Dynamic items rated 2 or 3 reflect a strong link to violence and should be considered treatment targets. Items rated 0 are areas with no problem (i.e., relative areas of strength), and those rated 1 suggest minimal concern. The sum of the ratings of the 26 items is the pretreatment level of risk. The VRS has demonstrated validity and reliability in the prediction of violence and in the measurement of change in risk as a result of treatment (Wong & Gordon, 2005, 2006).

Pearson correlations of the VRS total score with violent recidivism within 1-, 2- and 3-year windows of release were .28, .35, and .35 respectively (all at $p < .0001$). Computations of the area under the curve for the receiver operating characteristics analysis reflects the precision of prediction independent of the base rate of occurrence of the outcome. The areas under the curve for the VRS for violent reconvictions for all offenders with at least 1 ($n = 847$), 2 ($n = 758$), and 3 ($n = 571$) years of follow-up were .73, .74, and .72 respectively (all significant at $p < .0001$). In a sample of treated offenders, posttreatment VRS ratings were more strongly correlated with posttreatment violent recidivism than pretreatment ratings (Wong & Gordon, 2005).

All VRS ratings were conducted using extensive file information. Prior to making VRS ratings, an independent research assistant removed all information pertaining to posttreatment behavior or outcome to ensure that VRS ratings were conducted "blind" to the recidivism status of offender. To determine the interrater reliability of VRS ratings, a second rater randomly selected 13 cases for rerating. In the present study, 72% of VRS reratings were exact matches, and 95% were either exact matches or discrepant by a single point.

Results

Level of Psychopathy of NRPs and RPs as Measured by the PCL–R

The numbers of NRPs and RPs using 25 or 30 on the PCL–R as cutoffs are shown in Table 18–1. There were no significant differences in mean PCL–R scores of the NRP and RP groups using either cutoff; NRPs and RPs were not a function of PCL–R scores. The NRP group was not represented disproportionately by those with lower PCL–R scores. The mean PCL–R ratings in the 25 and 30 cutoff groups for both the RPs and NRPs were in the high 20s (28.7 and 29.6) and low 30s (32.2 and 32.4), respectively; all participants were highly psychopathic violent recidivists as indicated by their PCL–R ratings and criminal histories.

Level of Risk of NRPs and RPs as Measured by the VRS

Despite having virtually the same PCL–R ratings, the NRPs had a significantly lower violence risk than the RPs, as measured by VRS total scores, using either a PCL–R cutoff of 25 or 30 (see Table 18–1). The VRS Static and

TABLE 18–1.

Means and Standard Deviations of VRS Total, Static, and Dynamic Scores
and PCL–R Total Score, and *t* Test Comparisons for RPs and NRPs
using PCL–R Cutoffs of 25 and 30

Variable	RPs (n = 65)		NRPs (n = 58)		t (121)	p	RPs (n = 23)		NRPs (n = 24)		t (45)	p
	M	SD	M	SD			M	SD	M	SD		
VRS Total	59.9	8.2	54.6	10.4	3.2	.002	60.8	9.3	55.4	9.6	2.0	.05
VRS Static	14.4	2.8	12.1	3.1	4.3	.0001	14.4	3.5	12.2	3.6	2.0	.05
VRS Dynamic	45.5	7.1	42.6	8.3	2.1	.04	46.4	7.3	43.3	7.2	1.2	.22
PCL–R Total	28.7	3.1	29.6	3.3	0.9	.35	32.2	2.3	32.4	2.2	0.3	.79

Dynamic item scores also were significantly lower for NRPs than for RPs in the PCL–R 25 cutoff group (Table 18–1). In the PCL–R 30 cutoff group, both Static and Dynamic scores were also lower in the NRP group compared with the RP group, but the difference was only statistically significant for the Static scores.

Compared with the RPs, the NRPs have significantly lower ratings on five of the six VRS Static items. NRPs were rated as older than RPs at time of admission to treatment [Item 1[3]; NRP M = 2.36 (.77), RP M = 2.61 (.61); t (121) = 2.02, p = .046]. NRPs were older than RPs at their age of first violent conviction [Item 2; NRP M = 1.58 (.76), RP M = 1.86 (.73); t (121) = 2.09, p = .038]. NRPs had significantly fewer numbers of juvenile convictions than RPs [Item 3; NRP M = 1.78 (1.24), RP M = 2.42 (.98); t (121) = 3.18, p < .001]. NRPs used less violence throughout their life span than RPs [Item 4; NRP M = 2.17 (.80), RP M = 2.55 (.53); t (121) = 3.15, p = .002]. Finally, NRPs had more stability in their early family upbringing than RPs [Item 6; NRP M = 2.11 (.85), RP M = 2.50 (.77); t (121) = 2.61, p = .01]. In all, the results of VRS Static items indicated that, compared with NRPs, RPs were younger at admission, had a more chaotic upbringing, started offending and behaving violently at a younger age, and had a more violent lifestyle.

Criminogenic Need of RPs and NRPs as Measured by the VRS

The VRS uses the ratings of 20 Dynamic items to measure criminogenic needs linked to violence. Ratings of 2 and 3 indicate that the problem area measured by the item (e.g., Criminal Attitude) is directly or indirectly linked to the offender's use of violence, and, as such, should be considered a target for treatment to reduce the risk of violence. As noted earlier, the total dynamic scores of the RPs were higher than those for the NRPs using the PCL–R 25 and 30 cutoffs, but only the former was significantly different.

Figure 18–1 shows the percentages of NRPs and RPs who scored 2 or 3 on each of the 20 VRS Dynamic items, which gives a dynamic *risk profile* for the NRPs and RPs. As expected, both NRPs and RPs had many criminogenic needs linked to violence. With the exception of Mental Illness, about 70% or more of the sample were rated 2 or 3 across all VRS Dynamic items. For a number of items, such as Substance Abuse and Release to High Risk Situations, the percentages were well above 80%. Of note, Mental Illness appears to be a relatively uncommon dynamic risk item for both NRPs and RPs.

There were substantial differences between the NRPs and RPs in the ratings of the VRS Dynamic items. Overall, a smaller percentage of the NRPs than the RPs were rated 2 or 3 for the vast majority of the VRS Dynamic items. Comparisons of the mean ratings of the items indicated significantly lower ratings for the NRPs than for the RPs for Interpersonal Aggression

---

[3]VRS item number; lower ratings on this item indicate older.

[Item 6; NRP M = 2.49 (.65), RP M = 2.72 (.48); t (104) = 2.18, p = .03]. NRPs were rated as having a significantly less severe history of using Violence During Incarceration [Item 8; NRP M = 1.21 (1.11), RP M = 1.95 (1.08); t (121) = 3.72, p < .001]. Finally, NRPs were also less likely to be Released to High Risk Situations than RPs [Item 15; NRP M = 2.56 (.59), RP M = 2.80 (.49); t (121) = 2.02, p = .033]. Of interest, the Criminal Peers item, which measures the link between violence and the association with criminal peers and gangs, was the single item in which proportionally more NRPs then RPs are rated high (2 or 3). This suggests that RPs are more likely to commit crimes by themselves rather than being associated with a criminal group.

The dynamic risk profiles for the NRPs and the RPs are consistent with the general expectation that nonrecidivists should have proportionally fewer risk areas related to violence in comparison with recidivists. Among NRPs and RPs, these distinctions were observed along both static and dynamic risk dimensions.

Follow-Up Beyond the 5-Year Window. Follow-up for NRPs can exceed the 5-year window used as the criteria in this study to define NRPs. We extended the follow-up of the NRPs beyond the 5-year window to a mean follow-up time of 9.5 years (4.45) from the offender's release until the final data collection date. Three comparison groups of offenders were identified for exploratory analyses. The first group was the RPs previously identified (n = 65). The second group was labeled Pseudo-NRPs (p-NRPs) and consisted of NRPs who did not recidivate within the 5-year window but recidivated violently at some point beyond the 5-year window. The third group was labeled the True-NRPs (t-NRPs) and consisted of NRPs who did not have any criminal convictions (neither violent nor nonviolent) up to the end of the 9.5 years follow-up. If the likelihood of recidivism of the three groups of psychopathic offenders were associated with their level of risk, it would be predicted that the t-NRPs would have the lowest VRS scores and the RPs would have the highest, with the scores for the p-NRPs falling between the two groups.

Sixteen (28%) of the 58 NRPs violently recidivated after the 5-year window; these were the p-NRPs. Sixteen (28%) of the 58 NRPs did not recidivate with any type of offense up to the data collection date; these were the t-NRPs. The VRS total, dynamic, and static scores for the three groups supported our predictions (see Table 18–2), although none of the between-group comparisons were significant, most likely because of a lack of power, given the small group sizes. Similarly, the rate of pretreatment violent convictions was lowest for the t-NRPs, highest for the RPs, and in between these groups for the p-NRPs. These results are consistent with the view that speed of recidivism among psychopaths is similarly related to lower risk as measured by the VRS.

The risk profile of the t-NRPs (Fig. 18–1) would be predicted to be the lowest among the RPs and the NRPs if violent recidivism is a function of risk within psychopathic offenders. The prediction is generally consistent with

TABLE 18–2.
Mean Scores for RPs, p-NRPs, and t-NRPs

Variables	RPs (n = 65)	p-NRPs (n = 16)	t-NRPs (n = 16)
PCL–R Total score	28.7	28.9	28.4
PCL–R Factor 1 score	10.2	11.1	11.3
PCL–R Factor 2 score	14.6	13.5	13.2
VRS Total score	62.3	60.8	53.7
VRS Static score	14.4	12.8	10.9
VRS Dynamic score	47.9	48.0	42.8
Rate of preadmission violent convictions	0.49	0.38	0.27

the results. Of particular interest, the item Violence During Incarceration seems to most strongly distinguish the three groups.

Granting of Parole and Parole Violations Among Psychopathic Offenders

In the entire sample of 123 psychopathic offenders, 76 (61.7%) were granted parole sometime during the sentence they were serving at the time of admission to the RPC; 47 were not granted parole. There was no difference in mean PCL–R scores between the two groups. However, those who were granted parole had significantly lower VRS scores than those who were not (see Table 18–3). In addition, a significantly larger percentage of NRPs (72.4%; 42 of 58) than RPs (52.3%; 34 of 65) were granted parole ($\chi^2 = 4.24$; $p = .04$).

Of the 76 psychopathic offenders who were granted parole, 34 recidivated violently and 42 did not. There was no significant difference in mean PCL–R scores of those who violently recidivated and those who did not violently

TABLE 18–3.
Means and Standard Deviations of VRS Total, Static, and Dynamic Scores and PCL–R Total Score and t Test Comparisons for Offenders Not Granted and Granted Conditional Release

Variable	Not Granted Conditional Release (n = 47)		Granted Conditional Release (n = 76)		t (121)	p (Two-Tailed)
	M	SD	M	SD		
VRS Total	60.0	9.6	55.8	9.4	2.4	.017
VRS Static	14.3	3.1	12.7	3.1	2.8	.006
VRS Dynamic	45.7	7.8	43.1	7.7	1.8	.07
PCL–R Total	28.9	3.3	29.0	3.1	0.3	.80

recidivate. However, of those granted parole, mean VRS total scores of NRPs were significantly lower than those of RPs (see Table 18–4). Again, among those granted parole, the ones that recidivated violently had significantly higher VRS ratings, but their PCL–R ratings were virtually identical to the nonrecidivists.

Discussion

The propensity of psychopaths to violently recidivate is a serious concern for forensic professionals, correctional managers, parole decision makers, and community supervisors who are tasked to assess, manage, and provide services to these individuals. In addition, there are significant challenges to designing treatment programs for incarcerated psychopaths as they often sabotage or fail to complete such programs (Lösel, 1998; Ogloff, Wong, & Greenwood, 1990; also see Wong, 2000; Wong & Hare, 2005). However, psychopaths are not homogenous in terms of their risks to recidivate or violate parole and conditional releases; many of them did not recidivate or violate parole even after long follow-up periods. We investigated and presented results of the differences in risk and need profiles of highly criminalized and violence prone psychopaths who were treated in a forensic mental health facility and were then released to the community for at least 5 years. With this in mind, we provide a general guideline on the management of psychopaths while they are incarcerated.

Demographic, Risk, and Criminogenic Need Profiles

Compared with the RPs, the NRPs are older at release, older when they had their first violent conviction, had fewer juvenile convictions, and had an overall less violent lifestyle. The finding that these static risk variables discriminate the NRP from the RP are consistent with results that similar static risk variables also discriminated lower risk offenders from higher risk

TABLE 18–4.
Means and Standard Deviations of VRS Total, Static, and Dynamic Scores and PCL–R Total Score and t Test Comparisons for Offenders Granted Conditional Release

| Variable | RPs (n = 34) | | NRPs (n = 42) | | t (121) | p (Two-Tailed) |
	M	SD	M	SD		
VRS Total	58.4	7.7	53.6	10.1	2.27	.03
VRS Static	13.7	2.7	11.8	3.1	2.81	.006
VRS Dynamic	44.7	6.9	41.8	8.1	1.64	.10
PCL–R Total	28.2	2.7	29.4	3.6	1.58	.12

offenders in the general offender population (Gendreau, Little, & Goggin, 1996). Even among psychopathic offenders, variables that are linked to risk of recidivism can be used to distinguish NRPs from RPs.

As for criminogenic need or dynamic risk variables, compared with the RPs, the NRPs also had overall lower ratings, especially in the areas of violence while incarcerated, interpersonal aggression, and the likelihood of being released to high-risk environments. These are also criminogenic variables for offenders in general as identified in meta-analytic research (Gendreau, Little, & Goggin, 1996). In particular, previous research has noted a moderately strong relationship between institutional misconduct and recidivism in the community (Gendreau, Goggin, & Law, 1997). Taken together with the present results, it appear that those offenders (psychopathic or not) who are older, have short track records of violence, are less interpersonally aggressive, have less problematic behaviors during incarceration, and have better community support are less likely to recidivate violently. Given virtually identical PCL–R ratings, the fact that the NRPs did not recidivate within the 5-year window cannot be explained in terms of the NRPs simply being "less psychopathic" than their RP counterparts.

Speed to First Violent Reoffense

We also presented preliminary evidence to suggest that among psychopaths, the level of risk as measured by the VRS appeared to be related to the speed to first violent reoffense. The group of psychopaths with the highest total VRS scores reoffended within the 5-year window. The group with the next highest VRS rating reoffended between the end of the 5-year window and data collection date (9.5 years), and the group with the lowest VRS rating were conviction free up to 9.5 years after release. Although the differences in the risk ratings were not significant between the groups (probably because of lack of power associated with the small sample size), the trends for decreasing Static, Dynamic, and Total VRS ratings with decreasing likelihood of recidivism are worthy of further investigation. Other research has suggested that every 5 points of reduction in the VRS total score translates to about a 4%–5% reduction in the likelihood of violent recidivism (Wong & Gordon, 2005, 2006). The PCL–R scores of the three groups are almost identical, differing by no more than .5; a difference in psychopathy cannot account for the differences in the speed of reoffending. In other words, incarcerated offenders rated high on the PCL–R are not a homogeneous group in terms of their risk and criminogenic needs.

Parole Decision Making and Violation

Despite the psychopathic nature of the sample, decision makers seemed to be able to make decisions that reflected differences in risk. Psychopaths who were granted parole were at lower risk for violence than those who were not granted parole based on VRS ratings. The majority of psychopathic offenders who were paroled did not commit a violent offense, and those who successfully completed parole were at lower risk (as measured by the VRS) than those who recidivated.

Implications for Treatment

The results of this study have implications for risk assessment, treatment, and parole decision making for psychopaths. PCL–R scores of 25 or 30 are usually used as cutoffs to identify individuals as psychopaths. In forensic practice, a high PCL–R score is generally considered to be a strong indication of a high risk to recidivate, and treatment and disposition decisions are then made accordingly.

We have shown that NRPs are less likely to recidivate violently and have lower VRS ratings than the RPs. The results suggest that one approach to treating psychopaths with a view to lowering their risk of violent recidivism would be to address problem areas identified by the VRS dynamic risk variables. For example, if the VRS were used as the assessment tool in the treatment of psychopaths, the dynamic variables rated as 2 or 3 could be considered as treatment targets. Moderate decreases in risk across a number of VRS dynamic items as a result of treatment may be translated into a significant reduction in the likelihood to reoffend violently, even for psychopathic offenders. It is predicted that the larger the decrease in risk measured by the VRS, the lower is the likelihood to reoffend violently.

The empirical literature on the treatment of psychopaths is quite dismal; in a number of reviews it has been characterized as primarily consisting of poorly designed studies with a host of methodological problems (Wong, 2000; Wong & Hare, 2005; also see Salekin, 2002, for a description of the studies).

Our results indicate that there is a significant group of high PCL–R rated psychopaths that were treated and did not reoffend violently within 5 years. In addition, we identified a smaller group that did not reoffend with any criminal convictions for, on average, a follow-up of almost 10 years post-release. Our study did not establish a causal link between an absence of reoffending and treatment, but it did establish that not all psychopaths will inevitably reoffend over an extended period after release to the community. In addition, differences between the NRPs and RPs on dynamic items suggest that risk could be modified if treatment is prescriptive and intensive.

Even within a group of violent, criminalized, and highly psychopathic offenders, less serious criminogenic needs indicated by lower scores on VRS dynamic risk items were associated with a reduced likelihood of violent recidivism, just as they have been with nonpsychopathic offenders (Dowden & Andrews, 2000). These findings suggest that, with appropriate modifications, what works in violent risk reduction using contemporary correctional treatment approaches may also work for psychopaths. Obviously, interventions for psychopaths must incorporate appropriate modifications to address the special responsivity needs of the psychopath (see Wong & Hare, 2005). Recently, an outcome evaluation with a 2-year follow-up showed that high intensity in-patient treatment reduced the risk of criminal reconvictions and major institutional infractions of high-risk violent gang members compared with a carefully matched gang control group who received less treatment (Di Placido, Simon, Witte, Gu, & Wong, in press). In a separate evaluation, treatment was also associated with reduction of antisocial attitudes linked to non-sexual violence in sex offenders (Witte, Di Placido, Gu, & Wong, in press). These treatment programs are based on the What Works principles (see Andrews, Zinger, Hoge, Bonta, Gendreau, & Cullen, 1990; Harland, 1995; McGuire, 1995). It has been argued that similar approaches should be used as a foundation on which to design a program for treating psychopaths (Wong & Hare, 2005).

A recent meta-analysis showed that maximum reductions in violent re-offending were achieved when the principles of correctional treatment, i.e., the risk need, and general responsivity principles, were adhered to within the treatment program (Dowden & Andrews, 2000). Clinical approaches in the treatment of violence are efficacious with substantial effect sizes (see Dowden & Andrews, 2000). Also, the development of effective treatment approaches for violent and difficult-to-manage clients, such as members of gangs, could be generalized to treatment of psychopaths (Di Placido et al., in press). Guidelines for the treatment of psychopathy have been developed (Wong & Hare, 2005). These approaches, together with suggestions based on present research on NRPs and RPs, could be applied to the treatment of psychopaths by experienced and well-trained staff and with careful safeguards to ensure program integrity.

Conclusion

Forensic professionals, managers, and decision makers require information on the differences among psychopaths to be better informed about the assessment, treatment, and management of incarcerated psychopaths. Comparisons between psychopaths and nonpsychopaths do not provide them with the required information; rather such comparisons tend to reinforce the view that psychopaths are a rather homogeneous group. The results of our study provide some preliminary data on the heterogeneity of psychopaths in terms of their risk, need, and recidivism. Psychopaths are not all the same; they should not be treated and managed as if they are the same.

PART 2: GUIDELINES FOR THE MANAGEMENT OF INSTITUTIONALIZED PSYCHOPATHS

Psychopathy is a personality disorder and its association with affective, interpersonal, and behavioral dysfunction has been well established (see Herba et al., chap. 9 this volume; Newman, Brinkley, Lorenz, Hiatt, & Donal, chap. 8 this volume; Patrick, chap. 9, this volume). Psychopathy is also closely associated with antisocial behaviors, recidivism, escape risk, difficulties in management, and treatment resistance (see Hemphill, chap. 6, this volume; Jackson & Richards, chap. 15, this volume; O'Toole, chap. 11, this volume; Porter & Porter, chap. 10, this volume; Spidel et al., chap. 12, this volume; Thornton & Blud, chap. 20, this volume). Although there are a significant number of psychopaths in forensic institutions and there is a valid and reliable instrument to assess psychopathy (the PCL–R), a coherent set of general management guidelines for institutionalized psychopaths has yet to be developed for use by forensic personnel to manage this group of very challenging individuals and to address the heterogeneity among them. The following is a set of proposed guidelines.

Conceptualization of Psychopathy in the Forensic Context

- Psychopathy is a serious personality disorder. Consider psychopaths as a special population with special needs, no different from other special needs populations such as sex offenders and offenders with mental disorders.
- Do not demonize psychopaths; demonization will distort our understanding of them and will cause us to react to or reject them rather than to deal with them in a balanced and professional way.

Psychopathy is a personality disorder with well-defined affective, interpersonal, and behavioral characteristics. The proneness of psychopaths to aggression, manipulation, and intimidation and their lack of remorse and motivation to change (Ogloff, Wong, & Greenwood, 1990) often make life extremely unpleasant for those who are charged with the responsibility to manage or to treat them. Staff may personalize the negative behaviors of the psychopath and subsequently react and retaliate in a punitive or unprofessional manner. On the other hand, staff may avoid interacting with psychopaths for fear of being exploited and manipulated by them. Rather than trying to understand and appropriately manage, modify, and contain the behaviors using good treatment and correctional management principles, the behavioral and affective reactions of the staff can result in the labeling, demonization, and rejection of the psychopath. Alternatively, less experienced staff may be deceived by the charm and machinations of psychopaths and would be at risk to be exploited by them. In either case, a constructive working relationship or alliance becomes difficult if not impossible, and treatment failure is almost inevitable: a self-fulfilling prophecy for those already frustrated by the psychopath's resistance to change. We must understand the personality characteristics of the psychopath, an important responsivity factor, before we can appropriately manage and engage him/her in treatment (see Wong & Hare, 2005).

There is no doubt that a small number of highly psychopathic individuals with long histories of very violent and heinous crimes should be managed with extreme care for the safety of staff, other offenders, and society. As exemplified earlier, it is also important not to generalize "evil" from a few high-profile and extreme cases to all those who share some common personality and behavioral characteristics with their infamous counterparts.

In short, psychopaths should be regarded as a special needs group in corrections. We must try to understand their disorder, use best practice principles in their custody and treatment, work with them in a balanced and professional way, and take the necessary management and security precautions.

Assessment of Psychopathy: Use Appropriate Assessment Instruments, Such as the PCL–R Family of Instruments, to Identify This Population

The PCL–R family of assessment tools are widely accepted as valid and reliable means to assess psychopathy and to determine the seriousness of the disorder. For clinical purposes, a PCL–R score equal to or greater than 30 has traditionally been considered suitable to identify psychopaths (Hare, 2003).

Assessing the Psychopath's Risk, Criminogenic Needs, and Responsivity Factors

- Assess violent risk, criminogenic needs or dynamic (changeable) risk factors,[4] and responsivity factors in psychopaths. Understanding these factors are essential in case management and treatment decisions and in measuring changes in risk.

To reduce recidivism risk, the What Works literature indicates that treatment should be delivered to address the offender's risk and criminogenic needs and should be tailored to the responsivity of the client (see Andrews et al., 1990). Psychopaths are no different. The definition and implications of risk and needs of psychopaths are addressed in Part 1 of this chapter, and the treatment of psychopaths is discussed in detail elsewhere (Wong & Hare, 2005). A careful and in-depth assessment of the psychopaths risk, needs, and responsivity will assist service deliverers in formulating an objective and well grounded treatment plan that could be shared with the client and used to guide the delivery of treatment and to assess treatment change.

Security Classification

- Use an appropriate dynamic assessment tool to determine the appropriate security classification for the psychopath. Do not rely exclusively on the PCL–R rating because of the static nature of the tool and impor-

---

[4]The terms *criminogenic need* and *dynamic risk factors* are used interchangeably in this article.

tant heterogeneity among psychopaths (see Part 1 of this chapter; also see Hervé, chap. 17, this volume).

- Identify and appropriately manage psychopaths with high escape risk. The combination of psychopaths with histories of serious violence and high escape risk could have lethal consequences.
- Place psychopaths in institutions of appropriate security level; reassess as required. Although psychopathy is a personality disorder that is not likely to change over the short term, many factors related to institutional behavior are dynamic in nature. Updating and reviewing classifications are essential.

Psychopaths with histories of serious violent behavior and of escapes or other forms of unlawfully at-large behaviors should be carefully evaluated by correctional personnel in consultation with mental health professionals familiar with the assessment and management of psychopaths. Use the appropriate risk-based assessment tools to augment the classification decisions. Placement of these individuals in the appropriate security setting is paramount.

Case Management

- Make appropriate referrals to mental health professionals who are experienced and trained to work with psychopaths for specialized assessments, management, treatment, and release consultations and recommendations.
- Formulate structured and behaviorally based correctional and treatment plans for psychopathic offenders.
- Psychopaths who become "jail-house lawyers" could also become skillful manipulators of the system to serve their own narcissistic needs.
- Working with psychopaths is a challenge, not something to avoid; however, one has to be knowledgeable, skilled, realistic, and not naively gullible.

Consultation with knowledgeable professionals at key points in the offender's sentence is essential to providing quality services to address the assessment, management, and treatment needs of psychopaths. Psychopaths are more likely to function better within a structured correctional or treatment plan with clear goals, objectives, and evaluation strategies, rather than one with vague recommendations. The assessment and evaluation of progress is also easier within a structured, behaviorally based, and clearly worded correctional or treatment plan. Using clearly articulated and objective criteria to evaluate changes in the behaviors of psychopaths reduces the likelihood of staff being manipulated, exploited, or demoralized in working with them. The many manipulative behaviors of psychopaths must be managed in a professional and levelheaded manner rather than in a reactive way. The following are some examples of common "cons" perpetrated by incarcerated psychopaths, along with management suggestions:

1. Giving short-term good performances to lull others into lowering their vigilance towards him or her, thus enabling him or her to plan other illegal acts such as escape. At the same time, it is important NOT to put an offender into a Catch-22 situation; that is, damned if he or she does well and damned if he or she does not. Good performances that include a wide spectrum of appropriate behaviors sustained over a significant period of time and generalized to many different at risk and challenging situations should be given due recognition, reinforced, and supported, and are likely to be indicators of real changes.

2. Creating a smoke screen and impressions of change by performing well in areas that are NOT germane to his or her criminogenic factors. For example, a psychopath who had no problem in the academic or employment areas can become engrossed and take great pride in doing well in these areas. Given that the lack of academic achievements or employment skills are not his or her criminogenic factors, doing well in these areas does not translate into risk reduction. Any suggestions that a reduction of risk has occurred based on these positive performances are erroneous and may have serious consequences such as prematurely granting parole to a psychopath. A careful assessment of the presence of criminogenic factors and linking risk reduction to positive changes in the identified criminogenic factors will avoid these potentially very costly mistakes.

3. Wearing administrators down with frivolous complaints and mountains of paperwork until someone relents or reacts negatively to him or her. The latter would give the psychopath grounds for legal challenges or potential for sympathetic support from unsuspecting individuals in the community, the media, or advocacy groups. Again, a professional and level-headed approach to these situations is the best option.

4. Faking various illnesses and injuries to gain access to areas that may have lower security, a cache of medications, or even favorable assessments. Faking injury to obtain transfer to a general hospital where security is not as tightly maintained is a frequently used con. In an anecdotal case, a psychopath faked symptoms of mental illness to gain admission to a psychiatric facility for an assessment. An unsuspecting psychiatrist correctly assessed him as not suffering from any major mental illness or mental health problems. The "positive" assessment report was subsequently used as evidence to apply for lower security classification. The report was also submitted to the parole board in support of his contention that he no longer had any problems. Clearly, one must attend to manipulation and not lose sight of relevant risk factors when managing psychopathic offenders!

5. Lying to gain entry into witness protection programs and then use this special status as leverage to bargain for release considerations. Can we trust what a psychopath tells us in such circumstances when we know that he or she is prone to lying and deception?

Having a good understanding of the psychopathic personality and the associated behaviors will give staff a sense of self-efficacy and will empower them to work with, rather than to avoid or reject, this very challenging group of offenders.

Treatment

- Develop, deliver, and evaluate treatment programs designed specifi-cally for psychopaths. Many off-the-shelf programs are either inappro-priate or of insufficient intensity to address the very high risk and high needs of the psychopath.
- Reduce treatment attrition rates by conducting research to understand the reason for high treatment dropout and noncompliance (see Beyko & Wong, 2005).
- Assist staff to develop appropriate clinical skills to interact therapeuti-cally with psychopaths to increase treatment efficacy and reduce treat-ment attrition. Put in place procedures to debrief, supervise, and sup-port staff to avoid boundary violations and burnout.
- Conduct research to understand why some psychopaths do not recidi-vate and, where appropriate, use these factors in treatment.

A high-intensity treatment program for psychopathic offenders should be specifically tailored to their needs to maximize effectiveness. For a detailed discussion of the institutional treatment for psychopaths see the *Guidelines for a Psychopathy Treatment Program* (Wong & Hare, 2005). Briefly, treatment of psychopaths should focus on the reduction in the risk of violence rather than changing the psychopathic personality characteristics such as those indicated by the PCL–R Factor 1. The best practices of correctional treatment should be used as a foundation for the treatment program. Motivating the psychopath to engage in treatment should be a major component in the treatment pro-gram. Staff who are knowledgeable about psychopathy and are therapeuti-cally skilled to work with psychopaths should be enlisted to deliver the pro-grams to increase treatment efficacy and to avoid serious boundary violation issues (for other treatment guidelines pertaining to psychopaths, see Thorn-ton & Blud, chap. 20, this volume).

Staff Training and Supervision

- Include the construct of psychopathy in the staff-training curriculum for all mental health and correctional workers. Those who work in maximum-security institutions should receive additional training because of the likelihood that a relatively larger number of psychopaths could be housed in maximum-security institutions.

- Provide those who deliver specialized service to psychopaths with training in the assessment (including risk assessment), management, and treatment of psychopathy.
- Caution staff on the risk of becoming victims of the psychopath's manipulation, deception, and aggression, and equally important, to be attentive to the risk of overreacting to the negative behaviors of the psychopath. Provide staff with appropriate supervision and professional and collegial support to avoid the risk of boundary violation, burnout, and vicarious traumatization when working with psychopaths.

The amount and type of staff training should be contingent on the type and degree of contact that staff have with psychopathic offenders. All members of staff should be trained to a level of competency that will allow them to carry out their assigned duties. Assessment and treatment staff should receive the most intensive training because of their close therapeutic contact with the psychopaths (see Wong & Hare, 2005, for details). Staff should have appropriate (preferably postsecondary) training in theories, prediction, and treatment of criminal behavior, and they should be familiar with the clinical and empirical literature on psychopathy. They should receive instruction and supervised on-the-job training, overseen by someone who is experienced in working with psychopathic offenders. Staff should be provided with appropriate and on-going clinical supervision on intervention skills through in-program observations and evaluations by experienced senior clinicians according to preestablished criteria of good working alliances (e.g. see Horvath & Luborsky, 1993). Debriefing, close collegial support, and open communication are essential in maintaining staff morale and cohesion. Management must take staff selection, training, and supervision seriously if psychopathic offenders are to be managed appropriately and the welfare of staff valued and protected.

Community Supervision and Follow-up Services

- Develop effective community supervision strategies for psychopaths including follow-up treatment services, support, reestablishment of community linkages, and the identification of escape risk.

The planning of community supervision should begin while the individual is still incarcerated. See Wong and Gordon (2004) for discussions of the management of offenders who have had treatment before their release to the community. After the individual is discharged to the community (e.g., on parole), an intensive follow-up period can help psychopaths generalize to the community the knowledge and skills acquired during incarceration. The intensity of the follow-up services should be gradually decreased as the offender becomes more integrated into the community. The follow-up services must be accessible, relevant, and relatively frequent. That is, the offender should not have to overcome unreasonable obstacles (e.g., travel long distances) to access the service (see Wong & Hare, 2005). The follow-up services should be an extension of the services that the individual has been receiving in the institution. Often, the lack of interagency coordination leads to the fragmentation of service delivery such that the left hand does not know what the right hand is doing. The individual may be subjected to many rounds of unnecessary assessment and evaluation that serves to confuse rather than clarify the situation for all. Not only will this fragmentation compromise the efficacy of the service, it may set the stage for the psychopath to manipulate the system to serve his or her own needs. The supervision and follow-up services must be relevant to the life situation of the individual, and frequent enough for the individual to maintain a reasonable level of contact with the service providers. If the individual has been attending an institutional-based treatment program, the follow-up services could function as a community-based component of the program.

Psychopaths are more likely to pose a higher escape risk than nonpsychopathic offenders (Wong, 1984). The high-risk situation for escape can be assessed by examining the individual's history of institutional misconduct and compliance with community supervision. Research to gain a better understanding of psychopaths who have successfully completed parole should provide useful information on the appropriate supervision strategy to use for psychopaths.

Parole Decision Making

- Include the construct of psychopathy in the orientation and training of parole board members to assist them in their decision making.

The construct of psychopathy in parole decision making is important in at least two respects. First, the personality characteristics of the psychopath may have an impact on how the individual is perceived by members of the parole board. The glibness, charm, and manipulativeness of the psychopath may precipitate strong negative reactions and influence the board's decision making. On the other hand, less experienced or informed members may be deceived by the psychopath's impression management techniques. Decision makers must have a clear appreciation of the psychopathic personality to see beyond the façade of impression management behaviors that often accompany the presentations of psychopaths. Parole board members should also recognize that not all psychopaths recidivate and should avoid allowing personality features to disproportionately affect their judgment.

Second, although psychopaths are at higher risk to violate conditional releases than less psychopathic individuals, psychopathy is NOT synonymous with violence or parole violation. In fact, as indicated in the earlier part of this chapter, a significant portion of psychopathic offenders may not violate conditional releases or recidivate after their release. Clearly, a well-informed and balanced approach is paramount.

Conclusion

Research in the past three decades has identified affective, interpersonal, behavioral, risk, and other significant differences between psychopaths and nonpsychopaths. Many forensic and correctional personnel are tasked with providing appropriate services to address the needs of this group of very challenging clients. We must direct our attention to gain a better understanding of the similarity and differences among psychopaths, and we are just beginning the journey.

REFERENCES

Andrews, D. A., & Bonta, J. (2003). *The psychology of criminal conduct* (3rd ed.). Cincinnati, OH: Anderson Press.

Andrews, D. A., Zinger, I., Hoge, R. D., Bonta, J., Gendreau, P., & Cullen, F. T. (1990). Does correctional treatment work? A clinically relevant and psychologically informed meta-analysis. *Criminology, 28*, 369–404.

Beyko, M., & Wong, S. C. P. (2005). Predictors of treatment attrition as indicators for program improvement not offender shortcomings: A study of sex offender treatment attrition. *Sexual Abuse: A Journal of Research and Treatment, 17*, 375–389.

Blackburn, R. (1975). An empirical classification of psychopathic personality. *British Journal of Psychiatry, 127*, 456–460.

Canadian Psychological Association. (2000). *Canadian code of ethics for psychologists* (3rd ed.). Ottawa, Ontario, Canada: Author.

Di Placido, C., Simon, T., Witte, T. D., Gu, D., & Wong, S. C. P. (in press). Treatment of gang members can reduce recidivism and institutional misconduct. *Law and Human Behavior.*

Dowden, C., & Andrews, D. A. (2000). Effective correctional treatment and violent reoffending. *Canadian Journal of Criminology, 42*, 449–467.

Gendreau, P., Goggin, C., & Law, M. (1997). Predicting prison misconducts. *Criminal Justice and Behavior, 24*, 414–431.

Gendreau, P., Little, T., & Goggin, C. (1996). A meta-analysis of the predictors of adult offender recidivism: What works! *Criminology, 34*, 575–607.

Grann, M., Långström, N., Tengström, A., & Kullgren, G. (1999). Psychopathy (PCL–R) predicts violent recidivism among criminal offenders with personality disorders in Sweden. *Law and Human Behavior, 23*, 205–217.

Hare, R. D. (1991). *The Hare Psychopathy Checklist–Revised.* Toronto, Ontario, Canada: Multi-Health Systems.

Hare, R. D. (1996). Psychopathy, a clinical construct whose time has come. *Criminal Justice and Behavior, 23*, 25–54.

Hare, R. D. (1998). *Without conscience: The disturbing world of the psychopaths among us.* New York: Guilford Press. (Original work published 1993)

Hare, R. D. (2003). *The Hare Psychopathy Checklist–Revised* (2nd ed.). Toronto, Ontario, Canada: Multi-Health Systems.

Hare, R. D., Clark, D., Grann, M., & Thornton, D. (2000). Psychopathy and the predictive validity of the PCL–R: An international perspective. *Behavioral Science and the Law, 18*, 623–645.

Harland, A. T. (Ed.). (1995). *Choosing correctional options that work: Defining the demand and evaluating the supply.* Thousand Oaks, CA: Sage.

Hart, S. D., Kropp, P. R., & Hare, R. D. (1988). Performance of psychopaths following conditional release from prison. *Journal of Consulting and Clinical Psychology, 56,* 227–232.

Hemphill, J. F., Hare, R. D., & Wong, S. (1998). Psychopathy and recidivism: A review. *Legal and Criminological Psychology, 3,* 139–170.

Hervé, H. F., & Hare, R. D. (2002, March). *Criminal psychopathy and its subtypes:* Reliability and generalizability. Paper presented at the annual convention of the American Psychology-Law Society, Division 41 of the American Psychological Association. Austin, TX.

Horvath, A. O., & Luborsky, L. (1993). The role of the therapeutic alliance in psychotherapy. *Journal of Consulting and Clinical Psychology, 61,* 561–573.

Lösel, F. (1995). The efficacy of correctional treatment: A review and synthesis of meta-evaluations. In J. McGuire (Ed.), *What works? Reducing reoffending, guidelines from research and practice* (pp. 79–111). Chichester, England: Wiley.

McGuire, J. (Ed.). (1995). *What works: Reducing reoffending, guidelines from research and practice.* Chichester, England: Wiley.

Ogloff, J., Wong, S., & Greenwood, A. (1990). Treating criminal psychopaths in a therapeutic community program. *Behavioral Sciences and the Law, 8,* 181–190.

Salekin, R. T. (2002). Psychopathy and therapeutic pessimism: Clinical lore or clinical reality? *Clinical Psychopathy Review, 22,* 79–112.

Serin, R. C., & Amos, N. L. (1995). The role of psychopathy in the assessment of dangerousness. *International Journal of Law and Psychiatry, 18,* 231–238.

Serin, R. C., Peters, R. DeV., & Barbaree, H. E. (1990). Predictors of psychopathy and release outcome in a criminal population. *Psychological Assessment: A Journal of Consulting and Clinical Psychology, 2, 419–422.*

Skeem, J. L., Monahan, J., & Mulvey, E. P. (2002). Psychopathy, treatment involvement, and subsequent violence among civil psychiatric patients. *Law and Human Behavior, 26,* 577–603.

Wilson, N. (2001). The PCL Study 'false positive' offender group: Are they actually low risk and if so how did they do it (Report to Policy and Development). Wellington, New Zealand: Department of Correction.

Wintrup, A., Coles, M., Hart, S., & Webster, C. D. (1994). The predictive validity of the PCL–R in high-risk mentally disorder offenders [Abstract]. *Canadian Psychology, 35,* 47.

Witte, T. D., Di Placido, C., Gu, D. & Wong, S. C. P. (in press). An investigation of the reliability and validity of the Criminal Sentiments Scale using a sample of treated sex offenders. *Sexual Abuse: A Journal of Research and Treatment.*

Wong, S. (2000). Treatment of criminal psychopaths. In S. Hodgins & R. Muller-Isberner (Eds.), *Violence, crime and mentally disordered offenders: Concepts and methods for effective treatment and prevention* (pp. 81–106). London: Wiley.

Wong, S. C. P. (1984). *Criminal and institutional behaviors of psychopaths* (Programs Branch User Report). Ottawa, Ontario, Canada: Secretariat, Ministry of the Solicitor General of Canada.

Wong, S. C. P., & Gordon, A. (2004). A risk-readiness model of post-treatment risk management. *Issues in Forensic Psychology, 5,* 152–163.

Wong, S. C. P., & Gordon, A. (2005). *Violence Risk Scale: Research results.* Unpublished manuscript.

Wong, S. C. P., & Gordon, A. (2006). The validity and reliability of the Violence Risk Scale: A treatment friendly violence risk assessment tool. Manuscript submitted for publication.

Wong, S. C. P., & Gordon, A. (2001–4). Violence Risk Scale. Unpublished manuscripts.

Wong, S. C. P., & Hare, R. D. (2005). *Guidelines for a psychopathy treatment program.* Toronto, Ontario, Canada: Multi-Health Systems.

VII

PRACTICE CONCERNS

19

Psychopathy and Deception

Barry S. Cooper and John C. Yuille

In his lying, he is miles away from the confabulant, from the patient suffering from retrospective falsifications, or from the hysterical amnesic. He is
even far from the pseudologue. He is a pathological liar, his lying being
chiefly opportunistic and defensive and but little compensatory. Much of it
is at the conscious or near conscious level. [His] stories represent a conscious
attempt to deceive, coupled with a mental incapacity to appreciate the absur-
dity of his deceptions (Karpman, 1949, p. 521).

Deception is a cardinal component of psychopathy (Doren, 1987; Yochelson
& Samenow, 1976). Indeed, pathological lying and manipulation are two
items on the Psychopathy Checklist–Revised (PCL–R; Hare, 1991, 2003), the
gold standard in the assessment of psychopathy in forensic contexts (Fulero,
1995; Stone, 1995). Despite such centrality and the fact that there are large
independent bodies of literature on psychopathy and deception, relatively
little research has been done on the association between psychopathy and
deception. In this chapter, we review the relevant literature on psychopathy
and deception in forensic contexts to examine the following issues: (a) the
nature of psychopaths' use of deception; (b) psychopaths' ability to deceive
others; and (c) psychopaths' ability to detect deception in others. For the
purposes of this chapter, the general spirit of Ekman's (1997) definition of
lying (i.e., deliberate deception) was adopted. That is, deliberate deception
or lying occurs when an individual consciously attempts to mislead a target,
and the target is not informed about the liar's intention to mislead. This
definition includes both conscious falsification and concealment (Ekman,
1992) but does not include failures of memory, broken promises, or secrets
(Ekman, 2001).

In the next section, we review the nature of psychopaths' deceptive behavior, including their motivations to deceive others. Following, we discuss the
research investigating whether psychopaths are adept liars. We then discuss
research and theoretical speculations about psychopaths' ability to detect
deception in others. Finally, we offer implications for the criminal justice
system and provide suggestions for future research on psychopathy and
deception.

PSYCHOPATHS LIE A LOT AND
FOR A VARIETY OF REASONS

Everyone has lied at some point in his or her life (Wolk & Henley, 1970). Ekman's research with adults and children suggests most individuals lie primarily to avoid punishment or to obtain a reward (for reviews, see Ekman, 1989, 1997). His research indicates individuals also lie for the following, less frequent, reasons: to protect oneself from being threatened with harm; to prevent another individual from being punished; to gain the admiration of other individuals; to escape an awkward situation; to exercise power over other individuals; to keep a secret; and to prevent embarrassment.

In comparison with the general population, most criminals engage in deception much more frequently and for more self-serving reasons. Indeed, 50%–80% of incarcerated inmates have diagnoses of Antisocial Personality Disorder (APD; American Psychiatric Association, 2000), of which a cardinal component is the use of deception. As one convicted career criminal with APD stated to the first author in the context of a risk assessment, ". . . you can't commit crimes without lying." Although psychopathic criminals' use of deception is often in line with their nonpsychopathic counterparts in terms of general frequency, research suggests that they are more frequently motivated to tell certain types of lies than nonpsychopaths. We discuss these issues in more detail later.

Motivations to Deceive

According to Meloy (1988), psychopaths' use of deception is sometimes "endogenous," that is, compulsively fuelled to protect the narcissistic self. As an anecdotal example, Karpman (1949) noted the following about an idiopathic (i.e., primarily biologically based) psychopath: "in his presentation of the circumstances of the crime he wilfully forgets the true facts because they violate his egoism; he manufactures the false situation more because it flatters his egoism, than because the truth embarrasses him socially and ethically" (p. 502). He also commented that psychopaths' use of deception, although conscious, is "directed by unconscious motivations" (p. 505). As noted by Wolk and Henly (1970), as opposed to the "healthy liar," the pathological liar ". . . compulsively pyramids one untruth upon another, often in a conscious or unconscious attempt to hide his true personality" (p. 6). Although pathological lying is a hallmark characteristic of psychopathy, it is not synonymous with being a good liar or with being a natural liar. Ekman proposed the term *natural liar* (1985) and later *natural performer* (1992) to refer to individuals who appear credible while engaging in conscious deception and his research suggests that most of these individuals are not criminals or psychopaths.

Many psychopathic criminals' lies are motivated by the same factors as those of nonpsychopathic criminals (Hare, Forth, & Hart, 1989). For example, most criminals, irrespective of psychopathy diagnosis, lie to avoid trouble or punishment (e.g., incarceration). Such lies could be considered as arising from either an adaptational (i.e., based on a cost-benefit analysis) or a criminological motivation (resulting from APD-like characteristics; see Rogers, 1990a, 1990b; Rogers, Salekin, Sewell, Goldstein, & Leonard, 1998; Rogers, Sewell, & Goldstein, 1994). However, research indicates that some of the lies of psychopaths are more frequently motivated by intrinsic reasons. The following study is a case in point. Spidel, Hervé, Greaves, Cooper, and Hare (2003) examined a sample of 70 adolescent offenders, identifying real-life lies, that is, inconsistencies between their self-reports and file documentation. They demonstrated that psychopathic offenders lied to obtain rewards, to heighten self-presentation, and for *duping delight* (see the next section) significantly more frequently in comparison with nonpsychopathic young offenders. Similar findings have been demonstrated with adult offenders (i.e., Petitclerc, Hervé, Hare, & Spidel, 2000; Spidel, 2002), suggesting there are no age-related differences in motivations for deception across psychopaths' criminal careers. More importantly, Spidel et al.'s research indicated that psychopaths lie more frequently than nonpsychopaths when the motivation for deception involves positive affect (e.g., duping delight).

Duping Delight

As alluded to earlier, duping delight is an interesting type of deceptive behavior. Ekman (1992) discussed this phenomenon in reference to the positive feelings one may experience when "putting one over." The term appears to be tailor-made for the interpersonally skilled narcissistic psychopath. Karpman (1949) provided an interesting case example of an idiopathic psychopath who appears to have lied about most of his social and criminal history and demonstrated features of duping delight. In this regard, Karpman noted that the offender "thoroughly enjoyed writing about himself and his adventures . . . he possessed a lively imagination, from the exercise of which he derived considerable pleasure, entirely unrestricted by any regard from fact" (p. 497). Karpman speculated that part of the motive behind such lying is to "produce an effect" and to fuel "a form of fantasy which feeds his egoism" (p. 504; also see Meloy, 1988). Doren (1987) also reported the following: "once a clinician has come to suspect that the client is psychopathic, then it is probably a safe idea to believe little of the reported history until it is verified by outside sources. After all, many psychopaths simply enjoy lying for the sake of seeing what they can get past other people" (p. 142).

As a more recent example of duping delight, a psychopath who participated in a research project on memory discussed at length how he violently damaged his apartment in a LSD-induced rage state (Cooper, 2005). He talked about a number of acts including picking up his stove and hurling it across his apartment. He later discussed how, after he came down from his LSD "trip," his associate began cooking on his stove. Perplexed, the interviewer asked how his associate could have cooked on his stove after he finished informing her that he had thrown it across his room in his apartment. Undisturbed by his obvious inconsistency, the participant stated the following in a state of amusement: "Oh, that's weird, that's right, he was, how did that happen? See that's what I mean. That's why memories get screwed up when you're on acid, man. I don't remember how that worked" (p. 153). Similarly, another psychopath from the same research project claimed, with a smile on his face, to have committed more than one act of violence per day for approximately 20 years (Kendrick, Cooper, Hervé, Yuille, & Hare, 2004). Although possible, such a claim was neither credible nor verifiable. Often, as speculated by others, individuals engage in duping delight in part because it would be impossible to verify their accounts. Indeed, as Karpman (1949) noted, "it is characteristic, even typical, of the true psychopath to make statements which cannot be substantiated or verified" (p. 508).

As others have suggested, it is likely that psychopaths' deceptive behavior is at least partially situationally determined. This is somewhat akin to an adaptational motivation (Rogers et al., 1994, 1998). For example, consider the following statement by Karpman (1949) in reference to an idiopathic psychopath: his account "is tempered and colored by his narcissism, and by the practical consideration of what will do him the most good at the moment. He will deny an event or a series of events if, in his opinion, an admission of these is likely to reflect badly on him. To the same extent, he is likely to exaggerate or embellish his behavior if he thinks that this might lead others to think better of him" (p. 507).

Frequency of Deceptive Behavior

Some evidence suggests psychopathic criminals engage in deception more frequently than their nonpsychopathic peers (Hare et al., 1989). Such evidence is primarily extracted from clinical case studies and anecdotal reports (e.g., Cleckley, 1941; Hare, 1993). Research on the topic, however, has produced inconsistent results. That is, some research has shown that psychopaths' lie more than nonpsychopaths (e.g., Spidel et al., 2003), and other research has been equivocal (for a review, see Clark, 1997). One study, based on a correctional file review of 125 homicide offenders, demonstrated that psychopathic murderers were twice as likely as nonpsychopathic murderers to change their version of their homicide offenses over the course of incarceration (Porter & Woodworth, 2002). Contrasting results primarily stem from research and case studies on malingering. Although most psychopaths are not malingerers (Clark, 1997), some researchers have suggested that psychopathy is somewhat synonymous with malingering. Indeed, Ray (1983) proposed that the psychopathic deviate (Pd) scale on the Minnesota Multiphasic Personality Inventory (MMPI), historically used for psychopathy diagnoses, measures malingering as opposed to psychopathy per se. Similarly, Campbell (1943) argued that "the malingerer is . . . essentially a psychopathic personality" (p. 351) and suggested that psychopaths consciously pretend to have symptoms of physical and mental disorders for a variety of motivations (e.g., to avoid military duty). For example, similar to Ekman's definition of duping delight, Campbell suggested the psychopath or malingerer "derives a secret satisfaction in fooling others, or at least in being the center of attraction for a period of time" (p. 351).

The inconsistent pattern in the literature concerning psychopathy and lying may be a reflection of a general problem with much of the deception literature: too much of the research is laboratory based. In laboratory research, the participants are volunteers with only weak motivations related to lying. That is, there is often little at stake for the liar, and the liar is often given permission to lie. Interestingly, these features of laboratory-based work often remove the factors that improve lie detection (see Ekman, 2001). Our review of the literature suggests that studies reporting that psychopaths do not have higher lying rates are often laboratory based whereas field studies or anecdotal reports often show that the rate of deception in psychopaths is higher. Thus, the apparent contradiction in the literature may be a procedural artefact. Given the inherent shortcomings of the laboratory-based work on deception, conclusions concerning the rates of deception in psychopaths should be made on the field research and anecdotal evidence.

ARE PSYCHOPATHS GOOD LIARS?

Because of their experience in manipulation and deception and their lack of remorse for their actions, psychopaths have been routinely speculated to be good liars (Cleckley, 1941; Lees-Haley, 1986; Lykken, 1978). For example, Campbell (1943) suggested that psychopathic members of military troops have successfully pretended to have symptoms of mental and physical disorders to be relieved of military duty. It has been suggested that their deficit in processing emotions sets the stage for their ability to manipulate and deceive (Hare et al., 1989), and their lack of detection apprehension would lead to less emotional leakage (Ekman, 1992). Further, because of their hyposensitivity to arousal (Day & Wong, 1996; Hare, 1978; Hervé, Cooper, Yuille, & Daylen, 2003), it has also been suggested that psychopaths can "fool" the polygraph (Barland & Raskin, 1973). There has been scant research on this issue. The available evidence suggests psychopaths' use of deception is as easily detected by the polygraph as that of nonpsychopaths. For example, Raskin and Hare (1978) had 24 male offenders participate in a mock theft and an additional 24 participants not participate (there were 12 psychopaths in each subgroup). Both the *guilty* and the *innocent* participants were instructed to deny committing the mock theft. An examiner, blind to the experimental condition, used a control question polygraph examination on the participants. The results indicated that the guilty participants were not able to produce truthful responses to the polygraph, and psychopathic participants were just as easily detected as deceivers as the nonpsychopaths.

Although the Raskin and Hare (1978) study is not without criticism (e.g., due to lack of ecological validity and problems with the control question test; see Lykken, 1978, and rebuttal by Raskin, 1978), their results were replicated by Patrick (1987; see also Patrick & Iacono, 1989) using a threat, rather than a reward, paradigm. The participants in the Patrick and Iacono study were told that, if they failed the polygraph test, all of the participants would lose the monetary bonus, and the list of participants who failed the test would be made known to all participants. Hence, in contrast to the chance of winning money in the Raskin and Hare study, the participants in Patrick and Iacono's investigation were under the assumption that failing the polygraph test could have negative physical consequences. As with the Raskin and Hare study, half of the participants engaged in a mock theft, and it was again demonstrated that guilty psychopaths were as easily detected by the polygraph examinations as guilty nonpsychopaths.

The results from polygraph research are consistent with those from other research demonstrating that psychopaths are no better liars than nonpsychopaths (for review, see Clark, 1997). For example, Kropp (1994) showed that psychopaths were no better than nonpsychopaths at faking mental illness. Lindblad (1994) reported similar results. Furthermore, Cogburn (1993) demonstrated that psychopathy was associated with a lower perception of truthfulness in a study of interpersonal deception.

Regardless of the research on psychopathy and the polygraph and the research on malingering and psychopathy, indirect evidence suggests that psychopaths can be somewhat successful liars. For example, their use of correctional programs to impress the parole board that they have changed their antisocial attitudes, coupled with their often good performance at parole hearings, suggests that some psychopaths are able to fool people that their risk level is manageable in the community (Hare et al., 1989). However, the treatment research demonstrates that many psychopaths have not been true to their words (see Thornton & Blud, chap. 20, this volume). That is, a number of studies have shown that treated psychopaths reoffend at a higher rate than nontreated psychopaths. For example, Rice, Harris, and Cormier (1992) showed that untreated psychopaths had a lower rate of violent recidivism (55%) than treated psychopaths (77%). Similar results were reported by Seto and Barbaree (1999; also see Ogloff, Wong, & Greenwood, 1990), who suggested that psychopaths were likely to be able to deceive both their assessors and their victims. In some of the treatment studies, some psychopaths who violently recidivated posttreatment were the ones who were rated as having made the most treatment gains by their program facilitators. Although the treatment studies have been criticized on a number of grounds (e.g., lack of a true control group; see D'Silva, Duggan, & McCarthy, 2004) and some researchers in this area have produced null results (e.g., Barbaree, Seto, & Langston, 2001; Hare, Clark, Grann, & Thornton, 2000) and other researchers have showed that treatment is associated with a lowered rate of recidivism/ violence in individuals with psychopathic traits (e.g., Gretton, McBride, Hare, & O'Shaughnessy, 2000; Skeem, Monahan, & Mulvey, 2002), the fact remains that a substantial proportion of the psychopaths in all of these studies successfully "fooled" someone (e.g., clinical–forensic assessors or the parole board). It may be that psychopaths are not more effective liars when assessed in a controlled study (or via structured methods) but that, in certain contexts, in which their self-report cannot be easily verified (e.g., parole hearings, business, or sexual exploitation), they are more effective deceivers.

Converging evidence from the organizational context suggests that some psychopaths are "successful" in such environments, as they can easily use their deceptive and other interpersonal skills to exploit others and move ahead (e.g., Babiak, chap. 16 this volume; Person, 1986). Although most empirically examined psychopaths have a criminal history and are found in prisons, many psychopaths do not have a criminal history (Cleckley, 1941). Indeed, there is some anecdotal evidence suggesting that some psychopaths engage in white-collar crime (see Hare, 1993, for a series of case studies). As Sutherland (1940) noted, white-collar crime is found in every occupation including medicine, law, politics, business, and so forth, and, although often empirically overlooked, the financial costs of such crime is "probably several times as great as the financial costs of all the crimes" (p. 18). The white-collar or subcriminal psychopath appears to be attracted to occupations and situations in which access to power, prestige, and financial rewards is easily attainable (Hare, 1993, 1998). Positions that involve leadership and management seem to be particularly appealing to white-collar psychopaths, owing to their power and relatively high salaries (Babiak, 1995a).

Babiak's (2000) work on industrial psychopaths suggests that some psychopaths are able to successfully deceive and manipulate their colleagues as they strive to reach the top of the business world. Babiak (1995b) illustrates an interesting case of an industrial psychopath (i.e., high on Factor 1 and moderate on Factor 2 of the PCL–R; Hare, 1991) who was able to succeed in the business word by deceiving and manipulating his colleagues, subordinates, and superiors. According to Babiak (1995b), this industrial psychopath used the following strategy: he "identified powerful or organizational useful individuals necessary to his survival in the organization, and manipulated them more consistently and with more finesse than others whom he perceived to be either detractors, or obstacles. The ultimate outcome—a discrepancy in the perceptions of the subject between different members of the organization—is the core of the psychopath's ability to succeed in an industrial organization" (p. 184). Such discrepancies were caused by the psychopath through the use of deception and manipulation, a core interpersonal feature of white-collar psychopaths (Hare, 1998). That is, the psychopath used deception to facilitate a positive view of himself to his superiors (i.e., patrons), while badmouthing others (i.e., pawns) in the organization by spreading erroneous information about them (Babiak, 1995a). Although many of the individuals in the organization eventually realized they had been manipulated and deceived, it was far too late, and both the patrons and pawns became patsies to the psychopath as he moved to the top of the organization (Babiak, 1995b).

In addition to the business context, some psychopaths seem to be successful deceivers in the domain of casual sex, as many psychopaths are promiscuous and engage in trivial sexual encounters. Indeed, sexual promiscuity is an item on the PCL–R (Hare, 1991, 2003). As an example of sexual promiscuity, Karpman (1949) discussed the following in relation to an idiopathic psychopath: "in the choice of mates or partners, there is no great preference. Every woman teems with possibilities; the nearest is the most beautiful" (pp. 500–501). Unless many of psychopaths' sexual partners "are just into it for the sex," psychopaths are able to use deception to court unassuming partners into sexual activity. That is, it can only be assumed that some psychopaths are not steadfastly sincere in their seductions of their sexual partners. Stemming from a sociobiological framework, some have suggested that such a characteristic is an adaptive reproductive strategy (Harpending & Sobus, 1987). For example, psychopaths or those with APD may "cheat;" that is, ". . . misrepresent their status, access to resources, and intentions when forming relationships" (MacMillan & Kofoed, 1984, p. 703). Although their promiscuity is in line with a sociobiological framework, it is arguable their entire motive behind such behavior is solely determined by a "genetically influenced reproductive strategy" (p. 703). Psychopaths' promiscuous nature may be more a reflection of the characteristics of their sexual partners than their capacity to deceive. That is, clinical forensic experience suggests many psychopaths' target sexual partners with traits of Borderline Personality Disorder, and it is speculated that such individuals are vulnerable to being deceived. The effectiveness of a lie is clearly related to both the characteristics of the deceiver and the target (Ekman, 1992). As one psychopath commented, ". . . a good liar is a good judge of people" (Hare et al., 1989, p. 28). Indeed, many of the staff members who have been "set up" in prison contexts have been chosen on the basis of their vulnerabilities (e.g., naiveté or gullibility; see Allen & Bosta, 1981).

The discrepancy between the inability of psychopaths to be better deceivers than nonpsychopaths and the ability of some psychopaths to be adept at deceiving is explainable. Perhaps, psychopaths are adept at deceiving individuals in some contexts because, to the untrained observer, ". . . lying is just a matter of moving words around," an easily accomplished task for psychopaths due to their affective deficit (Hare et al., 1989, p. 34). In the business and sexual contexts, for example, the recipients of the psychopaths' lies are typically not trained evaluators. However, polygraphers are trained observers, and the research on that subject reviewed earlier indicates that, as a group, psychopaths cannot fool the polygraph. Another reason relates to the motivation of the recipient of the lie to believe the lie. That is, the effectiveness of the lie is increased by the recipient's motivation to believe it (Ekman, 1992). For example, a victim of fraud may have really wanted to believe the psychopathic hustler's claim that he or she could "get rich quickly." Similarly, a treatment facilitator probably wants to believe that his or her psychopathic client was being truthful about making gains in treatment. As another example alluded to earlier, a sexual partner probably wants to believe that his or her psychopathic partner wants a relationship as opposed to simply sexual relations.

Another reason for the discrepancy relates to psychopathic subtypes. As noted by Clark (1997), "plausibly, a portion of socialized sociopaths may be more adept than others at lying and dissimulation." (p. 74). That is, it is likely that certain types of psychopaths are better deceivers than other types. As discussed in an earlier chapter in this volume, not all psychopaths are the same (Wong & Burt, chap. 18, this volume). Indeed, Hervé (2000, 2002, chap. 17, this volume) has empirically demonstrated that there are four subtypes of psychopaths: the prototypical psychopath, the manipulative psychopath, the explosive psychopath, and the pseudopsychopath. Because of their interpersonal characteristics (e.g., manipulative, deceptive, and superficially charming), we propose that prototypical and manipulative psychopaths (Hervé, 2000, 2002) are more adept at deception than explosive psychopaths and pseudopsychopaths.

In short, the evidence on psychopaths' adeptness at deception is mixed. It appears that context (probably primarily defined by the skill of the lie recipient at detecting lies) is the major determinant of how detectable psychopaths' lies are. When facing someone trained in credibility assessment, the psychopath has no advantage in escaping lie detection. When facing a naïve person, the psychopath may be a more accomplished or successful liar.

ARE PSYCHOPATHS GOOD LIE DETECTORS?

John Wayne Gacy, a notorious serial killer, commenting on the detection of deception, stated: "no one can tell when you're lying and when you're not" (Cahill, 1986. p. ix).

Surprisingly, very little research has been done to examine whether psychopaths are adept at detecting deception in others. Indeed, this issue was specifically examined in only one study. In this study the Facial Deception Test (Ekman & Friesen, 1974) was used, and the results indicated that both psychopaths and nonpsychopaths were unable to detect deception at better than the level of chance, with no differences between the psychopathic and nonpsychopathic groups (Hare et al., 1989). This finding is consistent with the growing body of research on deception detection indicating that most individuals, irrespective of whether the detection of deception is central to their employment (e.g., judges or law enforcement professionals), are poor (i.e., chance level) at detecting deception in others (Ekman & O'Sullivan, 1991; Ekman, O'Sullivan, & Frank, 1999; Malone & Depaulo, 2001).

Research indicates that only a small percentage of individuals in the general population are very accurate in deception detection, a group referred to as *wizards* (for review, see O'Sullivan & Ekman, 2004). The wizards appear to be highly sensitive to nonverbal information (e.g., facial emotions) because of their training and experience (O'Sullivan, in press). Furthermore, they appear to be able to determine with high accuracy when someone is lying based upon a discrepancy between verbal and nonverbal information (i.e., emotions; O'Sullivan & Ekman, 2004). Indeed, according to Ekman (1997), most liars fail because their true emotions interfere (i.e., leak) with their goal (i.e., to hide the felt emotion). O'Sullivan and Ekman (2004) speculated that most wizards are introverted and are good at role playing and taking the perspective of others, and O'Sullivan (in press) suggested that they have a high degree of emotional intelligence.

The research and theoretical speculations on the nonverbal detection of deception coupled with the research on psychopathy, affect, and personality suggests that psychopaths' capacity to detect deception, particularly nonverbal clues to deceit, is poor. For example, as indicated earlier, it has been speculated that most wizards are introverted (O'Sullivan & Ekman, 2004). Although research does not indicate most psychopaths are extraverted, as a group, they are clearly not introverted. Indeed, sensation-seeking and a hyposensitivity to arousal, two core traits of psychopathy (Hervé et al., 2003), are not consistent with introversion (Blascovich, 1990, 1992; Eysenck, 1967; Feldman, 1995; Zuckerman, 1979). Moreover, psychopaths' limited capacity to empathize (Hare, 1991, 2003) suggests that their emotional intelligence is poor. Thus, they are likely to perform poorly in assessing other individuals' emotions, a necessary pre-requisite for the accurate nonverbal detection of deception (Ekman, 1992; O'Sullivan, in press). Further, generally speaking, they do not seem able to take the perspectives of others (Blair et al., 1995; Doren, 1987; Gough, 1948), which have been speculated to be a characteristic of the wizards (O'Sullivan & Ekman, 2004).

In short, whether psychopaths are adept at detecting deception in others has been examined in only one study. Consistent with the theoretical speculations offered earlier, the answer is no.

SUGGESTIONS FOR RESEARCH AND PRACTICE

One of the strengths of the PCL–R (Hare, 1991, 2003) is its reliance on collateral information. This reliance should be not viewed as a weakness of the measure as some researchers have suggested (e.g., Loza, 2003). Collateral information is needed for the assessor to not be deceived. Without independent collateral information to challenge the psychopath's account, individuals are susceptible to being duped (Hare et al., 1989). It is likely that subcriminal psychopaths are successful in the business context because no one is able to challenge their accounts, particularly at the beginning of their careers if their resumes are faked and not checked (Babiak, 1995a). Thus, in all contexts (e.g., from the research context to the correctional context to the business context), it is suggested that the assessor gather as much collateral information as possible. Assessors should attempt to assess offenders' interpersonal styles during interviews, as research suggests their presenting styles (e.g., social desirable vs. social nonconformist) can affect the assessment of their psychopathic attributes (Rogers et al., 2002). Collateral information is needed as offenders' response styles during interviews can drastically affect the assessment of their interpersonal or affective attributes.

In addition to collateral information, researchers and clinicians should use converging methods for the assessment of deception. Rogers et al. (1998) suggested that items from the Psychopathy Checklist: Screening Version (PCL:SV; Hart, Cox, & Hare, 1996) be used in conjunction with situational variables to facilitate the assessment of malingering. It has also been suggested that interviews such as the Structured Interview of Reported Symptoms (SIRS) (Rogers, 1992) be used to assess for malingering (e.g., Clark, 1997). Indeed, research on the SIRS has consistently demonstrated its ability to detect malingering and dissimulation in forensic contexts (for review, see Rogers, 1997). It has also been suggested that psychological measures, such as intelligence tests, could be used to identify malingerers, and peculiar responses on such inventories could be used to facilitate diagnoses of psychopathy (Hunt & French, 1952). To not be duped by a client, the clinical–forensic assessor should evaluate, among other variables, objective indicators of malingering, the motivation to feign, the context, and the presence of psychopathy (Clark, 1997).

On the basis of our experience working in forensic contexts, we believe that encouraging a psychopath to talk is an effective aid in credibility assessment. Our sense is that psychopaths often do not plan their lies. As a consequence, the more the psychopath elaborates his or her lie, the more likely inconsistencies, contradictions, and gaps will appear. Also, the more the psychopath talks about a lie, the more often the clues to duping delight will appear.

We know a great deal more about the independent areas of psychopathy and deception than we do about their intersection. Although the research literature clearly shows that the combination of verbal and nonverbal clues to deception facilitates a fuller understanding of deception (Memon, Vrij, & Bull, 1998), to date, little research has been done to examine nonverbal clues to deception in psychopathic offenders and none to investigate verbal clues to deception. We encourage others to conduct research in this area. To this end, we are in the process of evaluating the credibility of psychopathic and nonpsychopathic offenders' memories for their violent crimes though the use of Criterion Based Content Analysis, a technique to assess the credibility of statements (Undeutch, 1982; Vrij & Akehurst, 1998; Vrij, Akehurst, Soukara, & Bull, 2002).

Researchers and forensic practitioners are urged to incorporate the interesting and potentially informative area of psychopathic subtypes into their work on psychopathy and deception. As indicated earlier, Hervé (2000, 2002, chap. 17, this volume) has empirically shown that psychopaths differ in terms of their interpersonal and behavioral features. As alluded to earlier, we propose that certain subtypes are more likely to use deception, to use deception more successfully, and to be able to detect deception in others more accurately than other subtypes. Although it is an empirical question, we anticipate that prototypical psychopaths and manipulative psychopaths would be more adept at deception and the detection of deception than explosive psychopaths and pseudopsychopaths.

CONCLUSION

In this chapter we reviewed the relevant literature on psychopathy and deception. Clinical wisdom and anecdotal evidence suggest that psychopathic criminals lie a lot. The research in this area is flawed, but it is clear that deception is a major issue with psychopaths and that, more than individuals with any other personality disorder, these individuals will lie just for the pleasure of lying. How successful psychopaths are as liars appears to depend upon context: those well trained in credibility assessment (e.g., polygraphers) can detect lies in psychopaths at the same rate as they do in nonpsychopaths. However, psychopaths often seem to succeed in their lies when the recipient is naïve and/or ready to suspend his or her disbelief. Finally, although the amount of research is limited, theory suggests that psychopaths should not be good lie detectors.

Hare et al. (1989) made the following statement more than 15 years ago: ". . . although we know with certainty that psychopaths lie, deceive, and manipulate others, their performance on various tests associated with lying and deception is typically normal. Perhaps the most plausible reasons for this situation are that the various inventories and procedures currently in use lack ecological validity and are simply not sensitive to assess deception by psychopaths" (p. 44). Unfortunately, nothing in the subsequent research literature on psychopathy and deception has changed the value of this observation. As noted by Clark (1997), "at the present time, clinicians have no defensible basis on which to conclude that sociopathy, ipso facto, increases the likelihood of feigning" (p. 84). If we want to know more about psychopathy and deception, we need to develop sophisticated externally valid methodologies, utilize both verbal and nonverbal approaches to deception, and take into consideration the likely influence of psychopathic subtypes.

ACKNOWLEDGMENTS

Preparation for this chapter was supported by a doctoral fellowship to B. S. Cooper and an operating grant to J. C. Yuille from the Social Sciences and Humanities Research Council of Canada. B. S. Cooper was also supported by the Izaac Walter Killam Memorial Foundation and the Michael Smith Foundation for Health Research.

Although the first author is employed by the Correctional Service of Canada and gratefully acknowledges their support in preparation for this chapter, the views expressed by the authors do not necessarily reflect the official policy of the Correctional Service of Canada.

The authors thank Mike Stoian and Dr. Maureen O'Sullivan for their helpful comments on previous drafts of this chapter.

REFERENCES

Allen, B., & Bosta, D. (1981). *Games criminal play: How you can profit by knowing them.* Susanville, CA: Rae John Publishers.

American Psychiatric Association. (2000). *Diagnostic and statistical manual of mental disorders* (4th ed., text revision), Washington, DC: Author.

Babiak, P. (1995a). Psychopathic manipulation in organizations: Pawns, patrons, and patsies. *Issues in Criminological and Legal Psychology, 24*, 21–17.

Babiak, P. (1995b). When psychopaths go to work: A case study of an industrial psychopath. *Applied Psychology: An International Review, 44*, 171–188.

Babiak, P. (2000). Psychopathic manipulation at work. In C. B. Gacono (Ed.), *Clinical and forensic assessment of psychopathy: A practitioner's guide* (pp. 287–311). Mahwah, NJ: Lawrence Erlbaum Associates.

Barbaree, H., Seto, M. C., & Langston, C. M. (2001, November). *Psychopathy, treatment behavior and sex offender recidivism: Extended follow-up.* Paper presented at the 20th Annual Conference of the Association for the Treatment of Sexual Abusers, San Antonio, TX.

Barland, G. H., & Raskin, D. C. (1973). Detection of deception. In W. F. Prokasy & D. C. Raskin (Eds.), *Electrodermal activity in psychological research* (pp. 417–477). New York: Academic Press.

Blair, R. J. R., Sellars, C., Strickland, I., Clark, F., Williams, A. O., Smith, M., et al. (1995). Emotion attributions in the psychopath. *Personality and Individual Differences, 19*, 431–437.

Blascovich, J. (1990). Individual differences in physiological arousal and perceptions of arousal: Missing links between Jamesian notions of arousal-based behaviours. *Personality and Social Psychology Bulletin, 16*, 665–675.

Blascovich, J. (1992). A biopsychosocial approach to arousal regulation. *Journal of Social and Clinical Psychology, 11*, 213–237.

Cahill, T. (1986). *Buried dreams: Inside the mind of a serial killer.* New York: Bantam Books.

Campbell, M. M. (1943). Malingery in relation to psychopathy in military psychiatry. *Northwest Medicine, 42*, 349–354.

Clark, C. R. (1997). Sociopathy, malingering, and defensiveness. In R. Rogers (Ed.), *Clinical assessment of malingering and deception* (2nd ed., pp. 68–84), New York: Guilford Press.

Cleckley, H. (1941). *The mask of sanity.* St. Louis, MO: Mosby.

Cogburn, R-.A. K. (1993). A study of psychopathy and its relation to success in interpersonal deception. *Dissertation Abstracts International, 54*, 2191-B.

Cooper, B. S. (2005). *Memory for mayhem.* Unpublished doctoral dissertation. University of British Columbia, Vancouver, British Columbia, Canada.

Day, R., & Wong, S. (1996). Anomalous perceptual asymmetries for negative emotional stimuli in the psychopath. *Journal of Abnormal Psychology, 105*, 648–652.

Doren, D. M. (1987). *Understanding and treating the psychopath.* New York: Wiley.

D'Silva, K., Duggan, C., & McCarthy, L. (2004). Does treatment really make psychopaths worse? A review of the evidence. *Journal of Personality Disorders, 18*, 163–177.

Ekman, P. (1985). *Telling lies: Clues to deceit in the marketplace, politics, and marriage.* New York: W. W. Norton.

Ekman, P. (1989). *Why kids lie.* New York: Charles Scribner's Sons.

Ekman, P. (1992). *Telling lies: Clues to deceit in the marketplace, politics, and marriage* (2nd ed.). New York: W. W. Norton.

Ekman, P. (1997). Deception, lying, and demeanor. In D. F. Halpern & A. E. Vois-kounsky (Eds.), *States of mind: American and post-Soviet perspectives on contemporary issues in psychology* (pp. 93–105), London: Oxford University Press.

Ekman, P. (2001). *Telling lies: Clues to deceit in the marketplace, politics, and marriage* (3rd ed.). New York: W. W. Norton.

Ekman, P., & Friesen, W. V. (1974). Detecting deception from body or face. *Journal of Personality and Social Psychology, 29,* 288–298.

Ekman, P., & O'Sullivan, M. (1991). Who can catch a liar? *American Psychologist, 46,* 913–920.

Ekman, P., O'Sullivan, M., & Frank, M. G. (1999). A few can catch a liar. *Psychological Science, 10,* 263–266.

Eysenck, M. W. (1967). *The biological basis of personality.* Springfield, IL: Thomas.

Feldman, L. A. (1995). Valence focus and arousal focus: Individual differences in the structure of affective experience. *Journal of Personality and Social Psychology, 69,* 150–166.

Fulero, S. M. (1995). Review of the Hare Psychopathy Checklist–Revised. In J. C. Conoley & J. C. Impara (Eds.), *Twelfth Mental Measurements Yearbook* (pp. 453–454). Lincoln, NE: Buros Institute.

Gough, H. G. (1948). A sociological theory of psychopathy. *American Journal of Sociology, 53,* 359–366.

Gretton, H. M., McBride, M., Hare, R. D., & O'Shaughnessy, R. O. (2000, November). *Psychopathy and recidivism in adolescent offenders: A ten-year follow-up.* Paper presented at the 19th Annual Conference of the Association for the Treatment of Sexual Abusers, San Diego, CA.

Hare, R. D. (1978). Psychopathy and electrodermal responses to nonsignal stimulation. *Biological Psychology, 6,* 237–246.

Hare, R. D. (1991). *The Hare Psychopathy Checklist–Revised.* Toronto, Ontario, Canada: Multi-Health Systems.

Hare, R. D. (1993). *Without conscience: The disturbing world of psychopaths among us.* New York: Pocket Books.

Hare, R. D. (1998, October–November). *The psychopath: A dangerous domestic partner.* Keynote address presented at the IVth Love of Violence Conference, Seattle, WA.

Hare, R. D. (2003). *The Hare Psychopathy Checklist–Revised* (2nd ed.). Toronto, Ontario, Canada: Multi-Health Systems.

Hare, R. D., Clark, D., Grann, M., & Thornton, D. (2000). Psychopathy and the predictive validity of the PCL–R: An international perspective. *Behavioral Sciences and the Law, 18,* 623–645.

Hare, R. D., Forth, A. E., & Hart, S. (1989). The psychopath as prototype for pathological lying and deception. In J. C. Yuille (Ed.), *Credibility assessment* (pp. 24–49). Dordrecht, The Netherlands: Kluwer Academic.

Harpending, H. C., & Sobus, J. (1987). Sociopathy as an adaptation. *Ethology and Sociobiology, 8,* 63–72.

Hart, S. D., Cox, D. N., & Hare, R. D. (1996). *Manual for the Screening Version of the Psychopathy Checklist Revised (PCL:SV).* Toronto, Ontario, Canada: Multi-Health Systems.

Hervé, H. F. (2000, October). *Psychopathic subtypes: Issues in diagnostic specificity and sensitivity.* Paper presented at The Hare Psychopath: A Festschrift in Honor of Bob Hare, University of British Columbia, Vancouver, British Columbia, Canada.

Hervé, H. F. (2002). *The masks of sanity: A cluster analyses of subtypes of criminal psychopathy.* Unpublished doctoral dissertation. The University of British Columbia, Vancouver, British Columbia, Canada.

Hervé, H. F., Cooper, B. S., Yuille, J. C., & Daylen, J. (2003, July). *The psychopathic eyewitness: Perspectives from a biopsychosocial model of eyewitness memory.* Paper presented at the Society for Applied Research on Memory and Cognition conference, Aberdeen, Scotland.

Hunt, W. A., & French, E. G. (1952). The CVS abbreviated individual intelligence scale. *Journal of Consulting Psychology, 16,* 181–186.

Karpman, B. (1949). From the autobiography of a liar; toward a clarification of the problem of psychopathic states. *Psychiatric Quarterly, 23,* 497–521.

Kendrick, K., Cooper, B. S., Hervé, H. F., Yuille, J. C., & Hare, R. D. (2004, June). *Instrumental and reactive acts of violence as a function of psychopathy: An exploratory study with Canadian violent offenders.* Paper presented at the Canadian Psychological Association's Annual Convention, St. John's, Newfoundland and Labrador, Canada.

Kropp, P. R. (1994). The relationship between psychopathy and malingering of mental illness. *Dissertation Abstracts International, 54-B,* 5945–5946.

Lees-Haley, P. (1986). How to detect malingerers in the work place. *Personnel Journal, 65,* 106–110.

Lindblad, A. D. (1994). Detection of malingered mental illness within a forensic population: An analogue study. *Dissertation Abstracts International, 54-B,* 4395.

Loza, W. (2003). Predicting violent and nonviolent recidivism of incarcerated male offenders. *Aggression and Violent and Behavior, 8,* 175–203.

Lykken, D. T. (1978). The psychopath and the lie detector. *Psychophysiology, 15,* 137–142.

MacMillan, J., & Kofoed, L. K. (1984). Sociobiology and anti-social behavior. *Journal of Nervous and Mental Disease, 172,* 701–706.

Malone, B. E., & DePaulo, B. M. (2001). Measuring sensitivity to deception. In J. A. Hall & F. J. Bernieri (Eds.), *Interpersonal sensitivity: Theory and research,* (pp. 103–124). Mahwah, NJ: Lawrence Erlbaum Associates.

Meloy, J. R. (1988). *The psychopathic mind: Origins, dynamics, and treatment.* Northvale, NJ: Jason Aronson.

Memon, A., Vrij, A., & Bull, R. (1998). *Psychology and law: Truthfulness, accuracy and credibility.* London: McGraw-Hill.

Ogloff, J., Wong, S., & Greenwood, A. (1990). Treating criminal psychopaths in a therapeutic community. *Behavioral Sciences and the Law, 8,* 181–190.

O'Sullivan, M. (in press). Emotional intelligence and deception detection: Why most people can't read others, but a few can. In R. E. Riggio & R. S. Feldman (Eds.), *Applications of nonverbal communication* (pp. 215–253). Lawrence Erlbaum Associates.

O'Sullivan, M., & Ekman, P. (2004). The wizards of deception detection. In P. A. Granhag & L. A. Stromwell (Eds.), *Deception detection in forensic contexts* (pp. 269–287), Cambridge, England: Cambridge University Press.

Patrick, C. J. (1987). *The validity of lie detection with criminal psychopaths.* Unpublished doctoral dissertation, University of British Columbia, Vancouver, British Columbia, Canada.

Patrick, C. J., & Iacono, W. G. (1989). Psychopathy, threat, and polygraph accuracy. *Journal of Applied Psychology, 74,* 347–355.

Pearson, E. S. (1986). Manipulativeness in entrepreneurs and psychopaths. In W. H. Reid, D. Dorr, I. Walker, & J. W. Bonner (Eds.), *Unmasking the psychopath: Antisocial personality and related syndromes* (pp. 256–274). New York: W. W. Norton.

Petitclerc, A. M., Hervé, H. F., Hare, R. D., & Spidel, A. (2000). *Psychopaths' reasons to deceive*. Poster presented at the American Psychology and Law Society Conference, New Orleans, LA.

Porter, S., & Woodworth, M. (2002, May). *Investigation of impulsivity and sadistic violence by Canadian homicide offenders as a function of psychopathy*. Paper presented at the 63rd Annual Convention of the Canadian Psychological Association, Vancouver, British Columbia, Canada.

Raskin, D. C. (1978). Scientific assessment of the accuracy of detection of deception: A reply to Lykken. *Psychophysiology, 15*, 143–147.

Raskin, D. C., & Hare, R. D. (1978). Psychopathy and detection of deception in a prison population. *Psychophysiology, 15*, 126–136.

Ray, J. R. (1983). Psychopathy, anxiety, and malingering. *Personality and Individual Differences, 4*, 351–353.

Rice, M. E., Harris, G., & Cormier, C. A. (1992). An evaluation of a maximum-security therapeutic community for psychopaths and other mentally disordered offenders. *Law and Human Behavior, 16*, 399–412.

Rogers, R. (1990a). Development of a new classificatory model of malingering. *Bulletin of the American Academy of Psychiatry and Law, 18*, 323–333.

Rogers, R. (1990b). Models of feigned illness. *Professional Psychology: Research and Practice, 21*, 182–188.

Rogers, R. (1992). *Structured Interview of Reported Symptoms*. Odessa, FL: Psychological Assessment Resources.

Rogers, R. (1997). Structured interviews and dissimulation. In R. Rogers (Ed.), *Clinical assessment of malingering and deception* (2nd ed., pp. 301–327), New York: The Guilford Press.

Rogers, R., Salekin, R. T., Sewell, K. W., Goldstein, A., & Leonard, K. (1998). A comparison of forensic and nonforensic malingerers: A prototypical analysis of explanatory models. *Law and Human Behavior, 22*, 353–367.

Rogers, R., Sewell, K. W., & Goldstein, A. (1994). Explanatory models of malingering: A prototypical analyses. *Law and Human Behavior, 18*, 543–552.

Rogers, R. Vitacco, M. J., Jackson, R. L., Martin, M., Collins, M., & Sewell, K. W. (2002). Faking psychopathy? An examination of response styles with antisocial youth. *Journal of Personality Assessment, 78*, 31–47.

Seto, M. C., & Barbaree, H. E. (1999). Psychopathy, treatment behavior, and sex offender recidivism. *Journal of Interpersonal Violence, 14*, 1235–1248.

Skeem, J. L., Monahan, J., & Mulvey, E. P. (2002). Psychopathy, treatment involvement, and subsequent violence among civil psychiatric patients. *Law and Human Behavior, 26*, 577–603.

Spidel, A. (2002). *The association between deceptive motivations and personality disorders in male offenders*. Unpublished master's thesis. University of British Columbia, Vancouver, British Columbia, Canada.

Spidel, A., Hervé, H. F., Greaves, C., Cooper, B. S., & Hare, R. D. (2003). Psychopathy and deceptive motivations in young offenders. In M. Vanderhallen, G. Vervaeke, P. J. Van Koppen, & J. Goethals (Eds.), *Much ado about crime: Chapters on psychology and law* (pp. 265–276). Braxelles: Politeia.

Stone, G. L. (1995). Review of the Hare Psychopathy Checklist–Revised. In J. C. Conoley & J. C. Impara (Eds.), *Twelfth Mental Measurements Yearbook* (pp. 454–455). Lincoln, NE: Buros Institute.

Sutherland, E. H. (1940). White-collar criminality. *American Sociological Review, 5*, 2–10. Reprinted in J. E. Jacoby (Ed.), *Classics of criminology* (pp. 16–21). Oak Park, IL: Moore.

Undeutch, U. (1982). Statement reality analysis. In A. Trankell (Ed.), *Reconstructing the past: The role of psychologists in criminal trials* (pp. 27–56). Deventer, The Netherlands: Kluwer.

Vrij, A., & Akehurst, L. (1998). Verbal communication and credibility: Statement validity assessment. In A. Memon, A. Vrij, & R. Bull (Eds.), *Psychology and law: Truthfulness, accuracy and credibility*. London: McGraw-Hill.

Vrij, A., Akehurst, L., Soukara, S., & Bull, R. (2002). Will the truth come out? The effect of deception, age, status, coaching, and social skills on CBCA scores. *Law and Human Behavior, 26*, 261–284.

Wolk, R. L., & Henley, A. (1970). *The right to lie*. New York: Peter H. Wyden.

Yochelson, S., & Samenow, S. (1976). *The criminal personality: Vol 1. A profile for change*. New York: Jason Aronson.

Zuckerman, M. (1979). *Sensation seeking: Beyond the optimal level of arousal*. London: Wiley.

20

The Influence of Psychopathic Traits on Response to Treatment

David Thornton and Linda Blud

Psychopathic offenders present a particular challenge to professionals in correctional and health systems charged with their rehabilitation. They are widely accepted as both posing a substantial risk and being difficult to treat. The idea that they present a high risk is supported by most research studies. Psychopathy, at least as defined by the Hare Psychopathy Checklist–Revised (PCL–R; Hare, 1991), appears to be a robust predictor of both general offending and violence (e.g., Hemphill, Hare, & Wong, 1998). The treatability of psychopaths has aroused more controversy. Opinions seem to veer between those who (at least at the time) believed they were being treated effectively ("Here psychopaths are treated with success." from a Canadian government report on the Oak Ridge therapeutic community; Quinsey, Harris, Rice & Cormier, 1998) to those who believe they are untreatable (e.g., Treves-Brown, 1977; Vaillant, 1975).

A position somewhere between the two extremes has been expressed by Wong & Elek (1989) who examined the early literature on the treatment of psychopaths and concluded that there was virtually no real empirical evidence on the matter. Rather, they argued that the impression that these offenders are untreatable had come largely from clinical case studies. Hemphill and Hart (2002) suggested that although there is no good evidence that psychopathy can be reliably and effectively treated, neither is there any good evidence that it is untreatable. A more refined version of this "don't know" position has been articulated by Zinger & Forth (1998), who argued that the kinds of treatments to which psychopaths have been shown to respond poorly would have been ineffective with any kind of offender. A further variation on this position has been articulated by Hare (1998) who argued that although psychopaths are ill-suited for traditional treatment programs, they may be responsive to programs that have been designed specifically for them.

More empirical support for the idea that psychopaths are unusually difficult to treat effectively can be found if the definition of psychopathy is broadened beyond the Psychopathy Checklist and its variants. Garrido, Esteban, and Molero (1995) employed a broader conceptualization of psychopathy, using the American Psychiatric Association's *Diagnostic and Statistical Manual for Mental Disorders*, 4th ed. (*DSM–IV*) antisocial personality disorder, the Minnesota Multiphasic Personality Inventory (MMPI), the California Personality Inventory (CPI), and the PCL–R as indicators of psychopathic traits. Their meta-analysis showed that, on average, psychopaths responded more poorly to treatment than other offenders, especially when measures of recidivism were used as the outcome measure. In contrast, a meta-analysis by Salekin (2002) revealed an average rate of improvement of 62% with cognitive–behavioral treatment, 59% with psychoanalytic treatment, and 25% with therapeutic communities, compared with only 20% improvement in psychopathic traits or behavior without treatment. Additionally, Salekin reported that improvement rates were 96% for juveniles but 63% for adults; and 91% where treatment continued for longer than 12 months, but 61% when it continued for less than 6 months.

A key limitation of Salekin's study is the diverse ways in which improvement was defined, varying from recidivism rates to improved communication skills. Despite its obvious limitations, Salekin's review raises the possibility that treatments other than therapeutic communities may reliably produce some improvement for juveniles with psychopathic traits if they are treated intensively over longer than 12 months.

In this chapter we seek to make a contribution to the debate on the treatment of highly psychopathic offenders by combining a theoretical analysis of why these offenders are hard to treat with a review of studies examining the extent to which psychopathic traits moderate response to treatment. Our analysis also specifically addresses the following questions:

1. Do psychopathic traits lead to a different short-term response to treatment?
2. Are the short-term responses to treatment of offenders with psychopathic traits related to recidivism?
3. Is the effect of treatment interventions on recidivism altered by psychopathic traits?
4. Is the way psychopathic traits moderate the effect of treatment the same for (a) juveniles as for adults, (b) longer more intensive interventions as for briefer interventions, and (c) cognitive–behavioral as well as other forms of treatment?

We conclude with some recommendations as to how some of the treatment-interfering behaviors associated with psychopathy can be managed.

CONCEPTUALIZING PSYCHOPATHY

The model of psychopathy used here draws on the structural models developed by Cooke & Michie (2001) and Hare (2003). There is currently a bit of a controversy over whether psychopathy is best modeled with three or four dimensions. For the purposes of this chapter, the four-factor model has been adopted. The pragmatic reason for this is that in the research to be reviewed later the PCL–R Total score or the traditional Factor 1 and Factor 2 scores have been commonly used. These scores are well approximated by the hierarchical four-factor model but not by the three-factor model.[1]

To summarize, for the purpose of the following theoretical analysis we regard psychopathy as a broad factor composed of four partially independent facets that are conceptualized as follows.

1. *Interpersonal facet: An arrogant and deceptive interpersonal style*—grandiose, domineering, and manipulative; always seeking to control others through intimidation or deception.

2. *Affective facet: Deficient emotional connection with other*—emotionally cold, or shallow; labile emotions; callous, ruthless indifference to harm caused to others; lack of remorse; failure to accept responsibility for own actions; a lack of emotional bonds to other people.

3. *Lifestyle facet: An impulsive irresponsible lifestyle*—impulsive decisions that are not guided by any realistic long-term plan; persistently making irresponsible choices, ignoring commitments and obligations; and a predilection for parasitic financial exploitation of others.

4. *Antisocial facet: Persistent rejection of rules and restraints*—serious externalizing, "conduct" problems as a child, serious antisocial behavior as a teenager, and commission of a wide range of different kinds of criminal offenses; responding to frustration with threats, verbal abuse, or violence; serious violations of supervision rules (probation, parole, or conditional release).[2]

PSYCHOPATHY AS A MODERATOR OF TREATMENT IMPACT: THEORY

Theoretical implications for treatment will be considered separately for each of the four facets of psychopathy.

Implications of the Interpersonal Facet of Psychopathy

Five primary problems for treatment are implied by an arrogant, deceptive interpersonal style, together with three distinguishable impacts on staff.

---

[1]The superordinate general psychopathy factor emerging from the three factor model is not the same as the PCL–R total score as it excludes about a third of the items. Similarly, the traditional Factor 1 and Factor 2 scores used in the research to be reviewed do not play a part in the three-factor model.

[2]Our interpretation of the fourth factor gives it more of the quality of a personality trait and makes it something that goes beyond the mere commission of antisocial behavior. We see it as having elements akin to oppositional–defiant disorder in which there is a stubborn resistance to, and defiance of, any attempt to impose restraints.

1. *Failing to give accurate, personally relevant accounts of past history and functioning.* Offenders high on this interpersonal facet of psychopathy lie easily and frequently. They do this more easily than other people when there is some prudential function for deception (it might get me parole), but they also do it when there is no external motive for lying—just the fun of successful deception.

It is likely that all types of treatment will misfire if it depends on these offenders giving meaningful accounts of the thoughts and feelings that were involved with past behaviors or experiences. Of course, it is not being suggested that clinicians working with offenders simply assume that the offenders' account is truthful. Clinicians well understand that offenders may have practical reasons for concealing the truth, for example, making themselves sound less risky, emotional reasons such as shame, or fear that their family or others may reject them if they know the truth. Competent forensic clinicians are familiar with working through these problems. The particular difficulty with offenders high on the interpersonal facet of psychopathy is that their deception is also motivated by duping delight and is not deterred by having been caught lying. That is, they are likely to try to deceive even when there is no advantage to doing so.

The result is that the therapist may well end up accepting a largely fictitious account of the offender's motives, offense-precursors, and so on. Therapeutic procedures are then liable to be aimed to modify something that does not exist. Meanwhile, the offender experiences the therapist as just another person he or she has successfully conned.

2. *Having bogus intentions.* There is also a more subtle way in which psychopathic duplicity can undermine treatment. Treatment often involves discussing possible future ways of behaving. The most elaborate form of this discussion is probably relapse prevention. For ordinary offenders, these discussions can have some level of psychological reality. The offender may try out the behavior being discussed or at least seriously consider engaging in some of it. This discussion may sometimes lead to reluctance to agree to make various changes because a nonpsychopathic offender may be considering the real personal costs that such a change would require. Where high levels of interpersonal psychopathy are present, there will be no real intention to change the behavior. The psychopathic offender sees the discussion of behavioral options as just another way in which he or she can use language to manipulate others. This may lead to offenders high on the interpersonal facet of psychopathy to appear spuriously to do well as they can easily agree to change their future behavior, all without considering the real personal costs that would come from actually changing their future behavior. Such manipulative tactics are likely to be resistant to change, given that these types of offenders enjoy the effects that their fluent discussion of potential future behavior have on their listeners.

3. *Disrupting group processes.* A central part of the interpersonal facet of psychopathy is a concern to dominate others, and the offender will portray this characteristic in group treatment by trying to dominate both the therapist

and the other members of the treatment group. This behavior can thoroughly disrupt the ordinary group dynamic and lead the therapist to spend so much time dealing with this disruption that he or she is not able to attend to anything else. Naturally, the stress involved can easily lead to clinician burnout.

4. *Experiencing treatment as just another opportunity to con or dominate.* Offenders high on the interpersonal facet of psychopathy typically see group treatment programs as just another opportunity or challenge to con or dominate others. They organize their experience of treatment sessions in terms of these goals and not in terms of goals related to using the therapeutic experience to facilitate personal change. This way of focusing their attention means that they deprive themselves of the opportunity to learn from material that could otherwise have benefited them.

5. *Seeing no reason for personal change.* Grandiosity is one of the central features of the interpersonal facet of psychopathy. It is particularly hard for offenders who are high on this facet to see or accept the fact that there is any reason for changing themselves in any significant way. Because they "know" that they are superior, why should they give credence to suggestions from "lesser mortals." And for those individuals whose sense of superiority has the quality of fragile narcissism, contemplating the notion that they are in need of personal change will be deeply threatening and hence liable to be emphatically rejected.

Implications of the Affective Facet of Psychopathy

Shallow affect and lack of empathic engagement with others are central to the affective facet of psychopathy and render some forms of treatment pointless for offenders who are high on this facet. Two obvious examples are attempts to challenge distorted beliefs about the harm caused to victims of crime and conventional anger management programs.

The rationale behind treatment interventions that seek to modify distorted beliefs about harm to victims is that offenders possess a capacity for empathy with their potential victims that is blocked off by these distorted beliefs. If only offenders understood the harm their behavior causes, they would be motivated to behave differently. This kind of model, which is at least implicit in numerous sex offender treatments, is essentially misguided for individuals who show high levels of affective psychopathy. These offenders lack empathy for their victims, but this is not because a natural capacity for empathy is blocked off by cognitive distortions. Rather, they lack empathy for victims because they lack a capacity for empathy at all. Thus, therapeutic work undermining distorted beliefs that minimize harm to potential or past victims is essentially pointless with offenders who are high in the affective facet of psychopathy.

Similarly, interventions such as anger management with the assumption that angry behavior is the expression of an excess of poorly controlled emotion are pointless for offenders who are high on affective psychopathy. Conventional anger management programs assume that negatively biased interpretations of other people's behavior leads to persistent negative self-talk and that this hostile rumination of provocative thoughts leads to sustained and intense feelings of anger that motivate aggressive behavior. This model is therapeutically appropriate for some nonpsychopathic offenders. However, whereas offenders who are high on the affective facet of psychopathy may feign angry outbursts to intimidate people whom they wish to control, their violence is in fact predominantly instrumental (Cornell, Warren, Hawk, Stafford, Oram, & Pine, 1996). Fundamentally they do not feel the cognitively based, *sustained*, intense angry emotions assumed by conventional anger management.

The affective facet of psychopathy also contributes two other problems that make effective treatment difficult. First, the affective facet of psychopathy makes it harder for offenders to develop meaningful motivation to change their antisocial behavior. This is partly because altruistic motives based on empathic distress for the harm they have done are simply irrelevant to them. But additionally, their tendency to avoid taking responsibility for their own actions makes it harder for them to identify aspects of themselves that they might need to change. Second, their difficulty in affectively bonding with other people means that they are unlikely to be able to bond to a therapist working with them.

Implications of the Lifestyle Facet of Psychopathy

Effective treatment programs for offenders depend upon the active engagement of the offender. The offender has to work hard in a sustained way to develop new attitudes and behaviors, and these new ways of functioning have to be applied outside the treatment group itself. Offenders high on the lifestyle facet of psychopathy are particularly prone to getting bored, making impulsive choices, and blithely disregarding commitments. If these behavioral patterns are carried over into treatment, they may lead to homework assignments not being completed, sessions being missed, and, in general, a failure to reliably apply what has been learned if it does not work quickly and easily. Additionally, it may lead to an increased likelihood of withdrawing from treatment.

Implications of the Antisocial Facet of Psychopathy

Effective participation in treatment involves complying with sets of rules and conventions just as with any other social activity. An offender who is high on the antisocial facet of psychopathy is likely to have some difficulty complying with these rules. This lack of compliance is especially likely to occur if the treatment provider endeavors to impose some restrictions on behavior outside the group, for which the response is liable to be deliberate noncompliance. Moreover, the offender's oppositional style is likely to lead to a failure to complete treatment.

Additionally, in as much as the goal of is to encourage new behaviors that are an alternative to automatic defiance of rules, offenders high on the antisocial facet of psychopathy will have particular difficulty in sustaining these alternative behaviors and will more easily revert to their overlearned pattern of rule defiance.

Impact on Staff

The manifestations of the interpersonal and affective facets of psychopathy impact staff in three interrelated ways. First, the experience of working with this population may be damaging for staff. Staff may be conned or manipulated. In extreme cases, this may lead to fraternization, inappropriate sexual relations between staff and offenders, smuggling items into a secure facility, or even help with escape attempts. More commonly, staff will repeatedly experience being lied to or (unsuccessfully) manipulated in small ways that leave them unable to trust their own judgment. In the long term, staff may come to adopt a paralyzing conviction that these offenders always lie and can never be trusted. Combining this with having to resist the frequent attempts of the psychopath to dominate them can lead to a sense of emotional exhaustion and burnout.

Second, developing a therapeutic alliance becomes extraordinarily difficult. Because the psychopathic offender typically sees no reason to genuinely engage in personal change and experiences therapy as just another opportunity to con or dominate, there is no common ground or common objectives on which to build such an alliance. In normal psychotherapy, a patient bonds with the therapist. Commitment to this relationship and the trust that has been built up within it motivates and enables the patient to engage in difficult, painful therapeutic work. The therapeutic relationship may even allow the patient to develop more healthy attitudes and skills for other close emotional relationships. None of these processes are possible with offenders who are high on the affective facet of psychopathy.

Third, the same processes that operate within treatment groups will operate outside them in the wider environment of residential wings, recreational areas, and so on. There are constant attempts to intimidate or deceive staff. Small divisions between different members of staff are amplified and exploited. Staff groups are played off against each other. Individual staff members are psychologically isolated from their colleagues so that they become more vulnerable to other forms of manipulation. All of these factors can combine to destroy a therapeutic regimen.

Overall Effects of Psychopathic Traits

It should be apparent from the previous discussion that all four facets of psychopathy have a potential to disrupt effective participation in treatment, though the ways in which they affect therapy vary. Facets 1 and 2 and by implication the traditional factor 1 that is composed of these two facets, seem likely to have more profound effects. The interpersonal facet has the potential to particularly reduce treatment benefits, whereas the affective facet, although

less disruptive to the treatment process, seems likely to make certain interventions irrelevant. Facets 3 and 4 (lifestyle and antisocial facets) would both
seem likely to make compliance with the requirements of treatment less
likely and failure to complete treatment more probable and to imply a greater
likelihood of posttreatment relapse to well-established impulsive antisocial
behavior.

Might Treatment Make Psychopaths Worse?

Considering these difficulties, there are strong theoretical grounds for expecting treatment to have limited benefits for highly psychopathic offenders. But,
by themselves, the problems identified so far in this chapter do not suggest
that treatment would be actively harmful for highly psychopathic offenders.
There are, however, additional theoretical arguments that suggesting harm,
not just a failure to benefit, is possible.

There are three related lines of argument that might suggest that treatment
could be harmful for psychopathic offenders. The first is that the skills taught
during treatment might enable more psychopathic offenders to exploit others
more effectively. The argument would be that since highly psychopathic
offenders have a basically self-centered, antisocial value set, strengthening
their competence will merely enable them to offend more efficiently. Under
this view, any treatment that enhances competence could increase reoffending among highly psychopathic offenders.

A second line of argument would be that treatment programs have both
positive and negative elements for all offenders. For example, in many contexts, bringing a group of like-minded people together to share anecdotes
about their common behavior might be expected to encourage that behavior
through modeling, social support, and an opportunity to boast about
achievements. Perhaps this negative effect is outweighed for ordinary offenders by the positive benefits of treatment, but if highly psychopathic offenders are immune to the positive effects of treatment, then they might simply be
left with this negative effect.

A third possibility is that participation in treatment may provide richer
opportunities for getting away with behaving badly. Here the idea is that
highly psychopathic offenders are able to con therapists into helping them
avoid punishment for delinquent behavior. Thus, the experience of therapy
strengthens these offenders' belief that they can get away with anything; in
other words, it reduces their subjective probability of getting punished and
so strengthens their propensity to offend.

PSYCHOPATHY AS A MODERATOR
OF TREATMENT IMPACT: EMPIRICAL STUDIES

Some care is required in selecting studies for this kind of review. On the one
hand, studies need to meet some methodological criteria so that their results

are meaningful. On the other hand, if these methodological criteria are drawn too strictly, too few studies will be included for meaningful generalizations to emerge. The following three criteria were selected to try to balance these considerations.

1. *Measuring Psychopathy.* There can be little doubt that Hare's (1991, 2003) PCL–R presently is the preferred measure of psychopathic traits. However, it is not the only measure that can be used in assessing these traits. In addition to the PCL–R, three further methods were accepted as providing a usable way of distinguishing groups of offenders who differed substantially on psychopathic traits. These methods—use of the *DSM–IV* and of two offender typologies—are discussed below.

The *DSM–IV* provides criteria for antisocial personality disorder that clearly specify related traits. Differences between this and the PCL–R are in part that the former defines a category whereas the latter defines a dimension, but also a matter of emphasis, with the *DSM* placing less weight on the Factor 1 (affective and interpersonal) components of psychopathy. For this present review, the *DSM–IV* was regarded as being relevant in identifying psychopathy if it was combined with some other measure so that it better picked up Factor 1 components (interpersonal and affective). In the study included here, this was done by combining the diagnosis of antisocial personality disorder with assessment of depression, the argument being that the shallow emotionality that is part of affective psychopathy would make severe depression unlikely. Thus, offenders with antisocial personality disorder and severe depression would be unlikely to be exhibiting the full psychopathy syndrome.

Two offender typologies seem to include categories that approximate the psychopathy construct. The first of these is Knight and Prentky's (1990) typology of rapists. One of the dimensions underlying this typology is Lifestyle Impulsivity (Prentky & Knight, 1995). This dimension seems to distinguish rapists whose lifestyles show more evidence of impulsive, irresponsible decision making and who apply the callousness they manifest in rape across a broader range of crimes and victims (and who therefore show something more like the generalized callousness typical of affective psychopathy). It seems reasonable then to regard rapist types higher on lifestyle impulsivity as more psychopathic. Prentky and Knight's Pervasively Angry and Opportunistic Rapist categories are defined in a way that makes them high on this dimension and thus higher on psychopathy than other types of rapists. The second offender typology is the modification of Sullivan's Interpersonal Maturity System developed for young offenders as part of the California Community Treatment Project (Warren, 1983). This system identifies three major types of offender, two of which clearly differ markedly from each other on psychopathy. The Power-Oriented (conduct disordered and manipulative) type would seem to show substantially more psychopathic traits than the Neurotic (emotionally conflicted; developed conscience; interpersonally mature) type.

Studies in which psychopathy was assessed solely through self-report measures were not included in this review.

2. *Kinds of treatment outcome.* Three kinds of outcome measures were considered. The first, and weakest, outcome indicator was ratings of response to treatment based on case records. The second kind of indicator was change in psychometric indices or behavioral ratings. The third, and strongest, kind of outcome measure was indicators of recidivism in a follow-up period. Studies using self-report measures of recidivism were included in the review although their results were interpreted with caution

3. *Treatment moderator design.* To be included, a design had to have some measure of response to treatment for groups of offenders who were differentiated on some measure of psychopathic traits. The methodological challenge here is to have some way of estimating how the groups would have performed without treatment. Where some measure of change is used, in effect, each individual's pretreatment performance serves as a control against which his or her posttreatment performance can be compared. Where these are the outcomes of interest, there is no need for an untreated comparison group to be included in the design. The situation is more complicated when recidivism rates are compared. Where recidivism is the outcome of interest, some matched or randomized untreated group is necessary to provide a reference point because there is presently no known way of using the offender as his or her own control for this outcome variable.

This means that the following designs were included:

1.   A sample exposed to treatment that is broken down by level of psychopathic traits and the outcome variable is some measure of response to treatment such as rates of treatment completion, rated change in risk at the end of treatment, and changes in scores on psychometric instruments.

2.   Two samples, one exposed to treatment and the other untreated, where each sample is broken down by level of psychopathic traits and the outcome variable is recidivism rate. In this case (because subjects are not serving as their own controls) there will need to be some basis for assuming that the two samples had comparable levels of risk prior to one sample being exposed to treatment.

3.   Designs in which the focus is on whether psychopathic traits moderate the degree to which some measure of treatment performance relates to subsequent reconviction rates. Here, the concept is that if treatment reduces recidivism, then better participation, completion of treatment, or completion of more sessions ought all to result in reduced recidivism rates. Clearly, where the obtained data do show such a trend it will be open to an alternative explanation (that some unmeasured traits predisposes individuals both to better treatment participation and reduced recidivism). However, when this pattern of results is not obtained, for example, if treatment completers have higher recidivism rates than those who drop out of treatment, the results suggest that treatment is not beneficial. Thus, for example, if treatment completion related to

lower recidivism among less psychopathic offenders, but related to increased recidivism for more psychopathic offenders, this would suggest a differential response to treatment.

Two research designs were not included. The first of these was studies examining the reconviction rate of highly psychopathic offenders who participate in treatment, but for which there is no matched or randomized untreated group. The second group consisted of studies examining the reconviction rate of treated psychopathic offenders, combined with examining the reconviction rate of treated nonpsychopathic offenders. Whether the outcome is that psychopaths show a higher rate of reconvictions after treatment or their reconviction rates are more or less the same as those of less psychopathic offenders, we cannot make the inference that the effect of treatment has been moderated by psychopathic traits. In the first case, psychopaths may well have higher reconviction rates whether or not they participate in treatment. In the second, apart from the possibility that the result simply reflects sampling error (something that is especially likely if the sample is small), the interpretation of such a result depends critically on both the kind of recidivism being considered and on how the group of nonpsychopathic offenders was constructed.

Findings for Different Kinds of Treatment

The results of studies that met the above criteria are organized by the type of intervention employed and the age of the offenders concerned. Results for interventions that used behavioral or cognitive–behavioral techniques are reviewed separately from results for other kinds of intervention. The rationale for this is that behavioral/cognitive–behavioral interventions have generally emerged as being more effective with offenders (Andrews & Bonta, 2003). Equally, studies of adults are considered separately from studies of adolescents or younger children. The rationale for this separation is that psychopathic traits among juveniles may be less well established than in adults, and thus juveniles with these traits might potentially be more amenable to treatment.

Studies of Adults Treated With Cognitive–Behavioral Methods

In the studies of adults identified for this review, behavioral/cognitive–behavioral interventions appeared to involve three main components. These were as follows: (a) examination of offense-precursors including analysis of patterns of thoughts, feelings, and behaviors that preceded offending, together with identification of alternative ways of functioning; (b) cognitive restructuring of beliefs thought to predispose to offending, including both surface cognitions and schema-level beliefs; and (c) systematic skills training, usually focused on the development of self-control and problem-solving skills. Particular interventions involved these factors to varying degrees. For example, so-called cognitive-skills programs would not involve the first or second element, whereas some sexual offender treatments would not involve the third element.

Cognitive–Behavioral Treatment of Adult Sexual Offenders

Here the primary treatment elements were examination of offense-precursors and cognitive-restructuring focused on surface cognitive distortions. Bowers (1994) examined the response of rapists to a cognitive behavioral program of this type. She categorized them into the types distinguished by Knight and Prentky (1990). Progress was assessed using a combination of psychometrics and behavioral ratings administered before and after participation in treatment. Most rapist subtypes showed positive responses to treatment, but two types showed little progress. The poorly responding types were the Opportunistic and Pervasively Angry rapists. These two groups are distinguished from the others by having higher levels of lifestyle impulsiveness (i.e., higher psychopathy).

Seto and Barbaree (1999) related the quality of participation in treatment to rates of serious reoffending. Presumably those who cooperate with treatment get more real treatment than those who miss sessions or do not do exercises. Thus, if treatment is effective, poor participators should have worse recidivism rates than good participators (and, of course, you might also expect this if poor participation was a symptom of delinquent behavior). Seto and Barbaree examined the participation–recidivism relationship for those with higher and lower scores on the PCL–R (using their sample median, 15, to split the cases). Their results showed that, among the more psychopathic offenders, those rated as participating well in treatment were five times as likely to commit further serious (sexual or violent) offenses as those who were rated as participating badly. No such paradoxical pattern was apparent for low PCL–R cases.

Seto and Barbaree's results seemed to confirm Bower's finding that more psychopathic sexual offenders obtained little benefit from cognitive–behavioral treatment. Later results have, however, given a different and much more complex picture. When a more comprehensive source of information about reconvictions and a longer follow-up period were used with the same sample of offenders, the apparent interaction between quality of treatment performance and psychopathy disappears (Seto & Barabaree, in press). What is left is a general tendency of more psychopathic offenders to have higher rates of serious recidivism after treatment, and no relationship between treatment performance and recidivism, regardless of level of psychopathic traits. In this report there was some tendency for the more psychopathic offenders to be more likely to be rated as showing "bad" treatment behavior. Fifty-six percent of the more psychopathic offenders were rated in this way compared with 46% of the less psychopathic offenders.

A comprehensive follow-up of a much larger sample that included the original Seto and Barbaree sample has been reported by Langton (2003). There are a number of important differences between the studies. Langton used a PCL–R score of 25 to split his sample (much more appropriate in identifying a high psychopathy group). Langton used sexual recidivism rather than serious (sexual plus other violent) recidivism (more appropriate because treatment targeted sexual offending). Langton used the more comprehensive data source for recidivism (as used in the later Seto and Barbaree report), and the longer follow-up time. Additionally, Langton had nearly 500 offenders in his sample as opposed to just over 200 in the Seto and Barbaree reports. Thus, Langton's study is methodologically superior. In this larger study, a significant interaction was found between ratings of response to treatment and level of psychopathy, with better response to treatment being associated with less sexual recidivism specifically among the more psychopathic offenders. Langton put considerable effort into constructing more reliable measures of response to treatment and it is possible that this accounts for some of the differences between these results and the results reported by Seto and Barbaree. Langton also included offenders who failed to complete the program in his analysis; overall ratings of response to treatment turned out to be strongly influenced by this, with non-completers being rated as making very poor responses to treatment. Langton reports that, when those who failed to complete treatment were excluded from the analysis, the relationship between recidivism and treatment performance ceased to be reliable. Langton also found that both poorer response to treatment and failure to complete treatment were significantly associated with the presence of psychopathic traits.

These three reports are all based on a sexual offender program run at a particular correctional facility (Warkworth) in Canada. Langton's results are clearly more definitive given his superior methodology and, therefore, are reasonably taken as superceding the Seto and Barabaree reports.

A similar study has also been reported by Looman, Abracen, Serin, and Marquis (in press). Here, again, offenders in whom higher levels of psychopathy were combined with "good" treatment performance had worse rates of serious recidivism. The trend for ratings of good treatment behavior to be inversely related to serious recidivism was, however, similar for the more psychopathic offenders and the less psychopathic offenders. Thus, both this study and the later Seto and Barbaree results found that ratings of treatment performance do not relate to recidivism and that this is true regardless of level of psychopathy. Looman et al. also reported analyses for clinicians' ratings of reduction in risk. These ratings were based on the totality of institutional performance, not just in-session treatment behavior. These did show some relationship to serious recidivism (those rated as having reduced risk actually recidivated less) in the overall sample. When the sample was broken down by level of psychopathy, it became apparent that rated reduction in risk was particularly associated with lowered recidivism for the *more* psychopathic offenders. This trend was, however, suggestive rather than fully statistically reliable. Of importance, Looman et al. also found that the more psychopathic offenders were less likely to be rated as having reduced their risk.

Considering together Bowers' work, the Warkworth studies, and the Looman et al. results, it is possible to suggest a possible integration of seemingly diverse results. One consistent trend across these studies is for psychopathic traits to be associated with poorer response to treatment when this is defined in terms of ratings of failure to complete treatment, assessed reduction in risk, or lack of change on psychometric instruments. A second but less clear trend seems to be that if response to treatment is defined in more behavioral terms (failure to complete treatment or Looman et al.'s Rated Change in Risk), then offenders with more pronounced psychopathic traits who do show better response to treatment are also less likely to commit further (serious) offenses.

Treatment of More Diverse Groups of Adult Offenders

Woody, McLellan, Rubersky, and O'Brien (1985) studied the effect of schema-focused therapy on opiate-dependent patients. Schema-focused therapy uses cognitive–behavioral techniques to try to address the more central belief systems that underlie surface cognitive distortions. These researchers found that those without antisocial personality disorder responded well (including reduced offending), whereas those with antisocial personality disorder only benefited if they had severe depression. Given that a central feature of psychopathy is emotional deficiency, it seems unlikely that psychopaths would manifest "severe depression." Thus, the group that showed no benefit seems likely to have included all those in whom lifestyle impulsiveness was combined with Factor 1 type emotional deficiency.

Richards, Casey, and Lucente (2003) studied the response to substance abuse treatment of female offenders delivered in three different regimens. Treatment seems to have been broadly cognitive–behavioral in character, but the regimens differed in whether offenders participating in treatment were held together in dedicated housing or whether they were mixed in with the general inmate population. A no-treatment condition was not included in the study. Overall, psychopathy scores were associated with a poor treatment response, including nonretention, serious rule violations, evading urinalysis, and so on.

The most interesting analysis, however, focused on the relation between housing and how soon after release the offenders were charged with new offenses. Overall, dedicated housing for treatment participants was associated with a longer period before new charges were incurred. This effect seemed to be disrupted by Factor 1 (Interpersonal and Affective facets combined) traits. These traits were unrelated to speed of reoffending when the offender had been mixed in with the general population but were correlated with speed of reoffending when the offender had been held with others in treatment. Factor 2 (Lifestyle and Antisocial facets combined) traits showed an opposite pattern; they were associated with speed of re-offending for those offenders held in nondedicated housing but became less relevant when offenders in treatment were held together. The authors interpret their results as indicating that the structure and support provided by dedicated housing was specifically beneficial for offenders with Factor 2 traits but that Factor 1 traits nullified the benefit of dedicated housing.

The interventions considered so far all have in common a shared central concern with changing attitudes and beliefs. A different tradition in the cognitive–behavioral treatment of offenders is to focus on developing offenders' competence. The underlying assumption here is that reoffending often arises as the end point of a series of failures to solve everyday practical and interpersonal problems (Zamble & Porporino, 1988; Zamble & Quinsey, 1997). Strengthening offenders' competence should then interrupt the negative spiral that leads to reoffending. The purpose of cognitive skills programs, which are based on this model, is to strengthen offenders' skills in interpersonal problem solving and self-management. The degree to which psychopathic traits moderate the effects of cognitive skills programs has been investigated in several studies.

Hare, Clark, Grann, & Thornton, (2000) found that brief prison treatment programs of this type (mainly anger management or social skills training) were ineffective for those offenders scoring medium or low on the PCL–R Factor 1, but were counterproductive for those scoring high on Factor 1 (reconviction rates increased by nearly half).

Of course, one difficulty with short cognitive skills programs is their brevity. Highly psychopathic offenders can sensibly be regarded as "high-need" (in Don Andrews' sense) and consequently might be expected to require more treatment than is provided in these programs. Perhaps the same techniques applied more intensively over a longer period would produce better results?

This possibility has been investigated in two studies, in which intensive treatment over hundreds of hours was provided. Hughes, Hogue, Hollin, & Champion (1997) found that a highly intensive cognitive skills program run in a maximum security forensic mental health hospital produced substantial clinical improvement for patients scoring lower on the PCL–R (≤22) but those with higher scores showed no improvement. Mulloy and colleagues (Mulloy, McHattie, & Smiley, 1998; R. Mulloy, personal communication) evaluated the impact of 500 hours of cognitive behavioral treatment with a strong skills training element provided to high-risk offenders. Highly psychopathic offenders (PCL–R 27+ or 30+) showed little rated reduction in risk as opposed to the less psychopathic offenders who were rated as typically showing fair progress.

Summary for Cognitive–Behavioral Programs With Adults

These results may be summarized as follows.

1. The presence of marked psychopathic traits in adult offenders leads to worse short-term response to cognitive–behavioral interventions. This

is apparent in psychometric measures of short-term change, in ratings of treatment participation, in treatment completion rates, and in ratings of risk reduction.

2. When response to treatment is assessed more behaviorally, including defining it in terms of treatment completion, then offenders with marked psychopathic traits who show better response to treatment also show reduced recidivism.

3. No studies show adult offenders with marked psychopathic traits having reduced recidivism as a result of participating in treatment and one study shows increased recidivism after treatment participation. These moderating effects seem particularly derived from Factor 1 (interpersonal/affective) traits.

4. Although cognitive–behavioral treatment interventions are generally believed to be effective with less psychopathic offenders, the particular programs that produced a paradoxical increase in recidivism for the more psychopathic offenders were not beneficial for the less psychopathic offenders (they just had no effect). This raises the possibility that longer or more intensive programs would not have had this negative effect.

There is an apparent contradiction between treatment completion being associated with less recidivism but treatment participation being associated with more recidivism. It is possible that this contradiction reflects differences between briefer and more sustained interventions but it is also possible that psychopathic traits can lead offenders to respond to treatment in more diverse ways, with some increasing and others reducing their risk.

Studies of Adults Treated With Other Methods

The moderating effects of psychopathic traits on a number of non-cognitive–behavioral treatment methods have been examined. These studies include the use of therapeutic communities, expressive psychotherapy, prison education, and eclectic mental health treatment.

Therapeutic Communities

In democratic therapeutic communities, rather than having a hierarchical division between staff and patients, decisions are made about rules and disputes are resolved through meetings of the whole community. Both patients and staff are seen as equal members of the community. All members are expected to take responsibility for each other and for the running of the community. Therapeutic communities are more tolerant of outbursts and verbally aggressive behavior than a normal prison or hospital would be, but members get feedback both in small groups and in community meetings as to how their behavior is experienced by others. In addition, in the small groups, members initially help each other to identify the pathological patterns in their past behavior and then to recognize when these patterns are being enacted in the community. Offenders in a therapeutic community typically go through a sequence of adaptations that eventually lead them to try out new ways of behaving in the community (Genders & Player, 1995). Offenders who spend a short period in therapeutic communities seem to show little benefit, but those spending 18 months or longer have been found to have significantly lower recidivism rates compared with both matched untreated control subjects and those who spent less time in the therapeutic community (Taylor, 2000).

In its time, the therapeutic community that operated in Oak Ridge's Social Therapy unit was seen as an effective model for the treatment of psychopathic offenders. In the 1970s, both a Canadian government report and an independent panel of experts described the Oak Ridge regimen in the most positive of terms, claiming, "here psychopaths are treated with success" (Quinsey et al., 1998).

Some years later Quinsey and his colleagues carried out a reconviction study: Offenders who participated in the therapeutic community were matched to others who were assessed at the larger facility but served their time in prison. Both groups were scored on the PCL–R and classified into high versus low groups using a cutoff score of 25. During an average follow-up of about 10 years at risk, offenders scoring lower on the PCL–R appeared to have benefited from the therapeutic community as their rate of violent recidivism was about half that of matched offenders allocated to prison. For those scoring higher on the PCL–R, however, treatment appeared to have had an adverse effect: Treated offenders had a violent recidivism rate of 78% as compared with 55% for untreated offenders. An interesting supplementary result in this study was that the more psychopathic offenders showed more problem behavior in both their first and second years in the regimen but were given good ratings on soft variables based on clinicians' judgments.

There are a number of complications with this study, the most notable being that it depended on retrospective matching of cases. And, for the less psychopathic offenders, the selection process (referral for assessment at the psychiatric facility) meant that there was an over-representation of psychotic symptoms among the nonpsychopathic offenders. However, supplementary analyses showed that this did not account for the interaction between psychopathy and treatment; among the less psychopathic offenders, both psychotic and nonpsychotic offenders showed lower violent recidivism if they had participated in treatment (Quinsey et al., 1998).

Since the first publications describing these results, there has been a natural tendency for some to argue that the Oak Ridge therapeutic community was poorly conceived. There certainly were processes that seem bizarre to a modern eye (nude marathon encounter groups, for example). Nevertheless, the Oak Ridge regimen did seem to benefit ordinary offenders, reducing their rates of violent recidivism in a way that is comparable to those obtained with "more modern" treatment styles.

How psychopathy affects response to a therapeutic environment has been looked at in two other studies. Ogloff, Wong, & Greenwood (1990) found that those scoring higher on the PCL–R showed less improvement during their time in treatment, appeared to be more poorly motivated, and more often dropped out. Hobson, Shine, and Roberts (2000), studying responses to an English prison therapeutic community, found that the PCL–R, especially Factor 1, predicted difficult and manipulative behavior both during therapeutic community groups and in the regimen generally. There was some suggestion that Factor 2 had less impact when inmates had been in the regimen longer whereas Factor 1 continued to be associated with poor behavior regardless of time in the regimen.

Taken together these three studies suggest that the therapeutic community milieu is not effective in either engaging the motivation or controlling the manipulative behavior of psychopaths. Additionally, the results for the Oak Ridge therapeutic community are consistent with the idea that the increased opportunity for getting away with delinquent behavior strengthens the more psychopathic offenders' propensity to offend (the clinicians thought well of them despite their behaving badly).

Prison Education

The rationale for providing education to offenders is similar to the rationale for providing cognitive skills interventions: Offending is seen as being more likely when individuals have difficulty meeting their needs through legitimate means. Strengthen their ability to earn a living honestly, it is argued, and you reduce the need for them to resort to offending. In line with this argument, Hare et al. (2000) reported that prison education programs reduced reoffending (compared with similar inmates who did not participate in prison education) for those offenders identified (on the Level of Service Inventory–Revised [LSI–R]) as having difficulty getting work because of their limited educational opportunities. But this did not apply when the PCL–R Factor 1 score was high. In these offenders, education increased reoffending by nearly a half. This result held after controlling LSI–R scores, age at first conviction, current age, number of previous court appearances, and PCL–R Factor 2. Additionally, those with more marked psychopathic traits were much less likely to complete education or vocational programs.

This result is particularly striking for two reasons. First, it indicates that it is not just "therapy" in the narrow sense that can apparently be counterproductive for highly psychopathic offenders; other kinds of training programs can also have this paradoxical effect. Second, the more highly psychopathic offenders in this study were receiving an intervention that should have been directly relevant to their needs, yet their recidivism rate seems to have been increased by the experience.

Expressive Psychotherapy

Expressive psychotherapy is a form of intervention more normally used in general mental health settings than with offenders. Woody et al. (1985) examined the effects of this intervention with opiate-dependent patients with antisocial personality disorder. Similar to the findings for schema-focused therapy, expressive psychotherapy had no impact on further offending unless the patients were depressed. Additionally, treatment was beneficial for opiate-dependent patients without antisocial personality disorder regardless of whether they were depressed.

Eclectic Mental Health Services

Skeem, Monahan, and Mulvey (2002) examined the relationship between the amount of mental health treatment participated in and subsequent violence among civil psychiatric patients being treated in the community. In their study, they examined behavior and treatment received in successive 10-week periods. The general results from this project were that patients who participated in more sessions in the previous 10 weeks, on average, engaged in less violence in the subsequent 10 weeks. To this general finding, Skeem et al. (2002) added that this trend also seemed to apply to patients with more psychopathic traits. Specifically, for this more psychopathic group, they reported that those who participated in seven or more sessions in the previous 10 weeks showed reduced rates of violence in the subsequent 10 weeks. Additionally, they showed that this trend was similar in magnitude to that observed for their patients as a whole, except that for the general patient population there seemed to be some reduction in subsequent violence if the patients had participated in even small amounts of treatment in the previous 10 weeks. This pattern was not apparent for the more psychopathic patients who showed no benefit of small amounts of treatment participation.

These results are clearly more encouraging than any reviewed so far, but they are quite complex. First, at lower levels of treatment participation (less than seven sessions), Skeem et al. reported that psychopathic traits interfered with treatment benefits obtained by less psychopathic patients. Second, although Skeem et al.'s more psychopathic patients do seem to be reporting a reduction in violence if they participated in seven or more treatment sessions in the previous 10 weeks, this effect was most pronounced for the first 10 weeks of treatment after return to the community, present to a lesser extent for treatment participation in the next 20 weeks, and absent for treatment after that. The rapid fall-off in the effect of treatment here suggests that what is involved is treatment providing some cushioning of the immediate stresses of return to the community, rather than a modification of long-term propensities to offend.

Finally, some caution is warranted because both degree of treatment participation and violence during the follow-up periods were assessed through self-report. It is possible that the benefit of treatment for both more and less psychopathic patients was inflated by the effects of correlated measurement errors. A social desirability response set would, for example, be expected to lead to a patient claiming to have participated in more treatment and to have engaged in less violence.

Summary for Non-Cognitive–Behavioral Programs With Adults

These results may be summarized as follows.

1. The presence of marked psychopathic traits in adult offenders led to worse short-term response to these other programs just as it did with cognitive–behavioral interventions. This is apparent in poorer behavior during treatment and less retention in treatment.
2. Indices of behavior during treatment were related to recidivism whereas soft ratings by clinicians were not.
3. Offenders showing marked psychopathic traits responded in quite diverse ways to different kinds of treatment intervention. In two studies, provision of additional treatment services led to increased recidivism (a therapeutic community and prison education), in one study treatment made no difference to recidivism (expressive psychotherapy), and in one study treatment participation made no difference at a low dose but had a beneficial effect at a higher dose (eclectic mental health).
4. For all these interventions, treatment participation was associated with reduced recidivism for less psychopathic offenders.

The most consistent result here is that psychopathic traits lead to treatment having less beneficial effects on recidivism. This is true in four analyses and does not apply in one. The one in which it does not apply has a particularly weak methodology (self-report measures of recidivism).

Studies of Adolescents or Children Treated With Behavioral or Cognitive–Behavioral Methods

O'Neill, Lidz, and Heilbrun (2003) reported the results of a study examining the relationship between psychopathic traits and various aspects of response to a 3-month treatment program for adolescent substance abusers. This program is described as predominantly cognitive–behavioral. Total, Factor 1, and Factor 2 scores from the PCL: Youth Version (PCL:YV; Forth, Kosson, & Hare, 2004), were all negatively correlated with the number of days of active participation, quality of participation, and rated clinical improvement. Additionally, PCL:YV scores were positively correlated with subsequent abuse and arrests.

Catchpole, Gretton, and Hemphill (2003) reported an evaluation of a cognitive–behavioral program for adolescent violent offenders. For offenders high on psychopathy, rates of violent reconviction were 80% without treatment and 43% with treatment. For offenders low or moderate on psychopathy, rates of violent reconviction were 37% without treatment and 23% with treatment. The main effects of treatment and psychopathy were statistically significant and the interaction between them was not (although the trend was for a bigger treatment effect for the more psychopathic offenders).

Gretton, McBride, Hare, and O'Shaughnessy (2000) reported the results of a follow-up of adolescent sexual offenders who participated in a cognitive–behavioral treatment program. No untreated comparison group was reported, but a comparison was made between those who completed treatment and those who began but did not complete it. Among those high on psychopathy, sexual recidivism rates were 33% for completers and 30% for noncompleters. Among those low on psychopathy, sexual recidivism rates were 5% for completers and 50% for noncompleters. Taken at face value these results suggest that participation in the sexual offender treatment program made little difference to the more psychopathic offenders but was beneficial to the less psychopathic offenders.

Rates of recidivism for nonsexual violence showed a rather different pattern. Among those high on psychopathy, violent recidivism rates were 33% for completers and 80% for noncompleters. Among those low on psychopathy, nonsexual recidivism rates were 12% for completers and 19% for noncompleters. Taken at face value this second set of results suggested that participation in the sexual offender treatment program made a big difference for the more psychopathic offenders and only a small difference for the less psychopathic offenders.

It is useful to consider both sets of results together. The 80% violent recidivism rate for the psychopathic noncompleters is liable to have reduced the opportunity to commit sexual offenses for many of this group (if they were incarcerated after a violent offense). It may be better to consider the overall recidivism rate (for any offense). These figures were as follows. Among those high on psychopathy, recidivism rates were 78% for completers and 100% for noncompleters. Among those low on psychopathy, recidivism rates were 28% for completers and 69% for noncompleters. Overall, these results suggested that completion status reduced recidivism rates for adolescent sexual offenders, irrespective of level of psychopathy.

Summary for Cognitive–Behavioral Treatment with Adolescents or Children

These results may be summarized as follows.

1. The presence of marked psychopathic traits caused juvenile offenders to show a worse short-term response to cognitive–behavioral programs. This was apparent in poorer behavior during treatment and less retention in treatment.

2. Treatment completion was associated with lower recidivism for juvenile offenders with more marked psychopathic traits, just as it was for those with less marked psychopathic traits.

3. Participating in sustained cognitive–behavioral treatment was associated with reduced recidivism for juvenile offenders regardless of their level of psychopathic traits. Those with marked psychopathic traits showed a treatment effect that was as large as those with less psychopathic traits.

4. No studies indicated that intensive cognitive–behavioral treatment had adverse effects on juvenile offenders with marked psychopathic traits.

These findings are clearly much more encouraging than those considered so far but they are essentially based on just two studies from the same research group. There is, however, one other study clearly suggesting that cognitive–behavioral treatment can have a substantial effect on recidivism for adolescents with psychopathic traits. This study did not include results for nonpsychopaths so it is not a study of the moderating effects of psychopathic traits, but the results do relate directly to the efficacy of cognitive–behavioral treatment with adolescents with psychopathic traits. Two reports described recidivism rates for an extreme group of violent adolescent offenders treated at the Mendota Juvenile Treatment Center (Caldwell, Skeem, Salekin, & Van Rybroek, 2004; Caldwell & Van Rybroek, in press). These offenders had typically been too aggressive or difficult to treat in the community or normal juvenile correctional facilities and so had been referred to this specialized mental health treatment facility. Those released from this facility were compared with juveniles who were referred to it but were returned to the correctional system on the grounds that they seemed easier to treat (and so could be managed by the ordinary system). Both groups showed high levels of psychopathic traits (means of 33 for the treatment group and 32 for the comparison group on the PCL:YV) and were broadly similar on a variety of other offense-related characteristics. Violent recidivism rates were adjusted using a Propensity Score analysis to control for factors distinguishing those retained in the mental health facility. The treatment group here was 2.7 times less likely to be involved in violent recidivism in the community than the comparison group.

It is important to note that both the Mendota Juvenile Treatment Center and the juvenile correctional system to which the comparison group returned both provided services that were broadly cognitive–behavioral treatment. The differences between conditions were the intensity of treatment, richness of treatment resources, and response of treatment resources to aggressive behavior. The Mendota Juvenile Treatment Center was able to provide much more intensive treatment, ran smaller living units in which day-to-day management decisions were made by clinical staff, and maintained the intensity of treatment even when the offender acted out aggressively. By contrast, in the juvenile correctional system, aggressive behavior typically led to reduction or withdrawal of treatment services.

Thus, overall these results are consistent with the idea that cognitive–behavioral treatment can be effective for juveniles who have psychopathic traits so long as it is sufficiently intense and sustained.

Studies of Adolescents or Children Treated With Other Methods

For this review we located research into the effects on children or adolescents of two non-cognitive–behavioral kinds of treatment.

Early Correctional Treatment

The California Community Treatment Project involved a rigorous research design in which different types of young offenders were randomly allocated between intensive individual treatment matched to the personality of the offender and standard juvenile correctional treatment. For the "neurotic" type of offender individual treatment led to reduced reoffending in the 4 years after supervision ended. Neurotic offenders allocated to standard supervision were 81% more likely to be rearrested than those allocated to individual treatment. In contrast, for the more psychopathic, "power-oriented," individual, treatment led to increased reoffending. Power-oriented offenders allocated to individual treatment were 58% more likely to reoffend than their control subjects during the period after supervision ended (Warren, 1983).

Of interest, during supervision itself, the power-oriented offenders who received individual treatment had been more likely to be picked up by the police than their control subjects but were also more likely to be parole failures at 24 months; no such pattern of favoritism was apparent for neurotic offenders. This pattern is reminiscent of the Oak Ridge results. Again treatment seemed to provide the more psychopathic offenders with the opportunity to get away with behaving badly.

Parenting as a Form of Treatment

Parenting is probably the most sustained opportunity that one human being has to influence another. There is a well-developed body of literature on the features that distinguish parents who are effective (vs. ineffective) in helping their children grow up in a law-abiding way. Parental behaviors that increase the risk of delinquency are lack of involvement with the child, failure to use positive control strategies for discipline, poor monitoring and supervision of the child, inconsistency in discipline, and use of harsh physical punishments (Loeber & Stouthamer-Loeber, 1986). Effective parents combine love and warmth with consistent standard setting, supervision, and discipline. Does psychopathy moderate the effect of this very extended form of "treatment?"

De Vita, Forth, & Hare (1990) examined the relationship between family environment and age of onset of offending. For the less psychopathic individuals, bad environments led to early onset of delinquency. For more psychopathic offenders, the quality of the family environment had no influence on age of onset of delinquency. A similar result was also reported by Hare, MacPherson, & Forth (1984): A poor family background was associated with the emergence of criminality for nonpsychopathic offenders but not for psychopathic offenders.

Wootton, Frick, Shelton, & Silverthorn (1997) investigated the relationship between quality of parenting and degree of conduct disorder manifested by children. They found that for those with ordinary (nonpsychopathic) personalities, poor parenting led to more conduct disorder, but for those with high Factor 1 personalities (callous–unemotional), poor parenting was associated with less conduct disorder (although this paradoxical effect was small).

Thus, parenting strategies that are normally effective in socializing children are at best ineffective and may even be mildly counterproductive with children who show high levels of psychopathy—especially high levels of affective psychopathy.

Summary for Other Methods of Treatment Used With Adolescents or Children

These results may be summarized as follows.

1. The presence of marked psychopathic traits in juvenile offenders treated with non-cognitive–behavioral methods was associated with a paradoxical short-term response in which there was more actual delinquent behavior during treatment but treatment staff were more likely to make favorable decisions about the offender. This pattern can reasonably be summarized as treatment providing an increased opportunity to get away with behaving badly.

2. None of the studies directly examined the relationship between short-term response to treatment and later recidivism.

3. Juvenile offenders with marked psychopathic traits who were treated with non-cognitive–behavioral methods showed increased recidivism; this result contrasted with juveniles offenders for whom psychopathic traits were relatively absent who showed reduced recidivism. Analogous effects were obtained for children subject to different kinds of family environments. Parenting or family environment variables associated with reduced delinquency or conduct disorder in ordinary children had no such beneficial effect for children with callous–unemotional traits.

CONCLUSIONS FROM RESEARCH: SO WHAT DO WE LEARN FROM THIS LITERATURE?

There is a general pattern of psychopathic traits leading to poorer short-term responses to treatment. This poorer response includes less participation, poorer apparent motivation, worse behavior during treatment, less likeli-hood of completing treatment, and less rated reduction in risk subsequent to it. This overall pattern of poorer response to treatment seems to be true for adults and juveniles and regardless of whether cognitive–behavioral methods are used or whether the program is brief or lengthy. It is also not limited to traditional "therapy" but applies to other kinds of treatment ser-vices such as vocational training.

The way more psychopathic offenders respond during treatment does seem to be related to subsequent recidivism. At least when more behavioral indices are used (e.g., taking into account treatment completion or residential behavior), a better short-term treatment response seems to be associated with less recidivism. In contrast, softer clinicians' ratings, based solely on in-ses-sion behavior without regard to treatment completion, are not associated with recidivism rates. This finding, however, also seems to be true for offend-ers with less psychopathic traits. Thus, we do not presently know how to identify aspects of treatment performance that are associated with recidivism other than gross features such as completion or noncompletion.

With regard to non-cognitive–behavioral methods of treatment, it appears that these can be effective in reducing recidivism for less psychopathic offenders. However, participation in these kinds of treatment has been repeatedly associated with increased recidivism (three studies) or with no beneficial effect (three studies) for offenders with more psychopathic traits. In only one study for one dose of treatment was there an apparent benefit in terms of reduced reoffending for non-cognitive–behavioral treatment meth-ods; unfortunately, in this study recidivism was measured through self-report, which makes it less credible.

It is important to emphasize that the kinds of non-cognitive–behavioral treatment that have been reported as having no or negative effects for offend-ers with more marked psychopathic traits included therapeutic communities, individual therapy, prison education, and low-dose eclectic mental health ser-vices. Thus, this result applies to a range of modalities. It has also been observed for both adults and juveniles and for both brief and sustained, inten-sive forms of treatment interventions. This, of course, does not necessarily mean that there are not other forms of non-cognitive–behavioral treatment that would be more effective for this population. Salekin (2002), for example, claimed that psychoanalytic therapy consistently produced improvement in psychopathic offenders. It is notable, however, that in none of the studies of psychoanalytic therapy in Salekin's review was a reduction in recidivism used as the criterion for claiming that treatment had led to improvement.

The one combination for which the data are encouraging is the use of cognitive–behavioral methods with juvenile offenders. Here, there are two studies indicating that offenders with marked psychopathic traits show reduced recidivism if provided with treatment. Both programs provided relatively intensive and sustained treatment.

The picture is less clear with regard to the use of cognitive–behavioral methods for adults with marked psychopathic traits. Here, there were no studies indicating that treatment reduced recidivism, and one study indicated that it increased recidivism. The study that produced this negative result consisted of relatively brief interventions, a program that was not comparable to the programs that have been successful with juveniles. Thus, there is no direct evidence as to whether the kind of cognitive–behavioral programs that have worked for juveniles with psychopathic traits would be equally effective with adults.

It is, however, worth reflecting on the characteristics of the interventions that have produced no effect on recidivism or have increased recidivism, when used with offenders with psychopathic traits. The most striking distinguishing feature of these programs is that they were predominantly non-cognitive–behavioral programs for adults. Because cognitive–behavioral methods are generally recommended for use with offenders (Andrews and Bonta, 2003), it might be supposed that the interventions that led to increased recidivism for offenders with marked psychopathic traits were simply ineffective, poorly designed forms of treatment. It is important to emphasize that this is not the case. All of the non-cognitive–behavioral interventions that led to increased recidivism for psychopathic offenders were demonstrably effective in reducing recidivism for ordinary offenders. Additionally, the programs with juveniles that seem to have been effective all provided treatment over a relatively longer period. One of these programs had the feature of systematically ensuring that difficult/aggressive behavior by offenders with psychopathic features did not lead to a reduction in the level of treatment services provided to them.

One of the interesting features of two of the studies in which treatment led to increased recidivism by offenders with marked psychopathic traits is that these offenders behaved more delinquently during treatment, but the treatment process relaxed the extent to which they were held accountable for this. This happened in both the Oak Ridge program and the California Community Treatment project.

RECOMMENDATIONS

Taken together, the theoretical analysis provided in this chapter along with the studies reviewed makes a strong case for expecting highly psychopathic offenders to respond differently from less psychopathic offenders to commonly used treatment modalities. In light of this finding, what form should treatment services for offenders with marked psychopathic traits take? It is possible to make some cautious recommendations based on both the theoretical analysis of how the different facets of psychopathy are expected to moderate response to treatment and on the research findings that have just been reviewed. Implicit in this review and a good starting point for developing treatment services for offenders with marked psychopathic traits is the idea that treatment provision should be designed specifically for them rather than fitting them into treatment designed primarily for ordinary offenders.

Having said this, it is important to recognize that offenders with marked psychopathic traits do not form a homogeneous population. Hervé, Yong Hui Ling, and Hare (2000) reported cluster analyses of offenders with high overall scores on the PCL–R. Four meaningful types of psychopathic offender have emerged, profiled across the four facets. The prototypical type is high on all four facets, the manipulative psychopath is high on the interpersonal and affective facets, the explosive psychopath is high on the affective, lifestyle, and antisocial facets, and the pseudopsychopath is high only on the lifestyle and antisocial facets. These types are likely to present different problems and to have different treatment needs (see Hervé, chap. 17, this volume). Several studies found different effects of Factor 1 and Factor 2 traits with Factor 1 traits being more disruptive of positive treatment effects. This suggests that the pseudopsychopathic type, in particular, may be open to a much wider range of treatment modalities than the others, that the prototypical and manipulative types may be particularly resistant to treatment, with the explosive type falling somewhere in between.

With all this information in mind, it is possible to make a number of recommendations:

1. *Target potentially changeable factors linked to psychopathic offenders' criminal behavior for treatment.* This is a variant of Andrews and Bonta's classic Criminogenic Need principle, but it does differ from the general form of this principle in important ways. Some criminogenic factors may be so closely linked to underlying psychopathic traits that it is pointless to adopt them as treatment targets unless you believe you can change the underlying personality structure itself. For example, a lack of empathic connection to other human beings is a core feature of the affective facet of psychopathy. This means there is little point in trying to use treatment to increase empathy for others or empathy for potential victims for psychopathic offenders who are high on the affective facet (all except the pseudopsychopathic type).

Other generally criminogenic factors are unlikely to operate in their usual way when marked psychopathic traits are present. Cognitive distortions that minimize the harm produced by various criminal acts are certainly relevant for ordinary offenders because these distortions serve to neutralize the empathic reactions that would otherwise partially inhibit some of their criminal behavior. For psychopathic offenders who are high on the affective facet, changes in this kind of distortion may be essentially irrelevant since fundamentally they do not care whether someone else gets hurt.

Finally, some generally criminogenic factors may be largely absent in highly psychopathic offenders. For example, although they may often engage in angry intimidating behavior, this kind of behavior is largely instrumental in psychopathic offenders rather than being the product of overwhelming emotion. Similarly, violent crime engaged in by psychopathic offenders is more often "cold-blooded" (Woodworth and Porter, 2002). These authors report that 93% of the murders perpetrated by psychopaths were planned, unemotional, and motivated by an external goal. Along the same lines, Williamson, Hare, and Wong (1987) found that psychopathic violence was more often motivated by material gain or revenge, and that psychopathic offenders were less likely to have been in a heightened emotional state at the time of the act. This implies that there is little point in providing anger management or other strategies aimed to improve self-control over strong emotions as a way of reducing psychopathic offenders' propensity to engage in violence.

Thus, although it is sensible in selecting treatment targets to start with the factors that have been identified as generally criminogenic, it is essential to carefully consider how each of these factors will operate in the presence of psychopathic traits.

2. *Directly target treatment-interfering behaviors for treatment.* In the theory section of this chapter we provide an analysis of the particular treatment-interfering behaviors linked to psychopathic traits. These treatment-interfering behaviors are so habitual for most offenders with marked psychopathic traits that they will be automatically deployed without conscious awareness or reflection. In addition, unwary staff will be easily drawn into the dynamic of these behaviors. Thus, a process is required for helping both the offenders concerned and the staff who work with them to become more reflectively aware of treatment-interfering behaviors. Although it is likely that the underlying psychopathic traits will continue to predispose to these behaviors, it is proposed that in the right environment some highly psychopathic offenders can learn to reduce the severity of some of these behaviors, thus rendering the individuals concerned better able to learn.

Although they are habitually used, treatment-interfering behaviors serve various goals for psychopathic offenders, and if they are to consciously take control over these behaviors and develop new ones, they will have to be led to develop motives for doing so through the treatment environment. These motives will need to be short-term and to make sense from the offender's perspective. Motivation and awareness are not enough for change to take place; treatment should help the offender develop skills for reducing the frequency with which treatment-interfering behaviors are triggered and for interrupting them when they occur. Additionally, the offender will need to develop and practice alternative behaviors to use in circumstances in which the treatment-interfering behaviors would have previously been deployed. Although all of this will be hard work for both the offender and the staff concerned, in making progress in this area, the offender will have demonstrated a capacity for change that may be heartening to all involved.

3. *Avoid use of clinical methods that are particularly vulnerable to treatment-interfering factors.* The three common kinds of clinical methods that are especially vulnerable to the kinds of treatment-interfering behavior to

which psychopathic offenders are particularly prone are those that depend on uncheckable self-report, those that encourage these offenders to pretend to have emotional reactions that they do not have, and those that place offenders in positions of power and responsibility.

To avoid vulnerability to psychopathic offenders' propensity to duping delight, reliance on disclosures will need to be restricted to incidents about which there is sufficient collateral information. Treatment procedures requiring offenders to display emotions such as those commonly used in victim empathy work and many of the common self-help procedures designed for the "worried well" with low self-esteem should be avoided. Treatment methods that give particular opportunities for psychopathic offenders to exercise power over others, e.g., inmate or patient committees, democratic therapeutic communities, and any residential unit in which the residents get control over significant decisions or resources that are unmediated by staff should be avoided because offenders high on the interpersonal facet of psychopathy will come to dominate these venues and use them in ways that reinforce their power-oriented and exploitative tendencies.

4. *Use staff training, supervision, and operational procedures that maintain boundaries and reduce opportunities for manipulation.* Members of staff who work with significant numbers of psychopathic offenders are liable to be continuously tested by (psychopathic or interpersonally psychopathic) offenders seeking to draw them into accepting or participating in boundary violations. Staff training can offer some protection if it alerts members of staff to common tactics used by offenders and includes practice in effective ways of neutralizing these ploys. This training will need to be supplemented by an operational process with active supervisors who support staff members, are alert to detect the early stages of boundary violations, and encourage staff members to seek help when they have made mistakes in this area. Punitive management strategies are particularly counterproductive in this setting because the smallest mistake by staff can then provide an opportunity for blackmail and a lever that can force the staff member to engage in more serious fraternization.

Apart from straightforward boundary violations aimed at short-term gain, there may also be a continuous attempt to persuade staff members to make decisions in the offender's favor, not hold an offender accountable for his or her actions, and mistakenly credit the offender with improvements that have not in fact been made. One way to reduce the vulnerability of staff members in a therapeutic system to these effects is to reduce the degree to which important decisions are made by staff members who have substantial direct contact with the offender. In addition, it may help to have decisions strongly driven by rules and systems and to provide less opportunity for discretionary decision making.

5. *Deploy less reactive methods of assessment.* Because self-report and other easily manipulated channels of information are likely to provide misleading information about treatment needs, risk factors, or personal change, it will be important to develop an array of assessment methods that are less vulnerable to manipulation and dissimulation.

One key source will be very elaborate records of past behavior. Unfortunately, restrictions designed to protect patient or pupil confidentiality often make it difficult for a particular facility to access a suitable range of school and mental health records. Similarly, victim statements, police reports, and other information may sometimes be restricted because they were gathered for the purpose of a particular court procedure and are thought to be unusable for other purposes. These restrictions need to be overcome if psychopathic offenders are to be effectively assessed, managed, and treated. Sometimes, this will require alterations to relevant laws.

For those offenders residing in correctional or forensic mental health facilities, observations of their daily behavior will provide a potentially important source of assessment information. Making the most of this source requires staff training, rating, or recording procedures that capture relevant information in a cost-effective way, and methods of collating and assuring the quality of the staff observation and recording process. It will also depend on defining treatment concepts (such as "thinking errors") in more behavioral ways so that their occurrence can be observed by staff members rather than having to be self-reported by the offender.

A new development is the increasing availability of assessment tasks based on procedures used in experimental psychology laboratories. One obvious field in which they have been developed is neurocognitive psychology in which tasks are used to generate particular kinds of activity or test specific abilities and are commonly combined with physiological procedures designed to determine which areas of the brain are activated (Blair, 1999; Blair & Cipolotti, 2000; Blair, Jones, Clark, & Smith, 1995, 1997; Blair, Morris, Frith, Perrett, & Dolan, 1999). Similar but treatment-oriented tasks could prove of paramount importance in measuring treatment effectiveness for more psychopathic offenders.

6. *Appeal to motivations common among psychopathic offenders.* Motives based on altruism, empathy, deep emotional needs, or long-term self-interest are unlikely to be relevant to psychopathic offenders. Short-term self-interest, excitement, challenges, status, and a sense of power or control are all much more relevant. The motives to which psychopathic offenders are susceptible are all too easily gratified through crime, but it is possible to give these elements more play in treatment activities as well.

7. *Ensure that prosocial behavior during treatment leads to better consequences than antisocial behavior.* As noted earlier, one of the features of treatment programs that has led to increased recidivism for more psychopathic offenders was that involvement in treatment more often led to a reduc-

tion in the usual negative consequences of antisocial behavior. This seems likely to encourage the offenders' view that they can manipulate their way out of anything and hence increase their propensity to offend. It is therefore essential to establish a regimen in which prevailing contingencies encourage prosocial behavior and discourage antisocial behavior.

8. *Ensure that fluctuations in the quality of an offender's behavior do not lead to major reductions in the provision of treatment services.* Although psychopathic offenders sometimes show "miraculous" improvements in their behavior, they equally commonly show relapses into aggressive, impulsive, or manipulative behavior. It is all too easy for these negative behaviors to lead to a substantial withdrawal of treatment services. Treatment services, sanctions, and security processes need to be organized so that they do not interfere with each other; effective security, control of dangerous behavior, and sanctions for bad behavior need to be applied without necessitating the withdrawal of treatment services.

9. *Respond to diversity.* Offenders with marked psychopathic traits are commonly quite diverse in other ways. For example, deficits in executive functioning are reliably associated with antisocial personality disorder (Morgan & Lilienfeld, 2000); additionally, both poor performance on executive functioning tasks and measures of serotonin neurotransmission are associated with impulsiveness (Dolan, Deakin, Roberts, & Anderson, 2002). However, *psychopaths*, as defined by PCL–R scores of ≥ 30 or above, do not seem to show more marked executive functioning deficits than other offenders (Hare, 1984; Devonshire, Howard, & Sellars, 1988; Lapierre, Braun, & Hodgins, 1995). Thus, it is reasonable to expect some offenders who show marked psychopathic traits to show these deficits whereas others do not. Treatment of offenders with marked psychopathic traits is liable to be more effective if it includes assessments for and responses to this kind of diversity in choosing both treatment targets and in accommodating treatment methods to offenders' learning style.

10. *Use transitional facilities and extended supervision.* Too often highly psychopathic offenders are held in high-security conditions and then released without effective supervision into the community. This system gives little opportunity for gathering of behavioral evidence on the stability and generality of apparent progress of offenders before the community is exposed to risk. It is recommended that a graded series of transitions be used in which physical security and close supervision is gradually relaxed as apparent progress is made. These control measures will give much greater opportunity to both consolidate and test out the reality of this progress.

There are some hints in the literature (e.g. Tengström, Grann, Långström, & Kullgren, 2000) that close supervision is effective in partially suppressing psychopathic behavior. In this study, reoffending by psychopathic offenders only became markedly greater than that by nonpsychopathic offenders after supervision had been relaxed. Thus, institutional treatment should be followed by very extended, perhaps decade-long, supervision in the community.

11. *Use cognitive–behavioral treatment methods in a sustained manner*. Focusing only on treatment methods, without regard to the age of those involved, indicates that the sustained use of cognitive–behavioral methods is the only approach to produce promising results. For other methods, the general trend is for treatment to be ineffective or to increase recidivism. Thus, it is reasonable to cautiously recommend the sustained use of cognitive–behavioral methods for offenders with marked psychopathic traits.

12. *Prioritize work with juvenile offenders*. The most striking finding from our review is that reductions in recidivism for offenders with marked psychopathic traits have only been documented when cognitive–behavioral methods are applied in a sustained way with juvenile offenders. One possibility is that juveniles with these traits are more malleable than adults with them. If that proves to be the case, then there would be strong policy grounds for preferentially allocating resources to the treatment of juveniles with marked psychopathic traits. However, even if adults with these traits eventually prove to be responsive to treatment, there will still be a strong argument for interrupting psychopathic life paths at the earliest possible stage.

REFERENCES

Andrews, D. A., & Bonta, J. (2003). *The psychology of criminal conduct* (3rd ed.). Cincinnati, OH: Anderson Publishing Company.

Blair, R. J. R. (1999). Responsiveness to distress cues in the child with psychopathic tendencies. *Personality and Individual Differences, 27*, 135–145.

Blair, R. J. R., & Cipolotti, L. (2000). Impaired social response reversal—A case of "acquired sociopathy." *Brain, 123*(Pt. 6), 1122–1141.

Blair, R. J. R., Jones, L., Clark, F., & Smith, M. (1995). Is the psychopath morally insane? *Personality and Individual Differences, 19*(5), 741–752.

Blair, R. J. R., Jones, L., Clark, F., & Smith, M. (1997). The psychopathic individual: A lack of responsiveness to distress cues? *Psychophysiology, 34*, 192–198.

Blair, R. J. R., Morris, J. S., Frith, C. D., Perrett, D. I., & Dolan, R. J. (1999). Dissociable neural responses to facial expressions of sadness and anger. *Brain and Behavioral Sciences, 122*, 883–893.

Bowers, L. (1994) *Do different types of rapist respond differently to the sex offender treatment programme*. Unpublished masters thesis, University of London, London.

Caldwell, M. F., & Van Rybroek, G. J. (in press). Reducing violence in serious and violent juvenile offenders using an intensive treatment program. *International Journal of Mental Health and Law*.

Caldwell, M. F., Skeem, J., Salekin, R., & Van Rybroek, J. (2004). *Youth, psychopathy features, and treatment.* Unpublished manuscript.

Catchpole, R. E. H., Gretton, H. M., & Hemphill, J. F. (2003, April). *Is earlier better? The relationship between psychopathy and treatment outcome in adolescent violent offenders.* Paper presented at Developmental and Neuroscience Perspectives on Psychopathy Conference. Madison, WI.

Cooke, D. J., & Michie, C. (2001). Refining the construct of psychopathy: Towards a hierarchical model. *Psychological Assessment, 13,* 171–188.

Cornell, D., Warren, J., Hawk, G., Stafford, E., Oram, G., & Pine, D. (1996). Psychopathy in instrumental and reactive offenders. *Journal of Consulting and Clinical Psychology, 64,* 783–790.

De Vita, E., Forth, A. E., & Hare, R. D. (1990) Family background of male criminal psychopaths [Abstract]. *Canadian Psychology, 31,* 346.

Devonshire, P. A., Howard, R. C., & Sellars, C. (1988). Frontal lobe functions and personality in mentally abnormal offenders. *Personality and Individual Differences, 9,* 339–344.

Dolan, M., Deakin, W. J. F., Roberts, N., & Anderson, I. (2002). Serotonergic and cognitive impairment in impulsive aggressive personality disordered offenders: Are there implications for treatment? *Psychological Medicine, 32,* 105–117.

Forth, A. E., Kosson, D., & Hare, R. D. (2004). *The Hare PCL: Youth Version.* Toronto, Ontario, Canada. Multi-Health Systems.

Garrido, V., Esteban, C., & Molero, C. (1996). The effectiveness in the treatment of psychopathy: A meta-analysis. In D. J. Cooke, A. E. Forth, J. P. Newman, & R. D. Hare (Eds.), *Issues in Criminological and Legal Psychology: No. 24, International Perspectives on Psychopathy* (pp. 57–59). Leicester, UK: British Psychological Society.

Genders, E. and Player, E. (1995). *Grendon: A study of a therapeutic prison.* Oxford: Clarendon Press.

Gretton, H. M., McBride, M., Hare, R. D., & O'Shaughnessy, R. (2000, November). *Psychopathy and recidivism in adolescent offenders: A ten year follow up.* Paper presented at the 19th Annual Research and Treatment Conference, Association for the Treatment of Sexual Abusers. San Diego, CA.

Hanson, R. K., & Bussiere, M. T. (1998). Predicting relapse: A meta-analysis of sexual offender recidivism studies. *Journal of Consulting and Clinical Psychology, 66,* 348–362.

Hare, R. D. (1984). Performance of psychopaths on cognitive tasks related to frontal lobe function. *Journal of Abnormal Psychology, 93,* 133–140.

Hare, R. D. (1998). Psychopaths and their nature: Implications for the mental health and criminal justice systems. In T. Millon, E. Simonson, M. Burket-Smith, & R. Davis (Eds.), *Psychopathy: Antisocial, criminal, and violent behavior* (pp. 188–212). New York: Guilford Press.

Hare, R. D. (2003). *The Hare Psychopathy Checklist–Revised* (2nd ed.). Toronto, Ontario, Canada: Multi-Health Systems.

Hare, R. D., Clark, D., Grann, M., & Thornton, D. (2000). Psychopathy and the predictive validity of the PCL–R: An international perspective. *Behavioral Sciences and the Law, 18,* 623–645.

Hare, R. D., MacPherson, L. M., & Forth, A. E. (1984). *Early criminal behavior as a function of family background.* Unpublished manuscript, University of British Columbia, Vancouver, British Columbia.

Hemphill, J. F., Hare, R. D., & Wong, S. (1998). Psychopathy and recidivism: A review. *Legal and Criminological Psychology, 3,* 139–170.

Hemphill, J. F., & Hart, S. D. (2002). Motivating the unmotivated: Psychopathy, treatment and change. In M. McMurran (Ed.), *Motivating offenders to change: A guide to enhancing engagement in therapy* (pp. 193–219). Chichester: Wiley.

Hervé, H. F., Yong Hui Ling, J., & Hare, R. D. (2000, March). *Criminal psychopathy and its subtypes.* Paper presented at the biennial conference of the American Psychology-Law Society, New Orleans, LA.

Hobson, J., Shine, J., & Roberts, R. (2000). How do psychopaths behave in a prison therapeutic community? *Psychology, Crime, and Law, 6,* 139–154.

Hughes, G., Hogue, T., Hollin, C., & Champion, H. (1997). First stage evaluation of a treatment programme for personality disordered offenders. *Journal of Forensic Psychiatry, 8,* 515–527.

Knight, R.A. & Prentky, R.A. (1990). Classifying sexual offenders: The development and corroboration of taxonomic models. In W.L. Marshall, D.R. Laws & H.E. Barbaree (Eds.), *Handbook of sexual assault: Issues, theories and treatment of the offender* (pp 23–53). New York: Plenum Press.

Langton, C. M. (2003). *Contrasting approaches to risk assessment with adult male sexual offenders: an evaluation of recidivism prediction schemes and the utility of supplementary clinical information for enhancing predictive accuracy.* Unpublished doctoral dissertation. University of Toronto, Toronto, Ontario, Canada.

Lapierre, D., Braun, C. M. J., & Hodgins, S. (1995). Ventral frontal deficits in psychopathy: Neuropsychological test findings. *Neuropsychologia, 33,* 139–151.

Loeber, R., & Stouthamer-Loeber, M. (1986). Family factors as correlates and predictors of juvenile conduct problems and delinquency. In M. Tonry & N. Morris (Eds.), *Crime and justice* (Vol. 17, pp. 29–149). Chicago: University of Chicago Press.

Looman, J., Abracens, J., Serin, R., & Marquis, P. (in press). Psychopathy, treatment change, and recidivism in high risk need sexual offenders. *Journal of Interpersonal Violence.*

Morgan, A. B., & Lilienfield, S. O. (2000). A meta-analytic review of the relation between antisocial behavior and neuropsychological measures of executive functioning. *Clinical Psychology Review, 20,* 113–136.

Mulloy, R., McHattie, L. J., & Smiley, W. C. (1998, November). *A follow up of treated psychopathic and non-psychopathic sex offenders.* Paper presented at the annual conference of the Association for Sexual Abusers, Vancouver, British Columbia, Canada.

Ogloff, J. R., Wong, S., & Greenwood, A. (1990). Treating criminal psychopaths. *Behavioral Sciences and the Law, 8,* 181–190.

O'Neill, M. L., Lidz, V., & Heilbrun, K. (2003). Adolescents with psychopathic characteristics in a substance abusing cohort: Treatment process and outcomes. *Law and Human Behavior, 27,* 299–313.

Prentky, R. A., Knight, R.A., Lee, A. F., & Cerce, D.D. (1995). Predictive validity of lifestyle impulsivity for rapists. *Criminal Justice and Behavior, 22,* 106–128.

Quinsey, V. L., Harris, G. T., Rice, M. E., & Cormier, C. A. (1998). *Violent offenders: Appraising and managing risk.* Washington, DC: American Psychological Association.

Richards, H. J., Casey, J. O., & Lucente, S. W. (2003). Psychopathy and treatment response in incarcerated female substance abusers. *Criminal Justice and Behavior, 30,* 251–267.

Salekin, R. T. (2002). Psychopathy and therapeutic pessimism: Clinical lore or clinical reality? *Clinical Psychopathy Review, 22,* 79–112.

Seto, M. C., & Barbaree, H. E. (1999). Psychopathy, treatment behavior, and sex offenders recidivism. *Journal of Interpersonal Violence, 14*, 1235–1248.

Seto, M. C., & Barbaree, H. E. (in press). Psychopathy, treatment behavior, and recidivism: An extended follow up of Seto and Barbaree (1999). *Journal of Interpersonal Violence.*

Skeem, J. L., Monahan, J., & Mulvey, E. P. (2002). Psychopathy, treatment involvement, and subsequent violence among civil psychiatric patients. *Law and Human Behavior, 26*, 577–603.

Taylor, R. (2000). *A seven-year reconviction study of HMP Grendon Therapeutic Community* (Research Findings No. 115). London: Home Office Research and Statistics Directorate.

Tengström, A., Grann, M., Långström, N., & Kullgren, G. (2000). Psychopathy (PCL–R) as a predictor of violent recidivism among criminal offenders with schizophrenia. *Law and Human Behavior, 24*, 45–58.

Treves-Brown, C. (1977). Who is a psychopath? *Medical Science and the Law, 17*, 56–63.

Vaillant, G. E. (1975). Sociopathy as human process: a viewpoint. *Archives of General Psychiatry, 32*, 178–183.

Warren, M. Q. (1983). Application of interpersonal maturity theory to offender populations. In W. S. Laufer & J. M. Day (Eds.), *Moral development and criminal behavior.* Lexington, MA: Lexington Books.

Williamson, S. E., Hare, R. D., & Wong, S. (1987). Violence: Criminal psychopaths and their victims. *Canadian Journal of Behavioral Science, 19*, 454–462.

Wong, S., & Elek, D. (1989). Treatment of psychopaths: A review of the literature [Abstract]. *Canadian Psychology, 30*, 292.

Woody, G. E., McLellan, A. T., Rubersky, L., & O'Brien, C. P. (1985). Sociopathy and psychotherapy outcome. *Archives of General Psychiatry, 42*, 1081–1086.

Wootton, J. M., Frick, P. J., Shelton, K. K., & Silverthorn, P. (1997). Ineffective parenting and childhood conduct problems. *Journal of Consulting and Clinical Psychology, 65*, 301–308.

Woodworth, M., & Porter, S. (2002). In cold blood: Characteristics of criminal homicides as a function of psychopathy. *Journal of Abnormal Psychology, 111*, 436–445.

Zamble, E., & Porporino, F. J. (1988). *Coping behavior and adaptation in prison inmates.* Syracuse, NY: Springer-Verlag.

Zamble, E., & Quinsey, V. L. (1997). *The criminal recidivism process.* Cambridge, England: Cambridge University Press.

Zinger, I., & Forth, A. E. (1998). Psychopathy and Canadian criminal proceedings: The potential for human rights abuses. *Canadian Journal of Criminology, 40*(3), 237–276.

Author Index

Page numbers followed by f indicate figures
Page numbers followed by t indicate tables
Page numbers in italics indicate pages with complete bibliographic information

A

Abbott, A., 46, 49, *51*
Abracens, J., 517, *538*
Abramowitz, C. S., 98, *100*
Achenbach, T. M., 153, *166*
Ackerman, T. A., 134, *136*
Adolphs, R., 266, *276, 277, 279*
Adshead, G., 33, *51*
Ahern, G., 211, *250*
Akehurst, L., 497, *503*
Allen, B., 494, *499*
Allen, D., 67, *76*
Allen, J. J. B., 196, *203*
Allen, L. C., 99, *104*
Alpert, M., 188, *205*
Alterman, A. I., 46, *55*, 105, 108, *136, 138*, 374, *386*, 391t, 392, 393, 394, *409*, 449, 454, *455*
Amato, P. R., 344t, *362*
Ameli, R., 218, 237, *245*
Amos, N., 292, *297*
Amos, N. L., 396, *409*, 461, 462, *484*
Andershed, H., 6, 13, *23*, 256, *280*, 334, *340*, 369, 374, *382, 385*
Anderson, G., 153, *169*, 309, *324*
Anderson, I., 535, *537*
Anderson, I. M., 99, *101*
Anderson, R. E., 441, *456*
Anderson, S. W., 256, 266, *276, 277*
Andrade, A. R., 343, *365*
Andrew, C., 263, *281*
Andrews, B. P., *5*, *26*, 350, 351, *365*
Andrews, D., 380, *384*
Andrews, D. A., 59, 63, *72*, 162, *166*, 463, 474, 477, *482, 483*, 515, 530, *536*

Andrich, D., 134, *136*
Angrilli, A., 226, *250*
Anthony, B. J., 220, *243*
Anthony, V. L., 369, *386*
Anton, R. F., 268, *279*
Appelbaum, P. S., 11, 16, *28*, 60, *74*, 153, 162, *169, 170*, 447, *460*
Arce, E., 269, 275, *281*
Arieti, S., 32, 39, 40, 41, 44, 49, *51*, 431, 432, 433, 434, 435, 436, 437, 438, 440, 441, *455*
Arieti, Silvano, 4
Arnett, J. J., 373, *382*
Arnett, P. A., 181, 189, *202, 206*, 259, 260, *276*, 282, 442, *455, 459*
Aronen, H. J., 269, *280*
Austin, J., 86, 87, *102*
Avila, C., 160, *169*
Ayers, W. A., 68, *72*

B

Babcock, J., 328, 329, *338*
Babiak, P., 20, *23*, 51, *51*, 294, *297*, 413, 415, 417t, 420, 423, *426, 427*, 493, 496, *499*
Babiak, Paul, 413
Baca-Garcia, E., 404, *407*
Bagley, A., 98, *103*
Bagozzi, R. P., 93, *101*
Baker, F. B., 130, *136*
Baker, M. D., 371, *383*
Bakish, D., 404, *407*
Balaban, M. T., 225, 226, *243*
Bale, R., 391t, 399, *410*
Bandalos, D. L., 93, *101*

541

Subject Index

Page references followed by f indicate figure
Page references followed by t indicate table